DATE DUE

DE 18'98		
NO 4'99		

DEMCO 38-296

KEEPING
THE FAITH

KEEPING
THE FAITH

A CULTURAL HISTORY
OF THE U.S. SUPREME COURT

JOHN E. SEMONCHE

ROWMAN & LITTLEFIELD PUBLISHERS, INC.
Lanham • Boulder • New York • Oxford

ROWMAN & LITTLEFIELD PUBLISHERS, INC.

Published in the United States of America
by Rowman & Littlefield Publishers, Inc.
4720 Boston Way, Lanham, Maryland 20706

12 Hid's Copse Road
Cumnor Hill, Oxford OX2 9JJ, England

British Library Cataloguing in Publication Information Available

Library of Congress Cataloging-in-Publication Data

Semonche, John E., 1933–
    Keeping the faith : a cultural history of the U.S. Supreme Court /
John E. Semonche.
        p.   cm.
    Includes bibliographical references and index.
    ISBN 0-8476-8985-9 (cloth)
    1. United States. Supreme Court—History.   2. Constitutional
history—United States.   I. Title.
    KF8742.S444   1998
    347.73'26—DC21   97-32481
                                                              CIP

Printed in the United States of America

Design by Deborah Clark

∞ ™ The paper used in this publication meets the minimum requirements of American
National Standard for Information Sciences—Permanence of Paper for Printed Library
Materials, ANSI Z39.48—1984.

To all those whose faith

embraces a belief in individual freedom and responsibility,

including three strong women:

Anna, whose continued desire to learn kept her young;

Barbara, whose professionalism is only matched by her beauty;

and

Laura, whose perceptions of herself and her world have made her wiser than her years.

CONTENTS

ACKNOWLEDGMENTS

A single author certainly does not mean the absence of collaborators. Perhaps this is even more the case with a book that seeks to find meaning and significance in the words and rhetoric of a special body of public servants—the men and women who have served as justices on the nation's highest court. From its beginnings these very special judges not only decided cases but in the process of explaining their decisions shaped our culture as well. Many of the words that follow are their words, and athough they hardly can be held responsible for the purposes to which their phrases have been put, the author is indebted to them for their contribution.

The University of North Carolina at Chapel Hill has been a good place to teach and write, and I must thank my students who have probably taught me as much as I have taught them, especially in those seminars in which together we struggled with the concept of an American civil religion. Colin Palmer, a former chairman of the History Department, was instrumental in seeing that I got a semester off to get a large chunk of the first draft done and that my collection of Supreme Court opinions was brought up to date.

In addition two of my former students and now colleagues, Margaret A. Blanchard and Jordan M. Smith, went through the entire manuscript and gave me the type of feedback that I hope I have processed sufficiently so that this is a better book than it otherwise would have been. Furthermore, Jordan labored with me in those undergraduate seminars dealing with civil religion and law, and challenged my ideas by his probing questions.

Thanks also to my wife and daughter, Barbara and Laura, for their support and belief that the project I was engaged in was important and worthwhile. Barbara read the entire manuscript and pronounced my ability to communicate with the previously untutored a success. She also brought her talents to bear on the task of preparing the volume's index. Laura, also a lawyer and now legislative counsel, has shared my fascination with the role of the Court in American society.

Finally, to the folks at Rowman & Littlefield, especially Stephen M. Wrinn, the acquisitions editor, and Lynn Gemmell, the production editor, my thanks for their enthusiasm about this project and their professional competence in guiding it through the publication process.

THE TIES THAT BIND

At a time in American history when group seems to be pitted against group, when irradicable differences are stressed to the detriment of commonalities, when there seems to be no end to claims of victimization, and when social critics worry about the society falling apart, we need to take a fresh look at the ties that have bound a diverse people together.

Americans are united within a civic culture that is much stronger and more durable than current worries suggest. These ties that bind are primarily legal, political, and spiritual; they nurture and promote the interests of the individual within a national community; and they are institutionalized within the American constitutional system. The Supreme Court of the United States, which is at the apex of the country's legal system, plays a central role in explicating, reinforcing, and expanding the range of these ties. To show how and explain why this is so is what this book is about, but first we need to address some threshold matters relating to American society—the people who compose it and the nature and function of law within it.

From the beginning, Americans, lacking any traditional basis for nationhood, defined themselves in terms of ideas—liberty, equality, and republican government founded upon the people's consent—and embarked upon an experiment to determine whether a people so defined could constitute an enduring nation. Although many generations have passed since the founding of the United States, the experiment continues, and the unfinished nature of American society remains one of its most distinguishing characteristics.[1] So it must be, for this joining together on the basis of shared principles leaves much in a person's identity to be determined outside the parameters of this limited community. Those who seek to tighten the embrace of this community by attempting to read into it their cultural preferences as further tests of one's Americanism contradict the community's core principles. On the other hand, those who stress their diversity and attack the cultural grafts that their opponents would attach to being American too often fail to distinguish these vulnerable grafts from the core principles themselves. No matter how strident and seemingly total is the identification with a particular group, the American remains a member of the national community and both implicitly and explicitly works within its understood parameters.[2] For instance, "claims for tolerance, equality and justice must be based on the democratic principles of the national ideology," for by itself membership in any group "creates no claim on others for tolerance, respect, equality, or anything else."[3]

From the time of the Declaration of Independence, Americans were challenged to fulfill a founding myth that viewed the country "as a divinely inspired asylum for those who sought liberty and opportunity."[4] Blessings, therefore, were to be shared with new arrivals. The idealistic core of American identity was only strengthened as immigrants eagerly accepted "the universal norms of a moral and social order which gave them equality of status, liberty of expression, and the right to consider themselves citizens."[5] Throughout its history, the country staked its identity "on the peculiar faith that the One and the Many are not only mutually compatible but essential to freedom."[6]

As successive waves of immigrants peopled the new land, they quickly absorbed a legal tradition that responded to them as individuals. "It is this easily transferred and easily absorbed idea of a constitutional system that protects the individual . . . that harmonizes great social, economic and even ethnic differences in American society"[7] In the long run, this legal emphasis on the individual works against the stigmatization or subordination of any group of individuals.

When Thomas Paine exhorted Americans to shed their loyalty to King George III in 1776, he suggested that they crown law as their king.[8] And this is precisely what Americans proceeded to do. What eighteenth-century Americans had in mind when they spoke of the rule of law was the common law tradition, as they had interpreted it, with its emphasis on the protection of individual rights and its restraint on arbitrary authority. The rule of law sought to embrace all official conduct under standards of fairness, impartiality, and equality. Its legitimacy stemmed from a faith in procedures and reasoned justification.

This study proceeds from the assumption that law, itself, should be taken seriously. Those who see it as a tool of powerful interests or those who search for hidden motivations behind its text are refusing to come to terms with its significance in American culture, a significance it had at the time of national creation and a significance that it retains today.

Law, "as a community-defining totem,"[9] plays an important role in constructing and reconstructing the society. It is a defining language that seeks both to provide meaning and cohesion and to inform action within the community. To appreciate the definition of law as language, we need to escape from our common conception of speech and writing as transparent means of communication and view language "not as a set of propositions, but as a repertoire of forms of action and of life."[10] The law provides just one language out of many, and although it is artificial and bound by constraints, it reveals much about the culture. As elaborated by legal and literary scholar James Boyd White, law "is the constitution of a world by the distribution of authority within it; it establishes the terms on which its actors may talk in conflict or cooperation among themselves. . . . It makes us members

of a common world."[11] Since law "is continuous with ordinary language and politics, . . . [it] necessarily respects the culture it acts upon and out of; and it is
inherently idealizing, taking as its constant subject what we ought to do, who we
ought to be."[12]

To describe a rule of law without talk of justice, equality, and common decency—as has so often been done—is to purge that concept of the very ideals that
bind the diverse people called Americans together. The "single greatest achievement of Western political culture," White has asserted, is "the discovery that a
community can govern itself through a rule of law that attempts to create a fundamental moral and political equality among human beings."[13] This aspirational dimension of law is an integral part of an American creed.

American unity, however, is not based upon overwhelming agreement upon
substantive matters but rather on procedural and relational ones; that is, how are
differences among persons to be resolved and how can opposing parties be accorded the equal respect due them. The American legal system provides the arena
for resolving such disputes. In submitting the dispute to the resolution of courts,
opposing parties are subscribing to a substantial consensus. They believe that the
process will justly resolve their differences, that it respects them as individuals, and
that it gives them the opportunity to be heard.[14]

Such access to the judicial system provides an important means to present and
argue new claims and eventually to bring about changes in the law. In this adver-
sarial process lawyers play an important role. By transforming individual grievances
into legal issues, lawyers contribute indispensably to making judges both understand and respond to the claims presented. In undertaking this responsibility, courts
define and also educate a national community. The vocabulary of this conversation
provides "a rhetorical coherence to public life by compelling those who disagree
about one thing to speak a language which expresses their actual or pretended
agreement about everything else." By forcing litigants to speak the language of the
law, something new is created—"a place and mode of discourse, a set of relations,
that form a central part of our civilization."[15] The language and operation of the
law thus define the political community in which contesting parties find their
home.

Such a community cannot be created or maintained by force; this is why governmental repression, which seeks to replace difference with sameness, is so counterproductive. In fact, such diversity among individuals is the best testament to
unity. Within this national community "the most fundamental notion of legality"
requires that the government "justify, by reference to its legitimate interests and
concerns, any intrusions on the liberty and bodily integrity of its citizens."[16] The
legal system provides a structure in which the search for liberty and justice can
continue while managing conflict within the parameters of a prevailing consensus—precisely what the rule of law was designed to do. Conflict could not be

eliminated, but its disrupting potential could be reduced. The continued success of the American experiment rests upon the maintenance of this consensus.

The law provides so many roles that virtually all people in society have parts in the continuing drama, and over a lifetime the roles they play can and do change. First, we have the initial lawmakers—legislators and those administrators charged with formulating rules. Then, we have the initial law enforcers—the police and other governmental officials armed with the authority of the law. In the position of mediators between those who enforce and those who are the subject of enforcement are lawyers and arbitrators. And, finally, we have ordinary citizens, who are grand and trial jurors and who may be summoned as either civil or criminal defendants or who themselves, as plaintiffs, may summon others to the bar to redress some grievance.

Overseeing this drama and both directing and playing a complex major role, both as lawmaker and law enforcer, is the judiciary. The term "director" may be too limited, for it implies a script much more finished than the drama of the law provides. Perhaps the judiciary can be most usefully viewed as a dramaturge, that is, as a specialist in the art or technique of dramatic composition and theatrical presentation. This dramaturge's work is ongoing and can never be completed, but continually it must explain, justify, and develop the drama in the direction of the essential goals of a rule of law.

This is what makes the judicial opinion such a rich source for viewing law as a culture-shaping force. Judges are not necessarily wiser than the other legal players, but the task imposed upon them is appreciably different. Legal texts are not self-interpretive, and eventually the authority of the law must rest upon "the process of writing opinions by which the decisions reached by the courts are given their meaning." Judges must indeed respect the texts of the past, but they must also take responsibility for an interpretation that can only be their own. Regularly the meaning of the opinions is broader than first perceived, for underpinning the resolution are conclusions about who we are and what we do or should desire. In dipping into the past and establishing continuity with the present, the judge "establishes or modifies a discursive and political community with his readers."[17] In the process, generations are connected and so are different individuals and groups in the present.

The tradition of a rule of law is strong in the popular mind. All polls and surveys reveal a strong American commitment to obey the law that is not explained in terms of rational calculations of self-interest—the so-called instrumental approach. The normative approach, which suggests that people voluntarily obey the law because it is the right or moral or the just thing to do, continues to be a much more accurate description. There is a prevailing faith in the law, its relationship to common morality, and the essential fairness of its procedures.[18]

In fact, the law's protections are so ingrained in the popular mind that they become generalized standards of judgment. "Life in modern America," one legal historian has said, "is a vast, diffuse school of law."[19] Back in Jacksonian America the French traveler Alexis de Tocqueville had noted both the incorporation of legal language into everyday speech and a legalistic spirit pervading the whole society. In the century and a half since that time, public language has become even more legalistic in a continuing search for common values; it creeps "into the languages that Americans employ around the kitchen table, in the neighborhood, and in their diverse communities of memory and mutual aid."[20] Legal standards become minimum moral standards, and an American commitment to the rule of law becomes no less than a matter of fundamental faith, a subject to which we now turn.

Much of what we have been considering is part of an American faith structure, a creed, even a civil or public religion. This creed commands belief, operates as a vehicle for public discourse, becomes a spur to reduce gaps between belief and practice, and serves as a code that can be legally implemented. In 1967, Robert Bellah introduced the term "American civil religion" into the arena of contemporary scholarly debate, drawing his evidence from presidential addresses with their references to God, the nation's mission, and the transcendent standards to which the American people are held accountable.[21]

That a search for evidence of an American civil religion should seek out and find this God-talk in formal presidential addresses is understandable.[22] The nation has no other single spokesman, and the words of reference to divine providence are regularly found in such speeches. But such references get us only so far in an attempt to explore the viability of the concept of an American civil religion. Talk is cheap, and although such references seem to strike a popular chord, they provide limited evidence of an operative faith structure. Too often, such references seem to be a matter of political gloss, all surface and little substance. In fact, this search for God-talk may well lead us astray.

In the sociological search for a spiritual tie that bound the diverse people called Americans together, Bellah did fasten on a concept that has led to substantial debate and criticism.[23] The debate demonstrated that civil religion can be defined in diverse and contradictory ways, a result that called into question its serviceability as an analytical tool.[24] However, if Americans are defined in terms of their beliefs and if their actions are to be judged in terms of standards established by those beliefs, then the term civil religion may advance an understanding of what unites Americans.

Instead of beginning with an example of what we would agree was a religion and then measuring a claimant against the standards the example established, sociologists, cultural anthropologists, and even theologians have defined religion in terms of its functions. These definitions have stressed symbolism, meaning, transcendence, and wholeness as characteristics by which to grasp religion's place in the modern world. Although much in this world can be explained, "lingering contingencies" or the human being's need for holistic explanations that lie beyond the competence of empirical science remain.[25] Arguing that "any durable society seems to possess important collective religious aspects instrumental in its achievement of coherence and in its continuing viability,"[26] these writers have focused our attention on the many aspects of the culture that have religious characteristics. "A society acquires and maintains its legitimacy over time and through space on the basis of a meaning system which has been, empirically or historically speaking, most frequently religious,"[27] and "the possession of a common set of ideas, rituals, and symbols can supply an overarching sense of unity even in a society riddled with conflict."[28] One theologian has defined religion as a comprehensive interpretive scheme that structures "human experience and understanding of self and world," or alternatively "as a kind of cultural and/or linguistic framework or medium that shapes the entirety of life and thought."[29] A civil religion seeks to embrace the totality of public life and thought. To be more specific, the term "civil religion," as it is applied to the United States and used in this work, means "a public perception of our national experience, in the light of universal and transcendent claims upon human beings, but especially upon Americans; a set of values, symbols, and rituals institutionalized as the cohesive force and center of meaning uniting our many peoples."[30]

None of the critics of the concept of an American civil religion have denied that the adjective "religious" can and should be attached to various aspects of American culture. Look at the way Americans have glorified the origin of their nation and insisted upon their destiny. George Washington was deified before he died, and the practical politicians of the late eighteenth century who wrestled with the details of establishing governments are hallowed as "Founding Fathers."

One of the problems with the civil religion concept, however, is that it has been the preserve of academicians, who have paid too little attention to the everyday world that the faithful inhabit.[31] We need to look at the essentials of the American creed and see how they have become transcendent standards, not only for criticizing official action but also for promoting communication in the diverse society. To give more substance to the concept of an American civil religion, we eventually have to find some evidence of its social institutionalization.

American nationhood rests upon a common faith in a civil theology, largely composed of the principles of the Declaration of Independence, the Preamble to the Constitution, and the elaborated rights of the individual as found in the Constitution with its Bill of Rights.[32] All of this is housed within the concept of a rule of law, which promises fair, equal, and just treatment to all. Americans become, then, a " 'covenanting community' in which the commitment to freedom under law, having transcended the 'natural' bonds of race, religion, and class, itself takes on transcendent importance."[33] From the beginning, then, law for Americans was necessarily concerned with what can best be described as "religio-moral issues" and courts provided "a major arena for airing transcendental issues."[34] Sidney Mead, a historian of religion, has argued that Americans were adherents of a religion that "is essentially prophetic, which is to say that its ideals and aspirations stand in constant judgment over the passing shenanigans of the people, reminding them of the standards by which their current practices and those of their nation are ever being judged and found wanting."[35]

As Joseph Vining, a thoughtful legal scholar, has suggested, law within American culture can be most usefully perceived not in terms of science, economics, or even history, but rather of theology. First of all, lawyers and theologians tend to rely on "texts produced by hierarchical authorities." Second, for both professions, faith is a prerequisite; only then can understanding follow. This faith involves belief that human life has meaning and that it can be ordered to help individuals fulfill their destiny. Third, both studies encompass all of human life in the "effort to make sense of our experience and make statements that are consistent and understandable in light of it all." Finally, the parallels between the courtroom and the church are obvious, including the solemnity of both temples and the formality of the discourse between the supplicant "praying for relief" and the robed figures of priestly authority.[36]

To expand on Vining's first common characteristic—the existence of authoritative texts—the writing at the pinnacle of the civil religion's theological hierarchy is the Constitution. This document of fundamental law is unlike any other in that "it represents the lifeblood of the American nation, its supreme symbol and manifestation. It is so intimately welded to national existence that the two have become inseparable."[37] The Constitution is the official embodiment of the nation's values, which, when articulated, "provide an important part of the 'moral cohesion' that is the cement for our national community."[38] Supreme Court Justice Hugo L. Black went even further when he called the Constitution "my legal bible; its plan of our government is my plan and its destiny my destiny."[39] It binds the American people because they regard it as supreme and as having a capacity to answer the "most troubling national questions."[40]

This secular codification of fundamental law gains its predominant position because it flows from the mythical will of the whole people, the same way that the Bible represents the voice of God captured by His agents. Both texts contain most of the essentials of the theology and delineate the culture of believers. Priestly interpreters in both spheres rest their authority on their ability to extract meaning from the words and to draw conclusions in the form of judgments based upon the texts themselves. This task is far from a mechanical enterprise, for it involves the attempt to give moral structure to the world in which both the text and its interpreters live. As a rule of law seeks to define a culture, a society, and a world or cosmic view, it takes on a religious character. In drawing an analogy between a religious community and the American political community, one observer has said that the American constitutional text bears a close relationship to a sacred text in that the interpreter is charged with the responsibility of mediating "the past of the tradition with its present" for the purpose of infusing new life in the tradition. He adds that "for the American political community, the constitutional text is not (simply) a book of answers to particular questions. . . . It is, rather, a principal symbol, perhaps *the* principal symbol of fundamental aspirations of the tradition."[41]

Any interpretation is tentative and subject to change, for the community is afforded both room and encouragement to redefine itself. Others may interpret a constant search for the American character and national mission as evidence of self-doubt and insecurity, but such a search is revitalizing in that it forces Americans back to the basic principles that undergird their nation's foundation. As the founding generation so well realized, the nation was an experiment in the ability of very different people to find unity in a creed that respected individual differences. That generation saw in law a significant means to teach the lesson that national survival would depend on the people's ability to make that creed a practical reality. The Constitution has provided the arena for a people to find their unity in mutual respect as they "respond to the incessant prophetic call of the text"[42] in their continuing search for the liberty, equality, and justice promised by a rule of law.

What the concept of a civil religion does is widen the perspective so that what has usually been constricted by academic specialization can be seen in its cultural context. What makes the faith of Americans meaningful is its incorporation within the legal system in terms of the respect afforded the individual, the protection of basic rights, the recognition and toleration of diversity, and the provision for a unity that embraces all. The fundamental law establishes the parameters of the society and gives form, direction, and operative value to these elements of faith.

Both the civil religion and sectarian religions are based on theologies that establish transcendent standards by which to measure the acts of the faithful, but the most distinctive feature of the civil religion is its nonexclusive character. It, in fact, not only accommodates various private sectarian beliefs, it welcomes them as differences that do not compromise the essential equality of the individuals who make up the society. A primary function of the civil religion is to moderate the effect of sectarianism, and although all religions generally welcome converts, the civil religion rejects all boundaries and is potentially all-inclusive.

One, however, must be careful not to be seduced by a definition of "civil religion" as a distillation of Judeo-Christian beliefs that have become part of the nation's traditions over time.[43] To define "civil religion" as embodying the commonalities found in the country's dominant sectarian religions not only contradicts a core theological premise of the civil religion—its insistence that personal religious difference will not lead to exclusion—but also it trivializes and obscures the importance of the concept itself. Personal religion was to be excluded from the councils of government for the purpose of eliminating the potential for divisiveness that such religious differences inevitably would bring. The commitment of a majority of the people to certain sectarian religious symbols and practices cannot be controlling in a public faith structure.

As with other religions, the component parts of the theology of the American civil religion were forged into a whole within a relatively short time, in this instance in the latter quarter of the eighteenth century. Since that time when the theological core of the American civil religion was constructed, little has been added to it. Yet, during those years momentous change has taken place. Most of that change, as it relates to the equality of individuals comprising the society, however, has been premised upon its basic conformity with the civil religion's theological precepts.[44] This tendency to go forward by justifying the steps taken as a fulfillment of basic commitments long ago made gives the American people some common history, common identity, and common respect.

The basic theological principles are not so general that they lack any meaning or fail to provide a text that can be translated with some faithfulness to the original. For instance, take Thomas Jefferson's words in the Declaration, "All men are created equal." We know from human experience that not all persons are equally endowed with intelligence and material benefits. Were we God would we so create them? Or, less pretentiously, with our ability to allocate material benefits and our increasing ability to manipulate human matter, should we strive to achieve this goal? These are legitimate questions arising from the Declaration's text, and future generations may well take them quite seriously. Our history illustrates the way in which such fanciful questions of an earlier time can become real and demanding ones later.

To remain more faithful to Jefferson's text, clearly he was saying that all human beings are created with equal rights that their fellow creatures should respect and that government should protect. In Jefferson's time blacks were not considered the equal of whites, nor were women considered the equal of men. The problem, however, is not with the text but rather with the limitations of the times and of the translators of the text. Not all translators were equally circumscribed by such limitations. Abigail Adams warned her husband, John, of the rebellious potential of women who were denied the rights commanded by principles to which American males said they subscribed.[45] Many blacks as well wondered how their profound inequality could be supported by a text acknowledging that God had ordained a basic equality among all human beings. Such disparities lead us to a recognition that in the practice of any faith gaps exist between belief and action. Before any progress can be made in bridging the distance between the two, the faithful must perceive the gap. Inevitably, we more easily perceive our ancestors' failings than our own.

What we are dealing with, then, is not a changing American faith over time, but a remarkably consistent faith in which its practitioners contend with the task, first, of recognizing that gaps between faith and practice do exist, and, second, of attempting to close them. A nation founded by conscious political action that rests its continuing existence upon a set of principles incorporated in a constitutional order may seem fragile indeed, for survival depends upon its people keeping their faith. One might well expect that such a people could easily become cynical, hypocritical, complacent, or apathetic. When Americans could be so characterized, however, such attitudes have been exposed and condemned by fellow Americans in every imaginable literary and pictorial form. These critics ask no more than that their compatriots live up to the demands of their shared faith. In fact, most, if not all, internal criticism of American society is premised upon the critic calling attention to a discrepancy between belief and action. Challenges to the core beliefs themselves are indeed rare.

At times, these ever-present critics are successful in stirring the people to action.[46] As an illustration, the modern civil rights movement's success is in part explained by an identification of its aspirations with the civil theology. When Gunnar Myrdal, a Swedish social scientist, surveyed the condition of blacks in American society in the late 1930s and early 1940s, he found hope in what he called a spiritual consensus built around the ideas of dignity, equality, freedom, justice, and opportunity subscribed to by both "the rich and secure, out of pride and conservatism, and the poor and insecure, out of dire need." He concluded that the blacks and other disadvantaged groups "could not possibly have invented a system of political ideals which better corresponded to their interests." For Myrdal, these ideals constituted a creed that was "the cement in the structure of this great and disparate nation."[47] The ensuing civil rights movement was solidly anchored in the American creed. When Presidents John F. Kennedy and Lyndon B. Johnson sought to get the monumental Civil Rights Act of 1964 through Congress, their speeches were filled with references to the need for Americans to live up to the demands of their civil theology by making its benefits available to all.

These eras when creedal politics supplant interest-group politics are relatively rare, but the system does contain an ongoing institution that is at the heart of the civil religion—the United States Supreme Court. In recognizing and helping to close gaps between common belief and common practice, the Supreme Court has played a major role. The Court is the priestly interpreter of the holy writ, the one agency in government that has the assigned duty to respond to the claims of individuals that the rights they have been promised have not been realized. Those cases involving a claim of individual right interposed against governmental action are real-life dramas, in which seemingly trivial events are transformed "into narratives with meanings that touch our largest concerns as a people engaged in self-government under the law."[48] The Court's decisions reinforce a culture and speak to all about the integrity of the individual, the limits placed upon government, and how people should act.

In the process of writing opinions, the Court does far more than justify its decisions: it describes and defines American culture, it promotes unity, and it educates the people as to their responsibilities under the civil faith. All in all, the Court seeks to make the rule of law worthy of the faith a diverse people repose in it. This is as much a moral task as it is a legal one, and the Court has repeatedly insisted that it is the only agency that is both equipped and entitled to play the role of supreme priestly interpreter of the Constitution. In interpreting the holy writ, the Court not only describes, integrates, and preserves the law, it prioritizes, explicates, and then reinforces "the basic values . . . that make us a nation."[49] In its opinions the Court articulates and perpetuates "the ideals and aspirations that define the national character."[50] It explains both who we are and who we can be. As such, it maintains both the basic theology of the civil religion and the community it serves. As one longtime student of the Court has said, "it has remained true to its assumed role as our national conscience and our institutional common sense."[51] Another critic of the Court has defended judicial review as "one important way the American political community struggles to remain faithful to its" basic principles. That community, he continues, is one "of political-moral judgment" involving how people are to be treated and how their rights and liberties are to be secured.[52]

As any interpreter of the written word, the Supreme Court has considerable discretion; and in the task of interpreting, it is itself a creator. Precedent can, and at times should, be overruled, for the High Bench must enter into a dialogue with the past, not to accept its authority blindly but to inquire substantially into what has changed and what effect that change should have on the present ruling. In this dialogue with the past and with the advocates of the present, the Court explores "an enormous reservoir of intellectual and practical experience" and tends to make the law "a mode of communal self-education and self-constitution."[53] In their opinions, the justices constantly synthesize the old with the new, respecting tradition but reevaluating and reconstituting it in response to new problems. By summoning up the past and then reshaping it as they rationalize their decisions, they continually reconstruct the culture itself.

So, what follows is an attempt to draw out the Supreme Court's importance in American culture. Throughout this study the terms "conservative" and "liberal," as applied to both justices and Courts, have been avoided, as have been lamentations about the shift of the High Bench from one position to the other. This rejection of an analytical mode that characterizes so much of the literature on the Court is deliberate. Liberalism and conservatism, although hardly sharp and precise terms when applied to the judiciary, are used to polarize and separate, to overlook common ground and to focus upon differences. What the prevailing analytical mode overlooks, this book has sought to rescue in the belief that it illuminates a significant role that the High Bench has played and continues to play in nurturing a national identity.

This is not to say that all justices at all times were protective of individual rights and of a national unity that would overcome local particularism. Nor is it contended that the approach taken here embraces all the important decisions that constitute the respective canons of constitutional law and constitutional history. What is being argued is that, first, the Supreme Court viewed union as a precondition for the protection of individual rights; second, that from the very beginning the justices saw their role in terms of safeguarding these rights; third, that the current protection of individual rights builds upon a long, evolutionary process; and finally, that this emphasis throughout its history has made the Court an increasingly significant unifying force within the pluralistic society. To say that "the Supreme Court has established itself as a central institution for the self-conscious and authoritative reconstitution of our language, culture, and community" may not be an exaggeration.[54] Some of this work has been done quite consciously by the justices, and generally in both their decisions and their rhetoric they have lent credibility to their role as high priests of the American civil religion.

Just as the Court deals with legal texts and transforms them in the process, so, too, does any writer dealing with the public work of the justices. The quotations may be accurate, but the context into which they are put and the meaning extracted from them are new creations for which the author must accept responsibility. The hope, of course, is that what is created will strike a responsive chord and invite challenge and further discussion about the role of law in the shaping of American identity and culture.

"IN THE BEGINNING WAS THE WORD," 1620–1791

At the heart of American nationhood is an intractable religious core that has perplexed observers. In a country where official policy is to separate religion from the affairs of state, government and religion seem hopelessly blended. Not only does the great seal of the United States picture an eye that represents the all-seeing God, but it also contains the Latin inscription translated as "He has favored our undertaking." The coins of the realm are imprinted with the words "In God We Trust." Chaplains minister to legislatures, and presidents have always sprinkled their formal addresses with liberal references to God. Although strict separationists lament what they see as outmoded historical vestiges, and religious fundamentalists try to seize the opening to mold the society in their image, most Americans do not seem to be uncomfortable with the existing situation.

What is even more significant, however, is the way in which "a country that, despite its arbitrary territorial limits, could read its destiny in its landscape, and a population that, despite its bewildering mixture of race and creed, could believe in something called an American mission, and could invest that patent fiction with all the emotional, spiritual, and intellectual appeal of a religious quest."[1] The seedbed for these ideas can be found in Puritan thought and the colonists' experience in the New World.

The pervasive use of covenants and compacts, the emphasis upon the written word, the imagery of an errand into the wilderness for both God and his chosen people, and the rhetorical mode of blending censure for backsliding with promise of a glorious destiny are all elements of Puritanism that survived to become important components of an emerging American identity. Part of this heritage was the jeremiad, or, as the New England Puritans at times labeled it, the political sermon. In these sermons the faithful were condemned for their sins but then reminded of their special destiny. This self-critical mode of rhetoric moved beyond the pulpit and became a tool of American writers and speakers seeking to recall Americans to their mission and their ideals.

In fact, as the Eastern seaboard was further populated the concept of a chosen people on a special mission expanded to include all white Americans. As the controversy with Great Britain developed, ministers working from theological premises of revelation and divine sanction and secular figures, influenced by the Enlightenment and working from premises of human potential, reason, and the rule of law, reached the same conclusions.[2] Surveying the published sermons of ministers in the pre-Revolutionary period, one writer has concluded that "had ministers been the only spokesmen of the rebellion, had Jefferson, the Adamses, and [James] Otis never appeared in print, the political thought of the Revolution would have followed almost exactly the same line—with perhaps a little more mention of God, but certainly no less of John Locke."[3] Public discourse easily blended what seemed to be antithetical approaches in a rhetoric that mixed religious and secular voices. "An ideology of dissent that linked religious with civil tyranny created a common ground upon which rationalists and evangelicals alike could join to justify their opposition to England."[4] Some would call this strange mixture "peculiarly American."[5] Although battles had to be fought against sectarian religion, religion itself was an ally of the American cause. Even to Thomas Paine, the religious skeptic, the American Revolution was an event of no less than cosmic significance.[6]

Why such diverse streams of thought converge is in part explained by a single shared assumption that is basically religious—human dignity. Beginning with the Protestant Reformation, the idea that human beings were created in God's image takes on new and significant meaning. Without the need of any intermediary, persons could now find their way to heaven by reading God's word. Furthermore, humans could covenant with God and enter into agreements to found both churches and governments. By birthright, then, they had inalienable rights.[7]

This fundamental assumption about human dignity was central to both Protestant and Enlightenment thought, and when confronted with challenges to these rights, thinkers in both arenas responded in similar fashion. In fact, one could be insulated within the theological debate of eighteenth-century America and still learn a great deal about democracy, freedom, and the dangers of authoritarian control.[8] Furthermore, in the public arena religious and secular thinkers could be comfortable following the same path. Although Enlightenment thought about human perfectibility conflicted sharply with a religious view of inherent human sinfulness, the increasing personalization of sectarian religion minimized a potential conflict in the public arena during the revolutionary era. Furthermore, political leaders saw churches as schools in which the faithful could be educated to overcome their arrogance and selfishness, to develop concern for others, and to be ready to accept public responsibility.[9] Civic virtue, which republican theorists would so heavily emphasize, more readily sprang from sectarian religious training than from any other source.

Political leaders readily embraced religious terminology. In fact, one critic has suggested that they realized that the route to success was consciously to don the garb of the cleric.[10] This conclusion may go too far, but within the public discourse

of the time there was ready recourse to religious terminology, analogy, and justification. As the Revolution approached, the momentous step would have to be
reconciled with cosmic intentions. The old Puritan errand into the wilderness
would be redefined both to justify the break with Great Britain and to chart a new
mission.[11]

The Declaration of Independence, the first of the seminal documents underlying the nation's founding, accomplishes a number of purposes. In addition to sev-
ering ties to the king and presenting the case for independence to world opinion,
it seeks to constitute Americans as "one people" and outlines basic premises that
are the heart of the American creed and of the emerging American nation. These
premises are spelled out in the second paragraph:

> We hold these truths to be self-evident, that all men are created equal,
> that they are endowed by their Creator with certain unalienable
> Rights, that among these are Life, Liberty and the pursuit of Happi-
> ness. That to secure these rights, Governments are instituted among
> Men, deriving their just powers from the consent of the governed.[12]

What is so significant here is the primary focus on the God-given rights of the
individual.[13]

Despite the subsequent and at times overpowering worry about the threat that
government itself could pose to these rights, a clear obligation is placed upon
government to protect them. The colonials' recent experience was with government as oppressor; could it ever become the ensurer of those rights? Hope that
the protector would not become the violator was found in the premise that such
governments would be created by the consent of the people, who themselves
would be vigilant in safeguarding their own rights. Yet the dangers inherent in the
ability of majorities to override the interests of minorities were recognized. This
perception led republican theorists to believe that no less than a regeneration of
human nature was necessary. A government that rested upon the people required
citizens who would be publicly virtuous and place the public interest above their
private interests. How else could republican government, charged with protecting
the rights of all individuals, survive?[14]

This dilemma, posed at the outset of American national existence, would plague
political thinkers and actors as they coped with the task of erecting new governments. They recognized the uniqueness of their opportunity; they could draw
upon their rich and extensive colonial experience and what guidance they could
find in Western political thought and history, but in the end they would have to
work through their own solutions and hopefully profit from their own errors.

What was immediately clear was that the key premises of the Declaration had
set out the essentials of an American creed or civil theology, with its concepts of
equality, liberty, and popular consent.[15] In the act of inventing a nation and imbuing it with tradition,[16] Americans defined their character as political. They were

embarking upon the uncharted seas of republicanism, testing whether the principles of government by consent and of individual rights could form a lasting union.
Coping with modernity, where the old ties of the past had been dissolved, they
had to create new ties. A nation that had none of the attributes hitherto associated
with that designation, except for discrete geographical space, based its existence
on a creed. This is why "unAmerican" can carry a meaning that "unFrench" or
"unEnglish" never can. In this revolutionary environment, the American civil
religion was born.[17] It defined the American as a political animal sharing with
others a common faith with transcendent standards.[18]

A recent scholar summed up this religion as follows: "Theological doctrines of
equality, liberty, and justice—all derived from the sacred power and authority of
the divine Creator—were . . . integrated into a civil theology with deep biblical
roots." He then continued, characterizing the theology as "a rather loosely organized set of ideals and assumptions that have provided important religious resources
in shaping American self-understanding as nation. These elements create a theological vocabulary for achieving ideological consensus and for conducting ideological conflicts."[19] To call the creed a theology is not inappropriate, for this civil
religion brings with it the things we would expect of a sectarian faith: personal
commitment, sacred symbols and places, rituals, holy days, prophets, priests, saints,
and martyrs.[20] At times this creed so animates the political process that action is
taken to remedy the gaps between belief and practice, which one writer has characterized as periods of "creedal passion."[21] It also serves a primarily religious purpose by uniting the faithful around a common core of belief, no matter how
diverse they otherwise are.

That a civil religion, or a religion of the republic, was consciously created during the Revolutionary era is clear.[22] Religious pluralism was an incontrovertible
fact, and although many secular leaders felt that the churches were useful or even
indispensable in the moral training of republican citizens, the very fact of pluralism
meant that no sect could dominate and that sectarian religion would have to survive without governmental support. There was some local support of religious
establishments that extended into the nineteenth century, but the future of exclusively voluntary support for churches was clearly etched in the period of the Revolution. This development was the inevitable result of viewing religious freedom as
a right of the individual and religious institutions as the product of individual
consent and commitment.[23] The tendency has been to look back on the religious
pluralism of the eighteenth century and underestimate its importance. In fact, this
pluralism made toleration and individual religious freedom a necessity. That the
religiously different could agree on so much else provided hope for the founding
of a nation. If such fundamental differences could be accommodated, there was
hope that any other differences could be as well.

If traditional religion could not provide the glue to hold a diverse population together, then a new glue would have to be formulated. In the process of national creation, American political leaders used religious imagery as they interpreted current affairs and their history in terms of a cosmic plan. The Creator had been preparing a chosen people for the challenges that lay ahead. The people had been given rights; now could they live up to their obligations under them? Americans were embarking upon an experiment that would provide a model with worldwide implications. Americans tended to read their history in the light of this interpretation and to sacralize it. George Washington, who would come to be viewed as the new Moses leading his people to the Promised Land, emphasized this mission: "The preservation of the sacred fire of liberty and the destiny of the republican model of government are justly considered, perhaps, as deeply, as finally, staked on the experiment intrusted to the hands of the American people."[24]

In fact, Americans would become obsessed with their past, seeing it as the binding factor in their unity. Despite the lament of critics that Americans are ignorant of the specifics of their history, no country in the world has so celebrated its past. Nowhere else are there so many signs and plaques calling the traveler's attention to a historical site or personage. No nation has so consistently displayed its history on its postage stamps and coins as proud emblems of its identity or deified the political leaders who struggled with the problems of government in the wake of the Revolution. All of this speaks to the constant need to discover and then reaffirm an identity, a trait that still seems particularly American.

In the era of the Revolution, symbols[25] of the new nation had to be manufactured. The first and perhaps most enduring one was the flag, which was officially adopted on June 14, 1777. The American flag was and is more than a national emblem; as any useful symbol, its meaning is flexible, but its association with "the great faith to which we are born"[26] is not accidental. It is the preeminent symbol of the American civil religion.

Although such symbols were and are important in the American civil religious structure, the American civil religion that emerged from the Revolutionary period found its most significant transcendental reference point in the rule of law. Although law was expected to provide order, it was also seen as embodying essential principles of justice, liberty, and equality.[27] As Tom Paine had suggested, American colonials who earlier had found their unity in the Crown could now find it in their fidelity to the law.[28] The law provided not only the means to settle disputes but more significantly a meaning system that religiously diverse people could accept. When judges, as the agents of the rule of law, justified their decisions by talking of purpose, fundamental principles, equality, liberty, justice, and destiny, they would institutionalize this civil religious meaning system and educate new generations within it.[29]

As the Revolution was being fought, Americans were working to define themselves and forge some bonds of unity within the mechanism of the Second Continental Congress. This body would not gain legal status until the adoption of the Articles of Confederation in 1781, but in the meantime it acted in the name of all the colonies as it waged war and sought independence. That Second Congress suggested that the former colonies draft constitutions to put their governments on a legal footing. Eventually eleven colonies complied; Connecticut and Rhode Island simply modified their colonial charters. So began a seminal period of constitution making that would run through the framing and adoption of the federal constitution of 1787.[30]

Americans were well prepared to begin this process because of their colonial antecedents and recent struggle with British authorities. They had long asserted their rights based upon provisions of their colonial charters and their understanding of the unwritten British constitution.[31] The controversy leading up to the Revolution had conclusively demonstrated to them the problems inherent in a largely unwritten constitution. Its true nature, they felt, had been too easily corrupted by self-seeking ministers of the British crown. An emphasis on the written word, going back to the Bible, was deeply rooted in the American mind. Their new frames of government would be written, and they would seek to protect the freedom of the people by placing effective governing power in the legislative branch of the new governments. Worried that any government could be corrupted, they sought to check the governing power through frequent elections and an insistence upon individual rights.

These documents are significant in the form that they generally took. They tended to merge general political ideas and purposes and a delineation of rights with a description of the government created. In fact, the New York constitution used the Declaration of Independence itself as its preamble.[32] This tended to make much clearer the idea of the constitution as social compact. It also suggests a relationship between the Declaration and the Constitution of 1787 that makes the earlier document an integral part of the American constitutional tradition.

Most of these constitutions were framed by the new state legislatures and proclaimed in effect. If a constitution was to be fundamental law that placed an effective check on the government it created, there were real deficiencies in this early constitution-making procedure. Massachusetts provided the model that satisfied the theoretical demands of distinguishing the constitution from the ordinary work of the legislature. The first document drafted by the Massachusetts legislature was sent to town meetings for approval. A negative response forced reconsideration of a process that had already improved upon the common practice in other states. What the legislature devised was a special convention elected by the people for the sole purpose of writing the constitution. Its work would then be submitted to the citizens for their approval. In 1780, Massachusetts citizens ratified a state constitution drafted under this process.

What made the new model so compelling was its conformity with the notion that a constitution was higher law to which the established lawmaking authority had to conform. The constitution was legitimated in this superior position because it was the product of the sovereign people. In time, the Massachusetts practice became the norm.

As the states established their constitutions, the Second Continental Congress worked toward the construction of a national charter of government. Despite the ongoing war, there was understandable reluctance on the part of the individual states to entrust much power to a national government. The result institutionalized the Continental Congress system and established a confederation within which the states were recognized as sovereign entities. The drafters of the Articles of Confederation did label the new nation "the United States of America" and did seem to understand how powers should be distributed between state and confederate governments.[33] However, a single organ of government, Congress, was created that had no power to tax and no power to enforce its authority. Furthermore, any change in the Articles required the unanimous consent of all the states. Even before the Articles went into effect in 1781, critics questioned the Union's survival based, as it was, on such a weak foundation.

The war with Great Britain would be won, but the difficulty of waging it revealed the weakness of the central government under the Articles. In fact, national constitutional reform attracted those patriots who actively took up the national cause against Great Britain and had to endure the inability of the government to provide them with effective support. Those Americans who came of age during the Revolutionary struggle and identified themselves as Americans rather than Virginians or New Yorkers found real problems with a central government that, in fact, confirmed the primacy of local loyalties. The Articles had done little to create a national community.

Historians have long argued over whether national existence was truly threatened in the 1780s or whether nationalists exaggerated the situation to advance their own economic and political goals.[34] In the final analysis one's reaction must be based on the attractiveness of the concept that Americans constituted a single nation. The Articles had permitted the states to respond to the will of their citizens. But one could argue that even this governmental unit was too large and that truly responsible popular government was only possible within a small, well-knit community. Where one goes from this starting point is a matter of commitment to the larger grouping, for at each subsequent level some compromise and loss of control is extracted.

Although each state had its own distinctive history, the struggle with Great Britain had brought Americans together and broken down some of the old barriers. To argue that adjustments in the Articles could have provided the cement for the new nation seems naive. That charter of government contained the seeds of its own demise; it had little potential for winning the loyalty of the people, and it was too much the product of worrying about the past than of attempting to chart the future. If those who fought for a stronger central government were motivated by their own self-interest, so be it. Those who look for purity of motive in human action are bound to be frustrated. Obviously, in a largely agrarian society, some groups and interests would be served better by a continental union than others. But in time those men who sought to invest their time, energy, and reputation in the task of creating a nation were to be revered as founding fathers.

If state governments had acted as responsible partners in a common enterprise, the Articles might have survived. That, however, was no more likely than was the reformation of human nature that republican theorists sought. Political communities are like other communities; their very nature creates insiders and outsiders. Was, then, the political community the state or the nation? That was the key question of the 1780s. When the primary individual right, that of property, seemed under continual threat from state legislatures, with their ready issuance of paper money and their erratic economic policies, liberty seemed to be degenerating into license. Certainly the move to strengthen the central government was in part motivated by a desire to check state action that seemed detrimental to the property right. But a fundamental belief in its primacy among individual rights did not divide the society. Thomas Jefferson, in the Declaration, had substituted "the pursuit of happiness" for "property" in John Locke's formulation of the natural rights of man, but this change was hardly intended to downgrade the individual's property right. Few people felt that they could pursue happiness in the absence of legal protection for their property.[35]

The major achievement of Congress under the Articles was the establishment of a national land policy. Maryland had delayed ratification of the Articles by insisting that states, which under their colonial charters had land claims extending to the west, cede those claims to the new government. Virginia, the last holdout, finally acceded, thus giving to the new government the power to deal with the continental domain. By means of a series of land ordinances involving the Northwest Territory, Congress established the process by which new states, carved out of the area, could enter the Union on a equal footing with the older ones. The significance of this start cannot be overestimated. In the new American continental union, there would be no room for colonial dependencies, only equal states.

Aside from this lasting achievement, the new government under the Articles was foundering. It had little international respect, as its diplomats were unable to promise that the states would keep any bargains struck by the representatives of the confederate government. In part, the nationalists were able to grab the initiative because their potential opponents had vacated the national field, content with the bargain struck in the Articles.[36] And when localists realized that the confederation was under serious attack, they were placed in the politically untenable position of trying to defend an increasingly unsatisfactory status quo.

When the Philadelphia Convention met in 1787, with the delegates chosen by the state legislatures and with the blessing of the Congress, most of the members were charged only with the task of amending the Articles. Earlier attempts to give even limited commercial and taxing powers to Congress had foundered because of the requirement that unanimous consent was needed for any change in the Articles. Could a convention specifically called for the purpose of recommending amendments expect a different fate for its proposals? Anticipating a negative response, the Virginia delegation seized the initiative with a proposed plan of government that scrapped the Articles altogether and began anew. Such a bold move seemed necessary, for, both in public and private writing, many of the most prominent framers saw the fate of the Union and republican government hanging in the balance. Despite some grumbling, the delegates proceeded with their task of erecting a new structure of government.

At the outset, the members agreed on two points of procedure that would have great significance: the secrecy of the proceedings and the ability to reinspect and change any decision. The first rule permitted the members of the Philadelphia Convention to work relatively free from public scrutiny. The second rule allowed the delegates to change their positions and compromise their differences. What made secrecy palatable was the fact that any product of the Convention would indeed be made public in its entirety and widely discussed. Along with installing George Washington as the Convention's president, the two rules did much to keep the members working together toward a common goal.

In a little less than four months the delegates had put together a new framework of government. By the terms of its final article, the new constitution would go into effect when it was ratified by nine of the thirteen states. In a resolution passed on the Convention's final day, September 17, 1787, the constitution was to be sent to Congress, which in turn was asked to submit the document to the states for ratification. Furthermore, the suggested procedure called for special state conventions convened for the exclusive purpose of passing upon the new constitution. Although this procedure was obviously chosen to bypass entrenched state legislative interests that saw their existing power threatened, it also sought to base the new republican government on the people's consent. When Congress dutifully acceded to the request of the Convention, it put in process a movement that would lead to its own extinction.

Although the text of the draft constitution focused on what government could and could not do, the new frame of government rested, in part, upon basic notions concerning the relationship between the state and the individual. Although much of the wording was carried over from the Articles of Confederation, the constitution created a government that was quite different—a unique mixture of the elements of a confederation with those of a national government. Although the Constitution recognized and incorporated the preexisting states within the new

Union, it placed limitations upon their authority in favor of that Union. The clear thrust of the document was toward nationalism, not federalism, and toward a national community, not an assemblage of state communities.

Central governing power was separated in three, distinct branches—the legislative, executive, and judicial. Each branch was given checks and balances in relation to the others. This complicated system was designed to limit power and ensure, as much as any framework could, that the public interest would be served. If a new species of republican could not be created, then perhaps government could be so structured to restrain and impede self-interest in behalf of the public good. Corrupt executive or judicial officials could be removed from office by the House and Senate through impeachment and conviction. The president could veto legislation, and the Congress would have to pass it again with an extraordinary majority to make it law. The chief executive could nominate high executive officials and judges, but they could only receive their office with the consent of the Senate. And one house of the legislature would have to receive the concurrence of the other before any act could be passed. And so on. In fact, the obstacles placed in the way of effective government led some observers to conclude that the proposed government was unworkable. But its lack of efficiency was the price extracted to ensure that government operated without becoming a threat to the individual.

Speaking of the individual, one of the distinguishing features of the Constitution, in contrast to the Articles, was that it operated directly upon individuals. A relationship was thus created between the new government and the people themselves that did not exist under the Articles. The people had rights, responsibilities, duties, and burdens. As electors of the members of the House of Representatives, they were drawn into the orbit of the new government and would thereby give implicit consent for the passage of laws affecting them. Who could vote was left to the states to decide; therefore any democratization of the franchise in the states would make the new voters part of the electoral constituency of Congress as well. Although senators were elected by the state legislatures, nothing in the Constitution prevented the people from directing the choices of their state legislature by popular vote.

A general provision for equality or equal protection was not written into the Constitution, but many provisions seemed directed toward that goal. Payment was provided for members of the House and Senate, which meant that there would be no preexisting barrier of wealth that would disqualify potential candidates. Only requirements of age and residency were imposed. Naturalized citizens were eligible for all offices, except that of president. Congress was given the power and responsibility to treat residents of the various states equally with uniform naturalization and bankruptcy laws. Neither the United States nor any state could confer any titles of nobility, thereby preventing the formation of an inequality of status. Each state citizen was entitled "to all Privileges and Immunities of Citizens in the several

States." This latter language was carried over from the Articles, but as incorporated in a new, more potentially powerful structure of government, its promise was much greater. What the clause promised was the effective unification of the American people. Over time, the Constitution's interpreters would repeat again and again "that no provision in the Constitution has tended so strongly to constitute the citizens of the United States one people as this" one has.[37]

Finally, and among the most significant provisions, no religious test for federal office was permitted.[38] This prohibition, contrary to many state requirements, was obviously designed to enable all, despite sharp religious difference, to serve in the federal government and to identify with it. Equality was not only a principle but a necessity; differences would be harmonized by reducing their practical effect in terms of a common citizenship. Federal officeholders were asked to swear or affirm their loyalty to the Constitution, "but no religious Test shall ever be required."[39] The connective "but" seems to imply that the oath supporting the Constitution was a substitute for the traditional religious oath. If this is true, then there was a conscious attempt to have this pledged support of the Constitution displace the religious base for a commitment to public service. In any event, this pledge of loyalty had the effect of bringing religiously diverse officeholders into a single community.

In addition to these intimations of equality in the Constitution, protections of individual liberty were written into the document. Remember that the Declaration of Independence saw responsible government as a protector of, not as a threat to, individual liberty. The framers implicitly acknowledged that liberty had been endangered by the actions of state governments. From the time of framing forward, there has been concern that in a system of dual governments, protection from one might have to come at the hands of the other. The Constitution, then, restricted not only the new central government, but also state governments, from passing a bill of attainder (an act of legislative punishment) or an ex post facto law (an act making prior innocent conduct criminal). In addition, states could not impair the obligation of contracts, a prohibition obviously designed to give new federal protection to the holder of property. At the national level, the Constitution protected the rights of habeas corpus and trial by jury. It also tightly defined treason and limited punishment to the life of the person convicted.

As sent to the states for ratification, the Constitution contained both protections of individual rights and implications of equality, but the most significant compromise in this area concerned the institution of slavery.[40] The text did not contain the terms "slave" or "slavery" and consistently it alluded to slaves as persons. This wording was deliberate, as James Madison, speaking for other delegates at the convention as well, made clear when he said that he "thought it wrong to admit in the Constitution the idea that there could be property in men." Consciously seeking to give the Constitution a moral dimension, the Virginian protested against a twenty-year ban on congressional authority to suppress the slave trade. Arguing that in the interim period the damage would be done, he said that such a delay "will be more dishonorable to National character than to say nothing about it in the Constitution."[41] In the Constitution, then, slaves were persons, but definitely a special variety of human beings. They were "other persons" implicitly not free and distinguished from those who were bound to service for a term of years. One of these persons counted only as three-fifths of a whole person for purposes of representation and direct taxation.[42] Should such persons "held to Service or Labour in one State" escape to another state, they "shall be delivered up on Claim of the Party to whom such Service or Labour may be due."[43] In addition, the federal government was granted the authority to "suppress Insurrections," a power intended, in part, to provide federal assistance in suppressing slave rebellions.[44]

On the other side of the ledger, Congress was granted the power to abolish the slave trade beginning in 1808. When the final vote was taken on this provision, the four dissenting states, which included Virginia, were opposed not to banning the slave trade but to the delay in its interdiction. But even here the language read: "The Migration or Importation of such Persons as any of the States now existing shall think proper to admit, shall not be prohibited by the Congress prior to the Year one thousand eight hundred and eight."[45] This provision was cited by those who later sought to find some counterweight to the Constitution's condoning of slavery. Furthermore, the Constitution made the Union and the creed upon which it was built an ideal that would eventually lead to the emancipation of the slaves.

A national constitution that did not accommodate the interests of slave owners would have been an impossibility. If—as William Lloyd Garrison, the abolitionist, claimed later—the Constitution was a pact with the devil because of this accommodation, the strongest opponents of slavery saw no other way to provide for a more effective union. Clearly, in regard to what was commonly referred to as the fugitive slave clause, the Constitution sought to afford some protection to a property right in slaves. But beyond this point the fundamental law did not go. So, later both supporters and opponents of slavery found in the Constitution and its amendments evidence to reach opposing conclusions about the Constitution and slavery.[46]

The Constitution's judicial article was the shortest and least suggestive of the future course of constitutional development. James Madison wanted to write into the article an establishment of federal trial courts, but he and his supporters had to settle for a discretionary power in Congress to establish such courts. So, the Constitution vested the judicial power in a Supreme Court and such lesser courts as Congress chose to establish. Federal judges were to hold their offices "during good Behavior," which in fact meant for life. They were, of course, not exempt from the impeachment authority lodged in Congress. Federal jurisdiction was then detailed, and it included what has become known as diversity jurisdiction, that is, authority to hear a case when the contending parties are citizens of different states. The Supreme Court was given original jurisdiction only when a state was a party or when a case involved the representative of a foreign government. In all other instances, the Court's power was as a court of appeal, and in this arena Congress had the power to define the limits. In all criminal cases, a jury trial was guaranteed; and in regard to a charge of treason further protections were stipulated.

Although the checks and balances are easy to discern in the other branches, they are not in the judicial branch. As constitutionally explicated, that branch consists of a Supreme Court with potentially large appellate jurisdiction and limited original jurisdiction. Judges are appointed for life with salaries that cannot be diminished, thus providing for an independence found in no other federal office.

We might pause for a moment to reflect on life tenure in a society that believed in frequent elections and the need to hold decision makers politically responsible. Clearly life tenure was designed to ensure a rule of law freed from political pressure. Life tenure was a recognition of the cost of such independence. To so insulate decision makers from the political process seems dangerous, but judges were perceived as having special obligations under a rule of law. Both Thomas Jefferson and James Madison realized that, if the political branches responded too quickly to impassioned majorities insensitive to individual rights, the only hope for protection had to come from the judiciary.

Yet James Madison had been a reluctant convert to judicial review, which is premised generally upon a constitution conceived in legal rather than political terms.[47] Madison initially viewed a constitution as a political document to structure institutions. In the absence of a structure that, in part, would be self-corrective, constitutional commands would be no more than "parchment rules." As he said about the separation of powers, written admonitions were of limited value and separation was ensured by the document's "contriving the interior structure of the government, as that its several constituent parts may, by their mutual relations, be the means of keeping each other in their proper places."[48]

In so defending the Constitution, Madison suppressed his disappointment that some key provisions that he had proposed had not found their way into the finished document. He would have preferred to create a governmental structure that would have given the national legislature the power to invalidate "all state laws whatsoever." Second, he would have joined the president with members of the Supreme Court in a Council of Revision to review both federal and state laws. These measures, Madison felt, would limit the threat to individual liberty from both state and federal legislatures and protect the interests of the Union. These were political solutions to perennial problems, which the Convention rejected in favor of a legal solution when it stipulated that the Constitution, the laws made thereunder, and treaties "shall be the supreme Law of the Land," a directive that was to bind state as well as federal judiciaries.[49] The Convention itself, then, gave to the Constitution a legal status. This did not mean that the separation of powers and checks and balances were completely legalized; in fact there would be a reluctance on the part of the federal judiciary to get involved in what it would often refer to as political matters. But the potential for such involvement was present from the start.

Without judicial review, meaning the authority of the Court to pass on the constitutionality of legislative and executive action, the Court had no real check on the other branches. The limited discussion of judicial review at the Convention indicated that a number of delegates assumed that the Court would have such power, though many conceived of it solely as a means to defend the separation of powers.[50]

Some precedents for judicial review existed at the state level, although the supremacy of the legislative branches there made the questioning of statutes hazardous. A future Supreme Court justice, James Iredell, who had been involved in just such a case challenging the authority of the state legislature in North Carolina, saw judicial review as a logical deduction from a constitutional system. If an act of the legislature is unconstitutional, he said, "judges, consistently with their duties, could not carry it into effect."[51] In defending the Constitution in New York during the ratification contest, Alexander Hamilton called the judiciary "the least dangerous to the political rights of the constitution,"[52] because it had neither the power of the sword nor of the purse. Life tenure, he continued, was necessary to ensure the independence of the judicial branch, which, at times, would have to stand against the actions of other branches that threatened constitutional guarantees and the liberties of the people. Although Article III itself contains no specific provision authorizing judicial review, the deduction of the power from the text of the Constitution was nonetheless well recognized by both friend and foe of the new framework of government. What the Constitution clearly did was codify higher law and establish a single court at the apex of the nation's legal system.

Much of the Constitution's final wording is attributable to the Committee of Style and Arrangement and especially Gouverneur Morris. He wrote the Preamble, which was the only concession to the view that a well-drafted framework of government should acknowledge the purposes for which it was devised. The Preamble does summarize well the general ends of government that the founding generation had in mind. Also, it firmly restates the contractual nature of government and rests its claim on the sovereignty of the people. The Preamble reads as follows:

> WE THE PEOPLE of the United States, in Order to form a more perfect Union, establish Justice, insure domestic Tranquility, provide for the common defence, promote the general Welfare, and secure the Blessings of Liberty to ourselves and our Posterity, do ordain and establish this Constitution for the United States of America.

This Preamble, which would in time be memorized by schoolchildren, provides, as does the Declaration, a set of dynamic principles by which citizens could measure the actions of their government. It invites personal identification with the document itself, as it seeks to attract the loyalty of the citizens. The contrast with the Articles is indeed stark, for the Articles began with a recitation of the states agreeing to the subsequent terms of the "perpetual Union." Although the Constitution contains many of the same provisions found in the Articles, those very provisions take on new meaning and importance within the framework of a constitution that can only take effect when the people, in special ratifying conventions, make it their own. That the people are partners in a common enterprise is what the ratification process is designed to confirm.

Notice that the people, to achieve their stated purposes, not only establish the Constitution but ordain it as well. Although "establish" and "ordain" could be viewed as synonyms, the Committee of Style sought to eliminate redundancies in favor of precision and economy. Therefore, the use of the verb "ordain" should be read in its primary sense of investing religious authority. The Constitution, then, from its very formulation can be viewed as both a secular and a religious document.

Although the main text of the Constitution is often conveyed in authoritarian terms, it contains little in the way of specific directions as, for instance, how certain conferred powers are to be executed. In a very real sense, the Constitution "establishes a trust, placing complete confidence in others to do what should be done." In providing an authoritative text, it establishes both the roles and the basic terms for communication by constituting "a rhetorical community, working by rhetorical processes that it has established but can no longer control."[53]

The Constitution's general language gave the proposed fundamental law an unfinished character, which, when coupled with provisions for its amendment by the people, seemed to fit the community it was designed to serve especially well. That new national community was largely self-defining, and the Constitution provided the parameters within which that process could continue.

Self-styled Federalists, who appropriated this less than accurate appellation in urging the adoption of the Constitution, had the tactical advantage of proposing a ready alternative to the Articles. Ratification at first came easy, as three states adopted the plan unanimously and two others by decisive margins in the space of a little over a month. A union without the key states of Massachusetts, New York, and Virginia, however, would hardly be a viable entity, and in each of these states ratification was sharply contested.

Opponents who worried about the power lodged in the new government seized upon the absence of a bill of rights as a fundamental deficiency. Because Congress would be able to pass all laws "necessary and proper" under its delegated powers, did this authority not pose a real threat to the liberties of the people?

Realizing that they had found a vulnerable spot, the so-called Anti-Federalists seized upon this objection to funnel through it their anxiety about the expanded powers of the new central government. The matter of a bill of rights had come up near the end of the Philadelphia Convention, and the proposal to add such a bill had been unanimously rejected by the delegates. Now the Federalists were forced to justify that decision. They argued that, unlike the states where bills of rights were quite proper, the new federal government had only specifically delegated powers and therefore posed no threat to individual rights. But with congressional authority to pass laws that were "necessary and proper," that argument seemed disingenuous. A second major argument stressed the dangers that a specification of rights could involve. Such a list might not be all-inclusive, thus leaving the implication that nonlisted rights were unprotected.

By seizing upon the absence of a bill of rights in the Constitution, the Anti-Federalists had a popular issue that could sabotage the drive for ratification. Arguing that the state conventions had the choice only of ratifying or not ratifying the Constitution, Federalists in a number of states deflected the opposition by agreeing that a list of suggested amendments to the new Constitution accompany the state's ratification. James Madison had argued with Thomas Jefferson about the desirability and efficacy of such a listing of rights. Jefferson believed that with such rights incorporated in the Constitution there was hope that a learned and independent judiciary might be able to protect the individual.[54] Facing this ground swell, Madison accepted the idea of such a bill and gave his word in the Virginia ratifying convention that, if elected to the new Congress, he would work to remedy the defect. This strategy paid off in Virginia and in other states as well, and the Constitution was ratified. With the expected election of George Washington as president, the new government convened in New York in 1789.

Those friends of the Constitution who had seen it through the perils of the ratification process were less than enthusiastic about amending it. In the press of more urgent business, James Madison insisted upon keeping faith with the promises he and other supporters had made. He argued that with such provisions written into the Constitution

> independent tribunals of justice will consider themselves in a peculiar manner the guardians of those rights; they will be an impenetrable bulwark against every assumption of power in the Legislative or Executive; they will be naturally led to resist every encroachment upon rights expressly stipulated for in the constitution by the declaration of rights.[55]

Culling through the suggested amendments, many of which were attempts to limit federal power in behalf of the states, Madison overrode the apathy of his colleagues and proposed a bill of rights. As he sought to prepare a bill for inclusion in the federal constitution, Madison realized that such a move could silence the lingering Anti-Federalist protest about the new power at the center without really limiting the potential energy of the new government. Despite the political strategy involved, Madison devoted himself to the task and sought to protect individual rights as much as words on paper could.

One of the Federalist arguments that sought to counter the absence of a bill of rights maintained that the real threat to individual liberty came from the states, not from the new federal creation with its limited powers. And six of the thirteen states had no listing of individual rights in their constitutions. Central to his endeavor, Madison thought, was a blanket restriction on all states in favor of certain rights of the people. Because of varied wording and the absence of protection in certain states and because the Constitution had already placed certain restrictions upon the states in favor of individual liberty, such as prohibiting bills of attainder and ex post facto laws, Madison proposed the following amendment: "No State shall violate the equal rights of conscience, or the freedom of the press, or the trial by jury in criminal cases." Believing this addition to be the most important of all, he argued that "State Governments are as liable to attack these invaluable privileges . . . and therefore ought to be as cautiously guarded against." Although he convinced his colleagues in the House of Representatives, the Senate refused to support the addition. So, this early attempt to nationalize certain individual rights failed. Also of particular importance to Madison was the liberty of conscience; but the Virginian's attempt to protect what he called the "full and equal rights of conscience"[56] in the federal bill also died in the Senate.

Madison wanted to incorporate the new additions into the text of the Constitution. After all, it already contained some protection of individual rights; putting the new text into the old made logical sense. However, a number of congressmen disagreed, arguing that the Constitution should be preserved as it was signed by the convention delegates. They also noted that this approach would avoid the difficulty of determining where the new provisions would best fit into the original text. In the ensuing vote Madison lost. The result was to give to the Bill of Rights its collective form as the first amendments to the Constitution and to highlight their importance in the constitutional order.

The practice of adding changes in the form of amendments without any alteration of the original text has, in fact, preserved in the Constitution itself a record of formal change over time. For instance, the document records the legal protection of slavery and then its subsequent abolition, the acknowledgment of the error of prohibition, and the expansion of the franchise to women. What the Constitution becomes is an abstract of the nation's history. Although it has none of the compelling narrative of the Bible, it does, in a much abbreviated form, capture the history of a people. To have followed Madison's advice on the amending procedure, which over time would have added and deleted words, phrases, and sentences, would have produced a different Constitution, one less rich in symbolic and historical content.

By the end of 1789 twelve amendments had been sent to the states for ratification. What would become famous as the First Amendment was actually the third proposal; the first two, dealing with representation and salary matters, were not then ratified, thus leaving the place of honor for the third proposal.[57] To the often forgotten losers in the ratification struggle, the Anti-Federalists, must go the credit for adding a bill of rights to the Constitution. Critics have pointed to the agenda of the Anti-Federalists and claimed that their desire was primarily to limit the range of power delegated to the new government and that their concern for individual rights was at best secondary and at worst a smoke screen.[58] That the Anti-Federalists were worried about the new delegated powers is clear, but the concern for the protection of individual rights merged with a prime Revolutionary concern. Despite their mixed motives, the Anti-Federalists did put in motion the process that added a charter of individual liberties to the Constitution. The proposed amendments were sent to the states just about two years after the original document was drafted. In a little more than two years, the amendments were ratified. Not only do most Americans today assume that the Bill of Rights was always a part of the Constitution, but often they perceive the Constitution through the lens of these amendments. The long-run significance of the Bill of Rights is clear, and in the short run the amendments enhanced the appeal of the Constitution both as fundamental law and as something to be venerated.

What emerged from Congress in September 1789 and what was ratified by the end of 1791 was an impressive array of described rights expressed in clear and mandatory language. If words on parchment could rule, the people's rights appeared secure, at least from infringement by the federal government. The First Amendment read: "Congress shall make no law respecting an establishment of religion, or prohibiting the free exercise thereof; or abridging the freedom of speech, or of the press; or the right of the people peaceably to assemble, and to petition for a redress of grievances." The true significance of this amendment is that it promotes diversity and makes this diversity an integral part of the constitutional order. Paradoxically, one then can be loyal to the Constitution while fundamentally disagreeing with many of its provisions. Constitutional faith, then, does not necessarily imply an unthinking allegiance to a text.

The First Amendment is read as a prohibition upon Congress because it was from this body that the threat appeared to come. However, it has never been interpreted to mean that the other departments of the government were free to infringe the specified rights. From the outset, specific limiting language was read broadly as a prohibition upon all governmental activity. Among the suggested amendments coming from the states, no subject was of greater concern than religion.[59] The wording here is the result of compromise, but both religion clauses were designed to promote full religious freedom, first by prohibiting any federal governmental establishment of religion and second by a positive grant of religious freedom.[60] The protections of speech, press, peaceable assembly, and petition then follow. Just how these rights were to be protected during times of popular hysteria was unclear, but the text gave such claims substance. The First Amendment contains the rights that Americans were most concerned about, the rights that seem to lie at the heart of the republic.

Amendments Two and Three deal with the right to keep and bear arms as part of the militia's role in promoting security and with the bar to quartering troops in private homes. The protection of the sanctity of the home is also the subject of the Fourth Amendment's prohibition of "unreasonable searches and seizures."

The Fifth Amendment is another composite amendment; it begins with the requirement of an indictment by a grand jury in cases of serious crime and then goes on to provide protection against double jeopardy and self-incrimination. Then, shifting focus, it states that no person shall "be deprived of life, liberty, or property, without due process of law; nor shall private property be taken for public use, without just compensation."

Relating exclusively to criminal prosecutions, the Sixth Amendment provides for "the right to a speedy and public trial, by an impartial jury," communication of the offense, confrontation by accusing witness and compulsory process for obtaining favorable witnesses, and, finally, right to counsel. Extending rights to the accused, the Eight Amendment prohibits excessive bail and fines, along with "cruel and unusual punishments."

The Seventh Amendment bears the telltale signs of age in providing for a jury trial in a civil suit of more than twenty dollars, in many ways a clear reflection of the view that trial by jury was among the most prized rights. It also provides for the compulsory acceptance by the court of the facts as found by a jury.

The Tenth Amendment is what remains of the many suggested amendments outside the arena of individual rights that sought to limit the new powers of the federal government. On its surface, it seems to state the obvious—powers not delegated remain with the states or the people. But as constitutional language it could and would be reinterpreted over time.

What remains is the Ninth Amendment. Remember how the Federalists in their opposition to a bill of rights had argued that such listings could be unintentionally partial and thereby run the risk of inadvertently conceding governmental power that threatened individual liberty? The Ninth Amendment reads: "The enumeration in the Constitution, of certain rights, shall not be construed to deny or disparage others retained by the people." This amendment was an attempt to deal with the problem by, in effect, signing a blank check for later completion. It provides a constitutional target for claims that do not fit into the previous amendments but that raise similar issues of individual liberty. If any proof is needed that the Constitution was written for the future rather than to codify understandings of the present, the Ninth Amendment stands as excellent evidence.[61]

Progress toward the inclusion of a bill of rights in the Constitution brought North Carolina and Rhode Island into the Union, and the bill itself completed the Constitution, not only in the sense of remedying a deficiency but also in the sense of making it a symbol of unity and freedom. Although the Bill of Rights would not play an important role in constitutional adjudication until the twentieth century, its symbolic importance was both immediate and enduring. In a very real sense, modern constitutionalism arises from the American experience of placing individual rights at the heart of the fundamental law. The Bill of Rights "symbolized a new system of public morality" that enshrined the proposition that government held its power subordinate to the rights of the people.[62] In fact, one observer has argued that most of the original Constitution designed a state and government, while the Bill of Rights, along with similar clauses in the original text, constituted a civil society. It was a civil society that was diverse and pluralistic in which individuals had weapons of self-defense in these "entitlements to nonconformity and dissidence."[63] Just how well these rights would be protected and by whom remained questions to be answered.

Despite the often bitter ratification struggle, the Constitution rapidly worked its way into the fabric of the nation. Parades celebrated a new United States. Although the number of Americans who had voted for state convention delegates was relatively small, the celebrations confirmed a much more general approval. This fact lent fuel to the rising myth that the Constitution was a democratic document written by divinely inspired men who drew their authority from the sovereign will of the people, who, then, in democratic conventions accepted the framers' work as their own. The men at Philadelphia became founding fathers, who, as Madison himself said, were guided by "a finger of the Almighty hand,"[64] and who Jefferson had collectively labeled "an assembly of demigods."[65] So, from the very beginning the Constitution was not only a framework of national government, but also a symbol that attracted the people of the nation. Quickly the new constitution was seen as the anchor that would secure the people's liberties during the storms of political conflict. American Methodists praised "the most excellent Constitution of these States, which is at present the admiration of the world, and may in future become its great exemplar for imitation."[66]

A general improvement in economic conditions that coincided with the new government taking power tended to be attributed to the Constitution itself. Congressman Richard Bland Lee of Virginia, for instance, saw the Constitution solving the problems of the American government in dealing with foreign powers, in putting the financial and commercial situations in order, and in stimulating American agriculture. He wrote:

> In travelling through the various parts of the United States, I find
> fields, a few years ago, waste and uncultivated, filled with inhabitants
> and covered with new harvests; new habitations reared, contentment
> in every face, plenty on every board, confidence is restored, and every
> man is safe under his own vine and own fig tree, and there is none
> to make him afraid. To produce this effect was the intention of the
> Constitution, . . . and it has succeeded.

Such sentiments were so common that one contemporary critic was moved to comment that there was a tendency "to paint the state of the country under the old Congress as if neither wood grew nor water ran in America before the happy adoption of the new Constitution."[67]

Certainly the Constitution was no miracle elixir that could cleanse the body politic of all the old ailments and prevent the occurrence of new ones, but it did come to define the political world of Americans. The quick addition of a Bill of Rights, the organizational weakness of any opposition, the growing economic prosperity, and the people's trust in George Washington help explain the popular acceptance of the Constitution.

Just as the Philadelphia Convention was given credibility and stature by the election of George Washington as its president, so too would the government under the Constitution reap the benefits of Washington at its head. In fact, the general belief is that the office of chief executive was made more potentially powerful than experience under the crown would have made wise because of the understanding that Washington would become the first president. In Washington people trusted, and once more he reluctantly answered his country's call. Responding in part to religious leaders who lamented the absence in the Constitution of any mention of God or the Creator, the president, in his first inaugural address, tied the American experiment to God's holy plan. He asked of the "Almighty Being who rules over the universe . . . that His benediction may consecrate to the liberties and happiness of the people of the United States a Government instituted by themselves for these essential purposes." Acknowledging "the Invisible Hand" that had overseen the affairs of the United States, he offered "pious gratitude, along with an humble anticipation of the future blessings which the past seem to presage."[68] As with so much he did, Washington here established a tradition that subsequent presidents would follow. The nation's highest elected official would continue, in inaugural and other public addresses, to sanctify American exertions and beliefs.

Washington's prestige and precedent-setting administration would help launch the Constitution, but its success would hinge on the document's ability to command the loyalty of the people and its flexibility.

As political parties developed in the nation, the rival factions sought support in the Constitution. Remembering how the British constitution had been corrupted,

Americans saw as essential the maintenance of a constitutional balance of power. When under Alexander Hamilton's leadership, the Washington administration pushed a series of controversial economic measures through Congress, the opposition resorted to a traditional defense—that such measures were a distortion of the agreement spelled out in the Constitution. Political conflict in that new government thus led late-eighteenth-century Americans to a defense of constitutional limits. The document that had been attacked during the ratification campaign now became revered as no less than an embodiment of the "ancient constitution" that protected the rights of the people. Devoted to the concept of a fundamental law, the opposition to administration measures was expressed in terms of defending "a sacred constitution against an executive threat."[69] Political battles would continue, but the Constitution's worth and worthiness were accepted. Dispute centered largely on the interpretation of its words, and in explicating the words the translators were also describing and defining their culture.

As with any social symbol, but especially one that is the fundamental legal document as well, the Constitution's survival was closely linked to the flexibility that could be found within it. As Alfred North Whitehead, the British philosopher, wrote: "Those societies which cannot combine reverence to their symbols with freedom of revision . . . must ultimately decay either from anarchy, or from the slow atrophy of a life stifled by useless shadows."[70]

The framers of the Constitution and the Bill of Rights had faith in the ability of future generations to work within the broad framework and wording of the fundamental law. Although it reflected the existing social order, the Constitution interposed no real barriers to its change over time. If not a democratic charter, it clearly was a republican one. While the opponents of the Constitution in the ratification fight viewed the future with fear, supporters were willing to trust subsequent generations with the task of making the Constitution serve its purposes. No annotations were provided with the document as it was sent to the states to be ratified, and even ambitious explications of it, such as *The Federalist*, were more of an imaginative working out of the implications of its wording than an attempt to extract meaning from the debates.[71] Knowledge of the discussions at Philadelphia has largely come from the notes of James Madison, which were not published until fifty-one years after the Constitution went into operation. And when Thomas Jefferson contended with Alexander Hamilton over the constitutionality of a national bank, the knowledge that the Convention had rejected the inclusion of a general congressional power to charter corporations told the disputants no more than they already knew. The argument then had to shift to determining the legislative authority to choose the means by which to exercise its delegated powers.

At any rate, what was clear at the outset was that this fundamental law would have to be interpreted and reinterpreted over time. State and federal officials were all required to take an oath to support the Constitution, but this was more of a device to ensure its supremacy rather than one designed to leave constitutional interpretation to the varied judgments of a bevy of government officials. The whole idea of a higher law had an ephemeral quality until the era of American constitution making, when it became possible to enforce a codified higher law as part of the rules governing the community.[72]

In its codification of higher law the Constitution provides the forum for an evaluation of the most serious of legal claims. Yesterday's fancy can become tomorrow's constitutional law. This is so because interpretation of the basic law is not an abstract study but the result of resolving conflicting arguments in particular instances. In responding to such claims, interpreters of the Constitution are invited to make its words continually relevant and meaningful. It is this "living" Constitution that commands the faith of Americans. The basic charter is less that document on display in the National Archives than it is a set of principles continually tested by conflicting claims.

To seek the Constitution's place in American culture by an examination of the people's knowledge of its specific provisions,[73] or of their agreement on just how and by whom its words and phrases are to be interpreted,[74] is to follow the wrong trail. The Constitution's embodiment in the American faith structure, its civil religion, is what gives it such cultural importance. "Speaking from the past to the present and into the future in that scriptural voice that does not explain, embellish" or reveal its sources or the intentions of its framers, the Constitution invites believers to interact with the sacred text and puzzle over its meanings and values.[75] As a preeminent symbol of national unity, of the rule of law, and of the protection of individual rights, the Constitution became *the* fundamental article of a civic faith.[76]

The founding generation had made "a commitment to liberal justice that recognizes the moral worth of each person and embodies it politically in a commitment to fundamental rights."[77] The association of liberty with the Constitution has become a prime focus of constitutional law in relatively recent times, but that association was understood from the beginning.[78] The Constitution would be the people's "means by which to secure the Declaration's equal liberty for themselves and their posterity."[79]

By quickly finding in the Constitution a symbol of veneration, Americans were, in fact, paying tribute to themselves. They had endured their birth pangs and paved the way toward a new nationhood. The Constitution would be their rock, standing above the political turmoils of the day. It would provide "a uniquely American form of political rhetoric that allows one to grapple with every important political issue imaginable," no less than "a common language with which to carry on debate about the distribution and use of power in our society."[80] It would create a sense of community in pursuing the ends of justice and provide the means for broadening inclusion within the community. In one sense, the answer to just who are the people encompassed within this faith community is a progressive one.[81]

Whether Americans should venerate their Constitution is a question that critics feel uncomfortable answering in the affirmative.[82] As an act of free will and as a conscious attempt to construct a government responsible to the people and sensitive to their rights, the Constitution was a brilliant creation in which Americans can take rightful pride. An early Supreme Court justice on circuit called the Constitution "the most wonderful instrument ever drawn by the hand of man."[83] Most Americans would agree, then as well as now. When Barbara Jordan, a black congressional representative from Texas, one hundred and fifty years later, defended her vote to impeach Richard Nixon, she said: "My faith in the Constitution is whole. It is complete. It is total. I am not going to sit here and be an idle spectator to the diminution, the subversion, the destruction of the Constitution."[84] That Americans have revered their Constitution is not in doubt; the question has always been whether that reverence was justified, whether it was productive or counterproductive.

Part of the problem lies with what were later seen as defects in the document, such as its compromise with slavery, and with the way in which certain vested interests promoted the worship of the Constitution to freeze and glorify the status quo. But even those who decry the worship of the Constitution recognize its value as a symbol.[85] The meaning of the symbol would have to be reevaluated to better serve the needs of the society, but the Constitution's symbolic role became too ingrained to be dislodged. When the Great Depression stimulated new and often unprecedented federal government activity that was challenged as unconstitutional, critics saw this popular reverence for the Constitution as an obstacle that would have to be overcome. Although such profound respect might satisfy certain psychological needs, they said, such an attitude only furthered the rule of the privileged and deflected the people from their need to use the law as an instrument to improve their condition. Others pondered the effectiveness of a constitutional tradition committed to limited government with built-in restrictions on majorities to cope with the problems of a nationally planned economy.[86] But the Constitution would survive the New Deal largely intact up to the present day. Although the limits of power in the central government have been pushed outward and government at all levels has widened its concerns, the essence of a constitutional tradition of limiting majorities in behalf of the interest of individuals remains a key part of the tradition.

This tendency sanctified the Constitution and made it the Bible of an American civil religion.[87] The legal instrument became also a sacred symbol, starkly different from state constitutions and from the practice of other nations under a constitutional government. In a very real sense, the Constitution became Thomas Paine's charter that was to be crowned as representing the rule of law, a rule that would unite the diverse people called Americans into a national community and make possible the exercise of individual liberty. In part by embodying the higher law the

Constitution gave to the concept of a rule of law a new stature. Americans accepted law's rule as a check even on the people's will. Although the people were the source of power, the Constitution was increasingly viewed as the source of law.[88] As a, if not the, constituting agent of an American identity, the basic charter creates and maintains the American community and helps give the political system "a quasi-sacramental status."[89] Within this community a civil religion grounded in the Constitution provided "visions of good and evil."[90] The law was not the result of imposition upon the people but rather a product of their own sovereign will that merited their continuing faith.

Reflecting upon the basic charter of the nation, James Madison said in 1792 that nothing is more worthy of a people's reverence because it preserves both power and liberty. He went on to summon the people to "guarantee, with a holy zeal, these political scriptures from every attempt to add to or diminish from them."[91] And when George Washington delivered his Farewell Address on the ninth anniversary of the Constitution's signing at Philadelphia, he urged that the Constitution be recognized as "sacredly obligatory upon all."[92] Abraham Lincoln, a founding father once-removed and full-fledged prophet of the American civil religion, summoned the people to the "political religion of the nation" and strongly urged their reverence for the law. Such reverence would then lead to a religious obligation to obey the law,[93] which would, in turn, enable the people to enjoy the blessings of liberty.

With the Constitution as sacred text of the American civil religion in place, we can now turn to the establishment of the agency that, in time, would become not only the priestly interpreter of that text but a continuing force in promoting national unity and in securing and expanding the ambit of the protection of individual rights. More than any other single institution, the Supreme Court of the United States has been responsible for making the Constitution a vital document that continues to command the allegiance and faith of the American people.

ESTABLISHING THE PARAMETERS OF PRIESTLY DUTIES, 1790–1821

The U.S. Constitution was designed to accomplish two purposes: to establish and empower government and to protect individual rights. That the two purposes could collide was understood from the very beginning, and indeed the nation's history, in part, has been the continuing story of reconciling these twin purposes. But the Constitution was more than the sum of its provisions.

Maybe Americans of the founding generation were more aware of its specific language than their successors, but knowledge of the Constitution's details has always been less important than acceptance of its status as the seminal document of the social compact. In other words, what the Constitution says has been less relevant to understanding its place in the society than has been its symbolic importance—what it stands for. This is revealed even in the legal sources, as interpreters would read the text with concepts of liberty, equality, and justice in mind. Such an approach seemed premised on the theory that, in exchange for parting with some of their natural liberty to join together in a civil society, individuals received law that was just and that respected those rights that could be enjoyed without injury to others.

Confronting the First Congress under the Constitution was the task of fleshing out the outline of the fundamental law and providing for the construction of government under it. No matter was any more important than making the judiciary a functioning part of the new government, and Senate Bill Number 1 dealt with this matter. Left unresolved by the Constitutional Convention was the question of whether lower federal courts would be created, a matter that was left to the discretion of Congress. And, of course, no Supreme Court could come into existence until its composition was determined by the legislative body. Despite a general recognition that the judiciary was the weakest branch of the new government, the debate over ratification revealed much concern over the potential power of federal courts. On the most pressing issue—the creation of federal trial courts—the supporters of a strong federal government won the battle. But when it came to detailing the jurisdiction of these courts and their relationship to the state tribunals, substantial compromise was necessary.[1] Initially, except for matters of admiralty and federal criminal law, state courts had concurrent jurisdiction, which meant in practice that most cases involving federal law would be heard in state tribunals. Furthermore, when the jurisdiction of the federal courts could be invoked, the law that was to be applied by these courts, in the absence of conflict with federal law, was the law of the states.

Of most significance to those who saw a federal judiciary as a nationalizing force was section 25 of the act. This provision made clear what the "supreme law of the land" clause in the Constitution implied. The section provided for appeals from state supreme courts to the U.S. Supreme Court in cases where the decision rejected a claim based on the Constitution, a federal law, or a treaty. The nationalizing effect of the provision is apparent, and, although it would be the target of attack and attempted repeal, section 25 was always seen as an essential building block in the construction of the nation.[2] From the very beginning, then, the Court was charged with maintaining the national authority and, with it, the Union itself.

The Judiciary Act of 1789 created thirteen district courts, one for each of the states that had originally ratified the Constitution plus the areas of Maine and Kentucky. Next, it created three circuit courts, to be composed of two Supreme Court justices and one district court judge, any two of whom would constitute a quorum. Basically these additional courts were also trial courts, though they had some limited appellate jurisdiction from the district courts. At the apex of this federal judicial structure was the Supreme Court consisting of six justices, one of whom would be the chief justice. The number six was not an independent determination but the result of allocating two justices to each circuit. As the country and the territory encompassed by the federal judiciary grew, the number of district courts and circuits expanded, as did membership on the High Bench. Judicial organization was a continued subject of Congressional attention, but the basic outline of the federal structure was established in this first judiciary act.[3]

Also, the act acknowledged that the purpose of the judicial department was to protect the rights of individuals. The oath that federal judges took was specified by Congress and reads as follows: "I do solemnly swear that I will administer justice without respect to persons, and do equal right to the poor and to the rich; and that I will faithfully and impartially discharge all the duties incumbent upon me . . . according to the best of my abilities and understanding agreeably to the constitution and laws of the United States."[4]

One of the fears of opponents of the Constitution was that federal courts would become vehicles of oppression. George Washington sought to alleviate these fears by making appointments to the federal bench from the citizens of the state where the courts sat and by deliberately seeking geographical representation on the Supreme Court. This practice, designed to quiet some of the concern that "foreign" judges would fail to understand state interests, was generally followed by subsequent presidents. But the "domestic" judges so appointed would be assuming new, federal roles with new responsibilities, and this fact would partially counter their earlier identification with the states.

At the outset, the major task of the justices was not to assemble at the seat of the government—first New York City, then Philadelphia, and finally Washington, D.C.—and perform their collective duties as the Supreme Court, but rather to hold court in the wide-ranging circuits. On circuit, the justices were active, if often reluctant, trial judges. The southern circuit was especially onerous, requiring a justice to travel over a thousand miles on horseback in a single year. The reason for this added burden was found less in the light appellate workload than in a belief that justices should be brought in touch with common people at the trial level. They would be both learners and teachers, both informed by public opinion and shapers of it.[5]

Despite early and repeated protest from the justices, some circuit-riding responsibilities remained until 1891, when an intermediate appellate level of federal courts would be created. That some appointees balked at the heavy and hazardous travel and turned down the honor of appointment should come as no surprise. Still, the fact that the position had its disadvantages has probably been overemphasized. George Washington was able to staff the Court with well-qualified men who gave initial life, meaning, and direction to the role of the High Bench and its members in American culture.

In time observers would come to note the Court's role as the nation's schoolmaster, and any study that neglected the Court's educative function in the society would be deficient. This role was accepted by the justices early and can be seen most graphically in one important aspect of their circuit court work—their grand jury charges. These charges were far more than discussions of the relevant law; they were lessons on the nature of government and on the liberties and responsibilities of the people living under it. In such charges the justices brought home the primacy of the Constitution and the rule of law as the best security for individual rights. They taught the catechism of union and of responsible republicanism. As apostles of the civil religion, they spread the gospel as they moved from court to court. The audience for these grand jury charges was much larger than may at first appear, for often the charges were repeated as the justices traveled from circuit to circuit, and they were widely printed.[6]

Obviously Congress, in establishing circuit court duties for the justices, had assumed that the men would play a role in the political education of the citizenry. Such education was necessary in a republic where a favorable public opinion was the key to its survival. Because no defense was adequate when a majority resisted the law, the justices' task was to ensure that the people understood the basic political principles upon which their experiment rested. Over forty years later the perceptive French observer Alexis de Tocqueville asserted that the Supreme Court's power was dependent upon Americans viewing obedience to the law as a basic commandment. The justices, he said, had to be statesmen: "they must know how to understand the spirit of the age, to confront those obstacles that can be overcome, and to steer out of the current when the tide threatens to carry them away, and with them the sovereignty of the Union and obedience to its laws."[7]

Of the first Supreme Court justices, James Wilson of Pennsylvania was the most sensitive to the Court's need to accommodate public opinion. In his first grand jury charge in the circuit courts, he said that the will of the people first expressed in elections "ought to pervade all the subsequent progress and stages of the public business." This will preserve and secure the Constitution, for it "will be *always* accommodated to the dispositions, manners, and habits of those, for whom it is intended." Wilson concluded his general remarks with a tribute to Americans and the jury system: "We now see the circle of government, beautiful and complete. By the people, its springs are put in motion originally: By the people, its administration is consummated: At first, at last; their power is predominant and supreme."[8] Although our interest here is in the justice's acknowledgment of the importance of public opinion, notice also Wilson's belief in a constitution that is interpreted in response to changes over time.

In his first grand jury charge Chief Justice John Jay of New York took the opportunity to call for "good will, and good Temper, and the Progress of useful Truths among our Fellow citizens." As part of his lesson he talked about the improvements in the science of government, with the separation of powers and checks and balances, which prevent meddling "with the Rights reserved by the Constitution to the People." Defending the existence of the federal courts as a necessary result of the formation of a nation, the chief justice tied individual prosperity to national prosperity, which was dependent upon "a well organized Government, ruling by wise and equal Laws, faithfully executed." He reminded his listeners that such a government is a threat only to arbitrary power and licentiousness, not to civil liberty, which "consists in an equal Right to all the Citizens to have, enjoy, and to do, in peace Security and without Molestation, whatever the equal and constitutional Laws of the Country admit to be consistent with the public Good."[9]

While John Jay defended the role of the new courts as an indispensable part of the country's nationhood, his colleague James Iredell of North Carolina called attention to the "higher and more important" role of the federal judiciary "as a great constitutional guard of the constitution itself, since it is to carry into effect no laws but such as the constitution authorizes." Iredell speculated that this built-in restriction on the legislative power, although a unique characteristic of American government, was necessary to protect the "sacred bulwark" of "essential personal rights."[10]

The single most prevalent theme in these grand jury charges is the concept that the law must be obeyed. Although there is obvious self-interest in promoting this value as the foundation for judicial power and as an aid in emboldening grand jurors to bring in presentments and indictments, the concern of the justices was much broader. For Iredell, a republic rested on the proposition "that no one Man is superior to another, but the Law is superior to all. She is the Depository of the common happiness and security of all the Citizens."[11] James Wilson regarded obedience to law as the essential predicate of self-government. Citizens in a republic, he insisted, cannot "be true and faithful to themselves . . . unless they *obey* as well as *make* the laws—unless in the terms, in which a citizen has been defined, they partake of *subordination* as well as *power.*"[12] Wilson drew an analogy between education and law: "What education is to the individual," he said, "the laws are to the community."[13] For Justice John Blair of Virginia the social compact itself could only be preserved "by a dutiful obedience even to such laws (if such there be) as do not, in themselves, meet our approbation." Blair recognized the right of the people to seek the repeal or alteration of such laws, but until such change there was no exception to the duty of obedience.[14]

Perhaps no justice on circuit more directly addressed the need to educate a republican citizenry than did William Paterson of New Jersey. Labeling ignorance "freedom's worst foe," he called for the moral education of all. At the heart of this moral education Paterson saw the inculcation of a "uniform attachment to, and an habitual love and veneration for the constitution and laws." They

> contain the articles of our political faith; they point out the path we are to go, and the rule by which we are to walk. They are the work of the people, declarative of their will, and as such ought to be reverenced and obeyed. To fashion our temper, character, and conduct as citizens, by the principles and spirit of the constitution and laws is both our interest and duty; and while we do so, we shall insure internal order and repose, and be united at home and respected abroad.[15]

Oliver Ellsworth of Connecticut, who became chief justice in 1796, tied this obedience to law to the national fabric. "The national laws," he said, "are the national ligatures and vehicles of life." Among a diverse population in a widespread geographical area, "they give to the whole, harmony of interest, and unity of design. They are the means by which it pleases heaven to make of weak and discordant parts, one great people; and to bestow upon them unexampled prosperity." The future is bright indeed, he continued, "so long as America shall continue to have one will, organically expressed and enforced."[16]

Of all the early justices, James Iredell was most insistent in stressing the virtue of the Union, claiming that the unprecedented cession of state power to it had been successful beyond "the most sanguine expectations."[17] Because this union under the Constitution has "enabled us to reach our present envied situation, so, under the blessing of God, nothing but Disunion can in all human probability deprive us of it!"[18]

Talk of Union and the rule of law was often linked with the people's liberties. Iredell told his listeners that the Constitution "effectively protects each citizen in the enjoyment of all those essential personal rights necessary to secure his safety."[19] Such rights, in which he included life, liberty, property, and reputation, were worthy of "sacred protection."[20] James Wilson implied that government had a positive obligation to protect individual liberty through the enactment and enforcement of the criminal law, which he saw as a principal support for that liberty.[21] The Pennsylvania justice discoursed on the protection of personal property as a further responsibility of government.[22] William Cushing of Massachusetts summed up this sentiment, when he said that government's main purpose is to protect all individuals, "in the undisturbed enjoyment of their just rights, which are comprehended under a few, but important words—*security of person and property*, or, if you please, *rights of man*." Therefore government must hold in "sacred regard . . . the principles of justice, and . . . all moral obligations."[23]

Again it was James Iredell who put this individual liberty within its republican context, saying that liberty, "to be truly enjoyed, must submit to reasonable and considerate restraints," for the unbounded liberty of the strong oppresses the weak and the majority too readily can impose its will on the minority. "Unlicenced indulgence to all the passions of men is an impious rejection of the controul of reason which Providence has given for their government and direction."[24]

To reject reason was for Iredell no less than impiety, which indicates clearly how irreverence for law is seen in the republican nation as a fundamental rejection of the civil theology. Invoking divine sanction in this attempt to bridle passions, the justice continued: "Providence has designed man for society, and those who either from pride or vanity, or any worse motive, refused to yield to the conditions it indispensably requires, counteract so far as in them lies, the provisions of divine wisdom for the good order and government of mankind."[25]

Iredell's words provide an introduction to the frequent use of religious terminology in the charges. In these political charges, the justices used the common political rhetoric. They felt freer than in their opinions, where such references were far less frequent. The idea that the United States was a special nation charged with a unique responsibility to determine the survivability of a nation founded on the sovereignty of the people and their individual rights was implicit in most of the political charges. Chief Justice Jay said the blessings of Providence had been bestowed upon the nation, and the people must answer to Providence and mankind in general for their actions.[26] Iredell saw the "blessing of God" upon the American union.[27] And Chief Justice Oliver Ellsworth suggested: "let us rear an empire sacred to the rights of man; and commend a government of reason to the nations of the earth."[28] William Cushing urged Americans to "endeavor to secure the blessing of Heaven upon ourselves, and upon our country." And as the conflict with France in the 1790s divided the people and threatened war, Iredell concluded a charge with the following entreaty: "May that God whose peculiar providence seems often to have interposed to save these United States from destruction, preserve us from this worst of all evils! And may the inhabitants of this happy country deserve his care and protection by a conduct best calculated to obtain them!"[29]

Through John Adams's leadership the nation avoided war, but the political grand jury charge did not long survive the coming of the Jeffersonian Republicans to power. The charges had always had the potential of becoming vehicles of party politics, and Justice Samuel Chase of Maryland developed their full potential in this regard. Unwilling to accept the victory of the Republicans in 1800, he railed against the party in his grand jury charges, at times turning the constant theme of respect for law upon its head. Chase would be impeached but not removed from office.[30] The episode, though, sealed the fate of the political charge. To avoid accusations of political partisanship justices hereafter would give a wide berth to broad political issues and stick to the legal matters before the grand jury. This retreat did not cleanse the High Bench of politics, for the Court remains a political branch of the government. It did, however, leave the educating and revitalizing tasks more to the Court opinions themselves.

In its first decade the Supreme Court would do much to establish the viability and independence of the judicial branch of the government. For instance, when Secretary of the Treasury Alexander Hamilton wrote to Chief Justice Jay proposing a united front against Virginia's challenge to the constitutionality of the federal assumption of state debts, Jay counseled that such action was inadvisable.[31] But on the one constitutional issue that affected the justices most directly, they relied on their persuasive rather than on their institutional power. In response to President Washington's request for feedback on their experience with the Judiciary Act of 1789, they protested strenuously against their circuit-riding responsibilities.[32] The policy reasons for the protest were apparent, but the justices also addressed what they saw as a constitutional deficiency in the arrangement. They had been commissioned as members of the Supreme Court with limited original jurisdiction; the circuit-riding provision made them noncommissioned trial court judges with wide-ranging original jurisdiction, seemingly in violation of the Constitution itself. When cases they had heard at the trial level were appealed to the Supreme Court, they did not generally participate. Therefore, because of the additional congressional imposition placed upon them, they could not perform the task for which they had been commissioned. They concluded that the Constitution was "plainly opposed to the Appointment of the same Persons to both Offices."[33] Here, then, was an act affecting the judicial department that the justices considered in violation of the Constitution. When the issue finally came to the Court a decade later, the justices decided that their predecessors' willing service on the circuit courts had settled the constitutional issue.[34]

To have refused a responsibility imposed upon them by Congress seems not to

have been considered. But when Congress in 1792 passed a law requiring the
justices, as circuit court judges, to make decisions about the legitimacy of certain
pension claims that were then subject to reversal by the secretary of war and Congress, the justices resisted. All agreed that the law was unconstitutional in its attempted delegation of nonjudicial duties to the justices. Chief Justice Jay and
Justice Cushing said that they would interpret the act as appointing them to act as
commissioners outside of their judicial role, but Wilson and Blair refused to make
any such compromise and declined to proceed in such matters. Justice Iredell
agreed and doubted that the equivocation of Jay and Cushing was permissible
under the statute.[35] Although the popular press and some politicians of the day
interpreted these actions as constituting a declaration of the act's unconstitutionality, there was no formal ruling by the Court. And in the following year, despite
some grumbling, Congress changed the statute and eliminated the assigned duty.
What was clear, however, was that the justices were becoming protective of their
judicial role. And they received support from an unexpected quarter when opponents of the administration, who generally had been worried about the power of
federal judges, praised this initial act of judicial courage and looked forward to
further review of what they saw as unfortunate legislation.[36]

    That the Court would defend its particular and independent role was also made
clear when Secretary of State Thomas Jefferson, directed by President George
Washington, asked the Court to provide some guidance to the administration on
points of international law. Chief Justice Jay responded that the president could
consult his cabinet on such matters but not the Court, for the separation of powers
militated against "the propriety of our extra-judicially deciding the questions alluded to."[37] The refusal to provide advisory opinions not only established a guiding
precedent, but it divorced the Court in both time and function from the policy
decision. Only later when a party mounted a claim in the form of a case or controversy would such a decision be subject to judicial scrutiny. By so defining and
limiting its political role, the early Court was strengthening its authority within its
assigned sphere. In responding to individual claims, it might have to check the
operation of the other branches, but any such check was a subordinate result of
adjudicating a real dispute brought before the Court for resolution. As such, it was
an adjudicator of individual claims, not a partner in policy formation.

    By the end of 1793 the requirement of two justices for each circuit court was
reduced to one, and a separate and distinct branch of government was emerging
that would assert its independence of Congress and the chief executive. Although
the justices continued to address both political branches with considerable deference, this was more a matter of the nature of official discourse than a lack of
confidence in their independence.

    Although the Court throughout the first decade had few cases, the justices
quickly and clearly staked out a constitutional role that they would never relin-

quish. The Court would defend the Union based on the sovereignty of the people and would protect the rights of the individuals who composed that people. At the root of the theology of the American civil religion were the concepts of union and of individual rights, safeguarded by the rule of law.

These principles guided the justices in their first major case. What was at issue in *Chisholm v. Georgia* during the February term of 1793 was the question of whether a citizen of one state could sue another state. Article III of the Constitution provided that federal judicial power extends "to Controversies . . . between a State and Citizens of another State," and that "In all Cases . . . in which a State shall be Party, the Supreme Court shall have original Jurisdiction."[38] The suit for payment for goods supplied the state was instituted by Chisholm, and counsel appeared for Georgia only for the limited purpose of protesting the Court's jurisdiction.[39] What makes the four-to-one decision in favor of the plaintiff instructive is the broad-gauged way in which the justices defended it. Today, we might say that the plain language of the Constitution itself commanded a decision for the plaintiff, but that was insufficient for a number of reasons. First, Federalists had responded during the ratification contest to fears that the words of Article III would undermine state sovereignty by denying that such language meant that a state could be sued against its will, except by another state. Second, more than the principle of state sovereignty was involved, for a decision in favor of such a suit would result in a deluge of such suits, especially from former Tories, that would subject the states to substantial liability and confusion regarding property rights.

Although such politically charged practical concerns weighed on James Iredell who insisted that the bare words of the Constitution conferred no jurisdiction without the clear direction of Congress, his colleagues disagreed. However, they buttressed their interpretation of the constitutional wording with a fundamental exploration into the nature of the newly created union and the purposes for which it had been established.[40] The majority justices sought not only to educate the public but also to sanctify the Constitution by creating a myth about its origin. In this regard the opinions of Justice James Wilson and Chief Justice John Jay were the most significant.

The term "sovereign," Wilson began, is unknown to the Constitution and that where it could properly have been used—in referring to the sovereign people—the "ostentatious declaration" was unnecessary because Americans were "serenely conscious of the fact." He continued: "Man, fearfully and wonderfully made, is the workmanship of his all perfect creator: A state . . . is the inferior contrivance of man; and from his native dignity derives all its acquired importance." Resting upon these premises, Wilson asked, does justice not require that a state be held to same obligations of the people who compose it? The answer is obvious, he contended, asserting that the citizens of Georgia did not surrender their supreme power to the state. Condemning "haughty notions of state independence, state sovereignty, and state supremacy" as degrading man "from the prime rank, which he ought to hold in human affairs," Wilson said that the people are free to "extinguish or transfer" powers as they will.[41] By accepting the Constitution of the United States, he added, they have bound the state of Georgia to its provisions.

Then, seeking to buttress his decision, Wilson said that the purposes of the new government, as outlined in the Preamble, and "the general texture" of the Constitution lead to the same result: "that the people of the United States intended to form themselves into a nation for national purposes."[42] The justice added that the plain words of the Constitution clearly confer jurisdiction on the judiciary to adjudicate the claim before the Court.

Jay began his opinion by describing Americans at the time of the Revolution as a largely united people assuming their sovereign power. Recognizing their unified concerns, they established a confederation, which, when it frustrated their expectations, they displaced with the present government under the Constitution. "Here we see," Jay continued, "the people acting as sovereigns of the whole country; and in the language of sovereignty, establishing a constitution by which it was their will, that the state governments should be bound." Part of this collective desire was realized in the establishment of a federal judiciary that would "be responsible to the whole nation."[43]

Viewing the six aims of the Constitution as detailed in the Preamble, Jay said "that they collectively comprise everything requisite, with the blessing of Divine Providence, to render a people prosperous and happy." Federal judicial power, the chief justice continued, was essential "to the preservation of the tranquility, the equal sovereignty, and the equal right of the people."[44] To the claim that the constitutional provision should be interpreted to apply only when states were plaintiffs,[45] Jay said that such an interpretation of a Constitution established to do justice "would contradict and do violence to the great and leading principles of a free and equal national government." He defended the extension of federal jurisdiction to such cases

> because it leaves not even the most obscure and friendless citizen without means of obtaining justice from a neighboring state; . . . because it recognizes and strongly rests on this great moral truth, that justice is the same whether due from one man or a million, or from a million to one man; because it teaches and greatly appreciates the value of our free republican national government, which places all our citizens on an equal footing, and enables each and every one of them to obtain justice without any danger of being overborne by the weight and number of their opponents; and, because it brings into action, and enforces this great and glorious principle, that the people are sovereign of this country. . . . The people have reason to prize and rejoice in such valuable privileges; and they ought not to forget, that nothing

but the free course of constitutional law and government can insure
the continuance and enjoyment of them.[46]

In these remarkable opinions the sovereignty of the people and their essential
dignity is proclaimed; the Preamble, a key element of the American creed, is
viewed as providing direction in the interpretation of the Constitution; and the
people are encouraged to view the Constitution and the federal judiciary as the
protector of their rights. Here, then, at the very beginning of the new federal
government's history is a clear and forceful assertion of the special role that the
judiciary would play in American life. Based upon the mythic assertion that the
Constitution represents the will of the whole people, the Supreme Court defines
itself as the protector of the people's faith in a rule of law. It will not be dissuaded
from its appointed task of making sure that "the equal rights of the people" that
"are discernable in almost every sentence of" the Constitution are respected and
preserved.[47]

The political furor that Iredell saw on the horizon should the Court decide that
a state could be sued did indeed develop, and not only in Georgia where a state
legislator introduced a bill to condemn to death any federal marshal who sought
to execute process under the decision.[48] Yet, cooler heads prevailed and Congress
took up Justice Cushing's suggestion that if "the constitution is found inconvenient in practice in this or any other particular" it could be amended.[49] After final
judgment in the case was pronounced, Congress acted quickly to send an amendment proposal to the states. Within a year it was ratified by the required number
of states, though the official proclamation did not come until almost three years
later.[50] The Eleventh Amendment precluded suits by foreign citizens and citizens
of one state against another state.[51]

This action troubled John Jay, who believed that the amendment undermined
the Court's authority. The first chief justice concluded that the Court would never
amount to much within the American system of government.[52] Certainly his view
that the liberties of the people had been compromised by the amendment is clear,
but the amendment procedure, which requires three-quarters of the states to ratify
an addition to the Constitution, allows the people to make such compromises.

Jay, however, was a poor prognosticator not only about the future power of the
Court but, more immediately, about the effect of an amendment on the authority
of the Court. If Jay feared that each unpopular constitutional decision would result
in a successful amendment proposal, he was wrong. And if he felt that in some
way the Court's prestige and authority was compromised by this resort to the
people to change the Constitution, he was also wrong. Disobedience to a Court
decision, which indeed was forthcoming in this case, is a challenge to the Court's
authority. But recourse to the amendment procedure implies an acceptance of the
authority of the Court to interpret the Constitution as it then stands.

The fact that the decision in *Chisholm* led to a change in the Constitution has tended to obscure the significance of the opinions in that case. A majority not only boldly proclaimed national authority but rested that authority on its reading of the basic legal text to fulfill claims of justice and equality. In so doing, the Court staked out a role for itself within the American civil religion that would grow and develop over time. What is important here is the fact that the Court asserted its power primarily on grounds of its primary obligation to protect individual rights as the sacred underpinning of the American political culture.

Actually, the Eleventh Amendment did save the High Bench considerable work under its grant of original jurisdiction, which came to occupy less and less of the Court's time. And in the long run the new addition to the Constitution was circumvented by the Court's developing the fiction that a suit against a state official seeking to enforce an allegedly unconstitutional state law was not a suit against the state itself and therefore not barred by the Eleventh Amendment.[53]

In the relatively few constitutional law cases the Court heard in its first decade, the justices continued to describe the judicial role as one that enforced the mythic will of the people as codified in the Constitution. For instance, when dealing with Virginia's resistance to honoring the terms of the treaty ending the Revolutionary War, Justice Chase went behind the words of the Constitution to find the source of its power. He said: "There can be no limitation on the power of the people of the United States," who have declared "that every treaty made, by the authority of the United States, shall be superior to the constitution and laws of any individual state; and their will alone is to decide."[54] The Court, then, was the ongoing protector of the will of people frozen for the future in the text of the fundamental law.

Despite the problems the justices had with Congress in regard to circuit riding and the assignment of nonjudicial duties in the pension act, the Court was supportive of the federal legislature. When Congress levied a tax on carriages, the Court dismissed a challenge to the act that claimed it imposed a direct tax and therefore, in accordance with the Constitution, had to be apportioned. Justices Iredell and Wilson undercut the challenge to the act by concluding that, if a tax could not be apportioned in a reasonable manner, it could not be characterized as a direct tax. Chase added that only a "very clear" violation of the Constitution could justify the Court invalidating congressional action.[55]

The most interesting internal dialogue among members of the Court on the matter of just how the Constitution should be interpreted came in *Calder v. Bull.* States were barred from passing ex post facto laws; the question the case posed was whether all retrospective legislation fell under this ban. A unanimous Court said that only criminal laws were barred. Justice Paterson, however, took the opportunity to say that, while he agreed with this reading, he believed that all retrospective legislation was unsound and in violation of the social compact.

Had Justice Chase agreed with his colleague he might have dissented in the case, for his view on the nature of the federal constitutional limitation on the action of legislatures was much broader. Chase argued that a legislative act, "contrary to the great first principles of the social compact, cannot be considered a rightful exercise of legislative authority." This was so, he continued, because the binding nature of law "in governments established on express compact, and on republican principles, must be determined by the nature of the power, on which it is founded." Such power was informed by "vital principles," expressed in the Constitution's Preamble, that protected the individuals from "manifest injustice" and deprivation of their personal liberty or property. To argue, Chase continued, that a legislature could "change innocence into guilt" or violate "the right of private property . . . would, in my opinion, be a political heresy, altogether inadmissible in our free republican governments."[56]

Iredell, generally the most cautious of the early justices, boldly asserted the Court's obligation to declare invalid an act that transgressed the stipulated boundaries of legislative authority. However, he denied that the Court could rest such action on principles of natural justice. This is so, he continued, because the "ideas of natural justice are regulated by no fixed standard; the ablest and purest men have differed on the subject."[57] For Iredell, then, when the legislature violates the text of the fundamental law, the Court has the awesome duty of voiding its work, but when the legislature violates what some see as natural law, the Court has no authority to act. The policymaking body can only be called to account by the people it serves.

This dispute on the Court's proper constitutional role is quite illuminating. Chase's expansive concept of this role was much less politically sensitive than was Iredell's. This lack of sensitivity caused Chase to blend politics and law in a manner that gave credibility to the fear of judicial supremacy. Iredell, on the other hand, was quite aware that the power of the Court would have to rest specifically on the words of the Constitution. This conclusion would leave room for the other branches of government to abuse their discretion, but the remedy, he argued, was to be found in an aroused electorate, not a Court that exceeded its constitutional authority. Opinions of justices over the next generation would, at times, refer to natural law principles, often in conjunction with a textual explication, as reasons for a decision, but in time Iredell would be the clear winner.

Subsequent Courts would increasingly look to the words of the Constitution to support their determinations.[58] However, this development should not be viewed as eventually eliminating all vestiges of natural law in the Constitution's interpretation. There is a difference between reading words into the Constitution that are not there and reading the words that are with a view to promoting justice. For instance, a number of justices condemned the argument that the Court's jurisdiction extended only to suits instituted by states against out-of-state defendants as a reading of the Constitution that would frustrate expectations of justice.[59] The words themselves might establish parameters for an investigation of meaning, but the more general the word the more room there is for the interpreter. Also, the focus on text did not foreclose the investigation into relevant collateral matters, such as history, common law usage, and economic theory. However, this tendency was less an attempt to widen judicial power than it was a matter "of long-seated traditions in the technique of decision-making."[60] Essentially, the Court is limited by the requirements of reasoned discourse, where arguments on both sides are aired and considered, and where the judgment and its rationale are made public and subject to criticism. In the final analysis, this is the ultimate check upon the judiciary.

Chase was not alone in worrying about threats to the property right. That the Court from its beginning was intent upon protecting individual rights has been somewhat obscured by subsequent disparagement of what we know as the property right. Today, we distinguish among human rights and often oppose a right in property to other individual rights. We look back to the eighteenth century and find an absorption with the property right that seems to be misplaced. But it was the individual's right to property that seemed most in danger. To view private property as the creation of a civil society made it vulnerable to governmental control and disposition. In viewing property as a natural right, John Locke's primary purpose was to protect the individual's property from arbitrary invasion by government, and "his view that the right of private property is not dependent on the will of the State is likely always to appeal to the instincts and interests of mankind." Locke saw property as "the natural expression of human reason and personality."[61]

Within the Anglo-American tradition property and liberty tended to overlap, not as grants from a sovereign but as individual entitlements. "Property was an extension of the person, indeed in some ways a definition of the person, for the relations defined by property holding were political and social as well as economic."[62] And despite subsequent distortions, the fundamental desire to protect property was based on the process by which it was acquired—the efforts of the individual—and not an inordinate regard for what that work had produced.

Property was regularly conceived in a broad manner. For instance, libel and slander were viewed as crimes because they destroyed a person's good name. James Madison in 1792 saw property as an all-embracing concept of selfhood: "In its larger and juster meaning, it embraces every thing to which a man may attach a value and have a right; and *which leaves to every one else the like advantage.*" Thus, a man has property in his opinions and their communication, his liberty, and "in the free use of his faculties and free choice of the objects on which to employ them. In a word, as man is said to have a right to his property, he may equally be said to have a property in his rights." The threat, Madison claimed, came as much from an excess of liberty as from an excess of power. Believing that government's purpose was to protect these individual rights, Madison concluded that only "a *just* government . . . *impartially* secures to every man, whatever is his *own*."[63]

If the Court of the next century or so seems from a contemporary perspective to have been too centered on property in a narrower sense, that observation should not submerge the recognition that the Court was indeed protecting individual rights. We have made much of the changes of the twentieth century, but this should not be done at the expense of acknowledging that the Court from the very beginning saw its function in terms of protecting individual rights. Property was in the conventional sense the basis of independence and freedom; only when its security was assured could the other personal rights be enjoyed. When we redis-covered in the twentieth century that economic deprivation could make, for in-stance, the rights in the First Amendment hollow and irrelevant, we were again grasping the mindset of earlier generations who saw the property right as a neces-sary means to the true enjoyment of a full panoply of individual rights.[64]

How this concern for property was seen as the cornerstone of personal freedom and how it was early fit into the constitutional framework is well illustrated by a jury charge delivered by Justice Paterson on circuit court duty. In the case the plaintiff's title to land derived from the original grant to William Penn, the founder of the colony, and the defendant's case rested upon an act of the Pennsylvania legislature referred to as "the quieting and confirming act." The dispute centered on the authority of the Pennsylvania legislature to pass the act under its constitu-tion, which Paterson defined as "the form of government, delineated by the mighty hand of the people, in which certain first principles of fundamental laws are established." Although the justice was talking specifically about the Pennsylvania constitution, his words had a broader reach. After establishing the primacy of the constitution and detailing the relevant provisions of the Pennsylvania Declaration of Rights, Paterson concluded "that the right of acquiring and possessing property and having it protected, is one of the natural inherent and unalienable rights of man. . . . The preservation of property then is a primary object of the social compact, and . . . was made a fundamental law." To deprive a man of his property, as the act sought to do, was "inconsistent with the principles of reason, justice, and moral rectitude; it is incompatible with the comfort, peace, and happiness of mankind; it is contrary to the principles of the social alliance in every free govern-ment; and lastly, it is contrary both to the letter and spirit of the constitution." It is the sacred constitution's embrace of property, the justice continued, that "ren-ders it an holy thing."[65] He asked the jury for a verdict in favor of the plaintiff, and the jury complied.

Cases dealing with other individual rights were relatively rare in the 1790s, but the justices did deal with three other relevant matters. The first involved the ques-tion of expatriation. Under the British common law, a subject could not renounce his citizenship without the consent of the king. Although the justices unanimously ruled in a case that the individual was still an American citizen, none of them adopted the common law rule.[66] Justice Iredell saw the legitimacy of providing for a process of expatriation through statute, but all four justices acknowledged a right of expatriation.[67]

While the Constitution was silent on the question of expatriation, it was not on the subject of treason. Shay's Rebellion in Massachusetts in 1786 had convinced many that a stronger federal government was necessary. In 1794 that stronger government was confronted with an insurrection among western Pennsylvania farmers in protest against a federal excise tax on liquor. When they failed to disband in response to President George Washington's proclamation in which he called for fifteen thousand militia, he ordered the suppression of the rebellion. Two of the insurgents were brought to trial before Justice Paterson on circuit; the charge was treason. Obviously the insurgents were not giving aid or comfort to enemies of the country, so the only basis for the charge was that they were levying war against the United States. Paterson sought his definition in English law, which he said consistently held that "raising a body of men to obtain by intimidation or violence the repeal of the law, or to oppose and prevent by force or terror the execution of the law, is an act of levying war."[68] There had to be no general attack on the federal government or an attempt to topple it. Using this definition Paterson instructed the jury, all but directing it to find the defendants in the cases guilty. Eventually, President Washington pardoned the two men who had been convicted of treason and sentenced to death and issued a general amnesty proclamation to all insurgents.

Justice Iredell in 1799 accepted Paterson's definition of treason when he presided over the trial of insurgents who had participated in another Pennsylvania disturbance, this time over a federal property tax. He again said that any forcible opposition to a federal law constituted levying of war against the United States, adding that "opposition by force to one law . . . is of the same nature as opposition to all the laws."[69] The justices were so appalled by such uprisings that they were not sensitive to the fact that such a broad definition of treason would jeopardize the rights of the individual. Indeed, some crime may have been committed, but to call it treason and impose the death penalty seemed to narrow considerably the protection that the Constitution had intended. The treason clause would be reinspected in the next decade and given a reading that conformed to the intent of the Constitution's framers.

The third matter involved the First Amendment's protection of free speech and free press. In the 1790s the European conflict following the French Revolution divided Americans. Followers of Jefferson (the Republicans) were sympathetic to the French, while the supporters of the administrations of Washington and John Adams (the Federalists) were pro-British. These differences spilled over into domestic politics, as the Federalist administrations were increasingly attacked. Robust political criticism seemed subversive, and in 1798 the Federalist Congress passed legislation collectively called the Alien and Sedition Acts. Of most significance was the Sedition Act, which prohibited individuals from uttering or printing "any false, scandalous and malicious writing" about Congress or the president "with intent to defame . . . them."[70] Its primary political purpose was revealed in the stipulation that the act would expire with the end of the Adams administration.

The justices were drawn into the controversy on circuit where eager Federalist prosecutors brought Republican critics into court. Jeffersonians hoped that the federal courts would do their duty and strike down the hated Sedition Act on the basis of the First Amendment's command that "Congress shall make no law . . . abridging the freedom of speech, or of the press." But no such decision would be forthcoming. Although none of the other Supreme Court justices were as overtly partisan and overbearing as Chase, they were worried about the radical critics and sympathetic to the campaign to curtail seditious utterances.

As to free speech, Justice Iredell, in a grand jury charge, traced its meaning back to England and to that preeminent teacher of American lawyers, William Blackstone. What the First Amendment did was bar any previous restraint; it did not immunize individuals from subsequent punishment for what they had published or said. Iredell declared that "the will of individuals is still left free; the abuse only of that free will is the object of legal punishment." In fact, the justice pointed out, the act had liberalized the common law by stipulating that truth would be a defense to the charge. He could also have added that under the common law, there had been no provision for a jury trial in cases of seditious libel. Finding adequate room under the "necessary and proper" clause of the Constitution for such legislation, Iredell maintained that there was even more reason in a republic to protect the government from libel: "Take away from a Republic the confidence of the people, and the whole fabric crumbles to dust."[71]

Criticism, however, was not stopped by the Sedition Act, and the Republic did not crumble. What, in fact, the Sedition Act occasioned was a thorough-going exploration of the issues of free speech and free press in a republican society. The result was a broadened view of the permissible limits of political speech.[72] Lessons were learned, and more than a century would pass before Congress would again attempt to inhibit free political discussion.

The Court of the 1790s was immersed in the politics of the times. Presidents Washington and Adams saw nothing improper about pressing the chief justice into temporary diplomatic service. And when Jay finally resigned and Washington sought to make John Rutledge of Virginia his successor, the appointment foundered for political reasons. Rutledge had vehemently denounced the treaty that Jay had concluded with Great Britain in 1794, and the Federalist Senate refused to confirm his nomination. Washington then decided to elevate William Cushing to the position of chief, which could well have established a precedent that the senior associate justice would be moved to the chief's position once his predecessor had retired or died. Cushing declined the promotion, and Washington eventually appointed Oliver Ellsworth, an important contributor to the drafting of the Judiciary Act of 1789.

When Ellsworth resigned his post in 1800, John Adams wanted Jay to return to the post. Declining, Jay cited his health as a reason but left no doubt as to his worries about the Court's future. The Judiciary Act of 1789, he said, was less the result of sound policy decisions and more the result of "prejudices and sensibilities. . . . [E]fforts repeatedly made to place the judicial department on a proper footing have proved fruitless." Jay doubted "both the propriety and the expediency of . . . returning to the bench" when the views of the justices are disregarded. He said that little had changed since he left the bench "under a system so defective it would not obtain the energy, weight, and dignity which are essential to its affording due support to the national government, nor acquire the public confidence and respect which, as the last resort of the justice of the nation, it should possess."[73]

As Jay refused the appointment, Congress was moving to the enactment of a new judiciary act that would eliminate the circuit-riding responsibilities of the justices. It provided also for the appointment of new circuit court judges and the reduction of Supreme Court membership to five.[74] Prior to the bill's enactment, President Adams pondered the choice of a new chief justice. Federalists in Congress supported the elevation of Paterson to the center seat, but Adams suspected that the justice was an ally of Alexander Hamilton, who had criticized Adams's attempt to negotiate with the French. The president turned aside the suggestion by noting that Cushing was senior to Paterson. With Jay's refusal to accept the appointment, with Cushing having turned down the center seat earlier, and with time running out, Adams turned to his secretary of state, John Marshall. The president said, "I believe I must nominate you." Marshall, who earlier had rejected a seat on the Court, this time quickly accepted, saying that he was both pleased and surprised by the nomination.[75] There was some feeling in the Senate that a delay in confirmation might force Adams to chose Paterson, but Adams's steadfastness forced the Senate to approve the nomination.

Federalists, who had been responsible for setting the national government on a firm foundation, had worried that a Jefferson administration would erode this foundation. But what they found was that the radicalism of Jefferson in opposition was muted in Jefferson as president. In his inaugural address, he offered the olive branch, saying "We have been called by different names brethren of the same principle. We are all republicans, we are all federalists." And to those who questioned whether the government, which he called "the world's best hope," could sustain itself, Jefferson responded that it was "the strongest government on earth . . . [and] the only one where every man, at the call of the law, would fly to the standard of the law, and would meet invasions of the public order as his own personal concern."[76]

Although the new president and the new chief justice, John Marshall, were fellow Virginians with a commitment to the rule of law, they were political rivals. Jefferson, who had fled Monticello at the approach of the British in 1781 and who had entertained English and German officers who were technically prisoners, was not popular with Revolutionary veterans, such as Marshall. The two Virginians also clashed over a proposed state law to levy a tax to aid religion, over Hamilton's economic program, and over the proper stance to take toward France and England. It was Marshall's forceful defense of the constitutionality of Jay's Treaty that projected him forward as Virginia's leading Federalist. Even Jefferson, however, had a grudging respect for Marshall's argumentative skills.[77]

Marshall's first acceptance of national appointment came in 1798 when he had consented to be one of three ministers sent to France to resolve problems between the two countries. Despite the trio's inability to negotiate any settlement, the commissioners had held their ground against the French, and Marshall returned to the country a hero. Jefferson's comments about the failed mission did not reflect well upon Marshall and further estranged the two men. Jefferson's attack on the Federalists and on Washington himself only infuriated Marshall more. As a candidate for the House of Representatives, Marshall indicated his opposition to the Alien and Sedition Acts. And in responding to questions, he called the Constitution "the rock of our political salvation." After election to Congress, Marshall paid a call on Vice President Jefferson, who refused to return the call. And when the electoral vote in 1800 revealed a tie between Jefferson and Aaron Burr, Marshall lent some support to the idea that the House could choose another person as president. Jefferson resented this proposal, as he did the resignation of Chief Justice Ellsworth prior to the new administration taking office. But while still occupying the office of secretary of state and at Jefferson's request, Marshall, as chief justice, administered the presidential oath to his Virginia rival.[78] If the conciliatory tone of Jefferson's inaugural address seemed to indicate that both men could put their differences behind them, such was not to be the case.

John Jay saw institutional problems at the heart of the Court's weak position in the federal government,[79] but John Marshall would quickly demonstrate how strong leadership could remedy much of the perceived weakness. Marshall's agreeable personality, his willingness to shoulder a disproportionate share of the Court's burden, and the clarity and force of his reasoning gave him considerable influence on the Court's decisions. Among other things, Marshall was credited with the practice of announcing the decision of the Court in a single opinion.[80] He worked to resolve differences and seek unanimity among his brethren, even if it meant that he, at times, would have to defer to the judgment of others. A Supreme Court speaking with a single voice would lend weight to its authority. Because of his energy and the force of his personality, Marshall was able to craft and then deliver most of the significant constitutional opinions during what would become a thirty-four-year tenure on the High Bench.

The Supreme Court that John Marshall came to head was wracked by political controversy. In addition to the turmoil that the Sedition Act had unleashed, President Adams's appointment of Federalists to judicial positions late in his administration enraged his political opponents. Republicans were always wary of the federal courts; now they saw these last minute appointments as an attempt to reverse their recent victory at the polls. When in March 1802 Congress repealed the Judiciary Act of 1801 and dislodged the Federalist appointees from their circuit court seats, Republican leaders worried about the reaction of the Supreme Court. To head off any precipitate action, the act provided for a single session of the Court, to be held each year in February. Almost a year would pass before the justices could review the repeal act.

Late in 1801, however, the Court had decided to hear a case asking that the secretary of state, James Madison, be directed by a writ of mandamus, an order from the Court commanding the performance of an act, to deliver a commission as justice of the peace to William Marbury, who had been appointed in the waning hours of the Adams presidency. John Marshall, as secretary of state, had failed to make delivery of a number of such commissions. Now, as chief justice, he would have to address the delicate matter of whether the Court could try to force Madison to make such a delivery.

Marbury v. Madison[81] has been hailed as one of the most significant decisions in the history of the Court, primarily because it asserted the authority of the High Bench to pass on the constitutionality of federal legislation.[82] The decision takes a giant step in the direction of establishing, both theoretically and practically, the Constitution as an authoritative legal text subject to the interpretation of the Court. Marshall realized that in defending the power of judicial review he had to counter the argument that such a power would make the judiciary superior to the other branches. He did this, in part, by wedding the Court to the Constitution. As we have seen, the courtship began in the 1790s, but Marshall and his Court moved boldly through engagement to the wedding itself. The wedding meant that the Court was donning the mantle of the high priest charged with interpreting the holy writ of the American civil religion.

Marbury v. Madison is normally treated within the context of the conflict between John Marshall and Thomas Jefferson. The political environment should not be neglected, but our interest is centered on what the decision says about the Court and its role within the government. As the first instance of the Court invalidating a federal law, the case took on a life of its own and is still cited almost two centuries later as establishing judicial review—the authority of the Court to determine the constitutionality of legislation.

From the very beginning of the Court's history, we have seen how the justices had nurtured the myth that the Constitution was the product of the whole people's will. This gave the fundamental law a sacred character against which the results of the normal push and pull of the political process would be evaluated. Second, they saw their role in terms of protecting the rights of individuals. This latter view accorded with the common law tradition, but it was given new force and authority by the justices' interpretation of the Constitution.

Because Marshall would eventually deny relief to Marbury, who claimed that he was entitled to the office of justice of the peace, many critics of the opinion saw Marshall's confirmation of the claimant's right as gratuitous criticism of the administration. But much more is involved. The chief justice wanted to reemphasize the rule of law with its protection of individual rights from arbitrary action by the government. He sought to establish that the law could not be defied even by a popularly elected chief executive. As early as the 1780s, Marshall had sought to harmonize the majority will with what he called "maxims of democracy," among which he included a "strict observance of justice and public faith, and a steady adherence to virtue."[83]

In moving immediately to the decisive question of the Supreme Court's ability to grant relief, he would have missed a golden opportunity to associate the Court's work with the protection of the individual. So, as Marshall considered Marbury's claim, he first considered whether the appointee had a right to the office of justice of peace; in other words, did a commission properly signed and sealed vest a legal right in Marbury? The chief justice's answer was "yes." There must be a remedy for such a violation, he said, for the "very essence of civil liberty certainly consists in the right of every individual to claim the protection of the laws, whenever he receives an injury." Marshall, however, was careful to impose no barrier to the wide-ranging discretion of the executive department. He emphasized the distinction between law and politics, insisting that courts had no authority whatever to review political decisions. But here in Marbury's case all that remained to be done was a nondiscretionary administrative act imposed by the law. In such an instance, then, "where a specific duty is assigned by law, and individual rights depend upon the performance of that duty, it seems equally clear that the individual who considers himself injured, has a right to resort to the laws of his country for a remedy."[84] Marshall concluded that a writ of mandamus directing the secretary of state to deliver the commission was a proper remedy.

Such an order issued by the Court could be expected to be ignored by the administration. Confronted, then, with a battle the Court could not win, Marshall extricated the justices from the dilemma by ruling that a writ of mandamus could not be issued by the Supreme Court in this case. To reach this conclusion, he had to declare a section of the Judiciary Act of 1789 unconstitutional. In this brilliant maneuver Marshall used a case heavily weighted with political freight to issue a declaration of judicial independence.

Marshall read Article III of the Constitution as fixing the extent of the Court's original jurisdiction. Because Congress in the 1789 act had attempted to add to this jurisdiction by authorizing writs of mandamus in original cases, such as Marbury's, it had come into conflict with the text of the Constitution itself. This was not the only reasonable interpretation of the words in Article III,[85] but it was the one that enabled Marshall both to avoid a conflict with the administration and to assert the authority of the Court to review federal legislation.

Although the justices on circuit were popularly believed to have declared a federal pension act unconstitutional in 1792, the chief justice mentioned but did not rely upon this earlier episode to establish the case for judicial review of federal legislation. Seeking to deal with the Jeffersonian claim that such a right of review would establish the superiority of the judiciary over the other branches of the federal government, Marshall said such a power necessarily proceeded from "long and well established" principles. In fact, "the whole American fabric has been erected" on the right of the people to establish permanent and fundamental governmental principles to ensure their happiness. "Certainly all those who have framed written constitutions," he continued, "contemplate them as forming the fundamental and paramount law of the nation, and, consequently, the theory of every such government must be, that an act of the legislature, repugnant to the constitution, is void." When then such conflict occurs, "It is emphatically the province and duty of the judicial department to say what the law is. Those who apply the rule to particular cases, must of necessity expound and interpret that rule."[86]

Responding to the argument that the courts are to interpret only the law, not the Constitution—a remnant of the view that the Constitution is a political and not a legal document—the chief justice said that such an argument "reduces to nothing what we have deemed the greatest improvement on political institutions, a written constitution." The framers of that charter, now viewed reverently by Americans, "contemplated that instrument as a rule for the government of courts, as well as of the legislature."[87] By pointing to the specific restraints imposed by the Constitution on government, the oath taken by judges, and the fact that the Constitution is declared the supreme law of the land, Marshall sought to bolster the assertion that the Court is obliged to enforce the limits the Constitution places upon government.

Although this portion of the Judiciary Act of 1789 is the only federal law the Marshall Court invalidated during its long tenure, each time it upheld federal legislation in a contested case it reaffirmed its reviewing authority. An imprimatur by the Court meant more than the elimination of a potential obstacle to the law; it meant that the law had been sanctified under the Constitution. What is interesting about the assertion of judicial review in *Marbury* is that the negative reaction was quite minimal. Jefferson was able to withhold the commission from Marbury and deny him the office. More significantly, there was widespread political support, admittedly from different political interests and groups and at different times, for the Court to exercise such a power.

Marshall forcefully insisted that the Court's responsibility was to protect the rights of the individual in terms of the fundamental law established by the people. In the Anglo-American tradition, courts had long had the responsibility of adjudicating individual claims. What the Marshall Court significantly extended was the right of the individual to challenge governmental action by using the words of the written constitution. The Constitution's stature as a codification of the people's will, expressed in terms of fundamental principles, gave it a sacred character. Recognizing that the victory of the Jeffersonians had given force to the majority's will, Marshall sought to accommodate it without compromising the integrity of the fundamental law.

The explication of the constitutional text identified the Court with the fundamental law in a unique way that was unavailable to the other branches of the federal government. Although political interest groups can work through courts as well as through legislatures, the requirements for success are quite different. In the legislative arena, the formulation and nature of the claim is less important than the power that an interest group can bring to bear on the participants in the process. In the judicial arena, by contrast, the formulation and nature of the claim is a necessary prerequisite—the ticket of admission to a hearing. Power and money can indeed sustain a group's effort to work through the judicial process, but they cannot, by themselves, engage that process. A proper claim must be individually based, and it must summon the law to its service.

As Marshall sought to divorce the Court and the law from partisan politics, he had to weather another political storm that had been brewing since the Republicans came to power. Not only had the 1802 act disestablished the new circuit courts and removed federal judges by abolishing their seats, but it also forced the justices to resume their circuit court duties. Worry about how the Court would view this situation had led the Jeffersonians to put off the Court's next term for almost a year. However, a decision in favor of the act would be made implicitly if the justices held circuit court. So, John Marshall sought to collect the opinions of his associates on the matter prior to any circuit court sessions. Although his personal view echoed the opinion of the first justices—that a justice was not commissioned to hold circuit court—he said that he would defer to the judgment of his colleagues. Bushrod Washington, for whom Marshall had considerable respect and who had been appointed to the seat that Marshall had earlier refused, said the question had already been settled by the precedent established by earlier justices. Marshall, concerned about the appearance of justices not obeying existing law, warmed to Washington's position. Only Samuel Chase forcefully responded to Marshall in the negative, arguing that the independence of the judiciary needed to be asserted and that the Repeal Act of 1802 was unconstitutional. However, he also agreed to defer to the majority of his colleagues in the matter. The result was that the Supreme Court justices again took up their circuit court duties.[88]

When Marshall, on circuit court duty in Virginia, confronted a case that raised the question of the constitutionality of the 1802 act,[89] his decision had already been made. Upon appeal, his colleagues unanimously agreed in an opinion by Justice Paterson, who ruled that prior practice and acquiescence of earlier justices "affords an irresistible answer, and has indeed fixed the constitution."[90] Paterson certainly could not have been unaware that from the very beginning the justices had questioned the constitutionality of their being both circuit and Supreme Court judges. But, indeed, their actions had belied their words, and the decision the Court reached avoided another political battle that the Court could not win. Even Chase must have realized that this was not the place to make a stand.

Justice Samuel Chase, however, could suppress his criticism of the Republican administration only so long. In a grand jury charge in Baltimore in early May 1803, Chase chastised the Republicans for the Repeal Act and for their successful attempt to provide universal manhood suffrage in Maryland. Such measures, he continued, threatened the security of property, personal liberty, and the very foundation of society.[91] Obviously Chase had very different ideas of equal liberty and equal rights than did the Jeffersonians, who took his public diatribe as evidence of his unfitness for high office. Chase had stirred the wrath of Republican opponents by his high-handed enforcement of the Sedition Act, and when the new administration came to power, impeachment had been mentioned. Now this new outburst fueled the embers, and one year later the House of Representatives voted to impeach Chase.

The Constitution provided that a federal official could be impeached by the House of Representatives for "Treason, Bribery, or other high Crimes and Misdemeanors."[92] The trial on the charges brought by the House would be held in the Senate, where conviction would remove the official and disqualify him for further federal service. A rather loose interpretation of what was an impeachable offense was established on the very day that Chase was impeached, when the Senate voted to remove federal district judge John Pickering. Pickering was obviously unfit for his duties, but neither unfitness nor his alleged mental instability were embraced in the Constitution's specification of impeachable offenses. In many ways the Pickering removal was seen as a dress rehearsal for the movement against Chase, which, if successful, might pave the way for an attack on Marshall as well.[93]

As the House moved toward impeaching Chase, John Marshall worried about the future of the Court. Chase hardly was Marshall's model justice, for his colleague continually blurred the line between law and politics at the time when Marshall was working diligently to reinforce a barrier between the two. Yet, as the details of the charges were aired in the House, the chief feared that impeachment would become a device to undermine the independence of the judiciary. In a letter to Chase, Marshall confided that he would prefer, as an alternative to the constant threat of impeachment, that Congress be given the power to override what it considered "unsound" decisions of the Court.[94] This is an amazing concession from the writer of *Marbury v. Madison,* but it is stark testimony to his fear for the Court's future. Marshall agreed that Chase should be saved to protect the Court, but when the chief justice was called as a witness in the Senate impeachment trial, which began in February 1805, his testimony called into question some of Chase's behavior on the bench. In the final analysis, the Court was more important than any single member.

Conviction on the charges required two-thirds of the voting Senate, and in Chase's case this meant twenty-three votes. The closest that body came to removing Chase was on the count involving the Baltimore grand jury charge when nineteen Senators voted for conviction. At least six Republicans defected and voted for Chase on all counts. The charges had not been well drawn, and the prosecution was vulnerable because no crime had been alleged. Apparently the hope was that the Pickering conviction would be a precedent for a broad interpretation of what was an impeachable offense. But the defense insisted that impeachment required proof of the commission of a crime.[95]

The failure to convict Chase removed impeachment as a threat to the Court. Never again would a Supreme Court justice be impeached. But this consistent history may be somewhat misleading, for not only was Chase chastened by the experience, but blatant partisan politics disappeared from the federal bench. A Supreme Court that occupied a coequal status with the two other branches of the federal government and that had to resolve politically divisive cases, however, could hardly divorce itself completely from politics. At the heart of politics is the question of power, and because the Constitution seeks to distribute power, a decision to support the exercise of power is in that sense a political decision. At the very least, the justices had to have enough political sense to protect the position of the Court within the government. This involved determining the reasonable limits of its authority and creating an environment in which the justices' definition of the range of their power would be accepted. Although the Court would base its reasoning upon the law, the major constitutional decisions of the Marshall Court rested upon fundamental political principles, whose application could and did cause controversy. But the strategy the Court adopted of distinguishing between law and politics and between legal and personal discretion "was accepted as a respectable intellectual proposition by the Court's contemporaries."[96] So, the Court had weathered its stormy, early years and had begun the process of attaching itself to the sacred Constitution to ensure the rule of law.

Generally reading the Constitution as mandating a decision in favor of the federal claim, the Court expanded the judicial role until it was coterminous with the authority of the other branches. Primarily, it did this by reading section 25 of the Judiciary Act of 1789, which gave the justices power to review state court decisions, broadly. To reject the role of being an impartial arbiter of controversies between the states and the federal government, as the Marshall Court justices did, is hardly surprising. Clearly the role they occupied in the federal government dictated a commitment to prevent divisive state intrusions into the federal arena.

During Marshall's tenure, the major threat the justices encountered was state resistance to the claim of national supremacy. In 1809 one long litigated matter reached the Supreme Court. The case had its origin in a decision of the Committee of Appeals of the Second Continental Congress, which had sought to reverse a decision of Pennsylvania's admiralty court. The state resisted the decision for the next thirty years, bolstered by the legislature's assertion of power to resolve the matter itself. The High Bench considered the issue in terms of a writ of mandamus to compel federal district judge Richard Peters, who had affirmed the binding nature of the committee's decision, to enforce it. At a time when the New England states were becoming restive under a trade embargo imposed by Congress to deal with the problems stemming from the war in Europe, this challenge to national authority was closely watched.

"If the legislatures of the several states may, at will, annul the judgments of the courts of the United States, and destroy the rights acquired under those judgments," Marshall began, "the constitution itself becomes a solemn mockery, and the nation is deprived of the means of enforcing its laws. . . . So fatal a result must be deprecated by all." All people, including those of Pennsylvania, the chief continued, "must feel a deep interest in resisting principles so destructive of the Union, and in averting consequences so fatal to themselves." The issuance of the writ, Marshall concluded, is no less than the "solemn duty" of the Court operating under the law.[97]

The lesson of national supremacy was not easily learned, and in 1816, when Virginia resisted the enforcement of a Supreme Court judgment and asserted that section 25 was in violation of the Constitution, Justice Joseph Story spoke for the Court and spelled out this essential lesson once again. Citing the Preamble as indicating that the Constitution was established not by the states but by the people, he said that they had invested the federal government "with all the powers which they might deem proper and necessary." The general language, Story continued, "was to endure through a long lapse of ages, the events of which were locked up in the inscrutable purposes of Providence." And in Article III, the "whole American people solemnly declared" that the judicial department "was, in many respects, national, and in all, supreme." Congress's duty, then, was to vest this entire power in the federal judiciary. Only by enacting section 25 could Congress provide for appeals from final state court decisions and equalize justice for suitors in both state and federal courts. Ruling that the Constitution imposes its sovereign will on both persons and the states in their corporate capacities, Story found section 25 fully "supported by the letter and spirit of the constitution."[98]

When in *McCulloch v. Maryland* the state challenged the power of the federal government to charter a bank on grounds that such authority was not expressly delegated, Chief Justice Marshall spoke for the Court. Maryland had sought to tax the Second Bank of the United States, a bank chartered by the federal government. The Court had to assess the constitutionality of the bank's incorporation and the claimed authority of the state to tax its operations. Citing the Preamble and the state ratification conventions as evidence, Marshall said that the Constitution established "emphatically, and truly, a government of the people. In form and in substance it emanates from them. Its powers are granted by them, and are to be exercised directly on them, and for their benefit." Although the federal government is one of enumerated powers, it "is supreme within its sphere of action." In interpreting the power the fundamental law confers, he continued, "we must never forget that it is a constitution we are expounding." This Constitution was not designed to be a detailed legal code, incomprehensible to the public, the chief justice said, but rather a document marking out "great outlines" and designating "important objects." To read congressional power narrowly would hardly serve "a constitution intended to endure for ages to come."[99]

Only the Court, he concluded, was equipped to protect the whole people, whose constituting will is codified in the sacred text. The role Marshall is assuming is that of the priest, whose authority rests upon the will of the people as embodied in the Constitution. He is the defender of that will against the challenge from parochial interests that threaten to tear apart the fabric of union. The supremacy clause, he said, "so entirely pervades the constitution, is so intermixed with the materials which compose it, so interwoven with its web, so blended with its texture, as to be incapable of being separated from it without rendering it into shreds."[100]

Acknowledging that Congress was given no specific power to charter corporations, the chief justice ruled that the necessary and proper clause gave the legislature the authority to determine how to execute its delegated powers. "Let the end be legitimate," he continued, "let it be within the scope of the constitution, and all means which are appropriate, which are plainly adapted to that end, which are not prohibited, but consist with the letter and spirit of the constitution, are constitutional."[101]

Moving to the question of the tax, Marshall denied Maryland's ability to tax the operations of the bank. The fiscal institution, he continued, was among "those means which are employed by Congress to carry into execution . . . [the] powers conferred on that body by the people of the United States." Arguing that a power to tax was also a power to destroy, the chief justice voided the act because it taxed "the operation of an instrument employed by the government of the Union to carry its powers into execution."[102]

McCulloch is an important decision for what it tells us about the Court and the Constitution it interprets. Much of Marshall's defense of the bank echoes what Secretary of the Treasury Alexander Hamilton had said when he advised President George Washington on the constitutionality of the act chartering the first national bank. Although the chief justice cited a consistent history in favor of his position, he did not defer to it. Instead, he used the opinion to enhance the position of the Court. Many observers have noted that only in *Marbury* did the Marshall Court declare a federal act unconstitutional, thereby implying that it was a frail precedent upon which to build the practice of judicial review. What they miss, however, is Marshall's insistence that the Court independently exercise its constitutional judgment, so that even a decision in favor of congressional action is something much more than it first appears to be.

At the outset of the opinion Marshall noted the gravity of the federal-state conflict the case presented and then asserted that "by this tribunal alone can the decision be made."[103] The Court's responsibility, then, was not to defer to the judgment of Congress but to interpret the fundamental law for itself. Marshall's insistence upon federal supremacy as a principle adopted by the self-constituting people is a major part of his opinion.[104] As his predecessors had done, he emphasized that the Constitution was made supreme because it codified the will of "the People." And that will sought to create a new federal government with the power to eliminate the state squabbles that had plagued the decade of the 1780s. Marshall is educating a present generation and calling for its affirmation of the work of its predecessors.

As James White, a linguistic legal scholar, interprets Marshall's words, the Constitution "must be seen as an integral part of the culture of which it is made and which it, in turn, reconstitutes. This is indeed why it must be regarded not as a mere legal instrument, resting on some abstract authority, but as a true *constitution:* of language, of community, and of culture."[105] If that document and that culture are to be preserved, Marshall implies, the Court must do it, because only an independent judiciary can work within the parameters of a rule of law to produce reasoned judgments that are subject to scrutiny and debate. The discussion that results inevitably moves beyond the particular judgment and embraces the culture and community as well.[106]

Federal supremacy is further emphasized in *Cohens v. Virginia*, where once again the Court's authority to review state decisions is challenged. The Cohenses were indicted for selling lottery tickets authorized by the District of Columbia in Virginia. State authorities questioned the jurisdiction of the Court under section 25 of the Judiciary Act of 1789 and argued that the Cohenses' appeal to the High Court was, in effect, a suit against the state.

Marshall began by saying that the Court's jurisdiction extends to all cases arising under the Constitution or federal law and that any exception from this broad grant "must be so apparent as to overrule the words its framers have employed." Both the states and the people "have believed a close and firm Union to be essential to their liberty and to their happiness." To Virginia's contention that a sovereign state cannot be sued without its consent, Marshall again cited the Preamble and the supremacy clause as evidence that the American people intended to limit the sovereign claim of the states. In addition to specific checks on state sovereignty, the chief justice continued, the Constitution confers on Congress "a conservative power to maintain the principles in the constitution." And to maintain the purity of these principles, he declared, the Constitution provides in the judiciary an instrument for peaceful resolution of all such conflicts. From its general grant of jurisdiction, "no exception is made of those cases in which a state may be a party." Marshall made clear that the interest being protected was less the nation over the state than that of the individual over the government. He said of the individual claimant: "However unimportant his claim might be, however little the community might be interested in its decision, the framers of our constitution thought it necessary, for the purposes of justice, to provide a tribunal as superior to influence as possible, in which that claim might be decided."[107]

Were not the judicial power coextensive with the legislative power, Marshall argued, the Union would lay prostrate before the states. The preservation and fate of the Constitution, he maintained, rests with the federal judiciary. Although asserting that "a constitution is framed for ages to come, and is designed to approach immortality," he acknowledged the people's right to change it. But such power, he said, resides "in the whole body of the people; not in any sub-division of them."[108]

The decision in the case was anticlimactic, as the Court unanimously decided that the congressional provision giving Washington, D.C., power to authorize a lottery was a local measure that did not "limit the penal laws of a state." Sensitive to the states' control of the criminal law, Marshall said that an inroad upon it would have to "be clearly and unequivocally expressed."[109] So, once again the Court had carefully sifted the challenges to its authority and forcefully reasserted its jurisdiction under section 25 of the Judiciary Act of 1789, but then it rendered a judgment that allowed state control of the situation.

In these cases, the Court sought to base national supremacy on the ground that the American people had ordained it by ratifying the Constitution. This mythic view of the creation of the nation was nurtured and promoted by the justices. Their purpose was not to distort the complex history of the Constitution's formation and adoption but rather to call attention to its basic purpose—to create a Union of the American people, a national community that had to be protected against challenges that could imperil its very existence. Before the Constitution could effectively be interpreted to protect individual rights, the Union, over which it presided, had to be clearly established as fact. This is why the Court felt the need to reinforce the lesson that only in union is there both strength and adequate protection of individual rights.

As Edward White, a legal scholar, was summing up the Marshall Court after an exhaustive study, he said that "the function of law, in a republican society, was to inform the citizenry of their rights and responsibilities." Furthermore, although law could be a medium for change, it also promoted continuity. He continued: "One of the ways in which the Revolutionary experience was universalized and made permanent was through the promulgation of legal principles, principles that were conceived of as static in their nature but adaptive in their application." Then, citing the Constitution as a source of such principles, White concluded that such "legal principles were a mechanism for mediating between the past and the future, for accommodating the Revolutionary experience to the altered conditions of the early nineteenth century." He then added that judges, in "reconciling republican ideology with cultural change," were "serving as architects" of that change.[110] They based their claim to this role on their independence and on their ability to discern the principles of the law.

If we shear the historically limiting words from the above text, we have a useful description not only of the Marshall Court but its successors as well. First, the justices' judicial task has always been to accommodate change without undermining continuity. And included within continuity has been a strong disposition to the promotion of unity. Second, although terms such as "Revolutionary experience" and "republican ideology" have understood meanings in early-nineteenth-century America, they can be subsumed under the broader reach of such concepts as the American creed or civil theology. As such, then, they are less limiting and more long-lived than has generally been assumed. That popular consent provides the foundation of government and that government should serve the people and protect their rights are commandments at the core of the civil religion.

EXPOUNDING THE HOLY WRIT IN
TROUBLED TIMES, 1810–1860

Chief Justice John Marshall in his decisions asserting federal supremacy had made some headway in defining the priestly role of the Supreme Court, but that role had to be fleshed out and new generations had to be taught the essentials of the American faith with its reliance on a rule of law. In the process of doing this, the Court detailed its position in the constitutional order so well, in fact, that the High Bench itself would be sanctified and forgiven even the derelictions of its members.

One of the most nagging worries of Americans during the period of constitution making was that government, supposedly created to protect individual rights, would become the oppressor. That was the primary force behind the insistence upon bills of rights. Madison had failed in his attempt to include in the federal bill of rights a limited but uniform check on the states as well. But the creation of a potentially powerful federal government operating directly upon the people put in place a structure that would give to the Supreme Court the ability to protect at least some individual rights from state interference.

That the justices tended to focus on the individual's property right was the result both of the challenge posed by the cases generated by a growing economy and of specific constitutional language protecting this right. The fundamental law limited the rights an aggrieved individual could claim; the Constitution, at this time, contained no general language that afforded the Court the authority to check the much more active government of the states in their dealings with individuals. As a protector of individual rights, then, its authority was tightly circumscribed. Still, within these parameters the justices shaped the law.

This development is seen clearly in the Marshall Court's interpretation of the constitutional clause prohibiting any state from passing a "Law impairing the Obligation of Contracts."[1] The provision was an attempt to remedy the insecurity of property under the Articles of Confederation. In seeking to protect the individual interests involved, the Court would widen the reach of the prohibition. Entering a political thicket, the justices acknowledged a wide range of state discretion and sought only to interfere when individual rights were vested; that is, when a particular transaction had given to a party a clear legal right. If the right were vested, the Court would say, it was a proper subject for judicial resolution; if not, the states were free to regulate. This distinction was essential to the Court's definition of its own role, which prevented both undue interference with state discretion and a merger of politics and law. Of course, whether the contract clause applied in the first instance and whether the right was vested were decisions the Court reserved for itself. That political considerations could and would enter into this process seems clear. But once these threshold questions were answered and the Court proceeded to decide the individual case, the reasoning was continually sensitive to the need to distinguish between the realms of law and politics.

The contract clause cases directly pose a challenge to government action based on individual rights. In *Fletcher v. Peck*, the issue involved was whether the Georgia state legislature could rescind an earlier action granting state land to a company that, in part, had transferred it to innocent purchasers. Marshall first ruled that the original grant was a contract under the constitutional clause, which had been designed to protect private contracts. No limiting language, he continued, sheltered the state grant from the operation of the clause. Next, the chief justice put aside the contention that the original grant had been tainted with fraud, saying that the judiciary could not inspect the motivation of the legislature. This was a political matter over which the Court had no jurisdiction, its only task being to determine whether the rescinding act violated the rights of those who had purchased land from the company. And on this ground he ruled that the original grant had vested rights, which took the transaction out of the political mainstream where subsequent legislatures had the power to undo the work of their predecessors. Here, then, the Constitution had specifically shielded the people "from the effects of those sudden and strong passions to which men are exposed." Marshall concluded that the constitutional clause prohibiting bills of attainder, ex post facto laws, and laws impairing the obligation of contracts was no less than "a bill of rights for the people of each state," designed to restrain "the power of the legislature over the lives and fortunes of individuals."[2] At times the power of the states had to be limited to protect the authority of the federal government; at other times, as here, the limitation on state action was designed to protect the rights of individuals.

That such rights protected corporate entities as well, Justice Joseph Story made clear in writing for the majority in a subsequent case dealing with the authority of the Virginia legislature to confiscate land held by an Episcopal church. Not mentioning the contract clause, he said that neither the Revolution nor the state's disestablishment of religion affected the church's right to its property. Such assertion of state authority, Story ruled, was "utterly inconsistent with a great and fundamental principle of a republican government, the right of the citizens to the free enjoyment of their property legally acquired."[3]

The most famous of the contract cases was *Dartmouth College v. Woodward*, in which Marshall decided that a charter granted by the British crown was a contract that the state of New Hampshire could not abridge. The chief justice distinguished

between private and public corporations, saying that the former, such as Dartmouth College, were not subject to control by the legislature. He then responded
to a worry expressed by his colleague William Johnson in *Fletcher* that a broad
reading of "contract" would prevent the states from adapting the law to changed
circumstances. The chief justice rejected the argument, saying that the clause was
"intended to guard against a power of at least doubtful utility, the abuse of which
had been extensively felt; and to restrain the legislature in future from violating
the right to property."[4] In this way, Marshall felt, its application would be confined
to the very mischief that had given rise to its inclusion in the Constitution in the
first place. The chief justice brought the corporate charter within the protection
of the contract clause, ruling that the corporation had rights that are protected by
the Constitution.

Justice Story's concurring opinion in the case concluded with a revealing description of the Court's cultural role. He pronounced the High Bench's task "delicate, difficult, and ungracious" and found the Court's relation to the nation "full
of perplexities and embarrassments" as it coped with "jealousies and rivalries . . .
[and] with the most momentous interests confided to its care." The justices must
not listen, Story continued, "to the voice of persuasive eloquence or popular appeal" but instead must "pronounce the law as we find it; and having done this,
our justification must be left to the impartial judgment of our country."[5] For Story,
then, these priests on high serve the holy writ by insisting upon a rule of law that
seeks not popular acclaim but the careful, informed judgment of the people.[6]

In all of these cases, either explicitly or implicitly, the Supreme Court acknowledged that legislatures always had the opportunity to include in the original formulation of the contract a right to rescind or modify it. And as Marshall so clearly
conceded, the legislature had to be given room under the contract clause to regulate in the public interest. For instance, in clear anticipation of later decisions in
the area, Marshall said in 1830 that an immunity from taxation would not be
implied in a corporate charter. The "whole community" is interested in maintaining an undiminished taxing power, he asserted, and "has a right to insist that its
abandonment ought not to be presumed."[7]

A doctrine of vested rights seemed to make sense when a clear property interest
was invaded, but what would happen when rival property interests were involved—when even the absence of legislation could be seen as favoring one property interest over another?[8] Bankruptcy laws did just this. Although the
Constitution gave Congress the authority to pass a federal bankruptcy law, some
states enacted their own regulations. Marshall, for a unanimous Court, upheld the
right of the states to pass such legislation in the absence of a federal law in *Sturges
v. Crowninshield*. But the particular New York law presented in the case was ruled
unconstitutional because it sought to discharge a debt created before its passage.

Subsequent developments would indicate how precarious a precedent this unanimous decision was.

In *Ogden v. Saunders* a four-man majority, in individual opinions, ruled that a state bankruptcy law could discharge debts contracted after the effective date of the statute on the basis that the new law was a graft on the original contracts and thus did not impair them. Justices Joseph Story and Gabriel Duvall joined Marshall in the only dissent he penned in a constitutional law case. He said that the Constitution "intended to make us, in a great measure, one people, as to commercial objects."[9] To read the contract clause only retrospectively, the chief justice continued, invites a return to the chaos and insecurity of life under the Articles of Confederation.

Marshall was trying to use the contract clause to set national policy in the absence of a federal bankruptcy law, and Justice Robert Trimble countered by putting the contract clause in the context of Article I, Section 10 of the Constitution. There the contract clause is linked with the prohibition on bills of attainder and ex post facto laws, which Trimble read through the aims of the Preamble as protecting "personal security and private rights from the despotic and iniquitous operation of retrospective legislation."[10] This approach was consistent with Marshall's early reading of the clause as a constitutional provision designed to protect individual rights.

Despite the prevalence of adjudication involving property rights, other claims of violated personal rights were adjudicated by the Marshall Court. In *Ex Parte Bollman*, the High Bench decided that it had the jurisdictional authority to issue a writ of habeas corpus and that its issuance in the case was justified because of the paucity of evidence that the defendant had committed treason. Marshall partially relied upon a 1795 decision that had granted the writ without any published discussion of the jurisdictional question.[11] But he also asserted that the First Congress, which had organized the judiciary in the act of 1789, was fully cognizant of the constitutional protection of the writ of habeas corpus and "must have felt, with peculiar force, the obligation of providing efficient means by which this great constitutional privilege should receive life and activity." With this question settled, Marshall then proceeded to inquire into the allegations of treason. Saying that such charges excite men's passions, the chief justice added that the Constitution's framers "not only defined and limited the crime, but with jealous circumspection attempted to protect their limitation by providing that no person be convicted of it, unless on the testimony of two witnesses to the same overt act, or on confession in open court."[12]

The chief justice further elaborated the meaning of the Constitution's treason clause when he presided over the trial of Aaron Burr in circuit court in Richmond the following summer. President Jefferson had publicly proclaimed the guilt of Burr and subsequently held Marshall personally responsible for Burr's eventual acquittal. Despite the political furor, the two episodes did result in a tightly drawn definition of treason that would resist expansion and thereby protect individuals from political reprisal. The chief justice had curtailed the expansive interpretation of just what constituted "levying war" that had characterized the treason prosecutions of the 1790s.

With more wide-ranging effect, the Marshall Court also decided that there was no federal criminal common law. Criminal law was largely a state matter, and, even within its limited ken, Congress had been relatively slow to enact criminal statutes. Federal prosecutors had filled in the gaps by recourse to the common law. Remember how the Sedition Act of 1798 had proceeded on the assumption that there was a common law crime of seditious libel. After the 1798 act expired, prosecutions continued under the common law. In fact, it was one of these prosecutions that came before the Supreme Court in 1812. While on circuit duty, Justice William Johnson, the writer of the Court opinion, had refused to hear federal prosecutions based on the common law. He now declared that the matter had "been long since settled in public opinion."[13] Conceding that courts by their very nature must have implied powers, he said that jurisdiction over common law crimes was not one of these necessary powers. To confer jurisdiction, Congress must specify the crime, attach a punishment to it, and determine the court in which it could be prosecuted. Although Johnson's opinion did not talk of the protection of individual rights, clearly a statute would better protect the individual by providing notice of the offense and specifying its elements.

In shaping the contours of the law, John Marshall and his colleagues picked up their predecessors' worry about retrospective laws. The ban on ex post facto laws did not preclude retrospective legislation, but Marshall indicated the Court's continued distaste for such enactments. That law regulates future and not past acts he called "a principle which has always been held sacred in the United States."[14]

Late in its life, the Marshall Court tried to extend some protection to Native Americans. For years the chief justice had contended with Jefferson; now he would have to contend with President Andrew Jackson. An old Indian fighter, Jackson believed that the Cherokees in Georgia should either move west or submit to the authority of the state. In a suit for an injunction against Georgia seeking to restrain the state from enforcing its laws against the Cherokee Nation, Marshall, for the Court, denied that the Cherokees could invoke the jurisdiction of the Court. They constituted not a foreign state, he said, but rather a "domestic dependent" nation. Because their claim was political, he concluded, it was beyond the reach of the judiciary.[15]

Justice Henry Baldwin wrote a concurring opinion. He asserted that the Indians' right of occupancy "was as sacred as the fee-simple," a conclusion that the unanimous Court accepted four years later.[16] Most of Baldwin's opinion was devoted to attacking the dissenters in the case for bringing to the interpretation of the

Constitution "definitions of a State or nation by any foreign writer, hypothetical reasoning, or the dissertations of the Federalist." Such extratextual input, he argued, would "substitute individual authority in place of the declared will of the sovereign power of the Union in a written fundamental law." Furthermore, such action, which in effect amends the charter's words, is no less than "judicial sacrilege." Referring to the Constitution "as the rule and guide to my faith, my reason, and judicial oath," Baldwin said, "I will not take away from the words of this book of prophecy; I will not impair the force of its enactments, plain and unqualified in its terms." As the dutiful priest interpreting the sacred words, the justice concluded that neither public opinion nor strong moral views would tempt him to violate his "solemn conviction of duty."[17]

The dissent in the case that had provoked Baldwin was written by Justice Smith Thompson and joined by Story. Thompson said that the Cherokee Nation was a foreign state for constitutional purposes. Buttressing his definition, he cited the national government's practice of making treaties with the Indians. And to the majority's insistence that the matter was political and not legal, Thompson pointed to the Court's prior willingness to define its jurisdiction to embrace such matters.[18] Here, where the Indians' personal and property rights confirmed by treaty and federal law were threatened by Georgia, the justice saw jurisdiction clearly conferred on the Court by the Constitution. And since the state's action threatened "the total destruction of the whole rights of the complainants," an injunction against the state was the only proper remedy.[19]

Marshall had not generally hesitated since *Marbury* in finding federal judicial power coterminous with federal power, but here he was facing a situation in which a contrary decision would have been ignored both by Georgia and President Jackson. Yet, despite this tense political situation, two respected members of the Court were willing to do what they saw as their duty. To them, the Court, whether enforcement was feasible or not, had the obligation to perform its function, which was no less than trying to ensure justice by calling for decisions that would protect the rights of all individuals, even politically powerless noncitizens.

To have decided in favor of the Cherokee Nation would have protected no rights and would have weakened the authority of the Court. Present-minded critics tend to ignore the institutional and historical limitations that surround such cases. The Court must be continually sensitive to what is and what is not possible, given the potentially forceful opposition of both local and national governments. Only in this way can it both protect its position within the government and its role as a protector of, at least, some individual rights within the constitutional system.

Marshall had acknowledged in the Cherokee Nation decision that the Court might not be able to avoid a more discrete and focused individual challenge to Georgia law affecting the Indians. He had, in fact, encouraged Thompson and

Story to air their views in dissent and collaborated on a pamphlet giving the Cherokee Nation's claims wider publicity.[20] Such a discrete issue came to the High Bench in *Worcester v. Georgia*. The case involved the conviction of a white missionary for failing to obtain a license required by state law to work among the Cherokees. He was sentenced to four years at hard labor. To reach the issue of Worcester's confinement, Marshall, for the Court, had to deny Georgia's authority to impose its law on the Cherokee Nation. This time, Marshall traced the relationship of the Cherokees with the federal government and concluded that the Indians constituted "a distinct community, occupying its own territory, with boundaries accurately described, in which the laws of Georgia can have no force." They "are repugnant to the Constitution, laws, and treaties of the United States" because the task of determining the status of the Indians belongs "exclusively to the government of the Union."[21]

The next question was whether Worcester could benefit from this determination. In 1832 there was no federal constitutional bar on a state depriving an individual of liberty, but this would not stop Marshall. Saying that had Worcester asserted a property claim there would be no question of relief, the chief justice concluded that the same must be true "when the judgment affects personal liberty, and inflicts disgraceful punishment." In a concurring opinion, Justice John McLean added that state law repugnant to the Constitution and federal law cannot divest Worcester "of his property or liberty."[22] So, the Court for the first time found authority to protect the personal liberty of a defendant convicted under state law. Admittedly the conditions were unusual, but the assumption that personal liberty is as protected by the Constitution and federal law as is personal property marks a significant beginning.

Despite the fact that a white person's rights were at issue in *Worcester*, both Marshall's opinion for the Court and McLean's concurring words were broadly supportive of Cherokee claims. Although the removal policy continued, President Jackson, who had no intention of putting force behind Marshall's decision, was placed in a difficult position. Advocates for the Cherokees were planning to bring Georgia's failure to obey the earlier order before the Court. Meanwhile, Jackson was coping with South Carolina's attempt to nullify the operation of the federal tariff laws within its borders. How could he condemn South Carolina's claims to state sovereignty, while upholding Georgia's? A compromise was worked out. Worcester was pardoned by the governor of Georgia and released from prison. Two days later President Jackson asked Congress to authorize federal action against South Carolina. This conversion of the president to the doctrine of national supremacy won the plaudits of Marshall and Story.[23]

In *Worcester*, the Fifth Amendment's bar against depriving any person "of life, liberty, or property, without due process of law" was never mentioned. The reason seems obvious, for the Bill of Rights was designed to limit the power of the federal government, not the states. Still, there was some uncertainty, for unlike the First Amendment, which specifically barred congressional action, the other amendments were general statements of individual rights. Could it not be argued that the Constitution's status as the supreme law of the land made such general provisions binding upon the states as well? John Barron made just such a claim. He owned a wharf in Baltimore harbor that was rendered worthless when the city dredged the harbor and changed the flow of the water. Barron argued that Baltimore had violated his Fifth Amendment right by taking his property without compensation. Marshall, for a unanimous Court, found the answer to the claim in the history of the Bill of Rights, which clearly established that the amendments were to be restraints only on the federal government.[24] Some interpreters see this decision as reflecting the changing composition of the Court and the decline of the national supremacy doctrine, but the conclusion Marshall reached is historically sound. Earlier the chief justice had read certain provisions of the Constitution broadly and creatively without feeling bound by any historical context, but here the historical record was clear and insistent and could be neither ignored nor bypassed. Only in the post–Civil War years would the Constitution be amended to provide a basis for a much more wide-ranging protection of individual rights.

That a person's rights in the United States differed from state to state was clearly revealed in a case coming from New Orleans. A Roman Catholic priest violated a city ordinance that required funeral services to be held at a designated chapel and banned the transfer of the corpse to the church. A unanimous Court said that the "Constitution makes no provision for protecting the citizens of the respective States in their religious liberties; this is left to the State constitutions and laws."[25]

If states were free generally to define the rights of their citizens, clearly the Constitution did seek to override the interest of states in promoting a national economy. One of the primary reasons for dissatisfaction with the Articles of Confederation was its failure to entrust the central government with the authority to regulate commerce among the states. The pertinent clause in the Constitution read "The Congress shall have Power . . . To regulate Commerce with foreign Nations, and among the several States, and with the Indian Tribes."[26] From the beginning of the federal government under the Constitution, Congress had passed laws regulating commerce. And when President Jefferson, during the Napoleonic Wars, got Congress to pass an embargo act that sought to prohibit American trade with foreign nations, disgruntled New England opponents hoped the Court would find such a total ban on trade unconstitutional. However, the Court would not get drawn into the political controversy, and only later did it acknowledge the constitutionality of the act. So, strangely enough, the first case calling for an exploration of the meaning of the commerce clause did not arise until the Constitution had been in force for over a generation.

Gibbons v. Ogden involved a challenge to a New York law granting a monopoly over state waters to a steamboat company. In *McCulloch* the justices had to find power implied in Congress, but here the national legislature was clearly given power to regulate commerce among the states. *Gibbons* invited the Court to explore the dimensions of this commerce power and the related question of its exclusivity. Acknowledging that the task of constitutional interpretation is a matter of judgment and not mechanical application of text to situation, Marshall said that "the judges must exercise . . . that understanding which Providence has bestowed upon them, with that independence which the people of the United States expect from this department of the government."[27] Notice that in this formulation it is not legal learning or experience but "Providence" that brings understanding to the justices. From the very beginning of his tenure, John Marshall saw a special, constitutional role for the justices, but now he sees no less than divine inspiration in the doing of their duty.

Rejecting the argument that commerce does not encompass navigation, Marshall pointed to consistent congressional action, including the "universally acknowledged power of the government to impose embargoes." Broadly defining "commerce," he said that congressional authority does not stop at the state's borders. Although denying that prior practice had conferred any general concurrent right in the states to regulate commerce, he avoided the question of whether the grant of power to the federal government divests the states of any control in the matter. Instead, he said the question was whether the application of state law has "come into collision with an act of Congress, and deprived a citizen of a right to which that act entitles him." The chief justice then ruled that a federal coasting act, providing for the licensing of vessels involved in that trade, was in "direct collision" with the New York act that therefore must be invalidated. Having had to respond painstakingly to arguments that he felt were adequately answered by prevailing axioms, Marshall said that a tendency to expand the power of the states at the expense of the federal government would "explain away the constitution of our country, and leave it a magnificent structure indeed, to look at, but totally unfit for use."[28]

Justice William Johnson agreed with the decision but took issue with basing it on the federal coasting act. That legislation could be repealed and then individual rights would be vulnerable to state invasion. Insisting that the Constitution's words were precise and clear, he saw little room for misinterpretation. The clause's "great and paramount purpose," Johnson continued, "was to unite this mass of wealth and power, for the protection of the humblest individual; his rights, civil and political, his interests and prosperity, are the sole end; the rest are nothing but the means." Because a primary, if not *the* primary, purpose of the Constitution was "to keep the commercial intercourse among the states free from all invidious and partial restraints," Johnson believed that the grant to Congress had preempted any state regulation of such commerce.[29]

We may well wonder why Johnson's opinion, with its assertion of national supremacy and its promotion of union and the rights of individuals, did not attract his colleagues. Clearly it was much more consistent with Marshall's prior views. The answer lies in an issue not apparent on the face of the case but present in the background. On circuit Johnson had declared unconstitutional a South Carolina Negro seamen's act that sought to restrain Negro seamen coming into the port of Charleston. His decision, which illustrated how federal control over commerce might provide a threat to the domestic institution of slavery, met strong opposition, including talk of seceding from the Union.[30] So, in *Gibbons*, Johnson was seeking to vindicate his preemptive reading of federal commerce power. With talk of secession in the air, the Marshall Court had to proceed cautiously, especially when the advocates of concurrent state power brought to the justices' attention the analogy of state control over slavery.[31]

Unlike, then, the broad readings of the implied powers of Congress in cases such as *McCulloch*, the Court in *Gibbons* was treading lightly in the highly charged area of the commerce clause. Justice Johnson's circuit court decision invalidating the South Carolina seamen's act was never enforced, and the Court increasingly accommodated state action under the commerce clause.

Only in one instance, where New York and Massachusetts sought to tax immigrants coming into the ports of the states, did a narrow majority of the Court invalidate the laws on commerce clause grounds.[32] As a result, the justices did little before the Civil War to develop the commerce clause as a vehicle of both federal power and of national unification.

In the last five years of his life, John Marshall worried both about the future of the Court and the divisions in the country. He had created a legacy, and in the era of Jackson he questioned whether it would survive. Times indeed were changing. The foundation of national supremacy had been laid; the problems of a new era now called for accommodating the actions of the states, which were the centers of governmental activity, within the constitutional order. Marshall, who died in 1835, was succeeded in the center seat by Roger B. Taney, a Marylander who had served as a loyal lieutenant in Jackson's administration. As attorney general he had been primarily responsible for Jackson's message vetoing the recharter of the Second Bank of the United States. It challenged the Court's authority by denying that the justices' decision on the bank's constitutionality bound the chief executive. But Taney, now as chief justice, quickly became a defender of judicial power.

Under Taney, the Court would be much more divided and much more sympathetic to states rights, but such accommodations were made without undermining Marshall's major work.[33] Without much fanfare, the Taney Court increased the High Bench's scope of activity and expanded the range of its decision-making power. The contract clause would be interpreted to allow room for technological change by insisting that claims of vested rights would not be presumed; contracts involving governmental power would be construed strictly in favor of the public interest.[34] And in regard to the commerce clause, state regulation would be accommodated without really undermining the authority of federal power. Although Chief Justice Taney consistently supported state regulation of such commerce, he said such regulation had its limits. "Living as we do under a common government," he said, "charged with the great concerns of the whole Union, every citizen . . . is entitled to free access . . . to . . . every State and territory of the Union." The chief continued: "For all the great purposes for which the federal government was formed, we are one people, with one common country."[35]

More significantly than in the contract and commerce areas, the Court in a number of other areas expanded the range of its jurisdiction with a clear understanding that a vital judicial function was the promotion of national unity. Although undisturbed precedent negated a federal criminal common law, the justices in *Swift v. Tyson* found authority for federal courts to fashion their own common law rules, thus promoting national uniformity in commercial transactions.[36] Also, the Court ruled that federal courts were not bound by the equity practices of the states and that a corporation could claim the citizenship of the state in which it was chartered, thus discarding precedent and providing such businesses with easy access to the federal courts.[37] Finally, the Taney Court expanded the reach of admiralty jurisdiction, an exclusive federal preserve. Marshall had accepted the British rule of limiting such authority only to tidal waters. As interior commerce increased, Congress passed legislation extending admiralty jurisdiction to interior rivers and lakes. The Court noted the changes in interior waterborne commerce and concluded that the tidal waters limitation was "utterly inadmissible."[38]

Such decisions expanded both the reach of federal authority and the jurisdiction of the federal courts. Only in the admiralty matter had Congress acted; the extensions of federal judicial power over commercial transactions and corporate claims were the exclusive result of the Court's initiative in responding to perceived national needs. That the High Bench was doing far more than deducing results from the wording of the Constitution was made clear by Justice Peter V. Daniel of Virginia, who dissented in the admiralty case. Acknowledging that his view might "be contracted and antiquated, unsuited to the day in which we live," he nonetheless added that he could not agree to expand or contract the Constitution's original meaning on grounds of "expediency and necessity."[39] What has led historians to look generally with favor upon the Court that Taney headed from 1835 to 1864 was just what Daniel lamented—a flexibility of interpretation that adjusted the fundamental law to the economic and political currents of the democratic society. Change was accommodated by judicial translations of the fundamental legal text without sacrificing the continuity demanded by a rule of law.

The Taney Court was often divided, but generally it was sensitive to the political and social world in which it operated. It took two ideas that can be found in

Marshall's opinions and developed them into doctrines of constitutional law. The first was the doctrine of the state police power, a recognition by the Court of the wide-ranging governing power left to the states under the Constitution. When a state, for instance, passed a law that was challenged as infringing upon congressional control of interstate commerce, it argued that such authority was found within its police power. The Court, then, had to balance the competing interests. In generally upholding state action, the Court defined the local police power as "undeniable and unlimited" as that of any foreign nation, subject only to the checks imposed by the Constitution. Under this municipal regulation or internal police power, the Court continued, it is both the right and "the bounden and solemn duty of a State . . . to advance the safety, happiness and prosperity of its people, and to provide for its general welfare . . . by any and every act of legislation . . . conducive to these ends." This internal police power, the Court concluded, "is complete, unqualified and exclusive."[40]

The second idea that the Taney Court picked up from its predecessor and then further developed involved the divorcement of law from politics. Beginning in *Marbury*, Marshall had recognized that the Court had no authority to interfere with the political discretion entrusted to the other branches of government. From the raw material of this and other cases, Taney shaped the political question doctrine—a self-imposed and self-defined limitation on judicial power. There were certain questions that were not proper for judicial settlement and had to be left for the political branches to resolve. For example, when two rival governments were contending for recognition in Rhode Island, the Court deferred to Congress to decide which one was legitimate.[41] And when the Court decided that a railroad bridge could not obstruct the navigation of the Ohio River because "the great thoroughfares, provided by a beneficent Providence, should neither be neglected nor abandoned," Taney dissented. Such a judicial resolution, he said, comes "too near the confines of legislation."[42]

Providence not only gave the United States its waterways, according to the Supreme Court, it also checked the aims of foreign powers. So, when Spain ceded the Louisiana Territory to France and the latter power sought to frustrate American expansion, "It was not in the order of Providence that such intentions should be accomplished."[43]

Such acknowledgement by the Supreme Court of divine favor for the nation is limited, but the Court habitually sanctified American law and principles. For instance, the justices said that they would interpret a federal statute so as to never violate "those principles which we believe, and which it is our duty to believe, the legislature of the United States will always hold sacred."[44] Of course, the Constitution itself, the Court concluded, reflected the convention's intention to sanctify certain principles.[45] Vested property rights, the justices repeatedly said, survived even transfers of sovereignty over territory. The protection of such an individual right is "deservedly held sacred in the view of policy, as well as of justice and humanity."[46] Free government, they insisted, necessitates "that the rights of personal liberty and private property should be held sacred." No court, the justices continued, could assume "that the power to violate and disregard them . . . lurked under any general grant of legislative authority, or ought to be implied from any general expressions of the will of the people."[47]

Defending judicial sales of property, the Court said that "they are founded on the oldest and most sacred principles of the common law. Time has consecrated them. . . . Titles[,] acquired under the proceedings of courts of competent jurisdiction, must be deemed inviolable in collateral action, or none can know what is his own."[48] Counsel before the Court regularly sought to present their claims as "vested under the sacred sanction of the law."[49]

The repeated use of the term "sacred" in talking of law and individual rights was not idle rhetoric but a reflection of how the justices viewed both the status and purpose of law and their task within the confines of the American civil religion. And when the majority justices seemed to stray from their priestly responsibilities, their colleagues were there to point this out. For instance, when Justice Peter Daniel unsuccessfully sought to overturn the Court's decision that corporations were citizens who could invoke the jurisdiction of the federal courts, he said of the Constitution "that wherever the construction or the integrity of that sacred instrument is involved, I can hold myself trammelled by no precedent or number of precedents."[50] In similar attempts to overturn the Court's ruling, McLean called the Constitution "the sacred bark in which the safety both of the States and of the United States is freighted,"[51] adding in another case that his pledge of loyalty to the fundamental law resulted in "a sacred and solemn duty" that he would not compromise.[52]

By 1855, Daniel picked up some support on a related matter. This time Justice John A. Campbell of Alabama wrote a dissent that Daniel and John Catron of Tennessee joined. The case involved an Ohio tax on a bank that the majority ruled unconstitutional under the contract clause. Reciting the Preamble to the Constitution, the Court said that the case demonstrated the need for a judicial department in the federal government, for without it "neither the powers of the Constitution nor the purposes for which they were given could have been attained." As the majority asserted the Court's importance in the constitutional system, Campbell called attention to a distinction that the Court had evaded. Unlike human beings who come into society possessed of certain rights, he began, corporations are creatures of the state that "with faculties for good . . . combine durable dispositions for evil. They display a love of power, a preference for corporate interests to moral or political principles or public duties, and an antagonism to individual freedom."[53] Here, at a time when corporations were becoming a factor in the economy, some justices were worried about their potential power and its implication for human rights.

In a case involving the extension of admiralty jurisdiction, Daniel clothed himself in the garb of the Constitution, saying it was his "sacred duty" to check error before it assumed the power of precedent.[54] He was true to his word in a similar case when, again in dissent, he stood upon what he called "the sacred authority of the Constitution and the venerable dictates of the law."[55] What was behind this protest to a widening of admiralty jurisdiction was the absence of a jury in admiralty law. Earlier, Daniel had dissented in a case in which a federal judge, by commenting on the evidence, had all but dictated a verdict to the jury. Apparently this practice could be followed when federal trial courts were sitting in states that permitted such comment. Although the majority saw no problem, Daniel saw a violation of "a great principle lying . . . at the foundation of civil society itself: . . . the venerable, the sacred . . . trial by jury." Allowing such an inroad on this most basic right, he concluded, mocks and deceives "those who have been taught to revere and rely upon it as the best safeguard of . . . [their] rights."[56] That this denial of a right to a jury trial was at the root of Daniel's protest against a widening of admiralty jurisdiction is revealed in a dissent written by Justice Levi Woodbury that Daniel joined. Woodbury reminded his colleagues that Americans in the period prior to the Revolution were "indignantly remonstrating against . . . the smallest encroachment by England on that sacred trial."[57] Condemning the majority's willingness to make inroads on the hallowed right of trial by jury, Woodbury said such a departure from the past was a violation of the Constitution.

In his six years on the Court Woodbury demonstrated a keen sensitivity to issues of individual rights. In addition to the jury trial question, he was the lone dissenter in *Luther v. Borden*. The case involved a challenge to martial law proclaimed by the old government in Rhode Island. Although the majority dismissed the case invoking the newly developed political question doctrine, Woodbury condemned the state officials who had forcibly broken into a home and arrested its owner. He was incensed by the majority's callous disregard for individual rights: "The genius of our liberties holds in abhorrence all irregular inroads upon the dwelling-houses and persons of the citizen, and with a wise jealousy regards them as sacred." Noting that the Third, Fourth, and Fifth Amendments to the Constitution were conceived as necessary protections against such inroads, he denied that the state had any authority to take such action. War powers, in which martial law is included, he said, are preempted by the federal government. And legislative power at all levels is not authorized "to suspend or abolish the whole securities of person and property at its pleasure." No executive or legislature can so act, when "our social usages and political education, as well as our constitutional checks, are the other way." Government, he concluded, must exercise restraint in civil disturbances "under our boasted dominion of law and order . . . by enlightened and constitutional law, and the moderation of superior intelligence and civilization, rather than by appeals to any of the semibarbarous measures of the darker ages."[58] What incensed Woodbury was that his colleagues had shirked their priestly responsibilities under the commands of the civic faith.

Woodbury found no support for his claim that the federal government had a monopoly on declaring martial law, but a divided Court before his arrival did find one area where a delegation of power to the federal government precluded state action. The case arose in 1841 when the governor of Vermont sought to honor a claim by Canada for the return of a fugitive from Canadian justice. Rejecting the argument that the petition for a writ of habeas corpus was inappropriate in this case, Chief Justice Taney, for the majority, ruled that it, in effect, is a suit to recover liberty and is the proper remedy for a person who is "unlawfully imprisoned." Granting the writ, Taney said that "one of the main objects of the Constitution [was] to make us, so far as regarded our foreign relations, one people, and one nation." To allow states to make such determinations is "utterly incompatible" with this purpose and "would expose us to one of those dangers against which the framers of the Constitution have so anxiously endeavored to guard." Such centralized control also provides "the proper legal safeguards . . . for the protection of citizens."[59]

Notice, here, how Taney sought to protect the right of the individual to be freed from inconsistent state action by finding a monopoly of power in the federal government.

The chief executive of Vermont might be restrained in his attempt to be a good neighbor, but were there any limitations on the pardoning power of the nation's chief executive? Could a president under this power commute a death sentence to life imprisonment? A majority of the Court found no obstacle to the president granting a conditional pardon with the consent of the person affected. Justice McLean, in dissent, would have granted the claim urged in the case—that the condition was inoperative and the recipient of the pardon should be freed. What bothered the justice was that his colleagues had agreed to the displacement of the rule of law by a rule of unlimited executive discretion. In the circumstances, McLean found the prisoner's consent "a very inadequate protection for his rights." He concluded: "To speak of a contract by a convict, to suffer a punishment not known to the law, nor authorized by it, is a strange language in a government of laws."[60] Indeed it might be, but, ever since, the president's pardoning power has encompassed the conditional pardon.

As should now be clear, John McLean was a peppery figure on the Court. Writing for the majority in a land dispute case, he ruled in favor of the claimant who rested his title to the land on the basis of his settlement under a federal statute. The justice found preemption to be a legal right "founded in an enlightened public policy" designed to reward the enterprise of generally poor but adventurous citizens moving beyond the settled areas and encountering danger and hardships.[61] And when the Court decided that the extension of a patent redounded to the benefit of the assignee, McLean protested. Arguing that "all enlightened governments reward the inventor . . . [as] a public benefactor," he continued: "Many of the most splendid productions of genius . . . have been conceived and elaborated in a garret or hovel. Such results not only enrich a nation, but render it illustrious. And should not their authors be cherished and rewarded?"[62] The real matter in dispute was whose property rights were to be protected. While the majority saw the general welfare being served by protecting the assignee's rights, McLean saw that welfare being promoted by protecting the patent holder's rights.

Many of the Taney Court cases posed a similar problem—not whether to favor the property interest but, rather, which property interest to favor. So, for instance, in contract law cases, such as *Charles River Bridge v. Warren Bridge*, the Court had to decide between such rival claims.[63] Increasingly, the claim of a vested interest was rejected in favor of the more dynamic property interest. That the Court protected property interests was clear, but during the Taney years it increasingly provided the room for government to accommodate technological change.

If the Taney Court seemed to mirror the political change associated with the Age of Jackson, there were certain limits that even a popular administration could not transgress. Marshall had seen a real threat to the Court's authority in Andrew Jackson, whose assertion of power as a tribune of the people greatly expanded the office. The action of Jackson's postmaster general provided the occasion for the Court to deal in a limited way with what seemed to be an attack on the judiciary's role.[64] When a new appointee refused to make payments for which his predecessor had contracted, Congress passed a law directing that full payment be made. When the new postmaster general only partially complied, a suit was filed to compel him to make the full payment. Could a writ of mandamus be issued? Echoes of *Marbury v. Madison* were clearly heard, though the Court now was acting within its appellate jurisdiction. The argument before the justices was filled with rhetoric over the proper line between judicial and executive authority and with personal attacks as well. Attorney General Benjamin F. Butler was moved to condemn the "vehement invective and passionate appeals . . . as sounds unmeet for the judicial ear." This "holy ground," he said referring to the courtroom, "where questions of constitutional law could be discussed with calmness of mind and liberality of temper" has been desecrated.[65]

Over Taney's dissent and distinguishing between discretionary and ministerial duties, the Court majority upheld the grant of a writ of mandamus. To read a duty to execute the law to imply a power to supercede the law "would be clothing the President with a power entirely to control the legislation of Congress, and paralyze the administration of justice." The writ, the Court concluded, was necessary to prevent "a failure of justice."[66]

If the Court was the citadel of justice and if the Court had a priestly responsibility to protect threats to individual rights, why was it so insensitive to what we now see so clearly—the injustice of slavery in a society that professed a belief in the equality of human beings? First, we must struggle to overcome a moral condemnation that blinds us to the need to understand and work within a historical context where individual rights were protected by recognizing a property right in persons. When the justices confronted the conflict between the rival claims of liberty and property, they generally chose to safeguard the individual property right.[67] The acceptance of slavery by the Court, then, did not mean that the Court was not safeguarding individual rights; it simply was not giving proper weight to the countervailing right of personal liberty. Slaves, though consciously recognized as persons in the wording of the Constitution, were a special class of human beings. This was so because preexisting regulations establishing slavery in certain states were accommodated within the constitutional order. The sad effect was to dehumanize a portion of the American population.

Second, we must first recognize that the Court is limited by the Constitution. That Constitution does nothing to challenge the natural right to freedom, but it does contain certain concessions to the owners of slaves that were seen as a part of the cost of union. The Court could read natural law conceptions of equality into the Constitution only when there was a prevailing consensus, as there was on the importance of an individual right to property, and, after the early years, only when there was some specific wording to which natural law concepts could be attached as a guide to the text's interpretation.[68] Freedom was to a limited extent protected by the Fifth Amendment's admonition that "No person shall be . . . deprived of life, liberty, or property, without due process of law." But whatever protection is found here is only against the actions of the federal government, not against actions of the states. By necessity, the Constitution generally left the matter of slavery to state control. Even with the Bill of Rights the Constitution provided no means by which the Court could reach the larger issue of the freedom of the slaves.

Third, we need to be sensitive to the practical limits on the Court's power. At times critics have suggested that the justices have a moral responsibility to come to decisions independent of any concern for their enforceability. Were the justices to have succumbed to this temptation, they would have appreciably limited the Court's cultural role in American society. For example, Justice William Johnson believed strongly that the South Carolina seamen's act was an unconstitutional interference with Congress's control of interstate commerce. His decision to that effect was ignored. Whether he was right or wrong, the Court can hardly be faulted for not wading into such troubled waters, where decisions similar to Johnson's would only have exposed the inability of the Court to enforce its will. On the other side of the matter, when the justices tried to read into the Constitution greater security for a property right in slaves, in the infamous case of *Dred Scott v.*

Sandford,[69] it not only fueled the political fires of disunion and civil war, but it seriously undermined its role within the constitutional order.

Finally, we must resist a tendency to project our current sensibilities and priorities upon past generations. We need to add a wholesome historical perspective to our views—not to explain away the actions of past generations but to better understand how progress has been made and can be made toward the construction of a society that becomes more inclusive and more sensitive to the fulfillment of the grand principles announced at the founding of the country. Americans at their national inception had pledged their faith to a creed; that they did not live up to its commandments is clear, but equally clear is their own self-criticism leading to progress over time.

Perhaps the Constitution's compromise with slavery had ensured that the situation would be exacerbated over time, but in the late eighteenth and early nineteenth centuries the hope was that slavery would eventually be eliminated, not that it would find a secure lodging in an evolving Southern economic system. At that earlier time, there was a general understanding that slavery was an unnatural condition and that natural law made men free. Slavery was then a product of the enactment of positive law; in its absence all men and women were free. This is still our essential belief—that the absence of legal prohibition or special entitlement leaves individuals free to make their own choices. Law can positively assert and protect certain free choices from abridgement, but in its absence the assumption is the freedom of the individual. The incompatibility of slavery with basic American principles, however, was recognized at the outset, and until the 1820s there was some Southern support for emancipation.

In many of the cases that came before the Supreme Court slaves were treated as subjects of property disputes, but the Court did adjudicate fourteen cases involving a claim of freedom under its general appellate jurisdiction over federal trial courts in the period through 1861. They all involved interpretations of state law. Four decisions rendered the plaintiffs free, two gave them another chance to make their case at the trial level, and eight, including two episodes of the same case, confirmed their slave status.[70] Seven of the eight decisions favoring slavery occurred before 1828.

After that time, when the issue of slavery was stirring more popular dispute, the Court seemed more sensitive to the claim of freedom in this less noticed area of adjudication. For instance, in the earlier cases Justice Gabriel Duvall, a Maryland plantation owner, said that the majority was insisting upon a standard of evidentiary proof of emancipation that was not required in the state courts. Calling freedom "a natural inherent right," Duvall asserted that "the right to freedom is more important than the right of property."[71] He added that unless the majority was willing to make some reasonable accommodation as to proof, such claims would be impossible to substantiate. In another case, he would have found proof of descent from a free mother a sufficient basis for emancipation. The Court again disagreed.[72] Gradually, however, the Court moved in Duvall's direction and loosened the rules of evidence in such cases.[73]

Often the state statutes or decisions under inspection by the Supreme Court required that manumitted slaves be able to support themselves. Justice Duvall convinced his colleagues to follow a Maryland court decision that the grant by will of property to a slave served to emancipate the grantee.[74] The broadest decision in this area was written by another Southerner, Justice James M. Wayne of Georgia, after Duvall had left the Court. Clearly infants could not support themselves, but Wayne, brushing aside what seemed to be the rule in the state as not specifically covering a case where mother and child were freed at the same time, said that the Supreme Court can reach its own conclusion in the matter. Citing "those natural affections of a mother for her child which have always been found strong enough to cherish and sustain it," the justice ruled that the spirit of the law—not to burden the community with former slaves unable to support themselves—was not frustrated by the Court's decision in favor of freedom.[75]

These cases stirred little public attention, but there were others dealing both directly and indirectly with slavery that moved into the mainstream of public and political concern. They concerned the foreign slave trade, the state's ability to control the admission of slaves into the state, the enforcement of the Fugitive Slave Act, and a claim of freedom based upon residence in free territory.

In two cases the Court grappled with the result of Congress's interdiction of the foreign slave trade. Both times ships were seized off the coast of the United States by federal officers and brought into port. These cases gave the justices the opportunity to reflect on the institution of slavery generally without having to assess the implications of their ideas on domestic practice.

In *The Antelope* the federal government argued that the two hundred or so slaves on a ship brought into the port of Savannah by an American revenue cutter became free men. Rival claims were asserted by the Spanish and Portuguese, whose ships originally had housed the captive slaves. Chief Justice Marshall noted that the case presents "claims in which the sacred rights of liberty and of property come in conflict with each other." Agreeing with government counsel that the slave trade violates the law of nature, the chief justice said that "every man has a natural right to the fruits of his own labor, . . . and that no other person can rightfully deprive him of those fruits." But then distinguishing between the task of moralist and jurist, Marshall found slavery to be "a legitimate result of force" sanctioned by the actions of nations.[76] He concluded that there was some merit in the Spanish claim and provided for the return of some of the captives, but by decision of the Court the majority of the blacks were freed. They were eventually transported to Liberia, the colony established in Africa by the American Colonization Society.

The second case involving the slave trade excited great popular attention in 1841. It involved the schooner *Amistad*, which had been captured off Long Island by an American brig. The blacks aboard the ship had been seized in Africa by the crew of a Spanish ship, and during a voyage between Cuban ports the blacks rose up, killed the captain, and took control of the ship. Their intention was to return to Africa, but the Spanish crew sailed into American waters where the ship was captured. This time the United States, under certain treaty provisions, supported Spain's claim to the ship and the blacks. Former President John Quincy Adams argued extensively and forcefully for the freedom of the blacks, making sure that the Court would not miss the moral issue involved.

Joseph Story, writing for the unanimous Court, concluded that the blacks were never slaves because they had been seized in violation of Spanish law. And since they had been kidnapped and forcibly restrained, he continued, the blacks could not be considered pirates or robbers. Facing rival claims of property and liberty, Story said that a resolution must rest "upon the eternal principles of justice and international law." With life and liberty the issue, the Africans were entitled to assert their claim "before any of our courts to equal justice."[77] He ruled that the blacks were now free men, to the delight of those who had made the case a focal point for their antislavery campaign.

On the leftover question of the state's power over the admission of slaves into its jurisdiction, the Court implicitly condoned this authority in *Groves v. Slaughter* in 1841. But the volatility of the slavery issue was captured in the opinions of two justices, John McLean of Ohio, who concurred in the Court's resolution, and Henry Baldwin of Pennsylvania, who dissented from it.

McLean drew a distinction between slaves as property and slaves as persons, saying that the Constitution acts upon slaves only in the latter capacity. Although federal authorities are required to protect the property right in slaves, he asserted, their status as slaves derives exclusively from municipal law. In regard to the state's authority, the justice said that the commerce clause interposed no bar either to a state prohibiting or regulating the institution. The state, the justice continued, "has a right to protect itself against the avarice and intrusion of the slave dealer," a right that "is higher and deeper than the Constitution," for the "evil involves the prosperity and may endanger the existence of a State."[78]

Baldwin would have used the commerce clause to prevent a state from preferring the interest of its slaveholders over that of out-of-state residents. He said that the state law was "partial, anti-national, subversive of the harmony which should exist among the States, as well as inconsistent with the most sacred principles of the Constitution." After castigating the majority, he took aim on McLean, warning that to consider slaves as "persons merely, and not property, is . . . the first step toward a state of things to be avoided. . . . If the first step is a mistaken one, the successive ones will be fatal to the whole system."[79] There were those who saw the commerce clause as a threat to slavery, but notice how Baldwin would employ it to allow the unregulated transit of slaves among the slave states. At any rate, the colloquy here indicated the difficulty of formulating sound commerce clause doctrine in the face of strong, sectional passions.

Although the decision to allow the states discretion over the admission of slaves fit comfortably into a federal system that had to accommodate both free and slave states, more problems were apparent as the Court wrestled with the issue of fugitive slaves. In 1793 Congress had passed the first fugitive slave act, which it strengthened as part of the Compromise of 1850.[80] Without legislation, the performance of the duty to return escaped slaves would seem to lie within the discretion of authorities in each state. In time the Fugitive Slave Act spawned personal liberty laws seeking to protect free black residents from being unlawfully seized as escaped slaves. That federal-state conflict would result could be predicted, and in deciding the cases the Court would cast doubt on its previous characterization of the Constitution as the sacred embodiment of the united will of the whole people.

By the time the Court first confronted the conflict, antislavery sentiment had grown in the North. The most radical of such views challenged the legal order on moral grounds, advocating disobedience to the law. As William Lloyd Garrison, the fiery abolitionist, characterized the Constitution, it was " 'a covenant with death and an agreement with Hell' . . . and should be immediately annulled."[81] The second argument was equally broad in its implications, but it sprang from the text of the Constitution. Its proponents argued that the Fifth Amendment's protection of liberty declared slavery illegal and that the authority conferred on the federal government to guarantee to each state a republican government gave it power to outlaw the institution.

A more moderate view, early espoused by Salmon P. Chase, who would eventually become chief justice, was that the federal government lacked any power over the institution, which prevented that government from acquiescing in the extension of slavery into the territories and from aiding in the return of fugitive slaves. The controlling idea behind this position stemmed from a British case decided in 1772 that asserted that, in the absence of any positive law supporting slavery, freedom was conferred on those found within the realm.[82] This view had worked its way into the law of free states, posing real problems in a union half-slave and half-free. Was the obligation to return fugitive slaves, then, simply a matter of good faith or, as it is known in the law, comity? Were states free to legislate in protection of their domestic policies, despite the obligation to return fugitive slaves written into the Constitution and federal law?

That question came to the Court in *Prigg v. Pennsylvania* in 1841. The case involved a Maryland slave catcher who entered Pennsylvania and seized a woman and her newborn child as fugitive slaves. Edward Prigg was indicted in Pennsylvania for violating the state's personal liberty law, which had established procedural

safeguards that had been ignored in the seizure. Justice Joseph Story of Massachusetts began by saying that the Constitution in many respects must be viewed historically as a "compromise of opposing interests and opinions," which should be
interpreted "with all the lights and aids of contemporary history." This led the
justice to a discussion of the compromise necessary to bring the slaveholding states
into the new Union under the Constitution. Moving from this starting point,
Story essentially bypassed the wording of the fugitive slave clause and read into it
the "positive and absolute right" of slave owners with which states may not interfere. To give this right substance, the justice continued, Congress properly enacted
legislation to secure the protection that the clause intended. The fact that the
power is not specifically delegated to Congress is not conclusive, Story added, for
when an end is specified, it is "a just and necessary implication that the means to
accomplish it are given also." Before the Constitution the return of a fugitive slave
was "a matter of comity and favor," Story added, but now it was no less than "an
absolute, positive right and duty, pervading the whole Union with an equal and
supreme force, uncontrolled and uncontrollable by State sovereignty or State legislation."[83]

Earlier in his *Commentaries on the Conflict of Laws* Story had said that each state
had complete control over the law that would be enforced within its borders, but
in *Prigg* he carved out an exception for a right defined by the federal government.
The justice concluded that the power given the federal government was exclusive,
which meant that the federal government alone was responsible for providing a
remedy. But in attempting to strike a balance and indicate that the opinion was
not the first step toward nationalizing slavery, Story would not require any state
assistance in the federal effort to recover fugitive slaves. However, he was careful
to say that the state, in providing for the security of its citizens, was not precluded
from incidentally aiding the slave catcher. The opinion upheld the Fugitive Slave
Act and entrusted its enforcement to the federal government.

Wayne and Taney took issue with Story in concurring opinions. Wayne argued
for federal exclusivity as the means to ensure uniformity in enforcement, saying
slaveholders had been given a right to recovery in the Constitution that could not
be undermined by state action. Taney, on the other hand, argued that a protection
of individual rights by the federal government had not previously been interpreted
to mean "that the States could not uphold and maintain them." In fact, he said,
the reverse has been the consistent practice, as in the no-impairment-of-contract
cases, where the federal government acted only when necessary to prevent the
rule's violation. "I cannot understand," he continued, "the rule of construction
by which a positive and express stipulation for the security of certain individual
rights, of property in the several States, is held to imply a prohibition to the States
to pass any laws to guard and protect them."[84]

While most of the justices squabbled over the question of exclusive federal power, McLean sought to accommodate personal liberty laws with the Fugitive Slave Act. He acknowledged that the constitutional clause and act were compromises between slave and nonslave states in "an exercise of exalted patriotism."[85] But, he added, the Pennsylvania act only sought to prevent the forcible removal of any Negro or mulatto from a state in which all were presumed to be free. All the other justices said that the state law was inconsistent with the Constitution and the federal act, but McLean insisted that the law legitimately protected residents from forcible removal, a goal clearly within the state's police power. Although the federal act permitted the forcible capture of the alleged fugitive slave, the justice continued, it then required that the claim be presented to a judge before the fugitive could be removed. Prigg brought his captives before a state judge who refused to act. Then, rather than seeking out a federal judge, he removed the presumed slaves to Maryland.

Seeing no necessary incompatibility between the statutes, McLean would have allowed the state room to protect its residents. The justice went further than Story in asserting that the federal government, under its exclusive power, could impose a duty on state officials to hear the claim of the owner and accept the proof prescribed by Congress. But neither the Fugitive Slave Act nor the Constitution allowed the slave catcher, without establishing title, to remove a slave from the state. The whole purpose of the act, he continued, was to find a peaceful solution to a delicate problem "guarded by the forms of law." Pennsylvania, McLean continued, has not run into conflict with the federal law by "seeking to protect free persons of color within the State."[86]

McLean's reading of the fugitive slave clause and federal statute is sound; the majority avoids the Ohio justice's rationale by conjuring up a guiding historical intent that, in effect, rewrites the constitutional text to make slave property more secure. Story justifies his interpretation on grounds that such a reading is necessary to maintain a union of conflicting interests and of safeguarding the peculiar property right. To embellish the text with a judicially discovered intent, however, casts aspersions on the very notion of a rule of law and on the priestly authority of the Court.[87]

Furthermore, the lesson the opinions in *Prigg* teach about the Constitution vary considerably from those lessons taught by earlier opinions. Rather than presenting the fundamental law as an embodiment of the mythic people's will for whom the justices act as trustee in constituting and reconstituting the American community, Story finds the Constitution's supremacy resting upon a basic and necessary compromise of rival state interests. The aspirational reach of the document is all but eliminated, as the American people are reminded that their continued acceptance of that compromise is now mandated by the rule of law. The policy of free states, then, must yield to the demands of union based upon the founding compromise. Very much in the general spirit of the decisions of the Taney Court, McLean urged more flexibility in constitutional interpretation to accommodate both legitimate national and state interests. But he was also calling attention to the fact that the majority had read more into the law protecting slavery than the words themselves required.

In upholding the Fugitive Slave Act, the Court continued to remind Americans of their responsibilities under the Constitution. Writing for a unanimous Court in 1847, Justice Levi Woodbury of New Hampshire said that whether property existed in human beings was a political question answered by each state. Under the Constitution, he continued, "it is impossible to do justice . . . , or fulfill the duty incumbent on us towards all the members of the Union, . . . without sustaining . . . the statute of 1793." Whatever expediency we may now find in such "sacred compromises," he said, "this court has no alternative, while they exist, but to stand by the Constitution and laws with fidelity to their duties and their oaths. Their path is a straight and narrow one, to go where that Constitution and the laws lead, and not to break both, by traveling without or beyond them."[88] Woodbury acknowledged that the fundamental law could be changed by the people, but until then, the Court's and the people's duty was to live with the founding compromise on slavery.

In an earlier episode of the case in circuit court, Justice John McLean had expressed a similar idea: "The law is our only guide. If convictions . . . of what is right or wrong, are to be substituted as a rule of action in disregard of the law, we shall soon be without law and without protection." "Any departure . . . ," he continued, "inflicts a deep wound on society, and is extremely demoralizing in its effects."[89]

When Illinois sought to enforce legislation making "harboring and secreting a negro slave" a crime, the Court majority saw no conflict with federal legislation. States have the power, said Justice Robert C. Grier of Pennsylvania, "to repel from their soil a population likely to become burdensome and injurious, either as paupers or criminals." Illinois has the right to prohibit such conduct because it violates the duties imposed by the Constitution and federal law and tends "to destroy the harmony and kind feelings which should exist between citizens of this Union, to create border feuds and bitter animosities, and to cause breaches of the peace, violent assaults, riots and murder."[90] Grier saw the statute only indirectly aiding slave owners, and he said that whether the state could legislate in direct aid of federal fugitive slave policy was an open question.

Justice McLean dissented, objecting to the possibility that a single act could result in two offenses, one against state and the other against federal law. For the Ohio justice, such a conclusion was "contrary to the nature and genius of our government." Rejecting an explanation based upon dual sovereignties by saying both governments operate on the same people, he argued that no government under law punishes the same offense twice. He lamented the fact that the majority had provided "an exception to a great principle of action, sanctioned by humanity and justice."[91] McLean, among all the justices who served on the pre–Civil War Court, was the most sensitive to nonproperty individual rights.

The type of aid Illinois offered in support of the national policy on fugitive slaves was much less common than state legislation seeking to impede the operation of the federal law. The growth of the abolitionists' moral crusade against slavery threatened the maintenance of any political compromise, and the Court's plea to accept the bargain long ago struck to forge the Union was increasingly disregarded. But before getting to the final case in this area, which arose when the full authority of the state was interposed against the enforcement of the Fugitive Slave Act, we need to pick up the second thread of cases to put the final decisions in chronological order.

That second thread of cases begins with *Menard v. Aspasia*, which came from Missouri twenty-five years before a similar case coming from the same state would place the Court at the center of a political storm. The issue was whether a slave's prior residence in free territory operated to free her when she asserted that claim in a slave jurisdiction. She had been born to a slave mother in the Northwest Territory after it was organized by an act of Congress under the Articles of Confederation in 1787. That act, later confirmed by Congress under the Constitution, provided that there "shall be neither slavery nor involuntary servitude in the said territory."[92] This provision was carried over in the Illinois territorial government and into the constitution of the state in 1819. The claimant had lived as a slave in Illinois into her adulthood, when she was then sold by her master to the defendant in the case. He then gave her to his son-in-law in Missouri, who, upon commencement of the suit, returned her to his father-in-law. Missouri courts determined that her residence in free territory made her a free woman. The defendant appealed the case to the U.S. Supreme Court on the ground that the decision violated the protection of his property as provided for in the Northwestern Ordinance of 1787. He was seeking to bring the Supreme Court into the picture by claiming that the decision of the state was against a right founded on federal law and therefore within the Court's jurisdiction as provided by section 25 of the Judiciary Act of 1789.

The Court, speaking through John McLean, found the argument specious. Its acceptance, he said, would force the Court into the task of reviewing all challenged state action having any effect on property. Furthermore, McLean noted that the prohibition on slavery was specifically delineated in the ordinance and, as such, would override any generalized property protection. If it did not destroy a property right in slaves, he continued, it certainly did not strengthen any such right. So, the defendant's appeal was dismissed as not falling within the Court's jurisdiction. But, McLean then added, assuming that the 1787 Ordinance was an act of Congress and that the Missouri courts had decided against the freedom of the plaintiff, then the plaintiff herself could bring an appeal to the Court under section 25.[93] These words were *obiter dicta*—that is, not necessary to the decision in the case—but they made an appealing target for those opposed to slavery.

Actually much would happen in the twenty years between the decisions in *Menard* and *Strader v. Graham*. The comity shown by states, such as Missouri, in ruling that residence in free territory freed the slave broke down in the 1840s. In 1851 the Court finally addressed the effect of a slave's residence in the old Northwest Territory. A steamboat captain was being sued for the value of alleged slaves that he had transported from Kentucky to Cincinnati, Ohio. His defense was that the earlier transit of these individuals into Ohio, a state that had been carved out of the Northwest Territory, to perform as musicians had, in effect, made them free men. The Kentucky court decided that prior residence in free territory had not freed the slaves, and the defendant sought to appeal the decision to the Supreme Court.

Chief Justice Roger Taney, now deciding that the Northwest Ordinance could not be invoked to obtain the jurisdiction of the Court, dismissed the appeal. Because the early legislation had been supplanted largely by state law, the status of such slaves, Taney continued, was therefore exclusively a matter for the state to decide. Although all members of the Court now agreed that a claim based on the Ordinance of 1787 would not invoke the jurisdiction of the Court, Justice McLean suggested that the proper approach was to rest the case on the Ohio constitution, which carried over the federal ban on slavery.[94]

Antislavery forces were dismayed by a decision that gave slave states free reign to ignore claims of freedom. But a Court that had been consistently sensitive to the need to leave political decisions to the other branches of government could more than justify its opinion. The Taney Court had moderated the nationalistic doctrines of its predecessor and given the states room to act without fundamentally impairing national supremacy. It had demonstrated a sensitivity to the ongoing political process and gained a popularity denied to the Marshall Court. In fact, some hope was expressed that maybe the divisive slavery controversy could be moderated, if not solved, by a judicial resolution of the contentious issues. Enter Dred Scott, the most famous slave in the reports of the United States Supreme Court.[95]

Dred Scott sought his freedom initially in the Missouri courts on the basis of his residency in Wisconsin Territory and in Illinois as a servant to a military officer. Following *Menard*, the Missouri trial court granted Scott his freedom. Upon appeal, the state supreme court overruled its earlier decisions and held that Scott's status was determined by Missouri law, which pronounced him a slave. Six years later, in 1854, a new suit was instituted in federal court with Scott claiming to be a citizen suing an out-of-state owner. By this time the case was viewed by both sides as a means to obtain a reading from the Supreme Court on the constitutionality of Congress's power to ban slavery in the territories. A decision against Scott's claim in the trial court set the stage for the appeal to the U.S. Supreme Court.

Apparently the Court first decided to issue an opinion based on *Strader v. Graham* to the effect that Missouri courts had full authority to determine Scott's status. However, this solution broke down as some members of the Court were determined to confront the issue of slavery in the territories. The result was a welter of opinions in *Dred Scott v. Sandford*. Some conclusions, however, were clear: Scott could not sue in federal court for he was not a citizen of the United States; he was still a slave; and Congress did not have the power to proscribe slavery in the territories. The latter conclusion led to the declaration that the Missouri Compromise of 1820 that had divided the territories between slave and free was unconstitutional. So, although the Missouri Compromise had been scuttled by new congressional legislation in the early 1850s, the Court, for the second time in its history, invalidated a federal act.

The decision both undermined the Democratic Party's commitment to popular sovereignty, which sought to allow residents in the territories to make their own decision about slavery, and the new Republican Party's commitment to keeping the territories free. Rather than solve any questions, *Dred Scott* only made things worse by precluding any accommodation between the opposing forces. The Court had attempted to impose a proslavery solution on a divided nation, forgetting its inherent limitations and forcefully asserting the primacy of a property right in slaves to the detriment of liberty and of the Union itself. Strange, indeed, was the expectation that a Court pronouncement could settle a fundamental conflict that was increasingly tearing the nation apart. Yet, Justice James Wayne of Georgia asserted that because of differences involving "private rights of value, and constitutional principles of the highest importance, . . . the peace and harmony of the country required the settlement of them by judicial decision."[96] Earlier the justices had accommodated slavery as a necessary part of the compromise that had produced a nation; now the Court stirred fears that it was nationalizing the peculiar institution.

Members of the Court had recognized their delicate task of balancing individual rights of liberty and property, but now Chief Justice Taney trumpeted the triumph of the property right within an all-white constitutional order. Reading the Fifth Amendment to provide protection for both life and property, the chief justice neglected its liberty component. Within its terms, he found a constitutional right to own slaves that could not be abridged by denying slaveholders access to territorial land, which, he said, was held in equal trust for all citizens. In addition to enshrining this particular property right and elevating it to a new and superior status invulnerable to any invasion, Taney attempted to fix the inferior position of the black in the constitutional order. Not only was Dred Scott not a United States citizen, he said, but no black, whether free or enslaved, could ever be one. Reviewing the status of blacks in American society prior to the Constitution, Taney concluded that they had "been regarded as beings of an inferior order; and altogether unfit to associate with the white race, either in social or political relations; and so far inferior, that they had no rights which the white man was bound to respect; and that the negro might justly and lawfully be reduced to slavery." This prior history, he said, revealed that blacks were stigmatized with "deep and enduring marks of inferiority and degradation" and could not have been considered persons entitled to the liberties and rights of citizens.[97] States could and did confer their own citizenship, but who could be a citizen of the United States was fixed by the chief justice's idiosyncratic reading of American history. The communal terms of that order were fixed at the founding, and the past prejudice and the degradation of nonwhites was to be preserved in the present and into the future.

To save slavery, then, from the political process, Taney increasingly made the Constitution and the American community static and closed. The chief justice desperately tried to write an increasingly unpopular accommodation squarely into constitutional law despite the paucity of textual support. Perhaps, for the first time in its history, the Court had reached a decision that was broadly and personally felt by a large portion of the population. Instead of serving as a protector of union, the Court became, through Taney's opinion, the spokesman for a sectional interest. Why the decision has been described as a self-inflicted wound and why it has universally been characterized as the worst decision in the annals of the Court should now be clear. The majority justices put the force of the Constitution and the rule of law behind a particular propertied interest increasingly challenged in the society. They had sought peremptorily to close off the social dialogue. To have expected a bold decision in favor of liberty was unrealistic, but to have the justices wade into the political struggle as special pleaders for the slavery interest was a disaster for the Court and the nation.

Equally detrimental was Taney's assertion that the Constitution was a static document. The other decisions of the Court he headed for so long belied this conclusion, and his attempt to freeze full membership in the American community as of 1787 or 1789 was a fundamental violation of the spirit of the Constitution. In a very real sense, the constitutional history of the country can be seen in terms of expanding the benefits and protections of the fundamental law to those who had previously been excluded.[98] This history is what makes Taney's opinion so wrongheaded.

Justices John McLean of Ohio and Benjamin R. Curtis of Massachusetts dissented in *Dred Scott* and challenged the majority on all the major questions. Saying that "slavery has its origin in power, and is against right," McLean continued: "A slave is not a mere chattel. He bears the impress of his Maker, and is amenable to the laws of God and man."[99] Of course blacks could be U.S. citizens and of course Congress had full authority over the territories, propositions, he insisted, that are fully confirmed in the country's history. To allow Missouri's abrupt reversal of its own precedents freeing slaves who had resided on free soil to stand, McLean argued, is to deny that the law protects the liberty of a human being.

Curtis wrote the longest opinion in the case, and his views were widely circulated in pamphlet form. Citizens of states are necessarily citizens of the United States, he began, and "no power is conferred on the Government of the Union to discriminate between them, or to disenfranchise any of them." Challenging Taney's characterization of the founding fathers as virulent racists, Curtis said that it would be neither just nor true "to allege that they intended to say that the Creator of all men had endowed the white race, exclusively, with the great natural rights which the Declaration of Independence asserts." They were bound by circumstances, he continued, and not by any desire to limit the applicability of "universal abstract truths."[100] Then Curtis surveyed the action of Congress in regard to the territories and found no limitation on its power and certainly no duty to protect slaveholders. In the wake of the *Dred Scott* decision, Curtis, who had been appointed in 1851, resigned from the Court.[101]

The extensive opinions of the dissenters may have blunted some of the criticism of the Court. They provided a stark contrast to Taney's rambling and poorly developed opinion that sought to summon the Constitution to protect slavery. A heretofore limited protection of a peculiar form of property, seen as necessary to establish the Union, was transformed into a new, substantive, constitutional right. A natural claim to freedom that the Constitution did not deny by making necessary concessions to the slave interest was now swallowed up by an attempt to embed the right to own slaves more fully into the constitutional fabric. Slavery could not exist without legal recognition, for otherwise men and women were free.[102] McLean and Curtis in their *Dred Scott* opinions reveal themselves to be the proper conservators of the constitutional tradition—a tradition that requires a proper deference to the consistent exercise of congressional power and a sensitivity to the conflict of individual rights presented by the cases. Curtis, especially, sought to rescue the grand principles of the Declaration and reinforce their cultural importance as core elements of the American faith.

In the wake of *Dred Scott*, the Court was confronted with a forceful challenge to national authority based upon states' rights in the last of the fugitive slave cases. *Ableman v. Booth* involved an abolitionist newspaper editor, Sherman Booth, who had assembled a mob at the local jail to free a slave awaiting return to his owner. The slave had escaped from Missouri and had worked in Wisconsin for two years prior to his capture. When arrested for violating the Fugitive Slave Act, Booth was granted a writ of habeas corpus by the Wisconsin high court on grounds that the federal act denied a jury trial and took liberty without due process of law. As this decision was on its way to the United States Supreme Court, Booth was rearrested, tried and convicted. Once again, he was granted a writ of habeas corpus by the

Wisconsin high court and released. These cases were joined on appeal, and the justices announced their decision in March 1859.[103]

What gave Chief Justice Taney's unanimous Court opinion importance was its forceful assertion of national supremacy and of the authority of the Supreme Court. Although the opinion served the slave interest, its words go beyond the particular subject matter. Taney ruled that the federal government was endowed with a supremacy "to execute its own laws by its own tribunals" for the purpose of achieving "the ends for which the Union had been created," including the checking of "local passions or prejudices" that "would lead to acts of aggression and injustice by one state upon the rights of another."[104]

The federal judiciary, the chief justice continued, was to be "a common arbiter . . . to protect and guard the rights of all." At its apex, the Supreme Court was empowered by the Constitution to be the ultimate tribunal "to secure the independence and supremacy of the general government in the sphere of action assigned to it." Without such provision, the rule of law would have been supplanted by the rule of force. "So long, therefore, as this Constitution shall endure, this tribunal must exist with it, . . . deciding the angry and irritating controversies between sovereignties." The dignity of the states is not compromised in the process, Taney said, for "the highest honor of sovereignty is untarnished faith. And no faith could be more deliberately and solemnly pledged than that which every state has plighted to the other states to support the Constitution." Condemning the error of the Wisconsin judges, which he claimed "would subvert the very foundations of this government," he boldly asserted that the Constitution and the laws made thereunder confer power on "this court to decide, ultimately and finally, all cases arising under" them.[105]

In repulsing Wisconsin's challenge to federal authority, Taney had claimed ultimate authority for the Court in interpreting the Constitution. Earlier in the decade, the High Bench had provided the building blocks for the position so forcefully delineated in *Ableman*. In an 1853 decision, the majority said the Court's appellate jurisdiction is no less than "a bill of rights to the people of the State, incorporated into the fundamental law of the Union." Both national and individual prosperity, the Court continued, "depends upon a close adherence to the settled rules of law, and especially to the great fundamental law of the Union."[106] In another case, the justices had concluded that the framers of the Constitution intended to provide "one tribunal paramount to the rest, possessing a general superintendence, and authorized to settle and declare in the last resort a uniform rule of civil justice." Without such foresight, they continued, there would have been a diversity of interpretation that would have frustrated the equal application of the laws and made individual rights insecure. That foresight had provided for a "supreme tribunal" that in its sixty-seven years has "settled all differences which have arisen between the authorities of the States and those of the United States." Its appellate jurisdiction has been confirmed by history, the Court concluded, and it is now "rather late to question it."[107]

The broad assertion of federal supremacy and of the ultimate authority of the Supreme Court that came from Chief Justice Taney's pen in *Ableman* belied the fact that the *Dred Scott* decision, announced two years earlier, was hardly being respected as the final interpretation of the Constitution. Nor could it hide the fact that both the Constitution, itself, and its interpreter, the Supreme Court, had been tarnished in the raging conflict over slavery. A Constitution that was called sacred because it embodied the mythic will of a united people was exposed as a bundle of compromises, and the fundamental law's antiquity and longevity, by themselves, seemed insufficient to command the faith of a now badly divided people. The Supreme Court, still seeking to uphold the Union and protect individual rights, had overestimated its power. And despite its bold assertions, it was composed only of mere men whose claim to a priestly mission seemed especially hollow.

Neither the Constitution nor the Supreme Court held the solution to the perplexing problem of slavery in the nation. The original compromise with slavery was breaking down, and a Court that sought to preserve or strengthen that compromise was confronted by a growing moral outcry. The claims of the excluded were making inroads on the consciences of the included. Calls to obey law severed from its moral roots seemed, at the very least, misguided. Americans were being admonished to curb their moral views in behalf of a union that was becoming quite fragile.

When issues are perceived morally, compromise becomes difficult, if not impossible. What happens when law and morality are opposed? Is an obligation to obey the law in civil society sacred? Must good citizens swallow their moral disapproval until change can be effected? The existence of a union half-slave and half-free posed the ultimate challenge to the rule of law in American society. Repeatedly, the Court had acknowledged that just as it was the high servant of the law, the law was the servant of the people's will. The people had both the obligation to obey the law and the responsibility to change it when it lost touch with society's evolving views. To insist upon the rule of existing law is an obligation of the courts; both the common law and the American constitutional law tradition allows some judicial change in legal doctrine, but Taney and the justices were educated to the limits imposed upon such change by the resistance to *Dred Scott*. The Court, then, is forced to await the resolution of the political and social conflict, in hope that this resolution will extricate the justices from the impossible position of enforcing a rule of law that no longer commands respect.

As positions hardened, a mutually acceptable, peaceful resolution of the slavery issue seemed less and less possible. War would come, and from its ashes would arise no less than a new constitutional order. New words, designed to better ensure the civic faith outlined in the Declaration of Independence, would be added to the holy writ.

INTERPRETING NEW AND OLD HOLY BOOKS: PART I: BEGINNING TO WIDEN THE CIVIL RELIGIOUS COMMUNITY, 1860–1917

As late as 1859 the Court was insisting that recalcitrant states were constitutionally bound to accept the authority of the Union as created and fixed by the people of the founding generation, but a rival conception of union had been gaining favor. This view defined the Union as a compact among corporate states for whom the federal government acted as a trustee. Should the trustee fail to abide by the terms of its authority, the creators of the trust—the states—were free to sever the relationship.[1] Talk of seceding from the Union was heard in the South as early as the 1820s. Only the Compromise of 1850, which included Northern concessions on slavery in the territories and on strengthening the national Fugitive Slave Act, had avoided the real possibility of splitting the Union at that time.

Any hope of staving off a new secessionist threat in 1860 rested upon the Democratic Party's ability to keep together its Northern and Southern adherents. Its rival was the Republican Party, which at its inception in 1854 united around an antislavery platform. By 1860 that strong sentiment had moderated in the face of political reality, as the major plank of its platform called only for the banishment of slavery from the remaining federal territories. Even so, the Republican Party was a sectional organization. When the Democrats convened in late April 1860 and delegates from eight Southern states walked out of the convention, the remaining party members could not agree on a candidate and adjourned the convention. Subsequently, the Republicans nominated a one-term congressman from Illinois, Abraham Lincoln, who had come to public attention during his 1858 campaign for the Senate against Stephen A. Douglas, now the leading Democratic candidate for the presidency. Lincoln was chosen as his party's standard bearer because his views on slavery seemed more moderate than the better-known William H. Seward. When the Democrats met again in June and the Southern delegates once again bolted, the remaining delegates nominated Douglas. Those who left the convention convened later and nominated John C. Breckinridge of Kentucky. Clearly the split in Democratic ranks gave Lincoln and the Republicans an excellent chance to capture the presidency. Should this happen, some Southern leaders threatened, their states would leave the Union.[2]

Abraham Lincoln, in his debates with Douglas, had said that a house divided against itself cannot stand, but, as the Republican candidate, he was pledged only to uphold the platform's stand against the expansion of slavery into the territories. This was threat enough for the Southern firebrands, who saw his election as the first step to abolition.

When Lincoln received a winning margin of electoral votes from eighteen free states, South Carolina seceded from the Union. By the time he took office on March 4, 1861, Mississippi, Florida, Alabama, Georgia, Louisiana, and Texas had also seceded. Citing Northern aggression, the seceding states, in popular conventions, sought to sever all connection with the Union.

Lame-duck President James Buchanan had earlier said that the states could not secede from the Union, but if they did, the federal government was not empowered to do anything about it. Various attempts were made to find a compromise, including an amendment to the Constitution protecting the domestic institution of slavery by precluding the federal government from ever interfering with or abolishing slavery in the states. This proposed thirteenth amendment to the Constitution passed Congress, and Lincoln said that he had no objection to its enactment, for it was already implied in the Constitution. But this last ditch effort at compromise was overwhelmed by ensuing events that would eventually result in a far different thirteenth amendment that would accomplish just what the first proposal sought to prevent.

Lincoln came to the presidency with one goal in mind—the preservation of the Union. If this could be done without freeing a single slave, he said, he would accept the result. To simply call Lincoln a nationalist is to miss what the Union meant to him. It was the fundamental article of his civic faith. As he was to make so clear in his subsequent speeches, the Union had a transcendent meaning. For Lincoln it "tied together the nation, Constitution, and liberty in a trinity that he argued was inseparable. Together they made free government possible and worthwhile."[3]

Where his predecessor had found the Constitution deficient, Lincoln insisted that it was adequate to respond to any threats mounted against it. The new president had sworn to uphold the Constitution, and that he would do, consistently denying that any state could secede from the Union. So, when he determined to resupply Fort Sumter in Charleston harbor and informed South Carolina's leaders of his intent, he was ready for the consequences. Before the provisions could arrive shots were fired at the fort, and the commander was forced to surrender on April 13, 1861. The Civil War had begun. When Lincoln called for seventy-five hundred volunteers to defend the Union, Virginia, Arkansas, Tennessee, and North Carolina seceded and joined the Confederacy, which had been formed in February.

Lincoln called Congress into special session but set July 4, 1861, as the convening date. In the interim period of four months, Lincoln used his powers as commander in chief to prosecute the war. He raised an army, proclaimed a blockade of Southern ports, authorized arrests of civilians by the military, and suspended the writ of habeas corpus. Such unprecedented action was, in part, responsible for keeping Delaware, Maryland, Missouri, and Kentucky in the Union, but it raised substantial questions about the invasion of individual rights.

Historians have generally been sympathetic to Lincoln's problems and have acknowledged that such vigorous executive action seemed necessary in the prosecution of a full-scale civil war.[4] They also point to the fact that, despite the outspoken and continual criticism of Democrats, the president never interfered with the normal operation of the political process. As the war raged, elections took place as usual.

One outspoken and insistent contemporary critic of the administration was Roger Taney. The aging chief justice feared that Lincoln was instituting a military dictatorship in an attempt to force the Southern states back into the Union. Undaunted by the failure of the Dred Scott decision, he looked for opportunities to lecture the president and his supporters on their violations of the Constitution. When Lincoln suspended habeas corpus in the vulnerable corridor from Philadelphia to Washington, Union soldiers arrested John Merryman, a known secessionist. His lawyer sought out Taney, whose circuit responsibilities included Baltimore, for a writ of habeas corpus. The chief justice eagerly responded, saying that the president had usurped an authority conferred on Congress. But even Congress, he said, could not subject civilians to military trials because individuals were protected by the Fifth and Sixth Amendments to the Constitution.[5] Taney's view may be attractive, but it does not acknowledge the serious crisis facing the administration. Lincoln paid no attention to the writ but did eventually have Merryman indicted in a civil court.[6]

This episode in the bitterly divided state of Maryland evoked considerable discussion. Taney was reminded of his decision in *Luther v. Borden* in which he had said that the Court was both ill-equipped and ill-advised to deal with political questions.[7] Although the case here was posed in judicial terms, it involved questions of imminent danger to which political authorities had to respond. John Merryman was not an innocent civilian but an enemy of the Union cause.

Despite the hopes of Taney, the Supreme Court during the war years heard few cases dealing with individual rights. Events outside the Court were changing not only the social order but the constitutional order as well. A war that had begun to preserve the old Union was turning into a conflict that would forge a new one. Lincoln's view of the Union as one in which the Declaration of Independence was incorporated into the fundamental law would, in part, be written into the Constitution itself.

As the war dragged on, Lincoln realized that a fight for union was inadequate as a war aim. That the president was personally opposed to slavery is clear, but Lincoln was a politician who knew that he would have to develop support for a move against the peculiar institution. He waited for a Union victory before announcing, on September 22, 1862, that he would issue a proclamation on the first day of the new year freeing the slaves in areas that were then in rebellion against the United States. The delay was obviously designed to present the choice to the Confederate leadership of either preserving the domestic institution by abandoning secession or running the risk that a Union victory would make emancipation a reality. Despite the fact that the proclamation would not in fact free a single slave and that its reach did not extend to states loyal to the Union, this was the first step toward emancipation. Lincoln asserted his authority to take such action under his powers as commander in chief in prosecuting the war and under the authority of Congress, whose wartime legislation—preventing the return of fugitive slaves and confiscating rebel property—seemed to anticipate emancipation. On January 1, 1863, the Emancipation Proclamation was announced.

Politically, Lincoln had moved slowly, but his dedication to the principles of the Declaration of Independence made this first step to emancipation personally satisfying. In 1861, on his way to his inauguration, he had said that the Declaration "gave promise that in due time the weights should be lifted from the shoulders of all men, and that *all* should have an equal chance."[8] After the Emancipation Proclamation, he could speak much more confidently in terms of the nation fulfilling both its destiny and the promises its founders had made in 1776.[9]

In dedicating the Gettysburg battlefield, Lincoln began: "Four score and seven years ago our fathers brought forth on this continent a new nation, conceived in Liberty, and dedicated to the proposition that all men are created equal." The war, he continued was a test of "whether that nation, or any nation so conceived and so dedicated, can long endure." Concluding with a tribute to the men who died on the battlefield, he said "that we here highly resolve that these dead shall not have died in vain—that this nation, under God, shall have a new birth of freedom—and that government of the people, by the people, for the people, shall not perish from the earth."[10]

Lincoln had reclaimed the ideal of equality in the Declaration and made it an overriding national commitment. The Civil War would not bury states rights' arguments, but ever after they would be subordinated to Lincoln's vision of both the nation's spirit and its purpose. The Gettysburg Address encapsulated Lincoln's view of the guiding principle of American existence and became the authoritative reading of the Declaration accepted by scholars, citizens, and judges ever since.[11]

The emancipation of the slaves, brought about as a result of war, was a long-delayed fulfillment of the principles at the heart of the American civil religion. Lincoln assumed the role of a prophet, calling the American people to account for their sins. Nowhere is this more clearly demonstrated than in his Second Inaugural Address. The righteousness of God's judgment, he said, cannot be denied even if He wills that the war continue "until all the wealth piled by the bondsman's two hundred and fifty years of unrequited toil shall be sunk, and until every drop of blood drawn with the lash shall be paid by another drawn with the sword."[12]

Lincoln had injected into the American civil religion Christian themes of suffering and redemption.[13] The Civil War was not perceived as a fight between competing social and economic systems but as a struggle for the soul of the body politic. In his insistence on preserving the Union, Lincoln envisioned a nation that truly embraced the liberty that government had been established to protect. The founding generation had recognized the incompatibility of equality and slavery. If the price of union had been the accommodation of slavery, the price of liberty was the Civil War.

In less than six weeks after the Second Inaugural Address and less than a week after Robert E. Lee surrendered to Ulysses S. Grant, Lincoln fell prey to an assassin's bullet. He quickly ascended into the pantheon of American saints, taking his place next to the father of the country, George Washington. To use Christian terminology and follow the lead of clerics and secular writers, Washington was Moses and Lincoln Jesus Christ.

Inevitably, a new union would arise from the ashes of the Civil War. One-sixth of the nation's population had been freed. That union, however, as Lincoln had made so clear, would be redevoted to the same founding purposes outlined in the Declaration and in the Preamble to the Constitution. The ends had not changed, but there would be a substantial conference of new authority on the federal government designed to protect the rights of the individual—what we have referred to as the theological core of the American civil religion. New constitutional thinkers, arguing that for far too long the fundamental law had been interpreted primarily as imposing a series of "thou shall nots" upon the federal government, now redirected attention to that government's power "to act positively, as an instrument, to realize purposes that had inspired the creation of the nation."[14] Much of the country's subsequent constitutional history would be concerned with exploring the meaning and implications of the federal government's new authority, especially as codified in new amendments to the Constitution.

The period of American history following the Civil War and lasting until 1877, when the last of the federal military presence was removed from the South, has been referred to as "Reconstruction," a clear acknowledgement of the prime importance of the task of remaking the old union. That the task took so long can be attributed to Southern intransigence, and that the final results might be disappointing was the result of expectations outrunning the practical realities of the times.[15]

When the former states of the Confederacy responded to the end of slavery with black codes that restricted the liberty of the former slave, they exploded the myth that individual liberty in the American federal union was best protected by the states and invited intervention by the national government. For the first time, Congress had to define U.S. citizenship and the rights that it entailed.[16] This was the first step in the transformation of the national government from potential oppressor to protector of individual rights.

For our purposes, the most significant aspect of Reconstruction was the addition between 1865 and 1870 of three new amendments to the Constitution. Together they redefined the nature of the Union by placing in the federal government new power to ensure the protection of individual rights from violation by the states. Together they provided a secure textual foundation for a dialogue that had begun during the war and spread into the postwar period. Each of the amendments carried a concluding section conferring upon Congress the authority to enforce the new provisions. The first eleven amendments had sought to limit the range of federal governing power, and the twelfth dealt with a technical matter, separating the balloting for president and vice president. Now, for the first time since the adoption of the Constitution, new power was delegated to the federal government.

Had the Thirteenth Amendment, which abolished slavery and involuntary servitude except as punishment for the conviction of a crime, been fully accepted and its implications written into state law, perhaps no further constitutional change would have been required. A prevailing assumption was that there was no intermediate status between slavery and freedom; emancipation meant that slaves were now freemen with all the rights and duties conferred by that status. Senator John Sherman of Ohio, upon the ratification of the amendment, said that its enforcement clause gave Congress the power "to secure all . . . [Americans'] rights of freedom by appropriate legislation."[17] However, the success of this constitutional change rested initially less upon the federal government than upon the states' willingness to modify their laws and customs. Had they done this, Reconstruction would have ended quite quickly. However, the Southern states, which were ordered to ratify the Thirteenth Amendment as one requirement for their readmission to the Union, ignored the implications of the constitutional change and passed black codes that placed special and unequal burdens upon the former slaves.

As this resistance developed, members of Congress worried that the Thirteenth Amendment might not provide a secure constitutional foundation for such measures as the Civil Rights Act of 1866, which had attempted to delineate a host of individual civil rights. This concern led to support for another amendment to the Constitution, one that would clearly establish the basis for such legislation and write into the holy writ the implications of the Union victory.

The most significant section of the Fourteenth Amendment was the first: "All persons born or naturalized in the United States, and subject to the jurisdiction thereof, are citizens of the United States." Obviously, this part of the first section was designed to overrule *Dred Scott* by making the former slaves citizens, and to establish the primacy of federal citizenship, a subject on which the Constitution had hitherto been silent. Then the first section concluded with words that would become a prime focus of continuing litigation: "No State shall make or enforce any law which shall abridge the privileges or immunities of citizens of the United States; nor shall any State deprive any person of life, liberty, or property, without due process of law; nor deny any person within its jurisdiction the equal protection of the laws." The middle clause copied the words of the restrictions placed upon the federal government by the Fifth Amendment and made them applicable to the states. That the Declaration of Independence was the basic source of this portion of the Fourteenth Amendment would be reflected in subsequent opinions of the Supreme Court, when the justices addressing the clause often added "the pursuit of happiness" or substituted it for "property."[18]

This significant first clause also summoned up language from the original Constitution that had provided that "Citizens of each State shall be entitled to all Privileges and Immunities of Citizens in the several States."[19] Designed to prevent states from discriminating in favor of their own citizens, it did not reach the content of these privileges and immunities. States had been free to determine what benefits the clause conferred, the only limitation being that its reach had to encompass citizens of other states as well. Now, by terms of the Fourteenth Amendment, states were barred from abridging "the privileges and immunities of citizens of the United States." Clearly, then, what was a privilege or immunity of U.S. citizenship seemed to be a matter that would be determined by the national government.

A cottage industry has grown up among historians and legal scholars attempting to prove or disprove the proposition that the Fourteenth Amendment's first section was a shorthand way of making the Bill of Rights binding upon the states.[20] Clearly, the speeches of John A. Bingham of Ohio in the House and Jacob M. Howard of Michigan in the Senate, important figures in urging the approval of the specific text of the section, provide evidence for this hypothesis. Bingham, especially, talked of his intent to reverse *Barron v. Baltimore*, which in 1833 held that the Bill of Rights bound only the federal government. But beyond this, there is little hard evidence, not only in terms of what other representatives and senators understood the section to mean, but also in terms of what state legislators thought they were approving when they ratified the amendment. Nonetheless, new and potentially sweeping limitations were now imposed upon state action that eventually would have to be explicated by the Supreme Court.

The final clause in the first section of the Fourteenth Amendment—concerning the equal protection of the laws—was entirely new language for the Constitution. It harkened back to the Declaration's assertion that "all men are created equal" and was obviously designed to invalidate Southern black codes, which, by singling out blacks, had clearly denied the equal protection of the laws. For the first time, equality was specifically mandated by the Constitution in language that would clearly summon the attention of the federal judiciary.[21]

Sent to the states for ratification in 1866, the Fourteenth Amendment was added to the Constitution in 1868. Tennessee, as the only former Confederate state to ratify the amendment voluntarily, was welcomed back into the Union and its representatives seated in Congress. The remaining ten states were subjected to further congressional rule under "military reconstruction." Under these imposed governments, the remaining former states of the Confederacy ratified the Fourteenth Amendment.

Under military reconstruction, states were required to draft new constitutions and provide for universal manhood suffrage, thus enfranchising the former male slaves. The fear that this reform would not survive after the recapture of state governments by the Democrats led to the proposal of the Fifteenth Amendment in 1868. The new amendment did not, in itself, enfranchise the slaves or displace the states' general authority to set the qualifications for the franchise. It simply barred the states from using "race, color, or previous condition of servitude" to discriminate among potential voters.

These amendments and subsequent enforcement laws revolutionized the law of personal status and gave the federal government the constitutional power to define that new status. Equality had always been a prominent characteristic of the rule of law, but now that term was written into the Constitution itself and, as with liberty, clearly recognized as a fundamental principle of the social order. How well these ideals would be guaranteed, rather than simply proclaimed, subsequent history would tell.

If Reconstruction is to be evaluated in terms of how successfully it incorporated the former slaves into the American community as equal citizens, it was a failure. The Civil War saw a tremendous increase in federal executive and legislative power, but it was short-lived, as the federal structure continued to command the loyalty of citizens. After all, the Union, even as it fought rebellion, was composed of states that may have acquiesced in the short-term necessity of national power but were also more than ready to resume local control when the emergency ended. There was no support for a permanently enlarged federal government with a large bureaucracy intruding into the affairs of states. In fact, as we look back on the problems of the Civil War years, we are struck by the way in which reformers seem hampered by an implicit commitment to preserving state power. The federal system had been pushed to the brink by extremists, but that was the fault of the extremists and not the system itself. To have expected a long continued federal presence in the South to make the new guarantees written into the Constitution a reality is to expect too much of the times. Twentieth-century critics often have failed to understand the limitations of time and place.

Instead of rushing to grade Reconstruction in terms of its immediate accomplishments, we should recognize the huge commitment Americans made both to liberty and equality. In a clearly racist society, flawed men wrote more of the civil religious theology into the Constitution. They overcame their personal limitations to create an enduring legacy. The three Reconstruction amendments are legitimately recognized as a continuation of the founding experience. They continue a process begun with the Declaration and are integral additions to the holy writ. By expanding the constitutional vocabulary they also expanded the range of conversation in the society, creating new targets for the claims of individuals and adding new dimensions to the political culture. Almost ninety years had elapsed between the Declaration's promise of equality and the formal abolition of slavery. A little more than that span of time would again pass before the guarantees written into the Constitution from 1865 to 1870 would be made meaningful within American society. The historical process is slow because people are slow to assume their responsibilities under the American creed. Rather than blame past generations for their failures, though, we might be better advised to speed up the unfinished process of fulfillment in our own time.

We return now to the Supreme Court, which collectively had refused to be drawn into Chief Justice Taney's confrontation with the administration.[22] Critics have been surprised that the Court could recover from the disaster of *Dred Scott* within such a short period of time, but nothing was so wrong with an institution that a change in membership could not cure. The prize, of course, was the chief justiceship. Although ill, Taney would not retire. But there were other vacancies. Peter Daniel had died on May 31, 1860, and President Buchanan had failed to get a nominee approved by the Senate. Within two months of Lincoln's inauguration, John McLean died and John A. Campbell of Alabama resigned to join the Confederacy. Although three appointments at one time could have a dramatic effect on the Court's composition, this was not the case in late 1861. Of the remaining six members, five had joined the majority in *Dred Scott*, and Curtis's replacement, Nathan Clifford of Maine, was regarded as a Southern sympathizer. Early in 1862, Lincoln replaced McLean with Noah H. Swayne, also from Ohio, but he then waited for Congress to reorganize the judicial circuits.

Tradition called upon the president to appoint Supreme Court justices from the geographical circuit over which they presided. Those circuits had last been drawn in 1837, and five of them were located in the South. These circuits had a population of about eleven million and the Northern circuits had over sixteen million, with one Northern circuit having six times as many people as one Southern circuit, a reflection of the population and territorial growth over the intervening years. The *Dred Scott* decision had stirred some activity in Congress looking toward a reorganization of the circuits. But not until July 1862 did the national legislature pass an act, grouping all the Southern states into three circuits. Only after this change did Lincoln make the other two appointments. Samuel F. Miller of Iowa filled the seat that Peter Daniel of Virginia had long ago vacated, and David Davis of Illinois succeeded to the seat that John A. Campbell of Alabama had resigned. In addition, a tenth seat on the Court was created in 1863 to embrace a circuit consisting of California, Oregon, and Nevada. To this new seat, Lincoln appointed Stephen J. Field, a Union Democrat from California.

Roger Taney died in 1864, and he was replaced by Salmon P. Chase, Lincoln's secretary of the treasury and a prominent abolitionist. Reflecting upon Taney's death, Massachusetts Senator Charles Sumner credited Providence and said that the Constitution would now be read to promote liberty, not slavery.[23]

By the time Justice John Catron of Tennessee died in May 1865, Lincoln had been succeeded by his vice president, Andrew Johnson of Tennessee, a Union Democrat added to the Republican ticket in 1864 to strengthen its appeal. Johnson sought to reconstruct the Union on his own terms, only to run into opposition when Congress met in December 1865. The president sent a nominee to the Senate in early 1866, but Congress was then considering a reduction in size of the Supreme Court to at least nine to reestablish an uneven number. The final result, though, was an act in July 1866 that reduced the High Bench's membership to seven and that provided, in response to Chase's suggestion, that the title of his office be changed from Chief Justice of the Supreme Court to Chief Justice of the United States. This measure effectively precluded Johnson from making any appointments to the Court, and it met with no opposition from the sitting justices. In 1869, Congress raised the number to nine, where it has remained ever since. This latter act also provided for nine new circuit court judges and reduced the mandatory obligation of the justices to holding only one term of circuit court every two years.[24]

Even more significant for the future was the national legislature's action extending the jurisdiction of the federal courts. Although Congress, as it embarked upon reconstructing the former states of the Confederacy, was wary of potential judicial opposition, this fact did not prevent it from conferring new power on the federal judiciary. Jurisdiction may strike the reader as a technical matter of little public interest, but increased jurisdiction confers increased power on the judiciary—a power to widen the dialogue by bringing new parties into court and exercising authority over them. Congress was interested most in protecting blacks and federal officers in the South, but the jurisdiction once conferred could be used by all who fell within its parameters. "Congress had determined to expand the powers of the federal courts, sometimes at its own expense, more often at the states', to make them partners in implementing national policy."[25]

Prior to the Civil War no general jurisdiction was conferred on the federal judiciary to hear claims arising under the Constitution, federal law, and treaties. If the parties were citizens of different states, that gave them access to the federal courts and the federal claim could be asserted. Otherwise any federal claim had to be tried in the state courts, and only when a final decision against such a claim was reached could an appeal be had to the United States Supreme Court. Beginning in 1863 and culminating in the Judiciary Act of 1875, the jurisdiction of the federal courts was expanded to embrace such claims, either by removal from a state court or by bringing suit intially in a federal court. The federal trial courts now "ceased to be restricted tribunals of fair dealing between citizens of different states and became the primary and powerful reliances for vindicating every right given by the Constitution, the laws, and treaties of the United States."[26]

In addition, the writ of habeas corpus was given a broad, new meaning at the federal level. Prior to 1861 a federal writ of habeas corpus was available only prior to trial to test the issue of an individual's confinement. It could not be used to free prisoners who had been convicted by a state judicial tribunal. In 1867 Congress passed an act that gave federal courts the power to grant the writ of habeas corpus "in all cases where any person may be restrained of his or her liberty in violation of the Constitution, or of any treaty or law of the United States."[27] As we shall see, this legislation was repealed in the following year, but it was reenacted in 1885 and has ever since been an important addition to the federal courts' supervisory power over state courts.

This new conference of jurisdiction on the federal courts increased considerably the work of the Supreme Court as the primary appellate tribunal in the federal system. The justices' burgeoning caseload was finally relieved in 1890 when the Congress in the Circuit Courts of Appeals Act established intermediate federal appellate courts, whose decisions would be final in many cases instituted in the federal trial courts. This was the first in a series of acts that would culminate in 1925 in giving the Supreme Court almost complete control over what cases it would hear.[28] A Court that had begun its life as a passive recipient of appealed cases would finally become a tribunal that could choose the matters it wished to resolve.

Along with proposing three amendments to the Constitution, Congress had greatly expanded the jurisdiction of the federal courts, including the Supreme Court. New parts were put in place in the American constitutional order that would, in time, give the justices room and opportunity to perform their priestly role within the American civil religion by giving substance to the creed of individual rights.

Lincoln generally maneuvered successfully to prevent important wartime measures, such as habeas corpus, martial law, conscription, and emancipation, from coming before the Court. But two cases did come before the justices during the war that could have embarrassed the administration. The first involved Lincoln's proclamation of a naval blockade of the Confederacy, which the Court upheld in a five-to-four decision. Essentially the majority deferred to the president to make such vital political decisions, while the dissenters saw the need for congressional action.[29] The second case involved the military arrest and trial of a former Democratic congressman, Clement Vallandigham of Ohio, who was active in aiding the rebels. Lincoln commuted his sentence for confinement for the war's duration to banishment to the Confederacy. But Vallandigham returned and sought to have the Supreme Court annul his sentence on the basis that he was illegally arrested. Once again the Court, this time unanimously, avoided the issue by saying that it was without jurisdiction to hear an appeal from a military court.[30]

In the latter case, we might accuse the Court of shirking its prime duty—to protect individual rights. But the justices were not about to inject the Court into the path of the Union war effort. That, however, did not mean that the justices were either comfortable with the situation or insensitive to the constitutional claims presented. Habituated to looking at claims that individual rights were violated, the justices could face political realities and stay their collective hand, but all wars come to an end.

That the Court was eager to reassume its role as protector of individual liberties and as the public's constitutional educator can be seen in *Ex parte Milligan*. The case was argued from March 5 to 13, 1866, and the Court announced its decision on April 3, although opinions were not published until December. Lambdin P. Milligan was a militant citizen of Indiana who had been involved with Vallindigham in organizing a secret military society and planning the release of Confederate prisoners by armed force. Charged with a variety of treasonable offenses, Milligan was tried by a military commission and sentenced to death. A subsequent attempt to gain an indictment under the civil law failed. When President Andrew Johnson affirmed the death sentence, Milligan sought a writ of habeas corpus under the act of 1863.

Justice David Davis, for the majority, began by saying that Milligan's claim "involves the very framework of the government and the fundamental principles of American liberty." Acknowledging that the ongoing war had precluded a judicial evaluation of such claims, Davis now believed that the public safety had been secured and that the Court could resume its proper role in government by resolving "a purely judicial question." He accepted the argument that a suit for a writ of habeas corpus was the proper method to test the validity of the trial and then moved on to consider the authority of the military tribunal. Stressing that the matter before the Court concerns "the birthright of every American citizen[,] when charged with crime, to be tried and punished according to law," the justice said that only the law can secure human rights. Then, citing the protections afforded by the Fifth and Sixth Amendments, Davis praised "our ancestors" for making the Constitution "a law for rulers and people, equally in war and in peace,

. . . [that] covers with the shield of its protection all classes of men, at all times, and under all circumstances."[31]

Military tribunals, he continued, can have no constitutional authority over "citizens in states which have upheld the authority of the government, and where the courts are open and their process unobstructed." If it was dangerous to allow Milligan his freedom, Davis said, then the federal government should have sought his indictment in the civil court, which would have been sensitive to his right to personal liberty. And Milligan's right to a jury trial "cannot be frittered away on any plea of state or political necessity." Only with "the watchful care of those intrusted with the guardianship of the Constitution . . . can we transmit to posterity unimpaired the blessings of liberty, consecrated by the sacrifices of the Revolution." Acknowledging that the writ of habeas corpus can be suspended, the justice said that this does not mean that a person can be subjected to a military trial. Were this so, he continued, "it could be well said that a country, preserved at the sacrifice of all the cardinal principles of liberty, is not worth the cost of preservation." Although not denying that martial law could be proclaimed in certain wartime situations, Davis added that it "can never exist where the courts are open, and in the proper and unobstructed exercise of their jurisdiction."[32]

Davis's opinion should be viewed within the context of the Court's culture-defining role. Historians who have criticized the opinion for its lack of sensitivity to the realities of a civil war have missed what the majority justices sought to accomplish here and in similar subsequent opinions. The Court sought to rescue the society and its civil theology from the corruption of the war and to reclaim its priestly role as a protector of individual rights and as definer of the requirements of a just society.[33]

Four justices, led by Chief Justice Chase, agreed with the majority in *Milligan* on most matters, excepting only the conclusion that military courts cannot be established by the federal government. The majority's opinion, Chase said, tends "to cripple the constitutional powers of the government, and to augment the public dangers in times of invasion and rebellion."[34] He and his colleagues would allow Congress room under its war powers to establish such tribunals when deemed necessary.

That the difference was more than academic became clear shortly after the opinions in the case were delivered. Except for Tennessee, the former states of the Confederacy had refused to ratify the Fourteenth Amendment. Emboldened by the results of the midterm elections of 1866, Congress assumed control of the reconstruction process. Early in March 1867 Congress passed the first in a series of reconstruction acts providing for military control in the remaining ten states of the Confederacy. When the Court, in 1868, decided it would hear a case in which the petitioner challenged the authority of military trials in the South under the Habeas

Corpus Act of 1867, leaders of Congress worried that the Court might undermine reconstruction policy.[35]

In accordance with the constitutional provision that Congress determines the appellate jurisdiction of the Court, the legislature in March passed an act repealing the jurisdiction conferred by the special habeas corpus legislation of the previous year. Its intent was clearly to prevent the justices from deciding the case of William M. McCardle, charged with obstructing the reconstruction process in Mississippi. The Court had heard arguments in the case and was deferring judgment in anticipation of the repeal act. Despite the private protest of some of his colleagues, Chief Justice Chase delivered a unanimous opinion acknowledging that the Court could not proceed because its jurisdiction over the case had been withdrawn. "Jurisdiction is power to declare the law," he said, "and when it ceases to exist, the only function remaining to the court is that of announcing the fact and dismissing the cause."[36] Chase indicated, however, that the repeal of the expanded habeas corpus jurisdiction found in the 1867 act did not operate to deprive the Court of all jurisdiction in habeas corpus proceedings. Although he bowed to congressional authority here, Chase would not concede that the Court lacked power to consider all such petitions.

The justices gave force to this caveat six months later when they ruled that the Court possessed the authority to hear the habeas corpus petition of Edward M. Yerger, who was tried before a military tribunal for murdering a Union officer.[37] Worried that a decision in favor of Yerger would imperil congressional reconstruction, the government surrendered him for trial in the civil court.[38]

Clearly the Court was a force to be reckoned with, and its willingness to protect individuals from governmental overreaching embraced more than the censure of military justice. In January 1867, on the eve of military reconstruction and before McCardle and Yerger were known to the Court, the majority struck down by a 5–3 count both state and federal loyalty oaths, thus continuing the work begun in *Milligan*. Actually, the oral arguments before the Court in the cases followed on the heels of those in *Milligan*. Both state and federal oaths required persons to swear that they had always been loyal to the Union—the so-called ironclad test oath.

The first case involved a Missouri oath imposed upon ministers and priests. A Catholic priest, John A. Cummings, had been convicted of performing his duties without first taking the oath.[39] The federal case involved an attorney, A. H. Garland, who had been admitted to practice before the Supreme Court in 1860 and who subsequently joined the rebellion.[40] He received a pardon from President Andrew Johnson and refused to take the test oath on grounds that it was unconstitutional. Stephen J. Field wrote both opinions for the Court.

He began by noting that the state oath imposed by the Missouri constitution was unprecedented in its severity, its retrospectivity, its intent to reach "words, desires, and sympathies," and its failure to distinguish acts "springing from malignant enmity and acts which may have been prompted by charity, or affection, or relationship." Although recognizing that each state can determine the qualifications for office or for occupations, Field said that such authority cannot encompass "the infliction of punishment against the inhibition of the Constitution." American political institutions, the justice continued, rest on the inalienable rights of individuals, who in pursuing their happiness should find "all avocations, all honors, all positions, are alike open to everyone, and that in the protection of all these rights all are equal before the law." To suspend such rights or hinder this pursuit "for past conduct," he added, "is punishment, and can be in no otherwise defined."[41]

Quoting John Marshall to the effect that the restrictions on state power are no less than a bill of rights for the citizens of each state, Field cited the Constitution's ban on state enactment of bills of attainder and ex post facto laws. The former imposes punishment without a judicial trial, and the latter declares action criminal only after it has been committed. The failure to specify a particular person for punishment, Field continued, does not make the law imposing the oath any less a bill of attainder. But the requirement of the oath, he ruled, also runs afoul of the ex post facto law protection. Although no crime is defined nor penalty inflicted, the justice said, the laws imposing such oaths "produce the same result upon the parties against whom they are directed." They not only permanently bar individuals from practicing their profession, but they "subvert the presumptions of innocence, and alter the rules of evidence. . . . They assume that the parties are guilty; they call upon the parties to establish their innocence . . . by an inquisition, in the form of an expurgatory oath, into the consciences of the parties." Raising hypotheticals based on condoning such governmental conduct, Field concluded that a contrary decision would result in "individuals, and even whole classes, . . . [being] deprived of political and civil rights." Indicating that this punishment is also imposed without respecting the individual's sacred right to a jury trial, the justice, quoting Alexander Hamilton, concluded that it substitutes "a new and arbitrary mode of prosecution to that ancient and highly esteemed one recognized by the laws and Constitution of the State."[42] Condemning this inquisition into conscience, he ordered the discharge of Cummings.

In regard to Garland, Field returned to the effect of the oath as a perpetual exclusion from a profession and relied upon his reasoning in the prior case. He further addressed the pardoning power of the president, which he said "removes the penalties and disabilities, and restores him to all his civil rights; it makes him, as it were, a new man."[43] The justice then invalidated the federal oath required for attorneys and counselors.

The Court seemed more than ready to resume its role as both constitutional educator and the prime interpreter of the holy writ. Undoubtedly the majority was straining to find protection for the individual in these cases. Field's broad reading of the bill of attainder and ex post facto law prohibitions is an early instance of finding protection for individual rights by looking not at the historical definition of the terms but rather at their perceived intent and then applying that intent in protection of analogous invasions. It is an excellent illustration of the range of discretion left open to the interpreter of legal texts.

However, when challenges to congressional policy were directly mounted in suits to enjoin the president or secretary of war from carrying out reconstruction legislation, the Court gave a wide berth to the political branches.[44] On the touchy matter of whether the former Confederate states were in the Union or not, the justices, echoing Lincoln's view that the states could not secede from the Union, ruled that the "Constitution, in all its provisions, looks to an indestructible Union, composed of indestructible States."[45]

Stephen J. Field, the Court's spokesman in the test oath cases, apparently felt that the Court had not done enough in its decisions to instruct the government as to its responsibilities in protecting individual rights. He and Robert C. Grier had protested the Court's postponing a decision in *McCardle* to await legislative action on the High Bench's jurisdiction. They wanted the Court to confront the case and the congressional policy of military reconstruction; clearly they were prepared to rule in favor of McCardle.[46] Field took the opportunity in his opinions for the Court in the test oath cases to indicate that the justices would protect individual rights from government invasion. Their reach, however, was limited, and the California justice seemed to yearn for an opportunity to discourse on the limits of governmental power under the Constitution. He took the opportunity to do just that in a case that arose in Vermont during the war. A civilian had been arrested without warrant by a military officer and imprisoned without trial for aiding and abetting enlisted soldiers to desert. The civilian had actually procured substitutes for service in the Union army and had been paid a bounty; he was promised his release in return for his repayment of the bounty. When he refused, he was imprisoned for almost six months. The case arose when the military officer was sued for false imprisonment. When the Court reversed a substantial monetary judgment in favor of the plaintiff on grounds that excluded evidence should have been admitted, Field took the opportunity to chastise the government and provide a lesson on the sacredness of the rights of the individual.

In an earlier stage of the case, when the government argued that the military officer's action was immunized by Congressional act and presidential proclamation, Field had written for a unanimous Court in rejecting the argument.[47] Now, he chastised the attorney general for asserting the same justification, saying that the chief legal officer of a government constructed to assure the blessings of liberty surely could not contend that arbitrary arrest of individuals, far from any theater of war, could be justified in any manner. To maintain that war elsewhere within the country suspends "the guaranties of personal liberty . . . everywhere," he continued, "has no foundation in the principles of the common law, the teachings of our ancestors, or the language of the Constitution, and is at variance with every just notion of a free government." Although such principles are "universally recognized," Field said, "it is necessary at times . . . to restate them, in order to rescue them from . . . forgetfulness." To give credence to the claim that following the regular procedures of the law is too time-consuming, inconvenient, and harmful in a so-called crisis situation, Field added, seriously endangers free institutions. The processes of law "constitute the shield and safeguard of the honest and loyal citizen. They were designed not merely to insure punishment to the guilty, but to insure protection to the innocent, and without them everyone would hold his liberty at the mercy of the government."[48]

Field had taken this opportunity to slash away at the pretensions of the federal government and assert the pressing need of the Court to perform its solemn duty of protecting the rights of individuals. He was also explaining to a new generation the duties of the priestly interpreter of the holy writ. To fulfill this sacred responsibility the Court had to be vigilant against the claims of a government whose officials too often forget their obligation to safeguard the rights of the citizens.

None of these cases, however, addressed the new freedoms conferred by the Reconstruction amendments, a subject to which we now turn. Not only had these constitutional changes placed new responsibilities on the federal government to protect individual rights, they also confronted the Court with a new situation. The Court had protected individuals from state interference under specific constitutional provisions, such as the no-impairment-of-contract clause. But now it was faced with broad amendments and legislation that seemed to favor a particular class—blacks.

The concept of the rule of law within which the justices labored was built upon the premise that law shall have no favorites. Yet here was law that made blacks a special subject of federal interest and protection. The reasons for this are clear, for without such federal protection the former slaves would be left to the unfettered discretion of hostile state governments. Still, the need to view a claim through the lens of race led to some discomfort on the Court. However, what was involved was a matter of perspective. If the new law was perceived not as favoring a group but as demolishing the barriers that prevented individuals within the group from achieving the status of equal citizens, the discomfort should disappear. Law, then, becomes a remedy, not favoring some but rather making all equal.

From this perspective, the new law fits into old bottles, from which the justices had long filled their glasses. In initially defining the Union, the men on the Court saw it as a necessary vehicle for safeguarding individual rights. The old Union had proved defective, and the new one provided, in the Constitution itself, a strenthened foundation for the protection of individual rights. Not surprisingly, some justices who had matured within the old Union had difficulty grasping the contours of the new, believing that such a massive shift of power to the federal sphere ought to be slowed, if not halted altogether. Others, more adept at grasping and working within the new constitutional order, castigated their colleagues for not performing their assigned task within the expanding American civil religion.

Dissents during the Taney era were common in the work of the Court, but the post–Civil War era saw the birth of the dissenting opinion as a jeremiad, a political sermon instructing both colleagues and the people at large on their departures from the core elements of the faith.[49] Although only one of many potential models for dissenting opinions, the jeremiad, since its inception in the latter nineteenth century, has continued to attract the justices as they lecture their colleagues on the role of the Court within the civil religion.

This type of dissent not only dramatizes the work of the Court; it also filters into the culture itself, creating a dialogue focused on the articles of the faith. The result is that such dissenting opinions become far more than aired disagreements with the majority; they are preserved records asserting the primacy of basic values at the core of the civil theology. In the work that follows we will be paying more attention to such dissenting opinions because they capture well the role the Court and the justices play in maintaining the civil faith.

Much grist for the mill of such dissenters resulted from the Court's narrow reading of the Constitution's ban on slavery and involuntary servitude. Regularly, advocates for civil rights before the High Bench argued that the Thirteenth Amendment was framed to make the federal government the guarantor of the former slave's civil rights. The advantage of relying on this change in the fundamental law is that, unlike its successor the Fourteenth Amendment, it reached both private and governmental action.

Steadfastly, the majority of the justices refused to find such a wide-ranging ban on conduct in the Thirteenth Amendment. For example, when Congress passed a law conferring criminal jurisdiction on federal courts in matters involving civil rights, the majority ruled that a white man accused of murdering a black could not be tried for violating his civil rights. Only a living person, it said, could claim the protection of the statute. Nor did the fact that black witnesses were prohibited from testifying in the state trial bring the case under the statute, for such witnesses were not directly affected by the action of the defendant.

In dissent, Justices Joseph P. Bradley and Noah H. Swayne, berated their colleagues for perpetuating the vestiges of slavery. The Court, they concluded, had deprived witnesses of their rights and put a premium on murder by immunizing it from the reach of federal law. Reading the Thirteenth Amendment as a charter of freedom, the dissenters said that its enforcement clause gave Congress the "power to do away with the incidents and consequences of slavery, and to instate the freedmen in full employment of that civil liberty and equality which the abolition of slavery meant."[50]

This difference among the justices concerning the relative spheres of state and federal power also involved different conceptions of the Court's role in the society. The dissenters read the constitutional text as imposing upon the Court the task of helping to create a society of equal citizens, while the majority justices drew back from this expanded role and accommodated present political realities to the detriment of the common faith.

Again and again dissenting justices would echo this refrain, as the Court refused to read the Thirteenth Amendment to encompass any more than ridding the nation of the formal institution of slavery. When the Court finally addressed the meaning of "involuntary servitude" late in the nineteenth century, the majority tended to limit the reach of the words. The claim was made by seamen who jumped ship and were returned against their will to fulfill their contracts of service. Citing the history of the merchant service and its special requirements, the Court majority, in effect, read an exception for seamen into the Thirteenth Amendment. John Marshall Harlan of Kentucky in dissent said that runaway seamen were now in the perilous position that runaway slaves had been earlier. Boldly, he argued that a person forced to perform personal service in a private enterprise "places the person so held in custody in a condition of involuntary servitude forbidden by the Constitution."[51] He was using the words of the amendment to envision a society that deemed compulsory personal service, no matter in what form and in what situations, a form of slavery that a country of free individuals should not tolerate.

Only in the early twentieth century when the Court confronted prevalent Southern agricultural practices did it begin to see broader scope in the Thirteenth Amendment's ban on involuntary servitude. Actually, the federal statute involved was primarily directed at a practice, apparently prevalent in Spanish America and carried into the Territory of New Mexico, of forcing defaulting debtors to work for their creditors, a practice known as peonage. The cases that came to the Supreme Court, however, all concerned blacks in the South. Condemning peonage as involuntary servitude, the justices unanimously upheld the federal act's constitutionality under the Thirteenth Amendment.[52] In the major case, where an Alabama law compelled labor by presuming fraud when a person contracted to perform labor and then did not, the justices invalidated the state law. The state cannot do indirectly what it cannot do directly, the Court said, indicating its desire "to safeguard the freedom of labor upon which alone can enduring prosperity be based."[53]

Although the justices had not allowed the states by indirect means to institute compulsory personal service, the majority's narrow reading of the Thirteenth Amendment and enforcement statutes boded ill for its future significance in the new constitutional order. As a result, litigants usually resorted to the Fourteenth Amendment.[54]

In the Court's first consideration of the Fourteenth Amendment, the majority combined it with the other two Reconstruction additions to the Constitution and

said that their collective purpose was "the freedom of the slave race, the security
and firm establishment of that freedom, and the protection of the newly made . . .
[freedman] from the oppressions of those who had formerly exercised unlimited
dominion over him." But then in deciding the case, which did not concern blacks,
the Court distinguished between state and federal citizenship rights and ruled that
the Fourteenth Amendment still left "the regulation of civil rights, the rights of
person and of property," to the states.[55] The potential impact of such a ruling upon
blacks was obvious. Although the primary purpose of the amendment was to aid
blacks in achieving equal citizenship, the Court had clearly limited the range of
potential federal protection in this quest.

Under the Reconstruction governments, the former Confederate states enacted
laws that were designed to implement the federal amendments' command for the
equal treatment of blacks. As a result, the Supreme Court did not get relevant cases
seeking an explication of the meaning of new federal law until near the end of
Reconstruction. By that time the American people had tired of the task of remaking Southern society; and increasingly, the political decision was to leave the fate
of the blacks to the respective state governments. The fervor of the mid-1860s had
passed, and the question was how far could or would the Court go in trying to
enforce the Reconstruction settlement?

Working with enforcement legislation passed under the Fourteenth Amendment, the Court read the first section as barring only state, not private, action—a
ruling that limited federal protection of civil rights and forced the claimant to
seek redress under state law. The Fourteenth Amendment's due process and equal
protection clauses, the justices said, prohibited a state from violating "fundamental
rights," but those words add "nothing to the rights of one citizen as against another."[56] Thus, they concluded, an indictment containing charges that individuals
had conspired to deprive blacks of rights under the Constitution was too vague to
specify the elements of a crime. Nor did they find a specification of racially motivated action that might have brought the prosecution within the Thirteenth
Amendment, where formal state action was not required. In 1883 the Court struck
down the Ku Klux Klan Act of 1871 on grounds that the Fourteenth Amendment
did not allow Congress to penalize the action of private persons, absent any action
by the state. To the Thirteenth Amendment argument, the Court responded that
the language of the statute was so broad that it would encompass the situation
where two white men conspired against a third, a result that could not be supported by an amendment prohibiting slavery and involuntary servitude.[57]

Later that year in the *Civil Rights Cases*, the Court struck down the first federal
public accommodations law. Congress had sought to prohibit the denial of service
in public accommodations on account of race, noting in the preface to the act its
purpose of assuring "equal and exact justice to all." Addressing the Fourteenth
Amendment, the Court now said that, by its terms, Congress was only empowered

to remedy hostile state action, not to initiate legislation. The justices distinguished "fundamental rights which appertain to the essence of citizenship" and what they called "social rights," which, they claimed, the Civil Rights Act of 1875 sought to regulate. As for the Thirteenth Amendment, the majority justices ruled that translating the amendment as applying to all private acts of discrimination "would be running the slavery argument into the ground." So, the Court concluded, the discrimination involved here cannot be reached under the power conferred by the Reconstruction amendments, for such an interpretation of them would authorize the regulation of all private rights and substitute Congress for the state legislatures. Then the Court added: "When a man has emerged from slavery, . . . there must be some stage in the progress of his elevation when he takes the rank of a mere citizen, and ceases to be the special favorite of the laws."[58]

Actually this comment reflects the majority's unease in dealing with what we might call group rights, as opposed to individual rights. The Civil Rights Act of 1875 struck these justices as class legislation. Indeed, its singling out race or color as impermissible discriminatory factors did intend to make those who collectively fell into that category beneficiaries of the law. But, as the dissent would point out, Congress's intent was not to prefer a special group but rather to eliminate disabilities suffered by individuals because of their identification as members of a particular group. Blacks, whether slave or free, had been stigmatized as inferior. The purpose of the legislation of 1875, then, was to integrate blacks into society as equal citizens, not to compensate them for earlier wrongs.

In the first of many notable and usually lonely dissents, Justice John Marshall Harlan of Kentucky challenged the majority's opinion.[59] Harlan condemned its "narrow and artificial" distinctions. Constitutional provisions designed to ensure "rights inhering in a state of freedom," he said, "have been so construed as to defeat the ends the people desired to accomplish . . . and which they supposed they had accomplished by changes in their fundamental law." Finding adequate authority under the Thirteenth Amendment for Congress to eradicate the "burdens and disabilities which constitute badges of slavery and servitude," he saw the public accommodations law as furthering this purpose. Then, addressing the Fourteenth Amendment, Harlan declared that "exemption from race discrimination in respect of any civil right" is surely one of the privileges and immunities now conferred on U.S. citizens. Citizenship, he continued, must mean, at the least, equal rights, "unless the recent Amendments be splendid baubles, thrown out to delude those who deserved fair and generous treatment at the hands of the Nation."[60]

Justice Harlan berated the majority for ignoring precedents that acknowledged congressional power to "enforce and protect any right derived from or created by the National Constitution." Past Courts, he continued, had "always given a broad and liberal construction to the Constitution, so as to enable Congress, by legislation, to enforce rights secured by that instrument." Noting that before the Civil War Congress had passed laws protecting slavery, he insisted "that the National Legislature may, without transcending the limits of the Constitution, do for human liberty and the fundamental rights of American citizenship, what it did, with the sanction of this court, for the protection of slavery." Denying that this federal protection from discrimination would invade "the just rights of the States in the control of their domestic affairs," Harlan said Congress has primary responsibility for ensuring the possession of equal rights.[61]

He also noted that owners of inns, theaters, railroads, etc., are "instrumentalities of the State, because they are charged with duties to the public, and are amenable ... to governmental regulation." Lecturing the majority, Harlan said that the claim here is no more social than is the right to travel on a street or sit in a public building with others. And to the majority's assertion that blacks should not ask to be favored over other citizens, he responded that Congress had sought only "to compel a recognition of the legal right of the black race to take the rank of citizens, and to secure the enjoyment of privileges belonging, under the law, to them as a component part of the people for whose welfare and happiness government is ordained."[62]

Harlan would gain the reputation of being an eccentric on the Court, one who frequently chastised his brethren in his strongly felt opinions. His is the lonely voice of a prophet, passionately arguing that the holy writ now commands the complete inclusion of blacks within the American community as equal citizens. To condone their separation in spheres of public life, he insisted, denies them the equality promised by the Reconstruction additions to the Constitution. Only in the mid-twentieth century would his prophetic words be rediscovered and praised by a generation that had to recommit itself to the struggle for equal rights for blacks.

If the majority of the Court insisted upon hostile state action as a prerequisite for a valid Fourteenth Amendment claim, certainly state segregation statutes seemed to meet this standard. Lower federal courts had earlier upheld such legislation, but not until 1896 in *Plessy v. Ferguson* did the justices confront the matter. They had decided in 1878 that a Louisiana law that commanded the racial desegregation of public conveyances was an interference with interstate commerce.[63] But twelve years later they upheld a Mississippi law mandating segregation, ruling that, because the law was appropriately confined to intrastate commerce, it did not transgress upon national authority.[64] Neither of these cases, however, addressed segregation in terms of the Reconstruction amendments.

Now in *Plessy* the Court faced a law that required segregated seating on railroads within the state. Homer Adolph Plessy was ejected from a train and arrested for not complying with the 1890 statute.[65] Justice Henry B. Brown, for the Court, said that a distinction between races "has no tendency to destroy the legal equality of the two races, or re-establish a state of involuntary servitude." In regard to the Fourteenth Amendment, clearly state action was involved. Brown, however, saw no discrimination, saying that the amendment "could not have been intended to abolish distinctions based upon color, or to enforce social, as distinguished from political, equality, or a commingling of the two races on terms unsatisfactory to either." Calling fallacious "the assumption that the enforced separation of the two races stamps the colored race with a badge of inferiority," the justice said the act does not support this construction. Using a test of reasonableness, the Court, Brown concluded, "is at liberty to act with reference to the established usages, customs, and traditions of the people, and with a view to the promotion of their comfort, and the preservation of the public peace and good order." Saying that legislation was "powerless to eradicate racial instincts or . . . physical differences," he argued that such attempts only make matters worse. "If the civil and political rights of both races be equal, one cannot be inferior to the other. . . . If one race be inferior to the other socially, the Constitution . . . cannot put them upon the same plane."[66] The term "separate but equal," which inverts the wording found in the challenged statute, was not found in the Court's opinion, but its association with the decision does no violation to the position of the majority.

Harlan, dissenting alone, was even more irate than he had been in the *Civil Rights Cases*. Responding to the majority's characterization of the state regulation as reasonable, Harlan said no state, under the Constitution, has the authority to enact such unjust regulations. Such "legislation . . . is inconsistent, not only with that equality of rights which pertains to citizenship . . . but with the personal liberty enjoyed by every one within the United States." He castigated the majority for not acknowledging that the purpose of the statute was to remove blacks from the company of whites. Accusing his colleagues of caving in to the Southern practice of segregation, Harlan continued: "Our Constitution is color-blind, and neither knows nor tolerates classes among citizens. In respect of civil rights, all citizens are equal before the law. The humblest is the peer of the most powerful."[67] Contending with the majority's ruling that segregation treated individuals of both races equally, the Kentucky justice insisted that distinguishing among citizens on the basis of race was an egregious failure to live up to the commandments of the holy writ.

Condemning the Court's decision for being as pernicious as *Dred Scott*, he saw it permitting "the seeds of race hate to be planted under the sanction of law." The "thin disguise of 'equal' accommodations," he continued, "will not mislead anyone, or atone for the wrong this day done." He deplored his colleagues' acquiescence in state power "to interfere with the full enjoyment of the blessings of freedom; to regulate civil rights . . . upon the basis of race; and to place in a condition of legal inferiority . . . a part of the political community . . . of the

United States." The Court, he concluded, has been derelict in performing its "solemn duty to maintain the supreme law of the land."[68]

While his colleagues were acquiescing priests interpreting the holy writ to accommodate their Southern parishioners, Harlan was the prophet, reminding Americans of their creed and predicting troubled times ahead for an errant people. The Kentuckian's opinion was directed not only to his colleagues but to a people who had lost their bearings and apparently their interest in living up to the new and vital additions to the holy writ. But his invitation to open a dialogue among his colleagues and among the public at large on the obligations of the nation's faith was largely repulsed.

However, the justices work within the confines of the society they serve, and this inescapable fact tends to impose limitations upon them. *Plessy v. Ferguson* provides a good illustration. To us today, Harlan's opinion is unassailable, and we wonder why his colleagues were so unreceptive to his arguments. To condemn them as racist does not really provide an answer. We would get closer to understanding the decision by calling them realists working within both a governmental system and a society where segregation was seen as a necessary system of race regulation. A decision in Harlan's terms would have been impossible to enforce, given the state of the Union in the 1890s. It would have required active, ongoing and dedicated federal supervision, which would be possible only years later when the federal government had grown in power and bureaucratic strength. Indeed, a Court can lead, but as with any leader, it cannot move beyond the vision of those who are being led. That does not mean that there is no room for opinions that seek to educate rather than command the impossible; that, in fact, is precisely what Harlan often did so well. The decision in *Brown v. Board of Education*[69] would be possible almost sixty years later because the distance between leader and follower had been lessened. Then Harlan's dissenting opinion in *Plessy* would find the eager listeners denied it earlier.

Harlan, however, would not be stilled by his failure to win converts; his lack of success seemed to fuel his righteous indignation. When the Court in 1906 reversed the conviction of whites for harassing blacks by forcing them to leave their employment and invalidated the federal act authorizing such prosecutions, saying that the Reconstruction amendments did not "commit that race to the care of the nation," Harlan fumed. This time, at least, he garnered the vote of Justice William R. Day of Ohio. Accusing the majority of neutralizing the amendments, he condemned his colleagues for their hostility "to the freedom established by the Supreme Law of the land."[70]

Two years later, when the majority upheld a Kentucky statute making criminal the teaching of whites and blacks in a school or college on the evasive grounds that the state had the power to modify the charter of a corporation, the Kentucky justice passionately taught his lesson one more time. Asserting that the right to instruct students is "part of one's liberty as guaranteed against hostile state action by the Constitution," Harlan accused the state of laying its "unholy hands" upon a sacred right. Then he asked: "Have we become so inoculated with prejudice of race that an American government . . . can make distinctions between such citizens in the matter of their voluntary meeting for innocent purposes, simply because of their respective races?"[71]

Certainly his colleagues were, indeed, accommodating a practice that violated the American creed and that would stigmatize millions of Americans. But the gap between the civil theology and practice would be reduced with the passage of time. Individual freedom was both expanded and better protected in the early part of the twentieth century than it was in 1865, or for that matter, 1776 or 1791. If the Court did not always play a major role in this expansion of liberty, at least some of its members asserted that, in conformity with its anointed role, it should.

In the six years after Harlan's death in 1911, the Court decided a number of cases in a manner that the Kentuckian would have approved. From 1914 through 1917, the justices did begin to show more sensitivity to individual claims of racial discrimination.[72] For the first time, a majority of the Court addressed the separate but equal standard and insisted that the equality of accommodations in rail travel for blacks had to be provided irrespective of cost. Because the "essence of the constitutional right [to the equal protection of the laws] . . . is a personal one," it cannot be made to "depend upon the number of persons who may be discriminated against."[73] If certain accommodations are provided whites, the High Bench said, the railroad is constitutionally obligated to furnish equal accommodations to blacks.

In the same term of Court, the justices encountered a prosecution of election officials in Oklahoma for refusing to count the votes of blacks. They read the broad language of a much modified piece of Reconstruction legislation to authorize the prosecution. Words specifically dealing with elections had been dropped from the law, but, nonetheless, the justices did not hesitate in finding sufficient authority in the legislation to protect the rights of the aggrieved citizens.[74]

Finally, the Court struck down a residential segregation law. Apparently a black buyer and a white seller sought to test the validity of a Louisville ordinance seeking to prevent blacks or whites from moving into blocks in which the majority of residents was of the other race. Although the Court in *Plessy* had acquiesced in segregation, the justices now said there were limits and that such legislation, ostensibly enacted to promote the peace, cannot deprive "citizens of their constitutional rights and privileges."[75] Unanimously, they found the ordinance in violation of the Fourteenth Amendment. Although property rights were involved in the case, the right here came close to an essential component of liberty—the choice of a place to live.

Although the Court majority in *Plessy* did not distinguish between due process and equal protection arguments, the justices wrestled with that latter clause of the Fourteenth Amendment in a number of cases. A group of them dealt with jury service.

In *Strauder v. West Virginia*, the first of three cases resolved on the same day in 1880, the Court found that the exclusion by law of blacks from juries was a violation of the equal protection of the laws. This case, like a number of the others, arose on the criminal conviction of a black by an all-white jury. The issue here was whether the defendant could be indicted and tried by juries from which members of his race were excluded by law. In other words, was his individual right to the equal protection of the laws violated?[76]

For the Court, Justice William Strong of Pennsylvania said the Fourteenth Amendment "was designed to assure to the colored race the enjoyment of all the civil rights that under the law are enjoyed by white persons" under the protection of the federal government. To serve this purpose, the justice added, the Court must construe "the spirit and meaning of the Amendment, . . . liberally, to carry out the purposes of its framers." The prohibitive words, he continued, do assert a positive right—to be free "from legal discriminations, implying inferiority in civil society, lessening the security of their enjoyment of the rights which others enjoy, and discriminations which are steps towards reducing them to the condition of a subject race." The West Virginia law, Strong added, asserts racial inferiority and "is a stimulant to that race prejudice which is an impediment to securing to individuals of the race . . . equal justice."[77] To exclude by law all members of his race from jury service, the justice concluded, is a denial of the defendant's right to equal protection. He then overturned the conviction in the state court.

However, on the same day the justices, again speaking through Strong, denied that the mere absence of black jurors constituted a constitutional violation. What made this case different from *Strauder* was the lack of a discriminatory law.[78] The Court would consistently rule that blacks were not entitled under the Constitution to insist upon having members of their own race represented on their juries. Unfortunately, even in the absence of a law, local officials were able to keep black jurors from serving, and the Court did not explore this area in the absence of evidence of deliberate exclusion.[79]

In the third case, Strong, again for the Court, upheld the prosecution of a state judge for deliberately excluding blacks from a jury. Ample authority for the underlying federal criminal statute, he said, was found in the Fourteenth Amendment. The Reconstruction amendments, Strong asserted, were designed "to raise the colored race from that condition of inferiority and servitude in which most of them had previously stood into perfect equality of civil rights with all other persons within the jurisdiction of the States."[80]

The most interesting equal protection case involved not blacks but Chinese laundrymen; it demonstrated how evidence of the law's application could overcome its facial neutrality. A San Francisco ordinance required owners of laundries in buildings not constructed of brick or stone to obtain permission from a board of supervisors to continue their operations. On its face, the law seemed to be designed to protect the public from fire hazards. Yick Wo was convicted for operating his laundry after he and two hundred other similarly situated Chinese persons were denied permission by the board. Non-Chinese owners of laundries operating in wood buildings were regularly granted permission. Was this discriminatory treatment of the Chinese laundrymen a violation of the equal protection of the laws mandated by the Fourteenth Amendment?

Confronted by facts evidencing clear discrimination, the unanimous Court said yes. Justice Stanley Matthews found that the board acted arbitrarily and that Chinese aliens were "persons" protected by the Fourteenth Amendment. State claims of authority, he said, cannot justify "purely personal and arbitrary power." The Constitution, Matthews continued, provides relief, for "the fundamental rights to life, liberty, and the pursuit of happiness, considered as individual possessions, are secured by those maxims of constitutional law . . . securing to men the blessings of civilization under the reign of just and equal laws." The "very idea," the justice emphasized, "that one man may be compelled to hold his life, or the means of living, or any material right essential to the enjoyment of life, at the mere right of another" is the "essence of slavery itself." Appalled by the action of the board and characterizing it as applying the ordinance oppressively "with an evil eye and an unequal hand," he accused the administrators of "hostility to the race and nationality to which the petitioners belong, and which in the eye of the law is not justified."[81]

Notice how the Court delineates an individual right to choose and practice an occupation and then associates it with the pursuit of happiness. Regularly the Court accepted this guideline, at times seeming to write these words of the Declaration of Independence into the Constitution itself. And notice also how the action of the board is not simply characterized as unconstitutional but evil as well. The holy command of equal protection is being violated by those who have been tempted by the devil. The faith must be preserved, and the Court must answer the call.

Actually, the Chinese fared poorly in terms of equality in late-nineteenth-century American society.[82] For instance, when some Chinese persons were forcibly removed from the town in which they worked, the Court said that the whites involved could not be prosecuted under the Reconstruction enforcement laws because those statutes only protected citizens. Justices Field and Harlan protested against this miserly construction that left foreign nationals without adequate protection for their personal security.[83] Congress in 1882 had banned the immigration of Chinese persons, and subsequent legislation provided for the deportation of longtime residents. Generally, the Court accepted Congress's power to take such action as "an incident of sovereignty."[84]

Only when Congress, in its campaign against the Chinese, sought to provide that illegal residence in the country could subject the individual to a summary trial before a judge or commissioner leading to one year's imprisonment at hard labor did the Court invalidate the law. The justices ruled that aliens were indeed protected by both the Fifth Amendment requirement of indictment by a grand jury and the Sixth Amendment's guarantee of a trial by jury. That "the legislature should, after having defined an offense as an infamous crime, find the fact of guilt and adjudge the punishment by one of its own agents," they said, was totally inconsistent with basic principles of American government.[85]

Generally, the justices were content to defer to congressional authority in dealing with such aliens, but such deference did trouble some of their colleagues. When Justice Horace Gray, for the Court, approved an administrative procedure for the deportation of resident Chinese aliens, he denied that deportation was a criminal penalty and placed aliens beyond the reach of the Bill of Rights. Chief Justice Melville W. Fuller and Justices Stephen J. Field and David J. Brewer protested vigorously. Fuller saw in this latest installment of anti-Chinese legislation the assertion "of an unlimited and arbitrary power . . . incompatible with the immutable principles of justice, inconsistent with the nature of our government, and in conflict with the written Constitution by which that government was created and those principles were secured." Field was equally incensed by the majority's deference to such despotic power wielded against resident aliens, whom he saw fully protected by the Constitution. Stealing some of Harlan's prophetic thunder, Field said that the Court's decision "fills me with apprehensions." To hold "that Congress has the right to disregard the guaranties of the Constitution intended for the protection of all men, domiciled in the country with the consent of the government, in their rights of person and property" is a mighty blow "against constitutional liberty."[86] Brewer, the son of a missionary, asked how the country can, in good conscience, send missionaries to China to preach a Christian ethic that is blatantly transgressed by such legislation? To empower the federal government to disregard the liberties proclaimed by the Constitution as the Court has done here, he continued, makes other classes and other peoples vulnerable to similar oppression.

Of all the justices, Brewer was the most sensitive to the claims of the Chinese.[87] When the Court refused to hear one such case, the justice said that he could not "believe that the courts of this Republic are so burdened with controversies about property that they cannot take time to determine the right of personal liberty." Brewer concluded: If this anti-Chinese campaign undermines the friendship between the two countries, "the careful student of history will recall the words of Scripture, 'they have sown the wind, and they shall reap the whirlwind,' and for cause of such antagonism [we] need look no further than the treatment accorded during the last twenty years by this country to the people of that nation.''[88]

Increasingly, dissenting opinions warned of trouble ahead for a people that had lost touch with the essentials of their creed. Just as the political sermons of the seventeenth and eighteenth centuries, these opinions were designed to reach a much larger public audience.

Not until 1898 did the Court consider the status of Chinese children born of alien parents in the United States. The Fourteenth Amendment provided that "All persons born or naturalized in the United States and subject to the jurisdiction thereof, are citizens of the United States and of the State wherein they reside." Clearly, the language sought to void the *Dred Scott* decision by making citizens of former slaves. But did the broad words confer citizenship on every person born in the United States?

To get some bearing on this issue of citizenship, a subject central to the definition of community and to the idea of inclusion, we need to recognize that until the adoption of the Fourteenth Amendment state citizenship was primary in the American political system. Congress had the power to confer citizenship through the naturalization process, but this fact did not invert the normal relationship between state and federal citizenship. By becoming a U.S. citizen, a naturalized person also became a citizen of a state. Operating under its naturalization authority, Congress until 1870 only provided for the naturalization of "free white persons." In that year African aliens and those descended from them were also given access to the naturalization process. By treaty with China in 1868 the United States agreed that citizens of their respective countries would not be naturalized in the other country. And in 1882, Chinese were specifically made ineligible for naturalization by act of Congress.[89]

The first test of the citizenship clause in the Fourteenth Amendment came to the Court in 1882 and involved a Native American. John Elk had left the tribe, taken up residence among whites, and sought to vote. Was he not a citizen of the United States by the terms of the Fourteenth Amendment? Justice Horace Gray, for the majority, said no. That same amendment in its second section, the justice noted, excluded from the basis of representation "Indians not taxed." This provision, he continued, simply confirmed the common understanding that Indians were not citizens. And action subsequent to the amendment taken by Congress to naturalize certain Indians, he asserted, only lent further support to this conclusion. Then, departing from the Court's traditional role of inspecting the merit of the individual claim, Gray said that the matter of Indian citizenship should be addressed by tribes, "not by each Indian for himself."[90] Although Elk had severed his relationship with other Indians, he could not divorce himself from the tribal entity recognized by the federal government.

John Marshall Harlan, with William B. Woods, argued that the Fourteenth

Amendment conferred citizenship on Indians who "were subject to taxation and other public burdens." And to the majority's reference to naturalization acts making Indians citizens, Harlan responded that they had nothing to do with Indians who had severed their tribal allegiance and were now fully subject to the jurisdiction of the United States. Looking at the debates on the Fourteenth Amendment in Congress, the justice concluded that discussions there confirmed that Indians in Elk's position could claim citizenship under the amendment's terms. Accusing the majority of excising the "vital force" of the citizenship clause, he said that such a construction leaves "in this country a despised and rejected class of persons, with no nationality whatever" because they were born of tribal Indians.[91]

What made the decision so troubling was that it barred entry into the community to a Native American who sought identification with it.[92] Citizenship implies acceptance, and the refusal to grant it here stigmatized those individuals who wished to assimilate with the dominant culture.[93]

In his opinion, Gray had said that children born of aliens were not made citizens by the operation of the Fourteenth Amendment, but when that issue was squarely presented to the Court fourteen years later the justice took back these words. Apparently, such children, acculturated through the spreading system of public education, were generally assumed to be citizens. To banish them from the community to which they were assumed to belong was too much for Gray and the majority of his colleagues. But the precise issue before the Court in *United States v. Wong Kim Ark* was more complicated because it involved a claim of citizenship by a person born of alien Chinese parents in the United States. Chinese were subjects of the emperor, were forbidden by law to renounce their allegiance, and were deemed by Congress to be ineligible for naturalization. So, unlike the situation with European aliens, who were encouraged to become citizens, Wong Kim Ark's parents could not be naturalized.

Boldly, Gray interpreted the citizenship clause of the Fourteenth Amendment as declaratory of the common law rule that birth within the jurisdiction conferred citizenship on all, excepting only those children born of diplomats or of invading enemies. To the argument that citizenship by descent had replaced the feudal common law rule, he responded that there "is nothing to countenance the theory that a general rule of citizenship by blood or descent has displaced in this country the fundamental rule of citizenship by birth within its sovereignty." The Fourteenth Amendment, Gray continued, was not intended "to impose any new restrictions on citizenship." Any other rule, he said, would deny citizenship "to thousands of persons of . . . European parentage, who have always been considered and treated as citizens of the United States." The acceptance of congressional exclusion of the Chinese and of the denial of their access to the naturalization process, Gray added, cannot "constrain or permit the judiciary to refuse to give full effect to the peremptory and explicit language of the 14th Amendment." Statutes and treaties, he said, "must yield to the paramount and supreme law of the Constitution." Under its power to naturalize, Gray ruled, Congress can only "confer citizenship, not . . . take it away." Wong Kim Ark can indeed renounce his American citizenship, the justice concluded, for Congress in 1868 had declared expatriation "a natural and inherent right of all people," but until he does so, he is an American citizen.[94]

Taking almost two years to resolve the case and resisting societal and congressional pressure, the Court majority had asserted its authority under the Constitution to expand membership in the American community. As Congress moved with increasing illiberality in the arena of naturalization, the justices had imposed limitations upon the reach of this power. They had read the citizenship clause of the Fourteenth Amendment as a new emancipation proclamation that freed individuals from foreign bondage. In a generation in which the Court often temporized in confronting claims of individual right, here the justices assumed the full power of their priestly authority in making the holy writ operative in the society. The Court could not make prejudice disappear, but it could, and did, rescue American-born children from some of the racism that would have denied them membership within the community of their birth. Rarely has a decision of the Court personally affected so many people, including the yet unborn, whose freedom of personal choice would be enhanced by it.

The unconditional language of the first clause of the Fourteenth Amendment led to its broad construction by the Court, but the third of the Reconstruction amendments, the Fifteenth, was both written and construed quite differently.[95] Although the ban on "race, color, or previous condition of servitude" was expected to pave the way for blacks to the ballot box, in *United States v. Reese* the Court said that the amendment "does not confer the right of suffrage upon anyone." Only the state could confer that right. The justices, however, recognized that a new federal constitutional right had been created by the amendment— "exemption from discrimination in the exercise of the elective franchise on a account of race, color or previous condition of servitude."[96] When the Court then decided that congressional legislation was too vague to reach the conduct of state officials in Kentucky, Justice Ward Hunt of New York dissented.

Hunt directly confronted the issue of the statute's constitutionality, a matter the majority did not have to address. Reading the Fifteenth Amendment as embracing all elections in the United States, he asserted that the right to vote at the local level was even more important, because that government most intimately touches the individual. To place any limits on the freedmen's ability to participate in elections, Hunt continued, diminishes their security and importance and hinders their pursuit of happiness. He asserted that Congress possessed the power, free from judicial interference, to ensure that right. That power, Hunt added, encompassed the appointment of federal officials to administer the voting process in recalcitrant states, as the federal statute had provided. Accusing the majority of rendering the Reconstruction amendments impotent, he said that requiring the freedmen to combat "hostile legislation and personal prejudice" through the tedious and costly process of the state courts both ignores the purpose of the Reconstruction amendments and, in effect, denies relief to those whose rights have been infringed.[97]

Four years later, the whole Court confronted the issue of the constitutionality of the same but now amended federal law. The case involved the criminal prosecution of state officials for their resistance to the federal supervision of an election to the House of Representatives. The justices ruled that Congress had ample constitutional authority to protect the federal electoral process. They reminded the states that in jealously defending their rights they must not ignore the respect that is due the federal government: "Both are essential to the preservation of our liberties and the perpetuity of our institutions."[98]

A year later the Court held that the Fifteenth Amendment by itself operated to void any state law or constitutional provision that denied blacks access to the ballot. Furthermore, this meant that blacks were generally eligible for jury service, which was often limited by state law to registered voters.[99]

When a person convicted under federal law for interfering with a black's right to vote argued that according to *Reese* the Fifteenth Amendment did not create a federal right to vote that congressional legislation could protect, the unanimous Court disagreed. Unlike the Fourteenth Amendment, with its requirement of state action, the Fifteenth Amendment was interpreted as giving the federal government power to enact criminal laws punishing individuals, as well as state officials, for depriving persons of their voting rights in either state or federal elections because of their race. It further ruled that when racial restrictions are swept away and the black meets the other criteria for voting, Congress has the inherent power to protect that right to vote and to punish individuals who interfere with it. More broadly, it accepted congressional authority under Article I of the Constitution to prevent interference with the election of federal officials, whether or not race was involved. Surely, the justices concluded, the federal government must have "power to protect the elections on which its existence depends from violence and corruption." Without legal restraint against such evils, they added, the country is "in danger and its best powers, its highest purposes, the hopes which it inspires and the love which enshrines it, are at the mercy of the combinations of those who respect no right but brute force, on the one hand, and unprincipled corruptionists on the other."[100]

Black voting in the South continued into the 1890s, but by 1900 black voting had all but disappeared. How, with the interpretations of the Court, was this possible? Well, although holding that the Fifteenth Amendment had made race, color, and previous condition of servitude impermissible qualifications, the justices had left the general authority to determine who were qualified voters to the states. Because blacks were generally poor and inadequately educated in the South, de-

vices such as poll taxes and locally administered literacy tests often quite successfully removed blacks from the voting rolls. While the Supreme Court upheld these
methods of qualification,[101] one of the more blatant discriminatory devices, the
grandfather clause, did not survive the scrutiny of the High Bench.

When they first considered the matter in 1915 the justices unanimously struck
down such clauses in both Oklahoma and Annapolis, Maryland.[102] The grandfather
clause was a device to exclude blacks from the ballot by enfranchising only those
citizens who could vote, or were descended from those who could vote, prior to
the time when blacks were initially enfranchised by the Reconstruction governments. The Annapolis clause was an absolute bar, while Oklahoma's restriction
only exempted those who met this requirement from having to take a literacy test
to qualify for the franchise. In the latter instance, poorly educated whites were
admitted to the voting list and blacks were left to cope with the locally administered literacy tests. In both instances, the Court found these unsubtle devices in
violation of the Constitution because they recreate and perpetuate "the very conditions which the [Fifteenth] Amendment was intended to destroy."[103]

Despite such decisions, the Court's interpretation of the Reconstruction
amendments in behalf of civil rights seems cramped and distorted as we view its
work through late-twentieth-century eyes. The progress made in the early twentieth century seems slow and limited. We might be able to accept the proslavery
decisions of the justices before the Civil War on the basis that the fundamental law
allowed them little choice, but when that law was modified in favor of freedom,
liberty, and equality, why was a Court, with a tradition of safeguarding individual
rights, so reluctant to assert its new authority? Apart from its and the society's
devotion to federalism, the limited reach and resources of the federal government,
and antipathy toward class legislation, most of the justices could not square such
an abrupt break with the past with their idea of a rule of law. A second revolution
had indeed occurred, but as with the first, there was an innate tendency to moderate its effects on the society. So, in 1776 as the first revolution began, the Continental Congress called upon the states to draft constitutions and put their
governments on a sound legal footing. This was a conservative move, not only to
curtail the social implications of revolution but also to maintain the continuity
inherent in a rule of law. Equally conservative was the Court's reading of the
Reconstruction amendments, which had sought to write the results of the second
revolution into the Constitution. The majority of justices seemed temperamentally
unable to accept the implications of a radical restructuring of the Union. Working
within a framework of law, the judiciary tends to be conservative and suspicious
of abrupt change.

Through the dissenting opinions in many of these cases flow the winds of the
future. Their premises and deductions have become our own. They are enveloped
within the theology of the civil religion and their claim upon us is great. Despite

some Supreme Court decisions in the early twentieth century modifying the rigors of segregation, their inroad on the practice was small, and segregation would harden in the South after *Plessy*. A later generation would have to endure the agony of closing the gap between the premises of a common faith and existing discriminatory practices. And a Court that had condoned the disparity would be called upon to reinspect its earlier rulings and provide some leadership in this crusade.

The story told here of the limited application of the Reconstruction amendments is only part of the tale of their interpretation by the high priests of the Supreme Court. Although the justices were skeptical of wide-ranging claims of new federally protected civil rights, they were quite familiar with the property right and would encounter new and intriguing arguments about its protection under the Reconstruction amendments.

INTERPRETING NEW AND OLD HOLY BOOKS: PART II: PROTECTING PROPERTY AND OTHER INDIVIDUAL RIGHTS IN THE CHANGING ECONOMY, 1864–1917

In seeking to protect slave property in *Dred Scott*, Roger B. Taney was willing to interpret the due process clause of the Fifth Amendment in a new and intriguing way—as not simply a command for regularized procedures but rather as an absolute bar on legislation that would limit property in slaves. This part of the rambling decision seemed to be swept away with the decision itself, but the long tradition of the Court's special regard for the property right, which Taney's maneuver reflected, would survive *Dred Scott*, as would the attempt to find new federal protection for it.

Although the Court from 1861 to 1865 generally deferred to the political branches of the government to prosecute the war, the justices continued to assert their authority in promoting certain national aims and in securing the individual's right to property. One excellent example is *Gelpcke v. Dubuque*, which involved the Iowa city's attempt to repudiate bonds it had issued to aid railroad construction in 1857. In a rush to attract the Iron Horse, municipalities and states ran up huge debts that they later sought to repudiate. Here bonds had been authorized by a state statute that seemingly violated language in the Iowa constitution. Earlier state judicial readings of their validity were later reversed by the Iowa supreme court. The justices were not unmindful that a decision here had wide-ranging ramifications throughout the nation.

Justice Noah Swayne, who delivered the majority opinion in *Gelpcke*, two years earlier had put the Court on record as saying that it would follow the latest state high court decision,[1] but now he and his colleagues came to a different conclusion. Arguing that the repudiation decision of the Iowa court stood out "in unenviable solitude and notoriety" from the consensus reached in sixteen other states, he said this exceptional case called upon the High Bench to exercise its own judgment.

And justice, Swayne continued, demands that a state court be held to the same constitutional standard imposed on a legislature—not to impair the obligations of contracts. "We shall," he said, "never immolate truth, justice, and the law, because a state tribunal has erected the altar and decreed the sacrifice."[2] Here in 1864 Northern states were reminded by the Court of their basic obligations to protect the property rights of individuals by making their actions conform to a national commercial standard.

Gelpcke was only the first salvo in the Court's injection of its authority into the administration of state property law. When a creditor obtained a judgment against the city of Muscatine, Iowa, requiring the city to levy a tax to pay the award, the local officials responded that the maximum tax permitted by the city's charter had already been levied and committed. Upon appeal, the Supreme Court ordered the tax to be levied. Brushing aside the charter limitation, Justice Swayne, again for the Court, added that the law of "so enlightened a State" could not have been intended to frustrate the collection of a legitimate debt. After noting state judicial decisions that contradicted the one the Court was reaching, Swayne said the justices' task "cannot be performed . . . by blindly following the footsteps of others and substituting their judgment for our own." Were any other course of action followed, Swayne concluded, we would "abdicate the performance of a solemn duty, betray a sacred trust committed to our charge, and defeat the wise and provident policy of the Constitution which called this court into existence."[3]

In these two cases, the Court substituted its own reading of state law for that of the Iowa courts, resulting in orders to pay bonds that had been declared void and to levy a tax in excess of the limits prescribed by local law. This enlargement of the Court's jurisdiction was defended in terms of the priestly interpreter dutifully following the commandments of the holy writ.

This rationale is even more clearly presented in a later decision invalidating Virginia's attempt to modify the rights of its creditors. Pronouncing the offending act void, the Court said that the Constitution "speaks with sovereign and commanding voice, expecting and receiving ready and cheerful obedience, not so much for the display of its power, as on account of the majesty of its authority and the justice of its mandates."[4]

In this 1894 case, *Poindexter v. Greenhow*, state officials tried to use the Eleventh Amendment, barring suits against the state, to shield themselves from the consequences of what the Court saw as invasions of individual liberty. Justice Stanley Matthews, for the majority, said that officers "who falsely speak and act" in the state's name can be sued in their private capacity. In defending this conclusion, he wrapped the sacred Constitution around the Court's claim of authority. To deny the difference between the state and those who act under its pretended authority, Matthews continued, "obliterates the line of demarcation that separates constitutional government from absolutism." He asked: What would be the value of written constitutions protecting individual liberty "if their limitations and restraints upon power may be overpassed with impunity by the very agencies created and appointed to guard, defend and enforce them." The idea that courts were prohibited from imposing penalties upon such unholy conduct left Justice Matthews aghast, as he searched for words to convey his condemnation of such a claim. Finally, he said that those who assert it are urging "the doctrine of absolutism, pure, simple and naked; and of communism, which is its twin; the double progeny of the same evil birth."[5]

The Court was engaged in a holy battle against the forces of evil, including—for the first time in the annals of the Supreme Court—communism. It would not shirk its responsibility of protecting the individual against the wrongful exercise of authority by state officials, Matthews said. Only by rejecting such inroads upon individual liberty, the justice concluded, "can the supremacy of . . . [the] Constitution be maintained."[6]

What makes this decision even more significant is that it was the second salvo in the Court's battle to protect individual rights from governmental assertions of sovereign power. The first salvo, fired a little over a year earlier in *United States v. Lee*, was directed not at the state but rather at national government assertions that its actions were not reviewable by the courts. What was involved was land that had been owned by Confederate General Robert E. Lee that had been purchased by the United States at a tax sale. Two hundred acres were used to establish a national cemetery and a like amount was set apart as a military post. Lee's son, who claimed the property as his inheritance, sued the superintendent of the cemetery and the commander of the post to regain control of the property. Evidence was introduced that an agent of the general's wife offered to pay the tax but that the offer was refused because the payment was not tendered by the owner personally. The trial court found in favor of the claimant, over the protest of the government that this was, in fact, a suit against the United States.[7]

Contrasting the situation under the British crown, Justice Samuel F. Miller, for the Court, upheld the lower tribunal's ruling. He said that when an individual "has established his right to property, there is no reason why deference to any person, natural or artificial, not even the United States, should prevent him from using the means which the law gives him, for the protection and enforcement of that right." Although Miller cited precedent that upheld the right of an individual to sue the agents of government personally, he seemed to rely more on the Fifth Amendment's protection of the individual from being deprived of property without due process of law. The provisions of this amendment, he continued, "are of that character which it is intended the courts shall enforce, when cases involving their operation and effect are brought before them." To entertain a contrary view, Miller insisted, "seems to be opposed to all the principles upon which the rights of the citizen, when brought in collision with the acts of the Government, must be determined."[8] When government officials invade the rights of citizens, he continued, only the courts can protect them.

The executive department, Miller added, cannot confer any authority on its officials when the power it has attempted to exercise "is absolutely prohibited." Insisting that the Court's priestly authority is to enforce the commands of the sacred writ, he said: "No man in this country is so high that he is above the law. No officer of the law may set the law at defiance, with impunity. All the officers of the Government, from the highest to the lowest, are creatures of the law and are bound to obey it." Such must be the result, the justice continued, in any "government which has a just claim to well regulated liberty and the protection of personal rights." To the contention that this assumption of authority by the Court interferes with the legitimate and important powers of the executive branch, Miller responded that the "slightest consideration of the nature, the character, the organization and the powers of these courts will dispel any fear of serious injury to the Government, at their hands." Without control of either the purse or the sword, he said, the Court's "power and influence rest solely upon the public sense of the necessity for the existence of a tribunal to which all may appeal for the assertion and protection of rights guaranteed by the Constitution and by the laws of the land, and on the confidence reposed in the soundness of their decisions and the purity of their motives."[9]

In its first major decision in 1793 the Court had ruled that the Constitution permitted suits against the state by out-of-state citizens, employing language that bears a close resemblance to that used here.[10] That early decision was answered by the Eleventh Amendment, but, as we have seen, that bar was not interpreted by the Court to preclude a remedy for the invasion of individual rights. To deny recovery for a wrong was seen as a fundamental rejection of the rule of law and the special role of the judiciary. Although three generations had passed since that ruling and an industrialized society was now emerging, the justices' conception of their priestly role was strikingly similar—a clear acknowledgment of their duty to protect individual rights from hostile action by government at all levels.

The Court protected the right to property in these cases on the basis that state action had impaired the preexisting contract rights of individuals. But in the economically expanding society such a basis for protection was increasingly limited. In the latter third of the nineteenth century new security for property was sought, as the resources of the nation were now being privately tapped by growing corporate interests. Often such interests could find accommodating state legislatures, but at times the people demanded that their representatives exercise some control in the public interest. Increasingly, the Court would be drawn into this conflict, as lawyers urged upon the justices the view that the new constitutional order, arising from the Civil War, provided new protection for the property interest. The contract clause that had been used earlier in the Iowa cases was too limited to do the larger job; it required some specified prior commitment that was less and less the case as a new regulatory movement grew in various states. Increasingly this search for some type of federal constitutional check on the actions of states regulating the individual property right led to the Fourteenth Amendment with its generalized language protecting the right of property from abridgement without due process of law.

How an amendment primarily designed to ensure the rights of former slaves from discriminatory action by the states would be interpreted to provide new protection for the right of property in an industrialized society is one of the most fascinating stories in constitutional history. It begins with some irate butchers in New Orleans whose arguments confronted the Court with the task of determining the meaning and reach of the Fourteenth Amendment's significant first section. The Louisiana legislature in 1869 had established a corporation in New Orleans that was to have a monopoly on the slaughtering of animals for meat. All butchers, who earlier had done their own slaughtering, now were required to do this work within the facilities of the monopoly. Butchers, who were thus limited in carrying on their trade, brought action against the monopoly on the basis of the Thirteenth and Fourteenth Amendments.

Former Justice John A. Campbell, who had resigned his seat on the Court in 1861 to follow his state into the Confederacy, returned to argue the case for the butchers. In a wide-ranging argument, he insisted that the two amendments had revolutionized the constitutional order and made the federal government the primary protector of the rights of citizens. The Louisiana statute, he said, forced the butchers into involuntary servitude, denied them their privileges and immunities, due process, and the equal protection of the laws. He was asking the Court to affirm this new and sweeping interpretation of the reconstructed Union. That a majority of the Court recoiled from this invitation can be expected within a political culture where, despite the Civil War, there still was a profound attachment to a federalism in which states retained wide-ranging governmental authority.

Speaking through Justice Miller, the Court, in the *Slaughter-House Cases* of 1873, accepted the Louisiana regulation as a health measure, seeing no real interference with the butchers' trade. The Thirteenth and Fourteenth Amendments, he said, were designed primarily to protect the rights of former slaves and this purpose must guide "any fair and just construction" of their meaning.[11]

Distinguishing between United States citizenship as guaranteed by the Fourteenth Amendment and state citizenship, the justice said that the privileges and immunities of each were different. Noting that the privileges and immunities originally protected from abridgment by the states in Article IV of the Constitution were defined by the states themselves, he asked if the Fourteenth Amendment brought "within the power of Congress the entire domain of civil rights heretofore belonging exclusively to the states?" Without the guidance of clearer language,

Miller said that the Court would not depart "from the structure and spirit of our institutions" by radically changing "the whole theory of the relations of the state and Federal governments to each other and of both these governments to the people."[12]

Justice Stephen J. Field accepted what the majority could not accept—that the Reconstruction amendments had fundamentally restructured the Union. What makes his opinion so fascinating is its confirmation by subsequent history. Denying that the creation of the slaughtering monopoly was a health regulation under the state's police power, Field said that such a pretense "cannot be permitted to encroach upon any of the just rights of the citizen, which the Constitution intended to secure against abridgement." Although viewing the Thirteenth Amendment argument sympathetically, Field said the succeeding amendment clearly inhibits "any legislation which confers special and exclusive privileges like these under consideration."[13]

Castigating the majority for making the privileges and immunities section of the Fourteenth Amendment "a vain and idle enactment," Field argued that precedent had established clearly an "equality of right among citizens in the pursuit of the ordinary avocations of life . . . [as] the distinguishing privilege of citizens of the United States." Clearly the chartering of an "odious" monopoly, he added, interfered with the butchers' ability to practice their trade, thus denying them the "right of free labor, one of the most sacred and imprescriptible rights of man." And while Miller ended with a peroration praising the federalist system, Field said: "That only is a free government in the American sense of the term, under which the inalienable right of every citizen to pursue his happiness is unrestrained, except by just, equal, and impartial laws."[14]

Joseph P. Bradley, in his dissent, dealt more directly with the meaning of United States citizenship. The Fourteenth Amendment, he began, made it "a sure and undoubted title to equal rights in any and every state in this Union." An individual's choice of a lawful employment, the justice continued, is "one of his most valuable rights, and one which the legislature of a state cannot invade." Summoning up the Declaration of Independence, which he saw as the foundation of the nation's existence, he said "personal rights were deemed . . . sacred," and they belonged "to the citizens of every free government." The "right to choose one's calling is an essential part of that liberty which is the object of government to protect," Bradley insisted. He then condemned the majority's "narrow and insufficient estimate of constitutional history and . . . the rights of the American people." The Fourteenth Amendment, he continued, registered the people's intention "to provide national security against violation by the states of the fundamental rights of the citizen." Its language, Bradley asserted, embraces all citizens in seeking to rectify the problems of the past, which included not only slavery, but also disloyalty, intolerance of free speech, and the insecurity of property as well. The amendment, the justice concluded, "was an attempt to give voice to the strong national yearning for that time . . . [when] every citizen of the United States might stand erect in every portion of its soil, in the full enjoyment of every right and privilege belonging to a freeman, without fear of violence or molestation."[15]

Bradley also saw merit in the due process claim of the butchers, saying that the property right in their occupation had been unlawfully taken from them. He found meaning in that clause in the Fourteenth Amendment by expanding the long-standing interpretation that due process only mandated that regularized procedures must be followed. He now read it as conferring a substantive right that was immune from invasion. This view would receive more attention and support in the years to come.

Justice Swayne, in dissent, called the Reconstruction amendments "a new Magna Charta." The majority, he lamented, has turned "what was meant for bread into a stone." Rather than recoiling from the new accretion of federal power, Swayne continued, the Court should embrace it as both "beneficent" and as what "should exist in every well ordered system." Without authority to secure the equal rights and privileges of the people, "any government claiming to be national is glaringly defective."[16]

The dissents in this significant case are judicial jeremiads; they censure the majority for departing from the goal to which the people had rededicated themselves in the Reconstruction amendments. That goal, the dissenters insisted, was to ensure the protection of the essential rights of the individual from all governmental invasion. The Court majority just could not bring itself to accept the degree of centralized control that the dissenters felt was only just. Progress would be slow in the direction the dissenters charted, but they indeed had identified the course of the future better than they could have known. *Slaughter-House* had all but read the privileges and immunities clause out of the Fourteenth Amendment, and there it would stay, in part because the other pregnant clauses of the amendment would, in time, be summoned to serve the ends that the privileges and immunities clause had originally been designed to address.

Notice also how the pictures drawn by the opinions are so different. The majority hewed closely to a federal system that it saw imperiled by the new argument while the dissenters embraced the idea that the national government was now the fount of all important rights of individuals. A new dialogue had begun.

Four members of the Court had grasped the future, but only one of the four was willing to follow the logical implications of their finding—that a federal constitutional right protected an individual from state interference in pursuit of a lawful occupation. On the day after *Slaughter-House* was decided, the majority had no difficulty in ruling that a woman denied the right to practice law in Illinois because of her sex had no federal claim under the privileges and immunities clause of the Fourteenth Amendment. Women's rights advocates had made some headway during the Reconstruction years, especially in obtaining state legislation that would provide some protection for the property of married women.[17] But in this case only Chief Justice Salmon P. Chase, who would die just three weeks after the decision, dissented without opinion. The three remaining *Slaughter-House* dissenters concurred in the result, as they sought to distinguish a woman lawyer from a male butcher. Speaking through Bradley, they said the difference was justified because the role and character of the female sex, as fixed by the law of the Creator, "unfits it for many of the occupations of civil life." Noting that single women were exceptions to the general rule, they insisted that the "paramount destiny and mission of woman are to fulfill the noble and benign offices of wife and mother."[18]

The priests of the high court continued to read the holy writ through the assumed purpose of the Creator in allocating different roles to the sexes. When a prominent woman lawyer-reformer, who had been admitted to the federal bar and the bars of a number of states, was refused admittance in Virginia, the unanimous Court deferred to the discretion of the state and denied any Fourteenth Amendment claim. The legislation spoke only of qualified "persons," but the justices said that the state can decide for itself whether that term included female applicants.[19]

Unanimously, the justices similarly responded to a woman's claim that the Fourteenth Amendment precluded Missouri from denying her the right to vote. The Fifteenth Amendment had placed some restrictions on the state's discretion in determining who could vote, but, despite some lobbying by early feminists, sex was not included. Virginia Minor was thus reduced to arguing that as a United States citizen she had a right to vote. The Court rejected the claim, ruling that the franchise was not among the rights conferred by the Fourteenth Amendment.[20] In the justices' defense, the idea that voting qualifications are determined by the states was clearly established and was reaffirmed by the need for the Fifteenth Amendment, which banned only the use of "race, color, or previous condition of servitude" as qualifications for the vote.

So, even justices who accepted their role as a defender of individual rights against the actions of government excepted women from the full enjoyment of such rights. The words were broad and invited the arguments made, but the Court had no hesitation in narrowing the language through the lens of dominant social views. Distinctions, such as this one, could not stand the test of time, in part because the civil theological foundation supported no such distinction. But the society would have to change appreciably before the all-male bench would take such claims seriously. Some justices were more willing than others to protect the individual rights that lay at the heart of the American creed and they were willing to educate and lead the flock, but these priests remained bound within the limits of their own time, not ours. As the years passed, however, new justices would take a fresh look at the holy writ itself and shear it of the grafts that earlier translators had placed upon it.

Although the dissenters in *Slaughter-House* drew gender boundaries on their conception of a trade and its practice as a property right, their translation of the due process clause of the Fourteenth Amendment was appealing to those who sought some protection from state economic regulation. If, in the emerging industrial order, states threatened the property interest, at least a substantial minority of the Court seemed to believe that the Reconstruction amendments afforded some new protection.

Although the Court saw no bar to a state prohibiting the manufacture and sale of alcoholic beverages, it suggested that, if a case came to it involving a state attempt to confiscate such property owned before a prohibitory statute was passed, it might find a violation of the due process clause of the Fourteenth Amendment. Because the case of *Bartemeyer v. Iowa* was argued at the same time as *Slaughter-House*, the dissenters now lectured the majority about the essential differences in the two cases. Where the state's police power to regulate in behalf of the health and safety of the public is unchallengeable, there can be no right to pursue a calling deemed unlawful, Bradley said. Creating an "unconscionable monopoly" to limit a person's lawful trade, however, the justice continued, runs afoul of what has "become the fundamental law of this country that life, liberty, and property (which include 'the pursuit of happiness') are sacred rights, which the Constitution of the United States guarantees to its humblest citizen against oppressive legislation, whether national or local."[21]

Field continued the lesson by agreeing with the implications of the majority opinion that a state cannot broadly prohibit the sale, disposition, use, and enjoyment of property without violating the due process clause of the Fourteenth Amendment. Still, the justice continued, the state under its police power can regulate in the public interest. Then, returning to *Slaughter-House*, he said that under this power the state may not "farm out the ordinary avocations of life."[22] This is so, Field argued, because the Fourteenth Amendment, under the privileges and immunities clause, included as part of the individual's sacred right to pursue happiness the right to choose and practice a lawful occupation. The amendment, he concluded, has created a primary national citizenship that ensures the protection of all such individual rights.

Justices Bradley, Swayne, and Field had taken the opportunity in *Bartemeyer* to reemphasize their view that the Supreme Court now had a new and sweeping responsibility—to protect a great variety of individual rights from invasion by the states. A union that had been preserved by great sacrifice, Field said, would be "worthless if a citizen could not be protected in all his fundamental rights . . . throughout the limits of the Republic."[23]

Despite the majority's disagreement, the position of the dissenters fueled further dialogue and litigation. Clearly, the justices had expressed doubts that state discretion to regulate property was without limit. As the Court considered a number of laws passed by the states regulating property that had been spawned by the activity of the Grange, a farmers' organization, in the Midwest, the justices were forced to draw some lines. In *Munn v. Illinois*, owners of grain warehouses objected to regulation of their rates by the Illinois legislature. Were they being deprived of their property? No, said the Court majority. For the Court, Chief Justice Morrison R. Waite, who had replaced Chase in 1874, accepted that a taking of property would raise a federal constitutional question. But the state, he ruled, could regulate business "affected with a public interest." Finding the warehouses to be such property, Waite concluded that their owners could not invoke the aid of the courts. "For protection against abuses by Legislatures," the chief admonished, "the people must resort to the polls, not to the courts." Field in dissent, joined by Justice William Strong, saw the Constitution protecting individuals from just "such invasions of private rights."[24]

Changes in membership over the next twenty years made the Court more hospitable to the argument that the Fourteenth Amendment's due process clause provided some protection for property. What in 1878 the Court condemned as "some strange misconception of the scope of this provision as found in the XIVth Amendment,"[25] it would gradually accept as the basis for an expanded judicial role within which such regulation would be evaluated. Eight years later, for instance, the Court said that "the State cannot require a railroad corporation to carry persons or property without reward; neither can it do that which in law amounts to a taking of private property for public use without just compensation, or without due process of law."[26] And in that same term, Waite announced that no argument was necessary on the question of whether corporations were protected by the Fourteenth Amendment because the justices all agreed that such businesses were embraced by its language.[27]

The latter ruling was hardly a surprise, for corporations in American law had long been dealt with as artificial persons with standing to invoke the jurisdiction of the courts. To distinguish between parties on the basis of size or power would make a fundamental inroad upon the rule of law, something that no justice would countenance. The very nature of law was to protect all equally, and if individuals were to be immunized from state regulation, so, too, would corporations be.

The Court was mindful of this fact, and when well-financed corporate litigants continued to argue that their property should not be regulated at all, the Court rejected that challenge.[28] It responded similarly when the same litigants tried to use the technicalities of the federal system to escape regulation.[29]

Despite, then, the Court's gradual movement in the direction of finding some federal protection under the Fourteenth Amendment limiting state regulation of property, the claims had to be pitched to abuse of an acknowledged power to regulate—one that resulted in an implied taking of property by the government. In 1890, the Court, for the first time, invalidated a state law on grounds that in its attempted regulation it took property without due process of law. Minnesota had sought to make the rate decisions of a newly created railroad commission final by precluding any appeal to the courts. To prevent the judiciary from responding to a claim that the rate set was unreasonably low, the Court said, deprives the railroad "of the lawful use of its property, and thus, in substance and effect, of the property itself, without due process of law and in violation of the Constitution."[30]

Eight years later the justices unanimously took the final step and struck down a state law setting rates on grounds that it did not allow a fair rate of return on the property invested.[31] This drew the Court into the morass of determining just what was the invested capital upon which a fair rate could be calculated. Increasingly, the Court would be involved in second-guessing the state legislative or administrative process as part of its perceived duty to protect the individual's property right.

Of all the justices Stephen J. Field was the most persistent advocate for the protection of individual property rights under the Fourteenth Amendment. He considered his colleagues' concessions too grudging and limited. For instance, when the Court generally approved state regulation and prohibition of the manufacture and sale of margarine, ostensibly to protect consumers from fraud and an unhealthy product, Field protested. He said that the Fourteenth Amendment's protection of life, liberty, and property was designed "to secure to every person the essential conditions for the pursuit of happiness and is therefore not to be construed in a narrow or restricted sense." Field exposed the purpose behind such laws—the protection of the dairy industry—and he forcefully contended that a government that favors a competitor destroys the very rights that it was constituted to secure. "With the gift of life," he said, "there necessarily goes to everyone the right to do all such acts, and follow all such pursuits, not inconsistent with the equal rights of others, as may support life and add to the happiness of its possessor."[32] In another case Field joined in a dissenting opinion molded around his view that the Court had erred in its blanket ruling that property affected with a public interest can be regulated by government. "The utmost possible liberty to the individual, and the fullest possible protection to him and his property," the dissenters asserted, was "both the limitation and duty of government."[33]

In another case David J. Brewer, for a unanimous bench, explained the Court's predilection for giving to the words of the Declaration of Independence a constitutional importance. Although the Declaration is not part of the nation's fundamental law, he explained, "the latter is but the body and the letter of which the former is the thought and the spirit, and it is always safe to read the letter of the Constitution in the spirit of the Declaration of Independence." Then, he added: "No duty rests more imperatively upon the courts than the enforcement of those constitutional provisions intended to secure the equality of rights which is the foundation of free government."[34]

What makes these opinions instructive is a rhetoric that ties the American creed, as stated in the Declaration, to the language of the Fourteenth Amendment. The fact that at times corporate interests were protected from regulation has led critics to dismiss such language as window dressing. But how the window is dressed is itself a significant part of the story of the Court's place in American culture. These cases involve the question of how the protection of life, liberty, and property found in the Fourteenth Amendment is to be translated into practice. Field and Brewer answer, expansively, in keeping with the Declaration's promise that individuals will be protected in their pursuit of happiness. And that happiness is to be furthered, at least in part, by freeing individuals in their lawful economic pursuits from governmental interference. The dissenters are telling their colleagues that they are derelict in their essential duty of interpreting the holy writ to safeguard personal liberty to the fullest extent. Their errant colleagues are seeking justification for governmental action rather than ensuring the protection of individuals from an abridgment of their freedom.

The majority was sensitive to the need to allow government the room to cope with the economic and social problems following in the wake of the rapid industrialization in the latter nineteenth century. To enfeeble government at precisely the time it needed to be empowered seemed an unwarranted interference with the processes of democratic government. The prevailing social complaint was not that the property right was being threatened, but rather that it was so safeguarded that it precluded healthful and necessary change in the society. The majority generally recognized that the individual right to property should not be interpreted to preclude such change.[35] Yet, the dissents are appealing, largely because they view the cases not through the lens of social need but rather through the lens of individual liberty.

Often Field and his disciple and nephew, David J. Brewer, lost such battles, but the one that they clearly won demonstrated the pitfalls that the Court faced by enshrining the property right. One of the most dramatic Court battles of the 1890s saw that right pitted against the taxing authority of the national government. At issue was whether Congress had the authority to levy an income tax.[36] To redress the imbalance of a federal taxing system that left the fortunes of the wealthy largely untouched, Congress levied a flat tax of 2 percent on incomes in excess of the then princely sum of four thousand dollars. Advocates against the imposition argued that it would be the death knell of the capitalist system and would inevitably lead to "communism, anarchy, and then the ever following despotism."[37] The emotionalism of the arguments seeped into the discussions and the opinions of the justices themselves.

To invalidate the income tax the Court had to ignore precedent that had limited the definition of direct taxes to impositions that could reasonably be apportioned by population, as the Constitution required. To rule that an income tax had to be so apportioned would, in effect, rule out such a levy, but that is exactly what the majority did. Chief Justice Melville W. Fuller, who had replaced Waite in 1888, translated the constitutional requirement that direct taxes be apportioned as embodying the intent of the framers to prevent "an attack upon accumulated property by mere force of numbers." The direct tax limitation, he continued, is "one of the bulwarks of private rights and private property," implying that what the framers feared was just what the Court now faced.[38] To call the tax indirect, Fuller added, would undermine the protection and jettison the wisdom of the founding fathers.

The Court's eager response to the invitation to save the nation from calamity led Justice Edward D. White, a new arrival, to argue that the governmental system is best served when the Court stays within the parameters of its proper role. To subject the interpretation of the fundamental law to the personal whims of a bare majority of justices is to deprive it of its stabilizing value and make it "a most dangerous instrument to the rights and liberties of the people."[39] Another dissenter, John Marshall Harlan, worried that the Court's decision might well fan the flames of class warfare in the country, saying "that it is not possible for this court to have rendered any judgment more to be regretted than the one just rendered." He accused the majority of crippling "the just power of the national Government" and discriminating "against the greater part of the people of the country." Arguing that the decision is "inconsistent with the fundamental principles of our social organization," Harlan declared that the people have been placed in peril by so endowing certain property with power and influence. They "ought not be subjected to the dominion of aggregated wealth any more than the property of the country should be at the mercy of the lawless."[40] Justice Henry B. Brown echoed Harlan in saying that the decision approached being a "national calamity" fraught with danger to the society. "I hope," he added, "it may not prove the first step toward the submergence of the liberties of people in a sordid despotism of wealth."[41]

In these dissents the complaint was directed to the majority justices and the interests that they had so willingly accommodated. In the guise of protecting the individual property right, the majority used its interpretation of the Constitution to preserve the economic status quo by overriding the normal push and pull of the political process. To these justices, the Court was only doing what it had traditionally done—evaluating the claim of governmental authority against the protection of the individual right. But Harlan, who had no argument with the High Bench protecting the property right, insisted that the present case was quite different from ordinary fare. The property right was always conditioned upon the legitimate claims of government, he implied, and to argue that these claims should be honored by an overreaching Court both weakens its role in the constitutional order and casts aspersions upon its sacred duty to protect individual rights from the oppression of government.

To the dissenters, the majority had expanded the Court's role into the political realm to protect the powerful from paying their fair share for the maintenance of the government. What especially disturbed the dissenting justices was the fuel the decision provided to a growing class conflict in American society. As the people were suffering through an economic depression in the mid-1890s, the rule of law, as announced by the majority, was placed in the camp of the economically power-ful, who were immunized from obligations to contribute to the maintenance of the government. The Court was not simply protecting the property right but rather giving to certain types of property an inviolable character.

The federal income tax had been invalidated, but the decision could not weather the test of time. Although it obviously had powerful supporters, the cre-ation of largely untaxed wealth provided a target for reformers. Eager advocates wanted Congress to test the Court's resolve with a new statute, and as time passed the justices did seem to move away from the rigidity of the decision. But with encouragement from judicial supporters, who insisted that the proper route to change was a constitutional amendment relieving an income tax from the bar of the direct tax provision, the Sixteenth Amendment, empowering the federal gov-ernment to tax income, was added to the Constitution in 1913.

Americans had fought a civil war, made fundamental changes in their Constitu-tion, and industrialized their society; in the process the Supreme Court had grown considerably in power and visibility. As a branch of the federal government with an increasing ambit of authority, it was drawn into politics in a new way. The income tax decision was only one of a trio of resolutions reached by the Court in 1895; the other two narrowed the reach of congressional power over corporations that restrained trade and enlarged the use of the injunction to halt a strike threaten-ing the property of railroad owners.[42] From such decisions a picture of the Court emerged as a defender of the property interest against the perceived needs of a society trying to cope with dramatically changed conditions. When the Demo-cratic candidate for president, William Jennings Bryan, injected these decisions into the campaign and suggested that they could be changed by the appointments he, as president, would make to the High Bench, he brought the Court directly into the political arena.[43] Bryan lost the election to William McKinley, but he made the composition of the High Bench the political issue it has remained ever since.

The decisions to which Bryan alluded, however, did not typify the Court, though certainly some cases were resolved in a way that frustrated reformers. That the Court responded to claims that a right to property was being violated is to be expected, given its history and the society's focus on this particular right. But the justices were not blind to the fact that an industrialized society required govern-mental intervention to deal with the problems it brought in its wake. Moreover, a right to property had to be defined in relation to the society that afforded it protection.[44]

Despite the narrow reading of the taxing power in the income tax case and the commerce power in the restraint of trade area in the 1895 decisions, the Court generally found sufficient authority in Congress under both clauses to pass a wide range of federal regulatory legislation.[45] The justices had recognized that industrialization had made the sprawling geographical area called the United States a much more integrated economic unit. In the face of this reality and before Congress began to set new national policy, the Court had filled in the void. This can be seen both in the justices' new reading of the due process protection and in their interpretation of what the powers delegated to Congress encompassed.

None of these powers, with the possible exception of the authority to raise revenue, seemed more important to the framers of the Constitution than the power to regulate commerce. By the time the range of that authority was explored by the Supreme Court, the Southern insistence on protecting the institution of slavery had skewed the interpretation of that clause. State authority was accommodated and limitations were imposed on both the exercise and the interpretation of the range of this national power. Congressional inaction was taken to mean that local circumstances made a uniform policy unfeasible. The Civil War swept away the peculiar institution and its inhibitions on the potential of the commerce clause. What in the prewar years the Court had hesitated to proclaim, the Court now said boldly—that silence on the part of Congress was "equivalent to a declaration that interstate commerce shall be free and untrammeled."[46] States, which were bound by the Court's evolving interpretation of a new due process protection, now also were advised by the justices that only Congress could regulate the national common market.

Perhaps both the internal and external criticism the income tax decision received nipped the tendency of some justices to push the Court's authority further than society would tolerate. At any rate, the members of the High Bench would long hesitate to place themselves again in such a direct confrontation with the political authority of the federal government. If the majority had erred in overreaching, this error led to no reprisal against the High Bench, nor did it seem to have any effect on the preexisting ambit of the Court's general power to interpret the fundamental law and protect individual rights.

By the mid-1890s, the Court had come a long way since *Slaughter-House*, in finding that the Fourteenth Amendment had, indeed, created a federal property right enforceable by the courts. However, life and liberty were equally protected by the due process clause, and in *Allgeyer v. Louisiana* the Court created a new individual right that was to be preserved from state invasion—the liberty of contract.

For much of its history, the Court had been involved in the protection of preexisting contract rights but had said nothing about a right to enter into a contract. The Fourteenth Amendment's protection of liberty now provided a grounding for such a claim in the holy writ. Louisiana had sought to regulate the insurance industry by forbidding parties to enter into contracts with companies not authorized to do business in the state. When Allgeyer contracted with a New York firm to ensure his shipments out of the state, he ran afoul of the Louisiana law. In a unanimous opinion, Justice Rufus W. Peckham illustrated how completely the Court now accepted the dissenting opinions in *Slaughter-House*. The justice ruled that the Louisiana act violated the Fourteenth Amendment by depriving Allgeyer of his liberty without due process of law. This liberty, Peckham added, embraces the person's right to enjoy and employ his faculties; "to live and work where he will; to earn his livelihood by any lawful calling; to pursue any livelihood or avocation, and for that purpose to enter into all contracts."[47]

To extend the protection of the individual's rights was quite in keeping with the Court's tradition and its role within the American civil religion. Industrialization in the late nineteenth century, however, had reduced the bargaining power of the individual, and social critics worried about the justices' invention of a liberty of contract that in other applications could immunize the unequal bargaining power of the parties from regulation. Was the Court behind the times in emphasizing the individual during an age of increasing organization in labor, in business, and in so many other areas of life? Was the right to contract less a matter of protecting individual rights than a license to the more powerful party to exploit the weaker? Certainly, Allgeyer felt that the justices had properly protected his freedom to run his business as he saw fit, without interference by the state.

Did the Court's expansive language in *Allgeyer* now mean that states could not regulate the hours people worked in dangerous occupations on grounds that this was an interference with their liberty to contract? No, said the justices in the next term of court. The new liberty of contract, the majority ruled, "is itself subject to certain limitations which the state may lawfully impose in the exercise of its police powers."[48] The Court would impose no wholesale bar to state regulations of labor.

What seemed clear, however, was that the justices would decide for themselves whether the state interest overcame the protection of the individual's liberty to contract. When the New York legislature responded to union pressure to enact a law establishing a ten-hour day for bakers, the Court struggled with the decision. The trade of baker did not seem especially hazardous, and one of the advocates protesting the law was himself a former baker who had resented the law's interference with the hours he chose to work. Eventually, in a five-to-four decision, the Court in *Lochner v. New York* agreed with him and invalidated the law as a violation of the individual's freedom to contract. Denying that there was any state power to regulate a labor contract unless the health of the workers or the public welfare was involved, the majority condemned such "meddlesome interferences with the rights of the individual."[49]

To the majority's assertion of the need to protect the rights of individuals from

the overzealous reach of the state, the dissenters responded by accusing their colleagues of judicial overreaching by substituting their judgment for the people of
New York.[50] Justice Oliver Wendell Holmes Jr. said "that the word 'liberty,' in the
Fourteenth Amendment, is perverted when it is held to prevent the natural outcome of a dominant opinion, unless it . . . would infringe fundamental principles
as they have been understood by the traditions of our people and our law."[51]

Holmes was arguing against the use of the Fourteenth Amendment to protect
newly discovered individual rights from control by state legislatures.[52] Although
bucking a judicial tradition that only recently had focused on the amendment, his
opinion not only heartened reformers, who saw the labor contract skewed by the
imbalance in bargaining power between parties, but also led to second thoughts
on the Court in the next dozen years. Gradually, if somewhat reluctantly, the
justices found sufficient justification within the state's police power for legislation
prescribing hours of labor.[53] As late as 1917 they divided evenly on the issue of
whether this power encompassed the setting of a minimum wage.[54] The justices
did indeed respond to critics, not as Holmes would have the Court do by deferring
to the legislative will in all instances, but instead by blunting the sharp edges of
the new legal doctrine. In this way the Court accommodated change without
surrendering its authority.

Despite the difficulty the justices had in squaring wage-and-hour regulation
with the liberty of contract, the Court consistently upheld state laws designed to
aid workers in gaining compensation for their job-related injuries.[55] Common law
defenses to such suits had been formulated before the Civil War. Employee suits
to recover for injuries suffered on the job could be defeated by the employer on
grounds that employees assumed the risk with their employment, that the injury
was the result of the actions of a fellow employee, or that the employee's negli-
gence was in part responsible for the injury. Beginning in the 1870s, state legislatures began to chip away at these defenses in employee injury suits, thereby making
recovery more possible. The Court saw no federal constitutional bar to these statutory changes.[56] Even with this reform, the costly and protracted nature of the legal
process left many injured employees without an effective remedy. In the early
twentieth century, both the states and the federal government passed workmen
compensation acts that provided scheduled compensation for employee injuries.
Although the Court in such cases spoke in terms of governmental authority, it was
implicitly reinforcing the view that law can and should adapt to real-life conditions. If those conditions meant that legislation should ensure compensation for
injured workers, then the justices would interpose no bar to making both the law
and society more humane.

States generally would be given constitutional room to regulate the employer-
employee relationship, but the liberty of contract concept continued to attract the
justices. Over the protest of dissenting colleagues, they did uphold a Tennessee law

that required employers to redeem their usual payment in scrip or store orders for cash on grounds that state had a legitimate interest in eliminating the conflict caused by such payment.[57] And the majority also ruled that because insurance was a business affected with a public interest, the state's regulatory power encompassed the authority to set prices for individual contracts.[58] But when they confronted a federal law that barred the dismissal of an employee for joining a union, they balked. The statute had been passed in the 1890s by Congress under its power to protect the flow of interstate commerce from being disrupted by labor disputes.

The majority said the relationship between interstate commerce and the regulation was too attenuated, but it voided the legislation under the due process clause of the Fifth Amendment because it interfered with the liberty to contract. By dismissing the economic conditions that had given rise to the law, Justice Harlan, for the majority, found equality among the parties in that either party could terminate the employment relationship for any reason. Recognizing governmental power to regulate contracts in the public interest, he saw no such interest involved here and concluded that the statute was "an illegal invasion of the personal liberty as well as the right of property" of the employer.[59]

While the Court talked in terms of the liberty to contract, Justice Joseph McKenna, in dissent, saw necessary and legitimate governmental purposes in the law—to prevent strikes and the impoverishment of the workers and to preserve the public welfare by helping to establish a working relationship between labor and capital. "Liberty," he said, "is an attractive theme, but the liberty which is exercised in sheer antipathy does not plead strongly for recognition." Noting that the Court has accepted that Congress can regulate the railroads and proscribe collusion among them, he wondered why legislation regulating the labor contract, also clearly in the public interest, is met by "prejudice and antagonism" that is then read into the due process clause as an absolute bar to such legislation.[60]

McKenna's opinion illustrates well how the Court's inclination to protect individual rights can, at times, lead to decisions that seem oddly detached from the social and economic environment. The worlds pictured in the two opinions are radically different, and the question always is which world should the Court help shape.

Government's attempt to equalize the imbalance in bargaining power is perceived by the majority justices as an interference with personal liberty, when, in fact, the protection of the employer's liberty neglects that of the employee. Liberty, then, crowds out any meaningful consideration of equality. Behind this application of liberty of contract lurks an antiunion sentiment that would continue to characterize the Court until the later 1930s.[61]

As the Court modified the rigors of the doctrine in the regulation of hours cases, it steadfastly adhered to its condemnation of governmental interference with the employment contract as it related to union membership. When a state attempted to prescribe similar contracts, only four justices remained from the Court that had decided the federal case in 1908. Those four split evenly, and the five new arrivals split four to one in support of the due process bar on such legislation. States had long regulated the contract relationship on public policy grounds, and here Holmes, in dissent, said that protecting a liberty of contract makes sense only when the parties are relatively equal. Justice William R. Day added that the purpose of the state statute was to allow the employee the same freedom of action as that permitted the employer—the right "to make such lawful affiliations as he may desire with organizations of his choice." Then, accusing the majority of missing the point, he said the state statute did not require the employer to retain an employee against his will but simply to put "limitations upon the sacrifice of rights which one may exact from another as a condition of employment."[62]

In these cases the justices were less divided on the question of whether individual rights should be protected than on the proper role of government in the process. The justices more strongly attracted to the doctrine of liberty of contract tended to focus on government as interferer or oppressor, rather than on government as an ensurer of the equality of rights. This perspective seemed to blind them to what their colleagues saw so clearly—that in certain instances the protection of meaningful individual rights was furthered by governmental action redressing a bargaining imbalance.

The Court gave further credence to the view that its limited invocation of liberty in the Fourteenth Amendment was designed to further certain interests at the expense of others. For instance, when the voters in Washington used the initiative—a device of popular government that enabled them to propose and enact a law without legislative participation—to forbid employment agencies from charging fees to those seeking work, the Court struck down the law. The majority said that it "is arbitrary and oppressive, and that it unduly restricts the liberty of appellants, guaranteed by the 14th Amendment, to engage in a useful business."[63]

In interpreting the Fourteenth Amendment to provide protection for the right of property and liberty of contract, the Court was, in effect, weaving into the constitutional fabric key clauses of the amendment. Although those clauses were often interpreted to limit state interference with the property right, their words were general, and as some justices regularly reminded their colleagues, liberty was as fully protected as was property. This recognition in the formal record of the Court provided both a target and a dialogue that promoted consideration of other personal rights. That dialogue was conducted within the contours of the American civil religion, with its theological core being a steadfast commitment to protecting the rights of the individual.

Now and then the Court did find a different type of liberty protected, a liberty that brought to mind the claim of the butchers in *Slaughter-House*. Heavy immigration from eastern and southern Europe in the later nineteenth and early twentieth centuries had worried Americans. Could these immigrants be assimilated as Northern Europeans had been, and could the preexisting workforce handle the competition. In response to the latter threat, a number of states utilized their criminal law to enforce a preference for hiring citizens. In *Truax v. Raich*, the justices said that Arizona could not deny "to lawful inhabitants . . . the ordinary means of earning a livelihood." The "right to work for a living in the common occupations of the community," they continued, "is of the very essence of the personal freedom and opportunity that it was the purpose of the [Fourteenth] Amendment to secure."[64] Educating citizens as to their responsibilities under their creed, the justices said the statute must fall before the commandments of the fundamental law.

Unlike the situation in a number of the other cases under the Fourteenth Amendment in which government sought to protect or equalize the weaker party, here the state played the traditional role of oppressor in seeking to deny to new arrivals the benefits of fair and open competition. The message that the Court communicated in *Truax* about its role in the civil religion spoke unmuffled by concerns that in the search for liberty it was throwing its weight on the side of the more powerful. Freeing employers from the state regulation possibly gave them the opportunity to hire aliens at lower wages than citizens would demand. And from this perspective the vaunted protection of individual rights might seem no more than a glossy front behind which to conceal an agenda enhancing the employer's interest over that of the public.

By now, however, we should certainly take seriously the justices' expressed concern for the protection of individual rights from abridgment by government. We can indeed peer behind the opinions and attribute all sorts of motives to these judicial decision makers. But their published rationales are the foundation on which they must stand and on which they must continually defend their role in the democratic society. In *Truax* they widened the American community by saying that employment discrimination against aliens is not permissible within the confines of the civil religion. While others worried about assimilation, the Court here was willing to aid that process by sweeping away barriers that tended to make admission to the community more difficult. The protection of individual rights does not eliminate all discrimination but it does reach that portion of it that government seeks to embed in the law. All types of unfair discrimination may be equally abhorrent, but that which is written into the law has an especially debilitating effect because it becomes part of the structure of society. The hope that popular majorities will be sensitive to the commands of their faith has simply not been borne out in American history. This fact leaves the judiciary, and eventually the Supreme Court, with a continuing role to play, both in making law conform to the essentials of the civil theology that informs it and in continuing to teach new generations of Americans the catechism of their civic faith.

Although the Court was willing to explore the contours of the liberty protected from state interference by the Fourteenth Amendment, it was resistant to the wholesale idea that this constitutional change had now made the protections of the Bill of Rights binding on the states. Despite the Court's narrow reading of the dimensions of national citizenship in *Slaughter-House*, the claim had a certain plausibility. There was a basic legal text that could so be interpreted, and the idea that all Americans should have such fundamental rights recognized by all governments in the United States was a reasonable aspiration. The society it pictured seemed only just, for rights in a nation should not depend upon the borders of internal subdivisions. In their initial consideration of such claims, however, the justices unanimously rejected them. For instance, in 1876 they denied that the First Amendment's right to petition the government and peaceably assemble and the Seventh Amendment's right to a jury trial now bound the states through the due process clause.[65] And when a convicted murderer tried to argue that the newly implemented device of capital punishment, the electric chair, violated the Eight Amendment's ban on "cruel and unusual punishments," the Court showed no sympathy. No such change had been wrought in the federal union, the justices ruled, saying that the protection of life, liberty, and property still rested primarily with the states.[66]

Advocates for the nationalization of such rights, however, found a powerful ally when John Marshall Harlan came to the Court in 1877. Not only did he protest the Court's narrow reading of the rights of the former slaves under the Fourteenth Amendment, but he also castigated his colleagues for not interpreting its language to make the Bill of Rights binding upon the states.

In 1884, the opportunity to express his views came in a case of a convicted California murderer appealing to the Court on grounds that he had not been indicted by a grand jury, a requirement of the Fifth Amendment. The defendant contended that the due process clause of the Fourteenth Amendment had made this requirement binding upon the states. Upholding the conviction, the Court said that, although the clause does give the courts the right to protect the individual from arbitrary power exercised by the states, the due process required by the Fourteenth Amendment is afforded when "a trial is had according to the settled course of judicial proceedings."[67]

In lone dissent, Harlan saw much more meaning in the clause. Responding to the majority's view that the requirement of due process can be met by differing procedures, he said that due process, under the Constitution, "does not import one thing with . . . the States, and another with . . . the General Government." To the Court's view that the absence of specific language concerning indictment by a grand jury in the Fourteenth Amendment was fatal to the claim, Harlan responded that such a position "would lead to results that are inconsistent with the vital principles of republican government." In equating due process with "the law of the land" found in the Magna Carta, the justice said the words protect all the essential rights of the individual, including the right to a jury trial and an indictment by a grand jury. Noting the majority's concession that the due process clause "protects the fundamental principles of liberty and justice" and adding that the states uniformly in 1868 required such an indictment, Harlan could not fathom the grounds for excluding such a right from the reach of the due process clause.[68]

Sixteen years later, in *Maxwell v. Dow*, the Court reiterated its position that a state grand jury indictment was not necessary and gave its approval to a jury composed only of eight persons. Again Harlan was ready to do battle. Tracing the history of the Bill of Rights and how it fulfilled the purposes of the Preamble to the Constitution, the justice said that the Bill made "it certain that the privileges and immunities therein specified—the enjoyment of which, the fathers believed, were necessary in order to secure the blessings of liberty—could never be impaired or destroyed by the national government." That Bill, Harlan continued, "entrenched the right of trial by jury in the supreme law of the land." Assuming that a common law jury of twelve persons was generally required before the Fourteenth Amendment, he could not understand how the constitutional addition, which further limited the states, somehow left them free to invade the sacred right of trial by jury. At any rate, Harlan saw in both the privileges and immunities and due process clauses ample authority for requiring the states to employ a jury of twelve persons. The intention of the due process clause, he said, "was to prevent any state from infringing the guaranties for the protection of life and liberty that had already been guarded against infringement by the national government." Noting the Court's acceptance of the position that the Fourteenth Amendment precluded a state from taking property without compensation, Harlan concluded that "it would seem that the protection of private property is of more consequence than the protection of the life and liberty of the citizen."[69]

Again assuming the mantle of the prophet, Harlan pointed to the dire effects of the decision and its repudiation of the views of the apostles of the civil religion. Without the full protection of the Bill of Rights, he continued, the security of Americans is threatened and they cannot "enjoy real freedom." Detailing the protections found in the first ten amendments to the Constitution, Harlan said the Court opinion condones a wide range of state action extending from invasion of the freedom of religion to permitting a person to be burned at the stake. All this is possible, he asserted, because the Court continues to maintain an untenable distinction between state and national citizenship. "No judicial tribunal," he continued, "has authority to say that some of . . . [the specified rights] may be abridged by the states while others may not."[70] Harlan accused his colleagues of thwarting the solemn will of the American people who had made the Fourteenth Amendment part of their fundamental law.

To the argument that no state would countenance the fundamental inroads on the rights of citizens that his hypothetical situations envisioned, Harlan cited the position of the defendant in the case. He had been sentenced to the penitentiary after an imperfect jury trial that the justice contended would not have been tolerated in England at the time of American separation. "Liberty . . . ," he added, "depends, not so much upon the absence of actual oppression, as on the existence of constitutional checks upon the power to oppress." Accusing the majority of amending the Constitution by its niggardly interpretation, he saw only trouble ahead. Instead of maintaining a strong line of defense against invasion of individual rights, Harlan concluded, the Court has opted to permit the states to strike down "guaranties of life and liberty that English-speaking people have for centuries regarded as vital to personal security, and which men of the revolutionary period universally claimed as the birthright of freemen."[71]

Although Harlan could not convince his colleagues that their sworn duty as priestly interpreters of the holy writ commanded them to nationalize the Bill of Rights, he did force them to consider the dimensions of the liberty protected from state interference by the Fourteenth Amendment. Just as advocates and dissenters had earlier pushed the Court in the direction of recognizing the new property right, the majority here was forced to consider the argument and move in the direction of finding new meaning in the amendment's protection of liberty.

In 1907 the Court denied jurisdiction in *Patterson v. Colorado*, in which a newspaper publisher in Colorado was found in contempt of court for printing articles critical of the administration of justice in the state courts. Patterson claimed that his freedom of speech and press had been abridged in violation of the Constitution. The claim was founded on the view that the Fourteenth Amendment's protection of liberty had made the free expression provisions of the First Amendment binding upon the states. Holmes, speaking for the majority, did not reject the contention that free speech may be protected from state abridgement; he simply sidestepped the issue. All the First Amendment did, he continued, was to prohibit prior governmental restraint of expression, not subsequent punishment deemed necessary for the public welfare. Even if the protection of free expression did bind the states, Holmes implied, Patterson still could not escape the contempt citation.

Needless to say, Harlan returned to do battle in the cause of the core values at the heart of the civil religion. Arguing that both the privileges and immunities and due process clauses of the Fourteenth Amendment had made the rights of free speech and press binding upon the states as key incidents of national citizenship, he then confronted the majority's definition of what these rights entailed. To say that a person can be punished for speaking and publishing words of criticism, Harlan charged, is to allow vague conceptions of public welfare to "override constitutional privileges." He could not "conceive of liberty, as secured by the Constitution against hostile action, whether by the nation or by the states, which does not embrace the right to enjoy free speech and the right to have a free press."[72]

A year after *Patterson*, in *Twining v. New Jersey*, the Court confronted a claim that state criminal defendants had been denied their right against self-incrimination. As the trial judge was charging the jury, he commented adversely upon the fact that the defendants had not testified in their own behalf. Did not such comments invade their right against self-incrimination? Justice William H. Moody, for the Court, implied that if such a right were binding upon the states the comments of the judge would have violated it. He then asked: Was such a protection incorporated in the liberty protected by the Fourteenth Amendment? He said that a privilege against self-incrimination was not an integral part of what constituted the due process of the law. Recognizing more plausibility in Harlan's position than the Court had earlier, Moody said that the privilege against self-incrimination did not rank with "the right to hearing before condemnation, the immunity from arbitrary power not acting by general laws, and the inviolability of private property," which he referred to as "the inalienable possession of every citizen of a free government."[73]

With its rationale here the Court posted a clear target for advocates for a claim of individual right—associate the claimed right with immutable principles of justice as understood by people in the society. The right was fundamental not because it was included in the Bill of Rights but because it violated due process as protected by the Fourteenth Amendment. To determine what due process meant, the Court referred to a societal consensus, indicating that as that consensus changed more might well be included within the constitutional protection. Clearly, then, the Court is encouraging a dialogue in the democratic society in terms of basic concepts of fairness, justice, and universality that inform the due process clause's meaning. The Court is asking the people to determine the world in which they wish to live, to determine the principles that they wish to guide the rule of law. The justices may be cultural definers, but, as the opinion makes clear, the people themselves have a continuing input that can bring the rule of law into conformity with their aspirations. As high priests, the justices interpret the law, but that interpretation necessarily embraces more than the text itself.

Noting that the majority had recognized the importance of the right against self-incrimination as a safeguard against unjust prosecution and as a protection of political liberty, Harlan denounced the conclusion that it was not protected by the Constitution from state invasion. The justice insisted that the Fourteenth Amendment was generally understood to make a historically confirmed right of such "priceless character" available to the individual against invasion by the states. He concluded by saying that compelling a person to incriminate himself "shocks or ought to shock the sense of right and justice to every one who loves liberty."[74]

Until his death in 1911, Harlan would continue his crusade to protect individual liberty by nationalizing the protections of the Bill of Rights. In only one relevant case, when the Court ruled that the Fifth Amendment's provision that the government must provide compensation for the taking of private property is bind-

ing on the states, did Harlan ever command a majority of his colleagues.[75] However, one of the justice's examples of outrageous state conduct permitted by the
majority's view was presented in *O'Neil v. Vermont*. O'Neil took liquor orders
from citizens of dry Vermont and was found guilty of 307 offenses against the
state's liquor law. He was fined over $6,000; should he not pay the fine and costs,
he would have to serve three days for each dollar of the fine, which added up to
over fifty-four years. Overlooking the harsh sentence, the majority upheld the
conviction. But Stephen J. Field, who generally resisted Harlan's view that the
rights specified in the Bill of Rights bound the states, now saw the Fourteenth
Amendment protecting the individual against such a cruel and unusual punishment. Harlan, with whom David Brewer agreed, insisted that the Eighth Amendment's protection against such punishment was a fundamental right, the violation
of which was "inconsistent with the supreme law of the land."[76]

Harlan was what would later be called an incorporationist; that is, he believed
that all the rights specified in the Bill of Rights bound the states as a result of the
Fourteenth Amendment.[77] Field was content to fill in the content of the term
"liberty" on a case-by-case basis.

Despite the Court's hesitancy in making the protections of the Bill of Rights
available to state defendants, the justices dealt with both these protections and
others in responding to the claims of defendants in the federal courts. Increasingly
in the period, the justices, when asked to consider the rights of accused criminals,
revealed a tendency to construe their constitutional rights broadly. Criminal cases
had previously occupied little space on the docket of the Supreme Court; there
was relatively little federal criminal law, and the justices had no direct review
power even over capital punishment cases in federal circuit courts prior to 1889.
However, the Court's sensitivity to the rights claimed is revealed in two cases, one
federal and one state.

Prosecuted for the federal crime of appropriating postal mail bags worth $25, a
defendant was fined $200 and sentenced to a year in prison. After he paid his fine
and began serving his sentence, the defendant sought a writ of habeas corpus on
grounds that under the law either a fine or a jail sentence could be imposed, but
not both. The trial judge responded by resentencing the defendant to a year in
prison. Justice Samuel Miller, for the Supreme Court, equated the second sentence
with a second trial and ruled that the spirit of the Fifth Amendment's protection
against double jeopardy had been violated. Because the defendant had already satisfied one punishment under the statute by paying the fine, he "was forbidden by
the common law, by the constitution and by the dearest principles of personal
rights" from a second judgment. "There is no more sacred duty of a court," the
justice concluded, "than . . . to maintain unimpaired those securities for the personal rights of the individual . . . ; and in such cases no narrow or illiberal construction should be given to the words of the fundamental law in which they are

embodied."[78] The priestly role of the Court required the justices to move beyond a literal reading of the holy writ and fulfill the animating spirit behind it.

Just as the Court expanded the meaning of double jeopardy in the federal case, it expanded the range of the ex post facto law protection in a state case. Because laws making conduct criminal after the fact were so universally condemned, the appearance of such a case on the Supreme Court's docket was rare indeed. Charles Kring had been tried for murder in the first degree in Missouri three times without a legal result; on the fourth prosecution attempt he agreed to plead guilty to second degree murder and receive a sentence of ten years or less. When a sentence of twenty-five years was imposed, he appealed the conviction. It was set aside. On the fifth trial attempt, he sought to plead guilty to second degree murder, but the plea was not accepted because of Kring's insistence that the sentence be no more than ten years. A plea of not guilty was entered for Kring by the court. On trial before a jury, Kring was found guilty and sentenced to death. In rejecting the second degree murder plea, the trial court cited a change in the Missouri constitution that permitted the procedure. The change had been made long after Kring committed the crime but before his first plea of guilty. Was this constitutional change an ex post facto law? Missouri insisted that it concerned only a matter of procedure and that it therefore did not fall under the ban of the federal constitution.

Whatever the character of the change, Justice Miller began, "it is one which, to the defendant, involves the difference between life and death." Tracing the history of the ex post facto protection and its interpretation over time, the justice concluded that it has been interpreted liberally "in manifest accord with the purpose of the constitutional Convention to protect the individual rights of life and liberty against hostile retrospective legislation." An ex post facto law is any legislation after the commission of an offense that disadvantages the party. Labeling the change in Missouri law procedural does not shield the state from the ban of the federal constitution, Miller continued, for this would destroy "the value of the constitutional provision." After citing the Court's prior action on finding impairments of contract in procedural changes, he asks: "Why are not the rights of life and liberty as sacred as the right of contract?"[79] The Court's answer was that they were. And to Missouri's argument that the new law took effect before the plea of guilty, Miller responded that the time of the offense governs the matter. The judgment of the Missouri high court, he concluded, must be reversed.

In both of these criminal cases dissenting opinions were written in which some of the justices objected to the Court's broad reading of the double jeopardy and ex post facto law provisions. At times, these dissenters would gain the upper hand in denying relief to criminal defendants, but what remains important is that the Court was engaging in a substantial public dialogue about the individual rights that lay at the foundation of the American creed and the justices' role in protecting them. The majority justices in these two cases were describing a role for the Court within the American civil religion. Their task was to interpret the protections of individual rights in the holy writ, and in widening their reach they were fulfilling the Court's priestly role in making the individual secure from the oppression of government. They had to resort to the spirit of the constitutional guarantees, for the words, as they had been previously understood, seemed to frustrate the end the majority justices sought. In fact, they were redescribing the role of the Court and saying that individual protections in the Constitution must be construed broadly to effectuate their purpose. In this endeavor, the Court seems to be on solid ground and to be fulfilling its proper function within the civil religion. It is reinforcing the lesson that individual rights will be protected and that the Court is the one agency of government that will respond to such invasions.

Certainly one of the most important personal rights was freedom of religious belief, a view that the Court implicitly accepted in 1872 when it refused to be drawn into a controversy among rival Presbyterian groups over a Louisville, Kentucky, church. In announcing their decision, the justices proclaimed the individual's right to hold, practice, and teach "any religious doctrine which does not violate the laws of morality and property, and which does not infringe personal rights, is conceded to all. The law knows no heresy, and is committed to the support of no dogma, the establishment of no sect."[80]

The justices had no difficulty reading out of this protection the Mormon practice of polygamy,[81] but when a church seeking to hire a foreign minister was prosecuted and fined under a federal law prohibiting the importation of foreigners under a contract to perform labor or services, the Court read an exemption into the statute. Maintaining that the history of the United States proved it to be a religious nation, Justice Brewer said that the Declaration and the protection of religion found in the First Amendment "are organic utterances; they speak the voice of the entire people."[82] To punish a church for hiring a foreign minister, he concluded, could not have been in the contemplation of a Congress committed to religious freedom.

Although Bill of Rights protections offered to defendants would be most significant in the long run, the Court also dealt with other criminal matters as the national court of last resort. For instance, when prisoners in federal custody were attacked, the Court read Reconstruction enforcement statutes broadly to sustain a federal prosecution of the attackers. "The United States," the High Bench ruled, "are bound to protect against lawless violence . . . those held in custody on accusation of crime, and deprived of all means of self-defense."[83]

The Court's most insistent confrontation with the criminal law came in a series of federal cases imposing the death penalty. Prior to 1889 when the Court was given obligatory jurisdiction in federal capital cases, the only hope for a defendant was to obtain a commutation of a death sentence from the president of the United

States. What led to the new statute was the work of a federal judge in the Western District of Arkansas who had dispensed the death penalty with such liberality that it had become a national scandal. That federal district was unique in its criminal jurisdiction in that it embraced crimes committed by whites in Indian Territory, which would eventually become the state of Oklahoma. Judge Isaac C. Parker felt that society could best be protected by a court that deterred criminal action by the swiftness and certainty of its punishments. The 1889 statute made Parker all too familiar to the justices, who from 1890 to 1898 considered forty-four capital cases coming from Parker's court and only eighteen from all other federal tribunals.[84]

Reviewing Parker's cases, the Supreme Court reversed almost three out of every four, ruling that the judge had trampled upon the rights of the defendant, often finding that his improper instructions had probably led the jury to a finding of guilty. While the judge in Arkansas told the accused to look to the Christian God for mercy and forgiveness, the Supreme Court accepted its role as priestly interpreter of a civil religion that called on judges to protect individual rights. The justices reminded Parker that the accused was "to be tried upon competent evidence, and only for the offense charged."[85] And when Parker suggested that the defendant, in seeking to protect his life, had good reason to lie, the Court condemned the "hostile comments of the trial judge, whose duty it is to give reasonable effect and force to the law."[86]

Although Justice Brewer now and then accused his colleagues of searching for flimsy reasons to reverse the decisions, the majority was not deterred.[87] It lectured Parker on the "limitations inherent in and implied from the very nature of the judicial office"[88] and censured him for improperly tilting the very scales of justice he was charged with balancing.[89] These were not constitutional law cases, but the justices indicated their concern for the rights of the defendants, who, to their mind, had suffered at the hands of a judge who too often imposed his determinations of guilt upon the jury. In the next century the members of the Court would become heavily involved in defining the rights of the criminally accused under the Constitution,[90] but here, facing a new responsibility and with precious little prior experience, they were instinctively responding to the Court's role as a protector of individual rights.

That most of the justices saw as an essential part of their role the widening of the constitutional protections of individuals is apparent in their reading of the Fourth Amendment's protection against "unreasonable searches and seizures." In 1878, a unanimous Court said that this "great principle" protected the individual's letters and other sealed mail carried at the letter rate as if they were "in one's own household." In other words, a proper warrant, specifying what was to be seized and where, would be required for government officials to inspect the contents of such mail.[91] The Fourth Amendment could have been read as protecting only persons within their dwellings, but such a cramped reading did not appeal to justices who saw their role as extending rather than narrowing the ambit of individual rights.

Eight years later, in *Boyd v. United States*, the Court demonstrated that this judicial expansion of the meaning of the Fourth Amendment's protection was no aberration. After furnishing papers under the command of the customs laws, the Boyds were ordered to forfeit their imported property. They appealed on the basis of both the Fourth and Fifth Amendments, saying that they had been forced to furnish the evidence that led to the forfeiture. The case was not a criminal one, and no evidence had been seized. But Justice Joseph P. Bradley, for the Court, said that the amendments' history required that their spirit be implemented through liberal interpretation. He agreed that the Fourth Amendment's protection against unreasonable seizures and the Fifth Amendment's protection against self-incrimination dovetailed. Despite the civil nature of the suit, Bradley saw forfeiture akin to a criminal penalty and the compulsory production of papers akin to a seizure.

The "sanctity of a man's home and the privacies of life" are sacred rights, Bradley said, that are protected by the two amendments. They prevent "the invasion of his indefeasible right of personal security, personal liberty and private property." Such compulsory discovery, the justice continued, "is contrary to the principles of a free government. . . . It may suit the purposes of despotic power; but it cannot abide the pure atmosphere of political liberty and personal freedom."[92] Bradley was not only protecting the defendants' liberty, but he was also demarcating the proper relationship between government and all individuals.

Noting that there was no forced entry and that this was a relatively mild invasion of the Boyds' rights, Bradley nonetheless held that "illegitimate and unconstitutional practices get their first footing . . . by silent approaches and slight deviations from legal modes of procedure." To read the protective amendments too literally "deprives them of half their efficacy and leads to gradual depreciation of the right." He insisted that they must be liberally construed by judges, who must guard "against any stealthy encroachments" upon these rights.[93]

Bradley's words added new dimension to the Court's priestly role within the American civil religion. Earlier the justices said that their task required them to apply the spirit of the individual protections written into the Constitution. Now they seemed to say that this role also included being a watchdog for even the slightest incursions upon such rights; individual liberty was imperiled when any wedges, no matter how small, were driven into this sacred arena. That Bradley's formulation of the Court's responsibility struck a deep and responsive chord is born out by the constant quotation of his words in subsequent opinions.

This early application of the Fourth Amendment as a protection of privacy was followed by the Court when it refused to reverse the trial court and order a plaintiff in a personal injury case to undergo a physical examination. Over a dissent that argued that "truth and justice are more sacred than any personal consideration," the Court said: "No right is held more sacred . . . than the right of every individual to the possession and control of his own person, free from all restraint or interference of others, unless by clear and unquestionable authority of law."[94]

To dismiss the repeated use of the term "sacred" and the implied priestly role of the Court as mere rhetoric is to miss a matter of significance. The law, the Constitution, and the Supreme Court were key elements, an inseparable trinity, in the American civil religion. And, as teacher, the Court never grew tired of repeating this lesson.

Beginning with *Boyd*, the Court widened the orbit of the Fourth Amendment's protection. While it labeled the protection against self-incrimination in the Fifth Amendment a personal privilege and therefore unavailable to artificial entities, the majority ruled that a corporation could invoke a Fourth Amendment claim against an illegal search and seizure.[95]

Although *Boyd* had decided that an illegal search was a violation of a person's Fourth Amendment rights, not until 1914 did the Court determine that such evidence must be excluded from any subsequent trial.[96] The government's desire to catch criminals, the unanimous bench said, cannot be "aided by the sacrifice of those great principles established by years of endeavor and suffering which have resulted in their embodiment in the fundamental law of the land." To condone such governmental intrusion, the justices added, would be "a manifest neglect, if not an open defiance, of the prohibitions of the Constitution, intended for the protection of the people."[97]

These Fourth Amendment cases are of greater significance than might be initially realized, for far more was involved than the relief of certain defendants from government overreaching. Americans were alerted to the proper relationship between their claims to privacy and the authority of government. The conclusion that "one's freedom of person and place is an essential precondition to the exercise of all other rights, including those of expression and association, upon which our democratic system of self-government rests" does not seem exaggerated.[98] Although the Court did not carry its analysis this far, its strong and forceful rhetoric highlighted the importance of this individual right.

As the words in *Boyd* indicated, Fifth Amendment self-incrimination claims likewise received a sympathetic hearing by the justices. Unanimously in *Counselman v. Hitchcock*, they held that a governmental promise of immunity from prosecution did not satisfy the individual's right against self-incrimination because it did not preclude the use of other evidence subsequently unearthed as a result of such testimony.[99] When Congress passed a statute purporting to grant absolute immunity in return for testimony, a majority of the Court, assuming that it would protect the individual from any state prosecution as well, upheld its constitutionality. The dissenters questioned whether the individual could be immunized by federal statute from state law and argued that the strong and certain constitutional protection should not be displaced by "the doubtful and uncertain provisions of an experi-mental statute."[100]

Justice Field was even more sensitive to the cost extracted from an individual who accepted immunity from prosecution in exchange for his Fifth Amendment right. It is a poor trade, Field continued, for the individual's dignity and self-respect is substantially undermined by the "essential cruelty of compelling . . . [him] to expose his own guilt." He categorically rejected "the efforts of any individual or tribunal to weaken or fritter away any of the provisions of the Constitution . . . intended for the protection of the private rights of citizens."[101] Here, in his waning days on the Court, Field accused his colleagues of failing to uphold the command-ments of the holy writ.

Later the unanimous Court did rule that a presidential pardon cannot be forced upon an unwilling witness who refused to testify on grounds of self-incrimination. The justices agreed with the defendant that, unlike the acceptance of a grant of immunity, the acceptance of a pardon implies the guilt of the recipient. Individuals could stand upon their Fifth Amendment right and maintain the silence that the Constitution afforded them.[102]

Clearly the Bill of Rights bound the actions of the federal government domesti-cally, but did these individual protections follow the federal governmental presence overseas? The Court was drawn into this arena by the colonial adventures of the United States at the turn of the century. Hawaii had been annexed, and the Span-ish-American War had brought into the orbit of national control some former colonies of Spain. The justices had difficulty in determining how closely the Con-stitution followed the flag. Eventually, they would defer to congressional judgment on whether the colony was formally incorporated into the United States, in which case, they said, the Constitution fully applied.[103]

This conclusion most disturbed Justices Brewer and Harlan. Condemning "leg-islative absolutism," Harlan said the federal government is fully bound by the Con-stitution; the "idea that this country may acquire territories anywhere on earth . . . and hold them as mere colonies or provinces,—the people inhabiting them to enjoy only such rights as Congress chooses to accord to them,—is wholly inconsis-tent with the spirit and genius, as well as with the words, of the Constitution."[104] Brewer, who agreed with Harlan, tended to save his condemnation for the off-the-bench public speeches he made attacking the administration's imperialistic venture and condemning it for its wholesale violations of the principles at the heart of the American creed.[105] However, as they confronted the local law prevailing in the overseas possessions, the justices wrestled both with the application and the meaning of certain protections of accused criminals as delineated in the Bill of Rights.

The first case, from Hawaii, presented the claim that a criminal proceeding in which there had been no indictment by a grand jury and in which a finding of guilty could be made by the concurrence of nine of the twelve jurors violated the guarantees of the Fifth and Sixth Amendments. Reversing the lower court, the High Bench in a 5–4 decision upheld the conviction on grounds that the "rights alleged to be violated in this case are not fundamental in their nature." It ruled that the sixty-year-old procedure was well "suited to the conditions of the islands, and well calculated to conserve the rights of their citizens to their lives, their property, and their well being."[106]

Harlan was incensed, arguing that the majority had shirked its responsibility by deferring to congressional legislation that permitted such unconstitutional practices. To deny that the Constitution in its full protection came with the exercise of sovereign power, he stated, would empower the legislative branch of government to exercise absolute and arbitrary authority over the life and liberty of the inhabitants. Responding to the majority's conclusion that the individual rights claimed here were not fundamental, Harlan said that "no Federal civil tribunal, existing under the Constitution, and under a solemn obligation to maintain and defend it, can properly or safely ignore them."[107]

Harlan and his dissenting colleagues had only limited success in urging the Court to provide some Bill of Rights protection to overseas inhabitants. A unanimous Court concluded that Spanish trial law had been superceded in the newly established trial courts in Puerto Rico and that an indictment by a grand jury was required in prosecuting an individual for an infamous crime.[108] In the same term, the Court applied the Fifth Amendment's ban on double jeopardy to the trial of a Philippine lawyer charged with embezzling client funds. Prior practice had allowed the government to appeal a jury acquittal, and here the appeal had produced a judgment of guilty. The majority ruled that double jeopardy bars not only two punishments for a single offense but also what in fact amounted to a second trial.[109]

In the next term the Court reconsidered the double jeopardy protection and came out the other way. Unlucky defendants had appealed their conviction of assault and battery only to encounter a Philippine supreme court that pronounced them guilty of murder. Equating the procedure to one that ordered a new trial in which the charge of murder was reintroduced and then successfully prosecuted, the majority said the defendants' appeal waived any right they might have to claim double jeopardy. The dissenters saw no essential difference between this case and the preceding one, but Justice Harlan added words of his own. Accusing the majority of substituting "the law of convenience for the written fundamental law," he attacked the whole system of Philippine justice and condemned the denial of rights to a people subject to the protections of the Constitution.[110]

Generally the Court would continue to reject claims of double jeopardy coming from Philippine defendants, upholding the finding of two offenses in the same act and continuing to subject the defendant to the hazards of an increased sentence on appeal.[111] By the latter case, Harlan was gone, and a new arrival, Joseph R.

Lamar, picked up the attack on the exclusion of persons under the jurisdiction of the United States from the protections of its fundamental law.

The badly divided Court returned to the subject of Philippine justice in *Weems v. United States*, this time considering just what was barred by the Eighth Amendment's ban on cruel and unusual punishment. A Coast Guard officer was convicted of falsifying an official document and sentenced to pay a fine almost seven times the amount allegedly involved and to serve fifteen years in confinement "at hard and painful labor." Although the issue of cruel and usual punishment was not raised immediately after the sentence was levied, the Court said it had discretion to "notice a plain error not assigned." Justice Joseph McKenna, for the majority, explained that the purpose of the ban on cruel and unusual punishments was not meant to fix their content at some time in the historical past but rather to place limits on the government's power to prescribe punishment. The Court's duty, he added, is to give vitality to a principle embedded in the fundamental law by widening its application beyond "the mischief which gave it birth." Finding support in his reading of the Court's history, the justice continued: "Under any other rule a constitution would indeed be as easy of application as it would be deficient in efficacy and power. Its general principles would have little value, and be converted into impotent and lifeless formulas. Rights declared in words might be lost in reality."[112]

McKenna is saying that the priestly interpreter who parses the holy writ rather than follows its spirit is failing to do justice both to it and to the people it is designed to guide. The Court, he implies, must be a creative translator in making the protection of individuals meaningful in a much changed world, one in which new threats are mounted to the dignity and security of the individuals who inhabit it. We maintain faith with the civil theology not when we accept past illustrations as exhaustive of its reach but rather when we translate the basic text with an understanding of this past and a sensitivity both to the present and the future. The survival of the holy writ, then, relies not upon its longevity but rather upon the Court's role in making its commandments fit changed circumstances in the society. The claim the *Weems* case makes to conscience should not be rejected but accepted and served with an interpretation of the fundamental law that protects the individual's rights. Instead of arrogating power to itself, the Court is simply exercising the discretion it must have to reinforce the dictates of the civil religion.

Primarily, the Fourteenth Amendment had given the Court the means to ensure the national protection of individual rights. Although the High Bench initially seemed to respond most often to the claim that a right to property was being violated, this right was the one most often brought to the Court. And when the majority seemed to suffer from myopia in regard to other rights, usually dissenters spread upon the record the need of the Court to respond as positively and forcefully to the deprivation of these other individual protections as well. This tradition, dating back to the Court's formation, continues to justify its role in limiting governmental action.[113]

The argument here is not that the Supreme Court's work is adequately summarized by focusing upon the cases involving individual rights, but rather that these cases provide the lens through which we can see both how and why the High Bench plays such a significant role in the operation of an American civil religion. It educates in the faith and maintains and implements the precepts of the civil theology. Although cases in which there is a claim of violation of individual rights form only a portion of the Court's caseload, they constitute the most significant and revealing portion. How well the justices grasp this function differs with the individual, but colleagues are educators of new arrivals as well as the public. And so the tradition continues.

Accepting the Court's role as the priestly interpreter of the holy writ does not mean that citizens are required to blindly accept all its rulings as commandments of the writ itself. Education is a two-way street, as James Wilson acknowledged during his circuit-riding days. The justices are educated both before and after the fact. Before the decision, they are exposed to the written and oral arguments of advocates, who frame the contested issues within the vocabulary of the law. After the decision, the Court's work is evaluated by legal and popular critics. This largely legal dialogue filters into the society and expands both the language and perception of the community. It widens the parameters of thought and discussion and reinforces a sense of community among very different people. Working within a Protestant tradition of reading the holy writ for oneself, American citizens can then seek to correct the Court's judgment in a number of ways available to them both directly and indirectly within the political process.

Despite strong dissents that flew in the face of an innate judicial conservatism, the Court would move slowly in finding protection for an increasing assortment of individual rights within the constitutional framework. The evolving modern mass society only made more urgent the need to safeguard the individual. Clearly this process of defining individual rights was under way in the late nineteenth and early twentieth centuries, as the justices initiated a dialogue that spawned new claims of individual right and widened the public's sensitivity to the Court's primary task of protecting such rights from governmental invasion.

This new receptivity at a time of substantial immigration, primarily from eastern and southern Europe, tended to acclimate the immigrants to the concept of a rule of law by which they were told that they were equal and that the law had no favorites. That this was obviously not always the case underscores the inevitable discrepancy between theory and practice and not that the theory itself had been compromised or modified. Nativists feared the new immigrants and wondered about their capacity for assimilation into the society, but fairly quickly these new arrivals understood that they were living in a country in which law, as enforced by the courts, offered them protection as individuals. This lesson was quickly absorbed, and it was placed at the core of their concept of being an American.

RESPONDING TO NEW CRISES AND EXPLORING THE IMPLICATIONS OF THE CIVIL THEOLOGY, 1917–1941

A nation composed of such a mixture of ethnic groups always posed challenges, but at no time did such challenges cause greater concern than during a time of foreign war, when ancestral backgrounds would inevitably place Americans on opposing sides. When war broke out in Europe in the summer of 1914, President Woodrow Wilson proclaimed American neutrality in the struggle between Great Britain, France, and Russia on the one side and Germany and the Austro-Hungarian Empire on the other. Neutrality seemed the best option for Americans, some of whom condemned both sides. Direct participation by the United States would have to come knowing the difficulty of uniting the American people behind any decision. When Wilson tried to play the role of honest broker between the contending forces, he was rebuffed, and he increasingly favored the British in his policies. The result was a drift toward war, which came shortly after Germany launched unrestricted submarine warfare to break the British naval blockade of the European continent. After some American ships and lives were lost, Wilson obtained a declaration of war from Congress in April 1917.

Seeking to draw from a reservoir of American principles, the president announced that the country would have to go to war to save democracy, to make this the war to end all wars. He promised a peace without victory, one which would not punish the people who had been led astray by aggressive leaders. This resort to principle struck a responsive chord with many Americans, who seemed ready to help remake the world in their image. But, to others, it had a hollow ring, and internal division would not melt away.

Wilson realized that American participation would pose dangers to the society, but this concern did not stop him and his administration from seeking, through force if necessary, to bring some semblance of unity to the war effort. Men were drafted to obtain the necessary manpower to prosecute the war; a preexisting army of two hundred thousand would grow to almost five million, over half of whom were conscripted. In addition, Congress sought to limit dissent to the war effort by passing the Espionage Act, which punished conduct aiding the enemy and interfering with the draft. This statute was then amended to ban abusive language dealing with the government, Constitution, flag, and military. Not since the Sedition Act of 1798 had such a repressive ban on speech been enacted. While Senator Robert M. LaFollette of Wisconsin could rail against the war from the floor of the Senate with impunity, other public critics were subject to prosecution.

In addition to the legal action instituted by the Justice Department under the new laws, eager patriots went further in their campaign to make dissenters suffer. Such repression became commonplace, as the newly formed Committee on Public Information enlisted writers and artists to paint an inhuman picture of the German Hun and to promote 100 percent Americanism. The effects of this deliberate attempt to stimulate emotions did not come to a close with the cessation of hostilities, and in the postwar period the hatred was directed rather indiscriminately at many aliens, including those who espoused communism and anarchism. In response to such wholesale violations of individual rights, the American Civil Liberties Union was born—an organization devoted to the protection of such rights.[1]

Sooner or later claims of the infringement of individual rights would be submitted to the judiciary, and eventually to the Supreme Court. The first such issue concerned conscription. Although there had been a Civil War draft, the nature of such a conflict was quite different from the one in which Americans were asked to participate in 1917 and 1918. That earlier draft had sparked violent protest, and now opponents had recourse to the argument that the Thirteenth Amendment's ban on involuntary servitude precluded conscription. Was not the draft involuntary servitude? Early in 1918, the Court gave no credence to this argument, saying that it "is refuted by its mere statement." Instead, the justices referred to the citizen's "supreme and noble duty of contributing in the defense of the rights and honor of the nation."[2] The High Bench was no more sympathetic to the argument that allowing only members of pacifistic sects to qualify as conscientious objectors violated the First Amendment rule that government may show no religious preference. The idea that the Court would enter the political arena and declare the draft unconstitutional was always rather fanciful.

A more justiciable issue did seem to be posed by the claim that, in its zealousness to stamp out dissent, the federal government had gone too far in interfering with a person's right to speak freely. Just as the first sedition act had stimulated discussion about the meaning of free speech in American society, so, too, would this new legislation. The Court would have to determine what the individual right of free expression embraced and how far its range extended. Out of the repression of the war period would come a new and urgent dialogue on free speech.

After the war had ended, the Court heard arguments that the Espionage Act violated a person's right of free expression. In *Schenck v. United States*, Oliver Wendell Holmes, for a unanimous Court, upheld the conviction of Charles T. Schenck for printing and circulating leaflets sent to men who had been called up under the draft. The leaflets reprinted the Thirteenth Amendment and called upon their recipients not to be intimidated and to assert their rights. Conceding that freedom of speech may mean more than freedom from prior restraint and that the defendant's constitutional rights would protect such speech "in many places and in ordinary times," Holmes then added that "the character of every act depends upon the circumstances in which it is done." Citing the example of a false cry of "fire" in a theater, the justice ruled that the "question in every case is whether the words used are used in such circumstances and are of such a nature as to create a clear and present danger that they will bring about the substantive evils that Congress has a right to prevent."[3] Calling the matter one of "proximity and degree" and rejecting any need to find that Schenck was successful in his campaign, Holmes said that in the midst of war no court could find a constitutional right protecting the utterance of such words.

The clear and present danger test, as outlined by Holmes, clearly placed limits on the individual's free speech right; furthermore, it placed that right in a social context and acknowledged that the context was crucial in determining the scope of protected speech. The philosophy of individual rights always carried with it a fundamental limitation—that the exercise of one's rights not endanger others. If the clear and present danger test, then, was only an acknowledgment of this inherent limitation on individual rights, it might be a useful test. The danger, of course, was that the current threat would be exaggerated to the detriment of the individual right. Some would argue that this was done in *Schenck*, but the Court's subsequent decisions in the area made it clear that the test would not be applied with any presumption in favor of the individual right.

One week later the unanimous Court upheld two more convictions, including that of the prominent socialist, Eugene V. Debs. Holmes, writing for the Court, however, said we "do not lose our right to condemn either measures or men because the Country is at war."[4] And in the *Debs* case, he questioned the wisdom of such prosecutions and the prevalent jingoism of trial judges.[5]

Eight months later when the Court, in *Abrams v. United States*, affirmed a conviction under the Sedition Act of 1918, Holmes and Louis D. Brandeis dissented. Five Russian Jews had protested President Wilson's decision to send troops into Russia to overthrow the Bolsheviks, questioning how such hypocritical action was designed to promote democracy.[6] The majority disposed of the case by citing *Schenck*, but Holmes proclaimed that only imminent danger could justify such a restriction on free speech. He denied that Congress could "forbid all effort to change the mind of the country." Contending that the defendants were punished for their ideas and not for any crime, the justice now said that they "had as much right to publish as the government has to publish the Constitution of the United States now vainly invoked by them." That Constitution, Holmes continued, is premised upon the "free trade in ideas—that the best test of truth is the power of the thought to get itself accepted in the competition of the market. . . . [W]e should be eternally vigilant against attempts to check the expression of opinions that we loathe." He pictured an American community of various voices and reminded the public that "all life is an experiment."[7]

Instead of widening the discussion of free speech on the Court, as it did in legal and popular literature, Holmes's dissent seemed instead to push the majority in the direction of substituting for the "clear and present danger" test a "bad tendency" test; that is, did the words have a tendency to cause harm? In *Schaefer v. United States*, the Court did free two defendants because of the absence of evidence, but then, using the new test, it upheld the conviction of three others. The justices called free speech "that great ordinance of government and orderly liberty" and saw its invocation by "enemies of the United States" as "a strange perversion of its precepts." But again Holmes and Brandeis carried on the dialogue about the importance of free speech. This time Brandeis wrote the dissenting opinion. In this era of the first "red scare," he said such convictions threatened an already endangered press. Calling attention to the fact that people differ on what loyalty demands, he said "an intolerant majority, swayed by passion or by fear, may be prone in the future, as it has been in the past, to stamp as disloyal opinions with which it disagrees. Convictions such as these, besides abridging freedom of speech, threaten freedom of thought and of belief."[8]

Brandeis's belief that the press was endangered stems from a section of the Espionage Act that gave the postmaster general the authority to deny second-class mailing privileges to a newspaper that violated the law. When the Court received a case in which a newspaper publisher claimed that such a denial violated his right to a jury trial and his rights of free speech and free press, it rejected the claims. The First Amendment, the majority said, was not designed "to serve as a protecting screen for those who while claiming its privileges seek to destroy it." Brandeis, in dissent, argued that the denial of second-class rates and the subsequent banning of all issues of the paper from the mails, in effect, made the postmaster general "the universal censor of publications." The issue, he insisted, is no less than whether "our press shall be free." Accusing the majority of eviscerating the Bill of Rights, the justice reminded his colleagues that "in every extension of governmental functions lurks a new danger to civil liberty." Brandeis's forceful argument that condoning such administrative authority posed a grave danger to the freedom of the press led Holmes to change his mind in the case, as he now concluded that the postmaster general's action interfered "with very sacred rights."[9]

One week after *Schaefer*, the Court concluded its scrutiny of these wartime cases with the same predictable result. Again Brandeis wrote a dissent, calling attention to the absence of any governmental proof that the words of the defendants posed a clear and present danger. The fact that the defendants saw American participation in the war stemming not from principle but from the need to protect loans made to the Allies, Brandeis said, is hardly a crime, given the fact that even historians cannot agree on what leads a nation to war. Seeing no clear and present danger in the writings, the justice argued that the freedom to seek change by appealing to one's fellow citizens cannot be characterized "as criminal incitement to disobey the existing law—merely because the argument presented seems to those exercising judicial power to be unfair in its portrayal of existing evils, mistaken in its assumptions, unsound in reasoning, or intemperate in language."[10]

In these cases the majority justices, despite their special responsibility to protect individual rights, shared the mindset of those who staffed the other branches of government. In that mindset, criticism of the government during a time of national crisis was a disloyal act that should be punished. This is precisely the situation eighteenth-century Americans worried about—a neglect by the very government they created to protect and nurture individual rights at precisely the time when the threat posed to their rights was greatest. Here, the majority justices were not inviting but rather suppressing discussion. The portrait of the democratic society had been skewed to accommodate national policy.

On the other hand, the dissenters, although acknowledging that unusual situations may necessitate some restriction on speech, insisted that any exception to a right of free communication be very tightly construed. Otherwise, as Brandeis explained, the very nature of the society as composed of a people free to challenge and change their institutions would be imperiled.[11]

If war brings with it a search for superficial conformity, it also spawns a more generalized questioning of the underpinnings of the society, its faith, and its goals. The way in which the political system, the society, and the legal system had to cope with free speech during the era of American participation in World War I provides an excellent example of how a dialogue is begun, of how its limits are tested, and of how change comes about.

Behind the bleakness of the Court upholding the convictions of dissenters to the war effort, there were glimmers of hope. Brandeis and Holmes urged the public to maintain the tolerance for difference that lay at the heart of their society and to distance themselves from the emotions and passions of the moment. What seemed even more disturbing to them was the fact that judges themselves, sworn to uphold the protection of individual rights, seemed to have become agents of repression rather than preservers of the social compact. Repeatedly Holmes and Brandeis argued that the Court's rulings discouraged healthful and necessary public debate on governmental policies. They might have added that the unity of the diverse people called Americans was, in fact, more threatened by repression than by the tolerance demanded by the holy writ.

As the justices struggled with the claim of individual rights when the wartime society disparaged considerations of individuality, the dissents of Holmes and Brandeis were significant. A beginning had been made in the direction of exploring the domain of individual rights in a society where government was becoming more involved in the daily life of Americans. As long as government had limited arenas of activity, the threat to the individual's rights was small, but as those arenas expanded, so also did the threat. In response, courts, and especially the Supreme Court, would be increasingly drawn into the task of defining the individual's place in a mass society.

Education takes place on the Court as well. For instance, the difference between Holmes's opinion for the Court in *Schenck* and his dissent in *Abrams* reflects the personal education that took place in the eight months between the two decisions.[12] The worlds pictured in the majority and dissenting opinions in *Abrams* are almost diametrically opposed. For the majority, the individual's freedom must be curtailed because of the national commitment; for the dissenters, the world is much more open with all views equally entitled to a hearing in the competitive marketplace provided by the Constitution. There is in the latter case a respect afforded the individual and a recognition, largely new for Holmes, that the fundamental law must be interpreted to allow room for this exercise of freedom.[13] In the Court opinions in this area, the picture painted is quite different: it is of an authoritarian world in which individuals must defer to forces, policies, and institutions over which they are denied control.

In addition to the repressive measures of the federal government, the states also passed legislation designed to cleanse the body politic of subversive speech. In *Gilbert v. Minnesota*, the defendant was prosecuted for violating one of the most notorious of these state sedition statutes. Joseph Gilbert had said, among other things, "if they conscripted wealth like they have conscripted men, this war would not last over forty-eight hours." Finding no federal preemption of the area that would preclude such state statutes, the majority ruled that local government had "power to regulate the conduct of its citizens, and to restrain the exertion of baleful influences against the promptings of patriotic duty, to the detriment of the welfare of the nation and state." Without deciding the question of whether the First Amendment applies to the states under the due process clause of the Fourteenth, the justices said that it "would be a travesty" to protect such expression under the Constitution.[14]

Brandeis was left to carry on the fight for free speech alone, since Holmes had steadfastly maintained that the Fourteenth Amendment imposed no general impediment to the states doing as they wished. Brandeis argued that criticism of the federal government was a constitutionally protected right. Even "in times of great danger," he continued, "the most effective means of securing the support from the great body of citizens is to accord to all full freedom to criticize the acts and administration of their country." The justice saw in the Minnesota law a far greater obstruction to individual free expression than found in federal law, for the state had prohibited the teaching of doctrine and condemned pacifism as a crime.

Finally, Brandeis confronted the application of the free speech right as a bar upon state action, saying "I cannot believe that the liberty guaranteed by the 14th Amendment includes only liberty to acquire and to enjoy property."[15]

The majority wished to fix the history of American participation in terms of Wilson's principles, and agreed, almost enthusiastically, with the condemnation of those who would question officially announced national motives. Brandeis, as he had made clear earlier, thought any attempt to fix history was misguided and would be singularly unsuccessful. He reminded Americans that the attempt to suppress discussion violated a core principle of their civil theology—that in a democratic society government must respect the individual's right to criticize its actions. War had infected the minds of his colleagues, and Brandeis insisted that they had fundamentally departed from the very principles that had informed America's war effort.

Such decisions tumbled into a society convulsed by the first red scare, where aliens and political and labor agitators were the target of governmental repression. The war to end all wars had brought disillusionment. Wilson had inserted his hope for the peaceful resolution of conflicts, the League of Nations, into the peace treaties, only to fail to gain the support of the Senate for American membership in the organization. The search for conformity that the war had encouraged—what President Warren Harding would call "normalcy"—would continue throughout the decade. Drastic limits would be placed on further immigration, and the Ku Klux Klan would be reborn, finding new targets in aliens and Roman Catholics.

In fact this concern about the new immigrants who had come in droves to the United States in the twenty years prior to World War I fueled two quite different reform movements—prohibition and women's suffrage. Both crested during the war years and led to changes in the Constitution. The need to use grain to feed people rather than inebriate them gave the prohibition forces a new and compelling argument. And the middle-class belief that saloons of the working-class immigrants were dens of iniquity that drained off resources from the worker's family lent credence to the idea that the society would be better and healthier if prohibition were enacted. So, through the Eighteenth Amendment, the government sought to regulate personal behavior on a new scale; the error of its ways would be acknowledged when the amendment was repealed.

Women's suffrage, just as prohibition, had made some headway in the states prior to 1914, but what made the national goal reachable was the war. Women contributed greatly to the war effort. If they could do the jobs that men previously had done and if they were eager homefront "soldiers," then how could their exclusion from the political arena be justified? Although their inclusion in the political community would have to come through the votes of men, that became more possible when women's suffrage was seen also as a means to counter the votes of recent immigrants. If the vote of older stock Americans were doubled through the enfranchisement of women, then old institutions could be preserved from new attacks. On August 26, 1920, the Nineteenth Amendment, making sex an impermissible discriminatory factor in conferring the vote, became part of the holy writ.

So, two new amendments were added to the Constitution with very different impacts. In the first instance, the fundamental law now sought to limit individual freedom by removing the individual's choice to drink alcoholic beverages. In the second instance, women were now admitted to the political community as fully participating citizens. To have envisioned women voting as some kind of special-interest group, as some observers expected, is to miss the individual nature of this group empowerment. Gender, as race had been earlier, was now declared to be an irrelevant personal characteristic when it came to participating directly in the political process. The people had acted to double the electorate by recognizing individual capacity and ability irrespective of sex. At the least, women became the political equals of men at the polls.

Although some women then and especially later would question the primacy of the campaign to get the vote, suggesting that the other inequalities that remained in the society were more important targets,[16] the decision to make the acquisition of the vote the primary goal makes sense, especially in a society that has always been defined politically. The idea, of course, was that through the ballot all other reforms were possible. And to have expected an all-male electorate to have overcome its conditioning and addressed other forms of gender inequality in the society is rather far-fetched. The war years created just the right type of environment for a respectful hearing on the voting issue but not one to advance an agenda that is largely born of more recent times.

The Supreme Court had nothing to do with the enfranchisement of women, but it described in rather ideal terms the implications of the Nineteenth Amendment. Striking down a District of Columbia regulation seeking to establish a minimum wage for women, Justice George Sutherland distinguished a 1908 precedent in which the justices had upheld a maximum hour law for women.[17] There, women were described as physically inferior, maternal in their essential nature, and dependent upon men. Such a characterization of women he was personally happy to refute.[18] Pointing to the revolutionary changes in their legal status in the last decade or so, Sutherland said that the Court "cannot accept the doctrine that women of mature age . . . require or may be subjected to restrictions upon their liberty of contract" that are not equally imposed upon men. "To do so," he continued, "would be to ignore all the implications to be drawn from the present-day trend of legislation as well as that of common thought and usage, by which woman is accorded emancipation from the old doctrine that she must be given special protection or subjected to special restraint in her contractual and civil relationships."[19]

Sutherland ignored the fact that since that earlier decision the Court had approved maximum hour legislation for men as well,[20] but what is important here is the picture the Court is now painting of women in American society. Feminists would claim that the picture was far too rosy, that inequality still plagued women, and that the very Court that defined these equal rights could ignore them as new cases were decided.[21] Of course, this is true, but the Court was participating in the process of reconstituting that society in conformity with new ideals grounded on old ideas of equal rights. In one fell swoop, the Court seems to be discarding its nineteenth-century view that a constitutional right to choose and practice an avocation is an exclusively male right and instead suggesting that unequal laws based upon sex are now constitutionally suspect. Just as Sutherland sees a revolution in social views, he mirrors this revolution by putting the Court on the side of equal rights, irrespective of gender, and picturing a society in which sex is largely legally irrelevant. Whether that goal even now has been fully achieved is debatable, but the result of such rhetoric was to widen the community and find new meaning in the commandments of the holy writ.

William Howard Taft, who realized his goal of becoming chief justice in 1921, wrote a rare dissent on grounds that the Court had revived a precedent that it had earlier repudiated.[22] His main contributions to the Court are not found in his opinions or in his attempts to eliminate dissent, but rather in his success in lobbying on behalf of the institution he revered. A special building housing the Court was one of Taft's dreams. The highest tribunal of justice in the nation, the former president fervently believed, should be housed in a structure that represented its lofty position in the American system of government.[23] For its entire history in Washington, it had occupied various rooms in the Capitol. The holy writ should be interpreted by high priests residing in a temple that symbolized their special role within the American civil religion. Seventeen years of lobbying on Taft's part led to the passage of legislation in 1929, on the eve of the depression, appropriating almost ten million dollars to house the Court in "a building of dignity and importance."[24] Taft would die before 1935 when the Court held its first session in the imposing marble temple we now know as the Supreme Court Building.

For one hundred and forty-five years the justices had labored in the shadow of the legislative branches; now they had a building that seemed to capture their special place within the constitutional structure. It remains a most special institutional home within a city composed of governmental buildings. Its lavish use of marble and intricate ornamentation continue to impress visitors, and its impressive facade and spacious interior engender a respect accorded few other buildings in the capital city.

If the Supreme Court temple is the most publicly visible legacy of Taft's efforts, his most lasting contribution to the Court's work was the Judiciary Act of 1925. Called "The Judges' Bill" because it was drafted by Taft and his colleagues, the legislation gave the Court effective control over the cases it heard. The decisions of the Circuit Courts of Appeal, created in 1891, were now final in the vast majority of all cases. In cases coming from the state courts, a party had a right to appeal to the Supreme Court only when the decision below was against a claim based on the Constitution, federal statute, or treaty. From this point forward the Court's docket would be filled primarily by cases that at least four justices wanted to hear. More cases dealing with claims of a threat to individual liberty were being generated by the legal system, and the justices, in responding to a primary duty, would center more of their attention on making the liberty promised by the civil theology a practical reality in the society.[25]

A Supreme Court that had wrestled with the problems of government coping with the changes of an industrialized society had aged, and its new members were more hesitant to approve governmental action that seemed to intrude on the property right. In fact, the justices found what had so long evaded prior colleagues— businesses not affected with a public interest and therefore immune from governmental regulation.[26] With this less accepting attitude, however, the Court also began to look with more care at governmental regulation that intruded upon other individual rights. For instance, when state legislatures responded positively to the fear of alien influence in the education process, the Court was asked to judge claims of unconstitutional interference.

As part of the hysteria engendered by the war, Nebraska, Ohio, and Iowa forbad the teaching of any subject in any language other than English prior to high school.[27] In the major case, Robert Meyer, a teacher in a Lutheran school, was convicted of teaching reading in German to a student who was ten years old. The Nebraska Supreme Court said that the legislature had recognized that the attempt of foreigners to make their language the mother tongue of their children "was inimical to our safety." By thinking in that native tongue, students would be inculcated with "ideas and sentiments foreign to the best interests of this country."[28]

Justice James C. McReynolds wrote an opinion for the Court based upon a reading of "liberty" as found in the Fourteenth Amendment. Summarizing the Court's prior interpretation of the term as "encompassing those privileges long recognized at common law as essential to the orderly pursuit of happiness by free men," he then ruled that Meyer's right "to teach and the right of parents to engage him . . . are within the liberty of the Amendment." Although acknowledging the value of knowing English and fostering "a homogeneous people with American ideals," he said that this goal "cannot be coerced by methods which conflict with the Constitution" and "with rights long freely enjoyed."[29]

In many ways this is a surprising decision given the atmosphere of the times. The tight control of education by local government is loosened by finding, in the Fourteenth Amendment's promise of liberty, both a right to teach and a right of parents to determine how their children should be educated. The first had more prior standing in the law than the second, but what the decision reveals is a willingness of the justices to find new meaning in the term "liberty." Even more significant for our purposes is what the opinion teaches about the culture. A demand for conformity and homogeneity must yield to the core values at the foundation of that culture—a protection of individual rights. As McReynolds said, "a desirable end cannot be promoted by prohibited means."[30] The means are prohibited because they threaten a diversity that must be respected if the culture is to survive.

The novelty of the *Meyer* decision had stirred some dissent, but there was no dissent in 1925 when the Court considered an Oregon law requiring all students to attend public schools from age eight to sixteen. The revived Ku Klux Klan, worried about Roman Catholic parochial schools, had successfully influenced the legislative process in the state. A Catholic school and a military academy sought to enjoin the enforcement of the statute, and the cases were combined for decision. Although McReynolds was sympathetic to the threat to property that the law posed, again he anchored the decision on "the liberty of parents and guardians to direct the upbringing and education of children under their control." Illustrating the Fourteenth Amendment's nationalizing potential, the justice concluded: "The fundamental theory of liberty upon which all governments in this Union repose excludes any general power in the state to standardize its children by forcing them to accept instruction from public teachers only."[31]

This study has not generally focused on the personalities that compose the Court, although some members have been so important in terms of charting and delineating the Court's role within the American civil religion that they could hardly be neglected. But generally the thesis here proceeds on the assumption that the role they assumed made the justices more similar than different. In fact, that role tended to lead them to conclusions that seem, at times, quite different from those that might be deduced from their individual personalities or social and economic backgrounds.

An excellent illustration is James McReynolds, who penned the opinions finding a constitutional right to teach and a right of parents to control their children's education. McReynolds was appointed to the Court by President Woodrow Wilson in part to purge his cabinet of a truculent personality. Generally ranked by historians as one of the worst justices in the Court's history, McReynolds, who would serve from 1914 to 1941, was a constant irritant to his colleagues. He had strong prejudices and what Chief Justice William Howard Taft called a reactionary view of the Constitution. McReynolds was a bachelor, who excluded all married or engaged individuals from serving as his clerk. But then he excluded Jews and smokers as well. And he refused to attend social affairs in which Brandeis, his Jewish colleague, was present.[32] His dealings with his fellow justices showed a monstrous insensitivity to the feelings of others, and except for the protection of the property right, he was hardly a leader in the protection of other individual liberties. Yet, here he is writing opinions that broaden the arena of personal liberty and extol the very family life that he both implicitly and explicitly rejected. Although such opinions from McReynolds are rare, the fact that there are some is testament to the way in which the role assumed seemed to gain some control over the individual within it.

The decisions asserting individual liberty over the rights of states to control the educational process indicate a strong tendency to define liberty nationally, to reinspect and reevaluate a federal system where rights often were contingent upon where one lived within the country. Further confirmation of this tendency came a week after the Oregon decision in *Gitlow v. New York*. Benjamin Gitlow had been convicted under a state criminal anarchy statute for advocating the overthrow of the government. Three years earlier the Court had said categorically that the Fourteenth Amendment had not made the free speech guarantee binding upon the states,[33] but now the justices rejected that position and announced "that freedom of speech and of the press—which are protected by the 1st Amendment from abridgement by Congress—are among the fundamental personal rights and 'liberties' protected by the due process clause of the 14th Amendment from impairment by the states." However, this acknowledgment of the primacy of free speech in the national community did not help Gitlow. As in the cases after *Schenck* dealing with federal law, the majority sidestepped the clear and present danger test, with its talk of proximity and degree, and accepted the New York legislature's previous determination of "the danger of substantive evil arising from utterances of a specified character."[34]

Although accepting the majority's ruling on free speech as a fundamental right protected by the Fourteenth Amendment, Holmes, joined by Brandeis, dissented. Gitlow's words, the justice said, "had no chance of starting a present conflagration." Then in typical Holmesian fashion, he continued: "If in the long run, the beliefs expressed in proletarian dictatorship are destined to be accepted by the dominant forces of the community, the only meaning of free speech is that they should be given their chance and have their way."[35] The threat seemed unreal, but Holmes is quite right in recognizing that an acceptance of the individual's right to speak implies a commitment to what that process produces.

In *Gitlow* the Court found that states were bound to respect the individual's right of free speech, a most significant ruling in spite of the High Bench's limited reading of just what that right entailed. If the majority justices seemed to learn little in their six-year exposure to the free speech claim, that would change as the education process continued in cases coming from the states. Without this stream of cases that invited a continuing dialogue, perhaps the definition of free speech would have been fixed for the indefinite future, for federal prosecutions based on wartime legislation would eventually cease. So, as the Court now undertook to judge state action in terms of new fundamental rights, it would go through a process that we have seen earlier—constant argument that would lead to concession and then acceptance.

Two years after *Gitlow*, the Court issued two decisions on the same day regarding California and Kansas criminal statutes that were not appreciably different from the New York law. In the California case, Charlotte Whitney was convicted of violating the state law by joining the Communist Labor Party and subscribing to its goal of a proletarian revolution. The challenge to the constitutionality of the statute on free speech and association grounds was rebuffed by the justices. Such rights, the majority said, are abused "by joining and furthering an organization . . . menacing the peace and welfare of the state."[36] Although Brandeis, with Holmes joining, concurred on technical grounds, he used his opinion as an educational vehicle to widen the discussion on free speech and place it squarely within the nation's cultural heritage.

Brandeis described not the society that gave rise to the prosecution but one that would be true to its heritage. In words that have as much pertinence today as they did in 1927, he said:

> Those who won our independence believed that the final end of the state was to make men free to develop their faculties; and that in its government the deliberative forces should prevail over the arbitrary. They valued liberty both as an end and as a means. They believed liberty to be the secret of happiness and courage to be the secret of liberty. They believed that freedom to think as you will and to speak as you think are means indispensable to the discovery and spread of political truth; . . . that the greatest menace to freedom is an inert people; that public discussion is a political duty; and that this should be a fundamental principle of the American government. . . . [T]hey knew that order cannot be secured through fear of punishment for its infraction; that it is hazardous to discourage thought, hope and imagination; that fear breeds hate; that hate menaces stable government; that the path of safety lies in the opportunity to discuss freely supposed grievances and proposed remedies. . . . Believing in the power of reason as applied through public discussion they eschewed silence coerced by law—the argument of force its worst form.

Contending that the founding fathers "did not exalt order at the cost of liberty," Brandeis said only an emergency "can justify repression . . . if authority is to be reconciled with freedom." And the harm, he continued, must be to the society and not to individuals, who have other legal remedies without suppressing the offending speech. Appealing for judicial responsibility to investigate the surrounding circumstances of an alleged violation of law rather than deferring to a generalized legislative conclusion, the justice reminded all Americans that crime is deterred by "education and punishments for violations of the law, not abridgement of the rights of free speech and assembly."[37]

Brandeis's words would later be accepted by the Court as the "classic formulation" of the principle of free expression.[38] What made the words classic was the way philosophy and history were merged in an artful rhetoric that instructed the populace in enduring political values. It is as if Brandeis is simply the prophet through whom the founding fathers themselves speak to a distant generation.[39] The justice used his position on the Court to portray a society true to its origins and faithful to the commandments of the civil religion. John Marshall Harlan had been a forceful advocate for the nationalization of basic rights, but Harlan's dogmatism at times cut off ongoing dialogue. Brandeis always seemed to be sensitive to the need to stimulate such discussion as part of the process of cultural definition itself.

In the Kansas case, the justices did what they refused to do in the California one; that is, to consider the lack of evidence supporting the conviction under the state law. They justified this action on grounds that the facts were so intermingled with the constitutional claim that they had to be inspected to reach a just resolution. Harold Fiske had been convicted for distributing literature, speaking, and soliciting members for a branch of the Industrial Workers of the World (IWW). As evidence that the law had been violated, the prosecution introduced the preamble to the IWW's constitution. Finding therein no advocacy of unlawful acts or methods, the Court reversed the conviction on grounds that Fiske's right to liberty under the Fourteenth Amendment had been violated.[40] There was no talk of free speech or free association, just liberty itself. The Court's message seemed less than clear, but apparently after confirming Whitney's conviction against a free speech and association claim, the justices decided to rest their decision upon a general finding of a failure of due process as protected by the Fourteenth Amendment.

Four years later, in *Stromberg v. California*, the Court made clear that free speech was an integral part of the liberty protected by the Fourteenth Amendment. Yetta Stromberg was a supervisor at a summer camp for children. As a member of the Young Communist League she instructed the students on worker solidarity and made part of each day's exercises the raising of a homemade red flag in the image of the flag of the Soviet Union and of the Communist Party of the United States. This last activity led to her conviction under a California "red flag law." The legislation made criminal the public flying of such a flag as a symbol "of opposition to organized government or as an invitation or stimulus to anarchistic action or as an aid to propaganda that is of a seditious character." Although finding no difficulty with the second and third clauses of the law, the justices ruled that the first clause, referring to opposition to organized government, was so vague and indefinite that it interfered with "the opportunity for free political discussion." Such public speech, they continued, is "essential to the security of the Republic . . . [and] a fundamental principle of our constitutional system."[41] Because the conviction may have been based on that clause, it was reversed. As the two dissenters made clear, the majority seemed to be reaching to find reasons to reverse convictions that rested upon broad suppressive state laws. The Court was reminding popular majorities that the society would not be restructured to free them from ideas and practices that they deemed offensive.

If Americans were now being protected from hostile state action, did this protection of free speech expand to include those who wished to become Americans? In *United States v. Schwimmer*, the Court in 1929 had to address the openness of the national community in considering the denial of naturalization to a prominent feminist. Rosika Schwimmer had been born in Hungary and gained international attention during the recent war as a pacifist. In 1921 she came to the United States to lecture and decided to remain in Illinois and become an American citizen. This country, she said, was "based on principles and institutions more in harmony with my ideals."[42] Generally women were not required to respond to a question on the application form that asked if they would be willing to take up arms in defense of the country, but the woman's auxiliary of the American Legion had requested that she answer the question.[43] Her answer was no, but she saw no incompatibility between that answer and her wholehearted willingness to take an oath of allegiance agreeing to defend her adopted country. She recognized that women were not drafted in the United States or elsewhere and that all persons of her age of forty-nine were considered too old anyhow. But she said that if persons such as herself were subject to the draft, she would seek status as a conscientious objector like any man and perform the alternative service so required.

Viewing the naturalization procedure as one that is "to be construed . . . to favor and support the government," the Court majority saw "the duty of citizens by force of arms to defend our government against all enemies . . . as a fundamental principle of the Constitution." Worried that Schwimmer's views stressed the unity of the human family to the detriment of the nation, the justices said this sense of priority made her incapable of committing herself to the principles of the fundamental law. They concluded that she might well influence others and lessen their commitment to the country's defense. During the recent war, they continued, opponents of the American effort had demonstrated their lack of "the true faith and allegiance" that the naturalization act requires.[44] Because Schwimmer did not overcome doubts about her full and total allegiance to the United States, the majority upheld the decision to deny her citizenship. Ironically, only the previous year the United States signed the Kellogg-Briand Pact, which sought to outlaw war as an instrument of national policy.

Holmes, with Brandeis, dissented. Finding no sympathy on the part of the applicant for the "now-dreaded creeds" of socialism, anarchism, syndicalism, and communism, Holmes said that she clearly believes in democratic government. To think that the Constitution can be improved, he contended, does not show a lack of attachment to its principles. And although the justice could not personally agree with her optimistic view that war is absurd and will disappear as people become more civilized, he wondered why such optimism would not make her a better citizen than most. Ridiculing the majority's opinion by saying that it implied regret at our inability to expel Quakers and others who "believe more than some of us do in the teachings of the Sermon on the Mount," he returned to a core element of the civil theology. While the majority read the Constitution as imposing upon an individual the duty to take up arms when the government commanded, Holmes said that "if there is any principle of the Constitution that more imperatively calls for attachment than any other it is the principle of free thought—not free thought for those who agree with us but freedom for the thought that we hate." That principle, he argued, should guide both "admission into, as well as life within, this country."[45]

Far more than the fate of Rosika Schwimmer was involved in this dialogue.[46] It concerned the very definition of the community in which she sought membership. Repeatedly, the majority justices talked of allegiance to the government, implying the need for an uncritical loyalty to its policies. When the Constitution is then read to impose a duty to take up arms, and opponents, whether conscientious objectors or active lawbreakers, are lumped together as all but traitorous, the picture painted resembles a totalitarian society. The majority had not only succumbed to popular prejudice, it had given it the sanction of the fundamental law. Additionally, the majority sought to close the gates of admission to the faith-based American community by going even further than Congress, which in the 1920s had set quotas upon the admission of new immigrants. This type of cloture is even more disturbing, for it seeks to diminish and limit discussion within the community. Instead of fulfilling its priestly role of holding government to its duty of protecting both this dialogue and individual rights, the Court gave government a license to ignore its basic responsibilities.

In Holmes's dissent a very different American community is pictured. Rosika Schwimmer is excluded because her ideas stimulate thought and may make the government's task during an emergency more difficult. For Holmes, the Court's proper role, when confronted with an individual's claim of right, is not to oil the wheels of government but rather to exercise a brake upon them when their momentum poses a threat to the essential principles of the American faith. Schwimmer is being excluded because her professed pacifism is perceived to be a threat to uniformity. But such a search for uniformity has always been unsuccessful in the pluralistic society, and it has the paradoxical effect of undermining the unity by which Americans are brought together. Holmes put his finger on a much more essential ingredient of that unity—the freedom to be different. Seeing at the heart of the holy writ a fundamental commitment to free thought, he saw no reason to limit its benefits to prior arrivals to American shores. Instead, he insisted that the Constitution prevents government from closing the doors of the American community to those having different ideas. Also, the justice reiterated a lesson that continually has to be repeated—that free speech protects communication that others find offensive and hateful. His approach in the opinion is consistent with the tradition of the country, its civil theology, and the proper role of the Court. It seeks, even with an immigration quota policy, to say you, too, can belong.

Two years later, despite two new members, the Court again split five to four in dealing with less prominent applicants for naturalization, two Canadians, one a Baptist minister and chaired professor of divinity at Yale University and the other a nurse who had served with American forces in the recent war. The professor, Douglas Macintosh, said that he would bear arms in defense of the United States only if he believed the country was involved in a just war. However, he felt, as had Schwimmer, that he could take the required oath of allegiance. The nurse, Marie Bland, would take the oath only with the modification "as far as my conscience as a Christian will allow."[47] Reading the oath of allegiance, which talked of the defense of the country against enemies as requiring the applicant to be willing to bear arms, the majority justices rejected both applicants. Any doubt, they said, should be resolved in favor of the government.

This time the dissenters were led by the new chief justice, Charles Evans Hughes, who made clear how very different the assumptions of the two sides were in viewing American culture. Denying that Congress ever made a duty to bear arms a necessary condition for naturalization, he said the majority's implication of such a prerequisite "is directly opposed to the spirit of our institutions and to the historic practice of Congress." Reading the required oath in the way the majority does, Hughes added, makes it a religious oath banned by the Constitution as a violation of "freedom of conscience." While the majority viewed citizen pacifists as less desirable Americans, the chief justice paid them tribute as people of conscience who had made important contributions to the recent war effort. Hughes found no evidence that Congress sought to subordinate allegiance to God to the civil power, concluding that the "deplorable conflicts" that have been caused by such attempts have been avoided in this country by a firm commitment to the basic elements of the American creed.[48]

The Court majority sought to shift responsibility for such repressive decisions by saying that Congress had commanded the result. This attempt to escape a clear ethical and legal responsibility for its actions was not uncharacteristic of the Court during these interwar years, as the majority justices often sought to mask their discretion by saying the result was commanded by the text itself. Interpretation, by its very nature, is filled with choice and discretion, but even more important a claim that asserts that the text speaks for itself seeks to close discussion and fix the culture's boundaries in an ever-changing society.

Supreme Court decisions are not written in stone, and decisions such as those reached in these naturalization cases are vulnerable precisely because they are so out of kilter with the theological core of the civil religion. Ironically, it would take another war in which democracy was assailed and forced to defend itself against rival ideologies before a now more sensitized High Bench would chip away and then repudiate such decisions.

If an applicant for naturalization could be rejected because of a refusal to bear arms, could students be expelled from a state university for their conscientious refusal to take a compulsory course in military science and tactics? All the justices agreed that the University of California could take such action. The defendants certainly have a right to entertain and promulgate their views, the Court said, but they cannot assert the primacy of their opinions over the legitimate authority of the state to prepare citizens to defend their country. In a concurring opinion Benjamin N. Cardozo indicated his belief that the religious clauses of the First Amendment were now applicable to the states, but he denied that the requirement here was "so tied to the practice of religion as to be exempt, in law or morals, from regulation by the state."[49] Notice, however, how Cardozo opens up not only a legal but a moral discussion as well. In his opinion, which two colleagues joined, he also argues that the free exercise and no-establishment of religion clauses of the First Amendment should bind the states as they do the federal government.

Claims of government intrusion into the protected arena of individual rights went beyond free speech claims in the 1920s and 1930s. One such area involved the government's pursuit of violators of national prohibition policy, actually the first of many subsequent campaigns of federal law enforcement activity directed against evasive criminals. Earlier we have seen how the Fourth Amendment's protection against unreasonable search and seizure had been interpreted broadly and consistently to protect an individual's privacy. Now the Court, in opinions written by Chief Justice Taft, seemed to back away from this chain of precedent.

The first case posed the question of whether a suspicious officer could stop an automobile and search its interior for alcoholic beverages and, upon finding them, arrest the driver. Was this an unreasonable search and seizure? The chief justice drew a distinction between a dwelling and a vehicle, saying that the latter can be moved before a warrant can be obtained and that the suspicion of the officer in the case was sufficient probable cause. In addition, Taft gave weight to the nearness of the highway to the Canadian border and to its reputed use by smugglers.

The two protestors against this inroad on the individual's Fourth Amendment protection were Justices James McReynolds and George Sutherland, hardly remembered as forceful protectors of nonproperty individual rights. McReynolds wrote for the pair and reminded his colleagues that the "damnable character of the 'bootlegger's' business should not close our eyes to the mischief that will surely follow any attempt to destroy it by unwarranted methods." He continued: "If an officer, upon mere suspicion of a misdemeanor, may stop one on the public highway, take articles away from him, and thereafter use them as evidence to convict him of crime, what becomes of the 4th and 5th Amendments?"[50]

Because stopping vehicles and seizing the liquor being carried did little to interrupt the flow of such beverages to an eager American public, federal law enforcement officials sought other means to dismantle the criminal organizations that had been set up to cater to consumers' desires. As part of a surveillance system, government officials tapped telephone lines. The Court was asked to determine whether the use of the evidence thus obtained to convict individuals violated their Fourth Amendment protection. In *Olmstead v. United States*, a five to four decision, Chief Justice Taft, stressing the extent of the conspiracy to violate national law, said that there had been no search of defendants' premises and that no tangible thing had been seized; only speech had been intercepted. The state of Washington, where the wiretapping had taken place, had declared such taps illegal, but Taft ruled that the common law allowed the introduction of illegally procured evidence at trial. Precedent had created an exception only when there was an illegal search or seizure, something not present here. And finally to the claim that the government's hands should be clean or else the evidence should be excluded, the chief justice responded that a demand for "nice ethical conduct by government officials would make society suffer and give criminals greater immunity than has been known before."[51] Obviously the majority had enlisted on the side of the police and denied that law should have anything do with ethics or with encouraging regard for the individual rights that lay at its constitutional heart.

Among the four dissenters were neither McReynolds nor Sutherland but rather three justices who had acquiesced in the vehicle search—Holmes, Brandeis, and Pierce Butler. They were joined by the newest arrival to the High Bench—Harlan Fiske Stone—in their protest against what they saw as a clear violation of the individual's protection from unreasonable searches and seizures. Each of the four dissenters wrote opinions. Stone, however, simply said that he agreed with the others on the merits of the case. The aging and now mellowed Holmes, who in his early years on the Court had expressed no sympathy for the rights of accused criminals, now said that he considered "it a less evil that some criminals should escape than that government should play an ignoble part."[52] Butler added that the Court, in interpreting the Fourth Amendment, has always sought to further "the purpose or scope of its provisions," by protecting the individual "against all evils that are like and equivalent to those embraced within the ordinary meaning of its words."[53]

Brandeis, however, did the best job of exposing the majority's rationale and premises. The clauses protecting individual rights from governmental abuse, he began, must be read to adapt to a changing world. Brandeis buttressed his conclusion with an extensive quote from *Weeks v. United States*, in which the Court had fashioned the exclusionary rule to make the protection found in the Fourth Amendment effective.[54] In fact, consistent precedent, he continued, "has refused to place an unduly literal construction upon" the amendment. Wiretapping, the justice suggested, may be just the first step in technological and psychological developments that would be able to expose the individual's private thoughts. To use such evidence at trial, Brandeis insisted, violates the defendants' Fifth Amendment right against self-incrimination. Actually, the Bill of Rights, Brandeis continued, seeks to secure to the individual "conditions favorable to the pursuit of happiness." The constitutional framers, he added, "recognized the significance of man's spiritual nature, of his feelings and of his intellect. . . . They sought to protect Americans in their beliefs, their thoughts and their sensations." This they did, he said, by insisting that the government recognize the individual's "right to be let alone—the most comprehensive of rights and the right most valued by civilized men." The lack of physical invasion he pronounced immaterial, saying that the amendment commanded that the evidence be excluded from the trial. The "greatest dangers to liberty," he added, "lurk in insidious encroachment by men of zeal, well-meaning, but without understanding."[55]

Appalled by the majority's implicit condonation of the breaking of Washington law by federal officials, Brandeis reminded his colleagues of the essentials of a rule of law: "Decency, security, and liberty alike demand that government officials shall be subjected to the same rules of conduct that are commands to the citizen." Calling government "the potent, the omnipresent, teacher" that instructs by example, the justice said that a government that teaches that the law can be broken for the purpose of catching criminals "breeds contempt for the law; it invites every man to become a law unto himself; it invites anarchy."[56]

While the majority sneered at the contention that the law should accommodate ethical considerations, Brandeis insisted that a law that does not is unworthy of respect. And as the majority gave the most strained reading of the Fourth Amendment since the Court first interpreted it in 1886, the dissenting justice exposed the authoritarian premises behind the resolution. Those premises seemed to realize the worst fears of the founding generation—that government would lose sight of its primary responsibility of protecting individual rights and that the courts would provide a rationale supporting such invasions. *Olmstead* stands out not only because of its insensitivity to individual rights but also because it is such a sharp departure from the Court's earlier readings of the Fourth Amendment. When those earlier justices had said that the protection must be read in light of changed circumstances, they hardly had in mind a reading that the need to apprehend criminals was so urgent that the protection of individual rights had to be narrowed.

Since 1886, the Court had recognized that the Fourth and Fifth Amendments were designed to protect the privacy of the individual from governmental intrusion.[57] What Brandeis adds is a forceful assertion of the primacy of the individual within the civil theology. Formulating a new right in the language of the layman—"the right to be let alone"—he illustrates how the justices constantly remake the law and how their formulations connect "our own vernacular with the language of the Constitution and our past." Brandeis's opinion stimulates a democratic conversation within which "we can build, over time, a community that will enable us to acquire knowledge and to hold values of a sort that would otherwise be impossible" and recognize "that the essential conditions of human life that it takes as its premises are shared by all of us."[58] Harkening back to the Declaration of Independence, the justice insists that individuals should be free to pursue their happiness under a legal system that respects and protects their right of individual pursuit. If they are engaged in criminal conduct, certainly government may in turn pursue them, but it may not do so in disregard of their rights. To allow such activity, as Brandeis makes so clear, threatens the very foundation upon which the society rests.

Much of the free speech litigation that came to the Court in this interwar period actually involved publications that the justices peered through and treated as speech. Although the High Bench continued to blend the protections of speech and press into one, *Near v. Minnesota* forced the focus on the publication itself.[59] Ruling that the individual's rights of speech and press were protected from state invasion "by the general guaranty of fundamental rights of person and property" found in the Fourteenth Amendment, the justices then had to confront the claim of Jay Near. His paper, *The Saturday Press*, had been enjoined as a nuisance under Minnesota law for containing scandalous and defamatory matter; any subsequent publication would be viewed as contempt. Saying that the liberty of the press "has meant, principally, although not exclusively, immunity from previous restraints or censorship" and that the criticism of public officials is desirable in a democratic society, the Court held that the abuse of this right does not make it less necessary. And if a state had the authority to consider the possibility of even violent public reaction to publication, "the constitutional protection would be reduced to a mere form of words."[60]

Despite the attempt of the dissenters to narrow the ban of no prior restraint, *Near* wrote that standard into the evolving national fabric of individual rights. The majority had defended its action on the ground that a democratic society must allow its citizens to criticize their public officials. Libel and slander laws were untouched, but the decision did dismiss the contention that government could fashion new tools to deal with abuses of an individual right. Near was far from being a desirable model. He was an ill-tempered, irrational, headstrong, and vituperative man. What the majority justices are saying here is that so-called abuses of an individual right are an integral part of that right. Despite the attraction of preventing abuses, no one has ever found a means to do this without impinging on the right itself. The right must either be respected or compromised. There can be no middle ground where so-called abuses can be extracted safely. This is the price charged for protecting individual rights and maintaining a community of very different individuals. The result may not always be comfortable and orderly, but the resulting chaos can be managed and the community conditioned to expand the levels of its tolerance.

If a state could not enjoin the publication of a newspaper, could it impose a tax on its advertising revenue? That was the question the Court confronted in *Grosjean v. American Press Co.* George Sutherland, for a unanimous Court, began by acknowledging the importance of a free press in the building and development of the community. He said that "it goes to the heart of the natural right of the members of an organized society united for their common good, to impart and acquire information about their common interests." Sutherland then broadened the right beyond prior restraint to include freedom from "obnoxious taxes." Certainly newspapers are not sheltered from general levies, the justice added, but the one here is "a deliberate and calculated device in the guise of a tax to limit the circulation of information to which the public is entitled in virtue of the constitutional guaranties." Reading the nation's history as committed to the preservation of "an untrammeled press as a vital source of public information," Sutherland said the press has and does shed "more light on the public and business affairs of the nation than any other instrumentality of publicity." As "one of the great interpreters between the government and the people," he continued, the press informs public opinion, which "is the most potent of all restraints upon misgovernment." "To allow it to be fettered," the justice concluded, "is to fetter ourselves."[61]

Here the Court is fully measuring up to its priestly duties of checking the intrusion of government upon an important individual and social right. The corporations that published the periodicals are spared the exaction, but Sutherland makes clear that the right is protected because it is essential to the proper functioning of society and to keeping the sources of information open. In freeing the channels of communication the Court encourages the democratic dialogue and recognizes that the people and not their governors are the rulers. As an invitation to participate in the definition of their culture and acknowledge the rule of law as protector, the opinion is a model worthy of emulation.

Continuing to explore the range of the First Amendment rights as now protected from hostile state action, the Court next addressed the right to assemble peacefully. Dirk De Jonge spoke at a meeting, under the sponsorship of the Communist Party, that was called to protest certain activity of the Portland police. Labeling the right to assemble peacefully as fundamental as free speech, the Court reminded Oregon officials that such rights had to be preserved. Such protection was necessary in order "to maintain the opportunity for free political discussion, to the end that government may be responsive to the will of the people. . . . Therein lies the security of the Republic, the very foundation of constitutional government." The fact that the meeting was sponsored by communists, the justices concluded, afforded no excuse for state hostility, for "peaceable political action cannot be proscribed."[62]

Increasingly they tied protection of freedom of speech to its social usefulness: repressive measures were condemned because of their tendency to hamper the free exchange of ideas that both enhanced the freedom of the individual and provided the lifeblood of the Republic. In seeking to protect the government from radical attack, the Court said, such statutes restrict the parameters of healthful political discussion. By so doing legislatures ignore the genius of the American constitutional system, which allows room for the people to change their government if they so desire. Keeping such channels free reemphasizes the fact that free speech, a core tenet of the civil theology, is the best ensurer of order in the society. The justices recognized that respect for the rule of law, which could only be maintained by voiding regulations that limited speech, was perhaps the only practical way to maintain the general order in the face of attack.

This new willingness to scrutinize state violations of individual rights that the free expression cases illustrated pushed the Court beyond the boundaries of the guarantees found in the First Amendment. One especially notorious case involving the conviction of seven blacks for raping two white women on a freight train led the Court to inspect state criminal procedure. Known as the Scottsboro case because of its setting in that Alabama town, the trials became a national cause célèbre.[63] The charges were weak at best, and Southern justice in such cases was suspect. At the first trial, no counsel was appointed for the defendants until the trial was about to begin. The Supreme Court reversed the convictions on grounds that the defendants' Fourteenth Amendment right not to be deprived of their liberty without due process of law had been violated. Although counsel had been present at the trial, the accused had none in preparing their defense, which, the Court ruled, denied legal assistance at a crucial stage in the proceedings. It traced Anglo-American history and cited procedures throughout the nation providing for counsel in such cases. The Court then ruled that in a capital case, when a defendant is unable to employ counsel and cannot adequately defend himself, counsel must be appointed in a timely fashion as a matter of fundamental right.[64] In subsequent cases involving the federal courts, the High Bench broadened the right to counsel, saying that trial courts have a special responsibility to ascertain that any waiver of the right be both "intelligent and competent."[65] Subsequently, in 1945, the revision of the Federal Rules of Criminal Procedure codified this requirement of a right to counsel. In addition, many states had similar rules calling for the appointment of counsel in cases involving serious criminal charges.

Two of the Scottsboro cases came back to the Court three years later on the claim that the defendants had been denied the equal protection of the law, because all blacks had been excluded from both the grand and trial juries. Evidence showed that no black had served on a state jury for over thirty years, despite the fact that blacks had served on juries in federal courts in the state during the same time period. The justices reversed the conviction and justified their inspection of the evidence. Whenever facts are so intermingled with an asserted right, they said, "it is incumbent upon us to analyze the facts in order that the appropriate enforcement of the federal right may be assured." "Otherwise," they continued, "review by this Court would fail of its purpose of safeguarding individual rights."[66] Notice that the High Bench acknowledges its priestly function of safeguarding the rights of the individual, saying that it would not be impeded by technical considerations in the pursuit of this sacred duty.

The concern for the rights of black defendants expanded beyond this latest episode in the Scottsboro affair, as the justices now seemed more willing to look at jury selection in the South. The lack of discrimination in the formal law was not enough, said a unanimous Court, for equal protection must not simply be promised but actually given. Such deliberate and systematic exclusion of blacks, the justices said, not only "violates our Constitution and the laws enacted under it but is at war with our basic concepts of a democratic society and a representative government."[67] The Court's task was clear—to end this war by educating errant Americans to their responsibilities under the civil theology.

Equal protection demanded at least the opportunity of black defendants to be tried by juries that could contain members of their own race, but the Court did not stop there. When Missouri sought to preserve its all-white law school by offering to pay the tuition costs of an otherwise qualified black citizen to attend an integrated school in another state, the justices found a denial of equal protection. Approving and giving new force to a 1914 precedent that said cost and demand were irrelevant,[68] they ruled that the black applicant, Lloyd Gaines, had a personal right to insist that the state provide, within its borders, "facilities for legal education substantially equal to those which the State there afforded for persons of the white race, whether or not other negroes sought the same opportunity."[69] Missouri had the option of building a new law school, for what it claimed were the few qualified blacks, or eliminating the barrier that prevented blacks from attending the existing law school. The economic choice and the choice dictated by the American creed were the same. In this first of a significant line of cases dealing with equal access to education, the Court said that the submergence of the individual within a group, which the state then seeks to deal with as a group, fundamentally violates the essentials of the American creed.

This initial decision actually calls attention to the costly option of maintaining a segregated educational system, but Southerners would continue to resist, opting instead to spend limited resources in duplicating educational facilities. The New South that boosters were touting after Reconstruction was a long time coming, in part because so much money and effort was devoted to maintaining segregation. A New South would not truly arise until the region's economic resources were freed from the burden of maintaining a society that looked backward and not forward.

The old days in which the Court relegated claims of the violation of individual rights to the resolution of the states were waning. The justices were establishing the parameters of a new national dialogue: they translated due process to mean that all "state action . . . shall be consistent with the fundamental principles of liberty and justice which lie at the base of all our civil and political institutions."[70] In saying that its interpretation of the Fourteenth Amendment is to be guided by ideas of liberty and justice, the Court was inviting a discussion of what is just and what is not and implying that any such conversation must continue to reflect social change.

Applying this standard in *Brown v. Mississippi*, the Court reviewed physically coerced confessions and concluded that it "would be difficult to conceive of methods more revolting to a sense of justice."[71] Clearly, torture to extract a confession violated the due process clause of the Fourteenth Amendment, but the Court went further in subsequent cases to inspect the failings of Southern justice. In a number of cases, the justices ruled that prolonged and repeated questioning that wore down the resistance of the accused violates due process.

In *Chambers v. Flordia*, for instance, a unanimous bench, in an opinion written by Hugo L. Black, Franklin D. Roosevelt's first appointee to the Court,[72] zeroed in on the High Bench's role in protecting the rights of the accused. Four blacks had been convicted and sentenced to death for robbing and murdering an elderly white man. After being interrogated for a week without access to counsel, they signed confessions during an all-night session. Citing the Preamble's purpose of securing "the blessings of liberty," Black said the Constitution, in guaranteeing the individual due process, was designed to prevent government from using "dictatorial criminal procedure and punishment to make scape goats of the weak, or of helpless political, religious, or racial minorities and those who differed." It is those people, the justice continued, "who have suffered most from secret and dictatorial proceedings." For the Court to "permit human lives to be forfeited upon confessions thus obtained would make of the constitutional requirement of due process of law a meaningless symbol." In reversing the judgment, Black clearly described the responsibility of the High Bench under the rule of law: "No higher duty, no more solemn responsibility rests upon this Court, than that of translating the living law and maintaining this constitutional shield deliberately planned and inscribed for the benefit of every human being subject to our Constitution—of whatever race, creed, or persuasion."[73]

Black's final words carry a wealth of meaning about American culture, the rule of law, the relationship of past to present, and the role of the Court in a society with an institutionalized faith. The American community is composed of all human beings, their differences being irrelevant under the Constitution. They are united under the common protection of due process, with its insistence upon equality, fairness, and justice. Their faith in the rule of law is historically rooted and well placed, for it provides all of them with recourse against the dictatorial impulses of government. The Constitution was "deliberately planned" to embody the basic theology of individual rights. The evils that led to the written protections deserve attention and respect but less in the specifics that had informed them than in their value as illustrations of the generalized threat.

The Court's supreme priestly duty, then, is to maintain "this constitutional shield." And how are the justices to do this? By "translating the living law." A living law is an organism that evolves over time. So, the law is not fixed in meaning, but it changes as the society of which it is a part changes. And how is this change recognized and incorporated as part of the Constitution's text? The Court translates the basic wording—here the due process protection of individual liberty—and by the very nature of translation itself gives to those words a new meaning in the contemporary world. That the meanings will be changed or modified is assured, no matter how much the translator might protest, for translation involves a dialogue between past and present that leads to a creative transformation. What Black's words "translating a living law" do is call special attention to the evolutionary nature of constitutional law and the responsibility it places upon the justices. Here that responsibility seems even greater to Black, for it involves the powerless, the poorly educated—those continually subject to prejudice and discrimination. If law is to rule and the civil religion continue to maintain the allegiance of the faithful, then the Court must respond to the claims of just such individuals. Only by so doing can it play its anointed role as the creative and unifying priestly interpreter of the holy writ.

One further aspect of Black's opinion in this Florida case deserves attention, for it tends to mask the significant change that was taking place during this period. From the time the Bill of Rights was added to the Constitution in 1791, the Fifth Amendment protected individuals from federal governmental attempts to violate their liberty without due process of law. Not until the addition of the Fourteenth Amendment was a similar due process requirement imposed upon the states. We have seen how, prior to the 1920s, the prime focus of the Court was not on the liberty segment of the protection but rather on the property one. Of course there were exceptions, but prior to the 1920s there was relatively little investigation of the liberty component and great hesitancy on the part of the justices to get involved in state criminal procedure. That inhibition was now being overcome, as the Court responded to a growing number of cases under the due process clause of the Fourteenth Amendment. What *Chambers* illustrates is the Court's insistence that states now abide by national rather than local standards in enforcing their criminal law. This was true in regard to specific guarantees found in the Bill of Rights, which the justices now pronounced as so fundamental that they were included within the liberty protected by the Fourteenth Amendment from state abridgement. Due process, long before the Court read provisions of the Bill of

Rights into it, had always encompassed fair, regular, and just procedure. Florida courts had found nothing wrong with forced confessions, but they, and all other judges throughout the United States as well, had now been instructed otherwise. What the Court was doing was defining liberty nationally in bits and pieces as cases came before the bench. The ultimate goal now seemed clear. What had passed as liberty within the various states was increasingly being censored by a High Bench that saw its priestly duty clearly. If the privileges and immunities of United States citizens had been reduced to a nullity, the broader due process clause encompassing all persons was providing a textual base for an ongoing process of translation that was making freedom truly national.

Just how far the justices were willing to go to make sure that the state criminal process was not cheating individuals of their rights is made clear in the case of a state defendant who was apparently misled as to the charge against him and the extent of punishment that would be levied under it. When Nebraska authorities insisted that the defendant under state law had to appeal to the state parole board first, the justices refused to credit the authorities with a proper reading of state law. Accepting the appellant's allegations, the Court found a fundamental denial of due process. Informing individuals of the charges against them, the justices lectured, was "the first and most universally recognized requirement of due process."[74]

In the spring of 1937, a divided Court in *Herndon v. Lowry* insisted that the individual's right to free speech and assembly was not protected by a state law that allowed the jury to determine if the activity of the defendant might, sometime in the indefinite future, cause harm to the society. When Georgia convicted a paid organizer for the Communist Party, the Court divided five to four and determined that the evidence showed no threat to the state. The majority justices ruled that the state had licensed the jury to speculate on "future trends of thought and action" and the relationship of the defendant to them. The statute, they said, amounted to "a dragnet which may enmesh anyone who agitates for a change of government if a jury can be persuaded that he ought to have foreseen his words would have some effect in the future conduct of others."[75] Such vagueness, they ruled, condemns the law as a violation of the liberty promised by the Fourteenth Amendment.

The four dissenters in *Herndon*, Willis Van Devanter, James C. McReynolds, George Sutherland, and Pierce Butler, have been labeled the Four Horsemen for their opposition to New Deal reform measures. They had been together on the Court since early 1923, and their wariness about government intrusion in the economy antedated the Depression and the election of Franklin D. Roosevelt in 1932. The president's New Deal with its very substantial and in some cases unprecedented interjection of the federal government into the economy, found the Four Horsemen steadfastly defending the status quo against the executive and legislative initiatives that expanded federal governmental power to deal with the Depression and its underlying causes. For instance, when the government abandoned the gold standard and provided for payment in legal tender, a narrow majority upheld the measure against the impassioned dissent of the quartet. Accusing the government of annihilating its obligations and destroying the rights it was established to protect, they saw only "unending humiliation" and "impending legal and moral chaos."[76] But in 1935 and 1936 this was one of the few victories for the administration, for in eight of the remaining nine cases involving recent federal legislation, the Court—anchored by the Four Horsemen—decided against the government. Although the votes varied and some legislation was so poorly drawn that even those inclined to support the New Deal effort had to concede its unconstitutionality, generally Justices Louis D. Brandeis, Harlan Fiske Stone, and Benjamin N. Cardozo supported the government. That left Chief Justice Charles Evans Hughes and Owen J. Roberts on the fence. When both Hughes and Roberts voted with the Four Horsemen, the vote was 6–3.

This split on the constitutional limits of the federal government's regulation of the economy did not necessarily carry over into the domain of individual rights. For instance, when the governor of Texas proclaimed martial law in the state and ordered that the defendant limit his production of oil, a unanimous Court lectured the governor. To the argument that this was a political decision that the judiciary could not inspect, the justices responded: "When there is a substantial showing that the exertion of state power has overridden private rights secured by the Constitution, the subject is necessarily one for judicial inquiry in an appropriate proceeding directed against the individuals charged with the aggression."[77] Such words broadly asserted the Court's primary role—to penetrate facades of claimed governmental authority for the purpose of making meaningful the protection of individual rights enshrined in the holy writ.

The Four Horsemen's more confined view of the authority of government led them, whether they were always comfortable with the outcome or not, to scrutinize state regulations as they affected other individual rights. If they showed less sympathy than the majority toward Herndon, they were not always able to justify limiting government in one area—the property right—and ignoring such limits in other areas of individual rights. And all of them, except Van Devanter, felt strongly enough about liberty beyond the property right that they dissented in cases in which the majority ruled against the claim of an individual.

For instance, a dissenting quartet, composed of the fence sitter Roberts, Brandeis, and two of the Four Horsemen, Sutherland and Butler, protested when the majority deferred to state practice and refused to find that the defendant's absence during a viewing of the scene of the crime abridged his right to due process. In his opinion for the four dissenters, Roberts said due process in "the Fourteenth Amendment commands the observance of that standard of common fairness," the violation of "which would offend men's sense of the decencies and proprieties of civilized life." Essential to this standard, he continued, is the requirement of a fair hearing, which can only be described as fair "if it safeguards the defendant's sub-stantial rights."[78] The requirement that the defendant be present at all times during his trial, Roberts argued, is just such a fundamental right.

Although the Four Horsemen, then, could differ among themselves on claims of individual right, they had no trouble closing ranks against the economic reform measures of the New Deal. Franklin D. Roosevelt, who did not have a vacancy to fill during his first term, believed that the justices' obstruction to forceful govern-mental action had to be overcome. Shortly after his landslide reelection in 1936, he proposed a plan that would have enabled him to appoint six new justices to the Supreme Court. If a justice had served ten years and did not retire within six months of reaching the age of seventy, the president was empowered to appoint an additional justice to the Court. If the sitting justice retired, the president, of course, would appoint a replacement. Roosevelt presented his court-packing plan behind the facade of improving the efficiency of an aging High Bench. He argued that the fact that the justices chose to hear only about 20 percent of the cases under their discretionary review power was clear evidence of their incapacity. The facade was quickly penetrated, and the proposal was widely viewed as an attempt to un-dermine the independence of the Supreme Court.

In March 1937, in one of his fireside chats, the president acknowledged the reality behind the facade. He urged his listeners to read the Constitution as they did the Bible, again and again, and remember that it was framed to give the national government sufficient power to "promote the general welfare." Arguing that the Court's dissenters had made a convincing case for the sufficiency of the Constitu-tion to deal with the nation's problems, he said his plan was designed to reestablish a rule of law and not of men, "to save the Constitution from the Court and the Court from itself." Indicating that his real target was the Four Horsemen, he said that "we cannot yield our Constitutional destiny to the personal judgment of a few men who, being fearful of the future, would deny us the necessary means of dealing with the present." To counter the arguments of his opponents, who in-sisted that the plan would undermine the Court's role as a protector of individual liberty, Roosevelt responded: "This proposal of mine will not infringe in the slightest upon the civil or religious liberties so dear to every American."[79] Clearly the Court was obstructing economic policies that the American people desired and that the administration believed were necessary, but Roosevelt's initiative pro-voked bitter and sustained dispute and gave his opponents an issue that could garner the broader support earlier denied them.[80]

Roosevelt knew that his Republican and conservative critics would be allied against him, but he was unprepared for the defection of liberal Democrats. The most prominent of these defectors was Senator Burton K. Wheeler of Montana, who from the first public announcement of the plan indicated his commitment to its defeat. When the Senate Judiciary Committee voted against the proposed bill with a stinging rebuke of the president, Roosevelt asked Wheeler to come and see him. Unable to dent Wheeler's resolve, the president asked the senator to "keep the bitterness out" of the debate. Wheeler responded: "The Supreme Court and the Constitution are a religion with a great many people in this country, and you can't keep bitterness out of a religious fight."[81]

To many Americans, the president had launched an attack on the keeper of the faith. For instance, a Charleston publisher said that he had always been taught to regard the Court as a sacred institution, like a church, in which the justices "presided as Bishops should." Secretary of Interior Harold L. Ickes ridiculed such views, contending that all that remains is "to declare that the Supreme Court is immaculately conceived; that it is infallible; that it is the spiritual descendant of Moses and that the number Nine is three times three, and three stands for the Trinity."[82]

Despite Ickes's dismissal of such a pious attitude about the Court, Wheeler had been right in perceiving the religious overtones in the struggle. Although the imagery was often Christian, it had nothing to do with Christianity; rather the religion under attack was the civil religion. The Supreme Court had so anchored itself within that religion that the contemporary historian, James Truslow Adams, could call it "the sole bulwark of our personal liberties."[83] The Court and the Constitution are different, insisted Roosevelt, as he sought to expose the policymaking pretensions of the Four Horsemen. But the president had failed to realize that the Supreme Court had so attached itself to the Constitution that the American people saw the two as one, with the Court being the visible embodiment of the fundamental law. The public seemed willing to suffer bad decisions rather than support a plan to weaken the third branch of government—a branch that had become an integral part of a national faith structure. Roosevelt's initiative was perceived as no less than an attack on constitutional government and the rule of law. The president continued to push the plan, but changes were taking place on the Court that made the proposed legislation unnecessary.

In April 1937, Hughes and Roberts joined the three prior dissenters to uphold the National Labor Relations and Social Security Acts, two essential pieces of New Deal reform legislation.[84] Chief Justice Hughes had written a letter, signed by Brandeis and Van Devanter, disputing the purported rationale for Roosevelt's plan to increase the size of the Court. The chief knew, however, that the best defense would be for the High Bench itself to adopt the more flexible view of the Constitution urged by Brandeis, Stone, and Cardozo. Just as the Court had read the fundamental law to protect individuals from oppressive majorities, could it not now read the Constitution to allow room for the federal government to protect those individuals from economic exploitation? When no became yes, the Four Horsemen were reduced to lamenting the end of the Constitution and the federal system as they had known it.

Just prior to these decisions, Willis Van Devanter announced his decision to resign, giving the president his first appointment to the High Bench. The crisis had passed, and during his second term Roosevelt would have a steady stream of Court vacancies to fill. Although the president could be said to have lost the battle but won the war,[85] he had badly miscalculated popular sentiment and the place of the Supreme Court within the faith structure of the national community.

The change that took place on the Court in 1937 would prove to be decisive. The justices went out of the business of reviewing state economic and social legislation as it affected the property right. Hereafter a clear majority would presume the constitutionality of all such legislation. Also, the limited readings of the range of the taxing and commerce powers of Congress provided by the Court in 1935 and 1936 were repudiated, as the new majority rescued older precedents and conceded wide-ranging regulatory authority under these two reservoirs of power.[85]

Actually, since the early 1920s the Court had been treading two paths: the first was the older one that measured state and federal economic and social legislation against the justices' view of the Constitution's protection of the property right; and the second, relatively new path, involved a somewhat similar scrutiny of legislation affecting other individual rights, whether it be the parents' control of the education of their children or claims that free speech had been abridged by governmental action. In moving along that second path the Court came to the conclusion that the term liberty in the Fourteenth Amendment protected certain fundamental rights of the individual from state invasion. The justices moved hesitantly but consistently in the direction of holding local government to new national standards, some of which had been spelled out in the Bill of Rights. With that first path now closed by the Court itself, the justices explored the largely uncharted terrain into which that second path was leading them.

As the eventful year of 1937 waned, the Court used *Palko v. Connecticut* to take stock of its progress along that second path and its perception of what the vista ahead suggested. The case summoned up recollections of Philippine justice, as it involved a state procedure that allowed a defendant to be prosecuted for a more serious crime if a conviction on a lesser charge had been reversed upon appeal by the state. After the reversal of his conviction for second degree murder, Frank Palko had been tried for first degree murder, convicted, and sentenced to death. He claimed that this procedure violated his right to be protected against double jeopardy, a Fifth Amendment protection that he claimed was made binding on the states by the Fourteenth Amendment.

Rejecting the contention that all the Bill of Rights guarantees were now binding on the states, Justice Benjamin Cardozo, for the Court, attempted to make sense of what the High Bench had been doing in the past decade or so. The protection against double jeopardy, he began, is similar to the federal right to an indictment by a grand jury in that "they are not of the very essence of ordered liberty. To violate them is not to violate a 'principle of justice so rooted in the traditions and conscience of our people as to be ranked as fundamental.' " A just system, Cardozo continued, is quite possible without such protections. He contrasted such alleged rights with "a different plane of social and moral values" incorporated in certain other provisions of the Bill of Rights. These latter provisions were read into the Fourteenth Amendment because "neither liberty nor justice would exist if they were sacrificed." As an example, the justice cited "freedom of thought and speech . . . [as] the matrix, the indispensable condition of nearly every other form of freedom." Saying that political and legal history has provided "pervasive recognition of that truth," Cardozo added that the Court has found it logically imperative to protect "liberty of mind as well as liberty of action" from invasion by the states. What happened in Palko's case, the justice continued, is not so "acute and shocking that our polity will not endure it," nor does it violate those "fundamental principles of liberty and justice which lie at the base of our civil and political institutions."[87]

Justice Butler, one of the Four Horsemen, dissented in the case without opinion. In light of his spirited questioning of the state's attorney during oral argument, Butler apparently believed that a fundamental principle of justice had been violated in Palko's conviction.[88] Certainly, nothing could be more important to the defendant than his life. That Pierce Butler had a sensitivity to the invasion of individual rights that sometimes surpassed his colleagues was demonstrated a decade earlier when he alone dissented in the notorious case of *Buck v. Bell*. In upholding a Virginia law providing for the sterilization of so-called mental defectives, which would be utilized by the state until 1972, Justice Holmes, for the Court, dismissed the claim that the individual's personal liberty is being invaded and ruled that "society can prevent those who are manifestly unfit from continuing their kind."[89]

As early as *Twining v. New Jersey* in 1908, the Court seemed to be inviting a public debate on what due process should require.[90] The easy answer, that the liberty protected from state interference included all the provisions of the Bill of Rights, had been consistently rejected. Apparently the justices felt more comfortable with a much more open-ended approach that seemed designed to invite dialogue about just what was fundamental to the individual's protection in a democratic society. This approach not only preserved the justices' considerable discretion, but it seemed to say, here is constitutional language that must be reinterpreted over time to make the holy writ conform to the sensibilities of the society over which it presides. Although Cardozo in *Palko* seemed categorical about what was included in liberty and what was not, saying there is "a rationalizing principle which gives to discrete instances order and coherence," he could not hide the room left for changing interpretations over time. And, as the Court was redefining its role, Cardozo insisted on the relevance of "social and moral values" as a guide to its priestly responsibilities.[91]

If *Palko* was an attempt to rationalize the Court's checkered decisions on the content of liberty, it left open the question of how the Court was to draw another line—between governmental regulation that would now be presumed constitutional and other regulation that would not be accorded that accommodating presumption. In 1938, Justice Harlan Fiske Stone sought to deal with this matter in a footnote to a rather routine decision in *United States v. Carolene Products Co.* Stone suggested that there were three areas in which a claim of individual right should defeat the presumption of constitutionality. The first area involved claims based on specific language of the fundamental text, such as the Bill of Rights and the Fourteenth Amendment. The next area encompassed claims that access to the political process has been impeded. Finally, in the last area the justice grouped together statutes directed at particular religions and action based on "prejudice against discrete and insular minorities."[92] In the latter two areas, Stone believed that it was the Court's duty to cleanse the political process so that it could be expected to respond to legitimate grievances. In the first area, the justice simply implied that the Court, as interpreter of the holy text, had the duty to protect the individual rights therein specified.[93]

Stone had outlined a number of areas ripe for discussion and the bringing of claims, and, as subsequent history would demonstrate, the areas he staked out would attract his colleagues' special attention. The justice, who would be elevated to the center seat in 1941, had taken the opportunity to indicate that a Court willing to defer to legislative judgment in many areas was not about to abdicate its special role in both the constitutional system and in the civil religion. In delineating these special areas of judicial concern, Stone looked to a future in which each individual would be respected and would be welcomed as a full participant in the pluralistic national community. In protecting individual rights, the Court would be ever mindful that the threat to social unity was not difference but repression and exclusion.

In regard to ensuring access to the political process, Stone had cited two Texas cases in which blacks had been denied the right to vote in a Democratic primary. In what was then a one-party South, the real contest among candidates was the primary election. In the first case a unanimous Court allowed a suit to proceed for a black to collect damages for being deprived of his right to vote in a primary election. By law, Texas had provided that blacks could not vote in such elections. The unanimous Supreme Court decided that the state had violated the equal protection clause of the Fourteenth Amendment, saying that it was hard "to imagine a more direct and obvious infringement." "Color," the justices said, "cannot be made the basis of a statutory classification."[94]

When Texas sought to evade this decision by entrusting to party executive committees the determination of who could vote, and the Democratic committee stipulated that only whites could cast ballots, the Court divided, with a majority

condemning the evasion. Because these committees were "invested with an authority independent of the will of the association," the justices said that "they
become to that extent the organs of the State itself, the repositories of official
power." And as such, they continued, the parties must submit "to the mandates of
equality and liberty that bind officials everywhere." The Fourteenth Amendment,
the majority concluded, "lays a duty upon the court to level by its judgment these
barriers of color."[95]

The dissenters in the case were the Four Horsemen, who argued for the freedom of association, contending that political parties, which the majority had characterized as integral parts of the electoral process, are the "fruits of voluntary
association." Maintaining that exclusion "is essential to free government," the dissenters said that the instant case was no different from a women's party excluding
males and a black men's party excluding white men.[96] Of course, the difference
was a matter of power and effective control over the electoral process. While the
majority looked at the reality of politics in Texas, the minority asserted the abstract
right of association over the claim of being effectively excluded from participation
in the electoral process.

Texas again responded to the decision by placing full authority in the political
party itself to determine who could vote. When that law came before the Court,
a unanimous bench decided that the state had sufficiently divorced itself from the
party, and that the organization could determine for itself who could vote without
running into any constitutional problem.[97] So, the Court seemed to take a backward step by entrusting to the Democratic Party the composition of the electorate
that would make the effective choice of who would go to Congress.

That is where matters stood when Stone got the chance to reinspect the issue
of primary elections in 1941. By that time, the Four Horsemen had left the Court.
The issue was whether Louisiana election officials could be prosecuted under a
federal law for falsely counting ballots in a congressional primary election. Obviously, the officials sought to cancel out the vote of blacks. Stone, for the majority,
avoided the Reconstruction amendments and formulated the question in terms of
safeguarding federal elections. As such, the protection could be had against individuals as well as states, and it could reach primaries as well as general elections.[98]

Confronting the argument that the framers of the Constitution could not have
intended the result reached here, Stone launched into an exploration of how the
Constitution should be interpreted. Acknowledging that the framers could not
have envisioned party primaries any more than they could the telephone and tele-
graph, he said that determining whether a new subject falls within the commands
of the Constitution has nothing to do with the framers' ability to foresee the future.
Their "enduring framework," he declared, must be read "as the revelation of the
great purposes which were intended to be achieved by the Constitution as a continuing instrument of government." We maintain faith with them, Stone added,

by interpreting their words to "effectuate the constitutional purpose" in changing situations.[99]

Claiming that the purpose was "to secure to the people the right to choose representatives by . . . some form of election," the new chief warned that Congress would be "left powerless to effect the constitutional purpose" were its authority not extended to primary elections. "Words," he added, "are not to be read with . . . stultifying narrowness." And to deny citizens effective participation in the political process at its contested stage would hardly do credit to "the performance of the judicial function."[100]

Stone's view of the text of the fundamental law is quite instructive. Once we escape from confining notions of what was or was not intended by people long ago, then we can address the real question—how can the holy writ be made meaningful within changed circumstances? The chief justice's answer is commitment to its underlying and revelatory purposes from which the interpreters should not be distracted by either new devices or new technologies. Stone asserts the need to interpret the range of individual rights by discerning the primary purposes of the relevant text and then furthering the goals that these purposes envision. In many ways, his opinion responds to an invitation to take responsibility for the definition of the culture in which we live. This is what he seems to have had in mind in delineating the new areas of potential action in *Carolene Products*. A Court that does not seek to clear away obstacles to effective individual participation in government is shirking a fundamental responsibility under the terms of its priestly role within the civil religion.

Its growing sensitivity to individual rights, bolstered by new federal legislation, led the Court to view the claims of union members more sympathetically than it had in the past.[101] For years, going back to *In re Debs* in 1895, the Court had viewed the claims of organized laborers through the lens of the imperiled property interest. When state laws sought to protect unions, the Court struck down the protective legislation,[102] and when state laws sought to restrain union activity, the Court nodded its approval.[103] In 1932 Congress sought to overcome limiting Court decisions and gaps in prior law by seeking to protect unions from injunctions by passing the Norris-LaGuardia Anti-injunction Act. Three years later, in the National Labor Relations Act, Congress mandated the protection of union organization and collective bargaining. In addition, various states sought to protect peaceful picketing through the force of law. The New Deal had put the government on the side of organized labor, and armed with this new support, unions and their members gained a more sympathetic hearing from the Supreme Court.

The first in a series of picketing cases was decided by the Court just after Hughes and Roberts began supporting Brandeis, Stone, and Cardozo against the position of the Four Horsemen. As might be expected, the decision was five to four. At issue was a Wisconsin state law protecting peaceful picketing in labor disputes. A tile contractor sought to enjoin picketing of his business by members of a union who sought to obtain his promise that he would not personally lay any tile. When the Wisconsin courts refused to grant the injunction, the contractor appealed on grounds that the liberty protected by the Fourteenth Amendment ensured his right to work at his trade. Justice Brandeis said that, as long as the contractor did not sign the agreement, he was free to work as he chose but that the Fourteenth Amendment did not provide him immunity from legal competition or guarantee him any jobs. Even independent of the state law, the justice continued, union members can "make known the facts of a labor dispute, for freedom of speech is guaranteed by the Federal Constitution." Certainly, Brandeis added, the state can authorize union members to combine "as pickets, just as it permits capitalists and employers to combine in other ways to attain their desired economic ends."[104]

The question was whose liberty was to be protected? The state had made a prior determination that workers should be safeguarded in their ability to combine with others to achieve their economic goals through an appeal to the public by picketing. What the dissenters prior to 1937 had been arguing for was deference to the judgment of the state in such economic matters. But now the Court, for the first time, suggested that picketing, even in the absence of state statutory protection, could be considered free speech protected by the Fourteenth Amendment. So, the amendment, which had heretofore been read as protecting a person from interference in pursuing his trade, was now read to give to those who sought to limit this pursuit a free speech right to proceed.

Organization was the key to survival in the industrial society. The fact that a corporation pooled capital and thus created economic power had not led the Court to exclude the organization from the protective reach of the due process clause of the Constitution. Slowly the justices had come to the conclusion that simple fairness demanded that the pooling of workers into a union be treated in a similar way.

When organizers for the Committee for Industrial Organization (CIO) attempted to gain members in Jersey City, they ran into the implacable opposition of Mayor Frank Hague. Claiming authority under a city ordinance, the mayor directed that meetings be disrupted, leaflets confiscated, and the organizers driven out of town. Dissenting, Butler and McReynolds argued that an 1897 precedent confirming the authority of Boston officials to curtail speaking on the Common should control,[105] but the majority justices indicated how far the Court had traveled from that repressive decision. They differed on their rationales, with some of them seeking to find the conduct here protected by the privileges and immunities clause of the Fourteenth Amendment. But Justice Stone saw no reason to revive the dormant clause and thus limit the protection provided to citizens alone when the due process clause, which now guaranteed the rights of speech and assembly, embraced all persons. At any rate, a municipality could not use its alleged title to the streets and parks to suppress the discussion of public questions, for "they have immemorially been held in trust for the use of the public and . . . have been used for purposes of assembly, communicating thoughts between citizens, and discussing public questions."[106] And certainly, the majority said, there was nothing unlawful in soliciting workers for union membership.

In the next term, the Court considered an antipicketing law in *Thornhill v. Alabama* and now fully subscribed to the conclusion that picketing was speech protected by the Fourteenth Amendment. Over the dissent of McReynolds, the last survivor of the Four Horsemen, Justice Frank Murphy said that the abridgment of such free speech "impairs those opportunities for public education that are essential to effective exercise of the power of correcting error through the processes of popular government." He recognized the inherent value of "publicizing, without annoyance or threat of any kind, the facts of a labor dispute." Disseminating such information, Murphy ruled, was "within that area of free discussion guaranteed by the Constitution." To the state's claim that such a statute was necessary to preserve peace and public order, the justice responded that all speech has this potential. The law here, he continued, evidences no care "in balancing these interests against the interest of the community and that of the individual in freedom of discussion on matters of public concern."[107]

Notice how Murphy views freedom of speech as having both a social and personal value and how the fact that picketing involves more than speech is not addressed. In time, that question will receive more attention, but as the Court is defining the meaning of free speech in twentieth-century society, it is not inclined to make sharp distinctions between speech and accompanying conduct. In other words, the justices are looking at free communication in a nontechnical way. The question is not is it speech, or speech and something else, or just that something else. This common sense approach makes the educative value of such opinions more broadly accessible, a fact that the Court continually recognizes by putting its decision in a cultural framework that is designed to further the people's commitment to the theology of individual rights.

If peaceful picketing was now given immunity as free speech, did that immunity extend to picketing by union organizers of a business in which there was no existing employer-employee dispute? Yes, said Justice Felix Frankfurter, for the Court, as he recognized the "interdependence of economic interest of all engaged in the same industry." To limit picketing to employees, he said, would mutilate "the right of free communication."[108]

On the same day in a different case, Frankfurter continued the dialogue, calling peaceful picketing "the workingman's means of communication." In so doing the justice recognized that individuals in the industrialized society had different methods of communication, and that, to make freedom meaningful to all, the Court had to be flexible in its definition of free speech. As a product of the Enlightenment, he said, the guarantee was given "generous scope" for the purpose of averting "force and explosions due to restrictions upon rationale modes of communication."[109]

These final words led Frankfurter to distinguish this case from the others, finding in the facts as presented that the picketing "was set in a background of violence" that led to intimidation. The justice said that the state court's conclusion "that the momentum of fear generated by past violence would survive even though future picketing might be wholly peaceful" was not unreasonable.[110] Such an opinion would become increasingly typical of Frankfurter, as he boldly proclaimed the importance of individual rights but then tended to defer to the state's judgment on their applicability in specific situations.

Two dissenting opinions lamented the Court's retreat from the Thornhill decision. Certainly violence should be enjoined and picketers should be held responsible for any damage they cause, the dissenters said, but such grievances could be handled by the law without banning peaceful picketing. Calling the First Amendment "the foundation upon which our government rests and without which it could not continue to endure as conceived and planned," Justice Hugo L. Black said the injunction approved by the majority is so sweeping that it clearly invades protected constitutional rights. Justice Stanley F. Reed turned Frankfurter's accommodation on its head, saying if "the fear engendered by past misconduct coerces storekeepers during peaceful picketing, the remedy lies in the maintenance of order, not in the denial of free speech." To strip this right from the many for the misdeeds of the few undermines "the constitutionally protected ways in which orderly adjustments of economic disputes are brought about."[111] To give primacy to the assumed fear of those picketed, he concluded, in effect deprives the workers of their constitutional rights.

That the Court was struggling with the characterization of picketing as free speech is graphically demonstrated by two decisions on the same day in 1942. A majority overturned a New York injunction against the picketing of bakers who sold their goods to independent peddlers for resale. The union wanted these peddlers to hire a union driver for one of the seven workdays and sought to bring pressure on the suppliers of the goods. All the justices agreed that such picketing should be permitted, for otherwise the public that supported the system would not be apprised of the grievance.[112] But when the owner of a restaurant found his establishment picketed by union members after he had contracted with a nonunion employer to construct a building elsewhere in the city, a split Court went the other way. The justices upheld an injunction, saying that the state may constitutionally restrict "the area of the industry within which a labor dispute arises," for other avenues of communication remain open. The dissenters, led by Black, saw no appreciable difference between the two cases and accused the majority of weakening, if not undermining, the protected right. "In balancing social advantages," he concluded, "it has been felt that the preservation of free speech in labor disputes was more important than the freedom of enterprise from the burdens of the picket line."[113]

Black's comment sums up the conflict in this area. The Court had been fleshing out the contours of a right that was continually referred to as fundamental, the right from which others proceeded in the democratic society. When associated with picketing, however, the exercise of the right entailed a degree of coercion upon others. Black's preference for the speech right against the claims of enterprise was not fully shared by his colleagues. Although all agreed that property can be regulated, the strong pull of the property right was still felt.

These cases demonstrate graphically the problems involved in the adjudication of individual rights. And they invite discussion in the larger society. Some critics have suggested that the Court best performs its function not when it commands but when it sifts contentions and leaves room for decision making elsewhere. The High Bench, then, acting somewhat as a therapist, performs a vital service by setting the parameters of a continuing dialogue not only in other branches of government but in the conversations of the general public. Regularly, Felix Frankfurter maintained that the justices should stay their collective hands and allow the states to work through the major problems of governance. Within the democratic system, the High Bench, to his mind, should instruct and only when absolutely necessary command.

How attractive this view is depends upon one's faith in the administrative and legislative processes. When it was espoused by Holmes in an earlier period, it looked toward freeing government to cope with economic and social change. That battle was won in 1937. But Frankfurter, who saw himself as Holmes's worthy successor, applied this philosophy of judicial restraint to government regulations that posed a different threat—to a range of other personal rights.[114] The question was an old one, but the increased sensitivity of the justices to their responsibilities in this area was relatively new, in part because of the testing of the constitutional waters by new litigants and new claims.

Despite the activity of the American Civil Liberties Union in coming to the aid of litigants in free speech cases,[115] no group was more active in challenging state laws that limited the range of their activity than Jehovah's Witnesses.[116] They had been prosecuted for their opposition to American participation in World War I, and the claim that all members were ministers of the faith and therefore entitled to exemption from the draft was vigorously opposed by the government. Unlike Quakers, who were pacifists, the Witnesses were belligerent in their proselytizing and in their condemnation of other faiths. When they encountered hostile legislation they did not turn the other cheek; they fought such restrictions all the way to the Supreme Court. In the process, they would force the justices to contend with a great variety of state regulations that intruded upon the individual's freedom to speak, distribute literature, and proselytize.

When a Witness was found guilty of distributing religious literature without the permit required by a Georgia town, she appealed the conviction on various grounds, including its restraint on her free exercise of religion. A unanimous Court avoided the religious issue by talking in terms of freedom of speech and the press, where the path was much better grooved by prior decisions. The justices interpreted the liberty of the press to include the distribution of any written material and invalidated the local law as a "system of license and censorship in its baldest form."[117]

In four cases from cities in different states, only one of which involved a Jehovah's Witness, the justices, with only McReynolds dissenting, struck down all the ordinances on grounds that they violated free speech. The cities were not permitted to keep their streets free from litter or to save their citizens from solicitation in their homes by dimimishing individual "rights so vital to the maintenance of democratic institutions."[118]

How far the Court was willing to go to protect the individual's right of free speech is well demonstrated in *Cantwell v. Connecticut,* which involved Witnesses intent on communicating their views. Newton Cantwell and his two sons were convicted of not obtaining a license for their charitable solicitation and for breaching the peace. The second charge resulted from their playing a phonograph record attacking Roman Catholics for two men of that faith, who, upon hearing the attack, threatened to strike Cantwell unless he left the area. He left and was eventually charged with provoking others to breach the peace.

This time the unanimous bench did confront the free exercise of religion claim and ruled that it was part of the liberty guaranteed to individuals under the Fourteenth Amendment. Saying that action taken under the free exercise right is subject to regulation, the justices said such laws must not "unduly infringe the protected freedom." It is infringed, they continued, when a state official is given the power to determine if the cause for solicitation is religious. The state's interest in preserving order, the justices continued, has come "into fatal collision with the overriding interest protected by the federal compact," which they defined as follows: "that the free exercise of religion be not prohibited and that freedom to communicate information and opinion be not abridged." Also, the Court found no incitement to breach the peace—"no assault or threatening of bodily harm, no truculent bearing, no intentional discourtesy, no personal abuse."[119]

Notice how the justices see these individual rights as rooted in the social compact. They view their decisions as equally important both to the individual and to the survival of the pluralistic society. Acknowledging that the eager advocate can exaggerate, vilify, and seek to make the false true, the justices said that, despite abuses, the American public has ordained that "these liberties are . . . essential to

enlightened opinion and right conduct on the part of the citizens of a democracy."
They then added that "under their shield many types of life, character, opinion,
and belief can develop unmolested and unobstructed. Nowhere is this shield more
necessary than in our own country for a people composed of many races and of
many creeds."[120]

The Court is reminding the society it serves that a respect for such rights not
only nurtures individual development but also preserves the unity of a diverse
people. From the nation's beginning the new society was predicated on the premises that in diversity there is union and that only in union is there the strength to
protect that diversity.

As the justices are drawn more and more to the core of their responsibility—the
protection of individual rights—they seek to alert a new generation to the wisdom
of these premises and the ever-present danger posed by their neglect. Because the
Supreme Court can never save the people from themselves, they must be educated,
if not to applaud such decisions, then at least to accept them as the price for unity.
The hope, of course, is that the decisions and their rationale work their way into
a public conversation that enlarges people's sensitivities. The same is true of governmental bodies, which must be made to realize that order and security cannot
come at the cost of suppressing speech.

In *Cantwell*, the justices saw limits on the freedom of speech, saying that "epi-
thets or personal abuse is not in any sense communication of information or opinion safeguarded by the Constitution."[121] The Court put force behind these words
in another Witness case. A New Hampshire law sought to prevent persons in
public places from being called "by any offensive or derisive name." When a
Witness said that a public official was a fascist and racketeer and then included the
entire local government in his condemnation, he was arrested and convicted under
the statute. A unanimous Court found an exception to the free speech protection
for " 'fighting' words," saying that, as profane, libelous, and lewd expressions, they
"are no essential part of any exposition of ideas" and are therefore "outweighed
by the social interest in order and morality."[122] This is a strange decision, for it
does limit the range of individual expression and does submerge the free speech
right within the social context, implying that its protection is solely dependent
upon a perceived social value. To its credit, the Court has not built upon this
precedent.

If fighting words were beyond the protection of the free speech guarantee,
what about comments dealing with pending litigation in the state courts? Earlier
the High Bench had upheld contempt citations in such cases on grounds that such
criticism had the tendency to obstruct justice.[123] Now the majority looked closely
at the offending material and found it protected under the new and invigorated
right of free speech. Justice Hugo Black said that the majority decision was simply
giving effect to the will of the framers, who "intended to give to liberty of the

press, as to the other liberties, the broadest scope that could be countenanced in an orderly society." This goal is achieved, he continued, when the prohibition on any law "abridging the freedom of speech or of the press" is read as broadly as its "explicit language, read in the context of a liberty-loving society, will allow."[124]

Notice Black's logic as it affects the role of the Court in responding to claims of individual right. Rather than read the words therein in terms of prior British practice or original understanding, he deduces that the framers intended by their language to expand any prior understanding for the purpose of maximizing individual freedom. From this starting point, the task of the interpreter is not to balance the claimed right against some perception of governmental need but rather to read it as a command to give individual rights the "broadest scope" that the specifying words will permit. Black defines the society as "liberty-loving" and invites the people in the society to identify with that description. To the dissenters' belief that the contempt power in such a case was needed to ensure that judicial proceedings are respected as fair and impartial, Black responded that such a view "wrongly appraises the character of public opinion. For it is a prized American privilege to speak one's mind, although not always with perfect good taste, on all public institutions." Trying to silence such talk, the justice continued, "would probably engender resentment, suspicion, and contempt more than it would enhance respect."[125]

Felix Frankfurter, who spoke for the dissenters, contended that the majority's preempting of state discretion by finding an individual right, as it did in this case, prevents a democratic people from having their state government respond to their wishes. Black responded that courts earn the people's respect by protecting the basic rights of individuals, not by using their authority to curtail these rights. Courts gain the respect of the people not through their power but through their role in making the civil theology a reality within the society. As Black stated, a lack of sensitivity for the core rights within the American creed breeds resentment, certainly not respect. While Black invites democratic discussion, Frankfurter seeks to inhibit it.

The question boils down to whether the Court's essential task is to further the wishes of the majority, whether determined by state or national boundaries, and to defend the institutions created to serve those ends, or to view sympathetically challenges to the majority will based upon claims of individual right. It is this latter approach that, from the Court's inception, has characterized its work and given it a secure lodging within both the constitutional system and the civil religion. Black and Frankfurter would serve together for the next twenty years, providing critics with ample opportunity to assess their differing conceptions of the judicial role and of the cultures they thereby define.[126]

As the 1941 Term of Court began, the final member of the Four Horsemen, James C. McReynolds had retired, as had Chief Justice Charles Evans Hughes.

Harlan Fiske Stone was advanced by promotion by President Roosevelt to the center seat, and James F. Byrnes and Robert H. Jackson became the new associate justices. Byrnes would resign in a year and be replaced by Wiley B. Rutledge. What the president had failed to do by his court-packing proposal he was now able to do through the normal process of attrition. Roosevelt had made President Calvin Coolidge's appointment of Stone his own by advancing the senior member of the Court to the center seat; only the seat occupied by Justice Roberts, who had been appointed by Hoover, would escape the attention of Roosevelt.[127]

Much has been made of this transition of the old Court to the new, especially with regard to its approval of wide-ranging power, both local and national, to deal with economic conditions in the society. The commerce clause was now interpreted to be coextensive with the needs of a national economy, as the Court tossed aside limiting precedents of the past and looked with favor upon national regulation. However, in focusing upon this change we are apt to ignore a continuity between the Courts that the more dramatic shift has tended to obscure. Although the old Court read limitations into Congress's ability to regulate under the commerce clause, it insisted that the clause did operate to preclude state action that compromised national unity. In this sense, the old Court, as well as the new one, followed a long judicial tradition of safeguarding the Union from divisive state action.

To illustrate this continuity, we can look at two unanimous decisions of the Court, one in 1935 and the other in late 1941. In the first case the justices confronted a New York statute that prohibited the sale of milk bought outside the state for sale in the state at less than the stipulated minimum price. New York's argument that such control was necessary to protect the health and welfare of its citizens was rejected by the Court. In an opinion by Justice Cardozo, the Court recognized the plausibility in such an argument but said that its acceptance would "invite a speedy end of our national solidarity." The Constitution, Cardozo continued, "was framed on the theory that the peoples of the several states must sink or swim together, and that in the long run prosperity and salvation are in union and not division."[128] Reading the conferrence of power upon Congress as a constitutional mandate for the Court to safeguard the Union, the Court accepted its role both to repulse state incursions upon unity and to teach the civil religion. Believers are reminded again that they can be socially saved only through their continued commitment to national unity.

Six and a half years later only two members of that Court remained, as the justices confronted California's attempt to stem the influx of indigent persons by punishing citizens who brought such persons into the state. Fred Edwards had gone to Texas to bring his wife's brother, Frank Duncan, to California. Duncan was unemployed and eventually received assistance from the Farm Security Administration in the state. Edwards was prosecuted under the California law. A majority of the Court decided to resolve the case under the now far-reaching commerce clause, but it was not unmindful that the case involved not only Edwards but other indigent people as well. Although acknowledging California's attraction to migrants and "the problems of health, morals, and especially finance" that came in their wake, the Court said that the statute's whole purpose was to put an immediate and intentional burden on interstate commerce. This the state may not do, the majority continued, because such action violates the Constitution. Furthermore, any change in state policy is effectively precluded, for the people most affected "are deprived of the opportunity to exert political pressure upon the California legislature to obtain a change in policy." Summoning up the experience of the last ten years, the Court said that in an industrial society relief has ceased becoming strictly a local concern and instead "has become the common responsibility and concern of the whole nation." The matter the state has chosen to regulate, the majority continued, "does not admit of diverse treatment by the several States." Finally, dealing with an old precedent that seemingly acknowledged the right of a state to regulate the admission of paupers to save its citizens from "moral pestilence," the Court now insisted that "poverty and immorality are not synonymous."[129]

Although the majority expressed no judgment on the other constitutional claims the case presented, the four other justices protested the majority's reliance on the commerce clause. Justice William O. Douglas, in an opinion that Black and Murphy joined, insisted that the right of people to move freely within the nation is so fundamental that it must be addressed. Contending that our history establishes "that the right of free movement is a right of *national* citizenship," Douglas said to allow such state restrictions would "contravene every conception of national unity. It would also introduce a caste system utterly incompatible with the spirit of our system of government."[130] Such regulations, he continued, would stigmatize certain citizens as inferior, deny them freedom of opportunity, and seriously impair the equality promised all under our Constitution.

Jackson was even more disturbed, saying the majority's decision "is likely to result eventually in distorting the commercial law or in denaturing human rights." Instead he wanted to revive the privileges and immunities clause of the Fourteenth Amendment that had lain dormant since its reduction to a tautology in the *Slaughter-House Cases* in 1873. Surely, he said, if national citizenship means anything, it means the right to travel among the states and choose one's residence as one pleases. "We should say now, and in no uncertain terms," Jackson continued, "that a man's mere property status, without more, cannot be used by a state to test, qualify, or limit his rights as a citizen of the United States." To condition the mobility of our citizens on the basis of their property and thereby chain some to the locales of their misfortune "is not only at war with the habit and custom by which our country has expanded, but is also a short-sighted blow at the security of property itself." To make the possession of property "a pretext for unequal or exclusive civil rights," Jackson argued, is to invite a potentially devastating attack on property itself.[131] If indigent citizens are expected to defend their country, he concluded, certainly they must be free to migrate to any part of the country they are asked to defend.

All agreed that the California law could not stand under the Constitution, but the concurring justices believed that to subsume the precious rights involved in the case by treating human beings as commodities moving in interstate commerce evaded a prime responsibility of the Court—the protection of individual rights from invasion by government. The internal wrangling on the Court is significant for it focuses upon the importance of the rhetoric used to explain the decision. For the concurring justices, the majority reached the right decision but for the wrong reasons. The reasons were wrong because, although the majority accepted the priestly role of the Court, it had failed to educate the flock as to their responsibilities as equal citizens under the civil religion. Instead of censuring present citizens for attempting to deprive their brothers and sisters of the rights that they all hold, present citizens are told that such action is not permitted because a century and a half ago the Constitution had placed limits on the ability of states to regulate commerce. Such a rationale avoided the Court's educational function and, although it promoted unity, it did little to help define a society composed of equal citizens. To pass up the opportunity to insist upon the primacy of individual rights, no matter what the economic status of the individual, struck the concurring justices as no less than an abdication of the Court's responsibility to teach that differences in wealth matter no more in the civil religion than in many sectarian varieties.

Less than two weeks after the decision in the California case, the Japanese bombed Pearl Harbor and catapulted the United States into World War II. The war had begun in Europe over two years earlier, and from its onset the Roosevelt administration aided the Allies and prepared for war. The totalitarian and militaristic regimes of Germany, Italy, and Japan were seen as posing a threat to democracy itself. In August 1941 Great Britain and the United States agreed on a series of war aims that summoned up recollections of Wilson's Fourteen Points. What seemed clear was that the role of the United States in the world at the end of this second world war would change greatly.

Faced with serious challenges to their basic beliefs, Americans would have to inspect and contend with such threats during the war and into its aftermath. In this process, the Supreme Court, as expounder of the holy writ, would play a significant role, both priestly and prophetic.

SEARCHING FOR THE MEANING OF LOYALTY WITHIN THE AMERICAN CIVIL RELIGION, 1940–1959

The Japanese attack on Pearl Harbor and Germany's subsequent declaration of war involved the country in global hostilities. With a unity that Woodrow Wilson would have envied, the American people rallied to the cause of defeating the Axis powers. This national consensus, coupled with an administration intent upon distinguishing democracy from totalitarianism, tended to curb the violations of individual rights that had been so characteristic of the World War I period. In fact, as Adolf Hitler proclaimed the supremacy of Aryans, Americans seemed to revel in their polyglot ancestry and racial diversity, seeing only strength in a faith that theoretically embraced all.

That war creates strange bedfellows was illustrated by the alliance between the United States and the Soviet Union in the fight against Nazi aggression. Only in 1933 had the country established diplomatic relations with the Soviet Union, and the formal relationship did little to quiet a nagging fear of communism. During the depression, American communists actively sought recruits and had some success among intellectuals willing to consider alternatives to what appeared to be a failed capitalistic system. But when Joseph Stalin signed a nonaggression pact with Hitler in 1939, many of those American intellectuals who had been attracted to communism became disillusioned. When Hitler broke the pact in June 1941 and turned his forces against his former ally, the way was paved for the United States and the Soviet Union to join forces in fighting against a common foe.

This change in Soviet-American relations was reflected in the Supreme Court's decision in *Schneiderman v. United States*. William Schneiderman was a communist in 1927 when he was naturalized as a citizen; twelve years later a lower federal court stripped him of his citizenship on grounds that it had been "illegally procured."[1] The contention was that Schneiderman in the five years prior to his naturalization did not evidence a belief in the basic principles of the Constitution.

In writing for the majority Justice Frank Murphy defined American culture broadly.[2] Our judgment, he said, should be guided "by the spirit of freedom and tolerance in which our nation was founded, and by a desire to secure the blessings of liberty in thought and action to all those upon whom the right of American citizenship has been conferred by statute, as well as to the native born." He pictured American society as heterogeneous and in part composed of exiles from political and religious persecution. Such immigrants, Murphy said, have sought to become American citizens "in a free world in which men are privileged to think and act and speak according to their convictions, without fear of punishment or further exile so long as they keep the peace and obey the law."[3]

Pointing to the uniqueness of the government's challenge to Schneiderman's attachment to the Constitution a dozen years after citizenship was granted, Murphy said such a valued right should not be taken away "without the clearest sort of justification and proof." He added: "we certainly will not presume in construing the naturalization and denaturalization acts that Congress meant to circumscribe liberty of political thought by general phrases in those statutes." Then, exploring the meaning of "attachment" to the Constitution, Murphy concluded that it had reference to the behavior of the applicant. Using that standard, he found the conduct of Schneiderman "law abiding in all respects." The government's contention was that the applicant could not be attached to the Constitution because he advocated sweeping changes in the government it established and believed in the overthrow of government by force. The founding fathers, Murphy said, "did not forge a political strait-jacket for the generations to come." The provision for amendment of the Constitution and the First Amendment, he continued, "refute the idea that attachment to any particular provision or provisions is essential, or that one who advocates radical changes is necessarily not attached to the Constitution." Our task, the justice said, is "to uphold the right of free discussion and free thinking to which we as a people claim primary attachment." For judges to neglect this duty in a case scrutinizing one's "attachment to the Constitution would be ironical indeed."[4]

Citing "our tradition of freedom of thought," Murphy maintained that Congress could not have sought to restrict naturalization "to those whose political views coincide with those considered best by the founders in 1787 or by the majority in this country today." Although Schneiderman challenged prevailing views on private property, the justice asked if those who sought the elimination of slaves as property would be accused of not being attached to the principles of the Constitution. Asserting the primacy of the Bill of Rights in the constitutional order, he said that neither the Communist Party nor the petitioner clearly sought to abrogate such rights. Finding ambivalence in the political philosophy of the party and no advocacy of force to overthrow the government on Schneiderman's part, Murphy insisted that the government had not provided " 'clear, unequivocal, and convincing' evidence for setting aside a naturalization decree." Were such proof not required, he continued, "valuable rights would rest upon a slender reed, and the security of our naturalized citizens might depend in considerable degree upon the

political temper of majority thought and the stresses of the times." Such consequences he pronounced "foreign to the best traditions of this nation and the characteristics of our institutions."[5] These best traditions and characteristics were an
important part of the civil religious edifice that the Court was sworn to uphold.

William O. Douglas and Wiley Rutledge added to Murphy's words. Douglas
said that he would not imply that Congress had sanctioned a procedure whereby
a naturalized citizen could be divested of his citizenship because of political, social,
or economic beliefs. And when the controlling statutes can be read in more than
one way, he said, "we should choose the one which is the more hospitable to that
ideal for which American citizenship itself stands." A contrary decision, Rutledge
warned, would mean that "no naturalized person's citizenship is or can be secure."[6] He condemned a procedure whereby the decision of a competent court
that had granted citizenship could be reopened at some future time.

The majority justices were appalled by the government's attempt to purge the
American community of those whom its officials now deemed undesirable. Such
a fundamental threat to the inclusiveness of the American community, the majority
believed, demanded forceful words of rebuke. The Court majority had leaned
heavily in Schneiderman's direction, blessing an expansive conception of the
American community, if not the one that existed then the one that should be
formed. Although the majority may have blurred its message by arguing that communist ideology was not necessarily in conflict with the principles of the Constitution, at the core of the decision was the protection of the naturalized citizen.[7] To
allow the government to reopen the question of citizenship after such extended
time was deemed unconscionable. During a war in which the American people
were told they were defending individual liberty and representative government
against repression and totalitarianism, the decision was a healthy reminder of the
real differences in governmental systems. The basic difference rested upon a commitment to an institutionalized procedure in which the individual's claim would
receive a respectful and sympathetic hearing in a court of law.

When, a year later, a unanimous Court applied the *Schneiderman* precedent to a
naturalized citizen with Nazi sympathies, Frankfurter said that American citizenship brings with it "the right to criticize public men and measures—and that means
not only informed and responsible criticism but the freedom to speak foolishly and
without moderation." Now rejecting the narrower view of allegiance that he
voiced in dissent in *Schneiderman*, the justice embraced a definition with "a breadth
appropriate to the nature of the subject matter, being nothing less than the bonds
that tie Americans together in devotion of a common fealty."[8]

Three years after *Schneiderman*, the Court drew out the implications of its words
there and overturned its earlier decisions on the ineligibility of pacifists for naturalization. *Girouard v. United States* involved the petition for naturalization of a Canadian who was a Seventh Day Adventist and who had said he would refuse to serve

in the armed forces in a combatant role. Douglas, for the majority, now concluded that the earlier Court had erred. He said that those with religious objection to bearing arms have proven to be both loyal to the country and "unselfish participants" in the war effort. Noting that the applicant could, with his views, serve in Congress, Douglas said: "It is hard to believe that one need forsake his religious scruples to become a citizen but not to sit in the high councils of state."[9] Seeing the First Amendment as the legacy of a struggle to free religion from oppression by government, the justice stripped the required naturalization oath of the gloss that the Court had earlier placed upon it. And to the argument that Congress in making modifications to the naturalization law had left the oath untouched and thereby indicated its approval of the earlier judicial interpretation, Douglas said he would not impute the Court's earlier error to the people's representatives.

Less than two months after *Girouard*, however, the Court did rule, over the protest of Justices Rutledge and Murphy, that the government had carried the weighty burden of proof in a denaturalization proceeding. Paul Knauer had been a United States citizen for six years when the government moved against him. The majority found that the "ties with the German Reich were too intimate, the pattern of conduct too consistent, the overt acts too plain for us to conclude that Knauer was merely exercising his right of free speech either to spread tolerance in this country or to advocate changes here." Even the dissenters agreed that, if citizenship could be divested, a clear case had been made that the conduct shown here was incompatible with an oath of allegiance to the United States. However, Rutledge argued that Congress could not create an inferior class of citizens, saying that "any process which takes away their citizenship for causes or by procedures not applicable to native-born citizens places them in a separate and inferior class."[10] And to levy the harshest of penalties, deportation and exile, without the safeguards attendant upon a criminal trial, he continued, violated due process.

Congressional authority over naturalization, the dissenters said, did not encompass establishing a special category of citizenship vulnerable to subsequent attack. Such discrimination, they continued, was fraught with due process problems. Although the minority justices had little sympathy for Knauer himself, they saw him as a surrogate for "millions of naturalized citizens in their status and all that it implies of security and freedom."[11] To create different categories of citizenship was contrary not only to the Constitution but to the very core of the civil religious faith.

Frankfurter, himself a naturalized citizen, had strong feelings about what being an American meant, and he shared them with his colleagues. Acknowledging that his lack of traditional religious faith may well have caused him to endow American citizenship with a quasi-religious fervor, he said he knew hundreds of men and women who had willingly shed old loyalties to make themselves Americans. By believing in the United States and the principles enshrined in its constitutional order, they became Americans. Citizenship, Frankfurter said, "implies entering upon a fellowship which binds people together by devotion to certain feelings and ideas and ideals summarized as a requirement that they be attached to the principles of the Constitution."[12]

At the time when Frankfurter was describing the elements of his faith and urging his colleagues to decide against Schneiderman, the Court was reconsidering a decision that the justice had written three years earlier. At issue in that case was a Pennsylvania law mandating the pledge of allegiance in the state's schools. When the children of a Jehovah's Witness refused to participate, on grounds that their religion forbad them to pay homage to graven images, they were expelled from school.[13] The case came to the Court on a claim that their religious liberty had been infringed. Although conceding that "every possible leeway should be given to the claims of religious faith," Frankfurter said that "to affirm that the freedom to follow conscience has itself no limits in the life of a society would deny that very plurality of principles which, as a matter of history, underlies protection of religious toleration." One such limit, he continued, is that such scruples do not relieve "the individual from obedience to a general law not aimed at the promotion or restriction of religious beliefs."[14]

Viewing the law's purpose as promoting "national cohesion . . . [as] an interest inferior to none in the hierarchy of legal values," Frankfurter said that a free society is founded upon a unifying sentiment. Such a sentiment "is fostered by all those agencies of the mind and spirit which may serve to gather up the traditions of a people, transmit them from generation to generation, and thereby create that continuity of a treasured common life which constitutes a civilization." Asserting that a people lives by symbols, he said that "the flag is a symbol of our national unity, transcending all internal differences, however large, within the framework of the Constitution." The question for Frankfurter, then, was whether legislatures and school boards could develop "various means to evoke that unifying sentiment without which there can ultimately be no liberties, civil or religious." Instead of interfering with the "wisdom of training children in patriotic impulses by those compulsions which necessarily pervade so much of the educational process," the Court, he said, should leave the matter to the legislative process, which "serves to vindicate the self-confidence of a free people."[15]

Frankfurter's personal beliefs and public words highlighted the existence of a civil religion in the United States in which the flag was the preeminent sacred symbol. For his understanding of that symbol he cited words from an earlier Court decision, which included in part the following: "it signifies . . . liberty regulated by law; the protection of the weak against the strong; security against the exercise of arbitrary power."[16] Were such values being safeguarded by the Court's decision? The answer may well be no, and Frankfurter recognized this fact. In his infuriating way of distancing himself from the result he reached in the particular case, he acknowledged that perhaps "the deepest patriotism is best engendered by giving unfettered discretion to the most crotchety beliefs" and exempting members of a religious sect from compulsory civil devotion. He escaped the dilemma, if that is what it was, by deferring to the judgment of local authorities. Frankfurter believed the Court's role was to further the democratic process by empowering local government and hopefully educating its citizens, rather than impeding its operations. He sought to deny ethical responsibility by saying that the decision was not his to make. And despite the lip service he paid to individual diversity, the justice seemed comfortable with the view that schoolchildren could and should be indoctrinated in a civic faith that leads them to submerge their differences in "an attachment to the institutions of their country."[17]

By accommodating this attempt at coercive unity, Frankfurter had essentially ignored the individual rights at the core of the civil religion, but Justice Harlan Fiske Stone, in his lone dissent, brought the focus back to the religion's theological premises.[18] Calling the compulsory pledge law unique in Anglo-American history, the justice said that "the state seeks to coerce these children to express a sentiment which, as they interpret it, they do not entertain, and which violates their deepest religious convictions." There are other ways "to inspire patriotism and love of country" than to tread so heavily on the personal rights of its citizens. He recognized that, although state infringements on such rights are always justified "in the name of righteousness and the public good," they are almost always directed "at politically helpless minorities." The Constitution, Stone continued, "does not command such expressions or otherwise give any indication that compulsory expressions of loyalty play any such part in our scheme of government as to override the constitutional protection of freedom of speech and religion."[19]

To Frankfurter's admonition that the Court allow any correction to come through the legislative process, Stone responded that such an attitude surrendered "the liberty of small minorities to the popular will." While his colleague translated the Constitution as delegating to the democratic majority the authority to make policy, Stone interpreted it as "an expression of faith and a command that freedom of mind and spirit must be preserved, which government must obey, if it is to adhere to that justice and moderation without which no free government can exist." Where Frankfurter had seen conflict between a civil faith and a sectarian one, Stone saw the civil faith, as embodied in the Constitution, embracing the "freedom of the individual from compulsion as to what he shall think and what he shall say."[20] If there was conflict, Stone implied, it was because both the Pennsylvania legislature and his colleagues failed to understand and live by a key element of the American creed—respect for the individual's liberty.

This titanic battle over the essentials of the American civil religion and the Court's proper place within it was revived in 1943, when the justices agreed to hear a similar case, *West Virginia State Board of Education v. Barnette*. It was argued the day before *Schneiderman*, and a new majority, equally concerned with redefining the nature of the American community and its theological underpinnings, formed around Stone's earlier position. In the interim, two members of the former majority, Chief Justice Charles Evans Hughes and Justice James C. McReynolds, had left the Court. Stone had assumed the center seat, and Robert H. Jackson and Wiley B. Rutledge had ascended the High Bench. When three members of the old majority confessed their earlier error,[21] and when the new arrivals joined him, the new chief justice had a six to three count in his favor. Stone assigned the opinion to Jackson.

Perhaps to ease the abrupt reversal and to avoid carving out a religious exemption to valid civil law, Jackson grounded the opinion in the free speech clause of the First Amendment, made binding on the states through the Fourteenth Amendment. Piece by piece he undermined Frankfurter's rationale in the prior case. Saying that "history indicates a disappointing and disastrous end" for "officially disciplined uniformity," Jackson insisted that the preservation of individual rights does not weaken government. Nor, he said, does the striking down of the law interfere with the legitimate work of local school boards. The fact that "they are educating the young for citizenship is reason for scrupulous protection of Constitutional freedoms of the individual." Otherwise, the justice added, young minds are strangled at their source and students are implicitly taught that important constitutional principles are "mere platitudes." And to entrust the protection of individual rights to popular majorities, Jackson said, undermines the "very purpose of a Bill of Rights," which "was to withdraw certain subjects from the vicissitudes of political controversy, to place them beyond the reach of majorities and officials and to establish them as legal principles to be applied by the courts." Such fundamental rights "may not be submitted to vote; they depend upon the outcome of no elections."[22]

Jackson disputed Frankfurter's claim that the Court has no special competence to override such legislative decisions. He said that the recent tendencies of governments to expand their orbits of activity had deprived "precedents of reliability." We, Jackson continued, must exercise our own judgment, "not by authority of our competence but by the force of our commissions." History, he added, only validates the view that judges must protect individual liberty from aggressive governmental action. Then, tackling the rationale that the compulsory pledge promotes national unity, Jackson delved to the heart of the American experience. "Probably no deeper division of our people," he began, "could proceed from any provocation than from finding it necessary to choose what doctrine and whose program public educational officials shall compel youth to unite in embracing." Coercive attempts to end dissent, the justice warned, would exterminate dissenters and achieve "only the unanimity of the graveyard." The "First Amendment to our Constitution was designed to avoid these ends by avoiding these beginnings."[23]

"We apply the limitations of the Constitution," Jackson continued, "with no fear that freedom to be intellectually and spiritually diverse or even contrary will disintegrate the social organization." Then in words that capture well the crucial and transcendent position of individual rights in the American creed, the justice added

> If there is any fixed star in our constitutional constellation, it is that no official, high or petty, can prescribe what shall be orthodox in politics, nationalism, religion, or other matters of opinion or force citizens to confess by word or act of faith therein. If there are circumstances which permit an exception, they do not now occur to us.
>
> We think the action of the local authorities in compelling the flag salute and pledge transcends constitutional limitations on their power and invades the sphere of intellect and spirit which it is the purpose of the First Amendment of our Constitution to reserve from all official control.[24]

These eloquent words go far beyond the boundaries of the case and solidify the Court's commitment to the theological core of the civil religion.

What Jackson's opinion conveys so forcefully is that coercion is even more counterproductive to the civil religion than it is to sectarian religion. This is so because individual diversity is both respected and nurtured by the civil religion. As Justice Murphy added in his concurring opinion, "the real unity of America lies" in "preserving freedom of conscience to the full," relying only on persuasion and never on force or compulsion.[25]

Felix Frankfurter, who, as a Jew, acknowledged that he belonged "to the most vilified and persecuted minority in history," continued to urge judicial restraint upon his brethren. Although indicating sympathy for their view, he said he could not deny to government the power to promote "good citizenship and national allegiance." Coming back to the flag, Frankfurter argued that "it is not for this Court to make psychological judgments as to the effectiveness of a particular symbol in inculcating concededly indispensable feelings, particularly if the state happens to see fit to utilize the symbol that represents our heritage and our hopes."[26] Hiding behind the posture of judicial restraint appears to be Frankfurter's confession that the civil religion, as he defined it, was his personal religion as well. By privatizing the civil religion, the justice gave it the parochial characteristics of a sectarian faith. Rather than include, it tended to exclude, and instead of accommodating all private beliefs, it prescribed a catechism of its own. Although the justice said he believed that union and patriotism could flow from diversity, his words and rhetoric revealed a heart leading him in a different direction.[27]

Frankfurter's opinions in these flag-salute cases illustrate the dangers of transforming a public faith into a private one. In this form the civil religion becomes jealous, exclusive, and a rival of other sectarian faiths. As such, it loses all capacity to fulfill its essential function of unifying a people of widely differing private faiths in a single national community.

Fortunately, Frankfurter's attempt to privatize the civil religion was eventually repudiated by the Court. But the decision in the first flag-salute case had been inconsistent with the theology of the civil religion as both practiced and furthered by the Court over its long history. As Jackson made so clear in his eloquent opinion in the subsequent case, the Court has a unique role to play within the civil religion—a role that places effective limits on the inevitable tendency of the majority to seek conformity. The aim, of course, is to help preserve and nurture a society in which individuals with differing sectarian faiths still share fundamental beliefs, one of which is to allow individuals the room to search for their own personal salvation. The danger that the resulting diversity could fragment the society was there from the beginning, but that danger was best combatted by housing these personal differences within a constitutional system that gave to the civil theology a preeminent place in the rule of law. This rule of law recognized the dignity of individuals and mandated their toleration. The faithful were to be recognized not by the similarity of their personal beliefs but by their commitment to individual liberty and the diversity it spawned.

Although he took the position that the Constitution should be interpreted to promote federalism and the rule of the democratic majority and thus would have narrowed considerably the civil religious responsibilities of the Court, Frankfurter did not deny the priestly role of the High Bench. In fact, no justice spoke more plainly, directly, and eloquently of the sacred task with which he and his judicial colleagues were entrusted. For instance, in an opinion in another case, Frankfurter asserted that "the Founders knew that Law alone saves a society from being rent by internecine strife or ruled by mere brute power however disguised." In creating the judiciary, the justice added, these framers "set apart a body of men, who were to be the depositories of law, who by their disciplined training and character and by withdrawal from the usual temptations of private interest may reasonably be expected to be 'as free, impartial, and independent as the lot of humanity will admit.' " So committed were they to ensuring a rule of law, Frankfurter said, that the framers of the Constitution "endowed the judicial office with extraordinary safeguards and prestige." Then he continued: "The most prized liberties themselves presuppose an independent judiciary through which these liberties may be, as they often have been, vindicated." Such a judiciary, the justice insisted, was essential in a free and democratic society. "As the Nation's ultimate judicial tribunal," Frankfurter concluded, "this Court, beyond any organ of society, is the trustee of law and charged with the duty of securing obedience to it."[28]

Actually, the Court's reversal on the compulsory flag salute had been foreshadowed the previous month in *Murdock v. Pennsylvania* in which the justices overturned a decision they had made less than a year earlier. When the majority in

1942 ruled that local governments could demand a license fee from Jehovah's Witnesses selling religious books, Stone, Black, Douglas, and Murphy had vigorously dissented. Chief Justice Stone saw the exaction, "laid in small communities upon peripatetic religious propagandists," having the effect of suppressing "speech and press and religion despite constitutional guarantees."[29] In *Murdock*, one of the first cases heard by Wiley Rutledge, the new arrival joined the former dissenters to constitute a majority condemning such taxes as unconstitutional. Douglas, for the Court, took delight in overruling the earlier case and restoring "to their high, constitutional position the liberties of itinerant evangelists who disseminate their religious beliefs and the tenets of their faith through the distribution of literature."[30]

This new five-man block remained intact in a string of decisions upholding the claims of Witnesses that local regulations denied them their individual rights.[31] But that block was split when a five-to-four Court decided that state child labor laws could be applied to religious solicitation, a decision that led Murphy to protest. Recalling the religious persecution of the past, the justice argued that such religious minorities were "testing our devotion to the ideals and constitutional guarantees of religious freedom."[32] By using such a law to strike at a religious group, Murphy continued, the state has invaded a sacred right.

This willingness to defend the rights of individuals extended even to pulling the teeth of the Espionage Act of 1917, under which the Court earlier had so willingly approved the convictions coming before it. Elmer Hartzel had written a series of articles that he had mimeographed and sent to six hundred opinion leaders in the nation, including high-ranking military officers. In the pieces he condemned the American allies and Jews, cast aspersions on the patriotism of the president, and called for a union of all whites against the yellow races. Some of the copies were read by men eligible for the draft, and Hartzel was prosecuted for "willfully" seeking to obstruct the draft and to cause insubordination in the military. Murphy in announcing the judgment of the Court said that the government must prove both the specific intent to effectuate the harm contemplated by the statute and the existence of a clear and present danger that the writings would bring about that harm. The justice found no evidence of any such intent in the writings themselves, insisting that even reckless expression falls short of establishing the intent the prosecution must prove. Although acknowledging that the enemies of the country use propaganda to sow the seeds of disloyalty, Murphy ruled "that an American citizen has the right to discuss these matters either by temperate reasoning or by immoderate and vicious invective without running afoul of the Espionage Act of 1917."[33]

No longer could the administration rely upon the High Bench to rubber stamp such prosecutions. By the reversal of Hartzel's conviction, the Court said that not even total war would be allowed to put an end to a citizen's free speech. That such a decision was possible indicates just how far the justices had come since the decisions of 1919 and 1920.

Even a resident Japanese national found the Supreme Court hospitable to his claim for back wages and compensation for injuries suffered as a fisherman. The owners of the vessel sought to bar the suit on the basis that the plaintiff was an enemy alien barred from suing in American courts. Recognizing the severity of this old British common law rule, the justices said that such a policy "was clearly impossible for a country whose life blood came from an immigrant stream." "The doors of our courts," they concluded, "have not been shut to peaceable law-abiding aliens seeking to enforce rights growing out of legal occupations."[34]

The contest here was between private parties, but when the federal government moved against not only Japanese aliens but also Japanese American citizens, the justices were unwilling to presume their law-abiding character and insist upon their equal protection under the law. These people were concentrated in California, Oregon, and Washington and numbered more than one hundred and ten thousand, approximately two-thirds of whom were American citizens by birth. Rampant prejudice against Orientals dates back to the nineteenth century, and increasingly in the twentieth century this prejudice centered on the Japanese. Their clannishness and their resistance to the melting pot, along with their economic success, was resented by many white West Coast residents. When Japan launched the attack on Pearl Harbor, Californians found a national audience for their old prejudices. If Hawaii could be attacked, would not California be next? Was not the mainland especially vulnerable if even a portion of Japanese residents were willing to aid their ancestral homeland in its aggression? Spurred on by state politicians, including Attorney General Earl Warren, who would later come to preside over the Court as chief justice, the federal government, by order of the president, provided for the relocation of the entire Japanese and Japanese American population. Instead of seeking to determine loyalty on an individual basis, the whole ethnic group was pronounced suspect, ostensibly on the basis of military necessity. Some young Japanese escaped internment by enlisting in the military and serving admirably in the European theater, but the rest were relocated and confined in a number of interior camps.[35]

As cases were generated by individuals protesting the relocation and internment program, the Court faced the task of measuring the governmental action against the guarantees found in the Constitution. What possible justification could there be for submerging individual citizens and their rights into a racial group targeted for arbitrary treatment? Germans and Italians in the United States were allowed their liberty; why not the Japanese?

To the Court's discredit, the majority justices developed myopia and never fully confronted the enormous violation of civil liberties involved in this episode. The first case to come before the High Bench was *Hirabayashi v. United States* in 1943.

The Court restricted its consideration to the authority of the military commander of the area to order a curfew and avoided the matter of relocation. Gordon Hirabayashi, an American citizen and a student at the University of Washington, contended that his right to liberty under the due process clause of the Fifth Amendment had been violated.[36] Chief Justice Stone, for the Court, said that the war-making authority is placed in the political branches of the government and that "it is not for any court to sit in review of the wisdom of their action or substitute its judgment for theirs." Accepting the argument that the national defense required such action, the chief, after talking of the exclusiveness of the Japanese and their resistance to assimilation, suggested that many of them might still be attached to their native land. This Court, he continued, cannot pronounce as unfounded the military judgment that some of these Japanese, "whose number and strength could not be precisely and quickly ascertained," were not loyal to the United States. Acknowledging that distinctions based upon race "are by their very nature odious to a free people whose institutions are founded upon the doctrine of equality," Stone maintained that such distinctions could be made when they "are relevant to our national defense and . . . the successful prosecution of the war."[37]

Douglas, Murphy, and Rutledge, worried that the Court's deference to military authority might be read too broadly, added words of their own. Frank Murphy was most willing to contend with the larger issues involved in the case and their implications for the constitutional order. He argued that the individual guarantees of the Constitution were not suspended by war and that distinctions based on ancestry "are utterly inconsistent with our traditions and ideals . . . [and] at variance with the principles for which we are now waging war." Next, Murphy took issue with the majority's characterization of the Japanese as being resistant to assimilation, saying that such a conclusion would be an admission "that the great American experiment has failed." Then, equating the government's treatment of Japanese Americans to the Nazis' treatment of the Jews, he lamented the Court's unprecedented approval of such a massive assault upon personal liberty and the implicit creation of two classes of citizens. Although the justice acknowledged that the military situation on the West Coast in early 1942 might have justified the extraordinary treatment of Japanese American citizens, he said the validity of such treatment now was an entirely different question. Murphy concluded that the Court "has the inescapable duty of seeing that the mandates of the Constitution are obeyed," and he urged that the restrictions placed on Japanese Americans "be promptly removed and their freedom restored" as soon as possible.[38]

In the second case the Court considered, *Korematsu v. United States*, the majority again narrowed the issue, considering only the order excluding the Japanese from certain areas and ignoring their subsequent confinement in camps. Hugo Black, writing for the majority, acknowledged that racial classifications are suspect and must be closely scrutinized. But then he relied upon *Hirabayashi* and said that, although exclusion from one's home was more serious than a curfew, the threat to public safety from possible sabotage and espionage created an imminent danger that justified the action. Stating that war imposes hardships that may weigh more heavily on some than others, Black insisted that the "power to protect must be commensurate with the threatened danger."[39] To the argument that the Court must consider the constitutionality of the whole program, including the relocation to detention camps, the justice said that the provisions were separable and that the Court did not have to go any further in resolving the case.

Each of the dissenters, Murphy, Roberts, and Jackson, felt that the majority's evasion of the issues of Japanese detention and relocation was a violation of the High Bench's solemn responsibility. For instance, Roberts saw a clear violation of constitutional rights in punishing Korematsu for "not submitting to imprisonment in a concentration camp," solely because of his ancestry and without any inquiry into his loyalty to the country.[40]

Murphy was even more incensed as he accused the majority of falling "into the ugly abyss of racism." Seeing no " 'immediate, imminent, and impending' public danger" that could possibly justify such a total disregard of the Fifth Amendment's protections of individual liberty, the justice characterized the majority's decision as "one of the most sweeping and complete deprivations of constitutional rights in the history of the nation in the absence of martial law." He found "no reason, logic or experience" behind the assumption that all Japanese were potential saboteurs or spies. The claimed military necessity, Murphy concluded, was a facade behind which the Court imputed guilt to all members of a racial group. Suspicion of people of Japanese ancestry, the justice continued, is based on prejudice, "misinformation, half-truths and insinuations" that have "been discredited by independent studies made by experts." He charged the American government with adopting "one of the cruelest . . . rationales used by our enemies to destroy the dignity of the individual and to encourage and open the door to discriminatory actions against other minority groups in the passions of tomorrow." Finding no reason for the failure to treat the members of the group individually with full respect for their constitutional rights, Murphy condemned this "legalization of racism . . . [as] utterly revolting among a free people." He reminded his colleagues, government officials, and the American people that they are all "kin in some way by blood and culture to a foreign land. Yet they are primarily and necessarily a part of the new and distinct civilization of the United States." The Japanese, as all such persons, "must accordingly be treated at all times as the heirs of the American experiment and as entitled to all the rights and freedoms guaranteed by the Constitution."[41]

Jackson began by painting Fred Korematsu's situation in bold relief. Here was a law-abiding American citizen found guilty of a crime consisting "merely of being present in the state whereof he is a citizen, near the place where he was born, and where all his life he has lived." The nation's former chief law enforcement officer reminded his colleagues that "if any fundamental assumption underlies our system, it is that guilt is personal and not inheritable." Because Korematsu could not resign from his race, "a judicial construction of the due process clause that will sustain this order is a far more subtle blow to liberty than the promulgation of the order itself." In deferring to military judgment in such instances, Jackson continued, the Court does far more: it validates "racial discrimination in criminal procedure" and approves the compulsory transplanting of American citizens. Such principles, he warned, become cartridges in "a loaded weapon ready for the hand of any authority that can bring forward a plausible claim of an urgent need."[42]

The danger of embedding such principles in the constitutional order, Jackson said, has been illustrated in the Japanese relocation situation. In *Hirabayashi* the Court insisted that it was only upholding a curfew and nothing more; now in the instant case it relied on the earlier case to validate harsher and more indeterminate violations of individual liberty on the basis of the race. To defer to military judgment, Jackson continued, transforms the Court from an upholder of the Constitution into an instrument "of military policy." Conceding that the military power poses "an inherent threat to liberty" that the courts can do little to impede at the time, he believed that the justices must draw the line when they are "asked to execute a military expedient that has no place in law under the Constitution."[43]

On the same day the unanimous Court did free a Japanese American from an internment camp, but again the limited range of the decision pleased neither Roberts nor Murphy. Mitsuye Endo's loyalty was conceded by the government, and Justice Douglas, for the Court, refused to address any of the constitutional issues argued, simply holding that the War Relocation Authority, which had been established to operate the camps, had no power to detain a loyal citizen. In fact Douglas said that he would assume that detention in the camps was "justified." However, this justification, he continued, was based upon the need to protect against sabotage and espionage, not "community hostility to this group of American citizens." Murphy insisted that detention in the camps "is another example of the unconstitutional resort to racism inherent in the entire evacuation program." Roberts condemned the majority for avoiding the pressing constitutional issues in the case by "straining to conclude that Congress" did not intend that loyal citizens be confined in the camps.[44]

The day prior to the announcement of these final two decisions, the War Department announced its intention to free the majority of interned Japanese early in 1945, thus allowing them to return home and resume their full rights. Earl Warren, now the governor of California, and the governors of Oregon and Washington issued an appeal to their citizens to "maintain an attitude that will discourage friction and prevent civil disorder."[45]

How could a Court that seemed so sensitive to individual rights during the period of World War II have lent its support to such a wholesale violation of the rights of Japanese American citizens? Although the majority justices evaded confronting the full enormity of the detention and relocation program by narrowing the issues for decision, they could not escape charges of racism hurled from within the Court itself. They accepted the so-called military necessity of immediate removal of a racially identifiable and geographically concentrated body of American citizens without the normal due process requirement of individual hearings.

In this study we have been sensitive to the practical limits on the Court's power, indicating, for instance, that commanding the end of segregation in the 1890s or invalidating the draft in 1918 were decisions that a responsible Court could not make. But here, with the violation of constitutional rights so obvious, a decision against the constitutionality of the relocation scheme seems quite possible. The release of the confined Japanese Americans would hardly have damaged the ongoing war effort in 1944, and the Court had no reason to suspect that the administration would not comply with such an order. As the dissenters made clear, the majority justices were caught up in a form of racism that led them to submerge individuals in a stigmatized group. The evidence is spread upon the record: Japanese Americans are clannish; they do not assimilate; they maintain their own traditions and customs; and they maintain loyalties to their homeland that are appreciably different from other American citizens. To ask that they assume the burden of the war by being deprived of their property and their liberty in a way not demanded of other citizens was reprehensible.

Justice Murphy was right in pointing to the unprecedented nature of the Court's decisions in this area. Certainly other racial groups have been stigmatized, but by this time in the nation's history the justices were much more suspicious of racial discrimination. This huge backward step can only be attributed to a war in which the Japanese were portrayed in popular culture as being appreciably different from other peoples. Remember Hartzel contended that the United States was fighting the wrong war; the right one would see all Caucasians leagued against Orientals.

In terms of its role within the civil religion, the Court had been derelict in its duty, a conclusion reached by the dissenters. Prophetically, Jackson pointed to the loaded gun that the Court had placed in the hands of the government and the military by acquiescing in such a violation of the American creed. And Murphy sought to teach his colleagues and a people caught up in the emotions of war that the American experiment necessitated a respect for diversity free of the suspicion that the different were disloyal or a threat to national security. As the justice said, to accept the idea that ancestry precluded the full incorporation of individuals within the American community mocks the theological premises that lie at the very heart of the nation.

The suspicion of the dissenters that the Court majority had been hoodwinked by the government's plea of military necessity was eventually proved. For years those people who suffered in the camps followed a cultural tradition of keeping their feelings to themselves, but younger Japanese Americans sought redress and organized a movement that eventually led Congress in 1981 to appoint a committee to investigate the internment episode. In addition, television docudramas alerted a new generation of Americans to the shameful episode. The committee, after hearing 750 witnesses and reviewing a hoard of government documents, concluded that the excuse of military necessity was a sham and that internment was the result of "race prejudice, war hysteria, and a failure of political leadership." Also, the committee recommended that Congress pass legislation providing for compensation of $20,000 for each survivor of the camps, a suggestion that Congress enacted into law in 1988.[46]

Furthermore, the convictions of Japanese Americans sustained by the Supreme Court were all reversed in lower federal court proceedings by early 1988. All the defendants were still living, and they were able to reopen the cases by an ancient but seldom used device known as a writ of *coram nobis* (error before us). The writ can only be used after a final judgment by the courts and after individuals have served their sentences. The writ is granted only in cases where "manifest injustice" resulted from the concealment of facts by the prosecution. Government documents unearthed by the redress committee were supplemented with others that showed that during the trials the government had suppressed evidence. That evidence indicated that no sabotage or espionage had occurred and that the general military assessment was that no threat was posed to national security by the Japanese and the Japanese Americans living on the West Coast. The episode was finally closed forty-six years after it began, with the reversals of the convictions and the reparations act of 1988.[47]

Americans of Japanese ancestry in the continental United States had been confined during the war, but they made up about a third of the population in the Territory of Hawaii, where the entire population was placed under martial law. After the attack on Pearl Harbor the Hawaiian governor proclaimed martial law and suspended the writ of habeas corpus. The order was approved by the president, and the commanding general suspended normal court proceedings and set up military tribunals. Both defendants in the two cases the Court combined for decision were civilians, one a stockbroker charged with embezzling a client's funds and one a civilian shipfitter who got into a fight with some Marine guards. Tried and convicted by military tribunals, they challenged their convictions on statutory and constitutional grounds. Not until the war was over did the Supreme Court consider the legality of these proceedings, and then it anchored its decision on the grounds that the Hawaiian Organic Act of 1900 did not authorize the imposition of martial law.

Justice Black, for the majority, interpreted that act through the lens of the nation's Anglo-American heritage. The power of the military, he continued, is no greater in Hawaii than it would be in any of the states, and the people there are entitled to the same constitutional protections as all stateside Americans. "Courts and their procedural safeguards," the justice said, "are indispensable to our system of government. They were set up by our founders to protect the liberties they valued."[48]

Justices Stone and Murphy added words of their own. Stone simply asserted that the claim of military necessity must be scrutinized by the judiciary, and here, he continued, that scrutiny found no such necessity. Murphy addressed the constitutional issue, saying that "the unconstitutionality of the usurpation of the civil power by the military is so great in this instance as to warrant this Court's complete and outright repudiation of the action." The supremacy of civil over military power "is one of our great heritages," the justice said, as he insisted that the Court's duty was to maintain this heritage so "that it may be handed down untarnished to future generations." Murphy found no justification for the closing of the civil courts, which, he argued, could only be justified by an enemy invasion that deposed civil justice. Then, he added: "From time immemorial despots have used real or imagined threats to the public welfare as an excuse for needlessly abrogating human rights." To the argument that the civil process takes too much time, the justice responded that he and his colleagues "would be false to our trust if we allowed the time it takes to give effect to constitutional rights to be used as the very reason for taking away those rights." Finally, Murphy got to governmental claims of the doubtful loyalty of the heterogeneous population. Racism, he said, has no place either in our civilization or our Constitution, and its use as a rationale to deny basic individual rights results "in aggravating rather than solving the problems toward which it is directed. It renders impotent the ideal of the dignity of the human personality, destroying something that is noble in our way of life."[49]

Murphy's rhetoric was often an irritant to his colleagues, but he carried on a proud tradition of the Court, one that reemphasized the primary responsibility of the High Bench—the protection of the individual both from overreaching governmental action and from a tendency to submerge that individual within the stereotyped group. Those dangers would not lessen in the years ahead.

The two dissenters in the case, Harold H. Burton and Frankfurter, in an opinion written by the former warned "against the dangers of over-expansion of judicial control into the fields allotted by the Constitution to agencies of legislative and executive action."[50] Chiding the majority, they said their colleagues would not have decided as they did had the war still been raging, and if they had such temerity, they would have had a difficult time enforcing their decision.

Perhaps the dissenters were right, but to spread upon the public record a condonation of such an invasion of individual rights is precisely what made the Japanese

American cases so appalling. As made clear in *Ex parte Milligan* after the Civil War, peacetime gives the Court the opportunity to reassert the basic theology of the civil religion. To pass up that opportunity threatens future invasions of individual rights. If what has occurred cannot be immediately corrected, at the very least Court opinions can give pause to eager governmental and military officials contemplating future action. Putting the constitutional house in order is an important function of the Court, and justices have generally been aware of their responsibilities to the future in deciding the cases of the present.

Four years after these decisions, a somewhat chastened Court did decide a case under a California law that prohibited aliens ineligible for citizenship from owning agricultural land. Earlier the justices had upheld such laws against attack based either on the Fourteenth Amendment or a preexisting treaty with Japan.[51] The present case involved the purchase of land in the 1930s by a Japanese alien who deeded it to his minor son, an American citizen. California sought to obtain the land on the basis that the transfer to the son was an attempt to avoid the prohibition of the alien land law. A majority upheld the son's title, ruling that it could not be divested "because of his father's country of origin."[52]

Justices Black, Douglas, Murphy, and Rutledge would have preferred to rule the California law itself unconstitutional. In addition to finding such racial discrimination inconsistent with the Fourteenth Amendment, they also cited the United Nations Charter that called upon the signatory nations to promote "human rights and fundamental freedoms for all without distinction as to race, sex, language, or religion." Murphy, with whom Rutledge concurred, spread upon the record the history of California's persecution of the Japanese and condemned the land law as "a disheartening reminder . . . of the racial policy pursued by those forces of evil whose destruction recently necessitated a devastating war." Saying that most Americans, including Californians, rejected "racism and all of its implications," he warned that human liberty was imperiled if such statutes were not condemned under the equal protection clause.[53]

Murphy was inviting Americans to join with him in condemning racism in American society and in maintaining faith with the Fourteenth Amendment's codification of the civil religion's promise of equality. Racism was in league with the "forces of evil," and citizens, who had been willing to give their lives to triumph over such evil in war, should be equally committed to fighting for its eradication in times of peace. The United Nations charter with its commitment to human rights, Murphy added, only added emphasis to the nation's obligation to live up to its founding creed.

Late in the same term the additional vote needed to invalidate the California alien land law could not be found, but the Court did rule that a California statute forbidding the issuance of a commercial fishing license to a Japanese alien was a violation of the equal protection clause.[54] Earlier the High Bench had cited a treaty with Japan as the basis for a ruling against this type of discrimination.[55] Now in 1948 the justices confronted the constitutional issue: whether the federal ban on the naturalization of Japanese aliens allowed the state to impose such restrictions on the economic livelihood of such aliens. Torao Takahashi had been a commercial fisherman from 1915 to the time he was evacuated from the state in 1942. Upon his return he found a new law seeking to bar him from his life's work. The Court began by indicating its continuing commitment to a 1915 decision holding that the equal protection clause of the Fourteenth Amendment barred state and local governments from denying aliens the right to work for a living.[56] That amendment, the justices said, protected such aliens from states seeking to use discriminations written into the naturalization law to impose additional burdens upon aliens.

Murphy and Rutledge added words condemning the California law for codifying a racial antagonism that seeks to negate "all the ideals of the equal protection clause."[57] They were disturbed that the majority was willing to lend credence to California's claim rather than assert the incompatibility of such discrimination with both the Constitution and the American creed.

World War II also presented the Court with the first opportunity, since the early nineteenth century, to revisit the crime of treason. The two cases it considered arose from the same episode in which eight members of the German military had landed by submarine in the United States with the purpose of disrupting the war industries. They were caught and tried by a military tribunal, a proceeding that the Court approved under the war power.[58]

Two naturalized American citizens were also prosecuted for treason for aiding and abetting the Germans in their mission. In the first case the citizen met with two of the saboteurs and dined with them, actions that were testified to by two FBI agents. A narrow majority saw nothing in the meetings that gave aid and comfort to the enemy. By requiring the testimony of two witnesses to an overt act of treason, the Court said the constitutional provision was "framed by men who . . . were taught by experience and by history to fear abuse of the treason charge almost as much as they feared treason itself." The justices added that "the treason offense is not the only nor can it well serve as the principal legal weapon to vindicate our national cohesion and security."[59]

Two years later, the Court upheld the conviction in a second case in which the father of one of the saboteurs had housed his son, sought to get him a job in a defense plant, and helped him purchase a car. This time the justices found in these actions, which had been observed by FBI agents, what had been found lacking in the earlier case—a course of conduct "forwarding the saboteur in his mission." Murphy was the only dissenter, arguing that, because a father's aid to his son may spring from many nontreasonous motives, the aid here "cannot qualify as an overt act of treason."[60]

The rhetoric of the war in which the Allies said they were fighting for liberty and the dignity of the individual against the threat posed by the Nazis was not lost upon the justices. One theory that had earlier attracted many Americans—eugenics—was now subject to condemnation because of the Nazi persecution and extermination of the Jews. There had been no outcry when the Supreme Court in 1927 had upheld a state eugenics law providing for the compulsory sterilization of the mentally defective.[61] But in 1942 when the justices considered an Oklahoma law providing for the sterilization of certain habitual criminals, they found constitutional grounds for invalidating it. William O. Douglas, for the majority, now gave new respect and new life to an argument that had been rejected with disdain in the first case by relying on the equal protection clause of the Fourteenth Amendment. He said that the distinctions made in the law ran afoul of that constitutional protection. Then, the justice added that, since procreation "involves one of the basic rights of man," sterilization "may have subtle, far-reaching and devastating effects. In evil or reckless hands it can cause races or types which are inimical to the dominant group to wither and disappear."[62]

In two concurring opinions, Justices Stone and Jackson broadened the attack on the statute. Stone called "the wholesale condemnation of a class to such an invasion of personal liberty" a contradiction of the most fundamental notions of due process. And Jackson added: "There are limits to the extent to which a legislatively represented majority may conduct biological experiments at the expense of the dignity and personality and natural power of a minority."[63] Although the ruling here left the earlier decision untouched, the Court approached the matter with a sensitivity to the dignity of the human being missing in 1927.

That the law as interpreted by the Court had to be guided by a concept of human dignity, which lay at the core of the civil religion, was often made clear by the justices. In ruling that confessions obtained after repeated questioning by federal law enforcement officials must be excluded from the trial, the High Bench said: "A democratic society, in which respect for the dignity of all men is central, naturally guards against the misuse of the law enforcement process."[64] And when the Court tipped in favor of federal agents in their pursuit of crime, as it did in permitting the introduction of testimony intercepted through a device attached to the wall of an adjacent hotel room, a dissenting opinion could be expected. In this case, Murphy instructed his colleagues that "if men and women are to enjoy the full benefit of that privacy which the Fourth Amendment was designed to provide," the constitutional wording must be reinterpreted in the context of modern threats to that right. Reminding his colleagues that the nation was in the midst of a war to preserve democracy and liberty, he said that the Court "should not permit any of the essentials of freedom to lose vitality through legal interpretations that are restrictive and inadequate for the period in which we live."[65]

Murphy, along with Jackson, as former attorneys general, were forced to the sidelines when a dissenting trio again invoked the war to question the majority's resolution of a case. The four-man majority had decided that the Fifth Amendment's bar against self-incrimination did not preclude the federal government from using information that had been extracted from the defendant in a state proceeding. Black, joined by Douglas and Rutledge, said that "protections explicitly afforded the individual by the Bill of Rights represent a large part of the characteristics which distinguish free from totalitarian government."[66] Castigating the majority's reliance upon federalism as an excuse for the unprecedented decision, Black saw no such limiting language in the Fifth Amendment. He condemned the Court not only for violating its canon of broad construction in favor of individual rights but also for repudiating a fundamental principle of American law and the American civic faith—that the individual is not to be convicted on the basis of compelled self-incriminatory testimony.

President Franklin D. Roosevelt's reconstituted Court agreed on the legitimacy of governmental economic regulation but regularly divided in the area of individual liberties. For instance, when the question was whether a state could impose a registration requirement on a union leader coming into the state to speak, the High Bench split five to four against the regulation. Rutledge, for the majority, ruled that "the preferred place given in our scheme to the great, the indispensable democratic freedoms secured by the First Amendment . . . gives these liberties a sanctity and a sanction not permitting dubious intrusions." Any restrictions upon them, he continued, "must be justified by clear public interest, threatened not doubtfully or remotely, but by clear and present danger." Furthermore, he added, "the rights of free speech and a free press are not confined to any field of human interest."[67]

The Court continued to educate the public and governmental authorities about the meaning of free speech. When the postmaster general sought to deny favorable second-class mailing rates to *Esquire* on grounds that the privilege was available only to those magazines that were not immoral and served the public good, the Court condemned such censorship: "A requirement that literature or art conform to some norm prescribed by an official smacks of an ideology foreign to our system." Reminding the public that what some call "trash may have for others fleeting or even enduring values," the justices refused to unleash government officials to determine what material serves the public interest.[68] And when New York sought to punish sellers of crime magazines, the Court intervened and said of the free press guarantee: "The line between the informing and the entertaining is too elusive for the protection of that basic right. . . . Though we can see nothing of any possible value to society in these magazines, they are as much entitled to the protection of free speech as the best of literature."[69] Finally, Michigan's attempt to punish booksellers for selling material to adults that would tend to corrupt the morals of children also ran afoul of the Court. The justices said that such a general restriction of reading matter was an arbitrary curtailment of one of the individual liberties "indispensable . . . for the maintenance and progress of a free society.[70]

Obviously the protection of individual rights by the Court limited the ambit of state power, and in all these divided cases upholding the claimed right, the dissenters talked of the majority's insensitivity to the need to preserve a governmental structure that entrusted the states with substantial authority.

This deference to state authority attracted Justices Frankfurter, Roberts, and Jackson in the 1945 case of *Screws v. United States*. After law enforcement officers in Georgia arrested a black man and proceeded to beat him to death, federal prosecutors indicted the state officials under a Reconstruction statute that proscribed action, "under color of any law," that subjected "any inhabitant . . . to the deprivation of any rights, privileges, or immunities secured or protected by the Constitution and laws of the United States." Federal prosecutors acknowledged that this case represented the first attempt on the part of the government to prosecute defendants for a violation of the rights secured to individuals by the Fourteenth Amendment. Roberts, in the dissenting opinion, argued that "under color of any law" meant that the state law had to authorize such conduct, which it clearly did not do here. Second, he insisted that the interpretation of the law that the majority reached would displace state criminal law with federal authority, in contravention of the constitutional system. Furthermore, it would deny the defendants due process by forcing them to guess what the general language in the statute prohibited. The dissenting trio turned its back on the problems of racial injustice in the South, saying that the cure was not to be found in "an undue incursion of remote Federal authority into local duties with consequent debilitation of local responsibility."[71]

Justices Murphy and Rutledge voted to affirm the convictions, ridiculing the contention that the defendants did not know that they were violating a federally protected right of the person arrested by beating him to death. Murphy saw the black being deprived of life itself, a right afforded him as both a citizen and a human being. He was stripped, the justice continued, of "all the respect and dignity that is recognized and guaranteed by the Constitution." To resolve the case, Rutledge agreed to subscribe to the plurality opinion of Douglas, which sent the case back for retrial. The plurality agreed that the "under color of any law" requirement was met when the police officers arrested the black, for they acted under their lawful authority in making the arrest. But to save the statute from the vagueness that the dissenters saw as fatal, the plurality justices said the trial judge must charge the jury that the defendants can be convicted only if they acted willfully to deprive the arrestee of a federal right, "the right to be tried by a court rather than by ordeal."[72]

The case was difficult for the Court because it illustrated the failure of some states to safeguard the rights of certain members of minority groups. A majority of the justices were willing to find in the controlling statute a source of authority for remedying this problem. This fractured Court in 1945, by refusing to limit the "under color of any law" to statutes that were defective on their face and by refusing to be drawn into speculation on what impact such a decision would have on the federal system, took an important step in asserting national authority to remedy the problem.

Just nine years earlier, the Court had been telling the federal government that it could not take action that intruded upon the rightful domain of the states. But such decisions, as they pertained to economic regulation, were rejected beginning in 1937. The reconstituted Court was of one mind on the reach of federal governmental authority in the economic realm, but it proved to be a Court of many minds when other matters were involved. The lesson some justices drew from the court-packing crisis of 1937 was that just as the federal government was supreme in economic matters it was equally so in defining and protecting individual rights. Other justices seemed to feel that their earlier colleagues who had stood firm against the centralizing tendencies of the New Deal were sound in their attempt to protect the system of American federalism, which, they felt, tended to make government more responsive to the popular will. Their predecessors had erred only in their choice of the battlefield. As the issues in the post-1937 period increasingly pitted state authority to regulate against the claim of individual rights, some justices saw their primary role in protecting the federal system from further erosion.

The federal system was not an abstraction; it was a system to which some justices subscribed as the best embodiment of democracy, a reflection hopefully of the people's informed will. When in *Screws*, the dissenting trio was confronted with the claim that the state would not act to prosecute the lawbreakers, the justices said it should. It was not, to their minds, appropriate for the federal government to interfere. But such interference is the key to the role of the Court in both the constitutional system and the civil religion, for to permit such gross invasions of justice would make the Court itself a party to them.

To allow justice to hinge upon the determination of a majority in discrete cases as to whether due process had been afforded the individual especially disturbed Hugo Black, who saw such judgments as hopelessly subjective. For Black, the problem could be solved by reading the due process clause of the Fourteenth Amendment to bind the states to the individual protections specified in the Bill of Rights. By following this approach, what was then included in due process could be precisely determined. Black clearly outlined his position in *Adamson v. California* in 1947 and sought to buttress it in an extensive appendix designed to show that the framers of the amendment had sought deliberately the end he now was urging upon his brethren. Arguing that "the great design of a written Constitution" is frustrated when the Court substitutes "its own concepts of decency and fundamental justice for the language of the Bill of Rights," he said that liberty can be secure only "so long as a Bill of Rights like ours survives and its basic purposes are conscientiously interpreted, enforced and respected so as to afford continuous protection against old, as well as new, devices and practices which might thwart those purposes."[73] Although attracted to the idea of inserting definite content into the due process clause, Black was seeking to expand the protection of individual rights. Douglas agreed with him, and Murphy and Rutledge were willing to say that the due process clause meant at least that much.

Although Frankfurter was satisfied with the Court's decision that Adamson's rights had not been violated, he wrote a concurring opinion contending directly with Black's reading of Fourteenth Amendment history.[74] Of the forty-three members of the High Bench who had interpreted the Fourteenth Amendment, Frankfurter began, only one "eccentric exemption," the unnamed John Marshall Harlan, had ever lent support to Black's view. Justice Frankfurter argued that his colleague's "warped construction" would result in a denial of due process to individuals whose valid claims could not be fit into the first eight amendments to the Constitution and would deprive states of the opportunity to extend personal liberty beyond the Bill of Rights. Furthermore, Frankfurter saw nothing wrong with the Court exercising its considered judgment in reviewing all the circumstances of a conviction to determine whether "canons of decency and fairness which express the notions of justice" have been violated. The best check on the Court, Frankfurter contended, was "an alert deference to the judgment of the State court under review."[75]

Black would never win this battle, although, unlike Harlan, he would serve long enough to see the Court make most of the provisions of the Bill of Rights binding upon the states. Black was a civil religion fundamentalist: for him, the Court, as any priestly authority charged with the duty of interpreting the holy writ, had an obligation to respect the written text. And to Black this meant preferring the rights clearly delineated in that text to those that might be read into the general phrase "due process." The Fourteenth Amendment, he said, had filled a gap in the Constitution by making the listed guarantees found in the Bill of Rights now binding upon the states. The acceptance of Black's position in 1947 would have dramatically advanced the cause of individual rights, but his colleagues were wary, as fellow believers often are, of fundamentalists of their own faith.

In challenging Black, Frankfurter had relied upon a characterization of the Court that he derived from a critique of its work in the late nineteenth and early twentieth centuries. In this era the justices placed limits on governmental power to deal with social and economic matters. Frankfurter's role model, Oliver Wendell Holmes Jr., had railed against the use of the Constitution to interpose obstacles to matters that he believed properly belonged to legislative determination. When the Court went out of this business in 1937, Frankfurter, who came to the High Bench in 1939, deduced from this earlier experience a theory of judging that tended to

defer to the decisions of the legislative and executive departments. When his colleague Stone drew a new line that would focus the Court's attention on claims
that individual rights have been violated, Frankfurter resisted the development of
this double standard.[76]

The Court's role, he believed, was generally to educate the popular majority,
not frustrate it. To be fair, Frankfurter did embrace the Court's educative function,
often asserting what he called his personal view but refusing to enforce it upon
others, hoping that their view, in time, would coincide with his own. Although
this is a beneficial teaching approach and may have a positive effect in a one-on-
one situation, can it dent the resolve of determined majorities or governmental
officials? Does not acquiescence, no matter how explained, only reinforce such
views?

Despite Frankfurter's influence, the trend toward nationalizing the rights of
individuals had been established. It might be slowed, as it was in *Adamson*, but it
had a momentum that captured new members of the Court. It would have a much
more substantial history than would the few negative decisions that the Court
upheld as established precedent in *Adamson*.[77] In this process of nationalizing rights,
the Court was strengthening the bonds of the civil religion. If each individual was
possessed of rights recognized by all American governments, they were all dignified
participants in a changing and expanding American community.

That the Court was performing its task in nationalizing freedom and acknowledging its civil religious responsibilities is especially clear in a number of cases in
which the Court lectured lower courts on their duties. When the justices reversed
a contempt conviction of a newspaper editor and publisher for criticizing the local
courts, they said that otherwise "the constitutional limits of free expression in the
nation would vary with state lines." They added: "Free discussion of the problems
of society is a cardinal principle of Americanism." In a concurring opinion, Frankfurter added: "Judges should be foremost in their vigilance to protect the freedom
of others to rebuke and castigate the bench and in their refusal to be influenced by
unfair or misinformed censure."[78]

Such supervision of the work of the federal judiciary is part of the Supreme
Court's institutional responsibility. In reversing lower court decisions, the justices
took the opportunity to educate federal judges in regard to their role within the
civil religion. For instance, when a lower federal court dismissed a complaint,
thereby precluding a jury trial, the justices sternly reminded their erring brother
that "a right so fundamental and sacred to the citizen . . . should be jealously
guarded by the courts."[79] The High Bench's civil religious task was to protect the
sanctity of certain individual rights, which meant, as it did here, that lower court
decisions ignoring this responsibility had to be reversed and judges reminded of
their responsibilities in maintaining the faith.

The right to a jury trial was surely one of the most precious of individual rights and one of the most ancient lineage, but beyond the issue of racial exclusion the Court had said little about the composition of a jury. Then in 1946 the justices decided two cases in which that matter was directly addressed within the contours of both the civil religion and the society as a whole.

In *Thiel v. Southern Pacific Co.*, a plaintiff passenger seeking to obtain recovery from the railroad challenged the jury, arguing that the deliberate exclusion of all daily wage earners resulted in a jury with little sympathy for the problems of the working class. The justices said that the provision for a jury trial, in either criminal or civil matters, "contemplates an impartial jury drawn from a cross-section of the community." Although this requirement does not mean that "every jury must contain representatives of all the economic, social, religious, racial, political and geographical groups of the community, . . . it does mean that prospective jurors shall be selected by court officials without any systematic and intentional exclusion of any of these groups." To deny service to individuals because they are members of a group, the Court continued, "is to open the door to class distinctions and discriminations which are abhorrent to the democratic ideals of trial by jury." To the claim that the practice was designed to prevent hardship to the daily wage worker, the justices responded that such exclusion does "violence to the democratic nature of the jury system." Condoning discrimination against persons of "low economic and social status . . . would breathe life into any latent tendencies to establish the jury as the instrument of the . . . privileged."[80]

Later the same year the Court confronted the exclusion of women from participation in the jury system. Drawing upon their general supervisory power over the lower federal courts, the justices, reviewing a criminal prosecution for mail fraud, concluded "that the purposeful and systematic exclusion of women" from both the grand jury and trial jury panels necessitated the dismissal of the case. To the claim that the sex of the juror is of no significance, they responded that "the two sexes are not fungible; a community made up exclusively of one is different from a community composed of both. . . . To insulate the courtroom from either may not in a given case make an iota of difference. Yet a flavor, a distinct quality is lost if either sex is excluded." No showing of prejudice in the case was required, the Court continued, for the "evil lies in the admitted exclusion of an eligible class or group." Furthermore, the justices said, the "injury is not limited to the defendant—there is injury to the jury system, to the law as an institution, to the community at large, and to the democratic ideal reflected in the processes of our courts."[81]

In these two cases the Court was defining the community as inclusive, not only in terms of socioeconomic differences but those of gender as well. The jury was a microcosm of the community, and its inclusive character was necessary to afford individuals their rights under a rule of law. The federal courts were expected to conform to the high priests' interpretation of what the spirit of the civil religion commanded.

Although Frankfurter dissented in the jury exclusion cases, he did join his usual adversaries, Murphy and Rutledge, in protesting the Court's limiting the protection found in the Fourth Amendment's ban on unreasonable search and seizure. Although Frankfurter was hesitant to impose federal standards on state officials, he was ready to hold federal officials to high standards indeed. One such instance involved the question of whether a defendant had in fact consented to a search that revealed a cache of gas rationing coupons that the defendant was selling on the black market. The Court recognized that the purpose of the amendment was to protect the individual's privacy and to prevent the compulsory production of evidence that would be used against him. But it then ruled that the coupons were public and not private papers and that in opening the door to the business premises the defendant had consented to the search.

In a dissenting opinion that Murphy joined, Frankfurter saw importance in this "petty little case" in that it "put to the test respect for principles which the founders of this nation deemed essential for a free society." "History bears testimony," the justice continued, "that by such disregard are the rights of liberty extinguished, heedlessly at first, then stealthily, and brazenly in the end." No sympathy for the pursuit of the criminal should be allowed to hide the plain fact "that police excesses are inimical to freedom." Then, in conclusion, Frankfurter said: "In our democracy such enforcement presupposes a moral atmosphere and a reliance upon intelligence whereby the effective administration of justice can be achieved with due regard for those civilized standards . . . formulated in our Bill of Rights."[82]

Frankfurter demonstrated how an understanding of what the Fourth Amendment was designed originally to accomplish was frustrated by the majority's decision. As meaningful today as when it was added to the Constitution one hundred and fifty-five years ago, the amendment, he insisted, obligates the Court to protect the moral purpose for which it was designed—the protection of the individual. And, when in the following year, the majority again whittled away the protection Frankfurter saw in the amendment, he said that the Court's decision carried "implications which portend serious threats against the precious aspects of our traditional freedom." Seeing dangerous encroachments on the individual's privacy that the Fourth Amendment was designed to secure, he added: "Nothing less is involved than that which makes for an atmosphere of freedom as against a feeling of fear and repression for society as a whole."[83]

Again the picture of the society that Frankfurter presented is one in which individuals are protected from federal governmental officials invading their privacy. As he makes clear, one of the earliest worries of Americans was that government would trample upon their individual rights. Although Frankfurter was inclined to leave the definition of these rights to the states when local action was involved, he readily took the opportunity to provide an example for them in his interpretation of the rights individuals possessed under federal law.

Two years later, in *Wolf v. Colorado*, the Court was ready to make the Fourth Amendment applicable to the states. All the justices agreed that the protection against unreasonable searches and seizures was binding upon the states through the operation of the due process clause of the Fourteenth Amendment. That clause, Frankfurter said for the majority, acknowledges that a free society, by definition, advances "in its standards of what is deemed reasonable and right. Representing, as it does a living principle, due process is not confined within a permanent catalogue of what may at a given time be deemed the limits or the essentials of fundamental rights." Working from this premise, he then ruled that the "security of one's privacy against arbitrary intrusion by the police—which is at the core of the Fourth Amendment—is basic to a free society."[84] As such, it protects the individual against contrary state action. Then, however, Frankfurter distinguished the right to be free from such searches from the remedy of excluding the improperly seized evidence from trial. Exclusion, he said, is a federal remedy that the due process clause does not impose upon the states.

The dissenters argued that by failing to exclude illegally seized evidence the Court, in fact, confers a meaningless right and permits "what is indeed shabby business: lawlessness by officers of the law." After contrasting experience in states excluding such evidence with those that did not, they insisted "that this is an area in which judicial action has positive effect upon the breach of law; and that without judicial action, there are simply no effective sanctions presently available."[85]

The implication in *Wolf* is that exclusion of such tainted evidence is a remedy designed to deter the police from engaging in illegal practices and that other means might accomplish the same result. But the Court's prior reading of the Fourth Amendment reveals little support for the deterrence theory and much support for the view that exclusion is an integral part of the right to be free from unreasonable searches and seizures.[86] The Court's reading of the privacy protected by the amendment often relates to its desire to save individuals from being forced to divulge evidence that would lead to their own convictions. From the beginning of the High Bench's interpretation of the Fourth Amendment, the relation between it and the Fifth Amendment's privilege against self-incrimination was clearly recognized. To now say that the states must respect the individual's privacy as protected by the Fourth Amendment but then permit the admission of the evidence illegally seized is to deprive individuals of any meaningful protection of their right. A dozen years would pass before the Court majority came to the conclusion that a right without an effective remedy was no right at all.

If the Court concluded that the Fourth Amendment was now applicable to the states, was it ready to overturn *Palko* and make the protection against double jeopardy binding upon the states? No, the justices said in 1952, with only Douglas dissenting.[87] What made the dissent significant was its attack on the majority's assumption that it had a responsibility to maintain the federal structure of the Union and preserve the authority of the states.

No wording in the Preamble to the Constitution lent support to this assumed duty. Although the Tenth Amendment had been interpreted in the pre-1937 period to impose limits on federal governmental power or to create gaps in which neither state nor federal power could be exercised, the shift in the Court's decision making in 1937 ensured that the Constitution would not be interpreted to place certain matters beyond governmental control. One of the ideas that survived "the switch in time that saved nine," however, was the one that defined the Court's role, in part, as an arbitrator between state and federal power.

Under this theory, the High Bench was the honest broker of the constitutional system. Although the conditions of a modern mass society had aggrandized national power, the Court, in line with this theory, had a fundamental responsibility to protect democratic government in the states. This meant, in practice, that room should be given the states to experiment with different policies in response to the wishes of the democratic majority. Although the great majority of cases the Court was hearing and would hear in the future dealt with alleged state violations of constitutional rights, the majority justices, as late as 1948, generally agreed that the Constitution "sought to keep the control over individual rights close to the people through their states."[88] Of course, such a position assumed that the democratic people would be sensitive to the need to safeguard individual rights, a conclusion that was belied by the raft of cases on the Court's agenda claiming state infringement of such rights. Both Justices Felix Frankfurter and John Marshall Harlan, a new arrival in 1955 and the grandson of the earlier justice bearing the name, were strong exponents of the view that the justices should practice self-restraint and generally defer to the judgment of the people's representatives.

Justice Black, in his dissent in the second double jeopardy case, *Bartkus v. Illinois*, met this rival view of the Court's role head on. The Court had decided that a verdict of not guilty in a federal court did not preclude the retrial of the defendant for the same offense in a state court. As was his style, Black trotted out examples going back to the Greeks and Romans to establish the proposition that subjecting a person to a second trial for the same offense has been universally condemned. For the Court to acknowledge this fact but then nullify its significance on grounds of federalism, Black lamented, "is a misuse and desecration of the concept." Saying that the Court's decision obliterates "ancient safeguards," which provide "the bulwarks on which both freedom and justice depend," he derided a ruling that held "that individual rights deemed essential by both State and Nation were to be lost through the combined operations of both governments."[89]

We have seen how the early justices rejected the role of mediator or arbitrator between the states and the federal government in favor of a strongly nationalistic position, often finding their guide in the Preamble to the Constitution. They believed that the Court was empowered to aid the government that was established in achieving the described goals of union, justice, and liberty. Black, almost one hundred and seventy years later, was intent upon reminding both his colleagues and the public that the Court's priestly mission was to read the holy writ in light of its fundamental purpose of guaranteeing meaningful justice and liberty to the faithful.

The double jeopardy provision, unlike the protection against unreasonable search and seizure, did not leave the Court with an escape hatch. The right against double jeopardy and the remedy of invalidating the result of the second trial were so fused together that they could not be separated, and for ten years more the Court would resist making the protection of this individual right binding upon the states.[90]

Not so, however, with the First Amendment's ban on laws respecting an establishment of religion, which the justices in the 1940s proclaimed bound the states as well as the federal government. Drawing upon the fight for religious freedom in late-eighteenth-century Virginia and the words and actions of Thomas Jefferson and James Madison, all members of the Court agreed that the purpose of the establishment clause was to separate sectarian religion from government.[91] They disagreed, however, on whether the practice before them violated this principle. Citing Jefferson, Black, for the majority, described the constitutional barrier as follows: "The First Amendment has erected a wall between church and state. That wall must be kept high and impregnable. We could not approve the slightest breach."[92]

With its free exercise counterpart, the prohibition on establishment, Black said, was designed to ensure religious freedom by requiring "that no state could establish a church or aid religion or prefer one religion over another; that no government can force an individual "to profess a belief or disbelief in any religion"; that no tax can be levied to support "any religious activities or institutions"; and that neither government nor religion can participate in each other's affairs. Was, then, a New Jersey law that sought to reimburse parents for the cost of transporting their children to Catholic parochial schools unconstitutional? Surprisingly, Black said that such reimbursement of costs did not aid religion any more than did ordinary police and fire protection. "State power," he continued, "is no more to be used so as to handicap religions than it is to favor them."[93]

Justice Jackson, in dissent, was puzzled by a decision that seemed to violate the very premises upon which it had been constructed. Noting that the Court had strained to accommodate religious proselytizing in earlier decisions, he said: "Religious teaching cannot be a private affair when the state seeks to impose regulations which infringe on it indirectly, and a public affair when it comes to taxing citizens of one faith to aid another, or those of no faith to aid all."[94]

Rutledge, in an opinion that the three other dissenters joined, read the establishment clause as outlawing "all use of public funds for religious purposes." Otherwise, "the constitutional prohibition always could be brought to naught by adding a modicum of the secular." Insisting that the First Amendment's protection of free exercise and its ban on establishment were designed to make religion a wholly private matter, Rutledge believed that the majority's decision opened a door to religious conflict that the First Amendment was designed to seal tight. Implicitly summoning up one of the core elements of the theology of the civil religion, he said that "we have staked the very existence of our country on the faith that complete separation between the state and religion is best for the state and best for religion."[95]

Although all the justices subscribed to the principle that in the American constitutional order the spheres of sectarian religion and government were to be separated, they differed on the room this left for accommodation. The dissenters were worried that such a decision invited sectarian religious contests for governmental favor that would threaten unity.

In a very real sense, the Court was protecting the civil religion against the threat posed by sectarian religion. The American civil religion was based upon the existence of competing private faiths and was designed to fill a void by constructing a public faith to which those of varying beliefs could subscribe. Sectarian religions vying for governmental favor had a potential for undermining the unity of the American people and their built-in tolerance for competing private faiths. The demand of sectarians for public recognition has been ever present in the country's religious and political history, but the Court, even when it has accommodated such private faiths, has been ever mindful of the potential threat posed to the unity of the society.

No member of the Court wished to strike down a wall of separation, for the potential costs were too great. The question the Court began to wrestle with in 1947 is how much can government accommodate free religious choice without unleashing the forces of turmoil that the religion clauses in the First Amendment were designed to hold in check. From the dissenters' perspective, accommodation invites further accommodation, and the best guarantee for the future was to make no inroad on the First Amendment barrier. The majority, however, believed that accommodation could be made without opening Pandora's box.

In the next term, the Court confronted the action of an Illinois board of education that provided that thirty minutes of the school week be set apart for religious instruction provided by teachers selected by various religious groups. Those students who chose not to participate were required to remain in school and pursue their secular studies. Only Justice Stanley F. Reed voted to accommodate this not uncommon practice of "released time" within the Constitution as a "friendly gesture between church and state . . . embedded in our society by many years of experience."[96] Jackson worried about the precedent of the Court becoming a supreme school board and about the impracticality of attempting to purge all traces of religion from public education.

While Reed would have accommodated "released time" because it was in accord with the wishes of the people, Frankfurter, writing for the Court, said that history demonstrated the wisdom of separating religion and government. He continued: "Zealous watchfulness against the fusion of secular and religious activities by Government itself, through any of its instruments but especially through its educational agencies was the democratic response to the particular needs of a young and growing nation, unique in the composition of its people." Viewing "the public school as a symbol of our secular unity" and our democracy, the justice said divisiveness must be kept out of public education, for such schools provide "the most pervasive means for promoting our common destiny."[97]

Frankfurter saw a conflict between the civil religion and its sectarian counterparts. Indeed, the field of public education, as it had evolved, was a battleground in which so-called secular forces had to contend with those of sectarianism. The demarcation of the separate spheres of religion and government, one private and the other public, has always been untidy but no less necessary in a nation that from its beginning was composed of such diverse people.

In this first "released time" case, the Court invited further litigation by suggesting that other arrangements for religious instruction that did not so pervade the public education process might survive constitutional scrutiny. By the time such a case reached the High Bench, Murphy and Rutledge, strong believers in separating the two spheres, were gone. Over the protest of Black, Jackson, and Frankfurter, who saw no constitutional difference in the two cases, the Court accommodated a "released time" practice in *Zorach v. Clauson*. The case involved a program in the New York City schools in which the students who so desired were released to attend religious instruction off school grounds; the others remained in school. The religious organizations provided an attendance list to school authorities.

Defining Americans as "a religious people whose institutions presuppose a Supreme Being," Douglas, for the majority, said that the Constitution does not prefer "those who believe in no religion over those who do believe." To prevent governmental institutions from making "adjustments of their schedules to accommodate the religious needs of the people," he said, would read the Bill of Rights as hostile to religion.[98] And this he would not do.

Justice Black, who so often agreed with Douglas, was incensed that his colleague and the majority had abandoned the view that the First Amendment commanded government to be neutral toward religion. "The abandonment," he continued, "is all the more dangerous to liberty because of the Court's legal exaltation of the orthodox and its derogation of unbelievers." By denying equal justice to both believer and nonbeliever, Black argued, the Court invites "repression . . . great or small, by the heavy hand of government." Regarding the other side of the wall of separation, the justice said that governmental aid "to religion injects political and party prejudices into a holy field." Then, he concluded: "Government should not be allowed, under the soft euphemism of 'co-operation,' to steal into the sacred area of religious choice."[99]

What Black makes clear is that a tenet of the civil religion—equal justice under law—is compromised when a sectarian religious accommodation is made. To prefer religious belief to nonreligious belief places the Court, as the high priest of the civil religion, in a compromised position. The accommodation may seem innocuous, but its implications are substantial.

In the facts of the case Frankfurter saw what the majority denied—pressure placed upon the nonbeliever. If the proponents of the "released time" movement, he said, fought for the release of all students from school during a portion of the school day, there would be no constitutional problem. Their failure to do so, the justice continued, "betrays a surprising want of confidence in the inherent power of the various faiths to draw children to outside sectarian classes—an attitude that hardly reflects the faith of the greatest religious spirits."[100]

Jackson saw no essential difference in the "governmental constraint in support of religion" in the two cases. Contending with Douglas's suggestion that only the nonbeliever could find the accommodation offensive, Jackson, who acknowledged that his own children have attended Roman Catholic schools, said that his "evangelistic brethren confuse an objection to compulsion with an objection to religion." The justice reminded his colleagues that when "this country ceases to be free for irreligion it will cease to be free for religion—except for the sect that can win political power." For the Court to allow New York City authorities to recognize " 'duly constituted religious bodies' as exclusive alternatives for compulsory secular instruction" mixes "compulsory public education with compulsory godliness."[101]

Justice Jackson highlighted the problems involved when the Court attempts to accommodate sectarian religion within the constitutional order. Such accommodation inevitably divides the civil religious faithful and sidetracks the Court from its primary role of promoting unity and inclusion by respecting the individual rights of all. Any accommodation tends to draw boundaries that exclude some. Legislatures in making policy decisions do this all the time, but for a Court to respond to a constitutional claim by validating the discriminatory action of government is to compromise the neutrality essential to the civil religion.

Countering, the other side stresses the fact that the free exercise of religion is one of the most important of individual rights that the Court has an obligation to safeguard. To demand rigid separation between government and religion is to ignore the positive role, especially of the national government, in protecting individual rights. If a state wants to promote such freedom by accommodating sectarian religion, then does the Court, under its primary duty of protecting individual rights, not have the obligation to condone the accommodation? The answer goes back to the rationale for separating sectarian religion from government—to remove the potential divisiveness that a contest for governmental favor inevitably invites. To accommodate the religious beliefs of the many necessarily imposes some compulsion upon others. As Douglas realized later, relatively innocent accommodations connote agreement and a form of preference that lead to division within the society. To protect individual rights empowers the individual and protects that individual from the compulsive power of the majority. Unity in the nation comes from mutual respect, not such compulsion.

The issue of religion was also presented to the Court in a case involving the censorship of motion pictures. New York had authorized the censorship of movies that were judged to be "sacrilegious." First, the justices had to reverse a 1915 precedent that had written off motion pictures solely as entertainment with no claim to protection as free speech.[102] Now, they saw movies as "a significant medium for the communication of ideas . . . ranging from direct espousal of a political or social doctrine to the subtle shaping of thought which characterizes all artistic expression." As such, motion pictures clearly were protected by the First and Fourteenth Amendments. Although conceding that a state might be able to censor obscenity, the Court ruled "that the state has no legitimate interest in protecting any or all religions from views distasteful to them. . . . It is not the business of government to suppress real or imagined attacks upon a particular religious doctrine, whether they appear in publications, speeches, or motion pictures."[103]

So, the unanimous High Bench concluded that the state possessed no power to protect the religious sensibilities of its people. To find otherwise, the Court said, might run afoul of the religion clauses of the First Amendment. If the state does seek to protect certain religious believers from offense, it places the force of the state behind such belief to the detriment of the beliefs of other citizens. To permit such action would encourage a contest for government favor, divide the citizens, and threaten the unity found within the civil religion.

If sacrilege was a word that conveyed no clarity of standards for judgment, was obscenity, which the Court opinion sought to distinguish, any different? In 1957 the High Bench confronted this issue in *Roth v. United States*, which combined both a federal and state case for decision.[104] The majority dealt with the free expression problem by reading obscenity as a special category of speech not protected by the First and Fourteenth Amendments. This was so because it was "utterly without redeeming social importance." So, the Court proceeded on the assumption that protected speech had to have some social value, a position that inherently weakened the individual right. Still, this threshold decision left the Court with the task of separating such nonprotected speech from that which was clearly embraced by the First Amendment. Recognizing that discussion about sex and obscenity "are not synonymous" and that the effect of such speech on the most susceptible per-

sons could not be the proper standard, the majority agreed on the following definition: "whether to the average person, applying community standards, the
dominant theme of the material taken as a whole appeals to the prurient interest."[105] The Court then upheld both the state and federal laws.

Justice Douglas, joined by Black, castigated his colleagues for "giving the censor
free range over a vast domain," by allowing the censorship of thoughts not shown
"to be a part of unlawful action." The Court's precedents, he continued, have
established "that speech to be punishable must have some relation to action which
could be penalized by the government." To burden literary freedom by demanding
that it not encourage impure thought nor offend the community, Douglas added,
is a violation of the First Amendment. He urged his colleagues to have as much
faith in the individual's ability to "reject noxious literature as . . . in their capacity
to sort out the true from the false in theology, economics, politics, or any other
field."[106]

In this case of first impression, the Court limited the range of the right of free
expression and in sexual matters made it dependent upon the tolerance of the
community. This was strange First Amendment law, for to empower the community to judge the desirability of such material was to place a fundamental personal
right in jeopardy. The majority sidestepped the clear and present danger test by
claiming that obscenity was a form of expression that was not included within the
First Amendment.

The Court, however, could not avoid a variety of other free speech claims. At
times it was especially receptive to such claims, even to the extent of finding an
escape from the recently developed "fighting words" doctrine. The majority said
it did not have to consider its applicability in a Chicago case because the trial judge
had erred in instructing the jury that a conviction would be justified if the speech
"stirs the public to anger, invites dispute, brings about a condition of unrest, or
creates a disturbance." Justice Douglas, for the majority, said that the "vitality of
civil and political institutions in our society depends on free discussion." Free
speech, he continued, may "best serve its high purpose when it induces dissatisfaction . . . or even stirs people to anger." To define the right any more narrowly
"would lead to standardization of ideas either by legislatures, courts, or dominant
political or community groups."[107]

Attempts by local governmental officials to narrow the American community
by censoring public speech were often repulsed by the High Bench. The fact that
one Baptist minister had publicly denounced Roman Catholicism as "a religion of
the devil" and called Jews "Christ-killers,"[108] the Court said, did not justify denying him a permit to speak. At other times, however, the High Bench seemed
especially insensitive, such as when the majority approved the breach-of-peace
conviction of a student who called upon blacks to rise up and fight for their rights.
Black, in a dissenting jeremiad, castigated the majority for its refusal to inspect the

evidence, as it had done regularly in the past to ensure the protection of individual rights. The "partial abandonment of this rule," he said, "marks a dark day for civil liberties in our Nation." Even more has been lost, Black continued, for the Court has made "a mockery of the free speech guarantees of the First and Fourteenth Amendments" by taking "a long step toward totalitarian authority" in subjecting all speeches "to the supervision and censorship of the local police."[109]

That the Court could tip either way with the movement of a single justice was made clear in *Beauharnais v. Illinois*, which upheld the defendant's conviction under a state law punishing any exhibition or publication that "exposes the citizens of any race, color, creed or religion to contempt, derision or obloquy." Joseph Beauharnais, a white supremacist, had distributed material that vilified blacks as criminals. The majority simply ruled that just as traditional libel was not "within the area of constitutionally protected speech," neither was the Illinois variant.[110]

All four of the dissenters aired their views. Justice Reed condemned the statute for its "vague and undefined words." Douglas argued that the First Amendment codified our ancestors' choice to prefer even an abuse of liberty over any restriction on free speech. Seeing such laws reflecting "an influence moving ever deeper in our society," he castigated the majority for a decision that was "at war with the First Amendment—a constitutional interpretation which puts free speech under the legislative thumb."[111] The majority, he insisted, has clearly disregarded the individual rights that must take precedence over such naked governmental power.

Black was horrified that the Court had ignored the First Amendment problem in the statute, thereby giving the state license to experiment with the individual's liberties. He rejected "the holding that either state or nation can punish people for having their say in matters of public concern." "Whatever the danger, if any, in such public discussions," the justice continued, "it is a danger the Founders deemed outweighed by the danger incident to the stifling of thought and speech." Accusing the majority of violating this basic tenet of the civil religion by finding room for state censorship of certain views, he cautioned those minority groups that might be inclined to applaud the decision by calling to their attention "the possible relevancy of this ancient remark: 'Another such victory and I am undone.' "[112]

When the Court accommodates government power that compromises individual rights, Black was suggesting, it unleashes the unbridled discretion of the wielders of that power. Today's victory, then, can easily become tomorrow's defeat. To approve bartering away rights to protect sensibilities was, for this justice, a very poor bargain indeed. Just as the freedom of the nonbeliever must be protected to ensure the freedom of the believer, the purveyor of hateful speech must be protected to ensure free expression for all. Black could understand the misguided approbation of such a law by members of the affected minority, but his colleagues, he felt, should know better. They had lost touch with the very faith they were sworn to uphold and with their special responsibility within the civil religion that they were commissioned to serve.

This 1952 case summons up contemporary concerns, as groups in American society today seek to advance their agendas by seeking to stifle speech that offends the sensibilities of their members. To condone such legislative initiatives, however, is to threaten the unity of American society. When equal rights are compromised, the differences that draw Americans apart are emphasized. Fortunately, the Court was wise enough in the ensuing years not to build upon this group libel precedent any more than it had built upon the earlier doctrine of "fighting words." In both instances the potential for censorship that limits respect for the individual and makes inroads on the open society was great.

Although the Court never limited the applicability of the First Amendment to political speech—oral and written communication advocating different social and economic policies and even governments—clearly such speech was closest to the core of the amendment. In the late 1940s and 1950s the High Bench had to deal with a raft of legislation seeking to forestall communist subversion. The postwar period had not ushered in an extended era of peace but rather one of suspicion. Such suspicion led externally to the Cold War with the Soviet Union and internally to the attempt to cleanse American society of communists and fellow travelers. This was a time of loyalty checks, new test oaths, blacklists, and congressional witch-hunts. This second "red scare" in American history reverberated in the High Court, which was called upon to evaluate claims that in this campaign the fundamental rights of the individual were being violated.[113]

In 1945, before this new red scare would take hold, the Court did recoil from the federal government's attempt to deport an Australian, Harry Bridges, a prominent labor leader who had emigrated to the United States in 1920. When the government first tried to deport him in 1938 the controlling statute required that the person be a present member of, or be affiliated with, an organization seeking the overthrow of the government. When the attempt failed because present membership or affiliation could not be shown, the statute was amended to cover membership or affiliation at the time of entry or any time thereafter. Under this amendment, Bridges was ordered to be deported. The Court concluded that the literature published by him showed him to be "a militant advocate of the cause of trade unionism," but not a teacher or advocator of "the subversive conduct condemned by the statute."[114] The majority justices avoided passing on the constitutional issue of free speech. Instead, they decided that Bridges could not be deported because he had not had a fair hearing on the issue of membership and that the facts had not established his affiliation with the Communist Party.

Detailing the government's persecution of Bridges, Justice Murphy said that when one of the Constitution's "subjects is being excommunicated from this nation without the slightest proof that his presence constitutes a clear and present danger to the public welfare," the holy writ must be read to chastise such sinners. Condemning the government for its flagrant violation of Bridges's constitutional rights, the justice rejected the notion that the federal government had full author- ity, untouched by the Bill of Rights, to deport whomever it chose. Such a conten- tion he labeled "obnoxious and intolerable when viewed in the light of the supernal heritage and ideals of the nation." To make "constitutional safeguards transitory and discriminatory in nature," Murphy added, "would make "an empty mockery of human freedom."[115] To him, the deportation statute was invalid be- cause it found personal guilt in association and because there was no clear and present danger.

Murphy stood alone in challenging the government's authority to deport aliens, and the pattern established in this early case would characterize the Court's gin- gerly approach to these politically sensitive questions in the immediate future. Usually, though, some justices, in civil religious terms, reminded their erring col- leagues of their obligations under the fundamental law.

Especially illustrative of this approach were the opinions in the case of *American Communications Association v. Douds* in 1950. A six-man Court upheld the noncom- munist affidavit required of officers of a labor union as it applied to membership in the Communist Party or an affiliated organization. But the High Bench divided three to three on the requirement commanding a disavowal of belief in an organi- zation that sought the illegal overthrow of the government. The result was to uphold the lower court's ruling that the provision was constitutional. Justices Frankfurter, Jackson, and Black took Congress to task for seeking to censor belief.

In civil religious terms, Frankfurter declared that "the cardinal faith of our civi- lization is the inviolate character of the individual. A man can be regarded as an individual . . . only if he is protected to the largest possible extent in his thoughts and in his beliefs as the citadel of his person."[116]

Jackson continued the attack, as he reminded his colleagues and the public as well that the American Revolution clearly illustrated that the overthrow of an established government by force "is not Communist doctrine but an old American belief." Buttressing his conclusion with quotations from Thomas Jefferson, Henry Clay, and Abraham Lincoln, the justice argued that punishing such belief con- demns many undoubtedly patriotic individuals and seals off discussion about the very propositions upon which the country was founded. "Our forefathers," Jack- son continued, "found the evils of free thinking more to be endured than the evils of inquest or suppression." The Constitution, he said, "relies on our electorate's complete ideological freedom to nourish independent and responsible intelligence and preserve our democracy from that submissiveness, timidity and herd-minded- ness of the masses which would foster a tyranny of mediocrity." Calling the Con- stitution's protection of the individual's right to be different "essentially American," he cited this "recognition of the individual as a personality rather than as a soulless part in the jigsaw puzzle that is the collectivist state" as the most salient difference between democracy and communism.[117]

The specification of rights in our fundamental law, Jackson continued, was designed "to protect the individual in his individuality, and neither statutes which put those rights at the mercy of officials nor judicial decisions which put them at the mercy of the mob are consistent with its text and spirit." Acknowledging that the Court has a responsibility to bolster legitimate authority to preserve the society, the justice insisted that it must also be on guard that such claims of national security not "undermine our freedoms and open the way to oppression."[118]

In a final salvo Black protested that "the postulate of the First Amendment is that our free institutions can be maintained without proscribing or penalizing political belief, speech, press, assembly, or party affiliation." Such continued commitment should be ensured by the Court, for it "is the heart of the system on which our freedom depends." Then, seeking to educate the public, the justice said: "Fears of alien ideologies have frequently agitated the nation and inspired legislation aimed at suppressing advocacy of those ideologies. At such times the fog of public excitement obscures the ancient landmarks set up in our Bill of Rights."[119] The society that received the decision in *Douds* was one in which such fog was being deliberately generated. Black's call for increased sensitivity to individual rights was no more heeded by the public than by some of his colleagues on the High Bench.

A badly fractured Court, however, did decide that organizations labeled subversive by the attorney general did have authority to sue to determine the legality of the action and to have the name of the organization deleted from the list. Justice Douglas's concurring opinion explained that the order, security, and respect found in a rule of law involved more than whether the substantive law itself was just. "It is not without significance," he said, "that most of the provisions of the Bill of Rights are procedural. It is procedure that spells much of the difference between rule by law and rule by whim or caprice. Steadfast adherence to strict procedural safeguards is our main assurance that there will be equal justice under law."[120]

Because this decision was grounded on a denial of due process, the free speech claim could be avoided, but later in the term the Court had to confront the issue. The case involved the conviction of the leaders of the Communist Party of America for conspiring to teach and advocate the overthrow of the government by force in violation of the Smith Act of 1940.[121] Six members of the eight-person Court accepted the clear and present danger test as the standard for evaluating the constitutionality of the conviction, but only four of them believed that the requirements of the test had been met. There was no opinion for the Court in *Dennis v. United States*, although the conviction was upheld by a 6–2 count. Chief Justice Fred M. Vinson, for the plurality, said that discussion could not be stifled under the First Amendment but advocacy could. Second, he added, the government did not have to stay its hand, "until the putsch is about to be executed, the plans have been laid and the signal is awaited." The improbability of the defendants' success, Vinson said, was irrelevant, because of the "damage which such attempts create both physically and politically to the nation." Applying the clear and present danger test, he accepted the formulation of the court below: "In each case [courts] must ask whether the gravity of the 'evil,' discounted by its improbability, justifies such invasion of free speech as is necessary to avoid the danger."[122] The chief then concluded that the conviction here had passed this test.

Justices Black and Douglas dissented in separate opinions. Black first referred to his opinion in another case decided the same day in which the Court had upheld a restriction on uninvited peddlers and solicitors calling upon residents of a community. In that case he accused his brethren of ignoring the preferred status of First Amendment liberties, saying "that the freedom of the people of this Nation cannot survive even a little governmental hobbling of religious or political ideas, whether they be communicated orally or through the press."[123] Here, in *Dennis*, Black reproached his colleagues for transforming the First Amendment into a mere "admonition to Congress" and making it useless as a protection for anything more than orthodox views. Implicitly censuring his colleagues for being snared in the hysteria of the red scare, the justice hoped "that in calmer times, when present pressures, passions and fears subside, this or some later Court will restore the First Amendment liberties to the high preferred place where they belong in a free society."[124]

Despite the fear of communism in the American society of the early 1950s that would lend great popular support to the convictions here, Douglas eloquently reminded Americans and the federal executive of the essentials of a faith that had sustained them during the years of their nation's existence. He claimed that free and uninhibited discussion in the society, which the Court here sought to hamper, had, in fact, been responsible for the people's rejection of communism and the reduction of its domestic adherents to a small and insignificant band of "miserable merchants of unwanted ideas." We should have faith, Douglas continued, "that our people will never give support to these advocates of revolution, so long as we remain loyal to the purposes for which our Nation was founded."[125] The justice appealed to the government to have confidence in the people by entrusting them with the liberty promised them by the Constitution.

To turn speech, absent any act, into a seditious conspiracy, Douglas insisted, is "to violate one of the cardinal principles of our constitutional scheme." Free speech is rightfully exalted in American society, he insisted, because it "encourages the testing of our own prejudices and preconceptions . . . and . . . keeps a society from becoming stagnant and unprepared for the stresses and strains that work to tear all civilizations apart." Saying that the American political system is founded upon free discussion, the justice labeled it "the first article of our faith" and "the one single outstanding tenet that has made our institutions the symbol of freedom and equality." Douglas then added: "We have wanted a land where our people can be exposed to all the diverse creeds and cultures of the world." Arguing that the defendants' speech was protected because there was no clear and present danger, he sought to teach "that violence is rarely, if ever, stopped by denying civil liberties to those advocating resort to force"—a proposition he called "the great postulate of our democracy."[126]

Although the focus of the case led Douglas to concentrate on the social value of free speech, his opinion also was premised upon the ideal of individual liberty. What distinguishes American society, the justice implied, is a faith in individuals and their rights, which, if allowed unimpeded growth, will safeguard both liberty and order without the oppressive and counterproductive interference of government. Douglas is providing a lesson in the civil religion, reminding his audience of the relationship between a mutual respect for diverse individuals and the ties that bind the society together. His talk of faith is directly on point, for reason can always provide arguments for curtailing offensive or unpopular speech. At the heart of the American faith lies a belief in the dignity of the individual and a willing embrace of the social diversity that proceeds from such a belief.

Black and Douglas would serve on the Court long enough to see both the end of the red scare and changes in the makeup of the High Bench that would make it more receptive to its priestly obligations. For a while, though, they would have to spread on the record their objections to the Court's approval of the domestic war against communism. For instance, when the majority upheld New York's disqualification of public school teachers because of their membership in certain suspect organizations, Black and Douglas protested. Black said that "public officials cannot be constitutionally vested with powers to select the ideas people can think about, censor the public views they can express, or choose the persons or groups people can associate with." Accepting such authority, he continued, would turn public officials into "public masters." For the justice, the Constitution, itself, commanded "that government should leave the mind and spirit of man absolutely free." Douglas accused the majority of making teachers second-class citizens, stripping them of a right of free speech, and pronouncing them guilty by association. When "deadening dogma takes the place of free inquiry," he continued, our way of life is seriously threatened. Douglas said that the framers rejected dogmatism because they "knew the strength that comes when the mind is free, when ideas may be pursued wherever they lead." Although the state can probe the teacher's work, he added, it cannot invade "her private life, her political philosophy, her social creed."[127]

What is important here is that the dissenters were not unmindful of community considerations in their desire to protect the individual right. What the other members of the community had done was cast out one of their own, something the dissenters argue the Constitution does not permit them to do. Communities within the constitutional order have considerable freedom but that freedom must not ignore the restrictions that are placed on curtailing membership by ostracizing those who are different. While the dissenters embraced that difference, the majority recoiled from it.

Douglas and Black also picked up now-departed Justice Murphy's contention that there were constitutional limitations on the federal government's power to deport aliens. Absent any subversive conduct, they insisted, the government could not deport aliens simply because they adhered to the Communist Party.[128] Such banishment for former political views, the justices said, repudiates "our traditions of tolerance and our articles of faith based upon the Bill of Rights." Insisting that the "guarantees of liberty and livelihood are the essence of the freedom which this country from the beginning has offered the people of all lands," they contended that an alien's right to remain in the country "has a like dignity." Referring to the aliens' past party membership, Black and Douglas reminded Americans that "the principle of forgiveness and the doctrine of redemption are too deep in our philosophy to admit that there is no return for those who have erred."[129]

Although the Court voted to exile erring aliens from the American community, it did unanimously draw the line when a state sought to dismiss employees for refusing to take a loyalty oath denying membership in certain organizations. The Court found in the oath a presumption of disloyalty in that it assumed knowing membership. In this time "of cold war and hot emotions," the justices said, "when 'each man begins to eye his neighbor as a possible enemy,' " to fasten such "a badge of infamy" on an innocent person violates due process.[130]

Unlike the threat to free speech posed by the Sedition Act of 1798, when responsible leaders protested such inroads on the liberties of the people, Justice Black, in a concurring opinion joined by Douglas, said that today the danger is even greater because "few individuals and organizations of power and influence" raise their voices to defend unpopular views. Calling such test oaths "notorious tools of tyranny," Black insisted that freedom's preservation necessitates that they be suppressed by an "uncompromising application of the Bill of Rights."[131]

When the Court decided that a witness who claimed a Fifth Amendment right not to incriminate himself could be granted immunity under a federal statute and be forced to testify, Douglas and Black protested. They said that the protection against self-incrimination was not only designed to protect the individual from unjust prosecution and conviction but also to safeguard "conscience and human dignity and freedom of expression as well."[132] Regularly, these dissenters reminded their brethren to look at cases from the individual's perspective and the rights promised under both the Constitution and the civil religion.

In this same term of Court, Black and Douglas were joined in a number of their free speech dissents by Chief Justice Earl Warren, who had replaced Fred Vinson in 1953. When the Court avoided the constitutional question of whether an employer could dismiss an employee because of her membership in the Communist Party, the dissenting justices protested that she had been dismissed for her political ideas, a flagrant violation of the First Amendment.[133]

At the beginning of the 1956 Term of Court, William J. Brennan Jr., appointed by President Dwight D. Eisenhower, joined the dissenters to create a block that would make its influence felt on the determinations of the High Bench.[134] On June 3, 1957, in *Jencks v. United States*, the justices confronted the conviction of a labor leader for falsely swearing that he was not a member of the Communist Party. The Court reversed the conviction because the trial court had failed to provide the defendant with the FBI reports detailing the testimony against him. Either produce the reports or dismiss the prosecution, the Court said. Justice Brennan, for the majority, reminded the government that the interest of the United States was not in winning a case but in ensuring that justice was done.[135]

Two weeks later in *Watkins v. United States*, the justices clipped the wings of the House Committee on Un-American Activities. John Watkins had been a forthcoming witness before the committee, testifying freely about himself and those he knew to be communists. But he drew the line at responding to questions about others who, as far as he knew, had no present connection with the party. Watkins said: "I do not believe that such questions are relevant to the work of this committee nor do I believe that this committee has the right to undertake the public exposure of persons because of their past activities."[136]

Chief Justice Warren, for the Court, agreed with Watkins, and found "no general authority to expose individuals without justification in terms of the functions of the Congress." Warren said both parties had reciprocal obligations. Expecting individuals to respect and cooperate with congressional committees, he continued, "assumes that the constitutional rights of witnesses will be respected by the Congress as they are in a court of law." The chief justice was insisting that the rule of law requires mutual respect; its claim to rule is based on its essential justice and fairness. With sensitivity, he traced how abuses of the investigative process can erode protected freedoms: by dredging up the past to condemn those in the present; by seeking the names of others to subject to the same "public stigma, scorn and obloquy;" and by silencing others who wish "to avoid a similar fate at some future time."[137]

Inspecting the House action that had created the committee, Warren concluded that it "would be difficult to imagine a less explicit authorizing resolution." To the argument that the Court should defer to a coordinate branch of the government, the chief proclaimed that "such deference cannot yield to an unnecessary and unreasonable dissipation of precious constitutional freedoms." To hold witnesses in contempt, Warren continued, Congress must inform them of the subject of the inquiry "with the same degree of explicitness and clarity that the Due Process Clause requires in the expression of any element of a criminal offense."[138] In conclusion, the chief ruled that the conviction could not stand, because the committee refused to state the purpose of the inquiry and establish the relevance of the questions. It was time, Warren implied, to end this modern-day witch-hunt and reclaim the Court's role as a protector of individual freedom.

On the same decision day, a fractured Court decided in favor of a professor at the University of New Hampshire who had been held in contempt for refusing to answer certain questions posed by a state investigating committee. For a plurality of the Court, Warren found a violation of the professor's right to due process. The chief emphasized the "essentiality of freedom in the community of American universities" and the need for students and teachers to "always remain free to inquire, to study and to evaluate, to gain new maturity and understanding; otherwise our civilization will stagnate and die." Then Warren turned to the Bill of Rights and its provisions for the "political freedom of the individual." The absence of unorthodox and dissenting views, he added, "would be a symptom of grave illness in our society." In a concurring opinion, Frankfurter added that "the inviolability of privacy belonging to a citizen's political loyalties has so overwhelming an importance to the well-being of our kind of society that it cannot be constitutionally encroached upon on the basis of so meager a countervailing interest of the State."[139]

What made these decisions so significant was their long overdue reaffirmation of the proper relationship of government to the individual within the American governmental system. In the period of the red scare, many Americans, along with their political representatives, apparently believed that protection from an amorphous enemy was worth some sacrifice of individual liberty. In the darkest days, there were justices on the Court who, though defeated in particular cases, sought to educate the populace to the dangers that such a campaign posed. The danger was not only to their rights as individuals but to the essential faith that had tied Americans together. That the Court would now be thanked for its assertion of priestly authority that redirected the society to its basic faith would be too much to expect.

As predictors of the next few years, however, the decisions of June 1957 were not reliable. Despite gaining the support of Earl Warren and William J. Brennan, Black and Douglas were still in the minority when the Court upheld the power of local government to dismiss employees, including a teacher, for invoking the privilege against self-incrimination in testimony before a congressional committee. Both Black and Brennan in their dissents stressed the incompatibility of the majority's decision with the traditions of the holy writ. As Douglas outlined the constitutional guarantees protecting the individual, he said they "include the right to believe what one chooses, the right to differ from his neighbor, the right to pick and choose the political philosophy that he likes best, the right to associate with whomever he chooses, the right to join the groups he prefers, the privilege of selecting his own path to salvation." To penalize an individual for invoking a constitutional right, the justice continued, is a radical break with our tradition. Making the right belief a qualification for public office, Douglas added, is "a notion very much at war with the Bill of Rights." Brennan said that "each . . . man's honor and reputation is indelibly stained" by having been dismissed. He called his brethren to their duty, saying that "close judicial scrutiny is essential when state action infringes on the right of a man to be accepted in his community, to express his ideas in an atmosphere of calm decency, and to be free of the dark stain of suspicion and distrust of his loyalty on account of his political beliefs and associations."[140]

On the same decision day that the Court so closely divided on the issue of the legitimacy of the state inquiring into the associations of its public servants, it unanimously decided a case freeing the National Association for the Advancement of Colored People (NAACP) from a contempt citation in Alabama for failing to provide the state with a list of the organization's members. Justice John Marshall Harlan, the grandson of his namesake on the Court, wrote the opinion. Viewing the NAACP as an appropriate representative for asserting the rights of its members, the justice called attention to "the close nexus between the freedoms of speech and assembly," saying that controversial advocacy "is undeniably enhanced by group association." It matters not, Harlan continued, "whether the beliefs sought to be advanced by association pertain to political, economic, religious or cultural matters." Forced disclosure of membership, he argued, places a substantial restraint upon "the vital relationship between freedom to associate and privacy in one's associations." In fact, Harlan said, a failure to protect such privacy would erode any meaningful "freedom of association, particularly where a group espouses dissident beliefs." He rejected the claim that any reprisal against individual members would be the result of private and not state action, noting that the former stems from the latter. The Alabama order cannot stand, the justice concluded, for it is "so related to the right of the members to pursue their lawful private interests privately and to associate freely with others in so doing as to come within the protection of the Fourteenth Amendment."[141]

The inconsistency between the NAACP ruling with the previous ones in which a Court majority had upheld the state's inquiry into organizational membership was eliminated a little over two years later in 1960. The newest arrival on the Court, Potter Stewart, sided with the former dissenters to constitute a new majority in the case of *Shelton v. Tucker.* Teachers in Arkansas were required to list all organizations to which they had belonged or contributed in the last five years. A false affidavit could be punished with a fine up to one thousand dollars and a loss of the individual's license to teach. Maintaining that "the vigilant protection of constitutional freedoms is nowhere more vital than in the community of American schools," the new majority ruled that such "comprehensive interference with associational freedom goes far beyond what might be justified in the exercise of the State's legitimate inquiry into the fitness and competency of its teachers."[142]

What led to this protection of freedom of association was the fact that the states were not seeking to identify communists but rather those individuals who sought to reform the status quo. If certain Southern officials saw no difference between communists and civil rights advocates, the Court obviously did.

The Court, however, was far from consistent, and dissenters continued to criticize the majority for ignoring the commands of the holy writ. Black insisted on telling the tale of the evolution of the Bill of Rights again and again. He believed that the very evils that the Bill was designed to combat had to be faced again in the present and turned back with a continuing commitment to the philosophy embodied in its eternal truths.

For instance, when the Court upheld a contempt of Congress conviction of a teacher for refusing to testify as to his past and present activities concerning the Communist Party, Black, in a dissent joined by Warren and Douglas, reminded both his colleagues and the public about the nature of their society and the proper role of the Court within it. He characterized the majority's balancing the individual right against the social interest as a rigged test. Then, Black summoned up Madison's words on introducing the proposals that became the Bill of Rights to the effect that the judiciary would be expected to "resist *every* encroachment upon rights expressly stipulated for in the Constitution by the declaration of rights." Implicitly condemning his colleagues for dereliction of both their priestly and constitutional duties, Black said that, unless the Court accepts its inherent responsibility, "our great charter of liberty will be more honored in the breach than in the observance." Ridiculing the notion that the country could only be made safe by abridging the First Amendment, the justice called upon his colleagues to maintain faith with the founding generation. That generation, he continued, believed that "the people with the fullest possible freedom to praise, criticize or discuss, as they see fit, all governmental policies," will, themselves, be able to evaluate alternatives without the government placing the label "unlawful" on some of them. On this foundation, Black said, rests "the security of the Republic." Without the steadfast protection of all individuals to speak freely, he concluded, "we cannot honestly proclaim ourselves to be a free Nation and we have lost what the Founders of this land risked their lives and their sacred honor to defend."[143]

Black resented not that this lesson had to be taught and retaught but rather that a primary instructor, the Court, instead of fulfilling this historical role had accommodated popular fear. When, almost a decade earlier, Black had dissented in a case upholding the government's right to extract a noncommunist oath from union leaders, he expressed concern that the Court's decision might be interpreted to prevent individuals from "getting or holding any jobs whereby they could earn a living."[144] Now in his jeremiad he looked with regret at the accuracy of his early prediction, as "Communists or suspected Communists have been denied an opportunity to work as government employees, lawyers, doctors, teachers, pharmacists, veterinarians, subway contractors, industrial workers and in just about any job." How the primary protector of individual rights, the judiciary, can stand idly by as individuals are grouped in a class and subjected to inquisitions was beyond Black's understanding. Cutting to the core of the issue, he asked: do we adopt totalitarian measures or do we, "in accordance with our traditions and our Constitution . . . have the confidence and courage to be free[?]"[145]

The Court's decisions late in its term in 1957 had stirred just the political reprisal that at least some of the justices had implicitly feared. Most attention centered on *Jencks* as the most dangerous decision of the lot, because it seemed to demand the opening of confidential files to the detriment of the security of the nation. The attack on the High Bench, however, was broadened in the legislative arena. Activity in Congress was intense, as proposals seeking to limit the Court's jurisdiction wended their way through the legislative process. In the end, such legislation was derailed, in part through the skillful maneuvering of the Senate majority leader, Lyndon B. Johnson.[146]

Actually the attack on the Court in the period from 1957 to 1959, ostensibly stirred by the so-called procommunist decisions, was as much, if not more, fueled by an earlier decision. The unanimous ruling in 1954 that racial segregation in the public schools was unconstitutional had incensed traditionally powerful Southern representatives and senators. How and why the Court had stirred up this hornet's nest is a matter to which we now turn.

STRUGGLING TO EQUALIZE JUSTICE AND EXPAND THE CIVIL THEOLOGY'S REACH: PART I: THE MATTER OF RACE, 1954–1997

Brown v. Board of Education in 1954, which held that separate but equal public education did not meet the test of the Fourteenth Amendment,[1] should have occasioned less surprise than it did. In the two generations since the Court accommodated racial segregation in *Plessy v. Ferguson*,[2] much had happened to rescue Justice John Marshall Harlan's dissenting opinion from the limbo to which it had been consigned. The Kentuckian's jeremiad had made clear how the decision violated the nation's civil theology.

Too slowly for many, though consistently over time, the Court began to inspect the claims of blacks under the Constitution. Shortly before Harlan's death in 1911 the justices struck down an Alabama law that levied criminal penalties, mainly on blacks, for breaking employment contracts.[3] Then, in the next six years, they ruled that the requirement to provide equal accommodations for blacks in transportation could not be defeated by claims that it was too expensive, that grandfather clauses violated the Fifteenth Amendment, and that a residential segregation statute violated individual property rights protected by the Fourteenth Amendment.[4]

In the decades of the 1920s and 1930s, the Court took a closer look at the condition of blacks under Southern justice and the concerted attempts to deny them the franchise. In fact, many of the cases in which certain fundamental rights were nationalized concerned blacks. To allow a mob to poison the trial of black defendants, the Court ruled, was a denial of the due process protected by the Fourteenth Amendment.[5] So also was the extraction of confessions from defendants by both physical and psychological force.[6] And when black defendants in a capital case were not provided with effective counsel, the justices nationalized the right to counsel.[7] In addition, although black voting was limited in the South, the Court increasingly read the Fifteenth Amendment and Congressional power over federal elections broadly enough to find a protected right, extending even to primary elections.[8] Furthermore, the justices were willing to revive some Reconstruction legislation to find the requisite federal authority to punish state officers for violating the civil rights of certain individuals.[9]

For quite some time in the piecemeal fashion that the cases dictated, the Court had been inspecting evidence of the inequality suffered by blacks within American society.[10] Entrusting the civil rights and civil liberties of individuals to the states had been tried and found deficient. If the Court was to fulfill a responsibility to include all within the embrace of the civil theology, its role would have to expand in the years ahead.

Complementing this growing recognition were other developments in the society that coalesced to indicate that a system of apartheid could not survive much longer.[11] Profiting from their experience after World War I, blacks were much more conscious during World War II that their aim had to be a double victory, both over the Axis powers and over the forces of repression at home. If the end of this second worldwide conflict brought no immediate dramatic change, it did usher in a new national discussion that focused upon the denial of rights to a large portion of the black population. In 1944 Gunnar Myrdal, a Swedish social scientist, had published a comprehensive study of blacks in the United States that found hope for improvement in their condition because of a spiritual consensus he called the American creed.[12] Two years later President Harry S Truman appointed a Committee on Civil Rights to make recommendations to better secure the rights of all Americans. The committee's report in 1948 set the agenda for the future. Although Truman's call to Congress to fulfill the promises upon which the nation was built—its civil religious theology—was frustrated by an entrenched and resistant Southern leadership, the issue of civil rights had been given national visibility.

Finally, the end of World War II neither ushered in an era of peace nor afforded the nation the opportunity to leave the world arena and retreat to domestic concerns. The hot war was replaced with a cold war with the Soviet Union—a continuing contest between competing political and economic systems seeking to win favor in all areas of the world. To attempt to win other nations to the side of the United States, the American house would have to be put in order. To talk of the superiority of the American democratic system and its protection of individual rights when those rights were not accorded to all American citizens had more than an air of hypocrisy to it. If for no other reason than to give American propaganda greater credibility, the denial of basic rights to American blacks had to be addressed.

Obviously, as Truman found out, the difficulty of having Congress tackle this problem was a Southern leadership that resisted interference in what these senators and representatives believed was a matter of local concern. Earlier in the nation's history when Congress was likewise stalemated, then on the issue of the expansion of slavery into the territories, some political leaders believed that the impasse could be resolved by a decision of the Supreme Court. When that decision in *Dred Scott v. Sandford*[13] not only confirmed the position of the Southern slaveholders but

found new constitutional protection for their peculiar form of property, the conflict was only exacerbated and the political impasse could not be resolved short of
civil war. The *Dred Scott* decision had been described as a "public calamity" and a
wound inflicted by the Court upon itself,[14] but why was this so? Was more expected than any Court could deliver? Or was it simply a matter of deciding the
wrong way; that is, against the tenets of the civil religion rather than in conformity
with them?

The Court of 1954 had advantages not held by its predecessor almost a century
earlier. It was not immune from attack, but its place in the American constitutional
order was much more securely established. Increasingly over the past generation
the Court had asserted its authority to protect individual rights by characterizing
the constitutional order as being established just for this purpose. Unlike the situation earlier, the Court was not responding to a call to relieve a political impasse
but rather was responding to cases generated by individuals seeking equal protection for their rights.

In regard to the specific issue of unequal treatment of blacks in education, the
justices had been dealing with cases that the National Association for the Advancement of Colored People (NAACP) had selected specifically to challenge discriminatory state practices. By surveying these earlier decisions, we can sketch in the
necessary background to *Brown v. Board of Education*[15] and demonstrate how the
condemnation of racial discrimination can be seen as a partial fulfillment of the
Court's role as the high priest of the American civil religion.

In 1938 in the first of these cases, the Court dealt with Missouri's attempt to
keep its law school all white by providing that qualified blacks could seek admission to an out-of-state law school and, upon acceptance and enrollment, receive
payment for the tuition paid. Maintaining that the separation of the races in education is supportable only when "an equality of right" is afforded to individuals of
both races, the justices found the Missouri alternative in violation of the equal
protection clause. They ordered the admission of the applicant to the state law
school.[16]

Ten years later, however, the Court concluded that the earlier precedent did
not prevent a state from creating and maintaining segregated law schools. Justice
Wiley Rutledge, in dissent, wondered how a new law school, truly equal to the
established one, could be created overnight.[17]

When directly confronted with the hypothetical question that Rutledge had
posed, the justices in 1950 agreed with their colleague. In *Sweatt v. Painter* the
Court responded to the question of what room did the equal protection clause of
the Fourteenth Amendment leave for the state "to distinguish between students of
different races in professional and graduate education in a state university?" When
Heman Sweatt was denied admission to the law school at the University of Texas
in Austin because of his race, the state court found his equal protection claim valid

but then withheld relief for six months to provide time for the state to supply equal facilities for blacks. Although the state court subsequently ruled that the newly created facility was "substantially equivalent" to the one in Austin, Sweatt refused to attend it.[18]

By the time the case came to the Supreme Court the law school at Texas State University was on the road to accreditation; it had five full-time professors, a student body of twenty-three, a library of 16,500 volumes, and even one alumnus. Using only these measurements to compare the two schools, the justices found the University of Texas law school superior. Furthermore, they continued, the long-established school possessed "those qualities which are incapable of objective measurement but which make for greatness in a law school." The justices listed: "reputation of the faculty, experience of the administration, position and influence of the alumni, standing in the community, traditions and prestige." Maintaining that a law school "cannot be effective in isolation from the individuals and institutions with which the law interacts," they called attention to the new law school's exclusion of nonblacks. The excluded group, the justices continued, comprise "85% of the population of the State and include most of the lawyers, witnesses, jurors, judges and other officials with whom petitioner will inevitably be dealing when he becomes a member of the Texas bar." To the argument that had influenced the Court in *Plessy v. Ferguson*—that the separated races suffer equal disabilities—the justices said that this "contention overlooks realities." They concluded that Sweatt was entitled to "his full constitutional right: legal education equivalent to that offered by the State to students of other races."[19]

On the same decision day, the Court returned to the recalcitrance of officials at the University of Oklahoma to integrate higher education in the state. Conceding that a black seeking his doctorate in education was entitled to admission, University administrators sought to segregate the black student. At first G. W. McLaurin was required to sit at a designated desk in an adjoining anteroom to the classroom, sit at a table on the mezzanine floor of the library, and eat in the school cafeteria at a different time than the other students. Before the Court heard the case these conditions had been modified so that McLaurin could now sit in the classroom in a special row, at a table on the main floor of the library, and at a designated table in the cafeteria when the other students ate.

Even with these modifications the unanimous Court concluded that such "restrictions impair and inhibit his ability to study, to engage in discussions and exchange views with other students, and, in general, learn his profession." As a potential leader in society, the justices said, those he in turn trains "will necessarily suffer to the extent that his training is unequal to that of his classmates." Although the removal of these state-imposed restrictions "will not necessarily abate individual and group predilections, prejudices and choices," they continued, at "the very least the state will not be depriving appellant of the opportunity to secure acceptance by his fellow students on his own merits."[20] What the Court made clear was that race could not be used to justify unequal treatment.

Although the justices had refused to confront *Plessy*, they had made the task of providing equal facilities much more difficult. What they had introduced into the equation were factors that were impossible to equalize—number of alumni, prestige, tradition, excellence, and contact and exchange with the majority race. Perhaps the inclusion of such factors seemed especially necessary at the level of professional education, but clearly the Court had opened the door to a much more sensitive consideration of the position of the individual in these separated educational settings. Instead of comparing facilities and teacher-student ratios, the Court was now engaged in looking at the system of segregated education from the perspective of the minority students themselves. As the Court said in *Sweatt*, the rights involved are "personal and present,"[21] meaning that segregation would now be viewed increasingly in terms of its effects on the individual rather than on the outward equality of the facilities.

This new attitude represented a substantial change that focused the Court's attention on its long-standing obligation to ensure the protection of individual rights. The days when the rights of black individuals could be neglected by submerging these individuals into a group that could be regulated at the discretion of the states seemed to be numbered.

Although these cases dealing with segregation in higher education seem most pertinent to *Brown*, the Court was also developing new law in other areas in which the race of the defendant was hardly insignificant. Cases involving blacks tended to mount in the 1940s and early 1950s, and in their decisions the justices displayed increasing sensitivity to the rights claimed. For instance, though the Court had clearly ruled that a state could not exclude blacks from juries, the justices had never looked past the absence of a discriminatory statute. That was beginning to change. The issue generally came up in criminal trials in which black defendants argued that they had been denied the equal protection of the laws because members of their race had been systematically excluded from the jury pool. As early as 1939, the unanimous Court reversed a murder conviction in Louisiana, saying that its "solemn duty" required it to make an independent evaluation of the evidence to respond to a claim "that a citizen whose life is at stake has been denied the equal protection of his country's laws on account of race." This was so, the justices said, because "equal protection to all is the basic principle upon which justice under law rests." And that principle, they continued, is violated when particular groups are excluded from jury service. Notice the Court's use of "his" proceeding "country's laws."[22] The law that is *his* country's, the justices insisted, is a law that must recognize this individual's membership in a community premised upon equal rights for all. The Court was serving notice that its interpretation of the holy writ would encompass all, irrespective of their race.

In the following year when Texas claimed that its statute providing for jury selection was nondiscriminatory, the High Bench agreed but then found the law's application deficient, insisting that "equal protection to all must be given—not merely promised." To exclude persons from jury service because of race, the justices said, "not only violates our Constitution and the laws enacted under it but is at war with our basic concepts of a democratic society and a representative government."[23] Equal protection was more than a legal standard; it was part of the core theology of the American civil religion.

In 1942 the Court had found a prima facie case of racial discrimination, again in Texas, where blacks had been excluded from serving on grand juries for at least sixteen years. Justice Hugo L. Black, for a unanimous Court, insisted that every state must respect and "every person may demand" the equal protection of the laws. "Not the least merit of our constitutional system," he continued, "is that its safeguards extend to all—the least deserving as well as the most virtuous."[24]

When Texas authorities deliberately placed one black juror in a sixteen-person pool in a county where blacks made up about 15 percent of the population, the majority found no validity in the equal protection claim. Only one of the three dissenters, Frank Murphy, issued an opinion. He found the majority's approval of this quota system an evasion of "the fact that we of this nation are one people undivided in ability or freedom by differences in race, color or creed."[25] Five years later, after Murphy had left the Court, the justices seemed to agree with their departed colleague when they denied that such a quota system met the equal protection guarantee.[26] And when Mississippi officials argued that blacks were not found on state juries because of their failure to qualify as voters, the justices said that, as the state had conceded that the voting lists did contain some black voters, their exclusion from jury service could only result from impermissible discrimination.[27]

A 1953 decision revealed that the Court was now inclined to shift the burden of proof from the party claiming a violation of equal protection to the state by finding a prima facie case in certain circumstances. In Georgia the jurors were drawn from a box in which the names of whites and blacks could be identified by the color of the paper on which each name appeared. The state insisted that there had been no discrimination, but the all-white jury that resulted from the procedure convinced the Court that the state had to prove that there had been no discrimination, a burden the state could not carry.[28] With such opinions the justices believed that they had clarified the demands of the equal protection clause. It became increasingly common for the Court simply to reverse state determinations in the area without opinion.[29]

One related area where the justices did divide five to four was on the constitutionality of New York's system of creating "blue ribbon" panels and juries. A list of qualified jurors was reduced from about sixty thousand to three thousand, from which smaller panel the trial jury was chosen. Although only a little more than 20 percent of the Manhattan work force was composed of professionals, semiprofessionals, independent proprietors, managers, and officials, these groups composed more than 60 percent of the special jurors. One study had concluded that "blue ribbon" juries had a higher conviction rate, but the majority justices found no evidence of discrimination that would constitute a violation of the equal protection of the law. In two cases challenging the system, Murphy dissented, joined by Hugo Black, William O. Douglas, and Wiley B. Rutledge. They insisted that the Fourteenth Amendment "prohibits a state from convicting any person by use of a jury which is not impartially drawn from a cross-section of the community," which they defined as including "persons with varying degrees of training and intelligence and with varying economic and social positions." The New York practice, they continued, fails to honor the democratic principle that the defendant has a right to a jury "representative of all qualified classes of people." While the majority demanded evidence that the defendant had suffered discrimination, the dissenters said such prejudice "is so subtle, so intangible, that it escapes the ordinary methods of proof." To place in jeopardy such a basic right, which "may gradually and silently erode the jury system before it becomes evident," they argued, is to risk its irretrievable loss.[30]

A second case involved black defendants who pointed to the absence of persons of their race on the panel from which their jury was selected and the relative absence of blacks from "blue ribbon" lists. Murphy, for the dissenters, lamented that the two defendants in the case were to forfeit their lives because of conviction under such a defective system. "Such a basis for jury selection," he concluded, "has no place in our constitutional way of life."[31] For the dissenters this "constitutional way of life" demanded that the fundamental rights even of accused criminals be respected. Murphy implied that the Court majority had lost touch with its essential role of helping to nurture a "way of life" that demanded respect for a core precept of the civil theology.

On the eve of the *Brown* decision, the Court considered a case in which a Hispanic claimed that people of his ethnic background had been systematically excluded from jury service. Texas argued that the Fourteenth Amendment contemplated only two classes—whites and blacks. The unanimous Court rejected this limited reading and ruled that the equal protection clause protected individuals from discrimination based on ancestry or national origin as well. Although acknowledging that race and color have been historically the concern of the courts in ensuring equal treatment under the law, the justices said that "community prejudices are not static, and from time to time other differences from the community norm may define other groups that need the same protection." They continued: "When the existence of a distinct class is demonstrated, and . . . laws . . . single out that class from different treatment . . . , the guarantees of the Constitution have been violated."[32] This language seems to talk of the rights of a class, but the rights are those of individuals that have been abridged because of their submergence in a class. However, the effect of the opinion was to widen the protection of the fundamental law and bring into the civil religion those whose ancestry made them targets of discrimination.

The Court had come a long way in a relatively short period of time in insisting that states provide minority criminal defendants with a realistic chance of having some members of their own racial or ethnic group on their juries. Well before *Brown* the justices ruled that convictions would be reversed if they came from juries chosen from pools that excluded minority persons.

Another area, where the Court served notice that past precedents might not be a reliable guide as to how it would respond when blacks claimed discrimination, involved the interpretation of "state action." In the *Civil Rights Cases* of 1883 the Court had taken a narrow view, insisting that "state action" required finding agents of the state enforcing discriminatory legislation. In 1948, in response to a series of residential segregation cases, the justices took a much broader view. The cases involved restrictive covenants forbidding the sale of property to non-Caucasians. Did the courts in enforcing such covenants engage in the "state action" barred by the Fourteenth Amendment?

The unanimous Court in *Shelley v. Kraemer* began by saying that the framers of that amendment accepted equality "in the enjoyment of property rights . . . as an essential pre-condition to the realization of other basic civil rights and liberties which the Amendment was intended to guarantee." Although conceding that the restrictive agreements themselves were private, the justices ruled that their judicial enforcement did constitute the type of state action barred by the Fourteenth Amendment. No person, they continued, has any right "to demand action by the State which results in the denial of equal protection of the laws to other individuals." Realizing that the decision imposed new limits on the states, the justices added that the need to impose such restrictions in behalf of national constitutional guarantees was a problem "foremost in the minds of the framers of the Constitution." And regarding the Fourteenth Amendment, they said, the Court has for seventy-five years interpreted the primary purpose of its framers to be "the establishment of basic civil and political rights and the preservation of those rights from discriminatory action on the part of the States based on considerations of race or color." Within this constitutional tradition reaching back to the framers themselves, the justices concluded that the Court's solemn obligation was to pronounce such state action in violation "of the fundamental charter."[33]

A companion case involved the same situation in the District of Columbia, where the equal protection clause had no effect. Although grounding its decision in part on the Civil Rights Act of 1866, the Court also ruled that public policy could not permit federal courts to do what state courts could not do.[34]

In both of these decisions the Court had to overcome technical legal obstacles in order to reach a just decision. Increasingly the justices refused to interpose such obstructions to the claims of aggrieved parties, and in so doing they were fulfilling their priestly responsibilities. Just how far they were willing to go in impeding the effectiveness of restrictive covenants as tools of discrimination, for instance, is well revealed in *Barrows v. Jackson*. Olive Barrows, who had sold her house to non-Caucasians, was sued for damages under the controlling restrictive covenant. Could she be held liable or could she invoke the rights of other potential non-Caucasian buyers to defeat the action? The persons to whom she had sold the house were now the new owners and had no obligation to indemnify Barrows; neither could they be sued, because of the ruling in *Shelley v. Kraemer*.

Indicating their disdain for such covenants, the justices carved out an exception to a long-honored legal rule—that one cannot rely upon the invasion of the rights of others to defend one's own actions. They had to overcome a further objection because potential buyers could not be specifically identified. The Court pronounced the situation "unique" and proceeded to reach what it considered a just result. Damages, it said, would "sanction the validity of the restrictive covenant" and punish the defendant "for not continuing to discriminate against non-Caucasians." Making clear the Court's condemnation of such restrictions in a society committed to the equal protection of individuals under the law, the justices were happy to immunize defendants from such suits and thus "close the gap to the use of this covenant, so universally condemned by the courts." To the argument that they had created a group or class right under an equal protection clause that protects personal rights, the justices said that "it is not non-Caucasians as a group whose rights are asserted . . . , but the rights of particular non-Caucasian would-be users of the restricted land."[35]

Chief Justice Fred M. Vinson, the Court's writer in *Shelley*, dissented and accused the majority of making social policy, but could the Court have avoided the charge by deciding the case the other way? If the equal protection clause was designed to eliminate any state support for discrimination interfering with an individual's right to buy, sell, lease, and occupy property, as even Vinson agreed it did, should the Court take refuge behind general jurisdictional rules to look the other way as effective inroads are made upon the right? When such rules interfere with the Constitution's Preamble and its aim of establishing justice, should the rules prevail? The majority was willing to carve out an exception to fulfill a paramount responsibility under the civil theology—to protect individual rights.

Clearly the Court was becoming increasingly committed to providing equal justice under law. We see it in the demand that blacks be given equal opportunity in higher education. We see it in the reversal of criminal convictions, independent of any consideration of the evidence, because the constitutional right to be tried by a jury is contaminated by discrimination. Furthermore, we see it in these restrictive covenant cases, where the Court was intent upon teaching the society that racial discrimination is inconsistent with the American creed. The Court is both teacher and policymaker; the only question is what kind of teacher and policymaker will it be? And how willing is it to take the holy writ and make its promises meaningful in the society?

One further line of cases deserves exploration as the final link leading up to *Brown*. In 1941 the Court in *Mitchell v. United States* explored the practical meaning of a portion of the Interstate Commerce Act that made it unlawful for a common carrier "to subject any particular person . . . to any undue or unreasonable prejudice or disadvantage in any respect whatsoever."[36] The case arose when a black congressman from Illinois, Arthur W. Mitchell, bought a first-class ticket for rail travel from Chicago to Little Rock. As the train entered Arkansas the conductor not only refused to accept payment for a Pullman seat but forced Mitchell's removal to inferior accommodations in a segregated coach, apparently to conform to Arkansas's segregation statute. Mitchell sought a ruling on his complaint against the railroad from the Interstate Commerce Commission (ICC). The ICC dismissed the complaint, and a federal district court upheld the action. In appealing to the Supreme Court, Mitchell argued his own case. Despite the fact that one of the opposing parties was the United States government, the U.S. solicitor general joined Mitchell and argued against the ruling of the ICC and the lower court.

To add to this interesting situation, the writer for the unanimous Court was Chief Justice Charles Evans Hughes, who in his earlier tenure on the Court had written a decision in 1914 rejecting the contention that economic reasons could excuse a carrier from providing equal accommodations for members of different races.[37] Hughes now lectured the ICC, saying that the discrimination practiced here was clearly embraced by the authorizing statute, that state segregation statutes could not be applied to interstate commerce, and that the cost of affording equal accommodations was of no concern to the commission. Certainly a carrier was free to consider the demand for certain facilities, but once offered, Hughes said, they had to be offered to all persons. The chief added that the ICC's task was not to sympathize with the carrier's practical problems but rather come to the obvious conclusion that the discrimination against Mitchell "was palpably unjust and forbidden by the Act."[38]

Although the justices were simply interpreting the meaning of a statute and although they had the aid of the solicitor general against the ruling of the ICC, they indicated their commitment to the policy itself. As American citizens, Mitchell and others of his race, Hughes said, are entitled to travel by routes they choose free of the type of discrimination shown in this instance. The question, the chief continued, involved not segregation but "equality of treatment." Independent of the statute, Hughes ruled, the treatment of the congressman was "an invasion of a fundamental individual right which is guaranteed against state action by the Four-

teenth Amendment."[39] He concluded by reminding Americans that the equal protection clause safeguards the rights of individuals, not groups. Discrimination may
arise because the individual is part of a racially identifiable group, but the individual
right claimed cannot be evaded, as the commission did here, even if he is the only
person contesting the unequal facilities.

In our present era of persons identifying their interests with groups, we need to
pause to understand clearly how the civil theological principles of equal justice
under law and individual rights, when applied, can have both a liberating or eman-
cipating effect and set new social policy. Second, we need to realize how this
approach, practiced by the Court in *Mitchell*, had the potential to doom all officially
sponsored segregation. Interest groups contend with each other constantly in the
push and pull of the legislative process, and the key to success in this field is both
organization and appeal to those people outside the contending groups whose
sympathy can be garnered. The judicial arena focuses attention on the individual's
claim and forces upon judges the perspective of the individual. As Hughes insisted
in *Mitchell*, all other considerations must fade away as the Court determines
whether *this* individual in *this* situation was subjected to "undue or unreasonable
prejudice."[40] Any individual having a case adjudicated can represent the like interests of many, but the focus on the individual brings into play a rule of law that by
necessity can limit the range of social choice left to the political process.

This is what the Court was doing in many of these pre-*Brown* cases. Forced to
take the individual's perspective and apply equal justice under law, the justices
necessarily were challenging the social policy of segregation, which had been
enacted with relatively little concern for its effect on individuals. As the Court
confronted more and more challenges to the social system, segregation's incompatibility with the civil religion and the constitutional guarantees that translated its
theology into general legal principles became increasingly obvious.

When the right thing to do coincides with what is economically sound there is
added impetus for change. With the Court's insistence upon equality in practice
rather than just in theory, the cost of maintaining a segregated society was escalat-
ing. The railroad in *Mitchell* would be forced either to downgrade its service so
that equality is available at the lower level and run the risk of losing passengers, or
maintain cars and accommodations for which there was little demand. In other
words, the Court was making the maintenance of segregation too costly and therefore uneconomical. With new force and emphasis, the Court reiterated its earlier
ruling. That it would take yet another generation for economics and justice to
triumph over attempts to preserve an outmoded social structure is not the result of
the Court's failure to communicate.

In *Mitchell*, the power of Congress to control interstate commerce invalidated
the operation of a state segregation statute, but what if a state applied its civil rights
law to interstate commerce? That was the issue presented to the Court in 1948,

when a steamship company that regularly transported residents of Detroit to an amusement park located on a Canadian island denied that it was subject to Michigan's equal accommodations act. Two members of the High Bench were willing to strike down the law as an interference with Congress's ability to regulate commerce, but the majority disagreed. Not denying that the act regulated interstate commerce, the majority saw no conceivable national interest that could be interposed against Michigan applying "her long-settled policy against racial and creedal discrimination to this segment of foreign commerce, so peculiarly and almost exclusively affecting her people and institutions."[41]

Justices Douglas and Black, in a concurring opinion, said that the case is "controlled by a principle which cuts deeper than that announced by the Court." To envision the Court striking down a state law requiring common carriers to transport all regardless of race and color, they said, was "unthinkable."[42] Indeed, the state must bow to national regulation, the justices continued, but Congress has no power to distinguish among citizens on the basis of color that could lead to any imaginable conflict. Also, the application of such a law, they said, did nothing to burden commerce or undermine the uniformity that the clause was designed to promote. Finally, Douglas and Black concluded that there was no danger of inconsistent state laws, for *Mitchell* had clearly established that the individual rights protected here bind the states under the Fourteenth Amendment.

The Court earlier had come unanimously to the same conclusion when New York sought to apply its civil rights law to a union of post office workers. One of the arguments was that this action violated the Fourteenth Amendment rights of the union members. The justices found this a strange argument indeed, given that the amendment had been "adopted to prevent state legislation designed to perpetuate discrimination on the basis of race or color." And the fact that the federal government was the employer of the union members, the Court said, was immaterial. Felix Frankfurter added some telling words of his own in ridiculing the Fourteenth Amendment claim as "devoid of constitutional substance." That amendment, he said, does not prevent a state from widening the ambit of a policy of nondiscrimination beyond that which the Constitution mandates. In so expanding the individual's protection from racial or creedal discrimination, he continued, the state is placing "its authority behind one of the cherished aims of American feeling by forbidding indulgence in racial or religious prejudice to another's hurt."[43]

Even Frankfurter, who was acutely sensitive to the allocation of power within the American federal system, accepted the invitation to put the High Bench on the side of promoting equal justice under the law. Furthermore, as the justice clearly indicated, the High Bench's responsibility was to educate the public about the harm of racial prejudice and its incompatibility with the civil theological premises upon which the society rested.

These two decisions indicated that state policy promoting equal treatment would be accommodated and approved, while contrary state policy would be struck down and condemned. If states moved in advance of a divided Congress to ensure equal treatment for all, the Court would encourage, not obstruct, such action.

As the NAACP moved its judicial campaign attacking segregation from the field of higher education to primary and secondary education, no reader of the Court's recent opinions could fail to realize that the individuals the organization represented would receive a sympathetic hearing.[44] The case of *Brown v. Board of Education* would be argued twice, once before Fred M. Vinson as chief justice and once before his replacement, Earl Warren. Realizing the importance of the decision, Warren would work assiduously to mass the justices behind a single opinion for the Court.[45]

Warren came to the High Bench from the governorship of California. Before becoming state attorney general and then governor, he had spent his legal life as a prosecutor in Alameda County. He had no judicial experience, but he did have strong feelings about justice and fairness. Instinctively, he seemed to grasp and embrace the Supreme Court's civil religious role. "Warren repeatedly emphasized that he had a 'duty' under the Constitution to see its imperatives implemented, and he saw the Constitution's imperatives as ethical imperatives."[46]

His opinions had a common-sense quality and a vernacular style that tended to make them quite accessible to the general public. In *Brown*, he deliberately sought to write a short, easily comprehended opinion. In this especially sensitive area the task of the Court, in the face of expected opposition, was not only to decide the constitutional claim but also to gain support for both its resolution and the kind of society the opinion envisioned.[47]

Brown grouped together cases coming from Kansas, South Carolina, Virginia, and Delaware and forced the Court to reevaluate the conformity of the separate but equal test with the Constitution's guarantee of equal protection. This was so because the finding in the Kansas case was that the separate schools were equal in their tangible attributes. Faced then with the need to address *Plessy*, the Court ordered reargument on the matter of what had been the intent of the framers and ratifiers of the Fourteenth Amendment. After concluding that this history was inconclusive, the justices then moved on to inspect the equal protection argument from the perspective of the black students themselves.

Chief Justice Warren, for the unanimous bench, said that the Court could not "turn the clock back to 1868 . . . or . . . 1896" but must, instead, respond to the claim in the context of public education's "full development and its present place in American life throughout the Nation." Calling the provision for public education "perhaps the most important function of state and local governments," he maintained that such an education "is required in the performance of our most basic responsibilities, . . . is the very foundation of good citizenship[, and] . . . is a principal instrument in awakening the child to cultural values, in preparing him for later professional training, and in helping him adjust normally to his environment." Then picking up language from the recent higher education cases that he said now applied "with added force," the chief justice concluded that separating students "from others of similar age and qualifications solely because of their race generates a feeling of inferiority as to their status in the community that may affect their hearts and minds in a way unlikely ever to be undone."[48] Citing the work of recent social scientists to buttress this conclusion, Warren repudiated what he said had been the less informed perspective that had produced the result in *Plessy*.

This reference to "modern authority" listed in a footnote would draw considerable criticism by observers of the Court. They questioned the soundness of such studies and believed that they constituted a poor basis on which to ground such an important ruling. However, Warren was right. The Court in *Plessy*, without citation, had come to the psychological conclusion that any feelings of inferiority stemming from segregation were spun out of the fertile imagination of affected blacks and were not the result of the separation itself. So, *Plessy* was founded as much upon a psychological conclusion as was *Brown*, and even in 1896 its weakness was exposed in John Marshall Harlan's dissenting opinion. Whether "modern authority" did adequately support the new conclusion or not, its appeal to common sense was strong.

If some saw weakness in Warren's rationale, the conclusion he reached seemed clear enough. In "the field of public education," the chief justice stated, "the doctrine of 'separate but equal' has no place. Separate educational facilities are inherently unequal." The plaintiffs, and those similarly affected, he ruled, have been "deprived of the equal protection of the laws guaranteed by the Fourteenth Amendment."[49]

On the same decision day the Court responded to a similar case coming from the District of Columbia. Because the federal government, which maintained control over the District, was not bound by an equal protection requirement, the Court had to address the due process argument that the justices had ignored in the state cases. "It would be unthinkable, they said, that the same Constitution would impose a lesser duty on the Federal Government." Reading the Fifth Amendment to reach the situation, the justices ruled that segregation "imposes on Negro children of the District of Columbia a burden that constitutes an arbitrary deprivation of their liberty in violation of the Due Process Clause."[50]

All the controversy surrounding these decisions should not obscure the fact that the Court was doing what it should be doing in assessing claims that individual rights are being violated. From the very beginnings of its existence, this was the charge to which the Court consistently responded. Violations of individual right might be obscured by concentrating on the power of states to regulate, but the proper way to assess a claim that individual rights were threatened was to take the perspective of the claimant. This is what the Court did here so clearly and directly. The issue is not conceived in terms of the police power of the state but in terms of the rights guaranteed to the individual. *Plessy*'s error was in obscuring the claim by posing the question for decision in terms of the power of the state. How the issue is conceived tells us much about how it is to be decided. *Plessy* was always vulnerable and became much more so as the justices indicated their willingness to focus on claims of a denial of equal rights.

Despite its nonrhetorical tone, the Brown opinion is also significant as an attempt to define and enlarge the American community and make it conform to the fundamental theology upon which it rests. The Court in *Plessy* had allowed diverse states to define their own communities and erect whatever barriers they chose, but now the justices boldly reasserted their role in defining a national community in terms of equal justice under law. The inferiority that *Plessy* perpetuated was now recognized, confronted, and condemned. Agreeing with the Kansas court that segregated education tends to retard the mental development of those clearly denoted as inferior, the justices called a halt to their prior complicity in engendering in blacks "a feeling of inferiority . . . unlikely ever to be undone."[51] In protecting the rights of such children the Court was strengthening the civil religious faith.

Although the justices had decided that racially segregated public education was unconstitutional, they delayed a remedy and asked the parties to address this matter in the next term of Court. This departure from the High Bench's practice was an acknowledgment of the wide-ranging ramifications of the ruling in *Brown*. To mandate immediate relief, the usual practice, would ignore the practical difficulties involved in reorganizing public education in many parts of the Union. Perhaps, also, there was hope that peaceful, voluntary compliance with the ruling would begin.

In the supplemental ruling in the next term, labeled *Brown II* to distinguish it from what now was referred to as *Brown I*, Warren began by summarizing the first decision as holding that "racial discrimination in public education is unconstitutional." He continued: "All provisions of federal, state, or local law requiring or permitting such discrimination must yield to this principle." But after these broad generalities, he remanded the cases to the original trial courts to oversee the task of compliance. These courts were to maintain their jurisdiction in the cases and to use their power in equity, which "has been characterized by a practical flexibility in shaping its remedies and by a facility for adjusting and reconciling public and private needs." Insisting upon "good faith compliance at the earliest possible date," Warren charged the trial courts with the responsibility of overseeing the "transition to a racially nondiscriminatory school system" and of ensuring that the complaining parties involved in the cases are admitted "to public schools on a racially nondiscriminatory basis with all deliberate speed."[52]

What was significant here was not the mixed message the Court was sending as

CHAPTER EIGHT

to how quickly desegregation was to be achieved but rather how this difficult problem was to be resolved by expanding substantially the equitable powers of the trial courts. To achieve the end envisioned in *Brown*, trial courts would become heavily involved in evaluating and even drafting desegregation plans.

This beginning would have a dramatic effect on widening the role of the federal courts in implementing policies that carried out announced constitutional principles. As this door was opened, new litigants with new claims would pass through it, and cases would be retained by these courts as they sought to ensure that a decision reached much earlier was put into practice.

If the Court, as it indicated in the second opinion in *Brown*, saw evidence of good faith compliance with the new constitutional standard, it was reading the future badly indeed. For the latter part of the 1950s was characterized by such resistance that little desegregation took place in the Southern states. Often the legal process was used to obstruct rather than advance the desired end, and Southern state legislatures outdid each other in trying to devise means to overcome the Supreme Court's ruling.[53]

For the next three years the Supreme Court stood by as delay, obstruction, and resistance retarded any substantial advancement to the goal of a desegregated public educational system. In fact, in the year following the second *Brown* decision, over a hundred members of Congress signed a Southern Manifesto that condemned *Brown* as "a clear abuse of judicial power."[54]

The calm at the center of the storm was shattered in August 1958 when Chief Justice Warren called his colleagues into special session to consider resistance to desegregation in Little Rock. Actually, some peaceful progress in the direction of desegregation had been made in Arkansas, and Governor Orval Faubus had won reelection in 1956 over an uncompromising racist candidate. Contemplating running for a third term, however, Faubus felt that electoral success demanded dramatic action that captured the support of white opponents of desegregation. When Central High School in Little Rock was ordered by the federal court to admit nine blacks, Faubus dispatched the National Guard to the school on opening day to preserve the peace. The black students were blocked from entering the school. Only after the governor was enjoined from preventing their attendance was the Guard removed. The black students then entered the school and remained for a little over three hours before they were removed by police in response to the demands of the mob that had formed outside the school.[55]

Faced with this resistance to the legal process, President Dwight D. Eisenhower dispatched troops to Little Rock and nationalized the Arkansas National Guard. The students reentered the school. Although they were protected from serious harm by the military presence, they all were harrassed by white students. The local school board asked the district court for permission to reassign the students to a segregated school. Although the district court agreed, the Court of Appeals for the Eighth Circuit reversed the decision but then stayed the order pending appeal.[56]

Rushing to reach a decision in *Cooper v. Aaron* before the new school year, the Court expedited argument and met in special session. To highlight the importance of the decision and reaffirm the Court's continued commitment to its ruling of 1954, the opinion for the Court bore the signatures of all its members, including the three who had joined the Court since the Brown ruling. The justices rejected what they saw as an attempt to nullify *Brown*, which they now interpreted as imposing an affirmative duty on state officers "to devote every effort toward initiating desegregation and bringing about the elimination of racial discrimination in the public school system."[57] Arkansas legislators and executive officials who had interfered with the good faith attempts of the local school board to desegregate the school, the justices continued, were responsible for the resulting chaos and resistance at Central High.

Mincing no words, the unanimous bench said: "The constitutional rights of respondents are not to be sacrificed or yielded to the violence and disorder which have followed upon the actions of the Governor and Legislature." Law and order, the justices continued, "are not here to be preserved by depriving the Negro children of their constitutional rights." Condemning the evasive action of state authorities, the Court responded to the claim that Arkansas was not bound by the holding in *Brown*. Citing *Marbury v. Madison*, the justices said that the decision there had established the supremacy of the federal judiciary in interpreting the Constitution. "That principle," they added, "has ever since been respected by this Court and the Country as a permanent and indispensable feature of our constitutional system." Although conceding that public education was primarily a state concern, they ruled that all state action must be consistent with the Fourteenth Amendment. That amendment, the justices continued, "embodied and emphasized" the ideal of equal justice to which the government created by the Constitution had been dedicated. Reaffirming *Brown* and insisting that state officials are bound to obey the ruling, the Court said that the principles applied there "are indispensable for the protection of the freedoms guaranteed by our fundamental charter for all of us. Our constitutional ideal of equal justice under law is thus made a living truth."[58]

Despite his agreement with his colleagues, Frankfurter could not resist his own condemnation of the action of state officials in challenging the rule of law. What so disturbed the justice was the fact that "the process of the community's accommodation to new demands of law upon it, the development of habits of acceptance of the right of colored children to the equal protection of the laws guaranteed by the Constitution, had peacefully and promisingly begun." Then, he continued, the power of the state was used to thwart such compliance. "Our kind of society cannot endure," Frankfurter insisted, when the Court's declaration of what is the supreme law of the land is met with hostility rather than compliance. This is especially so when what that law "commands on an underlying moral issue . . . is the unanimous conclusion of a long-matured deliberative process." Acknowledging the Court's teaching role, the justice said that education can "vigorously flow from the fruitful exercise of the responsibility of those charged with political official power and from the almost unconsciously transforming actualities of living under law." And public officials in our democracy, he continued, have a responsibility "not to reflect inflamed public feeling but to help form its understanding." Finally, Frankfurter warned that attempts of state officials to obstruct the supreme law undermines "the maintenance of our federal system as we have known and cherished it for one hundred and seventy years."[59] A Court under attack responded with a vigorous defense of its priestly authority.

Despite its apparent intent to leave desegregation plans and details to the lesser priests in the federal judiciary, the Court could not avoid the challenge to its authority posed by Arkansas officials; neither could it escape forever the question of whether local officials could close the public school system. Actually Governor Faubus had closed the high schools in Little Rock for the 1958–59 school year, but he obeyed a lower court ordering their reopening in the following year.[60] The same was true in Virginia, which, except for Prince Edward County, gradually bowed to the inevitable and desegregated its public schools. Officials in Prince Edward County, however, decided to subsidize private schools in lieu of a public school system. With blacks refusing to participate in the new scheme, no public education had been provided for five years. Although an original suit to desegregate the schools of Prince Edward County was begun in 1951, not until 1964 did the Supreme Court finally confront the situation. The Court concluded that the county's action in closing the schools, while the other Virginia public schools remained open, "denied the petitioners and the class of Negro students they represent the equal protection of the laws guaranteed by the Fourteenth Amendment."[61] The justices directed the lower federal court to order the county to reopen its public schools.

As the Court was clearing this last hurdle, ten years after the initial *Brown* decision, some headway was finally being made not only in desegregating public schools but other public facilities as well. As President John F. Kennedy replaced Eisenhower, the Court widened the arena that its 1954 decision had opened.

Having determined that the ICC's ban on "any unjust discrimination or any unjust or unreasonable prejudice" embraced racial discrimination,[62] the Court in 1950 confirmed this interpretation and implicitly condemned the segregation that was practiced in a railroad dining car.[63] Now in 1960, when a black traveling on an interstate bus was denied service in the whites-only section of a restaurant in Virginia and arrested for trespassing, the Court reached for a solution under the Interstate Commerce Act. Although the bus company neither owned the terminal nor the restaurant, the justices ruled that the operators of these facilities must perform their services "without discriminations prohibited by the Act."[64] So, although the justices were not ready to tackle the constitutional claims of a denial of equal protection, they were willing to expand the range of the act to cover a privately owned business that was brought into the stream of commerce by its implicit arrangement with the bus company.

That the Court was ready to deal segregation a blow wherever it was found is even more clearly presented in a case decided three years later. Here, the fact that the restaurant was in a building owned by an agency of the state of Delaware was found sufficient to hold that the restaurant owner's refusal to serve a black patron violated the equal protection clause. "It is irony amounting to grave injustice," the Court said, "that in one part of a single building, erected and maintained with public funds by an agency of the State to serve a public purpose, all persons have equal rights, while in another portion, also serving the public, a Negro is a second-class citizen, offensive because of his race, without rights and unentitled to service." To correct such a "grave injustice," the majority held "that when a State leases public property . . . the Fourteenth Amendment must be complied with by the lessee as . . . [if it were] written into the agreement itself."[65]

Then, when Memphis authorities sought to delay the immediate desegregation of public parks, the unanimous Court reminded officials that a recognition in 1955 that some delay in creating a desegregated school system might be necessary meant neither that such delay would be countenanced today nor that "the same physical problems or comparable conditions" would be relevant in delaying the integration of other public facilities. Arthur J. Goldberg, a recent Kennedy appointee to the Court, called the public's attention to the general rule "that any deprivation of constitutional rights calls for prompt rectification." Addressing the claim for immediate access by blacks, he added: "The rights here asserted are, like all such rights, present rights; they are not merely hopes to some future enjoyment of some formalistic constitutional promise." And to the contention that the goodwill existing between the races might be eroded by proceeding too rapidly, the justice said that such goodwill "can best be preserved and extended by the observance and protection, not the denial, of the basic constitutional rights here asserted."[66]

Obviously Memphis officials and the members of the Court disagreed, with the Court saying that as soon as persons were not barred from the city parks because of their race the sooner will the community be appropriately enlarged so that all can embrace a common interest. In other words, a sensitivity to individual rights not only enlarges the community but it brings that community in conformity with the essential precepts of its civil religion.

When Virginia tried to maintain segregated seating in its courtrooms, the Court lectured the state that it was no longer constitutional to "require segregation of public facilities." Segregation, it said, was "a manifest violation of the State's duty to deny no one the equal protection of the laws."[67]

Then, in a number of sit-in cases, in which the participating blacks were convicted of criminal trespass after their refusal to leave restaurants when they were denied service, the Court further indicated that the end it sought was equal justice under the law. What made the cases difficult for the Court was the fact that the discrimination practiced by the owners of private businesses had to be, in part, imputed to the state before the equal protection clause could be applied. The ruling in *Shelley* that judicial enforcement provided the requisite state action had been criticized by legal scholars, and apparently there was no support on the Court for extending the reach of that precedent. In addition, Justice John Marshall Harlan, in a dissenting opinion covering four of the five cases, said such cases presented a constitutional conflict between what he called "competing claims of high order: liberty and equality."[68] When the majority found a statute commanding segregation, it cut off any further inquiry and found the necessary state action, saying that the law removes the decision to serve or not "from the sphere of private choice."[69] When there was no such law but only public statements of officials seeking to maintain segregation, the Court said such executive action was equally coercive and therefore unconstitutional.[70]

In a concurring opinion in the latter case, Justice William O. Douglas sought to strike down all such discriminatory conduct as unconstitutional. He characterized restaurants as instrumentalities of the state in that these so-called private businesses were licensed, regulated, and supervised by the state. "There is no constitutional way," he continued, "in which a State can license and supervise a business serving the public and endow it with the authority to manage that business on the basis of apartheid, which is foreign to our Constitution."[71]

Eighty years earlier the first John Marshall Harlan, in his dissent in the *Civil Rights Cases*, had read the Fourteenth Amendment's equal protection clause in the same way to justify the nation's first public accommodations act.[72] To both Harlan and now Douglas, businesses that served the public were always associated with the government, and to retreat to the concept that the liberty of the owner must be protected to the detriment of the patron's right to be treated equally was contrary both to the Constitution and the civil religion. Neither man was able to convince his colleagues in the particular case, but clearly the times had changed, and Douglas's words tumbled into a society much more sensitive to the incompatibility between such discrimination and the theology of the civil religion.

In another sit-in case the next year Douglas found some support from his colleagues when the Court remanded a case on the basis that the state law had changed since the time of the original conviction. Arthur Goldberg wrote a concurring opinion that both Douglas and Warren joined. He began by expressing his conviction "that the Constitution guarantees to all Americans the right to be treated as equal members of the community with respect to public accommodations." Citing the words of the Declaration of Independence as "the American creed," Goldberg said the denial to blacks of their freedom and equality was a departure from these fundamental principles "which it took a tragic civil war to set right." The Reconstruction amendments, the justice continued, are to be read in "light of this American commitment to equality, and the history of that commitment . . . 'as the revelation of the great purposes which were intended to be achieved by the Constitution as a continuing instrument of government.' " Insisting that the Constitution is color blind, he said that it left no room for the perpetuation of a caste system in the country. The equality of burden imposed by the Constitution, Goldberg continued, "insures an equality of public benefits." Not only had the state failed to protect the individual's right of equal access to public accommodations, he added, but it "is now prosecuting them for attempting to exercise that right." And to the dissenters' sympathy with the freedom of proprietors to choose their customers and summon police to preserve that freedom, the justice said that "the Fourteenth Amendment resolved this issue in favor of the right of petitioners to public accommodations."[73] Quoting Alexis de Tocqueville's comment that Americans are born equal and are equal before the law, Goldberg found that the amendment was designed to ensure this freedom and equality.

Douglas, in a separate opinion, chided his colleagues for failing to confront the challenge that such sit-in cases presented, reminding them that the "Court was created to sit in troubled times as well as in peaceful days." Quoting John Marshall's words that "the very essence of judicial duty" is to resolve conflicts brought before the bench, Douglas said the issue before the Court is clearly justiciable and "basic to our way of life and fundamental in our constitutional scheme." By avoiding decision, he continued, "the prestige of law in the life of the Nation is weakened." To deny service to blacks in a restaurant "is a badge of second-class citizenship. . . . When the state police, . . . prosecutor, and . . . courts unite to convict Negroes for renouncing that relic of slavery, the 'State' violates the Fourteenth Amendment."[74]

Goldberg, Warren, and Douglas saw the desegregation of public accommodations squarely within the Court's responsibility of widening the community of equal citizens. This was to be done by making the 1776 goal of equality, forcefully reasserted in 1868 with the addition of the Fourteenth Amendment, an obligation of the Court in the exercise of its priestly duties.

For more than two decades the Court had struggled alone in chipping away at racial segregation in American society, at times keenly aware of hostility in the other two branches of the federal government. But in June 1963 President John F. Kennedy urged Congress to enact a comprehensive civil rights act, including a public accommodations section. Calling the matter "a moral issue," which "is as old as the scriptures and is as clear as the American Constitution," he insisted that the question was "whether all Americans are to be afforded equal rights and equal opportunities, whether we are going to treat our fellow Americans as we want to be treated."[75] A nation that preaches freedom around the world, he continued, can no longer deny that freedom to its black citizens.[76]

After Kennedy's assassination, President Lyndon B. Johnson insisted that the civil rights bill would be a fitting memorial to the slain president. With skillful political maneuvering, Johnson got Congress to enact the Civil Rights Act of 1964, the most significant and far-reaching civil rights legislation in American history. As he signed the bill into law, the president saw the act as the generation's contribution to the quest for freedom and the establishment of "justice in the affairs of men." He continued: "This is a proud triumph. Yet those who founded our country knew that freedom would be secure only if each generation fought to renew and enlarge its meaning." He ended with a civil religious prayer:

> Let us close the springs of racial poison. Let us pray for wise and understanding hearts. Let us lay aside irrelevant differences and make our Nation whole. Let us hasten that day when our unmeasured strength and our unbounded spirit will be free to do the great works ordained for this Nation by the just and wise God who is the Father of us all.[77]

The Civil Rights Act of 1964 and the related legislation that would follow over the next four years are products of one of those relatively rare times in American life when the American creed comes to the fore and displaces the norm of interest-group politics. Such legislation is a tribute to an often condemned political system that at times does respond to the task of translating the core theology of the civil religion into practice.

By the end of 1964, after so many years of blazing the trail itself, the Supreme Court pronounced the act's public accommodations sections constitutional. The only controversy involved the basis for the decisions, as the majority found the act amply supported by Congress's authority to regulate commerce. In *Heart of Atlanta Motel v. United States*, the majority found that Congress had ample authority to pass the act "to eliminate the obstructions it found in interstate commerce caused by racial discrimination." The fact that Congress was also seeking to deal with "a moral and social wrong," the Court said, does not restrict its authority under the commerce clause.[78]

Douglas and Goldberg protested this reliance on the commerce clause. Not only should the constitutional rights of individuals be recognized, Douglas said, but a decision based on the Fourteenth Amendment would have the effect of "putting an end to all obstructionist strategies and allowing every person—whatever his race, creed, or color—to patronize all places of public accommodation without discrimination whether he travels interstate or intrastate." Goldberg agreed, insisting that the purpose of the act "is the vindication of human dignity and not mere economics."[79]

In a related case, the Court decided that the Civil Rights Act of 1964 had the effect of bringing to a close all pending cases under state laws inconsistent with the policy embedded in the new federal legislation.[80]

The Civil Rights Act of 1964 had as its aim the elimination of a segregated society, and it authorized the federal government to institute lawsuits, thus taking the burden off the shoulders of aggrieved private parties. It also empowered federal agencies to cut off funds if compliance was not forthcoming. What this act did was place more responsibility in the executive department, thus reemphasizing the idea that government can be the protector, rather than the potential violator, of individual rights.

In 1965 Congress passed the Voting Rights Act, again bringing the federal government directly into local affairs by suspending state qualifications for the franchise in areas where less than 50 percent of the adult citizens were registered to vote. Federal examiners were sent into these areas to register new voters. When South Carolina challenged the law, the Court readily repulsed the attack. "After enduring nearly a century of widespread resistance to the Fifteenth Amendment," the justices said, "Congress has marshalled an array of potent weapons against the evil, with authority in the Attorney General to employ them effectively." Now, with the legislative and executive branches enlisted in support of making the civil theology a reality for many in society, the justices did not hesitate to pronounce the disenfranchisement practiced by certain states "evil." "Hopefully," they concluded, "millions of non-white Americans will now be able to participate for the first time on an equal basis in the government under which they live."[81] The Court quoted the words of the Fifteenth Amendment and concluded that this recent legislative action was only seeking to accomplish what that amendment had long commanded. The dream of equal justice under law was coming closer to reality and with it the inclusion of all within the confines of the civil religion.

In accordance with this expanded view, the justices considered the effect of the Voting Rights Act upon Spanish-speaking persons in New York. A section of the legislation prohibited the state's denial of voting rights to persons who had completed the sixth grade in Puerto Rico but who could not read or write English. This prohibition had the effect of nullifying New York's voting requirement. Saying that Congress has the power to determine in its discretion "what legislation is needed to secure the guarantees of the Fourteenth Amendment," the justices read the section of the act "as a measure to secure for the Puerto Rican community residing in New York non-discriminatory treatment by government—both in the imposition of voting qualifications and the provision or administration of governmental services, such as public schools, public housing and law enforcement."[82] Although the Court here switched its concern from individuals to groups, it was simply recognizing that legislation, by its essential nature, is group oriented. The justices had not recognized group rights; rather they simply explored the purpose Congress had in adding this section to the Voting Rights Act of 1965.

Although the Court welcomed and supported congressional action in behalf of civil rights, it did not hesitate to subject its own relevant precedent to careful scrutiny. In the arena of voting rights, the justices reappraised the poll tax, which, as late as 1937, had been ruled constitutional.[83] Working from this ruling, civil rights groups had succeeded in obtaining an amendment to the Constitution, the twenty-fourth, that had banned poll taxes in all elections for federal office. Less than two years after the amendment took effect, the Court heard a case that challenged the imposition of all poll taxes as a violation of equal protection.

Douglas, for a six-person majority, invalidated the levy, saying, in response to the dissenters' worry over the overruling of precedent, that constitutional guarantees are "not shackled to the political theory of a particular era." He then added: "Notions of what constitutes equal treatment for purposes of the Equal Protection Clause *do* change." Times had indeed changed in the generation between the two decisions, but equally important was the Court's willingness to ask the question of what rational connection existed between the ability to pay a fee and the state's legitimate power to set voting qualifications. Once asked, the answer was obvious. Calling the ability to pay a fee "capricious or irrelevant," Douglas ruled that "the right to vote is too precious, too fundamental to be so burdened or conditioned."[84]

Although economic discrimination would remain an intrinsic part of the capitalistic society, the majority was determined that a right so fundamental as the franchise would not be tied to one's ability to pay. To fulfill its civil religious obligation to ensure a government that has the consent of the people, the Court had made the recently enacted Twenty-fourth Amendment superfluous.

The Court did something similar with regard to the last of the trio of significant civil rights measures, the Open Housing Act of 1968. In *Jones v. Alfred H. Mayer Co.* the majority ruled that freedom from racial discrimination in housing was already prohibited by the very first federal civil rights act, passed in 1866. Joseph Lee Jones had claimed that he was denied the opportunity to purchase a house in Saint Louis County, Missouri, because of his race. After having spent recent terms stamping their approval on the actions of Congress and the chief executive, the justices seemed eager to reclaim the initiative in the area of civil rights by reinterpreting the act of 1866. That legislation sought to give all citizens equal rights "to inherit, purchase, lease, sell, hold, and convey real and personal property." Extensively surveying the legislative history of the law, the Court said that Congress was authorized to enact such a measure under its power to enforce the Thirteenth Amendment's ban on slavery. Accepting what earlier Courts would not—that this amendment was designed not only to abolish the formal institution but its vestiges as well—the justices now ruled that it provided sufficient authority for Congress to protect individual rights both from public and private action. "Just as the Black Codes, enacted after the Civil War to restrict the free exercise of those rights, were substitutes for the slave system," the Court said, "so the exclusion of

Negroes from white communities becomes a substitute for the Black Codes. And when racial discrimination herds men into ghettos and makes their ability to buy property turn on the color of their skin, then it too is a relic of slavery." The Civil Rights Act of 1866 is fully justified by congressional authority granted under the Thirteenth Amendment, the justices continued, and it "operates upon the unofficial acts of private individuals, whether or not sanctioned by law." They insisted that the Thirteenth Amendment empowered Congress to ensure that the black had "the freedom to buy whatever a white man can buy, the right to live wherever a white man can live. If Congress cannot say that being a free man means at least this much, then the Thirteenth Amendment made a promise the Nation cannot keep."[85]

This reading of the Thirteenth Amendment and its empowerment of Congress to reach private discrimination indicated a Court committed to the precepts of the American civil religion. Not only would it interpose no obstacles to congressional action designed to achieve the practical implementation of the theology, it would read the Constitution and earlier legislation as an invitation to root out the remaining vestiges of segregation in the society.

The Court's new reading of the scope of the Thirteenth Amendment had wide-ranging implications.[86] The justices had continuously struggled with the Fourteenth Amendment's requirement that the state be involved in the act of discrimination; if the Thirteenth Amendment's general ban on slavery was interpreted to reach private, as well as public, discrimination, a new tool was available to Congress. In 1976, the Court extended its broad reading of the Civil Rights Act of 1866 to strike down racial discrimination in the admissions policies of private schools. The new civil rights legislation did not reach this area, but the justices read the earlier act's conference of the right "to make and enforce contracts" as imposing an obligation upon private schools not to discriminate on the basis of race among applicants seeking to contract for their children's education. Rejecting the claim that the rights of privacy and association should be protected and that such private discrimination was unreachable under federal law, Justice Potter Stewart relied heavily on *Jones* to say that such discrimination was "wholly inconsistent" with that case's interpretation of legislative history.[87]

Furthermore, the Court read the 1866 legislation to cover not only discrimination against whites[88] but ethnic discrimination as well. Both Arabs and Jews were Caucasians, but in two cases the justices said that mid-nineteenth-century thought had merged race and ethnicity. Legislative history, they continued, shows "that Congress intended to protect from discrimination identifiable classes of persons who are subjected to intentional discrimination solely because of their ancestry or ethnic characteristics."[89]

In a concurring opinion Justice William J. Brennan drew attention to the significance of the Court's resolution to the civil religion: "Pernicious distinctions among individuals based solely on their ancestry are antithetical to the doctrine of equality upon which this Nation is founded. Today the Court upholds Congress's desire to rid the Nation of such arbitrary and invidious discrimination."[90] Clearly the Court was expanding the sweep of the early civil rights legislation in behalf of those individuals who were suffering from similar discrimination. Whether the justices read congressional intent well or not, they surely were furthering the protection of individual rights and widening the embrace of the civil religion.

As things turned out, the civil rights legislation of 1968 was to be the last of its kind, as the active sympathy of the Johnson administration was replaced by the benign neglect of his successor, Richard Nixon.

In 1967, one year before Nixon's electoral victory, the Court finally confronted an issue that it had previously avoided in the wake of the furor over school desegregation—laws against interracial marriage. Such laws not only interfered with the most intimate of personal choices but they also were barriers to cultural assimilation. Mildred Jeter, a black, and Richard Loving, a white, were married in the District of Columbia. On their return to Virginia they were convicted for violating the state's antimiscegenation law and sentenced to a year in jail. The sentence was suspended on the condition that they leave the state and not return together for twenty-five years. All the justices agreed that such statutes were clearly unconstitutional. Potter Stewart simply said that laws that make criminality depend on the race of the people involved are invalid. Chief Justice Warren, for the rest of the Court, found such statutes in violation of both the equal protection and due process clauses of the Fourteenth Amendment. Noting that sixteen states had similar legislation, he rejected the argument that such laws passed the test of equal protection because they operated equally on the races. "There can be no doubt," the chief said, "that restricting the freedom to marry because of racial classifications violates the central meaning of the Equal Protection Clause." Furthermore, Warren continued, such laws also violate the liberty afforded individuals by the Fourteenth Amendment's due process clause. Calling the "freedom to marry . . . one of the vital personal rights essential to the orderly pursuit of happiness by free men," Warren declared that a denial of this freedom on racial grounds "deprives all the State's citizens of liberty without due process of law."[91]

There was no way such laws could stand once they were measured against the Court's reading of the individual rights it now found implicit in the Fourteenth Amendment. The case is an excellent illustration of how rulings change within the constitutional system. The High Bench simply said that earlier views of the equal protection clause had been "swept away" by more recent decisions.[92] Throughout its history, the Court has been engaged in this sweeping-away process. We may wonder why present sensibilities were not shared by past Courts, but the justices' continual task is to make the protection of individual rights effective as times change and different sensibilities develop.

Miscegenation statutes were vulnerable to attack because they imposed criminal penalties for no other reason than that the parties to the relationship were of different races. Striking down such laws would not change people's attitudes about racial mixing, and such attitudes might well insinuate themselves into other situations. When the Court got such a case, it proceeded with the same unanimity in striking down what it saw as impermissible discrimination. A Florida state court had ruled that a white mother's remarriage to a black constituted sufficient grounds to deprive her of the custody of her son. Being raised in such a racially mixed household, the state court concluded, was detrimental to the son's welfare. The unanimous United States Supreme Court said that the Fourteenth Amendment was designed "to do away with all governmentally imposed discrimination based on race." When the person is submerged in her race, as was the case here, the justices asserted that the decision reached is "more likely to reflect racial prejudice than legitimate public concerns." The Constitution, they added, "cannot control such prejudices but neither can it tolerate them."[93] As now interpreted by the justices, the sacred writ commanded not only that the law be purged of such bias but that its agencies not be employed to maintain private discriminatory attitudes. The law was read to teach the lesson of individual equality within a society characterized by mutual respect.

In many ways, this decision reveals the poverty of a critical approach that suggests that the Court should defer to judgments made at the state or local level, for otherwise it makes policy. What the justices say here rests upon the same basis that their earliest predecessors used—that deferring judgment to the state implicitly condones the discriminatory action. Although some justices have been sensitive to the charge that the Court is improperly making policy, the ultimate judicial decision maker cannot escape responsibility, even when its decision simply affirms a policy already made.

The momentum of the movement to a desegregated society, in which the American creed was being translated into practice, would survive new appointments to the Court. In Chief Justice Warren's last few terms, the Court rejected some plans that resulted in little desegregation. For instance, what was wrong with a system that allowed students to choose the school they wished to attend? Does such a plan not equally protect the rights of all students? The unanimous Court did not reject such freedom of choice plans in theory, but when in practice they essentially resulted in maintaining a segregated system, the justices said more affirmative action was required. The Virginia school district involved in one case was told that school boards are "clearly charged with the affirmative duty to take whatever steps might be necessary to convert to a unitary system in which racial discrimination would be eliminated root and branch." What the Court made clear was that the beneficiaries of the *Brown* decisions are all those persons who have been denied access to a racially nondiscriminatory public school system. The responsibility for creating such a system, the justices said, "Brown II placed squarely on the School Board."⁹⁴

Affirmative action is necessary because of the constitutional ruling that all persons in such segregated schools are being denied their rights under the Court's reading of the equal protection clause. After Warren E. Burger replaced Earl Warren as chief justice, he joined in a unanimous *per curiam* opinion that referred to the question for decision as "one of paramount importance, involving as it does the denial of the fundamental rights to many thousands of school children." The justices ruled that every school district is obligated "to terminate dual school systems at once and to operate now and hereafter only unitary schools."⁹⁵

Two years later, after another Nixon appointee, Harry A. Blackmun, joined the High Bench, the Court unanimously approved a lower court order commanding extensive busing of students in the Charlotte-Mecklenburg, North Carolina, school district for the purpose of desegregating the schools. The system embraced 550 square miles, and more than a hundred schools with approximately eighty thousand students. Citing segregation as "the evil struck down by Brown I as contrary to the equal protection guarantees of the Constitution," Chief Justice Burger, for the Court, said that, when school boards fail in their affirmative obligations to ensure a racially nondiscriminatory school system, the district court can use its "equitable powers to remedy past wrongs."⁹⁶

By the early 1970s considerable progress had been made in dismantling the dual school systems of the South, and where discrimination could be established in the drawing of school districts, considerable discretion was left in the lower federal courts to fashion effective remedies. But as the 1970s dawned, desegregation activity shifted northward, and substantial antibusing sentiment was aroused. Increasingly in urban America city school systems were predominantly black, and suburban school systems were predominantly white. Segregation as official policy was banned throughout the nation, but economic and social differences tended to result in segregated residential areas that were reflected in the nation's public school systems. If meaningful desegregation was to be achieved, this matter had to be addressed. Could a federal judge, responding to the discrimination that had infected a city's school system, seek a remedy by incorporating suburban school districts into the solution? That was the question posed in *Milliken v. Bradley*, which involved schools in Detroit and the surrounding suburbs.

Despite some minor differences, the justices for twenty years had been remarkably unanimous in their conviction that racially discriminatory school systems denied to blacks the equal protection of the law. Four members of the High Bench believed that the logic of these prior decisions and the Court's priestly role in interpreting the equal protection clause necessitated a decision upholding the lower court's order to merge suburban and city schools. But Potter Stewart joined the quartet of justices that President Nixon had placed on the Court to reject that remedy.

The claim of racial discrimination in the operation of the Detroit schools had been established, but any remedy faced the intractable problem that the city schools would remain predominantly black and not reflect the racial balance that was present in the larger metropolitan area. In other words, a Detroit-only remedy would tend to leave black schools surrounded by predominantly white schools and have no meaningful effect on the type of segregation that existed in metropolitan Detroit and, by implication, many other cities as well. There was no evidence that any of the fifty-three suburban school districts, which the trial judge sought to include in his remedy, had ever been guilty of racial discrimination. The crux of the resolution concerned the willingness of the justices to hold the state, which retained some control of public education, responsible for an effective remedy for the unconstitutional actions of the Detroit school board. Such a remedy subordinated the independence of school boards to the authority of the state. The majority conceded that preexisting school districts "are not sacrosanct and if they conflict with the Fourteenth Amendment federal courts have a duty to prescribe appropriate remedies." But the majority justices said that the scope of any remedy "is determined by the nature and extent of the constitutional violation." Finding the violation here confined to the city of Detroit, they ruled that the trial court, by including the suburban districts, had sought to impose "a wholly impermissible remedy." Although the majority did not dispute the fact that state authorities were implicated in the segregationist policy of Detroit schools, it denied that this participation afforded the trial court the authority to issue the sweeping order it did. To order interdistrict busing, the justices said, would expand the constitutional right drastically and without any support "either in constitutional principle or precedent."[97]

In dissent, Justice Byron R. White accused his colleagues in the majority of "crippling the ability of the judiciary" to deal with the violation of constitutional rights. To create impenetrable walls at school district lines, he said, frustrates the granting of appropriate relief and "leaves serious violations of the Constitution substantially unremedied." And because both lower courts agreed that an interdistrict plan would effectively remedy the violation and be less burdensome administratively, White argued that the plan meets "the goal of attaining the utmost actual desegregation consistent with restraints of practicability."[98]

Thurgood Marshall, who was nominated by President Lyndon B. Johnson and became the first black to sit on the Court, began his dissent by noting that "however imbedded old ways, however ingrained old prejudices, this Court has not been diverted from its appointed task of making 'a living truth' of our constitutional ideal of equal justice under the law." Accusing the majority of now taking "a giant step backwards" and of emasculating "our constitutional guarantee of the equal protection of the laws," he said the nation is ill served by the decision. He added: "Unless our children begin to learn together," he added, "there is little hope that our people will ever learn to live together."[99]

Marshall chided the majority for failing to confront the fact that the remedy for unconstitutional segregation of the Detroit schools cannot be found within the city school system. Seeing a dual system of public schools as "the product of purposeful and intentional state action," the justice pointed out that a remedy involving only Detroit would encourage white flight. It would also allow "the State to profit from its own wrong and to perpetuate for years to come the separation of the races it achieved in the past by purposeful state action." Marshall accused the majority of being diverted from its priestly task of enforcing the guarantees of the Constitution by a "public mood" that believes that this Court has "gone far enough in enforcing the Constitution's guarantee of equal justice." Then donning the mantle of the prophet, he concluded: "In the short run, it may seem to be the easier course to allow our great metropolitan areas to be divided up each into two cities—one white, the other black—but it is a course, I predict, our people will ultimately regret."[100]

The years since the decision have only confirmed the accuracy of Marshall's prophecy. In his own dissenting opinion, Douglas drew attention to how the majority's ruling inevitably led to a situation in which the state's schools would not even meet the old *Plessy* standard of separate but equal. This was so because the Court in the previous year had put its stamp of approval on a state public school financing system that allowed for considerable inequality between rich and poor districts.[101] The result, Douglas concluded, was to allow a state to violate the equal protection clause by supervising a school system in which the races are largely separated and in which there is substantial inequality in the education afforded to children of different races.

Although the majority of the Court rejected the affirmative action that trial courts had sought to enforce in the above cases, increasingly the justices would be drawn into the task of trying to accommodate affirmative action programs within the confines of the holy writ. Such programs proliferated in all areas of society in the late 1960s and 1970s, some stimulated by the federal government, others by state government, and still others voluntarily undertaken by private businesses. How could such programs be squared with both the Constitution's focus on individual rights and with the Court's priestly task of promoting unity and inclusion?

The Court had no difficulty, for instance, in supporting federal enforcement of the Voting Rights Act,[102] or in striking down employment tests that had the effect of discriminating against certain persons under the terms of the Civil Rights Act of 1964,[103] but race-conscious admissions policies divided the High Bench. In *Regents of the University of California v. Bakke*[104] the question was whether a white applicant who had been denied admission to the medical school at the University of California at Davis was denied his rights under the Civil Rights Act of 1964 and the equal protection clause in the Fourteenth Amendment. For the purpose of increasing minority presence in the medical profession, the school had set aside sixteen of the one hundred seats in its entering class for minority students. The school was relatively new and there was no evidence of prior racial discrimination in its admissions policies.[105]

Allan Bakke, a white applicant, claimed that this admissions process had prevented him from competing for sixteen of the available slots. The school could not refute Bakke's claim that he would have been admitted had the University not eliminated him from competition for the reserved seats. Four of the justices agreed with Bakke, and four others voted to uphold the Davis admissions procedure. The deciding vote was cast by Lewis F. Powell Jr., who agreed that the school must admit Bakke because of its violation of the nondiscriminatory provisions of the Civil Rights Act of 1964. The justice, however, decided to part company with the four colleagues who agreed with him on this issue and conclude that a consideration of race in the admissions process would violate neither the act nor the equal protection clause. On this matter, he had the concurrence of the other four justices, who were ready to accommodate the Davis procedure. In this very tentative way the Court gave its approval to affirmative action policies. In the absence of any prior discrimination, quotas could not be used, but race could be taken into account as one of a number of relevant factors.

Powell argued that attempts to distinguish benign from invidious discrimination under the equal protection clause would hitch its meaning to "transitory considerations" that could "vary with the ebb and flow of political forces." He then added: "Disparate constitutional tolerance of such classifications well may serve to exacerbate racial and ethnic antagonisms rather than alleviate them." Maintaining the immutability of the equal protection clause, the justice said, is necessary for both generational consistency and national unity. Furthermore, Powell stressed, the Court's task of upholding constitutional standards necessitates focusing on "the individual who is entitled to judicial protection against classifications based upon his racial or ethnic background because such distinctions impinge upon personal rights, rather than . . . because of his membership in a particular group."[106] To condone the discrimination as benign or as advancing the status of a hitherto disadvantaged group has the inescapable tendency to take the Court away from its proper focus on the individual's rights. He, however, did envision a legitimate state interest in devising an admissions program freed from such discriminatory quotas that included race and ethnicity as factors that could be brought into competitive consideration.

William Brennan, joined by his colleagues who would have approved the Davis admissions policy, said that neither the Constitution nor the Civil Rights Act of 1964 required that "color blindness become myopia" and obscure "the reality that many 'created equal' have been treated within our lifetimes as inferior both by the law and by their fellow citizens."[107] He saw no obstacle in either civil rights legislation or the equal protection clause to the University's desire to seek greater diversity through such an admissions process. And to Powell's acceptance of race as a legitimate admissions consideration but his condemnation of the Davis approach, Brennan saw no constitutional distinction between what the University at Davis did and other plans in which race is considered.

Justice Thurgood Marshall said that the Fourteenth Amendment was clearly designed to eliminate discrimination; "to hold that it barred state action to remedy the effects of that discrimination . . . would pervert the intent of the Framers by substituting abstract equality for the genuine equality the Amendment was intended to achieve." He had no qualms about responding to "several hundred years of class-based discrimination against Negroes" with class-based remedies. "It is unnecessary in 20th Century America," the justice continued, "to have individual Negroes demonstrate that they have been victims of discrimination; the racism of our society has been so persuasive that none, regardless of wealth or position, has managed to escape its impact."[108] Marshall, who had been a leading advocate in the NAACP's long campaign against the segregated society, saw the Court closing rather than opening doors that would lead to a truly integrated society.

For Harry A. Blackmun, affirmative action was needed to aid the transition to "a society that is not race conscious." He added that "the United States must and will reach a stage of maturity where action along this line is no longer necessary. Then persons will be regarded as persons, and discrimination of the type we address today will be an ugly feature of history that is instructive but that is behind us." Blackmun argued that such accommodation does wrest the Fourteenth Amendment "from its moorings and its original purposes." If it "conflicts with idealistic equality," he added, "that tension is . . . constitutionally imposed, and it is part of the Amendment's very nature until complete equality is achieved in the area." To bar considerations of race, the justice insisted, is to "perpetuate racial supremacy," something "we dare not" do.[109]

Strangely, this badly fractured decision of the Court held up, as admissions programs continued to take race into account. What made the case difficult was the long and solidly entrenched role of the Court as a protector of individual rights.[110] Usually those who bear the burdens of social change are anonymous and certainly not specifically identified, but here was the unchallenged claim that a particular person had been discriminated against because of his race. The bare majority wished to leave room for the operation of affirmative action programs to remedy past injustice. To remove the focus on individual rights, however, ran the risk of compromising the Court's traditional role as the best guarantor of the fairness, justice, and equality that lay at the core of the civil religion.

The problem in *Bakke* was posed by the language of the Civil Rights Act of

1964, which, by banning discrimination on the basis of race, seemed to operate to limit the range of affirmative action that could be undertaken to achieve the very goals of the act. In most cases the Court considered, however, the statutory language was cited as authority for the affirmative action. Although at times there was no opinion on which the majority could agree, the margin by which the justices upheld the legislation was quite comfortable. For instance, when California neglected to provide for the teaching of English to Chinese-speaking students in its schools, the Court found a violation of the Civil Rights Act of 1964. Only five members agreed with the Court opinion, but all reached the same conclusion that the state had the obligation to furnish such instruction. To require that a student acquire the basic skills before being admitted to a public school program designed to teach those skills, the majority said, "is to make a mockery of public education."[111]

In response to the claim that the school system's failure to provide such language instruction was not motivated by a discriminatory intent, the justices said intent was irrelevant and action that has a discriminatory effect is barred by the Civil Rights Act. And when New York reapportioned certain counties to assure districts in which certain minorities were in the majority, the Court rejected a challenge by Hasidic Jews that their Fourteenth and Fifteenth Amendment rights were violated. There was no Court opinion but only a single dissent from the ruling. In announcing the judgment of the High Bench, Justice White said that the amendments do not contain a "rule against using racial factors in districting and apportionment"; nor is the "use of racial criteria . . . confined to eliminating the effects of past discriminatory districting or apportionment."[112]

Brennan's thoughtful delineation of the problems involved in drawing clear lines between benign and invidious discrimination gave this last decision special importance. First, he said, "a purportedly preferential race assignment may in fact disguise a policy that perpetuates disadvantageous treatment of the plan's proposed beneficiaries." Second, the concerns that led the Court to view race as a suspect category for "classifying individuals are not entirely vitiated in a preferential context," for "basing decisions on a factor that ideally bears no relationship to an individual's worth or needs . . . may act to stigmatize its recipient groups." Third, in interpreting the equal protection clause "we cannot well ignore the social reality that even a benign policy of assignment by race is viewed as unjust by many in our society, especially by those individuals who are adversely affected by a given classification." Although approving the congressional action in this case, Brennan suggested that the above concerns have to be balanced "against the need for effective social policies promoting racial justice in a society beset by deep-rooted racial inequities."[113]

Brennan had doubts, but Chief Justice Burger dissented, arguing that "the mechanical racial gerrymandering in this case" cannot be squared with the Constitution.[114] Thirteen years earlier, Douglas, joined by Goldberg, had dissented in a similar case. Then, he said that when a state draws lines on the basis of race, "the multiracial, multireligious communities that our Constitution seeks to weld together as one become separatist," thereby generating antagonism and the type of racial and religious partisanship that "is at war with the democratic ideal."[115]

For years legislative bodies had been apportioned to deny a fair representation to minorities.[116] The Voting Rights Act of 1965 and its subsequent modifications sought to empower minorities by requiring a type of reapportionment that would afford some reasonable proportional representation to these minorities. That race or ethnicity would be a dominant consideration was clear. The Court seemed willing to approve such action in the absence of any finding that the action deprived any individuals of fair and equal participation in the voting process. In the case involving the Hassidic Jews, the majority justices saw no constitutional impediment to a division of that community between electoral districts for the purpose of giving Puerto Ricans a better opportunity to elect some of their own to the state legislature.

In 1993, however, the Court majority indicated that such ethnically or racially inspired reapportionment plans raised serious constitutional questions. At issue in *Shaw v. Reno* was a challenge to a North Carolina district, constructed in response to an objection of the United States attorney general rooted in the Voting Rights Act. Snakelike, the district passed through ten counties and extended over a hundred and sixty miles. The avowed purpose was to create a district that would increase the chances of electing a black to Congress. The majority, so disturbed by the strange shape of the district, felt that it was drawn to promote segregation and remanded the case. It wanted the state to justify the plan as "narrowly tailored to further a compelling governmental interest."[117]

Justice Sandra Day O'Connor, appointed by President Ronald Reagan and the first woman to sit on the Court, condemned as unconstitutional the state's action as an exercise in "political apartheid" and racial stereotyping. She sought to discredit the fragmenting notion that minorities could be represented only by their own kind. To the majority justices, this attitude seemed contrary to the realities of contemporary American politics and potentially quite harmful to the unity sought by the civil religion. Classifying people by race, O'Connor added, can cause "lasting harm to our society" by implying that skin color is significant. Furthermore, she continued, "racial gerrymandering . . . may balkanize us into competing racial factions; it threatens to carry us further from the goal of a political system in which race no longer matters—a goal that the Fourteenth and Fifteenth Amendments embody, and to which the Nation continues to aspire."[118]

O'Connor's adversaries did not espouse fragmentation of the society. Instead they pointed to the fact that, since the end of Reconstruction, North Carolina had not elected a black congressional representative until the state was forced by the

Justice Department to comply with the Voting Rights Act. When minorities are empowered by giving them the opportunity to elect one of their own to office, the dissenters implied, the result was not to fragment the society but to strengthen it. This was so because those who made the laws would truly be more representative of the entire population. White, joined by Blackmun and John Paul Stevens, said no preferential treatment was involved in the action taken here for it injures no other group or person and is no more than "an attempt to *equalize* treatment, and to provide minority voters with an effective voice in the political process."[119] Stevens drew a distinction between constitutional and unconstitutional gerrymanders saying that it "has nothing to do with whether they are based on assumptions about the groups they affect, but whether their purpose is to enhance the power of the group in control of the districting process at the expense of any minority group, and thereby to strengthen the unequal distribution of political power."[120] The dissenters argued that group interests have always been at the heart of the redistricting process. To deny that race is a legitimate consideration, they said, would be a perverse reading of equal protection, given the fact that the clause was added to the Constitution to aid blacks in claiming equal citizenship.

Two years later in *Miller v. Johnson*, four dissenters continued the refrain as the majority came to a similar conclusion in regard to a Georgia district. Although two of the dissenters in the North Carolina case—White and Blackmun—had left the court, their replacements—Ruth Bader Ginsberg and Stephen G. Breyer—appointments of President Bill Clinton, now joined their colleagues—Stevens and David H. Souter—in dissent. The majority had decided that the Justice Department's interpretation of the relevant voting rights law had been erroneous, and that Georgia's attempt to comply with it did not save the apportionment scheme from invalidation.[121]

Georgia's redistricting problems came back to the Court after the federal trial court established only a single black district when the state legislature could not agree on a redistricting plan. With the same majority that had rejected the earlier plan in *Miller*, the Court in 1997 approved the lower court's action. The quartet that had dissented in *Miller* did so again.[122]

In a companion case again challenging the court-ordered shaping of a district, four justices who had been in the majority in the Georgia cases now found themselves in the minority. Chief Justice William H. Rehnquist joined the earlier dissenters to compose a new majority that upheld the district.[123]

Despite the differences among the justices, they all desired to promote a unity in which race was irrelevant under the law. While one side saw empowerment in the redistricting that looked toward a more visible and thorough integration, the other side saw a new form of segregation that emphasized the position of the racial group to the detriment of a meaningful unity. Both sides shared the same objective, but they differed on how best to accomplish the agreed-upon goal.

Clearly, however, the Court generally did not want to stand in the way of the other agencies of the federal government in their attempt to move beyond the denial of rights to a degree of empowerment. When Congress, for example, provided that in projects funded by the federal government 10 percent of those funds must be set aside for minority-owned contractors, the justices decided 6–3 that the national legislature had authority under its Fourteenth Amendment enforcement power to pass such an act. In seeking to achieve "the goal of equality of economic opportunity," Chief Justice Burger said, "Congress has necessary latitude to try new techniques such as the limited use of racial and ethnic criteria to accomplish remedial objectives."[124]

Some state and local governments sought to follow the lead of Congress with similar programs, but when the justices inspected a Richmond, Virginia, plan, a majority of them found a constitutional violation. The majority wanted clear evidence of specific discrimination and rejected the notion that general societal discrimination could justify the set-aside program. The dissenters were satisfied that the evidence presented justified labeling the program remedial and not preferential.

Affirmative action programs had always caused difficulty for a Court that habitually focused on individuals as individuals and not as members of a group. In fact, Stevens, in a concurring opinion, argued that the judiciary and not the legislature was the proper forum for redressing past wrongs done to individuals. At any rate, those in the majority in *Richmond v. Croson Co.* were clearly suspicious of affirmative action programs, even in terms of their so-called beneficiaries. Justice O'Connor, in announcing the judgment of the fractured Court, said: "To whatever racial group these citizens belong, their 'personal rights' to be treated with equal dignity and respect are implicated by a rigid rule erecting race as the sole criterion in an aspect of public decisionmaking." Rejecting the notion that the Court had a responsibility under the Constitution and the civil religion to accommodate the preferential treatment of certain disadvantaged groups in society, she wrote: "The dream of a Nation of equal citizens in a society where race is irrelevant to personal opportunity and achievement would be lost in a mosaic of shifting preferences based on inherently immeasurable claims of past wrongs." Only when evidence is presented that specific discrimination has been practiced, she continued, can all citizens be assured "that deviation from the norm of equal treatment of all racial and ethnic groups is a temporary matter, a measure taken in the service of the goal of equality itself."[125]

In concurring opinions, Anthony M. Kennedy and Antonin Scalia, two of President Reagan's nominees, pursued the theme that the civil religion is best served by focusing on individuals and not groups. Kennedy saw the Richmond plan as a naked preference "which will cause the same corrosive animosities that the Constitution forbids in the whole sphere of government and that our national policy condemns in the rest of society as well." Scalia insisted that "we play with fire" when we depart from the principle of individual merit. "Those who believe that racial preferences can help to 'even the score,' " he continued, "display, and reinforce, a manner of thinking by race that was the source of the injustice and that will, if it endures within our society, be the source of more injustice still."[126]

The majority justices were concerned about ministering to the society they served. Their task was to promote equality under the law, which, they felt, could hardly be done by upholding preferences based upon vague allegations of past discrimination.

Equally interested in instructing and nurturing the society, the minority saw matters differently. Pointing to the irony that Richmond, the seat of the former Confederacy, was now led by officials acting forcefully to overcome the discrimination of the past, Thurgood Marshall, joined by Brennan and Blackmun, saw sufficient evidence of past discrimination. To condemn such state attempts to remedy injustice, Marshall said, "does a grave disservice not only to those victims of past and present racial discrimination in this Nation whom government has sought to assist, but also to this Court's long tradition of approaching issues of race with the utmost sensitivity." Blackmun, in a short dissent that Brennan joined, also saw the decision here as out of joint with the Court's work in the area. However, he said, he was confident that in time the High Bench "will do its best to fulfill the great promises of the Constitution's Preamble and of the guarantees embodied in the Bill of Rights—a fulfillment that would make this Nation very special."[127]

The dissenters were willing to accept that past discrimination still should weigh upon constitutional decision making. Individuals are not made equal by willing them so, and Marshall, Brennan, and Blackmun were convinced that the Court's role, at least since *Brown*, had been to promote societal and governmental action designed to overcome centuries of past discrimination. The arguments on the other side, however, are strong and persistent in their identification with the civil theology of individual rights.

Justice Stevens had joined the majority in the Richmond case, but a few years earlier he had penned a dissent that indicated his special sensitivity to the relationship of racial integration to the civil religion. His colleagues had decided that dismissed white teachers who had seniority over some retained black teachers had been denied the equal protection of the laws. To use race to fasten upon individuals a badge of oppression, he began, "is unfaithful to the central promise of the Fourteenth Amendment." However, Stevens continued, "in our present society race is not always irrelevant to sound governmental decision making." Then, making the case for a racially integrated faculty, the justice said that "one of the most important lessons that the American public schools teach is that the diverse ethnic, cultural, and national backgrounds . . . do not identify essential differences among the human beings that inhabit our land."[128]

Stevens saw a world of difference in using the factor of race to exclude minority teachers and in using it to include them. Exclusion, he continued, rests on the assumption that race reflects "real differences that are relevant to a person's right to share in the blessings of a free society. . . . That premise is 'utterly irrational,' . . . and repugnant to the principles of a free and democratic society." On the other hand, "inclusion of minority teachers in the educational process inevitably tends to dispel that illusion. . . . The inclusionary decision is consistent with the principle that all men are created equal; the exclusionary decision is at war with that principle. One decision accords with the Equal Protection Clause of the Fourteenth Amendment; the other does not." Stevens said the case presented is no different from any other negotiated breach of the rule of seniority to serve important public ends, such as giving preference to a football coach or to instructors teaching the use of computers. Economic conditions, he added, force hard decisions upon administrators, and their willingness to protect the results of an affirmative action program by agreement with the teachers' union is "justified by a valid and extremely strong public interest." In conclusion, the justice said that the narrowly drawn plan under consideration here "transcends the harm to petitioners, and . . . is a step toward that ultimate goal of eliminating entirely from governmental decisionmaking such irrelevant factors as a human being's race."[129]

Stevens is saying that the protection of individual rights has always occurred in a social setting. Making seniority in employment the sole criteria for deciding which teachers will go and which will stay and for evaluating the claim that individuals have wrongfully been deprived of their jobs, he argued, is to take a simplistic approach to a complex situation. The justice shifted the focus from the teachers to the students and looked at the educational setting. The arrangement here had been worked out between the administrators and the teachers, and Stevens felt that adequate notice of the preference had been given to all involved. He recognizes that schools are the basic teachers of the theology of the civil religion. Lessons based on the theological premises of the religion, Stevens believed, are taught most effectively not by reading or preaching but rather by example.

When the Court returned in 1990 to the subject of racial preferences in federal governmental action, it upheld the authority of Congress and the Federal Communications Commission (FCC) to increase minority "participation in the broadcasting industry." Moving away from the standard of strict scrutiny of racial distinctions, the majority held "that benign race-conscious measures mandated by Congress—even if those measures are not 'remedial' in the sense of being designed to compensate victims of past governmental or societal discrimination—are constitutionally permissible to the extent that they serve important governmental objectives." The dissenters, in a consolidated opinion, insisted that "the Constitution provides that the Government may not allocate benefits and burdens among individuals based on the assumption that race or ethnicity determines how they act or think." Kennedy, in additional dissenting words joined by Scalia, lamented "the return of racial classifications to our Nation's laws" and saw no room in the Constitution to stigmatize and stereotype citizens with a new standard of "unequal but benign."[130]

By the time the issue raised in the FCC case came to the Court again, four of the justices composing the majority there had retired. Although three of the new arrivals joined the holdover, Stevens, a new majority now insisted that the federal government meet the same strict scrutiny standards demanded of states in matters of racial classification.[131] The result, of course, was a setback for affirmative action programs.

In addition to condoning a minority preference in the awarding of broadcasting licenses, the Court in 1990 returned to the issue of school integration that it had largely neglected during the 1980s. More than three decades after *Brown*, many school desegregation cases were still on the dockets of the lower federal courts. In one of the last decisions in which Justice Brennan participated before his retirement, he helped form a bare majority that affirmed a rather bold trial court remedy. A trial judge had enjoined a state law that had imposed limitations on local taxes and had ordered officials in the Kansas City School District to raise taxes to cover the cost of a public school program necessary to remedy unconstitutional segregation. Four dissenters protested the Court's condonation of such broad-ranging judicial authority, saying that in the pursuit of "the demand of justice for racial equality, . . . the Court today loses sight of other basic liberties guaranteed by our constitutional system."[132]

After Brennan retired, his remaining eight colleagues addressed a major nagging problem—the existence in the nation of many public schools still mainly composed of a single race. The strongest proponents of maintaining a commitment to school desegregation—Justices Marshall, Blackmun, and Stevens—were clearly in the minority. Even before David H. Souter, President George Bush's nominee, took his seat on the Court, a majority charted a new course. Chief Justice Rehnquist, who had been elevated to the center seat upon Warren Burger's retirement in 1986, spoke for the Court in a case coming from Oklahoma. In the decision he placed the High Bench's approval on an end to busing and a return to largely single-race neighborhood schools. Considerable segregation still characterized the schools in the state, but Rehnquist said that the local school board had complied with the order for a reasonable length of time and that there was no need to preempt the authority of local officials in running the schools when the past discrimination that had led to the judicial order had been remedied. Marshall, for the dissenting trio, protested the Court's decision to condone racially segregated schools because "13 years of desegregation was enough."[133]

By the time the Court decided that the district courts supervising desegregation could withdraw their jurisdiction on a piecemeal basis, as the various elements of the desegregation plan were effected, Justice Marshall had left the Court, but four remaining justices—Blackmun, Stevens, O'Connor, and Souter—dissented. They argued that a more searching inquiry was necessary before such district court supervision should be withdrawn. Justice Blackmun, for the quartet, felt that the majority had accepted the explanation for less than integrated schools as being due to demographic change and that it had not inquired whether school policies contributed to such change.[134]

The Court's foray into the desegregation of secondary and elementary schools had been long delayed, but the delay in its scrutiny of the progress of desegregating public institutions of higher learning had been even longer. In 1992 the justices took a look at the Mississippi university system, and all agreed that the state had not eliminated racially discriminatory policies. In the opinion for the Court, Justice White denied "that a race-neutral admissions policy cures the constitutional violation of a dual system." A state system of admission based upon standardized test scores that resulted in maintaining historically white and black schools, he ruled, is traceable to de jure segregation and has a discriminatory effect. White also pointed to the duplication of programs, saying "surely the State may not leave in place policies rooted in its prior officially-segregated system that serve to maintain the racial identifiability of its universities if those policies can practically be eliminated without eroding sound educational policies."[135]

This new concern for the desegregation of higher education in the South seemed to promise a new round of decisions that would extend into the next century, but in another area the justices wrapped up their new work quite quickly. The subject again was an old one—jury selection and racial discrimination—but with a new twist. The ruling that blacks could not be excluded in drawing up jury pools was well established; equally so was the determination that defendants had no constitutional right to have members of their race on the particular jury that tried them. Beginning in 1986, however, the Court began to address the use of peremptory challenges under the equal protection clause. In *Batson v. Kentucky*, the Court overruled a 1965 precedent and held that a prosecutor's use of such challenges to remove blacks from the jury in the trial of a black defendant violated the equal protection clause.[136]

"Purposeful racial discrimination in selection of the venire," the Court began, "violates a defendant's right to equal protection because it denies him the protection that a trial by jury is intended to secure." Not only does a deficient process prejudice the rights of the accused, the justices continued, but it discriminates against those it excludes on a basis totally unrelated to their fitness to serve as jurors. Furthermore, they insisted that it both undermines "public confidence in the fairness of our system of justice" and stimulates a racial prejudice that compromises equal justice under the law.[137]

When, on the basis of the facts of the case, a defendant makes "a prima facie showing of purposeful racial discrimination in selection of the venire," the High Bench said that the burden of proving that the challenges have not been made as a result of racial discrimination shifts to the state. "By requiring trial courts to be sensitive to the racially discriminatory use of peremptory challenges," the justices continued, "our decision enforces the mandate of equal protection and furthers the ends of justice." Then they added: "In view of the heterogeneous population of our Nation, public respect for our criminal justice system and the rule of law will be strengthened if we ensure that no citizen is disqualified from jury service because of his race."[138]

The opinion here reveals the justices assuming the mantle of priestly interpreters of the sacred writ. Not only is the individual right of the accused to an impartial jury to be protected, but also the barriers that exclude individuals from communal and civic responsibility are to be eliminated—all to ensure equal justice under a rule of law. Clearly at stake are the essentials of a civil religion that has inclusion in the community and the protection of each individual's rights at its core. Equal protection becomes the doctrinal vehicle through which these ideals of the American community are to be realized.

Later in 1986, when the Court refused to hear a case asking the justices to expand the prohibition on peremptory challenges, O'Connor took the opportunity to expand on the significance of *Batson* and spoke in the language of the civil religion. The decision there, she said, "depends upon this Nation's commitment to the ideal of racial equality, a commitment that refuses to permit the State to act on the premise that racial differences matter." Referring to "the painful social reality" that, at times, belies "the deep faith that race should never be relevant," O'Connor then explained the symbolism associated with *Batson*: "That the Court will not tolerate prosecutors' racially discriminatory use of the peremptory challenge, in effect, is . . . a statement about what this Nation stands for."[139]

Working within the racial context of *Batson*, the Court subsequently widened the reach of its ruling. Although the Court in 1990 rejected the claim of a white defendant that he had been denied a fair trial by the prosecutor's use of peremptory challenges to remove blacks from the jury,[140] the High Bench in the following year found merit in an equal protection claim against the same alleged injury. Calling service on juries "an exercise of responsible citizenship by all members of the community, including those who otherwise might not have the opportunity to contribute to our civic life," Justice Kennedy, for the Court, said that "racial discrimination in the qualification or selection of jurors offends the dignity of persons and the integrity of the courts." So, he ruled, "a criminal defendant may object to race-based exclusions of jurors effected through peremptory challenges whether or not the defendant and the excluded juror share the same race." He continued: "Jury service preserves the democratic element of the law, as it guards the rights of the parties and insures continued acceptance of the laws by all of the people." To disqualify an individual on the basis of race, he added, "forecloses a significant opportunity to participate in civic life."[141]

Seeing the jury "as a vital check against wrongful exercise of power by the State and its prosecutors," Kennedy said that a prosecutor's active racial discrimination "invites cynicism respecting the jury's neutrality and its obligation to adhere to the law." To the argument that the defendants should not be able to claim the rights of an excluded juror, the justice responded that they have a common interest in purging the courtroom of racial discrimination. A juror so rejected, he continued, "suffers a profound personal humiliation heightened by its public character . . . [and] may lose confidence in the court and its verdicts, as may the defendant if his or her objections cannot be heard. The congruence of interests makes it necessary and appropriate for the defendant to raise the rights of the juror." The Fourteenth Amendment, Kennedy added, "makes race neutrality in jury selection a visible, and inevitable, measure of the judicial system's own commitment to the commands of the Constitution." He expected the trial courts "to develop rules . . . to permit legitimate and well-founded objections to the use of peremptory challenges as a mask to race prejudice."[142] The justices seemed as insistent upon using the claim of racially biased jury selection to promote inclusion of blacks in the community as they were to protect the rights of the accused.

Two months later the Court, with only one defection from its previous seven-person majority, applied its new rule to civil cases as well. Clearly a prosecutor's action is attributable to the state, but how is state action involved in a private suit? Again writing for the Court, Kennedy said that private parties are subject to constitutional restraints when the government dominates "an activity to such an extent that its participants must be deemed to act with the authority of the government." Here, the justice said that "a private party could not exercise its peremptory challenges absent the overt, significant assistance of the court." When the bench lends its support to a racially determined use of peremptory challenges, he insisted, it "in a significant way has involved itself with invidious discrimination." Selecting jurors, Kennedy maintained, "represents a unique governmental function delegated to private litigants by the government and attributable to the government for invoking constitutional protections against discrimination by reason of race." He continued: "If peremptory challenges based on race were permitted, persons could be required by summons to be put at risk of open and public discrimination as a condition of their participation in the justice system."[143]

To permit such discrimination in the courtroom "where the law itself unfolds," Kennedy said, "mars the integrity of the judicial system and prevents the idea of democratic government from becoming a reality." For the justice, the courtroom, no less than the schoolhouse, had to be safeguarded as a place where the civil religion can be taught best by example. A multiracial democracy, he added, "must recognize that the automatic invocation of racial stereotypes retards . . . progress and causes hurt and injury." Law, Kennedy continued, should dispel fears and preconceptions respecting racial attitudes. The quiet rationality of the courtroom makes it an appropriate place to confront race-based fears or hostility by means other than the use of offensive stereotypes. "Whether hostility or fear is the cause," he said, "neither motive entitles the litigant to cause injury to the excused juror." If bias in the case is feared, the justice added, "the issue can be explored . . . with respect for the dignity of persons, without the use of classifications based on ancestry and skin color."[144]

As a result of these rulings, the only remaining matter left for decision was the ability of criminal defendants to use their peremptory challenges to remove blacks from the jury. In the case that came before the High Bench, white defendants were accused of assaulting two blacks. Again, the Court demonstrated that its new reading of the equal protection clause was a two-way street, as it concluded that criminal defendants were as limited as prosecutors in their use of peremptory challenges in the process of selecting a jury. In the first of the peremptory challenge cases, the dissenters were Rehnquist and Scalia. In the subsequent civil case, O'Connor joined them. Chief Justice Rehnquist and new arrival Clarence Thomas,[145] whom President Bush had nominated to replace Thurgood Marshall, bowed to the earlier precedent and agreed with the result. Scalia, who had consistently opposed the Court's new rulings in this area, took pleasure in pointing out that the latest decision "gives the lie once again to the belief that an activist, 'evolutionary' constitutional jurisprudence always evolves in the direction of greater individual rights." Here in an effort to improve race relations, he added, "we use the Constitution to destroy the ages-old right of criminal defendants to exercise peremptory challenges as they wish, to secure a jury that they consider fair."[146]

Scalia seemed content to take litigants and defendants as they were—prejudices and all—and accommodate them within the law,[147] while the majority sought to redefine the culture of the trial and make it an example for the society as a whole. In this foremost drama of the law, the civil theology should be given more than lip service; it should be both practiced and taught. To accommodate prejudice and allow racial stereotyping by permitting such wholesale peremptory challenges, the Court said, would belie the nation's ideals and deny equal justice under the law. Even if one's prejudices could not be eradicated by the law, the majority believed that the law can demand that those who invoke its agency recognize the mutual respect at its core.

In dealing with matters of racial discrimination the justices had fashioned a jurisprudence based upon the equal protection clause that advanced the civil theology with its goals of equal justice and inclusion in the community. In opening this new legal arena, the Court invited new claims from new litigants.

STRUGGLING TO EQUALIZE JUSTICE AND EXPAND THE CIVIL THEOLOGY'S REACH: PART II: OTHER MATTERS, INCLUDING GENDER AND SECTARIAN RELIGION, 1962–1997

The Court's new reading of the requirements of the Fourteenth Amendment's equal protection clause in the civil rights area led other litigants to seek the embrace of its protective range. One of the most unusual of such claims came not from persons who were part of some minority but rather from individuals who laid claim to being part of the democratic majority. Population in the twentieth century had shifted from rural to urban and suburban areas, but rarely had apportionment in state legislatures or in the U.S. House of Representatives kept pace.[1] Responding to aggrieved voters who argued that Tennessee had denied them the equal protection of the laws by diluting their votes through malapportioned voting districts, the justices in 1962 concluded that their argument had constitutional merit.[2] The majority in *Baker v. Carr* characterized the claim as one of political right, the adjudication of which it pronounced "a responsibility of the Court as ultimate interpreter of the Constitution."[3]

Concurring, Justice Tom C. Clark drew out the underlying premises of the majority's decision and rhetorically tied them both to the theology of the civil religion and to the Court's role under it. This was not a political question, he argued, because "the people of Tennessee are stymied and without judicial intervention will be saddled with the present discrimination in the affairs of their state government." Citing John Rutledge, a delegate at the Constitutional Convention from South Carolina, Clark declared that a fundamental purpose of the establishment of the Supreme Court was "to secure the national rights," among the most important of which was that government must be truly representative of the people. To the dissenters' claim that the Court should be self-restrained and cautious,

Justice Clark responded that "national respect for the courts is more enhanced through the forthright enforcement of those rights rather than by rendering them nugatory through the interposition of subterfuges." "The ultimate decision today," Clark concluded, "is in the greatest tradition of this Court."[4]

Felix Frankfurter and John Marshall Harlan protested the decision, arguing that the Court should stay its hand and not get involved in a conflict between state government and its electorate. Their colleagues, however, were convinced that the Court had both the authority and the duty to make government responsive to the consent of the governed. To the dissenters' lament that the Court could not set all things right, the majority responded that, in this instance, the High Bench could not shirk its priestly responsibility to make the fundamental articles of faith a reality in the republican society. Indeed, the issue involved not only the rights of individuals but the very integrity of representative government.

That the justices recognized this fact was made clear in subsequent decisions. In *Baker*, the Court had simply determined that the claim of unconstitutional apportionment should be heard. Unlike what followed *Brown* when the High Bench left the lower courts to proceed as best they could, the justices repeatedly took cases in the next two terms to sketch in the guidelines for reapportionment under the equal protection clause.

Less than a year after *Baker*, the Court contended with Georgia's system for electing candidates in a Democratic primary for the U.S. Senate and statewide offices. A voter in sparsely populated Echols County had as much weight in the nomination of candidates as ninety-nine voters in populous Fulton County. The Court read the equal protection clause to mandate that when elections are held statewide "all who participate in the election are to have an equal vote . . . wherever their home may be in that geographical unit." Saying that the Constitution "visualizes no preferred class of voters," the Court concluded: "The conception of political equality from the Declaration of Independence, to Lincoln's Gettysburg Address, to the Fifteenth, Seventeenth, and Nineteenth Amendments can mean only one thing—one person, one vote."[5]

In the next year the Court responded similarly to another claim from Georgia citizens who resided in a congressional district that had more than twice the population of the average Georgia congressional district. The justices now said that substantial equality of population among the districts was the standard required under the equal protection clause. Responding to the argument that Congress alone had the authority to protect the rights of citizens to vote for federal officials, Hugo L. Black, for the Court, said that Article I cannot be read to "immunize state congressional apportionment laws which debase a citizen's right to vote from the power of courts to protect the constitutional rights of individuals from legislative destruction." He continued: "The right to vote is too important in our free society to be stripped of judicial protection by such an interpretation of Article I."[6]

Black then launched into a discussion of the Constitutional Convention and its "tenaciously fought for" decisions to base representation in the House solely on population and provide for popular election. Calling the right to vote "precious," he said that all "other rights, even the most basic, are illusory if the right to vote is undermined."[7]

The justice sought to make clear that the longtime deviation in the states from a standard of equal representation was contrary to the intent of the Constitution's framers and a clear violation of the principle of consent. To give to the rule of law its stature, force, and moral authority, Black insisted, no less than equal participation in the process of its making was necessary.

Later in the same term, the Court put the finishing touches on its reapportionment guidelines. *Reynolds v. Sims* held that both houses in a state legislature had to be apportioned solely on the basis of population. Viewing the right to vote as "the essence of a democratic society," Chief Justice Earl Warren, for the Court, said that "the right of suffrage can be denied by a debasement or dilution of the weight of a citizen's vote just as effectively as by wholly prohibiting the free exercise of the franchise."[8] To create classes of favored and disfavored voters, whose votes have differing weight, he declared, is to engage in prohibited discrimination.

"Diluting the weight of votes because of place of residence," the chief continued, "impairs basic constitutional rights under the Fourteenth Amendment just as much as invidious discriminations based upon . . . race." He then continued: "Our constitutional system amply provides for the protection of minorities by means other than giving them majority control of state legislatures." Responding to the critics of the earlier decisions, Warren simply said that "a denial of constitutionally protected rights demands judicial protection; our oath and our office require no less of us." The chief insisted that the principle announced here—that where people live cannot justify differences in the weighing of their votes—was established early in the nation's history. "To the extent that a citizen's right to vote is debased," Warren concluded, "he is that much less a citizen."[9]

These decisions did stir political activity that sought a constitutional amendment permitting at least one house of a state legislature to consider factors other than population in apportionment. The proposal, however, never emerged from Congress. One reason for this failure was that, as the states reapportioned their legislatures, enough of the people elected were, in fact, beneficiaries of the recent decisions.[10] The Court had entered an area; taught a lesson about consent, representation, and republican government; established guidelines; and in less than a decade did much to make representative government more viable and more responsive to contemporary problems.

By 1962, when the Court was ready to contend with malapportionment in the states, it had decades of experience with claims of voting discrimination—the effective denial to individuals of the right to participate as consenting actors in the political process.[11] In the reapportionment decisions these earlier cases were drawn upon to justify intervention in terms of the Court's responsibilities under the civil theology. If one person's vote counts less than another's, that person is not equally protected by the law, and the people's consent to their government is proportionately diminished. Contrary to the position of the dissenters, the majority justices realized that remedying apportionment problems in the states was a task clearly imposed upon them by their role within the civil religion. At the heart of its theology was not only the protection of individual rights but also the central idea that government was only legitimated by the consent of the governed. To remove the obstacles to that meaningful consent was in the best tradition of the Court.

Although the reapportionment decisions dislodged entrenched minorities to protect the rights of those individuals who could now compose an empowered majority, the Court has been far more involved in protecting the rights of individuals who have been members of real or virtual minorities. Women, who in fact comprised more than 50 percent of the nation's population, began to focus the Court's attention on gender discrimination. Only in 1920 did women throughout the nation gain the franchise. Those who fought so hard to reach this goal in the hope that enfranchisement would pave the way to greater equality under the law were initially frustrated.[12]

As recently as 1961, on the eve of new federal legislation designed to prevent sex discrimination, the Court had found no constitutional obstacle to Florida's absolute exemption of women from jury service.[13] Women could serve, but only if they voluntarily registered for jury service. A criminal defendant argued that her conviction for the murder of her husband was in violation of the Fourteenth Amendment because of this wholesale exclusion of women from the jury pool. Rejecting the claim, the Court said that because women remain "the center of home and family life," a state is not constitutionally barred from concluding "that a woman should be relieved from the civic duty of jury service unless she herself determines that such service is consistent with her own special responsibilities."[14] Apparently the woman in this case felt that a jury composed of husbands, former husbands, and would-be husbands might be less than impartial in judging her.

A decade later, in *Reed v. Reed*, the justices seem to have awakened to a growing woman's movement that had become more vocal and insistent in its assertions of equal rights. Confronting an Iowa law that gave preference to men in selecting administrators of decedents' estates, they unanimously struck down the preference. Administrative convenience, the Court said, cannot justify the making of "the very kind of arbitrary legislative choice forbidden by the Equal Protection Clause of the Fourteenth Amendment."[15]

As with cases claiming racial discrimination, the justices here were taking the perspective not of the state but of the person bringing the claim. Was Iowa law not telling the claimant that she was less qualified than a male to administer the estate? Before the civil rights revolution, the Court had routinely upheld such discrimination because there was some rational basis for the state's action.[16] The question earlier was can the state's action be rationalized; now the Court asked if the discrimination violated the individual's federal right to equal protection under the law? This latter perspective not only reveals the justices' sensitivity to protecting individual rights, but it also tends to promote decisions striking down inequality in the law, which, in turn, promotes the full inclusion of women in the national community.

When the sex discrimination claim was levied against the federal government, the justices applied the *Reed* precedent. *Frontiero v. Richardson* involved a difference in the way members of the armed services could claim a spouse as a dependent for purposes of housing allowances and fringe benefits. A married male could claim his wife as a dependent without further inquiry; a married female, on the other hand, had to prove that she was contributing over 50 percent of her spouse's support. The justices had little sympathy for the military's argument of administrative convenience in that most of the female spouses were truly dependent and most of the male spouses were not.

What caused the rift in the Court was not whether this system was constitutional or not but rather was sex a suspect category, thereby placing a greater burden on government to justify different treatment of the sexes. Four members of the Court, Justices William J. Brennan Jr., William O. Douglas, Byron R. White, and Thurgood Marshall, were ready to place sex in the same category as race. In announcing the Court's decision in the armed services case, Brennan confronted sex discrimination in American society, something the justices had not done earlier. He acknowledged "that our Nation has had a long and unfortunate history of sex discrimination . . . which, in practical effect, put women, not on a pedestal, but in a cage." Saying that "gross, stereotyped distinctions between the sexes" in the nineteenth century tended to make "the position of women . . . comparable to that of blacks under the pre–Civil War slave codes," Brennan argued that, as with race, sex is highly visible, and "statutory distinctions between the sexes often have the effect of invidiously relegating the entire class of females to inferior legal status without regard to the actual capabilities of its individual members."[17] Noting the statutory condemnation of sex-based classifications in the Civil Rights Act of 1964, Justice Brennan insisted that governmental action must be subjected to strict scrutiny when gender is the basis for distinguishing between similarly situated persons.

The four other justices supporting the resolution felt that no such elevated standard was required. Because the nation was then deciding whether to ratify the proposed Equal Rights Amendment, the quartet believed that the judiciary should not preempt the ongoing political process. Should the amendment pass, freedom from sexual discrimination would become a fundamental right, and states would have to establish a compelling interest to justify any gender-based difference in treatment. The Equal Rights Amendment, however, would not be ratified, and the four members of the Court who wanted to hold government to a higher standard in gender-based discriminations would not be able to gain a fifth vote.

Although the justices refused to place gender in the same category with race, most of them did insist that governmental regulations in the area pass more than a simple rationality test. For instance, in assessing Oklahoma's decision to restrict the sale of 3.2 percent beer to females under eighteen and males under twenty-one, the majority said such discrimination was not justified in achieving any substantial governmental objectives. Brennan, for the Court, declared that "the principles embodied in the Equal Protection Clause are not to be rendered inapplicable by statistically measured but loose-fitting generalities concerning the drinking tendencies of aggregate groups."[18]

Generally the Court based its decisions in employment discrimination cases on Title VII of the Civil Rights Act of 1964, as when it ruled that blanket height and weight requirements for jobs were invalid because they tended to discriminate against women.[19] In fact, the justices proclaimed that Title VII "provides the exclusive judicial remedy for claims of discrimination in federal employment."[20] Three years later in 1979, however, the Court had to take back these words. The occasion was a claim of sex discrimination levied against Congressman Otto E. Passman of Louisiana. Congress had specifically exempted itself from the provisions of the Civil Rights Act of 1964, a not uncommon practice. Shirley Davis had been refused promotion on Passman's staff because the congressman said that the position's heavy and diverse workload demanded a man. Faced with the exclusion in Title VII, Davis sued under the Fifth Amendment, contending that the equal protection requirement had been read into the amendment's due process guarantee and that she could sue under its provisions.

Justice Brennan, for the majority, agreed that the amendment's due process clause now included an equal protection component that "confers on petitioner a federal constitutional right to be free from gender discrimination." Next, he admonished the lower court for failing to distinguish between a constitutional and statutory right. Congress may indeed determine who may enforce a statutory right, Brennan continued, but "justiciable constitutional rights are to be enforced through the courts." This is so because there is "no effective means other than the judiciary to enforce these rights."[21] Notice here, almost two centuries after Thomas Jefferson expressed hope that the judiciary would guard individual rights, how the majority accepted this very responsibility.

Clearly, Shirley Davis had been the victim of sexual discrimination. The majority's insistence upon reading the fundamental law to protect her from such discrimination was a furtherance of the Court's primary function and a further reduction of barriers that obscure the merit and the qualifications of the individual. In finding a private justiciable right to be free from gender discrimination in the Fifth Amendment the Court had to push beyond its precedents, but the majority's solicitude for individual rights was in keeping with the Court's best tradition.[22]

Although the Court did uphold a statutory rape statute that penalized only the man and a draft registration requirement for men only,[23] its tendency was to strike down laws that either discriminated against men or imposed unequal burdens upon them. For example, when the Mississippi University for Women denied a male applicant the opportunity to prepare for a career in nursing, the Court concluded that the school had violated the equal protection clause of the Fourteenth Amendment. Acknowledging that the Court had allowed such discrimination when members of the favored sex had actually suffered a previous disadvantage,[24] the majority found no such excuse here. In fact, the justices concluded that the school's denial of admission to the male applicant was actually perpetuating the stereotype that nursing was woman's work. Any "gender-based classification . . . ," they said, "must be applied free of fixed notions concerning the roles and abilities of males and females." Lewis F. Powell Jr. in dissent accused the majority of rejecting an American tradition of diversity that he saw as "the essence of our democratic system."[25]

When the majority in 1996 applied the rule of the Mississippi case to the Virginia Military Institute, Powell had left the Court and only Antonin Scalia dissented. For the majority, Ruth Bader Ginsberg, President Bill Clinton's first nominee to the High Bench, responded to Virginia's attempt to justify the single-sex institution by telling the state that the Court no longer would condone the sexual stereotyping that limited the potential of individual females. "Generalizations about 'the way women are,' estimates of what is appropriate for *most women*," the justice said, "no longer justify denying opportunity to women whose talent and capacity place them outside the average description."[26]

Generally, the Court ruled that men must receive the same benefits challenged laws conferred upon women. For instance, a man in Alabama attacked the constitutionality of a system in which women were excluded from ever paying alimony. The Court agreed that the statute violated the equal protection clause. Although the woman in the case could hardly have applauded the Court freeing her former spouse from making the alimony payments earlier ordered, the justices saw the decision as furthering the quest for individual equality. "Legislative classifications which distribute benefits and burdens on the basis of gender," they said, "carry the inherent risk of reinforcing stereotypes about the 'proper place' of women and their need for special protection." Insisting upon gender neutrality, the Court condemned the statute for carrying "the baggage of sexual stereotypes."[27]

In one decision, however, a majority did uphold a financial preference for a widow, saying that the Florida law did not stigmatize females but, instead, simply recognized that in "a male-dominated culture, the job market is inhospitable to the woman seeking any but the lowest paid jobs."[28]

Justices Marshall and Brennan protested when the Court upheld a Massachusetts preference for veterans in staffing its civil service against a claim that it discriminated on the basis of sex. Pointing to the fact that under this law women occupied the less responsible and lower paid positions in state service, Marshall concluded that this type of "statutory scheme both reflects and perpetuates precisely the kind of archaic assumptions about women's roles which we have previously held invalid."[29]

The justices would have had to embrace a social engineering role to have invalidated the Massachusetts preference law,[30] and they felt much more comfortable in dealing with discrimination that was more clearly the result of prevailing sexual stereotypes. For example, when Illinois made the children of an unwed mother, who had died, wards of the state without any hearing on the fitness of the unwed father to raise them, the Supreme Court invalidated the law. "The private interest here, that of a man in the children he has sired and raised," the justices said, "undeniably warrants deference and, absent a powerful countervailing interest, protection." To presume the unfitness of unwed fathers, they continued, is not justifiable. Responding to the state's defense of the presumption on grounds of speed and efficiency, the Court spoke of its special responsibility to protect the rights of individuals as part of its civil religious duty. The justices ruled that the Bill of Rights and the due process clause "were designed to protect the fragile values of a vulnerable citizenry from the overbearing concern for efficiency and efficacy that may characterize praiseworthy government officials no less, and perhaps more, than mediocre ones." Cheapness and ease, they said, cannot be accepted as an excuse for "running roughshod over the important interests of both parent and child."[31]

The Court had highlighted an arena of conflict between citizen and government: the citizen's desire to be evaluated as an individual and the government's desire to establish rules that were to be applied generally. As indicated in the unwed father decision, the justices were well aware that their task was to prevent government in its search for convenient solutions from treading upon the rights of the individual.

With this sensitivity the High Bench considered school regulations that forced pregnant teachers out of the classroom at an appointed time in their pregnancies and mandated when, after the birth of their children, they could return to work. Jo Carol LaFleur was required to take maternity leave five months before the expected birth of her child and could not apply for reinstatement until three months after the birth. Maintaining that the "Court has long recognized that freedom of personal choice in matters of marriage and family life" is protected by the due process clause, the majority ruled that such "restrictive maternity leave

regulations can constitute a heavy burden on the exercise of these protected freedoms." Not only does "an irrebuttable presumption of physical incompetency"
have no rational connection to the individual teacher, but also such a presumption,
the justices continued, violates the due process clause by unduly penalizing a
woman who chooses to bear a child.[32] The regulation requiring the woman to
wait three months after the birth of her child to reapply for employment was
invalidated on the same grounds.

Generally, however, the Court looked with suspicion upon claims that affected
only women. For instance, when California refused compensation to a woman
whose disability resulted from pregnancy, six members of the Court upheld the
policy and said that it did not violate the equal protection clause. The three dissenters, Brennan, Douglas, and Marshall, believed the policy was discriminatory in that
it covered men "for all disabilities suffered, including those that affect only or
primarily their sex."[33] When the claim was based on Title VII of the Civil Rights
Act, the Court reached the same conclusion. In dissent, Justice Brennan, joined by
Marshall, argued that "today's labor environment warrants taking pregnancy into
account in fashioning disability policies." Contending with the majority's view
that such policies are based on risk allocations not discrimination, he said that they
"are not creatures of a social or cultural vacuum devoid of stereotypes and signals
concerning the pregnant woman employee." Justice John Paul Stevens insisted
that "the rule at issue places the risk of absence caused by pregnancy in a class by
itself" and therefore "discriminates on account of sex."[34]

Congress agreed with the protesting justices and passed the Pregnancy Discrimination Act of 1978 that wrote the dissenting position into law. Earlier, a unanimous Court had held that an employer cannot deny a woman, required to take an
unpaid leave for pregnancy, her seniority upon her return to work. Although there
was no requirement that a benefit be conferred upon women that men did not
share, the justices said, neither can "a substantial burden" be placed upon women
"that men need not suffer."[35] The Court confronted the new federal legislation
indirectly when it sought to decide whether California could supplement the federal act by providing for a qualified right of the woman to reinstatement. Although, as the dissenters noted, state legislation had imposed this requirement upon
all employers, even those with no disability policy, the majority found ample room
for states to supplement the federal law.[36]

Acknowledging the growing number of women in the workplace, the justices
consistently insisted that they be treated equally with men. For instance, the Court
said that the Social Security Act's provision for benefits to widows but not widow-
ers was a preference that could not stand. The Constitution, it ruled, "forbids the
gender-based differentiation that results in the efforts of female workers required
to pay social security taxes producing less protection for their families than is produced by the efforts of men."[37] Despite their greater longevity as a group, the

Court mandated that women could not be charged more to fund their pensions because Title VII of the Civil Rights Act of 1964 prohibited discrimination "against any *individual* with respect to this compensation, terms, conditions, or privileges of employment because of such *individual's* race, color, religion, sex, or national origin."[38]

The Court's insistence on distinguishing the individual from the class in the pension case was especially significant. Including individuals in classes tends, necessarily, to stereotype them and to submerge their individuality. Stevens, for the majority in the pension case, said that the controlling legislation's "focus on the individual is unambiguous. It precludes treatment of individuals as simply components of a racial, religious, sexual, or national class." Here, he continued, "there is no assurance that any individual woman . . . will actually fit the generalization on which the . . . policy is based."[39] Because this is so, Stevens concluded, the unequal compensation that results from the larger pension deduction violates the Civil Rights Act of 1964.

Notice the way in which the majority focuses its gaze on the particular woman claimant. While the dissenters were willing to hold the woman to statistical averages predicting that her pension years would be longer than those of male workers, thus rationalizing the difference in take-home pay, the majority said statistics have little value in dealing with any one member of a class. To deny the individual woman's claim because of certain characteristics of the class, the majority ruled, discriminates against her on the basis of her gender.

Courts are able to respond to individual claims because of the system that they serve—a system designed to hear and address an individual's claim for equal justice. The result is to make the judiciary a key factor in maintaining the respect for the individual within the diverse society, where the tendency both to stereotype and to see the society in terms of contending interest groups is strong. This insistent focus of the Court on the individual claim is what gives to that institution such a key role in maintaining the civil religion.

That the Court seemed insistent on purging the workplace of paternalistic attitudes that have hampered the economic potential of woman workers is well illustrated in the subsequent decisions of the Court. For instance, the majority insisted that a male challenger to an affirmative action plan had to prove its unconstitutionality. In the case of the advancement of a woman to a supervisory position over the claims of a male, the majority justices saw no obstacle to "voluntary employer action" seeking to eliminate "vestiges of discrimination in the workplace."[40] In another case, *Automobile Workers v. Johnson Controls*, the company had instituted a policy that barred female workers "who are pregnant or who are capable of bearing children" from jobs in which they would be exposed to lead. Fertile men were given a choice as to whether to risk such exposure that was denied to fertile women. Clearly, the Court said, this was discrimination based on sex that was prohibited by Title VII as modified by the Pregnancy Discrimination Act. To claims of the company that allowing women to make such a choice could expose it to a liability that would threaten the company's existence, the majority simply said that such facts were not present here. Making clear that it saw its task in terms of providing equal opportunity for both sexes by recognizing the capacity of all workers to make their own choices, the Court concluded that Congress had empowered the woman to decide whether her "reproductive role is more important to herself and her family than her economic role."[41]

The justices realized that distinctions between the sexes were embedded in the culture and that those that hampered the practical equality of women would take time and effort to root out. By the mid-1970s, however, they were eagerly grasping opportunities to strike laws that embedded such notions. For instance, when the Court considered a Utah law providing for parental support of males to age twenty-one and females to age eighteen, the justices condemned the distinction. They declared that forcing a female to bring "her education to an end earlier coincides with the role-typing society has long imposed."[42] No longer, they seemed to say, would law as a definer of the culture be an ally of those who sought to perpetuate sexual stereotypes. As interpreters of that law, the justices would seek to make the equality promised by the civil theology a reality.

Earlier in the same term in 1975, the Court was ready to reconsider the 1961 decision approving a wholesale exemption of women from jury service. This time the issue was raised by a male defendant in Louisiana, who argued that the general exclusion of women from jury service denied him a fair trial. In the jurisdiction females comprised 53 percent of the population but only 10 percent of those eligible for jury service. Women had to specifically offer themselves for service, and no woman had been included in the defendant's jury pool. Much had happened over the last decade or so, and now seven members of the High Bench found that the defendant had standing to raise the issue. Noting that the Court had made the Sixth Amendment's requirement of an impartial jury binding upon the states in 1968,[43] the justices ruled that the requirement that a jury be chosen from a cross section of the entire community was an integral part of this right. The purpose of the jury trial, they said, "is to guard against the exercise of arbitrary power." Such protection, they concluded, is missing when "the jury pool is made up of only special segments of the populace or if large distinctive groups are excluded from the pool."[44]

Notice here how the individual's right to a fair and impartial jury is deemed violated because a large group of potential jurors are excluded from service solely on the basis of their sex. The fact that the individual is male and those excluded are female is irrelevant as far as the Court is concerned. Fairness demands the end of any type of wholesale exclusion. Although the Court had taken almost thirty years to impose upon the states the same rule of jury selection that it had imposed upon the federal courts,[45] in the interim it had worked through a series of cases in which the essential individual rights protected by the Bill of Rights were increasingly made available to individuals at the state level. The inherent injustice of excluding women was seen earlier, but the barriers against nationalizing rights had only slowly been eroded. The Constitution had been designed to secure the blessings of liberty; now the Court was diligently working toward that end.

With the path so well blazed, it was only a matter of time before the claim of sex discrimination in the use of peremptory challenges would seek the Court's attention. And in 1994 the Court said that the use of peremptory challenges by the prosecutor to exclude, in this case, males from a jury was constitutionally impermissible. In a case seeking to establish paternity and gain child support, the prosecutor had used nine of ten peremptory challenges to remove males, the result being an all-female jury.[46]

Justice Harry A. Blackmun, for the Court, found the sex discrimination practiced here a violation of the equal protection clause. Such action, he said, "serves to ratify and perpetuate invidious, archaic, and overbroad stereotypes about the relative abilities of men and women." After analogizing the exclusion of women with that of blacks, Blackmun condemned the state's view that gender was a reliable predictor of a juror's attitudes. Exclusion based upon sex, he continued, "causes harm to the litigants, the community, and the individual jurors who are wrongfully excluded from participation in the judicial process."[47] In regard to the community, Blackmun said it would lose confidence in a system that perpetuates unjust stereotypes, encourages cynicism, and implicates the judiciary itself in gender discrimination.

Jurors themselves, the justice continued, have a right to a nonexclusionary selection system, and men as well as women are equally protected. Blackmun said that such exclusion "denigrates the dignity of the excluded juror," asserts the person's inferiority, and sends a message that simply because of gender a person is "presumed unqualified by state actors to decide important questions." The justice stressed the importance of the Court's new work in constitutionalizing the jury selection process.

> Equal opportunity to participate in the fair administration of justice is fundamental to our democratic system. It not only furthers the goals of our jury system. It reaffirms the promise of equality under the law— that all citizens, regardless of race, ethnicity, or gender, have the chance to take part directly in our democracy. . . . When persons are excluded from participation in our democratic processes solely because of race or gender, this promise of equality dims, and the integrity of our judicial system is jeopardized.[48]

The way to protect the status and the authority of the courts, Blackmun implied, was to ensure that the players in the courtroom drama were not either directly or indirectly contradicting the message of sexual equality that the High Bench was sending.

Anthony M. Kennedy added an opinion of his own in which he sought to reemphasize what he saw as crucial to the Court's ruling and to its civil religious role. Insisting that the equal protection clause mandated that government not submerge the individual in a class, he concluded that the harm of such challenges "is to personal dignity and to the individual's right to participate in the political process."[49] Cautioning that individual jurors sit not as representatives of a class but as representatives of the community, Kennedy highlighted an important function of the Court's work—proclaiming the dignity of individuals and their importance in the society.

Accusing the majority of obscuring its legal reasoning "by anti-male-chauvinist oratory," Scalia, writing for the three dissenters, denied that a peremptory challenge sent the same message that exclusion did.[50] What Scalia missed was the majority's sensitivity to the Court's role as a definer of the culture. In its envisioned culture, lingering historical stereotypes are banished and individuals are seen as truly equal under one law. To argue, as the dissenters did here, that this should not be the role of the Court is to argue against two hundred years of history. As an expositor of the nation's law, the Court cannot escape its cultural and civil religious role.

If law is the important ingredient in the cement holding the society together, then indeed it is important that those who practice law put their own houses in order by seeking the very diversity that characterizes the society. Therefore, a unanimous Court had no difficulty concluding that a law partnership was covered by Title VII of the Civil Rights Act of 1964 in a suit by a female associate who claimed that she was not made a partner because of her sex. Justice Powell, in a concurring opinion, said that race and sex are both widely and properly regarded as irrelevant factors in such decisions. "This is demonstrated," he continued, "by the success of women and minorities in law schools, in the practice of law, on the bench, and in positions of community, state, and national leadership. Law firms— and, of course, society—are the better for these changes."[51] Powell might also have mentioned that the High Bench itself was no longer a men's club with the appointment of Sandra Day O'Connor three years earlier in 1981.

Title VII, the Court also said, covered instances of sexual harassment. The statute "makes it 'an unlawful employment practice for an employer . . . to discriminate against any individual with respect to his compensation, terms, conditions, or privileges of employment, because of such individual's race, color, religion, sex, or national origin.'" Accepting Equal Employment Opportunity Commission (EEOC) guidelines, the justices concluded that sexual harassment encompassed "a hostile or abusive work environment." A lower court holding that, because the plaintiff had voluntarily engaged in a sexual relationship with her supervisor, she could not claim sexual harassment was rejected. "The correct inquiry," they said, "is whether respondent by her conduct indicated that the alleged sexual advances were unwelcome, not whether her actual participation in sexual intercourse was voluntary."[52]

The fight for equal access to the workplace was a part of women's basic struggle for equal rights, but a workplace that becomes uncomfortable and hostile for reasons of sexual harassment hardly comports with the equality that is promised. Here the Court put its stamp of approval upon the view that this equality meant not only that women should have access to all jobs and be evaluated fairly in terms of salary and advancement but that they should not have to compete under the burden of resisting the advances of supervisors. Congress in Title VII may not have considered the problem of sexual harassment, but both the EEOC and the Supreme Court saw this issue encompassed by the act's goal of removing sex discrimination from the workplace.

In 1993 the Court sought to clear up some confusion among the circuits as to whether a work environment had to result in damage either to the individual's physical or psychological well-being in order to be judged "hostile." A unanimous bench said no. Although something more than offensive conduct was required, a case could be made when a reasonable person could judge the working environment to be abusive or hostile.[53]

Earlier the Court had decided that Title IX of the Civil Rights Act of 1964, as amended in 1972, which prohibited discrimination based on sex in any educational program receiving federal funds, did give a private cause of action to a woman denied admission to a medical school on grounds of her gender.[54] That case did not involve a claim for damages based on the alleged sex discrimination, but that matter arose in 1992 when a female student in the Georgia public schools alleged sexual harassment and sued for damages. All the justices agreed, but three, including Clarence Thomas, whose confirmation hearing had been made a subject of great public attention by charges of sexual harassment, questioned whether the Court should continue to find private causes of action when Congress had not specifically provided for them.[55] The majority, however, was inclined to provide a judicial forum for a claim by one of the intended beneficiaries of such legislation. Congress could always overrule the Court, but in recent years the federal legislative branch was more apt to correct the High Bench when it failed to respond to an individual claim, such as with its passage of the Pregnancy Discrimination Act of 1978.

Just as Douglas, Brennan, and Marshall had been willing to pronounce sex a suspect category, which would force the state to meet a higher burden in justifying distinctions, they now were willing to characterize the right to an education as fundamental. Such a categorization would force the state to establish a compelling interest to justify the denial of equal educational opportunities. The specific issue presented in *San Antonio School District v. Rodriguez*,[56] was whether wealth could also be considered a suspect category. Texas supplied a basic dollar amount to each district based on the number of children enrolled that was then supplemented by local property taxes, which varied considerably from district to district. A bare majority of the justices, recognizing the widespread employment of such a system of financing in public education, saw no violation of the equal protection clause.[57] The dissenters, however, were convinced that educational opportunities were denied to children in the poorer districts. Looking at the case through the perspective of the state and local districts, the majority had found an acceptable system of financing. Looking at the situation through the perspective of the children in the various districts, the dissenters saw a clear case of discrimination. The widespread nature of such economic discrimination in the society led the majority to accommodate its results. On the other hand, the minority felt that in the crucial area of public education the effects of such economic discrimination were detrimental to the national interest.

Brennan argued that the majority's view that education could not be a fundamental right because it was not so specified in the Constitution was myopic. In instances like the present one, the justice continued, the Court should consider "the right's importance in terms of the effectuation of those rights which are in fact constitutionally guaranteed," among which he listed the right to vote and the right to free speech.[58]

In a separate dissenting opinion joined by Douglas, Marshall picked up Brennan's refrain, insisting that "the fundamental importance of education is amply indicated by the prior decisions of this Court, by the unique status accorded public education by our society, and by the close relationship between education and some of our most basic constitutional values." To find protection in the Fourteenth Amendment for "discrimination against important individual interests with constitutional implications and against particularly disadvantaged or powerless classes," Marshall added, is to make effective "the guarantees of our Constitution."[59] To deal with the matter simply in commercial terms, the justice warned, is to obfuscate the issues involved and abdicate the responsibility placed upon the Court both to educate and to make the Constitution's protection of individuals meaningful.

Potter Stewart, in a concurring opinion, took the opportunity to contend with the dissenters' willingness to find new individual rights within the equal protection clause. That clause, he insisted, "confers no substantive rights and creates no substantive liberties." Its function "is simply to measure the validity of classifications created by state laws."[60]

Despite Stewart's protest and the contrary decision in the San Antonio case, his colleagues were increasingly inclined to view such claims of unconstitutional discrimination with far more sympathy than had their predecessors on the bench. Part of the reason for this was the adoption of the claimant's perspective rather than that of the government. The question increasingly was whether, from the individual's perspective, the law operated to deny him or her the equality promised. *Brown v. Board of Education* had denied that equality under the law could exist when individuals were classified in terms of their race and dealt with in a manner disrespectful of their individuality. The Court would repeatedly be invited to view similar claims that illustrated how respect was denied individuals by subsuming them within a group and then imputing to them the claimed characteristics of the group.

One of the bases upon which the majority had relied in the San Antonio case was that the state's funding of the school districts had fulfilled the basic obligation to provide for the education of all children.[61] Two years after the decision in this case, Texas decided not to provide an education for some persons within the state—the children of illegal aliens. Funds for the education of these children were cut off, and local school districts were authorized to deny them admission to the schools.[62]

The High Bench faced this state policy in *Plyler v. Doe* and divided five to four. Justice Brennan, for the majority, rejected the claim that illegal aliens were not persons protected by the equal protection clause. Second, he said, that clause "was intended as a restriction on state legislative action inconsistent with elemental constitutional premises." Recognizing that illegal immigration had created an underclass that challenges "a Nation that prides itself on adherence to principles of equality under law," Brennan proclaimed that "legislation directing the onus of a parent's misconduct against his children does not comport with fundamental conceptions of justice." Pointing "to the pivotal role of education in sustaining our political and cultural heritage," he said that its denial "to some isolated group of children poses an affront to one of the goals of the Equal Protection Clause: the abolition of governmental barriers presenting unreasonable obstacles to advancement on the basis of individual merit."[63]

Brennan realized that the failure to provide an education for such children would deny them the "ability to live within the structure of our civil institutions" and make their contributions to the nation.[64] Brushing aside considerations of cost, length of residence, and claims that the public education system would be impaired, he said that extracting such a social and individual cost hardly seemed rational. The Court would not allow a primary facility for instructing persons in the American civil religion—the public school system—to bar the innocent victims of the conduct of others. Such attempts to restrict the community had to be repulsed if the Court was to fulfill its priestly function.

Despite the Court's rejection of the claim based upon the inequality of educational resources in Texas, the justices had lent a sympathetic ear to some claims of economic discrimination. So, the poll tax in Virginia was struck down because distinctions "drawn on the basis of wealth or property, like those of race, are traditionally disfavored."[65] When states refused to provide trial transcripts or counsel for the appeal of indigent defendants, the Court condemned such actions. In the first of these cases Justice Black, in announcing the judgment of the Court, said that the Constitution's due process and equal protection clauses are designed to address the "age-old problem" of ensuring "equal justice for poor and rich, weak and powerful alike." When "the kind of trial a man gets depends on the amount of money he has," Black concluded, there can be no equal justice for all.[66] In regard to the appointment of counsel on appeal, the majority said that "where the merits of *the one and only appeal* an indigent has as of right are decided without benefit of counsel, we think an unconstitutional line has been drawn between rich and poor."[67]

One of the most significant of these economic discrimination cases involved the right of women on welfare to obtain divorces. To file a suit for divorce in Connecticut costs $60, money that the claimants did not have. The lower court had dismissed the complaint, but the Supreme Court reversed. "Perhaps no characteristic of an organized and cohesive society," the justices said, "is more fundamental than its erection and enforcement of a system of rules defining the various rights and duties of its members." Due process, they continued, is central to the operation of this system and makes "the State's monopoly over techniques for binding conflict resolution . . . acceptable." To ensure that the ordered society is just, "this Court has through years of adjudication put flesh upon the due process principle." A state, they concluded, may not "pre-empt the right to dissolve this legal relationship without affording all citizens access to the means it has prescribed for doing so."[68]

If local governments could not make the ability to pay a prerequisite for equal justice, could they impose certain restrictions on recipients of welfare payments? When state and District of Columbia governments sought to make such benefits contingent upon a period of residence in the jurisdiction, Brennan, for the Court in *Shapiro v. Thompson,* invalidated the attempts. He ruled that their "purpose of inhibiting migration by needy persons into the State is constitutionally impermissible." The justice found a consistent acceptance by the Court of a fundamental right of the individual to travel throughout the country, despite the absence of any such written guarantee in the Constitution. "This Court," Brennan said, "long ago recognized that the nature of our Federal Union and our constitutional concepts of personal liberty unite to require that all citizens be free to travel throughout the length and breadth of our land uninhibited by statutes, rules, or regulations which unreasonably burden or restrict this movement." Seeing a one-year time limit as just such a burden, he pronounced such regulations unconstitutional. Quoting from an earlier Court opinion, Brennan said that government cannot "chill the assertion of constitutional rights by penalizing those who exercise them."[69]

If those drawing welfare benefits were not going to be denied their membership in the American community or their dignity before the law, how about those persons born out of wedlock—the so-called illegitimate? When the Court was confronted in *Levy v. Louisiana* with the denial by the state of the right of such children to sue for the wrongful death of their mother, the split on the Court clearly reflected the differing perspectives of the justices. Douglas, for the majority, looked at the distinction from the perspective of the illegitimate children and saw the state classifying them as "nonpersons." From this vantage point, he saw Louisiana law violating the equal protection clause, saying that it invidiously discriminates "against them when no action, conduct, or demeanor of theirs is possibly relevant to the harm that was done the mother."[70]

What is revealed clearly in the handling of such cases is the way in which unspoken assumptions lead inevitably to different results. Harlan, for the three dissenters, approached the case from the perspective of the state's ability to regulate the area and found justification for the distinction made. Douglas, on the other hand, saw the case from the perspective of the children and the alleged violation of their rights to be treated equally under the law. Illegitimacy carried its own social stigma and, from the majority's perspective, the law had an obligation to triumph over this stigma, not succumb to it. The decision here illustrates how a focus on individual rights tends to erode barriers that work against the establishment of a community under a rule of law.

When less than three years later in 1971, with some changes in its membership, the Court left some room for a state to prefer legitimate children, Justice Brennan protested. He accused the majority of excluding illegitimate children from the reach of the equal protection clause and subscribing to "the untenable and discredited moral prejudice of bygone centuries which vindictively punished . . . hapless, and innocent, children."[71]

Slightly over a year later, each side had lost an adherent, and two more Nixon appointees joined the Court. Only one of them, William H. Rehnquist, however, objected to the Court's rescue of *Levy* as the controlling precedent governing the case the High Bench now faced. What was at issue was Louisiana's preference for legitimate over illegitimate children in recovery for the death of their father under the state's workmen's compensation law. The other new arrival, Lewis F. Powell Jr., wrote for the majority, saying that *Levy* stood for the proposition that there must be "equality of treatment under the statutory recovery scheme." He said the pertinent question was whether the state's classification could stand when measured against the "fundamental personal rights" endangered by the classification. Where the majority the previous year had been attracted to the rationale that the state had a legitimate interest in promoting marriage, Powell now said to penalize a child for being born of an illicit union "is illogical and unjust." Recognizing that they could not reach "the social opprobrium suffered by these hapless children," he said that they certainly could "strike down discriminatory laws relating to status of birth where—as in this case—the classification is justified by no legitimate state interest."[72]

Powell's opinion was joined by six other members of the Court, a firm majority committed to eradicating the stigma of illegitimacy under the equal protection of the law. What is significant here is that within the space of four years the Court had announced a decision that protected individual rights and by law refused to honor social prejudices that had resulted in inequality of treatment. Then, as the first two Nixon appointees found the dissent in *Levy* more attractive than the majority opinion, the Court backed away from its belief that illegitimacy did not provide an excuse for the discrimination found in state law. The discomfort that resulted from this decision led all the prior members of the majority, with the exception of Blackmun, to change their mind and rescue *Levy* as the controlling precedent in the area.[73] Changes in Court membership can have a decisive effect in regard to particular decisions, but the strength and logic of inclusionary decisions that protect individual rights have the effect of triumphing over momentary aberrations. Only so long can reasonable state action obscure compelling claims for equal protection. The thrust of the underlying civil theology with its suspicion of such discrimination is simply too great.

Clearly, the Court was using the equal protection clause to demand of the states that they not ignore the individual in wholesale determinations of preference. Strict scrutiny was demanded when a fundamental right was involved or when the classification was suspect. The justices never determined that illegitimacy was a suspect classification and at times recognized a legitimate governmental interest in the orderly administration of estates, but the thrust of the decisions was in the direction of removing the law's reflection of the social opprobrium of illegitimacy. The picture of society the Court offered was one in which individual dignity and equality were not to be subordinated to matters over which the individual could exercise no control.

The High Bench, however, did pronounce alienage a suspect category, placing it in the arena with race.[74] The Constitution's due process and equal protection clauses protected persons, not simply citizens. The use of "persons" in the Fourteenth Amendment was designed to make the protection conform to the Fifth Amendment's wording. The reason for the difference in the privileges and immunities clause of the Fourteenth Amendment can be found in its antecedent in Article IV, Section 2 of the Constitution, which was designed to prevent discrimination in a state's treatment of citizens of other states. That use of "citizens" was carried over into the privileges and immunities clause of the Fourteenth Amendment. Some of the chief sponsors of the amendment and of this formulation had expected that this clause would provide the constitutional basis for protecting new national rights of citizenship. The Court's decision in the *Slaughter-House Cases* sapped the vitality of this provision and forced the focus on the two other protective clauses of the amendment, which did not limit their embrace to citizens. The result of all this was to expand the potential range of those who were protected as members of an American community. While other nations continue to discriminate between citizens and aliens, the provisions in the American holy writ work in the direction of incorporating aliens under the broad protection of the American rule of law.

Over its history, the Court had sought to balance the federal government's control over aliens with the fundamental law's protection of equal justice. For instance, we have seen how Justices Stephen Field and David Brewer protested, often unsuccessfully, against the federal government's campaign against the Chinese on the basis of the Fifth Amendment. We have also seen how the justices accepted the fact that facially neutral regulation by local government could operate to deprive such aliens of their rights under the Fourteenth Amendment's equal protection clause. That the Court in 1971 would find that classification based upon alienage was inherently suspect, thereby requiring the state to prove a compelling interest, seemed but an inevitable development of the justices' new focus on the equal protection clause.[75]

Eight justices agreed that state attempts to distinguish between citizens and aliens for the purpose of receiving welfare benefits ran afoul of the equal protection clause. Conceding that no one had a fundamental right to welfare payments, they said the deficiency here was that alienage was a suspect category and that the requirement of a compelling state interest was not satisfied by the "State's desire to preserve limited welfare benefits for its own citizens."[76]

Where important government functions were involved, such as in staffing a police force, the Court was willing to uphold a discrimination by a state against aliens.[77] When the majority agreed that that such discrimination could extend to the hiring of public school teachers, four members of the Court dissented. The majority had justified its approval, in part, on the basis that the public schools were "an 'assimilative force' by which diverse and conflicting elements in our society are brought together on a broad but common ground" on which "fundamental values necessary to the maintenance of a democratic political system" are inculcated. The dissenters wondered how such a common ground for diversity could "be achieved by disregarding some of the diverse elements that are available, competent, and contributory to the richness of our society and of the education it could provide."[78]

This was a typical civil religious debate on the High Bench. Both sides agreed that the schools play a vital role in teaching the essentials of the civil religion and provide an arena in which diversity should be both respected and accommodated. The dissenters were eager to welcome and embrace that diversity, while the majority accepted state authority to limit and confine it. The civil religion values diversity, and it seeks to ensure it by protecting individual rights. By viewing teachers

as governmental functionaries, the majority sought to overcome the equal protection rights of alien teachers. But as the dissenters made clear, an earlier six-to-three
decision of the Court prohibiting states from discriminating against alien applicants
to the state bar could hardly be squared with the decision here.[79] They condemned
the majority's decision for failing to acknowledge the Court's special role in ensuring the protection of individual rights in the pluralistic society. When the Court
in 1984 held that states could not refuse alien applications for the position of notary
public, only Justice Rehnquist dissented.[80]

Clearly, the Fourteenth Amendment has been viewed as an invitation to the
Court to evaluate carefully the claims brought under it and provide "Equal Justice
Under Law."[81] Well before the addition of the equal protection clause to the Constitution in 1868, the Court had accepted a certain responsibility to provide equal
justice and protect individual liberty. What the addition of the clause did, however,
was add to the sacred text this foundational element and further incorporate this
tenet of the civil religion into the constitutional fabric. Here we have seen how
the Court responded to claims brought under the equal protection clause, how it
widened the scope of the American community, and how it not only maintained
but also furthered its ordained role in American society.

A new emphasis on equality, however, did not mean that individual liberty was
now subordinated in the constitutional order. One of the most important of those
rights involved religious liberty, which the First Amendment sought to secure in
two clauses, one protecting the free exercise of religion and the other seeking to
bar government from intruding in religious matters. Obviously, religion backed by
the authority of government had the potential to burden the conscience of the
individual. We have seen earlier how the Court interpreted the First Amendment's
establishment clause to place a barrier between government and religion. That
barrier, however, was not interpreted to prohibit certain forms of indirect support,
such as the state paying for the bus transportation of parochial students or releasing
students early for the purpose of religious instruction.[82]

In 1962, for the first time, the Court confronted prayer in public school classrooms. The New York Board of Regents had composed a twenty-two word prayer
and required that it be recited by students at the beginning of each school day. A
challenge to this state-prescribed activity was rejected by New York courts on the
basis that students were not forced to join in the prayer. Black, for the Court, said
that New York's action "breaches the wall of separation between Church and
State," a wall created by the establishment clause in the First Amendment that is
made binding upon the states by the Fourteenth Amendment. This protection, he
continued, "must at least mean that in this country it is no part of the business of
government to compose official prayers for any group of the American people to
recite as a part of a religious program carried on by government." Citing the
history of religious persecution, Black said that by the time the Constitution was

drafted Americans knew "that one of the greatest dangers to the freedom of the individual to worship in his own way lay in the Government's placing its official stamp of approval upon one particular kind of prayer or one particular form of religious services."[83] Neither denominational neutrality nor the fact that dissenting students may remain silent or leave the room, the justice continued, can cure the constitutional defect.

In addition to the implicit pressure upon religious minorities to conform, Black insisted, "a union of government and religion tends to destroy government and to degrade religion." On the latter point, the justice said that such mergers tend to encourage religious persecution. The founders of the nation, he added, recognized "that religion is too personal, too sacred, too holy, to permit its 'unhallowed perversion' by a civil magistrate." Then, responding to the claim that the decision here was hostile to religion, Black insisted that having the people rely upon themselves and their spiritual advisers for guidance in religious matters was "neither sacrilegious nor antireligious." And to the argument that New York's action was no real threat to religious liberty, the justice quoted James Madison's admonition that "it is proper to take alarm at the first experiment on our liberties."[84]

Stewart, the lone dissenter, pointed to many instances in which God's blessings were sought in governmental practice. He would accommodate them, as well as the New York prayer, as part of a long tradition of "deeply entrenched and highly cherished spiritual traditions of our Nation."[85]

Despite Black's careful opinion, the furor the decision caused had not subsided when in the subsequent term the justices ruled that readings from the Bible came under the same ban. Tom Clark, for the Court, said that the establishment clause requires that a challenged practice must have a clear secular purpose and neither advance nor inhibit religion. Furthermore, he continued, to prove a violation of the establishment clause requires no showing of coercion; government interference by itself constitutes the violation. Recognizing that a study of religion is a proper part of education and that the Bible can indeed be analyzed as a literary and historical source, Clark said that such secular study is clearly distinguished from the practices involved in the cases before the Court. The government, he insisted, can neither "aid or oppose" nor "advance or retard" religion. And to the argument that such rulings hinder the majority's religious freedom, the justice responded that the free exercise clause "has never meant that a majority could use the machinery of the State to practice its beliefs."[86]

In these opinions the justices said that religion's importance in the lives of the people meant that it must be protected from the coercive force of government. Neutrality, as Justice Clark sought to make clear, was a policy designed to accomplish this end. In allowing individual human beings to determine for themselves their place in the cosmos, the Court hardly intended to belittle the importance of such a determination.

The human being's place within the constitutional system, however, is an entirely different matter. In fact, we have pictured the justices as serving a civil religion by treating individuals with dignity and protecting their rights, equality, and personal choice. We have suggested that law is a language through which the culture is defined and redefined and that the Court plays a primary role both in this process and in nurturing a sense of common identity. As high priests, the justices guard, teach, and implement the civil theology. Civil religion, as that term is used here, is defined largely in functional terms. Its task is to provide unity for an expanding community of very diverse people. It seeks not to supplant traditional religions but to ensure them the room they need to fulfill the demands of their believers. To separate public faith from private faith may not be easy, either for individuals or societies, but civil religion is premised on both the ability and necessity of doing just that. In fact, civil religion is a response to the fact that many diverse religions exist in American society. This pluralism of private religions necessarily invites the creation of a public faith that can both house and unify diverse people. It can succeed in its fundamental task not by seeking to homogenize the many private faiths but by affording them and their adherents respect and a promise that they will be free to follow their own paths to salvation.

In a very extensive concurring opinion in the Bible-reading cases, Justice Brennan sought to disassociate the decision from the question of whether the framers of the Constitution and the First Amendment would have condemned such practices. In what was now even more obviously a nation of diverse believers, he said, the Court's task must be to look at what the First Amendment's religion clauses were designed to do and the substantive evils they sought to guard against in order to be "responsive to the much more highly charged nature of religious questions in contemporary society." Then, burrowing to the heart of the matter, Brennan said that late-eighteenth-century Americans could not envision the development of free public education in which these "schools serve a uniquely *public* function: the training of American citizens in an atmosphere free of parochial, divisive, or separatist influences of any sort—an atmosphere in which children may assimilate a heritage common to all American groups and religions."[87]

Here was the essence of the problem, for indeed the function of the public schools was seen not only in terms of teaching basic skills but of teaching the civil religion itself. The Court could reinforce and make operative the civil theology, but the school system itself was a primary transmitter of the civil religion to the young. Pointing to the fact that state prescription of religious exercises in the public schools was a relatively recent development, Brennan said such laws cannot be justified as serving a secular purpose. Drawing upon the civil theology, he suggested that readings from great American speeches "or from the documents of our heritage of liberty, daily recitation of the Pledge of Allegiance, or even the observance of reverent silence at the opening of class may . . . adequately serve the solely secular purposes of the devotional activities." This alternative, the justice added, would not jeopardize "either the religious liberties of any member of the community or the proper degree of separation between the spheres of religion and government."[88]

To the contention that the application of the establishment clause in the First Amendment to the states was not justified because that clause does not protect the freedom of the individual, Brennan responded that it was designed to bolster religious liberty in a way that the free exercise clause alone could not accomplish. Although denying that any common core of theology from all religions could be extracted and used in the classroom, Brennan said that even if it were possible, the result would still be offensive to those who reject any form of public communion. In regard to the noncompulsory features of such state requirements, the justice agreed that this was not relevant in an establishment case. Brennan explained that "the excusal procedure seems to me to operate in such a way as to discourage the free exercise of religion on the part of those who might wish to utilize it, thereby rendering it unconstitutional in an additional and quite distinct respect."[89]

In the wake of these decisions certain religious groups and their political supporters sought to get Congress to propose an amendment to the Constitution to legitimate school prayer.[90] But no such resolution has emerged from Congress, and the Court has continued to strike down various attempts to inject religion into the public school classroom. In 1968, the justices unanimously rejected an Arkansas law forbidding the teaching of the doctrine of evolution in the public schools.[91] Almost twenty years later, the Court was no more favorable to a Louisiana statute that required equal time for balancing the teaching of evolution with the religious theory of creation, now labeled "creationism."[92] Also, the Court ruled that the Ten Commandments could not be posted in public school classrooms as required under Kentucky law.[93]

Despite the consistency here, the Court in the years since the school prayer decisions had accommodated certain governmental actions dealing with religion. In 1970 eight members of the Court decided that state tax exemptions for churches could survive constitutional challenge. In writing for the Court, Chief Justice Warren E. Burger saw no advancement of religion or governmental entanglement in the exemption scheme, for churches were grouped with other nonprofit institutions, all of which received the same benefit. He noted that all states provided for such tax exemptions and that the tradition went back to pre-Revolutionary times.

Brennan added that such consistent and long-established practice "is a fact of considerable import in the interpretation of abstract constitutional language." But rather than stop here he assessed the rationale behind the practice. First, the justice said, churches "contribute to the well-being of the community in a variety of nonreligious ways, and thereby bear burdens that would otherwise either have to be met by general taxation, or be left undone by the community." Then to counter

Douglas's dissenting opinion, which saw in the exemption a direct subsidy to religion, Brennan responded that such exemptions are justified because religious organizations, as other nonprofit organizations, contribute "to the diversity of association, viewpoint, and enterprise essential to a vigorous pluralistic society."[94] Seeing clear secular purposes in the exemption, he read the consistent history into the Constitution.

In 1983 Brennan's implicit worry that his colleagues might seek to shortcut constitutional analysis by deferring to past societal practice was borne out when the Court upheld the use of chaplains in legislative bodies. A six-person majority held that the Nebraska legislature's employment of a chaplain was consistent with federal practice that had started with the very Congress that had sent the Bill of Rights to the states for ratification. "In the light of the unambiguous and unbroken history of more than 200 years," the Court said, "there can be no doubt that the practice of opening legislative sessions with prayer has become part of the fabric of our society . . . ; it is simply a tolerable acknowledgment of beliefs widely held among the people of this country."[95]

Although Stevens found the state legislature's practice inconsistent with the ban on religious preference imposed by the First Amendment, Brennan, in a more extensive dissent joined by Marshall, lectured the majority for ignoring the Court's responsibility within the constitutional order. The establishment clause, he said, commands that "religious issues, precisely because of their importance and sensitivity, not become the occasion for battle in the political arena . . . and that no American should at any point feel alienated from his government because that government has declared or acted upon some 'official' or 'authorized' point of view on a matter of religion." Finding "that legislative prayer violates both the letter and spirit of the Establishment Clause," Justice Brennan attacked the Court's historical justification and its view of the Constitution as a static document.[96]

To label the prayer involved " 'nonsectarian,' " Brennan warned, "will inevitably and continuously involve the State in one or another religious debate." He continued: "It is simply beyond the competence of government, and inconsistent with our conceptions of liberty, for the State to take upon itself the role of ecclesiastical arbiter." To the claim that his strict separationist view would rob "the Nation of its spiritual identity," the justice responded that, in fact, a contrary decision here would "have invigorated both 'the spirit of religion' and the 'spirit of freedom.' "[97]

Brennan highlights a fundamental difference among the justices. The majority justices saw the Court's task in terms of accommodating the religious beliefs of the dominant number, despite the obvious opposition of some individuals to the official incorporation of such views into the social fabric. On the other hand, the minority justices believed that any popular outcry stimulated by a contrary decision was based upon a misconception of the purpose of the establishment clause and the proper role of the Court. The establishment clause was designed to keep government out of religious affairs because such interference caused division and compromised religious freedom. Brennan reminded his colleagues and the American people that the spiritual core of their nation was personal freedom, which could only be ensured by freeing religion from the potentially chilling hand of government.

In the following year, 1984, the Court confronted the case of a municipality incorporating a Christian religious symbol, the crèche, in a Christmas display. Among other things, the display included a Santa Claus house, a Christmas tree, and representations of animals and human figures. A bare majority of the justices accommodated the practice by draining the crèche of its religious significance. Speaking for the majority, Chief Justice Burger referred to "an unbroken history of official acknowledgment by all three branches of government of the role of religion in American life from at least 1789." He noted that the nativity scene "depicts the historical origins of this traditional event long recognized as a National Holiday." Responding to the claim that the display would lead to social divisiveness, Burger said "that this Court has not held that political divisiveness alone can serve to invalidate otherwise permissible conduct."[98] In conclusion, he ruled that the city had a secular purpose for including the crèche and that its inclusion neither advanced religion nor excessively entangled government in religious affairs.[99]

O'Connor added some words of her own. She read the establishment clause to say that government is prohibited "from making adherence to a religion relevant in any way to a person's standing in the political community." It violates this command when it endorses religion, the justice continued, for it "sends a message to nonadherents that they are outsiders, not full members of the political community, and an accompanying message to adherents that they are insiders, favored members of the political community." Here, O'Connor concluded, the city cannot be said to have endorsed religion by simply celebrating the "public holiday through its traditional symbols."[100]

Brennan disagreed and wrote for the four dissenters. "Neither the character of the Christmas holiday itself, nor our heritage of religious expression," the justice began, "supports this result. Indeed, our remarkable and precious religious diversity as a Nation, . . . which the Establishment Clause seeks to protect, runs directly counter to today's decision." To find a secular purpose in the display of the crèche, Brennan continued, ignores the clear evidence that "demonstrates that a narrower sectarian purpose lay behind the decision to include a nativity scene." Clearly, municipal authorities sought to convey the message that the views of minority religious groups and atheists "are not similarly worthy of public recognition nor entitled to public support." A failure to heed the command of the establishment clause, he warned, means that, "because communities differ in religious composition, the controversy over whether local governments may adopt religious symbols will continue to fester." For persons to be excluded by their government "is an insult and an injury that, until today, could not be countenanced by the Establishment Clause."[101]

Five years later the Court returned to consider the display of a crèche and of a menorah during the holiday season. The crèche was surrounded by flowers on the grand staircase of a county courthouse with a banner proclaiming "Gloria in Excelsis Deo." The menorah was displayed with a Christmas tree outside a government building with a sign reading: "During this holiday season, the city of Pittsburgh salutes liberty. Let these festive lights remind us that we are the keepers of the flame of liberty and our legacy of freedom."[102] The justices could not agree on an opinion. Four of them argued that whether the government could be said to endorse the displays was not relevant to a decision under the establishment clause, a proposition that the other five rejected. However, when the votes were counted, six members of the Court found the display of the menorah in its context acceptable under the First Amendment, but five justices found the display of the crèche unacceptable. Four members of the Court would have upheld both displays, and three would have rejected them both.

Blackmun, in announcing the judgment of the Court, did have the support of four of his colleagues in rejecting the minority's attempt to exclude government endorsement from an inquiry of whether the establishment clause had been violated. In fact, he called "offensive" and "absurd" the charge that the majority was hostile or indifferent to religion. He accused the minority of misperceiving "a respect for religious pluralism, a respect commanded by the Constitution, as hostility or indifference to religion. No misperception could be more antithetical to the values embodied in the Establishment Clause." There was no escape, he said, from the conclusion that the display of the crèche resulted in the endorsement of the Christian religion. In regard to the menorah, however, Blackmun sided with his adversaries and concluded that "the city's overall display must be understood as conveying the city's secular recognition of different traditions for celebrating the winter-holiday tradition."[103]

O'Connor also contended with the minority's attempt to confine the reach of the establishment clause to cases of coercion or attempts to proselytize. That view, she said, would not fully "protect the religious liberty or respect the religious diversity of the members of our pluralistic political community."[104]

Brennan and Stevens, in dissenting opinions joined by Marshall, saw no essential differences between the display of the crèche and the menorah. Brennan attacked the view that the Christmas tree was exclusively a secular symbol and Stevens the view that the menorah could be viewed as something more than a religious symbol. Stevens saw the second display as endorsing two religions, "the very kind of double establishment that the First Amendment was designed to outlaw."[105]

Behind all these opinions was the one by Kennedy that Rehnquist, White, and Scalia endorsed. Accusing his colleagues of "an unjustified hostility toward religion," he argued that the establishment clause "permits government some latitude in recognizing and accommodating the central role religion plays in our society." The justice maintained that "the risk of infringement of religious liberty by passive or symbolic accommodation is minimal." Such noncoercive action, Kennedy continued, "does not violate the Establishment Clause unless it benefits religion in a way more direct and more substantial than practices that are accepted in our national heritage." Viewing the establishment clause only as barring government coercion or proselytizing, he said that "the principles of the Establishment Clause and our Nation's historic traditions of diversity and pluralism allow communities to make reasonable judgments respecting the accommodation or acknowledgment of holidays with both cultural and religious aspects."[106]

Three years later, in 1992, when the Court addressed a prevalent school practice with definite religious overtones, however, Kennedy had apparently changed his mind. In *Lee v. Weisman*, the Court in a five-to-four decision found prayers offered during the invocation and benediction of a public school graduation ceremony unconstitutional. The Reagan and Bush administrations had given support to a constitutional amendment permitting prayers in the public schools, but that proposal was still stalled in Congress. However, in this Rhode Island case, the United States attorney general received permission both to file an *amicus curiae* brief and to participate in urging the Court to approve the practice, apparently a good-faith effort of the administration to repay religious groups for their political support.

The Court looked broadly at the practice permitted in Providence schools that allowed principals to invite a member of the clergy to participate in graduation ceremonies. A rabbi was invited to a middle school graduation and given a memorandum with suggestions about prayers for civic occasions. The actual prayers thanked God for a country in which diversity is celebrated, for liberty, for the American political and judicial process, and for the potential fulfillment of the aspirations of the graduates.

Kennedy, now for the majority, accepted the conclusion that such prayers had "profound meaning to many students and parents," but he ruled that precedent condemns such activity. The justice held that "government involvement with religious activity in this case is pervasive, to the point of creating a state-sponsored and state-directed religious exercise in a public school." Kennedy maintained that the school's good-faith attempt to purge the prayers of sectarianism was irrelevant, saying that the result invited the social division that the establishment clause was designed to eliminate. "The potential for divisiveness," he said, "is of particular relevance here . . . because . . . subtle, coercive pressures exist and where the student had no real alternative which would have allowed her to avoid the fact or appearance of participation."[107]

"The First Amendment's Religion Clauses," Kennedy continued, "mean that religious beliefs and religious expression are too precious to be either proscribed or prescribed by the State." The Constitution, he added, commits the "preservation and transmission of religious beliefs . . . to the private sphere, which itself is promised freedom to pursue that mission."[108]

Contrasting the right of free speech, which often involves an attempt to stimulate government action, Kennedy said religious freedom necessitates that there be no governmental action.[109] The state's duty, he added, is "to guard and respect that sphere of inviolable conscience and belief which is the mark of a free people. To compromise that principle today would be to deny our own tradition and forfeit our standing to urge others to secure the protections of that tradition for themselves."[110]

To the argument that one who objected to the prayers could simply stay away from the ceremony, Kennedy responded that the ceremony was important in that its purpose was to impress "upon the young person the role that it is his or her right and duty to assume in the community." The state, the justice concluded, cannot force the individual from the community of scholars by requiring "one of its citizens to forfeit his or her rights and benefits as the price of resisting conformance to a state-sponsored religious practice."[111]

Kennedy's opinion is especially interesting for it represents the Court's first public grappling with "civil religion." The supporters of the Rhode Island scheme argued that nonsectarian prayers at public occasions have long been a part of the country's tradition and that their recognition of a common ethic and a transcendent reference point has and should continue to be accommodated as a means to promote a sense of community. Kennedy responded that the government may no more establish a religion, based upon some common theological ground that various traditional religions share, than it could any traditional religion. "That the intrusion was in the course of promulgating religion that sought to be civic or nonsectarian rather than pertaining to one sect," he said, "does not lessen the offense or isolation to the objectors. At best it narrows their number, at worst increases their sense of isolation and affront."[112] Notice that Kennedy implicitly rejects the notion that such prayers promote community, saying that they, in fact, work against the creation of an all-inclusive community.

What this discussion highlights is a use of civil religion as a term that houses certain generalities or commonalities of theistic faiths most often paid lip service in public addresses. That the Court should condone governmental support for its less specific content struck Kennedy as a contradiction of what the religion clauses mandated.[113] If the justices play an essential role in nurturing a civil religion, how can Kennedy's rejection of this role be explained? The confusion arises because of the identification of civil religion with traditional sectarian religion as simply an alternative way to summon God's blessings upon the faithful. In fact, in rejecting the invitation to accommodate such nondenominational religious exercises, the justice promotes the civil religion as we have defined it. By necessity, it must be more person-centered than any traditional religion, and its basic assumption is the dignity of the human being. It involves a faith in individual rights and in a rule of secular law; its thrust is toward inclusion and against exclusion. So, as the majority rightfully rejected the accommodation of a watered-down theistic religion, it was furthering the aims of the civil religion.

The Court's task is to interpret the holy writ, and here that text necessitates a decision not to exclude. What makes the civil religion different from traditional religion is the drive toward inclusion. Any community seeks to exclude in part to define its existence, but from the beginning, the civil religion has posited an ever-expanding community. The Court's ongoing task is to block this inherent tendency to exclude by reminding the faithful of the premises upon which their faith rests. All religions include a guide for living one's life, and the civil religion is no exception. What makes it different is that its theology is its code of conduct, a portion of which involves the individual's relationship to others, to the majority, and to the government. Belief is not enforced; it is elicited by example. One of the essential principles at the very heart of the civil religion is the individual's freedom from governmental intrusion into the domain of personal religious belief.[114]

Apparently only Kennedy among the majority justices felt that coercion to conform was necessary to a finding of unconstitutionality under the establishment clause ban.[115] The other members of the majority in two separate opinions denied that coercion was the controlling factor; to them the key element was the state's active involvement in promoting religion.

Blackmun, in an opinion joined by Stevens and O'Connor, assumed the civil religious responsibility of the Court when he said that "The Establishment Clause protects religious liberty on a grand scale; it is a social compact that guarantees for generations a democracy and a strong religious community—both essential to safeguarding religious liberty." Just as James Madison had done two centuries earlier, Blackmun called attention to the linkage between individual freedom and the need to remove religious differences from the public arena. "When government puts its imprimatur on a particular religion," the justice warned, "it conveys a message of exclusion to all those who do not adhere to the favored beliefs. A government cannot be premised on the belief that all persons are created equal when it asserts that God prefers only some." When government, he continued, "arrogates to itself a role in religious affairs, it abandons its obligation as guarantor of democracy. Democracy requires the nourishment of dialogue and dissent, while religious faith puts its trust in an ultimate divine authority." Because "religious freedom cannot thrive in the absence of a vibrant religious community and that such a community cannot prosper when it is bound to the secular," Blackmun concluded, "our cases have prohibited government endorsement of religion, its sponsorship, and active involvement in religion, whether or not citizens were coerced to conform."[116]

Justice David H. Souter, joined by Stevens and O'Connor, argued that a nonsectarian prayer was a contradiction in terms. The recent appointee of President George Bush sought to demonstrate how the decision here was both solidly anchored in precedent and in original intent. "We have not changed much since the days of Madison," he began, "and the judiciary should not willingly enter the political arena to battle the centripetal force leading from religious pluralism to official preference for the faith with the most votes." To critics who contended that the establishment clause only barred governmental favoritism among religions, Souter responded that such an inquiry would "invite the courts to engage in comparative theology," hardly a subject within the competence of the judiciary. Explaining the presence of religious sentiments in public addresses, he said that such words "inhabit a pallid zone worlds apart from official prayers delivered to a captive audience of public school students and their families."[117]

Scalia, in dissent with Rehnquist, White, and Thomas, reminded his brother, Kennedy, that only three terms earlier he had written that the establishment clause should not be used to "invalidate longstanding traditions" that are part of the nation's "political and cultural heritage." Now, Scalia accused his colleague of wiping out "a tradition that is as old as public-school graduation ceremonies themselves, and that is a component of an even more longstanding American tradition of nonsectarian prayer to God at public celebrations generally." The Constitution, he said, should be interpreted in accord with its "deep foundations in the historic practices of our people."[118]

"Maintaining respect for the religious observances of others," Scalia continued, "is a fundamental civil virtue that government (including the public schools) can and should cultivate." He said that the rabbi's prayers were "so characteristically American [that] they could have come from the pen of George Washington or Abraham Lincoln." Proceeding on the assumption that Souter condemned—that all religions are theistic—Scalia said that toleration is promoted by people of differing beliefs joining in prayer. "To deprive our society of that important unifying mechanism, in order to spare the nonbeliever . . . minimal inconvenience . . . ," the justice added, "is as senseless in policy as it is unsupported by law."[119]

What is interesting is that both sides in the controversy say that they are operating from the premise of respecting the diversity and pluralism of American society. However, Scalia and his cohorts see such diversity not in terms of the individual but in terms of majorities in different communities, who, through their governments, should be freed from judicial interference to reflect in action the dominant beliefs and traditions of those majorities. The idea that individuals of differing beliefs are thereby excluded represents to them the inevitable result of majoritarian government. The diversity and pluralism they recognize comes from different majorities in different local units. On the other hand, the justices in the majority here pay respect to what they see at the core of the establishment clause—the premise that government cannot use religion to narrow membership in the national community. The Court's task, according to their opinion, is to ensure that dissenting individuals not suffer exclusion based upon a difference in religious belief. In holding government to such a standard, the justices are responding to their duty under the civil religion. The civil religion is not designed to affirm dominant religious beliefs but rather to afford individuals the room to pursue their own beliefs without suffering the pain of exclusion.

Although Congress would not propose an amendment to the Constitution and the Court would not reverse its precedents on school prayer and Bible-reading, the forces seeking such change scored victories on the periphery of the main battle. Those victories included equal access to school facilities for religious groups and government prescriptions of moments of silence.

If the constitutional obstacle to school prayer was the participation of teachers and administrators, which gave official governmental sanction to the activity, might it not be accommodated if such sanction were severed or submerged in a neutral policy? That was the question posed in *Widmar v. Vincent* in 1981. Students at a branch of the University of Missouri had been denied the use of classroom space to hold religious meetings and discussions. The rationale was that the school in making such space available would be furthering religion in a manner forbidden by the establishment clause. The Court avoided the potential conflict of the religion clauses by resting its decision on the free speech provision of the First Amendment. Having created a forum generally open to student groups, the university could not discriminate against religious speech without running afoul of the free speech clause.[120] Congress responded enthusiastically to the decision by seeking to apply it to any public secondary school receiving federal funds in the Equal Access Act of 1984.[121]

Similarly, moments of silence were given congressional approval in the same year. Although the justices in 1985 struck down a state law prescribing such silence because evidence showed that the law was designed to promote prayer, they indicated that a regulation not so encumbered would be permissible.[122] They made good on the promise in 1990 when the Court upheld the new federal legislation.[123]

So, although the High Bench consistently ruled against officially sanctioned prayer in the classroom and in school exercises, it was willing to allow room for students, free from official sponsorship, to exercise their religion freely. The justices said that the establishment clause was designed to promote religious freedom by staying the hand of government in interfering in religious matters. The actual range of individual freedom in the society, however, depended more on the Court's interpretation of the free exercise clause.

There are a number of ways in which the Court can deal with a claim to free exercise of religion or conscience: first, the justices may reject the claim on the basis that the general law has a secular purpose and only indirectly burdens free exercise; second, they may invalidate the law as a direct burden; third, they may carve out an exception to the general applicability of the law; and fourth, they may broaden the exception to embrace all individuals with similar claims, whether grounded in religion or not.

Utilizing the first approach in 1961 the Court decided that state Sunday closing laws, despite their original purpose of protecting the Christian Sabbath, could now survive scrutiny under the establishment clause on the grounds that the state had a secular purpose in providing for a day of rest and recreation.[124] However, Jewish merchants, who had a different Sabbath, argued that their free exercise of religion was abridged as state law forced upon them a choice between observing their Sabbath and economic survival. The majority justices, who could not agree on a Court opinion, essentially saw the religious burden as indirect and therefore not unconstitutional.[125] Despite the difficulty they had with the claim, the idea that an otherwise valid law could be challenged because of religious belief had received no prior recognition by the Court. Apparently, if the law was not designed to burden free exercise, it would pass constitutional muster.

Three weeks after the decisions in the Sunday closing cases, the Court illustrated what a direct burden on free exercise meant with its decision in *Torcaso v. Watkins*. In many of the Jehovah's Witnesses cases of the late 1930s and 1940s the Court, responding to the free exercise claim, simply invalidated the laws that had the repressive effect. Now again invoking the second approach, as outlined above, the Court invalidated a provision of the Maryland constitution requiring that a state officeholder profess a belief in God. When Roy Torcaso was appointed to the office of notary public he refused to declare such a belief and therefore was denied the office. Unanimously, the Court rejected the state's argument that there was no coercion because Torcaso was not compelled to hold office. It said that a "religious test for public office unconstitutionally invades the appellant's freedom of belief and religion and therefore cannot be enforced against him."[126] The Constitution's prohibition on religious oaths was now read into the free exercise clause, which in turn was read into the liberty protected from state abridgment by the Fourteenth Amendment. This is an excellent example of how the community is widened by striking down a law that seeks to limit inclusion and participation.

Two years later, in 1963, the Court for the first time looked with sympathy upon a religious claim for exemption from the general reach of the civil law—the third approach. At issue was the right of Adell Sherbert to collect unemployment insurance under the rules of South Carolina. Because of her refusal to work on Saturday, which was her Sabbath as a Seventh Day Adventist, she was denied benefits. This was true for all applicants who, for whatever reason, were unwilling to work on Saturday. Was Sherbert's insistence that the state accommodate her day of rest more compelling than that of the Jewish merchants? Yes, Brennan answered for the Court in *Sherbert v. Verner*.

The decision not to pay Sherbert unemployment benefits, he said, "derives solely from the practice of her religion" and places "pressure on her to forgo that practice." To so condition benefits, the justice continued, "effectively penalizes the free exercise of her constitutional liberties." Because South Carolina law provided that an applicant would not be excluded from benefits for refusing to work on Sunday, Brennan held that the "unconstitutionality of the disqualification . . . is thus compounded by the religious discrimination which South Carolina's general statutory scheme necessarily reflects."[127] Asserting that the Court's ruling only reinforces the neutrality government must maintain toward religion, he glossed over the fact that an immunity from the operation of general state law had been granted for religious reasons.

Earlier free exercise claims had been upheld by declaring the offending statutes unconstitutional. What is different here is that the underlying law is unchanged, but an exception is written into it in favor of those who profess a religious objection. The effect is to safeguard the conscience of individuals who might otherwise have to compromise it to receive needed economic benefits. Such a reading of individual rights departs from precedent but is not inconsistent with the Court's close inspection of governmental action as it affects the individual in the decade of the 1960s.

In fact, Douglas, in a concurring opinion, focused clearly on what South Carolina's denial of benefits to Sherbert meant. "The harm," he said, "is the interference with the individual's scruples or conscience—an important area of privacy which the First Amendment fences off from government. . . . This case is resolvable . . . solely in terms of what government may not do to an individual in violation of his religious scruples."[128] Viewed from this perspective, the decision seems to be imposing upon government an affirmative duty to equalize the operation of law to eliminate discrimination among religions.[129]

This brings us to the last of the four approaches the Court can use in free exercise cases—that of expanding the range of the free exercise clause by bringing more people within the parameters of its operation. The justices used this approach in coping with conscientious objection to military service. In conscription laws Congress had always provided for conscientious objectors. The draft laws of the Civil War and World War I had required that conscientious objectors be members of religious sects that forbad their members from bearing arms. Legislation before World War II shifted the focus from the sect to the individual and required only that "the claimant's own opposition to war was based on 'religious training and belief.'" In 1948 Congress specified "that 'religious training and belief' was to be defined as 'an individual's belief in a relation to a Supreme Being involving duties superior to those arising from any human relation, but [not including] essentially political, sociological, or philosophical views or a merely personal moral code.' "[130]

Three cases were combined by the Court in *United States v. Seeger*, all of which involved individuals being denied conscientious objector status, either because they hedged on the question of whether they believed in a Supreme Being or because their objection to service stemmed from a personal moral code. Clearly, the Selective Service law distinguished between individuals on the basis of whether their objection to war was religious or not. Readings by the Court of the meaning of the establishment clause had called into question the constitutionality of a religious preference. However, an invalidation of this part of the law would have stripped the draft of any provision at all for conscientious objector status.

What the unanimous Court did was define religious belief broadly and find that all three individuals came within the new definition. Saying "that in no field of human endeavor has the tool of language proved so inadequate . . . as it has in dealing with the fundamental questions of man's predicament in life, in death or in final judgment and retribution," the justices formulated the decisive question as follows: "Does the claimed belief occupy the same place in the life of the objector as an orthodox belief in God holds in the life of one clearly qualified for exemption?" Draft boards, the Court said, must "decide whether the beliefs professed by a registrant are sincerely held and whether they are, in his own scheme of things, religious."[131]

Douglas concurred, saying that a broad understanding of what Congress meant by "Supreme Being" was necessary to save the provision from invalidation. "I would attribute tolerance and sophistication to the Congress," the justice added, "commensurate with the religious complexion of our communities."[132]

The unanimous Court had said that earlier preferences, first for pacifistic sects and then for narrowly defined religious views, would now have to be discarded if people similarly situated were to be treated equally in terms of qualifying as conscientious objectors. The approach to take was the perspective of the individual; it was that person's conscience that had to be safeguarded. But the Court was not through with the task of liberalizing the requirements for conscientious objector status.

Five years later, in *Welsh v. United States*, a fractured Court in fact rewrote the legislative provision for conscientious objection by excising the portion that precluded an exemption for a pacifistic belief arising from a personal moral code or from secular study.[133] Black announced the decision of the Court in an opinion that Douglas, Brennan, and Marshall joined. He explained that when Welsh denied that his beliefs were religious he was unaware of the Court's broad reading of "religious." Therefore, Black continued, his denial "is a highly unreliable guide for those charged with administrating the exemption." Contending with the exclusion of a personal moral code or of "essentially political, sociological or philo-

342

CHAPTER NINE

sophical" views, the justice said that this wording excluded "those whose beliefs are not deeply held and those whose objection to war does not rest at all upon moral, ethical, or religious principle but instead rests solely upon considerations of policy, pragmatism, or expediency." Finding Welsh to be one of those people "whose consciences, spurred by deeply held moral, ethical, or religious beliefs, would give them no rest or peace if they allowed themselves to become a part of an instrument of war," Black said the man was entitled to conscientious objector status.[134]

Harlan, concurring in the result, condemned the plurality's evasion of what the decision in fact did—rewrite a law of Congress. In the belief that such unusual action on the part of the Court must be justified, the justice proceeded to do just that. A law that "excludes from its 'scope' individuals motivated by teachings of non-theistic religions, and individuals guided by an inner ethical voice that bespeaks secular and not 'religious' reflection," Harlan said, "not only accords a preference to the 'religious' but also disadvantages adherents of religions that do not worship a Supreme Being." As such, it "offends the Establishment Clause and is that kind of classification that this Court has condemned." The key, he insisted, must not be the origin of but "the intensity of moral conviction with which a belief is held." Having established the validity of the constitutional claim, Harlan dealt with the remaining options: first, to invalidate the conscientious objector section, or, second, widen the class to which it is applied. He chose the latter as less disruptive. "The policy of exempting religious conscientious objectors," he continued, "is one of longstanding tradition in this country and accords recognition to what is, in a diverse and 'open' society, the important value of reconciling individuality of belief with practical exigencies whenever possible." Congressional policy can be best maintained, Harlan concluded, by the Court repairing the statute to cure "the defect of underinclusion."[135]

Although often accused of making policy through their interpretations of the Constitution, justices have rarely been as forthright as Harlan was in the Welsh case. Obviously Black and the plurality justices preferred to hide their decision under the guise of statutory interpretation, but Harlan's concurrence exposes that subterfuge. Because the law does not conform to the dictates of the civil religion, which mandates that claims of conscience be treated equally, the high priests must make it conform. The other option, to eliminate conscientious objector status from the law and force Congress to redraft the provision, only invites controversy and perhaps further litigation. What the Court in fact did was assert its priestly authority to safeguard perhaps the most precious of individual rights—the freedom of conscience.

The result of the fourth approach is to widen the class to include all those persons with strong beliefs, thus eliminating any possible preference for religion without endangering the protection of those who are religiously motivated. In fact, one scholar has argued that, although religious adherents have been important forces for beneficial social change, success often has been masked by the fact that their achievements have redounded to the benefit of the entire secular society.[136] We can see this outcome in the litigation of the Jehovah's Witnesses in which the Court often invalidated laws that burdened a wide variety of speech. What the majority justices came to see in the conscientious objector cases was that overpowering the individual conscience was no less morally wrong when that conscience had been formed on the basis of input not traditionally characterized as religious. Here the Court was doing just what the civil religion demanded of it—recognize the diversity of individuals in the society and insist that they be treated equally.

Employing this fourth approach, courts are not required to enter the arena of individual religious belief to assess whether that belief provides the basis for an exemption from otherwise valid civil law. Otherwise, judges risk becoming entangled in the very arena that was put beyond the ken of government for the purpose of building a community of diverse people.

Despite such potential problems, however, the Supreme Court was increasingly asked to build upon the *Sherbert* precedent that first accommodated a religious exemption from valid civil law.[137] This was so, in part, because of the general sympathy of the 1960s Court to claims that individual rights were being violated by the states. Although this concern, when focused on the rights of the accused criminal, has waned in subsequent decades, it has only increased in the free exercise area, where political liberals and conservatives find a rare meeting ground.[138]

The justices continued to insist that religious objections be accommodated within the states' unemployment systems. When a Jehovah's Witness refused to work on the production of armaments and quit when no other employment with the company was offered, Indiana denied him unemployment benefits. Because the sect of which the claimant was a member did not seem to interpose such an objection, the state court decided that the individual quit his employment for personal reasons. The Court found *Sherbert* controlling and reversed, seeing no compelling state interest that would justify the denial of benefits.[139]

In the next case, the employee became a Seventh Day Adventist and thereafter refused to work on Saturdays. Eventually, she was dismissed and the state refused to pay her unemployment compensation. To the argument that government was precluded from honoring such religious claims under the establishment clause, Brennan, for the Court, responded that "the accommodation at issue here does not entangle the State in an unlawful fostering of religion." Precedent, he continued, has established "that such infringements [of the free exercise right] must be subjected to strict scrutiny and could be justified only by proof by the State of a compelling interest."[140] Finding no such interest here, Justice Brennan concluded that the woman's free exercise had been burdened.

When, in an Illinois case, an employee refused to work on Sunday for religious reasons, though he identified with no particular church and simply identified himself as a Christian, the denial of unemployment benefits was again overruled by the Court. "We reject," the justices said, "the notion that to claim the protection of the Free Exercise Clause, one must be responding to the commands of a particular religious organization."[141]

Carving out such exceptions, however, has the potential of making sectarian religion a divisive issue, thereby endangering the civil religion itself. When the Court first encountered a claim of Amish parents that sending their children to public school violated their religious belief and practice, the justices dismissed the appeal and refused to hear the case.[142] But five years later, in 1972, in *Wisconsin v. Yoder* the Court decided to rule on whether Amish parents were entitled to an exemption from Wisconsin's compulsory school-attendance law. The law required attendance until the age of sixteen, but Old Order Amish refused to send their children to school after the eighth grade. Further schooling, they believed, "would not only expose themselves to the danger of the censure of the church community, but . . . also endanger their own salvation and that of their children."[143]

Exploring the record, the Court acknowledged that further education would hinder the incorporation of children into the religious community and "that the Amish have an excellent record as law-abiding and generally self-sufficient members of the society." Burger, writing for the Court, ruled that "only those interests of the highest order and those not otherwise served can overbalance legitimate claims to the free exercise of religion." Then, saying that the objection to continuing secular education must be rooted in religious, not philosophical nor merely personal, beliefs, the chief justice agreed that further public schooling "would gravely endanger if not destroy the free exercise of respondents' religious beliefs." To the argument that such an excursion into the nature of the Amish religious community brings the Court into conflict with the establishment clause, Burger responded that such concern "cannot be allowed to prevent any exception no matter how vital it may be to the protection of values promoted by the right of free exercise." Pointing to a tradition of "informal vocational education" that will continue in the Amish community, he said that the Amish have proved to be "a highly successful social unit within our society, even if apart from the conventional 'mainstream.' " They, in fact, exemplify Jefferson's ideal of the yeoman farmer, the chief continued, saying that "their idiosyncratic separateness exemplifies the diversity we profess to admire and encourage." To the worry that a decision in favor of the Amish undermined the state's compulsory attendance law, Burger replied that "probably few other religious groups or sects could make" a similarly successful claim.[144]

From one perspective the opinion is sensitive to nonmainstream religion, indicating that differing lifestyles can be accommodated within the broad reach of the nation's civil religion. But in stressing the history of the Amish community and implicitly approving its alternative way of life, the Court is clearly distinguishing this religion from others and giving its adherents the opportunity to resist the homogenizing process of public school education beyond the eighth grade. To pronounce these religious adherents worthy and to indicate that few others would be, the Court seemed to say that some world views are more deserving of protection than others.

Douglas in his partial dissent highlighted the fact that his colleagues had evaluated the claim through the lens of the group to which the individuals belonged. He argued that what may have been the contrary interests of the children were ignored in preference for those of parents and the community to which they belong. "Religion is an individual experience," the justice contended, noting that only one child involved in the case clearly subscribed to her parents' view. He maintained that "the student's judgment, not his parents', . . . is essential if we are to give full meaning to what we have said about the Bill of Rights and of the right of students to be masters of their own destiny."[145]

In the Yoder case, the majority sought to narrow the range of the free exercise clause by saying that only certain religions could possibly earn exemptions from the reach of clearly valid state law. In that sense the case, although it seems to further the reach of the free exercise clause, limits its availability to those adherents who commend themselves to the Court. So, a decision that on the surface seems to widen the arena for the exercise of protected individual rights contains, behind the surface, intimations of exclusion. This is what picking and choosing among religions inevitably involves; rather than extend individual freedom such an approach tends to circumscribe it.

Would the Court, for instance, be as accommodating when it encountered one of the many Native American religions? In 1986 in *Bowen v. Roy*, the Court heard the claim of a Native American father that the obtaining of a Social Security number for his two-year-old daughter, as a condition for her receiving welfare assistance, was an infringement of her free exercise of religion. He maintained that "the uniqueness of the Social Security number as an identifier, coupled with the other uses of the number over which she has no control will serve to 'rob the spirit' of his daughter and prevent her from attaining greater spiritual power." In rejecting the claim, Burger carried along all but one of his colleagues. "The Free Exercise Clause," he said, "affords an individual protection from certain forms of compulsion; it does not afford an individual a right to dictate the conduct of the Government's internal procedures."[146]

A majority of the Court, however, repudiated Burger's idea that a free exercise claim could never prevail over such governmental interests. What especially disturbed O'Connor was Burger's view that there could be no legitimate free exercise claim to a facially neutral law when the government demonstrates that the law is "a reasonable means of promoting a legitimate public interest." Speaking for Brennan and Marshall as well, O'Connor said: "Such a test has no basis in precedent and relegates a serious First Amendment value to the barest level of minimal scrutiny." Instead, she urged that the Court follow precedent and "hold that the Government must accommodate a legitimate free exercise claim unless pursuing an especially important interest by narrowly tailored means."[147]

Two years later the Court confronted another Native American religious claim, one involving federal governmental lands in a national forest that had historically been used by three Native American tribes for religious rituals seeking personal spiritual development. Of crucial importance in these rituals were "privacy, silence, and an undisturbed natural setting."[148] By the time the Court got the case, the only issue remaining was whether the government could construct a six-mile segment across the land to fill in the missing link in a seventy-five mile road connecting two California towns.

O'Connor, for the Court, acknowledged that the building of the road "will have severe adverse effects on the practice of their religion." She then found, however, that the Native Americans would not be "coerced into violating their religious beliefs; nor would . . . governmental action penalize religious activity by denying any person an equal share of the rights, benefits, and privileges enjoyed by other citizens." Even accepting the most disastrous result that the road will "virtually destroy the . . . Indians' ability to practice their religion," O'Connor added, "the Constitution simply does not provide a principle that could justify upholding" the free exercise claim. What the Native Americans are claiming, she asserted, is a form of beneficial ownership, and whatever rights they possess "those rights do not divest the Government of its right to use what is, after all, *its* land."[149] With this statement O'Connor recognized the fundamental differences between the two cultures in regard to their conceptions of land and its ownership.

She contended that the government, throughout the whole controversy, had been guided by the American Indian Religious Freedom Act of 1978[150] and had changed its plans in an effort to respect and preserve the religion of Native Americans. Although the study commissioned by the Forest Service recommended that the plans for the road be abandoned, O'Connor insisted that the government had proceeded with sensitivity to the claims of the Native Americans. To find in the provisions of the legislation the conference of any special rights, she insisted, was contrary to the intent behind the act. She then turned her attention to the dissent that maintained that the free exercise clause prohibits any government action that interferes with one's practice of religion. O'Connor maintained that such a position could not be squared with the Constitution, precedent, and "a responsible sense of our own institutional role."[151]

The dissent was written by Brennan and joined by Marshall and Blackmun. Justice Brennan rejected the majority's narrow reading of the free exercise right, saying that the individual guarantee "is directed against any form of governmental action that frustrates or inhibits religious practice." Seeing in the action of the federal government a dire threat to the very survival of the Native American religion, Brennan drew attention to the differences between traditional Western religions and that of Native Americans. Instead of creation being attributed to a deity, he said, "tribal religions regard creation as an ongoing process in which they [the adherents] are morally and religiously obligated to participate." And whereas "dogma lies at the heart of western religions, Native American faith is inextricably bound to the use of the land," which is specifically identified and "is itself a sacred, living being." Relying upon the lower court's finding that the construction of the road would "virtually destroy respondents' religion," Justice Brennan said that, whatever the form of governmental restraint on religious practice, the key question was the effect such action has on the free exercise of religion.[152]

Brennan read precedent to say that "laws that frustrate or inhibit religious practice . . . trigger the protections of the constitutional guarantee." Attacking the majority's use of *Bowen v. Roy* to hold that only government action that coerces conduct in conflict with religious faith can violate the free exercise clause, the justice said such a reading narrows "both the reach and promise of the Free Exercise clause." Then Brennan addressed the crux of the matter by acknowledging that the rival claims to land presented here "are fundamentally incompatible, and unless they are tempered by compromise, mutual accommodation will remain impossible." Relying upon *Yoder* and the express wording of the American Indian Religious Freedom Act, Brennan ridiculed the majority's conclusion that, although the practice of a religion may be destroyed, the Native Americans are fully protected in their beliefs. After quoting from the 1978 legislation, the justice called the proposed road only "marginally useful" and said that the majority "makes a mockery of the 'policy of the United States to protect and preserve for American Indians their inherent right of freedom to believe, express, and exercise the[ir] traditional religions.' " The Court's decision, Brennan concluded, "fails utterly to accord with the dictates of the First Amendment."[153]

Two years later, when the Court was reviewing a denial of unemployment benefits to some Native Americans, it drew a new line and questioned the religious exemption, contending that the compelling-state-interest test, earlier used by the justices in such cases, would invite anarchy. What was involved in *Employment Division v. Smith* was the firing of two Native Americans from a private drug rehabilitation organization for their use of peyote in religious ceremonies. They were denied unemployment benefits, but the Oregon supreme court decided that, although peyote was a drug banned by state law, its use for sacramental purposes was covered by the free exercise clause and that the two claimants were entitled to unemployment compensation.

Scalia, writing for the Court, reversed, saying that the applicants had been denied benefits because there was no religious exemption "from a generally applicable criminal law." Recognizing that states can and have made exceptions for sacramental peyote use, the justice said that such exceptions are not constitutionally mandated. "To make an individual's obligation to obey such a law contingent upon the law's coincidence with his religious beliefs, except where the State's interest is 'compelling'—permitting him, by virtue of his beliefs, 'to become a law unto himself' . . .—contradicts both constitutional tradition and common sense."[154] In fact, the majority was simply reviving the standard that had been used by the Court up until *Sherbert* in 1963: general legislation not passed with an intent to hinder free exercise imposed an indirect burden and was constitutional.

Justice O'Connor, in a concurring opinion joined by Brennan, Marshall, and Blackmun, protested the majority's inroads on the "Nation's fundamental commitment to individual religious liberty." She castigated the majority for holding that no generally applicable law that incidentally infringed on religious practice could be challenged successfully under the free exercise clause. Insisting that the decision here did not require scrapping the compelling interest test, O'Connor said that "the essence of a free exercise claim is relief from a burden imposed by government on religious practices or beliefs." It makes no difference, she continued, whether the state interferes directly by compelling or prohibiting religious practices or indirectly by causing persons to abandon their religion or conform "to the religious beliefs of others" to obtain "an equal place within the community."[155]

The free exercise clause, she insisted, not only protected individual belief but also protected a person from ostracism from the civil religious community. She took issue with the Court's view that minority religions are inevitably disfavored as an "unavoidable consequence of democratic government." Instead, she argued that "the First Amendment was enacted precisely to protect the rights of those whose religious practices are not shared by the majority and may be viewed with hostility."[156]

In dissent, Blackmun, carrying along Brennan and Marshall, argued that, given the contours of the Native American religion, the state of Oregon did not prove a compelling interest that enabled it to override the free exercise claim here. The framers of the First Amendment, he said, considered "freedom from religious persecution . . . an essential element of liberty—and . . . they drafted the Religion Clauses precisely in order to avoid that intolerance." Although acknowledging that "the American Indian Religious Freedom Act, in itself, may not create rights enforceable against government action restricting religious freedom," Blackmun insisted that the Court "must scrupulously apply its free exercise analysis to the religious claims of Native Americans, however unorthodox they may be. Otherwise, both the First Amendment and the stated policy of Congress will offer to Native Americans merely an unfulfilled and hollow promise."[157]

When a religious objection is honored, the Court runs the risk of treating people similarly situated unequally and thereby compromising the rule of law. In *Sher-*

bert the Court found an inequality in the state law's respect for differing Sabbaths that outweighed the inequality of treating all those who chose not to work on Saturday quite differently. Here in *Smith*, despite the apparent sympathy that caused some states to exempt sacramental peyote use from its criminal drug law, the claim for an exemption from otherwise valid law seeking to reach social harm presents a dilemma. If the civil religion is based on a rule of law and a respect for individual rights, what happens when the two principles conflict, especially when the honoring of the religious claim gets the courts involved in determining what is or is not a valid religious objection?

Scalia's conclusion in the Smith case that fringe religions and their adherents, by necessity, will be less protected by the free exercise clause than the mainstream sects and their followers struck four of his colleagues, including O'Connor, as an abdication of the Court's primary role. Furthermore, the result spawned a movement of diverse interest groups to get Congress to pass legislation insisting that the Court adopt its previous interpretation of the free exercise clause.

This campaign for overriding legislation brought together a wide array of often bitterly opposed interest groups ranging from the American Civil Liberties Union to the National Association of Evangelicals and the Traditional Values Coalition. All seemed to agree that the Court should protect the free exercise of religion by individuals and narrow the possibility of any governmental intrusion upon this right. Congress responded with an overwhelming vote that swept along its most conservative and most liberal members to pass the Religious Freedom Restoration Act. It was signed into law by President Bill Clinton on November 16, 1993.[158] The legislation sought to write into all law—federal, state, and municipal—the Court's prior test of requiring government to prove "a compelling interest" before burdening the free exercise of religion. No longer could government successfully defend an enactment as generally applicable and not directed toward burdening any religion or religious exercise.[159] Only thirty years earlier had the High Bench first upheld a personal religious objection to the imposition of an apparently neutral civil law;[160] now Congress sought to make that ruling universally applicable. The new personal religious defense that the statute sought to confer apparently made no law immune to such a challenge.

Congress indeed had often corrected the High Bench's reading of federal law, but it was unprecedented for the legislative branch to insist that the Court follow an apparently discarded precedent in its interpretation of the Constitution itself.[161] The protection of other individual rights by the Court had often divided the very interest groups that joined together to support the Religious Freedom Restoration Act, but here they agreed that the Court should be directed to check even inadvertent intrusions upon religious practices.[162]

Just how would the high priests take to this legislative attempt to correct their reading of the holy writ? Three justices—O'Connor, Souter, and the latest arrival,

Stephen G. Breyer—wanted to reinspect *Smith*, the ruling that had precipitated the furor and had led to the Religious Freedom Restoration Act, correct its ruling, and avoid, for the present, any judgment on the statute. The other six justices, however, did not hestitate to strike down the act as a invasion of judicial authority.[163]

This sparring over the extent of the right of free exercise might suggest that the legislative branch has become more solicitous of protecting individual rights than the Supreme Court itself. Furthermore, such a conclusion seems to reinforce a prevailing view that the appointments to the Court made by Presidents Reagan and Bush have resulted in a bench less sensitive to individual rights and civil religious responsibilities and more inclined to defer to legislative determinations. Before we climb aboard this bandwagon, however, we need to recognize that the right of individuals to freely exercise their religion is, of all individual rights, one which can be interpreted to divide rather than unite the diverse American people. Distinctions can be drawn that may seem different from those based on race or sex, in that belief seems to be a matter over which the individual can exercise some control. Such distinctions, however, are no less discriminatory and no less divisive. The inevitable result of preferring a religious over a nonreligious view of the world is what led the Court to rewrite the law of conscientious objection.[164] Equally sincere individuals who came to the conclusion that war was wrong should not, the justices concluded, be treated differently because one route to that conclusion was traditionally religious and the other was not. A government preference for religion over nonreligion, from the beginning of the Court's modern inspection of the religion clauses, struck the justices as contrary to the establishment clause's prohibition.[165] Government may not interfere with free exercise, but neither should it promote it. Of the nine justices who contended with the Religious Freedom Restoration Act only one, John Paul Stevens, saw it violating the establishment clause in that it clearly preferred the believer over the nonbeliever.[166] Implicitly, Stevens saw the civil religious responsibility of the Court and with it the danger inherent in interpreting the free exercise right as an invitation to the government to ignore the restraining effect of the establishment clause.

The other guarantees of individual rights found in the Constitution contained no such limitation and therefore a shift from prohibition to action affirmatively protecting such basic rights encountered no obstacle and only furthered the goals of the civil religion. To this part of the story, we now turn.

MAKING THE SCRIPTURES ON INDIVIDUAL RIGHTS NATIONALLY OPERATIVE, 1960–1997

By 1960 the members of the Court had survived the attacks based upon their desegregation and allegedly procommunist decisions with no diminution of confidence that they were discharging their priestly responsibilities. In all likelihood, the justices did not realize the implications of the pathway they had opened with their new reading of the equal protection clause in *Brown v. Board of Education*, a pathway that would branch out into many different directions and lead to new protections for individual rights. They were, however, quite aware of the ongoing evolution in protecting individual rights that came from their reading of the due process clause of the Fourteenth Amendment. By the end of the decade they would succeed in making most of the protections found in the Bill of Rights binding upon the states.[1] Also, they would be responding to arguments that these protections did not exhaust the liberties that individuals had a right to claim. Before the 1962 term of Court, the new president, John F. Kennedy, had replaced Felix Frankfurter and Charles E. Whittaker with Arthur J. Goldberg and Byron R. White. Those justices who looked with sympathy upon claims that the due process clause of the Fourteenth Amendment protected the individual liberties found in the Bill of Rights from state invasion now had a clear majority.

Prior to 1961, the Court had made the clauses of the First Amendment binding upon the states to the same extent that they bound the federal government. In regard to other significant provisions of the Bill of Rights, the majority had found that certain protections were binding upon the states not because they were to be read in their entirety into the Fourteenth Amendment's due process clause but generally because they were essential for a fair trial. So, by making this distinction the Court could hold, for instance, that a right to counsel, listed in the Sixth Amendment, was a part of the due process that must be made available to defendants in capital cases but not to defendants facing less serious charges.[2]

The battle continued between Justices Hugo L. Black and Felix Frankfurter over the meaning of due process, with the former seeking its content in the provisions of the Bill of Rights and the latter being willing to determine on a case-by-case basis what the requirements of a fair trial necessitated.[3] Black had William O. Douglas's support,[4] and two new arrivals in the 1950s—Chief Justice Earl Warren and William J. Brennan Jr.—seemed increasingly sympathetic. On the other side, Frankfurter was always able to attract some support and now found an able ally in Justice John Marshall Harlan, who joined the Court in 1955. Harlan steadfastly held to the position long after Frankfurter left the Court. Ironically, Harlan's grandfather, who had sat on the High Bench from 1877 to 1911, was the first justice to take the view now associated with Black.

Just how these two views divided the Court can be seen in the aftermath of *Wolf v. Colorado*, the decision in which Frankfurter, for the majority, applied the Fourth Amendment's protection of the individual against unreasonable searches and seizures to the states as a requirement of due process.[5] However, he then ruled that the federal remedy of excluding such evidence from trial did not survive the transfer. Over the next dozen years, the justices struggled with the implications of this ruling.

In 1952, the Court confronted a situation in which law officers, without either an arrest or search warrant, broke into the bedroom of Antonio Rochin. When Rochin took two capsules off a nightstand and sought to swallow them, the officers attempted to extract them from his mouth. Being unsuccessful, they rushed him to a hospital and obtained a doctor who pumped Rochin's stomach. Two capsules of morphine were extracted, and Rochin was arrested and convicted of violating the state law prohibiting the possession of narcotics. Clearly this was offensive governmental conduct, but following *Wolf* the evidence so seized would not be excluded. However, Frankfurter, who wrote the Court opinion in *Rochin v. California* as well as the one in *Wolf*, saw a distinction that empowered the Court to reverse Rochin's conviction.

In his *Rochin* opinion, Frankfurter portrayed the High Bench as the conscience of the national community and described its priestly attributes. The due process clause in the Fourteenth Amendment, he began, imposes an obligation upon the Court to exercise its judgment upon the trial proceedings "to ascertain whether they offend those cannons of decency and fairness which express the notions of justice of English-speaking peoples even toward those charged with the most heinous offenses." This responsibility, Frankfurter continued, does not leave justices free to consult "merely personal and private notions," but rather they must draw upon "considerations deeply rooted in reason and in the compelling traditions of the legal profession." He added: "To practice the requisite detachment and to achieve sufficient objectivity no doubt demands of judges the habit of self-discipline and self-criticism, incertitude that one's own views are incontestable and alert tolerance toward views not shared." These are the "qualities society has a right to expect from those entrusted with ultimate judicial power." Then, addressing the facts of the case, Frankfurter called the action of the law officers "conduct that shocks the conscience." States, he concluded, must "respect certain decencies of civilized conduct." To condone such action would "discredit law and . . . brutalize the temper of society."[6]

Frankfurter explained that due process cannot be given a fixed meaning but must be interpreted by judges "duly mindful of reconciling the needs both of continuity and of change in a progressive society."[7] The justices, he implied, have established their qualifications as high priests charged with the responsibility of interpreting the holy writ to ensure justice, decency, and civilized behavior. Few opinions in the history of the Court have been so self-conscious in their delineation of the civil religious role of the justices. Due process is seen as an invitation for the Court to give meaning and effect to the individual's constitutional rights. Only the justices have the training and experience to enforce the morality found implicit in the fundamental law.

Black and Douglas condemned the wide-ranging discretion that Frankfurter's opinion invited and would have replaced it by reading into the due process clause all of the essential guarantees of the Bill of Rights. What Frankfurter's opinion does, however, is reveal clearly the room left to the definitive interpreter of the Constitution to determine how vagueness in its wording will impact upon individual rights. Here, all the justices agreed that the Constitution must be interpreted to accord with basic conceptions of justice and fairness; they disagreed only on how this end could best be accomplished. Both approaches merged the moral with the legal and were premised on a priestly role for the Court.

Black and Douglas picked up converts as the decade progressed and new justices were added to the Court. The rule announced in *Rochin* was that evidence in state prosecutions would be inadmissible if the conduct of the officers in obtaining it "shocked the conscience"; if not, *Wolf* remained the guiding precedent. The difficulty the justices had with the *Rochin* exception was revealed in 1954 in *Irvine v. California*. Police officers had a key made to Irvine's house and entered four times to install microphones in various rooms, including the bedroom. Conversations were monitored and on the basis of the information so obtained Irvine was tried and convicted for gambling. Four members of the Court, including the then relatively new chief justice, Earl Warren, concluded that precedent did not bar such evidence. Tom C. Clark indicated his displeasure with precedent but then cast the deciding vote in favor of the admissibility of the evidence.[8]

Frankfurter saw the situation governed by *Rochin*. He accused his colleagues of misreading that decision, saying that its holding "is that a State cannot resort to methods that offend civilized standards of decency and fairness." Denying that *Rochin* was based upon the physical violence involved, he said here there was "a more powerful and offensive control over the Irvines' life than a single, limited physical trespass." Such "infringements of the dignity and privacy of the individual," the justice insisted, are indeed embraced by the due process clause. Frankfurter argued that imprisoning "due process within tidy categories misconceives its nature and is a futile endeavor to save the judicial function from the pains of judicial judgment."[9]

Three years later, when the Court decided that a blood sample could be drawn from an unconscious accident victim and its alcoholic content then used against him in a criminal prosecution, Warren, in an opinion joined by Black and Douglas, saw no real difference between a stomach pump and an involuntary blood test. The dissenters accused the majority of building constitutional doctrine "on shifting sands." Douglas added for himself and Black that the invasion "by the police of the sanctity of the body of an unconscious man" to procure by force evidence with which to convict him certainly affronted "the decencies of a civilized state." But the majority, in an opinion by Clark, simply said that "so slight an intrusion as is involved in applying a blood test . . . is far outweighed by the value of its deterrent effect" on driving while under the influence of alcohol.[10]

Frankfurter had accepted the lack of certainty in the law of search and seizure that would result from this case-by-case inspection of particular facts, but generally the justices believed that certainty was essential to the maintenance of a rule of law. Whether *Wolf* could survive in such an environment was questioned in *Elkins v. United States*. Until this decision of 1960, federal courts had accepted into evidence material illegally seized by state officials under the theory that the Fourth Amendment bound only the federal government and its agents. However, the Court had insisted upon the exclusion of such evidence when federal officials were implicated in such state seizures.[11] In *Elkins* the High Bench reinspected what had been called the silver-platter doctrine. Logically, the majority now said, *Wolf* is incompatible with that doctrine because the decision there placed the individual's protection against such unlawful seizure on constitutional grounds that bound the states as well.

Looking at the situation from the perspective of the individual, the Court said that whether the violator is a state official or a federal official is of no real importance. Then switching to the supervisory role of the Court in the administration of criminal justice in the lower federal courts, the majority saw requisite authority to enforce the exclusionary rule. Zeroing in on the reason for such exclusion, the justices said: "The rule is calculated to prevent, not to repair. Its purpose is to deter—to compel respect for the constitutional guaranty in the only effective available way—by removing the incentive to disregard it." The Court said that the main purpose of the rule was to protect the rights of defendants. Furthermore, the majority continued, the silver-platter doctrine must go because it compromises judicial integrity. For courts to participate by admitting evidence secured by illegal means, the justices now acknowledged, is dangerous to the maintenance of a rule of law. The federal courts cannot "be accomplices in the willful disobedience of a Constitution they are sworn to uphold."[12]

Frankfurter, writing for four dissenters, correctly drew out the incompatibility between the nonexclusion rule in *Wolf* and the *Elkins* decision. In the next year, the Court overruled *Wolf*, and, for the first time, made one of the criminal procedure provisions of the Bill of Rights fully binding upon the states.

Black and Douglas had been holdouts in *Wolf*, and they were now joined by Warren, Brennan, and Clark to compose the new majority. Justice Clark's opinion for the Court in *Mapp v. Ohio* centered on the High Bench's responsibility in protecting individual rights. The case involved an apparently warrantless search of Dollree Mapp's residence for a fugitive and for gambling paraphernalia. Instead, the search produced a cache of pornographic material, for which Mapp was subsequently prosecuted and convicted. What appeared to be a case that called for a ruling on the constitutionality of the private possession of obscene material was turned into a definitive ruling on the applicability of the exclusionary rule to the states. Tracing the history of the Fourth Amendment's interpretation by the Court back to 1886,[13] Clark referred to the Court's "jealous regard for maintaining the integrity of individual rights." He cited James Madison's hope that "independent tribunals of justice . . . will be naturally led to resist every encroachment upon rights expressly stipulated for in the Constitution by the declaration of rights."[14]

Repeatedly referring to the amendment as a protection of the individual's right to privacy, Clark said that, by overruling *Wolf* and making the exclusionary rule binding upon the states, the Court was closing "the only courtroom door remaining to evidence secured by official lawlessness in flagrant abuse of that basic right, reserved to all persons as a specific guarantee against that very same unlawful conduct." Just as the exclusionary rule was necessary to prevent the protection against unreasonable federal searches and seizures from being only a " 'form of words,' valueless and undeserving of mention in a perpetual charter of inestimable human liberties, so too, without that rule the freedom from state invasions of privacy would be . . . ephemeral and . . . neatly severed from its conceptual nexus with . . . freedom." To deny the only effective remedy for such invasions of privacy, Clark insisted, would confer a right without a remedy. "The ignoble shortcut to conviction left open to the State," he added, "tends to destroy the entire system of constitutional restraints on which the liberties of the people rest." Claiming that the new ruling is based "on reason and truth," Justice Clark declared that it "gives to the individual no more than that which the Constitution guarantees him, to the police officer no less than that to which honest law enforcement is entitled, and, to the courts, that judicial integrity so necessary in the true administration of justice."[15]

This first step in making the full protection of the criminal procedure sections of the Bill of Rights fully binding on the states is as significant for its rhetoric as for the ruling itself. First of all, Clark ties the Court's opinion to James Madison's words in introducing the proposal for a Bill of Rights to Congress in its first session. He thus establishes a link between the present and the hallowed past and submerges the novelty of the opinion within the view that a primary function of the judiciary was to ensure the protection of the listed rights from government overreaching.[16] Expanding their reach to bind the states as well served only more completely to protect individual rights from governmental abridgement.[17]

To the dissenters' plea that the authority of the states be respected, the majority responded with a sermon on the sanctity of individual rights as ordained by the holy writ. As Clark said, not only did common sense and reason dictate the result, but so did truth as discerned by the high priests of the Court. With the majority willing to read the Constitution broadly as "a perpetual charter of inestimable human liberties,"[18] it obviously had little patience with the structural arguments of dissenters Frankfurter and Harlan. And if respect for federalism had convinced earlier Courts to be wary about intruding upon state criminal justice, the majority proudly pointed to Founding Father Madison's charge that the judiciary has a special responsibility to ensure the protection of individual rights.

Clark's vote to make the exclusionary rule binding on the states had been crucial, and he became the Court's writer six years later when the High Bench brought electronic surveillance under the protections of the Fourth Amendment. Back in 1928 Justice Louis D. Brandeis in *Olmstead v. United States* had taken his colleagues to task for their view that the Fourth Amendment did not protect the individual from having his words electronically intercepted.[19] Now, the majority struck down a New York statute that permitted such "electronic eavesdropping" without protective procedures or adequate judicial supervision. Responding to the argument that in the war against crime such tactics, as used by New York police, are necessary, Clark said that "we cannot forgive the requirements of the Fourth Amendment in the name of law enforcement." Compliance with its strictures, he concluded, is necessary "before the innermost secrets of one's home or office are invaded. Few threats to liberty exist which are greater than that posed by the use of eavesdropping devices."[20]

Later that same year the Court finally put the Olmstead precedent to rest. Advocates for the federal government had defended the admissibility of wiretapping evidence on the basis that a person in a phone booth with glass sides open to public view could hardly expect privacy. Justice Potter Stewart, for the Court, said that the uninvited eye was not the same as the "uninvited ear." A person who makes a phone call, he continued, "is surely entitled to assume that the words he utters into the mouthpiece will not be broadcast to the world. To read the Constitution more narrowly is to ignore the vital role that the public telephone has come to play in private communication." Then, vanquishing the ghost of *Olmstead*, Stewart ruled that "the Fourth Amendment protects people, not places,"[21] thus reminding both government and the public of the significance of the protections found in the Bill of Rights and the Court's role in making them effective.

Mapp in 1961 had signaled the appearance of a new Court majority willing to focus substantial attention on claims of state deprivation of individual rights. What afforded further evidence of this new sensitivity was the willingness of the justices to scrutinize the many irregular petitions for review of state criminal convictions, some of which were handwritten. When merit was found in the claim, the Court allowed these petitioners to proceed *in forma pauperis*, which meant that most of the technical and costly printing requirements for appeal were waived and that counsel was appointed to present the claim to the Court. This willingness to sort through such claims only emphasized the justices' commitment to ensure that the full protection of an individual's rights would not be submerged under a yoke of poverty.

Such was the situation in *Robinson v. California*, a case the Court decided a year after *Mapp*. A man had been convicted and sentenced to a jail term of ninety days for violating a state statute making addiction to narcotics a crime. The justices pronounced the sentence cruel and unusual in that it was imposed not upon a criminal but upon a person acknowledged to be ill. Although with less than complete clarity, the Court seemed to be writing the Eighth Amendment's protection against cruel and unusual punishment into the due process guarantee of the Fourteenth Amendment. In a concurring opinion, Douglas was much more forthright: "We would forget the teachings of the Eighth Amendment," he said, "if we allowed sickness to be made a crime and permitted sick people to be punished for being sick. This age of enlightenment cannot tolerate such barbarous action."[22]

In the following year, 1963, the Court was ready to address the issue of legal representation of indigent defendants. A generation earlier the Court had ruled that the due process clause of the Fourteenth Amendment required that such representation had to be provided in state prosecutions that involved the death penalty.[23] Then, a decade later in *Betts v. Brady*, the Court concluded that counsel need not be furnished in noncapital cases.[24] Instead, the Court embarked upon a case-by-case consideration of the ability of defendants to conduct their own defense. The story of Clarence Gideon, an indigent defendant forced to defend himself, who petitioned the United States Supreme Court asking that he be released from custody, has been well told.[25] Gideon had been charged with breaking and entering a poolroom with the intent to commit a crime, a felony under Florida law. The state had denied any obligation to provide him with counsel. To argue the case for Gideon, the Supreme Court chose the well-known Washington lawyer, Abe Fortas. He was asked to address whether *Betts*, which required states to furnish counsel only in special circumstances, should be overruled.[26]

Unanimously, the Court in *Gideon v. Wainwright* decided that counsel had to be provided for indigent criminal defendants. The Sixth Amendment's provision for counsel was now made binding upon the states. Justice Black, for the unanimous bench, said that the Court had erred in *Betts* when it refused to classify the

right to counsel as "fundamental and essential to a fair trial." He now so characterized it. The justice continued: Pre-*Betts* precedents joined by "reason and reflection require us to recognize that in our adversary system of criminal justice, any
person haled into court, who is too poor to hire a lawyer, cannot be assured a fair
trial unless counsel is provided for him." Such a trial, he concluded, is mandated
by our system, for from the very beginning "our state and national constitutions
and laws have laid great emphasis on procedural and substantive safeguards designed to assure fair trials before impartial tribunals in which every defendant stands
equal before the law."[27]

That the Court took so long to face the reality that equal justice under law was
a mockery if a criminal trial pitted the legal expertise of the prosecutor against the
layman defendant was now clearly regretted by the justices. They all agreed that a
system that so disadvantaged a criminal defendant was not in accord with the
American faith.

On the same decision day, the Court also ruled that a state had the obligation
to furnish counsel for indigents appealing their convictions. California law required
the appellate court to make an initial determination from the record as to whether
there should be an appointment of counsel. This procedure, the justices said, drew
"an unconstitutional line . . . between rich and poor."[28]

In these two decisions the Court gave new meaning and effect to the basic civil
theological premise that sought to afford individuals equal justice under law. To
the widely held notion that the economically favored have, in practice, more rights
than those who are not so favored, the Court responded with a ruling that the
ends of justice are not to be dependent upon the individual's ability to employ
counsel.

The picture of the society and of the relationship between the enforcement of
the criminal law and the individual painted by the Court is one that reinforces
both human dignity and the protection of individual rights. A third decision
handed down on the same day only sharpens the image. At issue was the right of
a person convicted of felony-murder in a state trial to petition the federal courts
for a writ of habeas corpus. The prevailing rule was that a failure to appeal the
conviction and assert the constitutional claim precluded any later consideration of
the claim through habeas corpus proceedings.

Now, however, six justices made further inroads on state administration of its
criminal law by granting the writ. Citing the role of habeas corpus in "the unceas-
ing contest between personal liberty and government oppression," Justice Brennan, for the majority, said the writ's "history is inextricably intertwined with the
growth of fundamental rights of personal liberty. . . . Its root principle is that in a
civilized society, government must always be accountable to the judiciary for a
man's imprisonment." Here, the two other defendants had been freed because, on
appeal, their confessions were found to have been coerced. This fact did not go

unnoticed, as Brennan said that "surely no just and humane legal system can tolerate" such a result. "For such anomalies, such affronts to the conscience of a civilized society," he concluded, "habeas corpus is predestined by its historical role in the struggle for personal liberty to be the ultimate remedy."[29]

Notice how the Court here demands accountability from government, as the justices clearly assert that their solemn responsibility under the rule of law requires that they protect the rights of the individual. If in performing this task they have to break down barriers earlier imposed to prevent federal interference in the operation of state criminal justice systems, the price is simply the cost of fulfilling the priestly functions of the High Bench. In the process, the Court is also describing what it sees as the characteristics of a civilized society.

In 1964, the Court returned to the task that it had begun with *Mapp* and *Gideon*, which was nationalizing the protections of accused criminals found in the Bill of Rights through the medium of the Fourteenth Amendment. Brennan, for the Court, did not hesitate to overrule precedent and hold that the Fifth Amendment's protection against self-incrimination was also binding on the states. Earlier decisions, he asserted, had accorded "the Fourteenth Amendment a less central role in the preservation of basic liberties than that which was contemplated by its Framers when they added the Amendment to our constitutional scheme." Justice Brennan was insisting that the present decision did no more than recover the meaning that the amendment was designed to have within the remade constitutional system after the Civil War. "The same standards," he added, "must determine whether an accused's silence in either a federal or state proceeding is justified."[30]

On the same decision day, the justices widened the reach of the individual's protection against self-incrimination by ruling that a state grant of immunity forecloses the use of the forthcoming testimony in a federal prosecution and vice versa. Justice Goldberg, for the majority, said that such a result was necessary to promote the "policies and purposes" of the individual protection. The privilege, he said,

> reflects many of our fundamental values and most noble aspirations: our unwillingness to subject those suspected of crime to the cruel dilemma of self-accusation, perjury, or contempt; . . . our fear that self-incriminating statements will be elicited by inhumane treatment and abuses; our sense of fair play . . . ; our respect for the inviolability of the human personality . . . ; and our realization that the privilege, while sometimes "a shelter to the guilty," is often "a protection to the innocent."[31]

One week later on the last opinion day of the term, the Court looked at the implications of the Sixth Amendment's right to counsel. Danny Escobedo, during interrogation on a murder charge, had been denied his request for counsel and had not been informed of his rights, including the right to remain silent. Subsequently, he made incriminating statements that were used in his trial. Was he denied his right to counsel? Goldberg, speaking for four of his colleagues, answered yes. Escobedo had not been indicted, but when "the process shifts from investigatory to accusatory—when its focus is on the accused and its purpose is to elicit a confession—our adversary system begins to operate, and, under the circumstances here, the accused must be permitted to consult with his lawyer." To the argument that such a requirement would hamstring the police and hinder law enforcement, Goldberg answered that history teaches us "that no system of criminal justice can, or should survive, if it comes to depend for its continued effectiveness on the citizens' abdication through unawareness of their constitutional rights." If so informing the accused "will thwart the effectiveness of a system of law enforcement, then there is something very wrong with that system."[32]

The focus in *Escobedo v. Illinois* had been on the denial of the right to counsel, but two years later, by the same five-to-four count, the Court shifted its attention to the Fifth Amendment's protection against self-incrimination. Chief Justice Warren, for the Court, began by saying that the cases collected under the title *Miranda v. Arizona* "raise questions that go to the roots of our concepts of American jurisprudence: the restraints society must observe consistent with the Federal Constitution in prosecuting individuals for crime." Acknowledging the "spirited legal debate" that *Escobedo* had caused, the chief sought "to give concrete constitutional guidelines for law enforcement agencies and courts to follow." Noting that "precious rights were fixed in our Constitution only after centuries of persecution and struggle" and quoting Court decisions stretching back to the time of John Marshall, Warren said the decision today accords with the spirit of protecting individuals from "overzealous police practices" and is "consistent with our role as judges."[33]

He detailed the new mandate: "Prior to any questioning, the person must be warned that he has a right to remain silent, that any statement he does make may be used as evidence against him, and that he has a right to the presence of an attorney, either retained or appointed." Then tracing the record of the cases before the Court, the chief justice said they all "share salient features—incommunicado interrogation of individuals in a police-dominated atmosphere, resulting in self-incriminating statements without full warnings of constitutional rights." Noting that the cases present psychological and not physical coercion, Warren added that "concern for adequate safeguards to protect precious Fifth Amendment rights is, of course, not lessened in the slightest." A hostile environment, the chief continued, "is equally destructive of human dignity. The current practice of incommunicado interrogation is at odds with one of our Nation's most cherished principles—that the individual may not be compelled to incriminate himself."[34]

Recognizing that the privilege against self-incrimination has evolved over time, Warren said that it is an integral part of a person's right to privacy, which itself "is the hallmark of our democracy." He then continued: "The constitutional foundation underlying the privilege is the respect a government—state or federal—must accord to the dignity and integrity of its citizens." Such respect "for the inviolability of the human personality" requires the government to proceed against an individual by producing "evidence against him by its independent labors, rather than by the cruel, simple expedient of compelling it from his own mouth." The defendant, Warren ruled, "must be adequately and effectively apprised of his rights and the exercise of those rights must be fully honored." Because the privilege against self-incrimination "is so fundamental to our system of constitutional rule and the expedient of giving an adequate warning . . . so simple," the chief concluded, no inquiry will be made into whether the defendant had prior knowledge of such rights or whether the defendant's education and experience would imply such knowledge.[35]

What Warren makes clear in this decision is that the effective protection of individual rights is the Court's business and that those rights are designed to curtail the actions of government that fail to respect the dignity of the individual. Cries of imperiling the social order by overly protecting the accused criminal were rampant in the post-*Miranda* years. Whether critics agreed with the Court's detailing of state criminal procedure or not, the justices' concern for the effective protection of individual rights was well anchored in both precedent and the civil theology.

In the year between *Escobedo* and *Miranda* the Court had ruled "that the Sixth Amendment's right of an accused to confront the witnesses against him is . . . a fundamental right and is made obligatory on the States by the Fourteenth Amendment." All the justices agreed "that the right of confrontation is an essential and fundamental requirement for the kind of fair trial which is this country's constitutional goal." They differed, however, on how the conclusion should be justified. Although Harlan agreed with the result, he wanted to leave room for the states as laboratories to experiment. Goldberg responded that, although social and economic experimentation was fine, it certainly should not include "the power to experiment with the fundamental liberties of citizens safeguarded by the Bill of Rights."[36] No legitimate power has been taken from the states, the justice added, for the state no more than the federal government can deny a fundamental constitutional right under the Constitution.

Although most claims alleging a transgression of individual right were levied against state action, some did concern the actions of the federal government as well. For instance in 1965, for the first time, the justices found a federal law unconstitutional as an abridgement of free speech under the First Amendment. A postal service regulation labeled non–first class mail from communist countries as "communist political propaganda" and provided that addressees be notified and asked whether they wished to receive the mail. If they failed to return an enclosed card requesting delivery, the mail was destroyed. Seven members of the Court saw the requirement to return the card "as a limitation on the unfettered exercise of the addressee's First Amendment rights." They recognized that the need to request the delivery of mail labeled "communist propaganda" would inhibit a number of addressees. "The regime of this Act, the justices ruled, is at war with the 'uninhibited, robust, and wide-open' debate and discussion that are contemplated by the First Amendment."[37]

Brennan added a concurring opinion that Goldberg and Harlan joined, expressing his belief that the "right to receive publications is . . . a fundamental right." He continued: "The dissemination of ideas can accomplish nothing if otherwise willing addressees are not free to receive and consider them. It would be a barren marketplace of ideas that had only sellers and no buyers." And to the government argument that the issuing foreign governments are being subsidized in their propaganda campaigns, Brennan responded: "That the governments which originate this propaganda themselves have no equivalent guarantees only highlights the cherished values of our constitutional framework."[38]

The First Amendment was also implicated in a case in which the Court passed upon the authority of Congress to revoke the passports of American citizens who were members of the Communist Party. In response to the government's argument that a right to travel would be respected once the complaining parties relinquished their membership in the party, the justices reminded government counsel that the First Amendment protects a freedom of association. Six years earlier in 1958 the Court had avoided passing judgment on such a legislative restriction by denying that the secretary of state had been given authority to deny a passport on ideological grounds.[39] Now, the majority confronted such legislation and declared it unconstitutional on grounds that it interfered with the individual's liberty as protected by the due process clause of the Fifth Amendment. Freedom to travel, the justices said, defines who the individual is as much "as the choice of what he eats, or wears, or reads." Travel is no less than a part of our national heritage and "scheme of values."[40]

Restricting a citizen's right to travel may make that person less than an equal citizen, but seeking to strip a person of citizenship effectively ostracizes that person from the national community. In fashioning naturalization law over the years, Congress had provided for the divestment of American citizenship when a citizen did certain things, such as voting in a foreign election. In just such a case in 1958 the Court upheld the law, maintaining that the individual's consent or intent was irrelevant and that there was a rational relationship between such a rule and the need to avoid foreign policy problems.[41]

In 1967, the Court, with its acute sensitivity to claims of individual right, found a barrier to such federal governmental action in the Fourteenth Amendment's citizenship clause. A majority of five, taking the individual's rather than institutional or governmental perspective, overruled precedent. The birthright declaration of citizenship in the amendment, Black ruled, "can most reasonably be read as defining a citizenship which a citizen keeps unless he voluntarily relinquishes it." Such a reading, he continued, is much more in tune "with the principles of liberty and equal justice to all that the entire Fourteenth Amendment was adopted to guarantee."[42] To hold that temporary legislative majorities could deprive others of their citizenship, Justice Black insisted, was incompatible with free government. American citizens, he concluded, are protected from legislative divestiture and remain immunized as long as they so choose.

Obviously the majority had read into the sparse words of the citizenship clause new protection for the individual, but such a reading was all but necessitated by the civil religious responsibility of the justices. In the process of widening the American community to embrace those who had been excluded earlier, the Court certainly could not allow vague assertions of national interest to override the individual's choice to retain membership in the community.

As the Court was ensuring the protection of the individual's citizenship from divestiture, it was continuing to read provisions of the Bill of Rights into the Fourteenth Amendment's due process clause. For instance, it unanimously struck down a Texas rule holding that testimony from an alleged accomplice was not admissible. The Sixth Amendment's provision for securing witnesses in the accused's favor, the Court said, was as fundamental as the right to confrontation. "The Framers of the Constitution," it continued, "did not intend to commit the futile act of giving to a defendant the right to secure testimony he had no right to use."[43] In the same year, the Court decided that the Sixth Amendment's protection of an accused's "right to a speedy . . . trial" was now also binding upon the states, labeling it "as fundamental as any of the rights secured by the Sixth Amendment."[44]

In 1968, after years of addressing related rights, the justices finally confronted the issue of whether there was an individual right to trial by jury in a state criminal case. Saying that such a trial "is fundamental to the American scheme of justice," they found it required by the due process clause. "Community participation in the determination of guilt or innocence," they added, protects the individual from "unfounded charges," a "corrupt and overzealous prosecutor," and "judges too responsive to the voice of higher authority."[45]

The majority was nationalizing the standards that the Bill of Rights contained, something that would have been impossible prior to the enactment of the Fourteenth Amendment. Frankfurter earlier and now Harlan argued that the question of whether the standards of due process were met could and should be adjudicated on a case-by-case basis. But even Cardozo in *Palko v. Connecticut* looked for guidance in the Bill of Rights when he sought to describe what rights were an essential part of due process and which were not.[46] Those rights that were fundamental were to be applied equally to both the federal government and the states. This left open the door to enlarging the category of fundamental rights, which is precisely what the 1960s Court majority was doing.

That this approach would run full circle and reach the specific individual claim of right that Cardozo had deemed nonfundamental—the protection against double jeopardy—could have been expected. This reversal occurred in *Benton v. Maryland*, the last of the Warren Court decisions reading specific provisions of the Bill of Rights in their full force into the Fourteenth Amendment's due process clause. Finding the protection against double jeopardy "deeply engrained in . . . the Anglo-American system of jurisprudence," the justices now decided that the right was fundamental and, as such, binding upon the states.[47]

Constitutional rights, including the fundamental rights of the First Amendment, were always viewed in a setting where their rationale was tied to ensuring the integrity of the individual. Although free political speech was often defended in terms of serving the democratic society, other protections of speech were usually buttressed with reasoning that emphasized the freedom of individuals to explore the realm of their being within space that could not be invaded by the government.

One especially sensitive area was the public schools, where free discussion seemed especially needed and yet where majoritarian preferences were strong and at times oppressive. During the second red scare, as with the first following World War I, teaching had been an especially vulnerable profession, as American "patriots" sought to cleanse the classroom of subversive ideas. Loyalty oaths were commonly required, until the Supreme Court found such oaths too vague to meet the constitutional standard.[48] For example, in 1967 the Court responded to nontenured employees of a branch of the state university of New York in Buffalo who were seeking a declaratory judgment against the validity of an oath they were required to sign. Characterizing "treasonable" and "seditious" as vague terms, the majority justices said: "Our nation is deeply committed to safeguarding academic freedom, which is of transcendent value to all of us and not merely to the teachers concerned." Quoting an earlier decision, the Court reiterated that "Teachers and students must always remain free to inquire, to study and to evaluate, to gain new maturity and understanding; otherwise our civilization will stagnate and die."[49]

Maintaining that constitutional doctrine has advanced since the contrary decisions of the 1950s, the Court further ruled that knowing membership "without a specific intent to further the unlawful aims of an organization is not a constitutionally adequate basis for exclusion from such positions as those held by the appellants."[50] The justices brushed aside arguments that there was no right to be employed as a teacher and that the privilege could be restricted as the state chose, saying that such arguments did not justify infringing the right of free expression.

In the following year, the Court decided that a state could not dismiss a public school teacher for criticizing the board of education and the school superintendent for their failure to urge voters to increase the school tax. The justices said that "a teacher's right to speak on issues of public importance may not furnish the basis for his dismissal from public employment."[51]

In 1972 all the justices agreed "that the nonrenewal of a nontenured public school teacher's one-year contract may not be predicated on his exercise of First and Fourteenth Amendment rights."[52] What divided the Court was the extent of the state's obligation to furnish reasons to the teacher who was not rehired. Douglas, in dissent, in the first of two cases, argued that in all instances where a person is not rehired school authorities should supply their reasons and give the person the opportunity to rebut them. Thurgood Marshall went further in imposing an obligation upon government as employer, saying its "agencies are restrained from acting arbitrarily with respect to employment opportunities that they either offer or control." Government employment, he continued, must be regulated by procedural due process as "our fundamental guarantee against arbitrary, capricious, and unreasonable government action." Marshall dismissed the argument that government resources would be taxed by explaining to the affected persons the reasons for the termination of their employment. And to the claim that devious minds will always be able to come up with a satisfactory rationale, the justice responded that "procedural regularity . . . renders arbitrary action more difficult. . . . When the government knows it may have to justify its decisions with sound reasons, its conduct is likely to be more cautious, careful, and correct."[53]

The Court and the nation had traveled a long way from the time in which the privilege-versus-right dichotomy had left claimants bereft of a remedy for action infringing upon their rights. All the justices agreed that government employees had a right to due process. Government was no unrestrained benefactor doling privileges and favors as it pleased; it had a special responsibility to provide a model for how employers were to deal with their workers.

Not only were teachers in public institutions better protected in their exercise of individual rights guaranteed by the Constitution, but so, too, were students. In 1969 in *Tinker v. Des Moines Independent Community School District*, the Court ruled that the right to free speech embraced minor students as well as adults. Three teenagers wore black armbands to school to protest the Vietnam War. Aware of the anticipated protest, school principals agreed that, if the students did not remove the armbands when asked, they would be suspended. Although the display did not cause any disturbance, the children refused to remove the armbands and were suspended.[54]

Justice Abe Fortas, President Lyndon Johnson's appointee, spoke for the Court and said that neither students nor teachers "shed their constitutional rights to freedom of speech or expression at the schoolhouse gate." Finding no speech or action that was disruptive, the justice added that "in our system, undifferentiated fear or apprehension of disturbance is not enough to overcome the right to freedom of expression." Indeed any words or display could conceivably cause a disturbance, he continued, "but our Constitution says we must take this risk . . . ; and our history says that it is this sort of hazardous freedom—this kind of openness—that is the basis of our national strength and of the independence and vigor of Americans who grow up and live in this relatively permissive, often disputatious, society." Noting that the Vietnam protest had been singled out for disciplinary action, Fortas reminded school officials that "state-operated schools may not be enclaves of totalitarianism. School officials do not possess absolute authority over their students." As "persons" under the Constitution, he concluded, students "are possessed of fundamental rights which the State must respect."[55]

One of these rights, a subsequent decision of the Court in 1975 determined, was that students be afforded procedural due process. All four appointees placed on the High Bench by President Richard M. Nixon dissented, as White wrote the Court's opinion in a case concerning suspensions from school for ten days that were authorized by Ohio statute without notice or hearing. "Having chosen to extend the right to an education . . . ," he ruled, "Ohio may not withdraw that right on grounds of misconduct, absent fundamentally fair procedures to determine whether the misconduct has occurred." At stake, the justice continued, is not only the temporary denial of an education but also "the liberty interest in reputation, which is also implicated."[56] In conclusion, White barred the school system from suspending pupils under the statute and ordered it to remove references to past suspensions from the students' records.

Two years later in a Florida case involving paddling incidents in the Dade County schools, Justice Stewart joined the four Nixon appointees to reject the claim that the students' right to be free from cruel and unusual punishment made the disciplinary action unconstitutional. The majority justices saw the Eighth Amendment's prohibition applying only to the criminal law, not to school discipline. "The openness of the public school and its supervision by the community," they said, "afford significant safeguards against the kinds of abuses from which the Eighth Amendment protects the prisoner." As to the need for procedural due process before the punishment takes place, the majority accepted the argument that the cost of affording such safeguards "would significantly burden the use of corporal punishment."[57]

White, for the dissenters, was incensed, first because the majority had confined the Eighth Amendment, in the absence of any qualifying language, only to the criminal law. He noted that "in this case the record reveals beatings so severe that if they were inflicted on a hardened criminal for the commission of a serious crime, they might not pass constitutional muster."[58] The social condemnation of reprehensible punishment, he said, surely must apply equally to misconduct in school. Second, the justice berated the Court for distinguishing between suspension and paddling in terms of the due process required.

In 1982, White provided the swing vote when a fractured Court contended with a growing phenomenon in the country—attempts of local school boards, concerned parent groups, and others to remove certain books from school libraries or from the curriculum. No book was safe from these would-be censors, but the Court agreed to hear a case when four of its members, intent upon confirming the authority of school officials, voted to hear the matter.[59] Eight of the justices split evenly on whether a valid First Amendment claim had been raised. White did not address this issue, but he voted with the four who saw a valid First Amendment claim to overrule the summary judgment that had protected the school board's action.

The Court had earlier gone on record as holding that the First Amendment contains a right to receive as well as to transmit information and opinions.[60] Now, four justices would have expanded the earlier holding to stop school authorities from withdrawing certain books from school libraries on the basis of an objection to the content of the books. Harry A. Blackmun would only interfere when books were removed for the purpose of censoring social and political ideas. Brennan announced the judgment of the Court and wrote also for Marshall and Stevens, and Blackmun in part. Although recognizing the discretionary authority conferred on local school officials, Brennan insisted that they "must discharge their 'important, delicate, and highly discretionary functions' within the limits and constraints of the First Amendment."[61]

The justice added that "the right to receive ideas is a necessary predicate to the *recipient's* meaningful exercise of his own rights of speech, press, and political freedom." Such access to ideas, Brennan continued, "prepares students for active and effective participation in the pluralistic, often contentious society in which they will soon be adult members." Furthermore, "the special characteristics of the school *library* make that environment especially appropriate for the recognition of the First Amendment rights of students," for the library "is the principal locus" of a search for knowledge and understanding.[62] In exercising their important function of providing a library, Brennan insisted, school officials may not remove books to suppress ideas and promote orthodoxy. The task of inculcating community values must not, he concluded, ignore the predominant value of free inquiry.

Although the justices were deeply divided on the authority of school officials to remove books from the library, they all agreed that the Fourth Amendment's prohibition on unreasonable searches and seizures applies through the Fourteenth Amendment to students in the public schools. Such agreement, however, did not preclude differences when the question was whether a particular search met the constitutional standard. A fourteen-year-old student was found smoking in the restroom in violation of school rules. A teacher demanded her purse, a search of which produced not only cigarettes but also marijuana, along with information that she had been selling it to her classmates. With this evidence introduced, the student was found guilty as a delinquent. The state court ruled that the incriminating evidence had to be suppressed under the student's Fourth Amendment right. The Supreme Court reversed, saying that "a search will be permissible . . . when the measures adopted are reasonably related to the objectives of the search and not excessively intrusive in light of the age and sex of the student and the nature of the infraction."[63]

Brennan and Marshall dissented from the ruling. "It would be incongruous and futile," Brennan began, "to charge teachers with the task of imbuing their students with an understanding of constitutional democracy, while at the same time immunizing those same teachers from the need to respect constitutional protections." He said the search of the student by the vice principal "was undoubtedly a serious intrusion on her privacy," which "is the very purpose for which the Amendment was thought necessary." Criticizing the majority for rejecting the probable cause standard and balancing away the privacy of the student in favor of the authority of school officials, Justice Brennan said: "Moved by whatever momentary evil has aroused their fears, officials—perhaps even supported by a majority of citizens— may be tempted to conduct searches that sacrifice the liberty of each citizen to assuage the perceived evil."[64] Even if the vice principal had cause to search the purse for cigarettes, Brennan concluded, he had no authority to pursue the search any further.

Stevens's dissenting opinion, joined by his two other dissenting colleagues, expressed alarm at what he believed was the Court's invitation to school officials "to search students suspected of violating only the most trivial school regulations and guidelines for behavior." Reading the Fourth Amendment to deter illegal official behavior, he added: "In the case of evidence obtained in school searches, the 'overall educative effect' of the exclusionary rule adds important symbolic effect to this utilitarian judgment." Citing Louis D. Brandeis's words that "Government is the potent, the omnipresent teacher," Stevens said "that rules of law also have a symbolic power that may vastly exceed their utility."[65]

Recognizing the way in which law, especially constitutional law, can assume a sacred character, Justice Stevens indicated his awareness of the civil religious responsibilities of both the Court and the public schools and their relationship. "Schools," he said, "are places where we inculcate the values essential to the meaningful exercise of rights and responsibilities by a self-governing citizenry. If the Nation's students can be convicted through the use of arbitrary methods destructive of personal liberty, they cannot help but feel that they have been dealt with unfairly." Excluding such evidence "makes an important statement to young people that 'our society attaches serious consequences to a violation of constitutional rights.' " Accusing the majority of making Fourth Amendment "virtually meaningless in the school context," he argued that, because public schools educate "every citizen and public official, from schoolteachers to policemen and prison guards," they should not be allowed to scorn the values they supposedly teach.

"One of the most cherished ideals," the justice concluded, "is the one contained in the Fourth Amendment: that the government may not intrude on the personal privacy of its citizens without a warrant or compelling circumstances."[66]

While the majority called for the Court to be deferential to school authorities as they coped with their responsibilities, Stevens insisted that this authority could not be exercised to contradict civil religious teachings. More than lip service paid to individual rights was required. Students, the justice insisted, had to be taught by example that they, too, were beneficiaries of the rule of the law embodied in the civil religion's theology.[67]

Three years later, in 1988, the Court returned to the question first posed in *Tinker:* What limits can be imposed on students' free expression in the public schools?[68] In a student newspaper, written and edited by a high school journalism class in Missouri, articles dealing with three pregnant students and with the impact of divorce on students were withdrawn from publication by order of the principal. A statement of policy printed in the paper declared that "Spectrum, as a student-press publication, accepts all rights implied by the First Amendment." The Court majority distinguished *Tinker,* saying that the question here was "whether the First Amendment requires a school affirmatively to promote particular student speech." Answering no, it held "that educators do not offend the First Amendment by exercising editorial control over the style and content of student speech in school-sponsored expressive activities so long as their actions are reasonably related to legitimate pedagogical concerns."[69]

Brennan, with Marshall and now Blackmun joining him, continued to insist that the elements of the civic faith must be taught by example. He described the episode in terms of school authorities breaking a promise and violating "the First Amendment's prohibitions against censorship of any student expression that neither disrupts classwork nor invades the rights of others, and against any censorship that is not narrowly tailored to serve its purpose." Brennan continued: "Public education serves vital national interests in preparing the Nation's youth for life in our increasingly complex society and for the duties of citizenship in our democratic Republic." To serve this end, the justice added, "public educators must accommodate some student expression even if it offends them or offers views or values that contradict those the school wishes to inculcate." Accusing the majority of subverting *Tinker,* he said that school authorities have no "general warrant to act as 'thought police' stifling discussion of all but state-approved topics and advocacy of all but the official position." The principal's high-handed censorship, Brennan continued, demonstrated "unthinking contempt for individual rights. . . . It is particularly insidious from one to whom the public entrusts the task of inculcating in its youth an appreciation for the cherished democratic liberties that our Constitution guarantees."[70] As a civics lesson taught to youngsters, he concluded, the principal's action, now confirmed by the Court majority, was a poor one indeed.

In all of these school-related cases, there was an implicit recognition of a substantial amount of discretionary local control. With that local control often came majority prejudice seeking to limit and curtail freedom of discussion and thought. All the justices seemed to recognize that the public schools were the primary vehicle for teaching the essentials of the civil religion, but when the Court sought to isolate students from the diversity that characterized the society it served or when it found a respect for individual rights too burdensome, some justices felt the need to protest.

Reluctantly the Supreme Court had entered the world of the public schools, first through desegregation, then through the banning of officially sponsored prayer. Inevitably, as individuals sought to test their rights, the majoritarian emphasis of the schools provided a vulnerable target. In the final analysis, what is practiced becomes more important than what is taught. In this series of cases, certain justices were acutely aware of the effect of the discrepancies in what the students were actually being taught.

The landmark *Tinker* decision came two years after the Court had decided that its new protection of adults accused of crime would have to be made available in juvenile court proceedings. The process in such forums had lagged considerably behind the new national standards, and in deciding *In re Gault* the justices considerably reduced the distance. For making an obscene phone call, Gerald Gault, a fifteen year old, was convicted and committed to the Arizona State Industrial School until he reached the age of twenty-one.[71]

Fortas, for the Court, found the commitment almost totally void of due process. He ruled that written notice of the offense had to be communicated to the boy and his parents, that they should be informed of their right to counsel and the boy's self-incrimination protection, and that witnesses had to be sworn and cross-examination allowed. "Due process of law," the justice said, "is the primary and indispensable foundation of individual freedom. It is the basic and essential term in the social compact which defines the rights of the individual and delimits the powers which the state may exercise."[72]

Maintaining that the application of due process requirements will not impair the supposed benefits of the juvenile process, Fortas argued that "the condition of being a boy does not justify a kangaroo court." Then noting that an adult guilty of such a crime would face a fine of no more than $50 or imprisonment for up to two months, the justice remarked that such disparity of treatment "requires a bridge sturdier than mere verbiage, and reasons more persuasive than cliché can provide." To call the proceedings civil, Fortas continued, cannot mask that a person is deprived of liberty when incarcerated against his will. Finally, addressing the self-incrimination claim, he added that this protection is "a command which this Court has broadly applied and generously implemented in accordance with the teaching of the history of the privilege and its great office in mankind's battle for freedom."[73]

The result of these cases was to incorporate minors within the guarantees of the Constitution. Although the Court would continue to allow states to protect and regulate children, it gave notice that it would not place under that umbrella the ability to deny fundamental rights to persons simply because they had not reached their majority.

As the paternal role of government was being narrowed by the Court's delineation of the individual's rights, including those of minors, the justices repeatedly had to deal with laws purportedly enacted to protect children. In seeking to limit the access of children to sexually explicit material, states imposed regulations often with wide-ranging effects that invited legal challenge.

The Supreme Court's test for what was obscene,[74] even as subsequently restricted,[75] left considerable room for the distribution of erotic literature. And a state could not seek to protect "juvenile innocence" by depriving adults of reading matter, for that would be akin to burning "the house to roast the pig."[76] What was clear to the censors, however, was that carefully drafted restrictions on the access of children to such material could be sustained, a position the Court accepted in *Ginsberg v. New York* in 1968.[77]

Since *Ginsberg*, the tactic of would-be censors has been to use the wedge the Court had given them to make inroads on the general availability of sexually explicit material. When a father driving with his young son complained to the Federal Communications Commission (FCC) about a monologue by humorist George Carlin titled "Dirty Words" that he and his son had heard on their car radio on a Tuesday afternoon, the FCC found the broadcast violated the statutory provision against indecent broadcasts. It issued a declaratory order that would be made part of the station owner's licensing file. The FCC relied in part on the fact that the time the monologue was broadcast made it likely that children would hear it. The question was, could indecent, not obscene, material be banned from the airwaves? Five members of the Court said yes, on grounds that a radio broadcast could be thrust upon unwilling listeners, among whom could be children.[78]

Brennan, in dissent and with Marshall joining the opinion, accused the majority of ignoring the commands of the First Amendment and imposing "its notions of propriety on the whole of the American people." The Court errs, he continued, when it seeks to exclude from the protection of the Constitution those from "different socio-economic backgrounds" that do not respect "majoritarian conventions" regarding "which words or expressions are acceptable." The decision, then, is no less than "another of the dominant culture's inevitable efforts to force those groups who do not share its mores to conform to its way of thinking, acting and speaking."[79] What seemed to especially appall Brennan was the majority's deference to such majoritarian tendencies, when, he firmly believed, the Court's role,

the one at the heart of the civil religion, was to forbid exclusion and extend tolerance by rightfully applying the First Amendments's protections.

Brenan also contended with the majority's concern for the tender sensibilities
of children. Inspecting the monologue, which was inserted as an appendix to the
opinion, Brennan found no "erotic appeal to the prurient interests of children"
and condemned the censoring of nonobscene material.[80] He reminded his majority
colleagues of a three-year-old decision in which a Jacksonville, Florida, ordinance
prohibiting drive-in theaters from showing films containing nudity on a screen
visible from a public street was invalidated. There the Court had said that "speech
that is neither obscene as to youths nor subject to some other legitimate proscription cannot be suppressed solely to protect the young from ideas or images that a
legislative body thinks unsuitable for them."[81] The children-in-the-audience rationale, Brennan concluded, has no limits and would provide a basis for banning "any
'four-letter words' regardless of their context."[82]

If the would-be censors in American society were cheered by the "dirty words"
decision and convinced that children were to be the stalking horse to accomplish
their goals, subsequent attempts were viewed less charitably by the Court. In fact,
Justice Stevens, the newest member of the High Bench when he wrote for the
Court in the "dirty words" case, increasingly distanced himself from the rationale
of that opinion. For instance in 1989, in a case involving sexually explicit telephone messages, commonly called "dial-a-porn," he demonstrated his change of
mind. When the Court struck down a federal statutory ban on indecent messages,
ostensibly enacted to protect children, but left the ban on obscene messages stand,
Stevens joined Brennan and Marshall, his earlier antagonists in the "dirty words"
case, in arguing that the Court should also have struck down the ban on obscene
messages as well. Now realizing that the protecting children argument was often a
smokescreen, Stevens had no trouble agreeing that the criminal sanctions imposed
in all cases on the transmission of obscene speech by telephone "curtails freedom
of speech far more radically than the Government's interest in preventing harm to
minors could possibly" justify.[83]

In the dial-a-porn case the statute involved had been hastily enacted, but Congress learned little from this episode when it tacked the Communications Decency
Act onto a comprehensive law, titled the Telecommunications Act of 1996. This
addition was not much discussed during the extensive hearings, and, in fact, the
provisions challenged were offered as amendments on the Senate floor. Those
provisions sought to criminalize the transmission of indecent or patently offensive
messages to any recipient under the age of eighteen over the Internet, an international network of computers that enables millions of people around the world to
communicate in cyberspace.[84]

This time Stevens wrote for the Court and invalidated the challenged provisions
for running afoul of the First Amendment. He had no trouble understanding how

technology had created a global marketplace of ideas and images to which individuals were gaining access at a phenomenal rate and how very important it was not to obstruct this new democratic channel of communication. Rebuffing all attempts to limit First Amendment protection in cyberspace, Stevens lectured Congress, saying that it cannot seek to protect minors by suppressing "a large amount of speech that adults have a constitutional right to receive and address to one another." Although not as clumsy as the wholesale ban on indecent telephone communication, the new law, he declared, casts "a far darker shadow over free speech." Calling the breadth of the law's coverage "wholly unprecedented," he concluded that "the interest in encouraging freedom of expression in a democratic society outweighs any theoretical but unproven benefit of censorship."[85]

One did not have to wait for the Supreme Court to act to conclude that the two recent pieces of congressional legislation ostensibly passed to protect children were incompatible with the First Amendment. The explanation for their emergence from the legislative hopper rests with the nature of the political process and majoritarian government. If some eighteenth-century political thinkers believed that legislatures could be trusted with the job of protecting the people's liberties, time has proved them wrong. These early pundits based their prediction on the belief that legislators would be short-term officeholders who would instinctively identify with the people and jealously preserve the rights of the individual, because in so doing they would be protecting their own rights. Although early congressmen and senators took their oath to support the Constitution to mean that they had an obligation to assess the constitutionality of their actions, this concern has dissipated with the passing years. Apparently, the people's representatives have found greater comfort and far more security in succumbing to the perceived desires of voters than in engaging in the risky process of educating them.

That educational task has fallen to the federal judiciary, and especially, because of both its visibility and its place within the hierarchy, the Supreme Court. If legislators and the democratic electorate stray from their constitutional moorings, the Court's task is to bring them back and refasten the bonds. These bonds are not simply constitutional precepts; they are the articles of faith of the civil religion.

Without a doubt the preeminent symbol of this religion is the flag.[86] Reflect for a moment on its primacy in the culture. *What* object do Americans annually celebrate? *To what* do Americans, alone among all nationals of the world, pledge allegiance, *with what* do Americans drape the coffins of those who have died in service of their country, and *upon what* object is both the American national anthem and the national march focused? Only by understanding the position of the national emblem in this civil religious structure can we begin to make sense of the heated debate that the issue of flag burning ignited. Few on either side of the ensuing controversy denied the symbolic importance of the American flag, least of all the burners themselves.

Gregory Johnson had burned the flag in Dallas at the meeting of the Republican National Convention in protest against the policies of the Reagan administration. What his conviction posed was a conflict between society's interest in protecting the sanctity of the flag and Johnson's individual right based upon a key commandment in the holy writ—the right of individual self-expression. The battle would be fought among the faithful.

Few Court watchers in 1989 could or would have predicted the result in *Texas v. Johnson*. During his two terms in office, President Reagan had sought to place individuals on the Court who would be inclined to defer to the policymaking authority of the legislative branches. He had promoted William H. Rehnquist to the center seat and placed three others on the High Bench. But, true to its history, the Court surprised, ruling that flag burning was protected speech. Brennan's majority opinion gained the support of Marshall, Blackmun, and two Reagan appointees, Antonin Scalia and Anthony M. Kennedy.[87]

Brennan ruled that Johnson had been engaged in the type of expressive conduct that came within the embrace of the First Amendment. To Texas's claims that its statute protected against breaches of the peace and sought to preserve the symbolic nature of the American flag, the justice responded: "We hold that the first interest is not implicated on this record and that the second is related to the suppression of expression." The lesson of our prior decisions in the area, that the government may not prohibit expression simply because it disagrees with the message," he remarked, "is not dependent on the particular mode in which one chooses to express an idea." Brennan continued: "To conclude that the government may permit designated symbols to be used to communicate only a limited set of messages would be to enter territory having no discernible boundaries." He accused the dissenters of seeking to carve out "an exception to the joust of principles protected by the First Amendment." The Court's decision, the justice insisted, did not weaken "the flag's deservedly cherished place in our community"; rather it was strengthened by reaffirming "the principles of freedom and inclusiveness that the flag best reflects." Tolerating such criticism, he argued, "is a sign and source of our strength." The flag's special role in our society, Brennan added, is preserved through persuasion, not punishment. "We do not consecrate the flag by punishing its desecration," he concluded, "for in so doing we dilute the freedom that this cherished emblem represents."[88]

Kennedy added some words of his own in which he captured the spirit of the Court's work. Indicating that the High Bench can neither share nor escape its responsibility in such cases, he confessed: "The hard fact is that sometimes we must make decisions we do not like. We make them because they are right, right in the sense that the law and the Constitution, as we see them, compel the result." Stating that "the flag is constant in expressing beliefs Americans share, beliefs in law and peace and that freedom that sustains the human spirit," Kennedy said that the decision here "forces recognition of the costs to which those beliefs commit us. It is poignant but fundamental that the flag protects those who hold it in contempt."[89] Kennedy's opinion eloquently acknowledges that the role of high priest of the civil religion imposes obligations upon the interpreter of the holy writ that cannot be avoided. Although his personal inclinations follow the dissenters, his obligation does not.

Chief Justice Rehnquist, joined by White and Sandra Day O'Connor, President Reagan's appointee, dissented. Tracing 200 years of the worship of the flag in prose and verse, the chief argued that this history, in which the emblem "has occupied a unique position as the symbol of our Nation," should be a sufficient answer to Johnson's claim. "Millions and millions of Americans," he continued, "regard it with an almost mystical reverence" despite their differences in political and social views. The act of flag burning was not expression, Rehnquist added, but rather "the equivalent of an inarticulate grunt or roar . . . indulged in not to express any particular idea, but to antagonize others." Accusing the majority of delivering "a regrettably patronizing civics lecture," he said that the Court oversteps its bounds when it acts "as a platonic guardian admonishing those responsible to public opinion as if they were truant schoolchildren." Counseling deference to democratic majorities, Rehnquist said: "Surely one of the high purposes of a democratic society is to legislate against conduct that is regarded as evil and profoundly offensive to the majority of people—whether it be murder, embezzlement, pollution, or flag burning."[90]

Apparently Stevens, who wrestled like Kennedy with a painful choice, wanted to separate himself from Rehnquist's hyperbole. He also sought to extract the flag from other symbols and, despite his broader view of its meaning, turn it into a sacred object. Seeing the flag as "a symbol of freedom, of equal opportunity, of religious tolerance, and of good will for other peoples who share our aspirations," Stevens argued that a governmental "interest in preserving that value for the future is both significant and legitimate." The decision permitting its burning, he continued, "will tarnish its value—both for those who cherish the ideas for which it waves and for those who desire to don the robes of martyrdom by burning it." Insisting that the case is not about the communication of ideas, Stevens said that, instead, it "involves disagreeable conduct that . . . diminishes the value of an important national asset." A flag symbolizing the motivating power of ideas such as equality and liberty, he concluded, is certainly "worthy of protection from unnecessary desecration."[91]

In a very real sense, the conflict among the justices took place within the arena of the American civil religion. The strong feelings of the dissenters in seeking to promote community by protecting the flag from desecration easily fits into this context.[92] A prime motivation for the delineation of the nature of such a religion has been the search for the bond that holds a diverse people together. On the other hand, the cool rationality of the majority opinion might hide the fact that it is no less civilly religious than the opinions of the dissenters. Working from a text—the First Amendment—that lies at the heart of the theology of the civil religion, Justice Brennan's task was quite different from that of the dissenters. While they had to wrap the flag in two hundred years of history and try to rescue it from the ambit of the First Amendment, all Brennan had to do was apply the free speech provision in a relatively conventional manner.

The conflict in the flag desecration cases was not between believers and heretics, but rather between believers who differ in three instances: first, how is the flag's symbolic value maintained; second, what does the civil religion command; and third, what is the role of the Court within it. Whether consciously or not, the majority's opinion had the effect of preserving the symbolic value of the flag from the threat of the minority to turn it into an object of limited symbolic significance.[93] To the dissenters, the individual's right to burn the flag was not protected speech, and the Court's role should be a priestly one—to soothe the faithful with assurances that the sacred nature of the flag will be ensured by law. To the majority, the Court's role should be a prophetic one—to call the faithful back to an understanding of what the theological text mandates.[94]

Furthermore, the furor that greeted the decision can only be understood within the contours of the civil religion. Members of Congress were besieged to do something about the Court's ruling, and the proposal for a constitutional amendment prospectively overruling the decision began to pick up steam. What the sharply etched differences and emotional fog and rhetoric tended to conceal was the basic agreement that both sides shared. Both sides accepted the Supreme Court's authority to adjudicate the claim of free speech by interpreting the First Amendment. Opponents of the decision did not claim that free speech should not be safeguarded; rather they argued that the Court had erred in calling this act of flag desecration "speech." And they could point to four members of the Court who agreed with them. There were no calls for the impeachment of the majority justices; in fact the most insistent opponents accepted the five-to-four decision as no less than what the Constitution itself had ordained. Implicitly working from this premise, they pressed for changing the Constitution to remove flag desecration from the reach of the First Amendment. Only in this way could the most sacred of symbols of the American faith structure be preserved from defilement. Despite the raging battle over the flag as symbol of the national faith, undergirding that struggle was a substantial ideological consensus about both process and content. Despite the harsh words and bitterness, it was still a quarrel among the faithful.

Something had to be done to placate the aroused constituency. Enough of the people's representatives were worried about the wisdom of modifying the text or the reach of the First Amendment, and they therefore sidetracked the amendment proposal. Instead, Congress passed the Flag Protection Act, which simply sought to protect the physical flag from desecration.[95]

When the new statute came before the Court, nary a mind was changed, and Brennan denied that the statute was or ever could be content-neutral. First of all, he began, "the Government's desire to preserve the flag as a symbol for certain national ideals is implicated 'only when a person's treatment of the flag communicates [a] message' to others that is inconsistent with those ideals." Second, Brennan continued, the statutory wording "connotes disrespectful treatment of the flag and suggests a focus on those acts likely to damage the flag's symbolic value." Quoting his earlier opinion, the justice said that an exception in the statute to permit worn-out flags to be burned allows the state to promote orthodoxy "by saying that one may burn the flag to convey one's attitude toward it and its referents only if one does not endanger the flag's representation of nationhood and national unity."[96]

Despite the broader language of the new federal act, Brennan ruled, it "still suffers from the same fundamental flaw: It suppresses expression out of concern for its likely communicative impact." To the government's request that the Court reconsider its earlier decision because of a " 'national consensus' favoring a prohibition on flag burning," the justice answered: "Even assuming such a consensus exists, any suggestion that the Government's interest in suppressing speech becomes more weighty as popular opposition to that speech grows is foreign to the First Amendment." Acknowledging that "Government may create national symbols, promote them, and encourage their respectful treatment," he ruled that "the Flag Protection Act of 1989 goes well beyond this by criminally proscribing expressive conduct because of its likely communicative impact." Making desecration of the national emblem criminal, Brennan concluded, "dilutes the very freedom that makes this emblem so revered, and worth revering."[97]

Stevens, now writing for all dissenters, did not disagree with the proposition that government cannot censor offensive speech, but he argued that the protesters had alternative means of conveying their views. The government, he insisted, has a valid societal interest in maintaining the flag as a symbol, for the emblem "uniquely symbolizes the ideas of liberty, equality, and tolerance . . . and . . . embodies the spirit of our national commitment to those ideals." This message, the justice continued, "does not take a stand upon our disagreements, except to say that those disagreements are best regarded as competing interpretations of shared ideals." He agreed that protection of the individual's right of free expression was "one of the critical components of the idea of liberty that the flag is intended to symbolize," but he asserted that the right was not absolute. In conclusion, Stevens condemned the majority for damaging the flag as symbol, but he also castigated those "who seem to manipulate the symbol of national purpose into a pretext for partisan disputes about meaner ends."[98]

Stevens's dissent is a worthy response to the majority opinion. It is firmly rooted in the civil religion and is concerned about promoting and encouraging the unity that the religion seeks. The dissent does not deride the majority's respect for wide-ranging political speech; instead it empathizes with the view and associates the flag with it. In other words, the opinion does not promote unity to the detriment of diversity; it simply finds room for the government to preserve an important unifying symbol.

Because a more carefully drawn statute could not pass constitutional muster, Congress in the wake of the second decision voted on a resolution proposing an amendment that would exclude flag burning from the reach of the First Amendment. Although majorities in both houses voted in favor of the constitutional change, the vote was considerably short of the two-thirds required by the Constitution to send the resolution to the states.

Were this a single episode we might conclude that supporters of broad First Amendment protection were lucky, but the history of the last half century or so demonstrates that this episode is one of many that have failed to limit either the Supreme Court's authority to interpret the scope of individual rights or the Constitution itself. Throughout the 1950s and 1960s, especially, many legislative initiatives were mounted to curb the Court's wide-ranging protection of such rights.[99] Defenders had to be found within the legislative arena, but they have always appeared, convinced that these rights are never definitively won and that each generation must be ready to do battle to preserve them. These defenders are stronger than they first appear, in large part because they draw upon key articles of the civil theology. The public may have to be reminded of these basic principles, but they are the stuff of a common American faith.

At the heart of the flag-burning controversy was the question of just who defines the meaning of a symbol. The chief justice argued that it was not government that had given the flag its symbolic meaning but rather the people over 200 years. Any such distinction, however, only highlights the threat to individual liberty posed by the majority will. And in regard to symbols, "human experience has shown that there is always danger that a system of order, a framework of unambiguous signs, will become ends in themselves to be rigidly imposed and preserved from any possible deviation."[100] Brennan saw only danger in allowing any government to establish the orthodox meaning for a symbol; its variable meaning makes it a unifying agent for a diverse people.

In the final analysis, such decisions—as the Court reached in the flag-burning cases, insisting that the protection of individual rights triumph over a societal desire to be free of offense—tend to resanctify the law.

Although in the flag-burning cases four justices would have allowed government to proscribe the conduct involved as not protected by the First Amendment, all members of the Court agreed in 1992 that the burning of a cross on the property of a black homeowner was speech protected under the amendment. The case arose within a society that was increasingly interested in promoting a degree of civility through the medium of rules and regulations. Whether the arena was the nation's colleges and universities or city councils or state legislatures, what was called "hate speech" was targeted. "Political correctness" and "cultural diversity" were code words that captured some of the movement's attempt to ensure civility through threat of punishment. Could students be expelled from school or could individuals be punished because they insulted others on the basis of their race, religion, or ethnic background? The desire in a pluralistic society for civility is laudable, but the problem is that such regulations threaten one of the basic theological premises, the right of free speech. Repeatedly the Supreme Court had said that injured feelings and resentment are insufficient reasons to limit free expression. Both lower state and federal courts struck down regulations, ordinances, and statutes that clearly invaded this key theological area. Some of these attempts were such blatant attempts to censor expression that appeals were not pursued. The case the Court took seemed to pose a more difficult problem.

A teenager was tried and convicted for burning a crudely constructed cross on the property of a black homeowner in St. Paul, Minnesota. The relevant ordinance prohibited, among other things, the burning of a cross "which one knows or has reasonable grounds to know arouses anger, alarm or resentment in others on the basis of race, color, creed, religion or gender."[101] Ruling the ordinance unconstitutional under the First Amendment, the trial court dismissed the charge. The Minnesota high court, however, reversed and said that the language was to be read to embrace only the "fighting words" that the United States Supreme Court had placed beyond the pale of the First Amendment.

Although all the justices concluded that the ordinance was unconstitutional, only five of them joined the Court opinion—Scalia the writer, Rehnquist, Kennedy, and President Bush's two appointees, David Souter and Clarence Thomas. What the majority decided was that the ordinance in proscribing only certain fighting words had made an impermissible content discrimination. "The government," Scalia held, "may not regulate use based on hostility—or favoritism— towards the underlying message involved." Selecting messages of racial, gender, and religious content for proscription, he continued, clearly indicates "that the city is seeking to handicap the expression of particular ideas."[102]

White, Blackmun, Stevens, and O'Connor concurred in the result but attacked the majority's reasoning. Stevens was most outspoken in support of such a law if it were drafted more tightly to overcome the objection the four of them found in the St. Paul ordinance.

The Minnesota court had sought to rely on *Chaplinsky v. New Hampshire*, the "fighting words" precedent, to justify its decision,[103] and *Chaplinsky* has often been summoned to lend support to governmental attempts to punish offensive speech. Wisely, the Court has refused to build doctrine upon this peculiar precedent. Most speech that has been the target of suppression can readily be labeled offensive and provocative; if it were not, who would care? During the protest over American military involvement in Vietnam, California sought aid from *Chaplinsky* in labeling as offensive conduct a person's wearing a jacket bearing the words "Fuck the Draft." The majority justices took the opportunity to explain the civil theological foundation for free speech:

> The constitutional right of free expression is a powerful medicine in a society as diverse and populous as ours. It is designed and intended to remove governmental restraints from the arena of public discussion, putting the decision as to what views will be voiced largely into the hands of each of us, in the hope that use of such freedom will ultimately produce a more capable citizenry and more perfect polity and in the belief that no other approach would comport with the premise of individual dignity and choice upon which our political system rests. To many, the immediate consequence of this freedom may often appear to be only verbal tumult, discord, and even offensive utterance. . . . That the air may at times seem filled with verbal cacophony is, in this sense[,] not a sign of weakness but of strength. We cannot lose sight of the fact that, in what otherwise might seem a trifling and annoying abuse of a privilege, these fundamental societal values are truly implicated.[104]

These words, written by the second Justice John Marshall Harlan, were designed not only to teach the basic beliefs of the civil religion but to justify them in terms of the pluralistic society that the religion serves. Of note also is Harlan's emphasis not only on the social order but on individual dignity as well. We have seen how some supporters of free speech base their support on its social benefit and how others see free speech as a recognition of individual freedom. Harlan blends these two foundations in the above quotation in large part to forestall either judges or other governmental officials from determining the social interest for themselves. Individuals are left to determine for themselves what views they will express, both out of respect for their dignity and as a protection against oppression.

Just as social pressures have led some rule makers to target "hate speech," political campaign abuses have led to legislation seeking to regulate campaigning. One common mode of regulation engaged in by the federal government and every state but California has been to insist that campaign literature be identified by the name of the individual or organization circulating it. The purpose is to cleanse the process of anonymous charges and countercharges. When the Court looked at such regulation through the lens of an Ohio statute, it struck it down. Stevens, for the Court, said that "anonymity is a shield from the tyranny of the majority." The First Amendment's purpose, he continued, was "to protect unpopular individuals from retaliation—and their ideas from suppression—at the hand of an intolerant society."[105] Stevens might have noted that this was a society that regularly had to be informed of the articles of its civil religious faith.

Although all students of the Constitution would agree that the free speech clause protected political utterances, including campaign literature, commercial speech, as such, was not brought under the protection of the First Amendment until the mid-1970s. In the major case of *Virginia Pharmacy Board v. Virginia Consumer Council*, the Supreme Court ruled that a state ban on advertising prescription drug prices could not stand. Saying that from the consumer's perspective the price of a needed drug may be of more interest than any political utterance, Blackmun, for the Court, added that "society also may have a strong interest in the free flow of commercial information." To the state's alleged interest in protecting the public, the justice responded that the First Amendment has already made the choice "between the dangers of suppressing information, and the dangers of its misuse if it is freely available."[106] Over the ensuing years commercial speech has been given a secure lodging within the protective reach of the First Amendment.[107] These decisions, though solicitous of certain business interests, continually stress the need to provide individuals with information so that they can make informed and thoughtful decisions.

One interesting recent case arose when a community, seeking to preserve its aesthetics, actually made an exception for a type of commercial speech when it placed a general ban on signs placed on residential property. "For sale" signs were the only exception to the Ladue, Missouri, ordinance. When a woman put a small sign in a second floor window reading "For Peace in Gulf" during the Gulf War, she was charged with violating the Ladue ordinance. The unanimous Court, speaking through Stevens, ruled that Ladue sought to foreclose "a venerable means of communication that is both unique and important." He reminded the town leaders of their civil religious responsibilities: "A special respect for individual liberty in the home has long been part of our culture and law . . . ; that principle has special resonance when the government seeks to constrain a person's ability to *speak* there."[108]

Stevens might also have added as a part of this special liberty the right to read and to listen in one's home free from such interference. The individual's privacy had been an insistent concern from James Otis's protest against writs of assistance in the early 1760s through the addition of the Fourth and Fifth Amendments to the Constitution in 1791, the Court's tribute to sanctity of the home in *Boyd* in 1886, and Brandeis's dissent in *Olmstead* in 1928, up to the application of the exclusionary rule to the states in 1962.

Justice Hugo Black, who had long been an advocate of reading the Bill of Rights into the Fourteenth Amendment, had no difficulty protecting the privacy associated with the Fourth and Fifth Amendments, but when his colleagues sought to widen its ambit he balked. The claim of a right to privacy, not specifically embraced by words in the Bill of Rights, was presented to the Court in 1965, when a Connecticut law proscribing the use of contraceptives was challenged. The director of the state Planned Parenthood League and a physician were prosecuted for giving advice to married persons on how to avoid conception. When the majority of the Court invalidated the law, Black accused his brethren of reading natural law principles into the Constitution. Those justices who disagreed with Black in *Griswold v. Connecticut* insisted that they were doing no more than fulfilling the Court's responsibility to protect individual rights. The interference of the state with individual choice was blatant, and the majority justices worked to find a way to define and then protect the infringed right.

Justice Douglas wrote for five members of the Court as he sought to square the new right with the now-familiar terrain of the Bill of Rights. Saying that the Connecticut law "operates directly on an intimate relation of husband and wife and their physician's role in one aspect of that relation," he cited the Court's protection of "peripheral rights" when it allowed parents to educate their children as they chose and to have their children exposed to the German language.[109] Such decisions, Douglas said, "suggest that specific guarantees in the Bill of Rights have penumbras, formed by emanations from those guarantees that help give them life and substance." Finding in these penumbras emanating especially from the Fourth and Fifth Amendments "rights of 'privacy and repose,' " the justice added that the case here "concerns a relationship lying within the zone of privacy created by several fundamental constitutional guarantees." Such a law, Douglas continued, "seeks to achieve its goals by means having a maximum destructive impact upon that relationship" in that it "would allow the police to search the sacred precincts of marital bedrooms for telltale signs of the use of contraceptives." As such, he concluded, it cannot stand. For the majority, then, a law that invaded the marital relationship invaded "a right of privacy older than the Bill of Rights."[110]

Goldberg, with Warren and Brennan, all of whom joined the Court opinion, focused on the Ninth Amendment, which provides that the enumeration of rights "shall not be construed to deny or disparage others retained by the people."[111] He argued that "the Framers did not intend that the first eight amendments be construed to exhaust the basic and fundamental rights which the Constitution guaranteed to the people." Responding to internal criticism that such an interpretation allows the Court to manufacture new rights, the justice insisted that what the majority had done here only "serves to support what this Court has been doing in protecting fundamental rights."[112] Then addressing the dissenters' constitutional literalism, Goldberg added that, accepting their reasoning, there could be no ban on a state forcing sterilization on couples who have already borne two children because the Constitution does not specifically address the matter.

Harlan and White both concurred in the result, feeling quite comfortable with invalidating the archaic law on due process grounds. Still contending with the dissenting Black, Harlan argued that his colleague's simple fundamentalism was no guarantee against justices reading their own preferences into the Constitution.

Actually Harlan would have come to the same decision on the Connecticut law four years earlier when the majority dismissed a similar case on grounds that prosecution under the law was not threatened. He was incensed that the majority had ignored its civil religious responsibility.[113] "Making it a criminal offense for *married couples* to use contraceptives," the justice insisted, "is an intolerable and unjustifiable invasion of privacy in the conduct of the most intimate concerns of an individual's personal life." The text of the Constitution, he added, must be read "not in a literalistic way, as if we had a tax statute before us, but as the basic charter of our society, setting out in spare but meaningful terms the principles of government." Maintaining that a definition of due process solely in procedural terms could threaten the very liberty it was designed to protect, Harlan said that the protection, as interpreted by the Court, represents "the balance which our Nation, built upon postulates of respect for the liberty of the individual, has struck between that liberty and the demands of organized society."[114]

Now, seven members of the Court in *Griswold* had decided that such state restriction on private choice could not stand. In the sense that the parties involved were a married couple and their physician, the state regulation seemed even more oppressive. But this decision protecting the intimacy of the marriage relationship was an opening wedge in dealing with a subject of increasing importance in the society—privacy. From the Court's early excursion into interpreting the Fourth Amendment's protection against unreasonable searches and seizures in 1886, the justices had talked in terms of protecting individual privacy. The dispute in *Griswold* centered on just how much privacy could be protected when not encompassed by specific wording in the Bill of Rights. What *Griswold* did was open a new dialogue that moved beyond the limited facts of that case into a much larger arena.[115]

In regard to the general availability of contraceptives, the Court pushed far beyond the marriage bed. In 1972 the Court, by a four-to-three count, ruled that a state could not distinguish between married and unmarried persons in regard to its laws concerning contraceptives. Recognizing that *Griswold* had dealt with marital privacy, Brennan, for the majority, now defined the protected union in terms of "an association of two individuals each with a separate intellectual and emotional makeup." Giving new scope to the right first recognized in 1965, he said: "If the right of privacy means anything, it is the right of the *individual*, married or single, to be free from unwarranted governmental intrusion into matters so fundamentally affecting a person as the decision to bear or beget a child."[116]

Five years later, the Court struck down a New York law that made it a crime for anyone to sell or distribute contraceptives to minors under the age of sixteen, for anyone but a pharmacist to distribute contraceptives to anyone over fifteen, and for anyone to advertise or display contraceptives. Four members of the Court said that "the right to privacy in connection with decisions affecting procreation extends to minors as well as adults." Concurring, John Paul Stevens found the state's rationale of enacting the law to discourage sexual relations among minors "irrational and perverse." The state, he said, cannot "attempt to persuade by inflicting harm on the listener."[117]

More important than the availability of contraceptives, however, was the further delineation of the right of privacy first accepted by the Court in *Griswold*. One of the targets of a revitalized women's movement in the late 1960s and early 1970s was restrictive state antiabortion laws.[118] Many women saw such regulation as an unwarranted invasion of their privacy. Some liberation of state abortion laws had taken place, but the attraction of litigation as a means of changing policy on a national level had steadily grown since *Brown v. Board of Education*.[119] In *Roe v. Wade*, which was reargued in 1972 to include two recent appointees of President Richard Nixon, the Court decided, seven to two, that the newly recognized right of privacy encompassed a woman's right to terminate a pregnancy during the first six months.

Harry Blackmun wrote the majority opinion in *Roe*, which involved a pregnant single woman challenging the constitutionality of a Texas law that prohibited abortion except when the woman's life was in jeopardy. Acknowledging that a right of privacy is not specifically mentioned in the Constitution, he cited a number of Court decisions going back to 1891 in which there was protection of "certain areas or zones of privacy . . . under the Constitution."[120] In the 1891 case, the Court had ruled that a plaintiff in a personal injury case could not be forced to undertake a physical examination at defendant's behest. The justices there said: "No right is held more sacred, or is more carefully guarded by the common law, than the right of every individual to the possession and control of his own person, free from all restraint or interference of others, unless by clear and unquestionable authority of the law."[121] Drawing upon this line of precedent, Blackmun deduced a right of privacy that "is broad enough to encompass a woman's decision whether or not to terminate her pregnancy."[122]

He then proceeded to qualify the right by recognizing that regulations can be imposed by the state to safeguard the health of the pregnant woman and to protect "the potentiality of human life." To accommodate these interests the justice divided the period of pregnancy into trimesters. In the first trimester, there could be no state interference with the decision of the pregnant woman and her physician. In the second, the state could regulate the procedure to protect the pregnant woman's health. Only in the final trimester could "the State in promoting its interest in the potentiality of human life . . . regulate, and even proscribe, abortion except where it is necessary, in appropriate medical judgment, for the preservation of the life or health of the mother."[123] In relying on the Fourteenth Amendment's due process clause, Blackmun exposed the Court to the claim that the justices were simply reading their personal views into the holy writ.

Douglas, in a concurring opinion, sought to tie the liberty protected by the Fourteenth Amendment to both the Ninth Amendment and the phrase in the Preamble that stated that the government, established under the Constitution, was to "secure the Blessings of Liberty to ourselves and our Posterity." Although neither the Ninth Amendment nor the Preamble created legally enforceable rights, he said, they do summon to our attention the "customary, traditional, and time-honored rights, amenities, privileges, and immunities . . . [that] come within the meaning of the term 'liberty' as used in the Fourteenth Amendment." Douglas then sought to sum up the essence of this liberty in three propositions:

> First is the autonomous control over the development and expression of one's intellect, interests, tastes, and personality. . . .
>
> Second is freedom of choice in the basic decisions of one's life respecting marriage, divorce, procreation, contraception, and the education and upbringing of children. . . .
>
> Third is the freedom to care for one's health and person, freedom from bodily restraint or compulsion, freedom to walk, stroll, or loaf.[124]

From these premises, the justice had no difficulty in finding a constitutional warrant for protecting a pregnant woman's choice.

The Court had not concluded that there was an absolute right to an abortion, but it did respond to arguments that the choice should be protected as a part of the liberty guaranteed by the Constitution. With this single decision the High Bench had nationalized a policy on abortion that overturned most state law in the area and that invited attack on the Court itself. Much of the criticism missed the point that the justices were responding to a claim that individual liberty had been invaded. The privacy that was protected here might be new, but the Court's recognition that constitutionally protected individual rights embraced privacy went back into the nineteenth century. Although the two dissenters, Rehnquist and White, would have deferred to state legislatures to make policy in this contested area, the majority found credibility in an individual's claim that her rights were being infringed.

Over the next twenty years *Roe v. Wade* would continually be challenged, and Presidents Ronald Reagan and George Bush considered appointments to the Court with an eye toward reversing that decision.[125] In this period the Court upheld certain limitations on the right of a woman to terminate her pregnancy, including a denial of Medicaid funds for abortions, waiting periods, and parental consent for minors. In 1986, however, the Court struck down a revamped Pennsylvania law in an opinion by the author of *Roe*, Harry Blackmun. "The States are not free," he said, "under the guise of protecting maternal health or potential life, to intimidate women into continuing pregnancies." Invalidating all six provisions of the law, Justice Blackmun declared "that they wholly subordinate constitutional privacy interests and concerns with maternal health in an effort to deter a woman from making a decision that, with her physician, is hers to make."[126]

Recognizing the spirited debate that *Roe* had provoked, Blackmun maintained that "controversy over the meaning of our Nation's most majestic guarantees frequently has been turbulent. . . . But those disagreements . . . do not now relieve us of our duty to apply the Constitution faithfully." Reading the holy writ to embody "a promise that a certain private sphere of individual liberty will be kept largely beyond the reach of government," Justice Blackmun said that it "extends to women as well as to men." He then continued: "Few decisions are more personal and intimate, more properly private, or more basic to individual dignity and autonomy, than a woman's decision . . . whether to end her pregnancy. A woman's right to make that choice freely is fundamental."[127]

Adding words of his own, Stevens said that *Roe* "presumes that it is far better to permit some individuals to make incorrect decisions than to deny all individuals the right to make decisions that have a profound effect upon their destiny." This is the way it should be, he implied, saying that "the lawmakers who placed a special premium on the protection of individual liberty have recognized that certain values are more important than the will of a transient majority."[128]

Stevens had written in part to contend with White's dissenting opinion that urged the Court to overrule *Roe*. To the general argument that the justices should follow their own precedents, the doctrine of *stare decisis*, White responded that a Constitution ordained and established by the people should be interpreted to facilitate and not frustrate their authority. In contrast to the idea that Chief Justice John Marshall had made a part of Court tradition—that the Constitution was the product of a mythic will of the people and that the justices' task was to interpret its protection of individual rights within that spirit and not defer to the contemporary majority will—White assumed a continuing constitutive will to which the Court should defer. Accusing the majority in *Roe* of having usurped the people's authority, the justice urged his colleagues "to restore authority to its proper possessors by correcting constitutional decisions that, on reconsideration, are found to be mistaken."[129]

Earlier in 1986 in a case that had nothing to do with abortion, the justices took the opportunity to discourse on the value and importance of following precedent. Justice Thurgood Marshall, for the majority, said that the doctrine of *stare decisis* allows law to "develop in a principled and intelligible fashion," and "permits society to presume that bedrock principles are founded in the law rather than in the proclivities of individuals, and thereby contributes to the integrity of our constitutional government, both in appearance and in fact." Precedent should be overruled, he continued, when "changes in society or in the law dictate that the values served by stare decisis [should] yield in favor of a greater objective." Marshall concluded that the burden of proving that the prior rule is "outdated, ill-founded, unworkable, or otherwise legitimately vulnerable to serious reconsideration" must be placed squarely upon those who seek a reversal.[130]

For the moment the majority was committed to *Roe*, but in 1989 when the Court again confronted a new set of state restrictions on the right to an abortion, William Rehnquist had replaced the retired Warren E. Burger as chief justice. Antonin Scalia and Anthony M. Kennedy had been appointed to fill the vacated seat of Rehnquist and the open seat caused by the retirement of Lewis F. Powell Jr. Powell had been with the earlier majority, and when both Scalia and his replacement, Kennedy, voted with the former minority, the Court's decision was to sustain state restrictions on the abortion right. Although not overruling *Roe*, the majority implied that *Roe* was vulnerable, as it discarded the trimester formula and cast doubts on the viability standard.

Blackmun, the author of *Roe*, was incensed, especially with the majority's implicit invitation to the states to place further restrictions on the basic right. He said: "I fear for the future. I fear for the liberty and equality of the millions of women who have lived and come of age in the 16 years since *Roe* was decided. I fear for the integrity of, and public esteem for, this Court." He accused the majority of being callous toward women and "profoundly destructive of this Court as an institution. . . . To overturn a constitutional decision that secured a fundamental personal liberty to millions of persons would be unprecedented in our constitutional history." Women can still control their own destinies, Blackmun concluded, "but the signs are evident and very ominous, and a chill wind blows."[131]

Stevens, in dissent, focused on the preamble to the Missouri law that said that life began at conception and that the unborn child had all rights available to other persons in the state. The justice said that it clearly "interferes with contraceptive choices," and it also offends the First Amendment's prohibition on establishing religion, because it serves "no identifiable secular purpose" and rests on "an unequivocal endorsement of a religious tenet of some . . . Christian faiths." Missouri, Stevens warned, "may not inject its endorsement of a particular religious tradition into this debate."[132]

Three years later, in *Planned Parenthood of Southeastern Pennsylvania v. Casey*,[133] the Court, by the narrowest of margins, upheld its earlier ruling that there was a limited right to an abortion safeguarded by the Constitution as a right of privacy. Although the decision sustained most of the state's restrictions on the right to choose an abortion, it was made significant by the majority's refusal to overrule *Roe v. Wade*. Remaining from the bench that had decided *Roe* were Rehnquist (now chief justice), White, and Blackmun. The first two had been dissenters and the third was the opinion's author. The one nomination that President Gerald Ford had made, John Paul Stevens, was a supporter of *Roe*. Before the Reagan and Bush appointments, the Court was divided two to two. The appointments of Sandra Day O'Connor, the first woman to take a seat on the High Bench, Antonin

Scalia, Anthony M. Kennedy, David H. Souter, and Clarence Thomas were made by Presidents Reagan and Bush. Scalia wrote for Rehnquist, White, and the new arrival Thomas, in scolding the majority for not overruling *Roe*. That majority was composed of Blackmun, Stevens, and a trio of O'Connor, Kennedy, and Souter who collectively authored an opinion announcing the judgment of the Court.

Responding to his colleagues who would have overruled *Roe* and returned abortion to the regulatory power of the states, Justice Blackmun condemned the "stunted conception of individual liberty" upon which they had based their reasoning. He pointed to the fact that a woman's right to privacy was in danger and that the public should be made aware that his successor would in all likelihood decide the future of this right. The justice warned that the society pictured by the minority, in which individual liberty was sacrificed to electoral results, was worlds removed from the one pictured by a majority that maintained faith with a long tradition that forcefully asserted "that there are certain fundamental liberties that are not to be left to the whims of an election. A woman's right to reproductive choice is one of those fundamental liberties."[134] Blackmun implied that his erring colleagues were pawns of a political movement that sought to limit the Court's civil religious role in protecting and defending individual rights.

The trio who announced the judgment of the Court clearly addressed the function of the High Bench within the civil religious order. This part of the opinion carried along Blackmun and Stevens and therefore became the opinion of the Court as well. What the highly politicized process of selecting nominees for the Court in the Reagan and Bush years had done was suggest that the law and the Constitution could be made to conform to a political agenda—that the interpretation of the fundamental law was simply a matter of placing on the Court those who seemingly shared the same political goals as the Republican presidents who appointed them.[135] According to this notion, the way to reverse *Roe v. Wade* was simply to fill the High Bench with enough members who believed that the range of choice available to a pregnant woman should depend upon the views of a majority of the people as expressed through their state legislatures. What O'Connor, Kennedy, and Souter sought to do was explain what the rule of law meant within the civil religious order and how it imposed obstacles to being captured by political majorities. In other words, although Blackmun confronted the politicization of the abortion issue, the trio explained more thoroughly the special role of the Court in American society and the centricity of individual rights in the constitutional order.

Recognizing their traditional responsibility to protect individual liberty, these justices said that "matters . . . involving the most intimate and personal choices a person may make in a lifetime, choices central to personal dignity and autonomy are central to the liberty protected by the Fourteenth Amendment. At the heart of liberty is the right to define one's own concept of existence, of meaning, of the universe, and of the mystery of human life." They assumed that the civil religion necessitated that the cosmic questions of existence be left to individual determination. Asserting that liberty was threatened by "a jurisprudence of doubt," they found in the Constitution a promise "that there is a realm of personal liberty which the government may not enter." Government is not equipped to define woman's role, they added, because the task is too personal and intimate, and her destiny "must be shaped to a large extent on her own conception of her spiritual imperatives and her place in society."[136]

Next, the trio addressed the propriety of overturning *Roe*, saying that the Court's task was "to test the consistency of overruling a prior decision with the ideal of a rule of law, and to gauge the respective costs of reaffirming and overruling a prior case." Finding the ruling that prior to the viability of the fetus the pregnant woman has the right to obtain an abortion neither unworkable, hardship-inducing, nor obsolete, the justices said it must stand. This is so because it "serves human values" and because it furthers the "ability of women to participate equally in the economic and social life of the Nation." Alluding to the Court's overruling of separate but equal in *Brown v. Board of Education*, the trio said that the decision there was an excellent illustration of where the facts and the understanding of them had changed over time, thus not only justifying but requiring that the Court overturn precedent. Here, however, despite continuing political furor, "neither the factual underpinnings of *Roe*'s central holding nor our understanding has changed." For that reason, "the Court could not pretend to be reexamining the prior law with any justification beyond a present doctrinal disposition to come out differently from the Court of 1973." To not have overturned the separate but equal standard, the justices continued, would have extracted a "terrible price. . . . In the present case, however, . . . the terrible price would be paid for overruling."[137]

Overturning *Roe*, they continued, "would seriously weaken the Court's capacity to exercise the judicial power and to function as the Supreme Court of a Nation dedicated to the rule of law." Succumbing to political pressure and reversing *Roe*, the justices said, would severely damage "the Court's legitimacy [which] depends on [its] making legally principled decisions under circumstances in which their principled character is sufficiently plausible to be accepted by the Nation." They then added: A people's faith in their ability to live under the rule of law "is not readily separable from their understanding of the Court['s] . . . authority to decide their constitutional cases and speak before all others for their constitutional ideals." Fully accepting the justices' role as definers of the culture, they continued: "If the Court's legitimacy should be undermined, then, so would the country be in its ability to see itself through its constitutional ideals. The Court's concern with legitimacy is not for the sake of the Court, but for the sake of the Nation to which it is responsible."[138]

For three justices, chosen by Presidents Reagan and Bush in the hope that they would vote to overrule *Roe* and curtail the Court's checks on state legislative discretion, to pen such words illustrates the power of the judicial tradition and the primacy of a concern for individual rights embodied in the commandments of the holy writ. What makes the opinion so revealing is its implicit recognition of the Court's civil religious function. First of all, despite the refusal to endorse the decision of 1973, the three justices recognize that the earlier ruling was based upon maximizing individual choice and limiting the imposition of majoritarian government upon that choice. The decision to have an abortion, no matter how much so-called pro-life supporters protest, is both private and within the control of the individual.[139] Abortion can be made more difficult, even illegal, but it cannot be stopped. To attempt to use law to impede this choice runs the risk of weakening the rule of law. The three justices put principled justification at the heart of the rule of law, but, as we have seen, it also embraces equal respect for individuals. Second, the trio sought to educate Americans about the Court's task in interpreting the holy writ. Current interpreters are not free, nor should they be, the justices said, to interpret the holy writ in a vacuum or in light of their own personal views. Deducing conclusions from the text of the Constitution itself, without any support from prior cases, would ill serve a Court whose task is to maintain the rule of law in a changing society.

The trio realized the hazards that the divisive issue of abortion posed to the integrity and role of the Court in American society. Blackmun saw the matter exclusively in protecting an individual right from the onslaught of those who denied its existence, but the trio, while accepting the right of privacy as part of the liberty protected by the Fourteenth Amendment, emphasized the Court's need to be a dutiful and consistent interpreter of the holy writ. Any other approach, the justices implied, would call into legitimate question the Court's special role within the civil religion. With acute sensitivity to the historical role of the Court, they concluded:

> Our Constitution is a covenant running from the first generation of Americans to us and then to future generations. It is a coherent succession. Each generation must learn anew that the Constitution's written terms embody ideas and aspirations that must survive more ages than one. We accept our responsibility not to retreat from interpreting the full meaning of the covenant in light of all our precedents. We invoke it once again to define the freedom guaranteed by the Constitution's own promise, the promise of liberty.[140]

Justice Stevens added some words of his own to the civil religious litany, calling the decision in *Roe* "an integral part of a correct understanding of both the concept of liberty and the basic equality of men and women." The state, he continued, must respect the woman's right to make such decisions, for the authority to choose is both empowering and "an element of basic human dignity."[141]

With the election of Democrat Bill Clinton later in 1992, the threat to *Roe* passed. The new president's support for the woman's right to choose would be reflected in his choices for the High Bench.[142] The clock would not be turned back to the mid-1970s, but *Roe* had survived the political onslaught. In the succeeding term four members of the Court were ready to read an old Reconstruction era statute to allow abortion clinics to collect damages from pro-life demonstrators who sought to close down their operation, but the majority rejected the claim. Two of the dissenters accused their majority colleagues of ignoring the clear purpose of the statute, which was the protection of "this Nation's citizens from what amounts to the theft of their constitutional rights by organized and violent mobs across the country."[143] While the majority worried about new federal interference with state authority, the dissenters lamented the Court's failure to live up to its responsibility to protect individual rights.

Many of the Court's critics questioned first the deduction of a right of privacy from the constitutional text and then the inclusion of a limited right of abortion within its ambit. But at the heart of the justices' century-old adjudication under the Fourth Amendment's ban on unreasonable searches and seizures was the protection of privacy. Only later did the justification switch to deterring illegal police conduct, and even then the bedrock reason for wanting to deter such action was that it improperly invaded the sanctity of the individual's living space.[144] The Fifth Amendment's protection against self-incrimination was also seen in terms of violating the integrity of individuals by forcing them to provide evidence of their guilt.

A right of privacy had more of a history in constitutional interpretation than its critics generally granted, and despite the fact that it was often identified with the abortion issue, its reach extended much further. For instance, the Court in 1969 confronted the issue that it had sidetracked in *Mapp v. Ohio* when it had made the exclusionary rule binding on the states.[145] In that case a cache of allegedly obscene materials that had provided the evidence for Mapp's conviction was excluded. Facing a similar situation in *Stanley v. Georgia*, three justices still preferred to avoid the privacy issue and decide the case on the *Mapp* precedent, but the five that subscribed to the Court opinion addressed the privacy right. In the course of a search for bookmaking paraphernalia, officers found some allegedly obscene films that led to the conviction of Robert Stanley. "The right to receive information and ideas, regardless of their social worth . . . ," the Court said, "is fundamental to our free society." Government, the majority continued, cannot make "mere possession [of obscene material] by the individual in the privacy of his own home" a crime. At the foundation of our society, the justices added, "is the right to be free, except in very limited circumstances, from unwanted governmental intrusions into one's privacy." They then concluded: "If the First Amendment means anything it means that a State has no business telling a man, sitting alone in his own house, what books he may read or what films he may watch. Our whole constitutional heritage rebels at the thought of giving government the power to control men's minds."[146]

If privacy is a constitutional right, then does not the private sexual activity of consenting adults fit under this protection? No, said a five-person majority on the Court in 1986 in the case of *Bowers v. Hardwick*.[147] Michael Hardwick had been discovered in his bedroom with a male friend by a police officer who had entered the house to arrest Hardwick for failing to appear in court on a charge of public drunkenness. The officer arrested Hardwick and his companion for violation of the Georgia law against sodomy.

The majority said the question for decision was "whether the Federal Constitution confers a fundamental right upon homosexuals to engage in sodomy and hence invalidates the laws of the many States that still make such conduct illegal and have done so for a very long time." To pose the question in such terms implies the answer. The justices announced that they would not assume "further authority to govern the country without express constitutional authority" by expanding the reach of due process. As to the privacy issue, the Court said that the decision in *Stanley* was anchored in the text of the First Amendment, but Hardwick's claim was not. They would not, the majority justices said, immunize the home from the reach of governmental authorities in this situation, for "it would be difficult, except by fiat, to limit the claimed right to homosexual conduct while leaving exposed to prosecution adultery, incest, and other sexual crimes even though they are committed in the home."[148]

Blackmun, in dissent with Brennan, Marshall, and Stevens, attacked the majority's characterization of the case, saying the issue was the privacy of both homosexuals and heterosexuals, since the statute encompassed both. The dissenters accepted Hardwick's claim that the state statute "interferes with constitutionally protected interests in privacy and freedom of intimate association."[149] Earlier in the year the dissenting quartet had gained Powell's vote and invalidated restrictions on abortion, and there Blackmun had said: "Our cases long have recognized that the Constitution embodies a promise that a certain private sphere of individual liberty will be kept largely beyond the reach of the government."[150] Now repeating these words, he said that they embraced two areas: the decisions that are to be left to the individual and the places in which the individual should not be disturbed. "The fact that individuals," Blackmun continued, "define themselves in a significant way through their intimate sexual relationships with others suggests, in a Nation as diverse as ours, that much of the richness of a relationship will come from the freedom an individual has to *choose* the form and nature of these intensely personal bonds."[151]

Blackmun derided the majority's talk of the issue in terms of a fundamental right to practice homosexuality, saying "what the Court really has refused to recognize is the fundamental interest all individuals have in controlling the nature of their intimate associations with others." He added that "the right of an individual to conduct intimate relationships in the intimacy of his or her home seems to me to be the heart of the Constitution's protection of privacy." And in contrast to the majority's admonition that the Court should not seek to extend its power in such a case, Blackmun responded: "It is precisely because the issue touches the heart of what makes individuals what they are that we should be especially sensitive to the rights of those whose choices upset the majority." Neither public interest nor the protection of the rights of others, the justice continued, "can justify invading the houses, hearts, and minds of citizens who choose to live their lives differently." He pleaded with his colleagues to reevaluate their "analysis and conclude that depriving individuals of the right to choose for themselves how to conduct their intimate relationships poses a far greater threat to the values most deeply rooted in our Nation's history than tolerance of nonconformity could ever do."[152]

Notice the jeremiadic nature of Blackmun's dissent. His brothers had erred and strayed from their responsibilities under the holy writ. By denying the individual the choice that the civil religion demands, they had assaulted their own professed values. Apparently on second thought, Powell, who had voted with the majority, agreed.[153]

Unanimously, the justices decided in 1995 that a Massachusetts public accommodations law did not preclude the organizers of a St. Patrick's Day parade in Boston from excluding a group of gays, lesbians, and bisexuals from marching as a unit in the parade,[154] but the Court split the following year in a decision that cast doubt on the precedential value of *Bowers*. The voters in Colorado had by referendum enacted a constitutional amendment that sought both to override and to prevent the passage of local laws protecting individuals from discrimination on the basis of sexual orientation. Writing for a majority of six in *Romer v. Evans*, Kennedy agreed with the state courts in striking down this attempted graft on the state constitution. Concluding that only "animus toward the class that it affects" could explain the imposition of such "a broad and undifferentiated disability on a single named group," the justice pronounced this attempt "unprecedented in our jurisprudence" and "not within our constitutional tradition."[155]

Kennedy said that the protections against discrimination enacted by certain Colorado cities that had been the targets of the amendment drive "are taken for granted by most people either because they already have them or do not need them; these are protections against exclusion from an almost limitless number of transactions and endeavors that constitute ordinary civic life in a free society." The amendment, he concluded, sought to make homosexuals "unequal to everyone else. This Colorado cannot do. A State cannot so deem a class of persons a stranger to its laws."[156] Blackmun's dissenting words in *Bowers* had been heeded, for the majority now implicitly recognized that the Court's civil religious task was to promote inclusion and repel threats to the citizen's meaningful exercise of rights.

That the Court majority had come to this conclusion with little precedent and much indignation did not escape Scalia, who, in dissent with Rehnquist and Thomas, accused his brethren of elitist hostility to democratic attempts to reinforce traditional values. Scalia said that the present decision and *Bowers* were inconsistent in that if certain conduct was subject to criminalization then certainly the state could disfavor it. Accusing the majority of frustrating the democratic will and subverting traditional morality, the justice insisted that the Court should not "take sides in this culture war."[157]

What Scalia seeks to avoid cannot be avoided; the Court is and must be a combatant in any culture war. A decision here overturning the Colorado high court and condemning the expressed views of the state's governor would hardly be culturally neutral. From its very inception, the Court has been a definer of American culture. In *Romer* the majority justices exorcised the ghost of *Bowers* and discharged their duty under the civil religion by promoting inclusion and unity.[158]

Any religion, including the American civil religion, must deal not only with the quality of life but with its end as well. Beginning with Abraham Lincoln, if not before, those who were willing to die to maintain its tenets were hailed as heroes whose sacrifice ensured that the nation with this theology at its core would survive. The civil religion consecrates such deaths by giving them meaning and honor. But most people die far removed from the public arena, and their demise is generally not a matter of great public attention. Advances in medical technology, however, have attracted attention, and physical life can be prolonged despite the cost to its quality. Given this situation, it was inevitable that the Supreme Court would eventually have to contend with an individual's right to die. In 1990 the high priests of the American civil religion first confronted the subject.

The case arose from the attempt of the parents of Nancy Beth Cruzan to order the hospital to withdraw the life support system that maintained their daughter in an unrecoverable, vegetative state. A Missouri trial court acceded to the parents' wishes but was overruled by a divided state supreme court. Missouri law, seeking to further a state interest in the preservation of human life, required that clear and convincing evidence of the patient's prior wishes not to exist in such a vegetative state be provided. Despite the presentation of some testimony to that effect, the Missouri supreme court found the evidence deficient in terms of the statutory standard. The appeal to the United States Supreme Court was premised on the due process clause of the Fourteenth Amendment.

Although splitting five to four in *Cruzan v. Director, Missouri Department of Health,* all the justices agreed that the liberty protected by that amendment encompassed a right to refuse unwanted life-sustaining medical treatment and, to that extent, a right to die. What the majority decided, however, was that Missouri's interest in preserving human life did allow it to impose its burdensome evidentiary requirement. Despite the parents having no interest adverse to that of their daughter and the daughter's appointed representative agreeing that Cruzan would best be served by discontinuing the forced feeding, the majority deferred to the state's decision.[159]

Brennan, joined by Marshall and Blackmun, protested a resolution that made Nancy Cruzan "a passive prisoner of medical technology." Asserting that she has a constitutional right "to choose to die with dignity," Justice Brennan said the role of the Court is to provide a framework for difficult and personal decisions by "delineating the ways in which government may and may not participate in such decisions." He continued: "The right to be free from medical attention without consent, to determine what shall be done with one's own body, *is* deeply rooted in the Nation's traditions." Maintaining that "the State has no legitimate general interest in someone's life, completely abstracted from the interest of the person living that life," Brennan argued that its only interest should be "in safeguarding the accuracy" of the personal decision. Accusing Missouri of adopting a rule that militates against "the likelihood of accurate determinations," he insisted that "a State generally must either repose the choice with the person whom the patient himself would most likely have chosen as proxy or leave the decision to the patient's family." Here in the case of Nancy Cruzan, Brennan concluded, both the state and the Court majority "have discarded evidence of her will, ignored her values, and deprived her of the right to a decision as closely approximating her own choice as humanly possible."[160]

Justices O'Connor and Scalia, whose votes helped constitute the majority, added words of their own that indicated the wide-ranging differences among members of the majority. O'Connor insisted that the due process clause would be violated if intrusive life-sustaining procedures were forced upon the patient, for the patient has the "liberty, dignity, and freedom to determine the course of her own treatment." Second, she insisted that the decision here "does not preclude a future determination that the Constitution requires the States to implement the decisions of a patient's duly appointed surrogate."[161]

Scalia, on the other hand, wrote an opinion that not only distanced himself from the other members of the majority but from the traditions of the Court as well. Equating a personal decision to refuse life-sustaining treatment with suicide, he would place both within the regulatory power of the state. The justice argued against finding substantive meaning in the due process clause, condemning his colleagues for creating "out of nothing (for it exists neither in text nor tradition) some constitutional principle" to limit discretion that properly belongs in the states. "Our salvation," he concluded, is "in the Equal Protection Clause, which requires the democratic majority to accept for themselves and their loved ones what they impose on you and me. This Court need not, and has no authority to, inject itself into every field of human activity where irrationality and oppression may theoretically occur, and if it tries to do so it will destroy itself."[162]

Scalia's opinion was based on premises that were not shared by his brethren and certainly not borne out in the history of the Court in American culture. Although O'Connor apparently wrote for the purpose of distancing the majority's decision from what Scalia said, Stevens called attention to his colleague's retreat from constitutional duty and placed the present matter within the confines of the civil religion with its regard for the sanctity of the individual.

"Our Constitution," Stevens began, "is born of the proposition that all legitimate governments must secure the equal right of every person to 'Life, Liberty, and the pursuit of Happiness.' In the ordinary case we quite naturally assume, that these three ends are compatible, mutually enhancing and perhaps even coincident." But at times, he implied, the state's preference for one of the three can intrude upon the sacred domain of individual choice. Accusing the majority here of elevating the abstract interest of the state over that of the best interests of one of its citizens, Stevens insisted that "the Constitution requires the State to care for Nancy Cruzan's life in a way that gives appropriate respect to her own best interests." To Scalia's warning that the Court is invading an area reserved to the democratic process, Stevens responded that "our responsibility as judges both enables and compels us to treat the problem as it is illuminated by the facts of the controversy before us." And to his colleague's curt dismissal of the due process clause, he said that the Missouri regulation was clearly "an unreasonable intrusion upon traditionally private matters encompassed within the liberty protected" by that clause.[163]

Because Nancy Cruzan had not written a "living will" or more clearly anticipated her eventual fate, the majority found what amounted to a waiver of her constitutional right, something Stevens called "a distressing misunderstanding of the importance of individual liberty." Maintaining that the liberty involved here was undervalued because public discussion has been rare, he said that modern medical science and its ability to prolong existence to the point where it is "an insult to life," necessitates public scrutiny. "Choices about death," the justice added, "touch the core of liberty." Death being so intertwined with faith "is reason enough to protect the freedom to conform choices about death to individual conscience." Then, tying Cruzan's interest in liberty "to an interest in how she will be thought of after her death by those whose opinions mattered to her," Stevens condemned the Missouri action as subordinating "Nancy's body, her family, and the lasting significance of her life to the State's own interests."[164] According to the justice, the premises of the civil religion necessarily allow the individual to consider the memories she will leave behind—how she will be embedded in the thoughts of those who mattered to her. The afterlife promised by the civil religion is what remains in the memories of those still living.

Accusing the state of making a mockery of life as protected by the Constitution, Stevens insisted that Missouri's "unflagging determination to perpetuate Nancy

Cruzan's physical existence is comprehensible only as an effort to define life's meaning, not as an attempt to preserve its sanctity." The state has no authority under the Constitution, the justice continued, "to circumscribe the liberties of the people by regulations designed wholly for the purpose of establishing a sectarian definition of life." Life and liberty are opposed in this case, he added, because "of Missouri's effort, and this Court's willingness, to abstract Nancy Cruzan's life from Nancy Cruzan's person." Stevens argued "that this Court cannot defer to any State policy that drives a theoretical wedge between a person's life, on the one hand, and that person's liberty or happiness on the other." He continued: "Our Constitution presupposes a respect for the personhood of every individual and nowhere is strict adherence to that principle more essential than in the Judicial Branch." For the state to preempt the authority of her parents to give "meaning and completion" to their daughter's life, results in "appropriating Nancy Cruzan's life as a symbol for its own purposes." If the state, the justice concluded, wants "to demonstrate its commitment to life [, it] may do so by aiding those who are actively struggling for life and health. In this endeavor, unfortunately, no State can lack opportunities."[165]

Stevens had to move to the frontier of the law, but what he says makes sense within the context of the Court's role within the civil religion. He added dimension to the civil religion by recognizing that the afterlife it envisioned was to be found in the memories of individuals and in the recorded memory that is history. The dissenters wanted to empower the individual, or those best equipped to know her wishes, to have some control over just how she would be remembered. For the state to superimpose its authority and reconfigure Nancy Cruzan's afterlife was to Stevens the ultimate affront to her dignity as an individual.[166]

This unique case is not an aberration but a preview of things to come as the American population ages and technological means are found to preserve some semblance of life. Increasingly, the Court will be drawn into adjudicating ultimate questions of life and death.[167]

If past practice provides reliable evidence, Stevens and the other dissenters can expect to see their position eventually become that of the Court. This prediction rests on two grounds: the tendency of the majority justices to err in cases of first impression when dealing with the impact of new technology on individuals and their rights and the fit of the dissenting view with the civil religious responsibility of the Court.

As examples in first area, the Court initially ruled that motion pictures were not speech but entertainment that could be censored,[168] that evidence seized by wiretapping was admissible because the premises were not physically penetrated,[169] and that television cameras so interfered with a trial that they were constitutionally barred from the courtroom.[170] These early decisions did not survive, for when the justices grasped fully the implication of the technology on individual rights, they realized their earlier errors.

Regarding the second area, the majority justices in *Cruzan* preferred an abstract state interest over that of the individual. Although some justices throughout the Court's history have been attracted to the governmental perspective rather than the individual's, in the vast majority of opinions written from that perspective, the state had some tangible interest at stake. Here, the dissenters reveal how the state's defense of a philosophical view of life impacts so disastrously on the dignity of the individual. To allow a state to superimpose its abstract interest and use the incompetent person for its own purposes reduces that person to a nonperson in both the civil religion and the constitutional house within which it is designed to thrive.

In 1997 the Court unanimously decided that neither the due process nor the equal protection clauses of the Fourteenth Amendment forbad states from legislating against physician-assisted suicide.[171] Five of the justices, who wrote or joined concurring opinions, however, were unwilling to defer in all possible cases to the way in which an ongoing public debate about physician-assisted suicide might be written into state law. Justice Souter, for instance, said that an individual's right to die with dignity was "within that class of 'certain interests' demanding careful scrutiny of the State's contrary claim."[172] He did not want to rule out the possibility that in future cases the state's claim might be overriden by the individual's. And Stevens, continuing the dialogue in which he so eloquently participated in *Cruzan*, asserted that the state's unqualified interest in preserving life "is not itself sufficient to outweigh the interest in the liberty that may justify the only possible means of preserving a dying patient's dignity and alleviating her intolerable suffering."[173]

The liberty of the individual, so central both to our constitutional system and to the maintenance of a binding civic faith, will continue to be challenged in the coming century, often by those groups who find comfort in conformity and only chaos in individual diversity. At times the majority of the Court will tip in favor of the challengers, citing the system of federalism or the ability of the democratic majority to enforce its will. However, there will always be justices to argue for the importance of the individual in the pluralistic society and the crucial role of the Court in keeping the faith, and there will always be decisions that reflect, sustain, and promulgate that faith.

THE BLESSINGS OF LIBERTY

If we are to be as a shining city upon a hill, it will be because of our ceaseless pursuit of the constitutional ideal of human dignity. For the political and legal ideals that form the foundation of much that is best in American institutions—ideals jealously preserved and guarded throughout our history—still form the vital force in creative political thought and activity within the nation today. As we adapt our institutions to the ever-changing conditions of national and international life, those ideals of human dignity—liberty and justice for all individuals—will continue to inspire and guide us because they are entrenched in our Constitution. The Constitution with its Bill of Rights thus has a bright future, as well as a glorious past, for its spirit is inherent in the aspirations of our people.[1]

Speaking from the perspective of almost thirty years on the High Bench, Justice William J. Brennan's words highlight the very special place the Constitution, as interpreted by the Supreme Court, has come to occupy within American life. His language is not that of a constitutional lawyer or scholar but rather that of a keeper of the faith. He reminds Americans that the role of the Court is to help shape a just society by making the premises of that faith a social reality. His words capture the sentiments of many of the public who view the Constitution as a protector of their rights.

As Brennan and many others who have served on the Supreme Court have recognized, the Constitution does embody substantive value choices. They involve the protection of individual rights and are based upon a fundamental conception of human dignity. When a claim of individual right is presented to the Court, Brennan implied, justices should not take refuge behind the ambiguities of the text but rather confront the claim in full recognition of the values that the Constitution seeks to preserve and promote. These protections of the individual to which Brennan alluded are so entwined with the contemporary understanding of the Constitution that there has been a tendency to elide the Bill of Rights, where many of them are located, into the original text. When celebrations were held in 1987 commemorating the 200th anniversary of the framing of the Constitution, for instance, the Bill of Rights became a primary focus, despite the fact that these amendments were not framed until 1789 and not made a part of the Constitution until late in 1791.

Although the story of the nationalization of the protections found in the Bill of Rights is largely a tale of the middle third of the twentieth century, the concern for safeguarding such rights was made manifest in the debate over the ratification of the Constitution in 1787 and 1788. And, from the inception of the federal judiciary, the justices, collectively and individually in their missionary work in the circuits, made the task of preserving and protecting individual rights a special responsibility. In its first important case, *Chisholm v. Georgia*, the Supreme Court interpreted the language of the judicial article to permit individuals in one state to sue another state. Its rationale was that otherwise individual rights would be abridged and the Constitution would have failed in establishing justice and providing for a more perfect union.[2]

In the new federal structure, where power and responsibility were dispersed, the possibility of one level of government interposing its authority to protect individual rights from impositions by the other was early recognized. The immediate fear, as illustrated in the Virginia and Kentucky Resolutions of 1798 and 1799, was of an aggrandizing federal authority threatening the freedom of the states' citizens. As the nineteenth century progressed and slavery increasingly divided the nation, Southern energy was directed toward safeguarding chattel slavery with its asserted property interest in human beings.

If the Constitution's accommodation of slavery seems inconsistent with what Justice Brennan proudly proclaimed as the "constitutional ideal of human dignity," the recognition of that incompatibility was never far from the surface. As President Abraham Lincoln so eloquently explained, slavery was a sin against the dictates of the civil theology for which the men and women of mid-nineteenth-century America would pay a terrible price.

The Union victory in the Civil War brought in its wake a reshaping of the constitutional order with the addition of the Thirteenth, Fourteenth, and Fifteenth Amendments. These collective changes might well be described in terms of the American people remembering and recovering "the narrative thread of their story . . . as a people" committed to ensuring a government of consent based upon a respect for individual rights.[3] For the first time, in the initial section of the Fourteenth Amendment, a wide-ranging generalized check was placed on state authority—a check designed to protect the rights of the individual from the very governments that earlier were viewed as steadfast protectors of such rights.

If there was some national backsliding in terms of making former slaves equal members of the reconstituted society, the national government had been empowered and the building blocks for such a future had been put in place. The accommodation of slavery had been purged, and the new Union was rededicated to the liberty and equality promised by the Declaration of Independence. These early articles of faith were now made part of the sacred text itself. The nation is still working through the implications of this dramatic change, but the potential for the nationalization of individual rights was solidly laid with the Constitution itself.

Although progress toward the goal of recognizing the dignity of all human beings has proceeded too slowly for some, that progress has been steady. Locating the animating spirit of the Constitution in the aspirations of Americans, Brennan predicted that the challenges of the twenty-first century would be met with the same steadfast faith that thus far has sustained the American experiment in self-government.

Here we have suggested that such aspirations are part of a civic faith that continues to be taught, learned, and applied within the society—a civic faith that promotes tolerance, diversity, and individual choice as the cement of union. In our historical survey we have seen change over time, not in the basic faith structure but in the working out of its precepts in an ever-evolving society.

When Justice Brennan delivered his "If we are to be as a shining city" speech in 1985, he was, in part, responding to the argument of President Ronald Reagan's attorney general, Edwin Meese, among others, that the Court should interpret the fundamental law in accordance with original intent; that is, what the words meant and what they encompassed at the time they were made part of the Constitution. Brennan called that view arrogant and presumptuous because it assumed that later interpreters could extract from the distant past something resembling a composite and consistent intent. He might well have added that such an approach only masks what always must be the substantial contribution of the modern interpreter to the task of extracting meaning from an ancient text. From Brennan's perspective, judges who read the text to make sure that the Constitution delivers on its promise of securing the liberty of individuals are, in fact, fulfilling the hopes of the framers.

Those who seek to characterize the Court in a fundamentally different way—as an umpire of the federal system or as an impartial arbiter between social and individual interests—must contend with a two-hundred-year history that has provided little evidence for such characterizations. For instance, when the Supreme Court by a five-to-four count in 1995 invalidated the Gun-Free School Zones Act of 1990 as beyond the reach of Congress's commerce power, two members of that majority—Justices Anthony M. Kennedy and Sandra Day O'Connor—searched the Court's record to find guidelines for judging questions of federalism. What they found, to their apparent surprise, was "much uncertainty respecting the existence, and the content, of standards that allow the judiciary to play a significant role in maintaining the design contemplated by the Framers." Although they then rejected one logical conclusion—"that the balance between national and state power is entrusted in its entirety to the political process," they recognized that it was "axiomatic that Congress does have substantial discretion and control over the federal balance."[4]

What is of interest to us in this concurring opinion is its acknowledgment of how little support exists in the Court's history to conclude that the High Bench's task was to ensure the preservation of the federal structure.[5] Although Felix Frankfurter repeatedly argued that the Court should be the umpire in a game of federalism, most justices saw themselves, from the very beginning, not as umpires but as committed players. They were striving to promote unity in a pluralistic society and working toward the inclusion of all by insisting upon the rights of each individual.

Debate over the Court's proper role in a democratic society has spawned a vast literature on judicial review in which writers seek either to limit the Court's role as a policymaker or explain that role in terms of reinterpreting the American political system. Some of these explanations see the judiciary as being the branch best equipped to protect individual rights, but much of the explanation is focused on the more modern work of the Court, and much of it is vigorously contested.[6] Yet clearly the protection of individual rights, even including the hotly contested right of privacy, is what has justified and continues to justify the role of the Court in the popular mind.

For instance, in 1987, when Chief Justice Warren Burger, who had resigned from the Court to head the bicentennial celebration of the Constitution, was seeking to stir up popular interest, he was upstaged by a contemporary drama that caught the public's attention. In midyear, President Reagan nominated Robert H. Bork for a seat on the Supreme Court, and interest groups on both sides engaged in a battle over the candidate's confirmation. Opponents gained a substantial advantage when they pictured Bork as hostile to the Court's activism in protecting individual rights. When the appointee questioned the civil religious role of the Court and took exception to viewing it as a culture-defining institution with a moral vision, he alienated himself from an American public quite comfortable with the justices' role as priests interpreting the holy writ in their behalf.[7]

When Robert Bork was responding to questions before the Senate Judiciary Committee, a friendly senator asked him why he wanted a seat on the Court. His response was that he saw it as an intellectual challenge, hardly the response that the questioner hoped would endear the candidate to the watching public.[8]

Indeed, constitutional law can be an intellectual challenge, but it is far more than that because it is informed by a moral perspective. One scholar has characterized the constitutional directives concerning individual rights as "constituents of a particular conception of human good" or "standards . . . of political-moral judgment" that do much to make the American people a political community.[9]

This study has suggested that the justices and the Court they serve operate within a civil religion, the theology of which provides them with certain fundamental moral assumptions that they bring to the task of interpreting the words of the holy writ. In a world where relativism rules and where it is fashionable to deny any common morality, the Court has continued to see the words of the text through a few basic moral principles that are quite clear: The human being is a creature of dignity worthy of common respect; this respect is ensured by recognizing that the individual possesses certain rights; an open American community is premised on the differences that a respect for the individual necessitates; government is justified only by the consent of the governed; government has a positive obligation to ensure the protection of individual rights; and, finally, that the law can be the common vehicle to achieve a consensus that otherwise would elude a pluralistic society.

Analyzing some of the important work of the Supreme Court through the lens of an American civil religion succeeds only as the perspective furthers an understanding of the High Bench's place within the life of the society, its relative invulnerability to attack, and its policymaking role. The construct of a civil religion seeks to highlight the moral dimension that the Court brings to its task of interpreting the words of the fundamental law. In these pages we have seen justices performing priestly and prophetic roles within the civil religious structure. We have seen the Court they serve defining the culture in terms of its aspirations and goals, promoting unity through the nationalization of individual rights and through the recognition of what Americans share in common, educating the citizenry as to core values, and working to reduce the gaps between what should be and what is. Finally, the Court has repulsed threats to exclusion and widened membership in a national community that remains an important component of the identity of all Americans.

Accepting the Court's role as the priestly interpreter of the holy writ does not mean that citizens are required to blindly accept all its rulings as commandments of the writ itself. Education is a two-way street, as Justice James Wilson acknowledged during his early days as a circuit rider. The justices are educated both before and after the fact. Before the decision, they are exposed to the written and oral arguments of advocates, who frame the contested issues within the prevailing culture. After the decision, the justices' opinions are critiqued by legal scholars and popular writers. This dialogue filters into the society and expands both the language and perception of its members. It widens the parameters of thought and discussion and reinforces a sense of community among very different people. Working within a Protestant tradition of reading and interpreting the words for oneself, American citizens can then seek to correct the Court's judgment in a number of ways available to them both directly and indirectly within the political process.[10]

When members of this community are so critical of rulings that neglect or subordinate the civil theology, as they sometimes are, they can change them prospectively. As illustrations, we need look no further than the Pregnancy Discrimination Act of 1978 or the Civil Rights Act of 1991.[11] This is as it should be if the teaching of the civil catechism has been successful, for the Court is not infallible. It probably functions best when the faithful are alert and concerned.

Still, the Court plays a most significant role as an actor within the culture. In Brennan's speech, which he delivered as a contribution to a seminar on interpreting texts at Georgetown University, he distinguished the justice's task from that of the literary interpreter by calling attention to its public, obligatory, and consequential character.[12] Unable to avoid ambiguity or indeterminacy, the justices must reach a conclusion that not only decides the issue between the parties but often sets wider social policy as well. Their constant recourse to the civil theology to legitimate this process is, then, quite understandable. The Supreme Court has long played a crucial role in maintaining a national community built upon a theology that animates and explains change. If not all its members all of the time, many of its members much of the time have acknowledged this special duty.

If the Court is so busily and consistently engaged in such an endeavor, why is the unity it seeks to promote more hidden from view than the sharp differences that divide Americans? First, we may tend to expect more from a national American community than it can possibly deliver, for that community is premised upon a respect for difference that militates against both sameness and conformity. Furthermore this community has little of the warmth and comfort that so often is attached to the word "community." To make the American national community more comfortable, its people more alike, would be no less than un-American. What is American is a respect for difference, a willingness to accept the implications of the principles of liberty and equality in social development, and a faith in law as the means to accomplish these ends. Second, the fact that Americans are most aware of unity when confronting national crises should not be taken to mean that unity does not exist at other times. In fact, were it not there, it could hardly be summoned up with such alacrity and success. And, third, Americans today may be both more aware and more sensitive than earlier generations to the diversity that has always characterized their society. This is so because of our continuing commitment to a civil theology that stresses toleration and acceptance of the different. If Americans did not believe what they say they do, their society would exhibit more surface conformity.

The very success of minority groups in advancing their causes probably comes less from their electoral strength than from the advantage they gain from operating within a common faith structure that commands practitioners to respect the rights and differences of others.[13] In this faith, intolerance becomes a sin, and often the outcast becomes a prophet.[14] If the many different voices that characterize American society do not always make a harmonious chorus, we can still appreciate that they are singing together in the same hall. The Court's success in its civil religious role is not measured in terms of the elimination of diversity among Americans but rather in the society's acceptance and embrace of it.[15]

Of all the branches of government, the Supreme Court maintains a continuity and tradition that gives real substance to the concept of a rule of law. In a federal governmental structure in which the entire House of Representatives and one-third of the Senate is elected every two years, in which one-term presidencies have become common, and in which those chief executives who do survive to fill a second term have fared poorly, the Supreme Court maintains a continuity of personnel undisturbed by the restlessness of voters. New arrivals are welcomed to the fold and embraced by the traditions of the judicial branch. Judicial independence has created not only an immunity from electoral reprisal but a maverick quality that has made the Supreme Court neither subservient to the other branches of that government nor institutionally inclined to favor the governmental interest over that of an individual.

From the beginning the Court carved out for itself a special role within this government: It would be the branch that clothed itself in the Constitution and interpreted that document to further the aims of the Preamble—the most important of which has been to secure "the Blessings of liberty to ourselves and our Posterity." The Court has been made essential by the nature of a society based upon the individual and by the diversity that such a foundation encourages. Groups and coalitions dominate the political process, but the Court's business is to respond to the claims of individuals within a tradition that explains the success of government in terms of its ability to secure the rights of human beings.

That the Court is antimajoritarian is a given within the system established, and easy explanations of its decisions in terms of the ruling coalition or emerging majorities miss the genius of its special role. Perhaps the Court's nonelective character poses problems for those who see majoritarian government as the norm, but increasingly in the twentieth century Americans have voted in fewer and fewer numbers and have shown little confidence in those candidates who do emerge victorious. That confidence has been increasingly placed in the judicial branch and in the Supreme Court. The Court is the institution that survives dramatic electoral changes; it is the ongoing preserver of the national faith, and it is anchored in the soul of Americans. As long as the individual counts, the Court will continue to play a most significant role in ministering to the pluralistic society.

When Robert Bellah wrote his seminal article in 1967 discovering an American civil religion, he found his evidence in presidential addresses.[16] The way in which a president summoned God to the American experience, for instance in an inaugural address, seemed revelatory to Bellah. His focus, however, tended to mask what may, after all, be the best evidence of the existence of an American civil religion—the opinions of the Supreme Court of the United States. Such mentions of God in public addresses seem far less significant than the way in which certain transcendent values are brought to bear in the resolution of particular cases—often involving the individual challenging action by government. We may be disturbed that these transcendent values at times are read differently by various members of the High Bench or that the Court majority is at times less sensitive than it is at other times, but the disagreement among the members most often takes place within the confines of the civil religion. Although a president may seek to energize the citizenry to fight a battle to defend a core value, the critic cannot shake a certain suspicion that the rhetoric is being used to serve certain political ends. The Court has no such political agenda, and, when it reads the fundamental law to advance the civic faith by bringing its reading to bear on a specific case, it not only speaks but acts as well.

For a long time, we have failed to realize that behind what we thought was no more than a clever metaphor—that the Supreme Court Building is a temple and that the robed persons who inhabit it are priests—is a fundamental truth that illuminates not only the work of the Court but the society that has entrusted it with such a heavy and continuing responsibility.

NOTES

INTRODUCTION

1. Michael Walzer, "What Does It Mean to Be an 'American'?" *Social Research* 57 (Fall 1990): 614.
2. "The very assertion of the ethnic dimensions of American culture can be understood as part of the rites and rituals of this land, as an expression of a persistent conflict between consent and descent in America. . . . The symbolic construction of American kinship has helped weld Americans of diverse origins into one people, even if the code at times requires the exaggeration of differences." Werner Sollors, *Beyond Ethnicity: Consent and Descent in American Culture* (New York: Oxford University Press, 1986), 15.
3. Philip Gleason, "American Identity and Americanization," in *Encyclopedia of American Ethnic Groups*, ed. Stephen Thurnstrom (Cambridge: Harvard University Press, 1980), 57. This piece provides a good historical sketch of American identity.
4. Lawrence H. Fuchs, *The American Kaleidoscope: Race, Ethnicity, and the Civic Culture* (Hanover, N.H.: University Press of New England for Wesleyan University Press, 1990), 31.
5. Yehoshua Arieli, *Individualism and Nationalism in American Ideology* (Cambridge: Harvard University Press, 1964), 345.
6. Arthur Mann, *The One and the Many: Reflections on the American Identity* (Chicago: University of Chicago Press, 1979), 179.
7. John E. Semonche, "The Tie That Binds: A Bicentennial Appraisal of the U.S. Constitution," *North Carolina State Bar Quarterly* 34 (Summer 1987): 5.
8. Thomas Paine, "Common Sense," in *The Thomas Paine Reader*, ed. Michael Foot and Isaac Kramnick (New York: Penguin Books, 1987), 92.
9. Kenneth L. Karst, *Belonging to America: Equal Citizenship and the Constitution* (New Haven: Yale University Press, 1989), 229.
10. James B. White, *Justice as Translation: An Essay in Cultural and Legal Criticism* (Chicago: University of Chicago Press, 1990), xi.
11. James B. White, *When Words Lose Their Meaning: Constitutions and Reconstitutions of Language, Character, and Community* (Chicago: University of Chicago Press, 1984), 266. Linguistic studies of the law have been abundant in recent years, but there is no more perceptive and thoughtful work than White's two books, to which I am substantially indebted in the discussion that follows.
12. James B. White, *Justice as Translation: An Essay in Cultural and Legal Criticism* (Chicago: University of Chicago Press, 1990), 80.
13. Ibid., 66.
14. In one study of small claims court litigants, the researchers were surprised to find that

unsuccessful parties did not generally blame the law, which they continued to believe was fair and just. John M. Conley and William M. O'Barr, *Rules versus Relationships: The Ethnography of Legal Discourse* (Chicago: University of Chicago Press, 1990), 174–75.

15. James B. White, *Justice as Translation: An Essay in Cultural and Legal Criticism* (Chicago: University of Chicago Press, 1990), 179, 202. See also, Lawrence Rosen, "Continuing the Conversation: Creationism, the Religion Clauses, and the Politics of Culture," *Supreme Court Review* (1988): 61–84. Rosen writes: "When . . . the Court . . . invokes constitutional principles as symbolic unifiers, it displays what is arguably its single greatest power, the power to capture the terms of the discussion. And where the Court demonstrates that the principles lie in the overall process—in the willingness of the losers to accept contrary results yet continue to acknowledge the rules of contestability themselves—it demonstrates just how deeply the logic of its thought is bounded and suffused by the assumptions that characterize much of the larger culture." (Ibid., 84).

16. James B. White, *Justice as Translation: An Essay in Cultural and Legal Criticism* (Chicago: University of Chicago Press, 1990), 195.

17. Ibid., 217, 222.

18. For instance, see Tom R. Tyler, *Why People Obey the Law* (New Haven: Yale University Press, 1990).

19. Lawrence M. Friedman, "Law, Lawyers, and Popular Culture," *Yale Law Journal* 98 (June 1989): 1598.

20. Mary Ann Glendon, *Rights Talk: The Impoverishment of Political Discourse* (New York: Free Press, 1991), 3.

21. Robert N. Bellah, "Civil Religion in America," *Daedalus* 96 (Winter 1967): 1–21.

22. For a fuller treatment of the presidential role within the civil religion, see Robert V. Pierard and Robert D. Linder, *Civil Religion & the Presidency* (Grand Rapids, Mich.: Academie Books, Zondervan, 1988).

23. See for instance, Russell E. Richey and Donald G. Jones, eds., *American Civil Religion* (New York: Harper & Row, 1974).

24. For a recent round of thoughtful criticism along these lines, see "Forum: American Civil Religion Revisited," *Religion and American Culture* 4 (Winter 1994): 1–23.

25. Robert Wuthnow, *The Restructuring of American Religion: Society and Faith Since World War II* (Princeton: Princeton University Press, 1988), 302.

26. John F. Wilson, *Public Religion in American Culture* (Philadelphia: Temple University Press, 1979), 24, 25.

27. Ibid., 25.

28. Robin M. Williams Jr., *American Society: A Sociological Interpretation*, 3d ed. (New York: Knopf, 1970), 366.

29. George A. Lindbeck, *The Nature of Doctrine: Religion and Theology in a Postliberal Age* (Philadelphia: Westminster Press, 1984), 32–33.

30. This definition comes from Michael Novak, *Choosing Our King: Powerful Symbols in Presidential Politics* (New York: Macmillan, 1974), 127. For an analysis of the problem of defining the term "civil religion" that reaches a conclusion similar to Novak's, see Ellis M. West, "A Proposed Neutral Definition of Civil Religion," *Journal of Church and State* 22 (Winter 1980): 23–40.

31. See Russell E. Richey and Donald G. Jones, eds., *American Civil Religion* (New York: Harper & Row, 1974).

32. For a useful discussion of these documents, plus Lincoln's Gettysburg Address, as part of the nation's faith structure, see Mortimer J. Adler and William Gorman, *The American Testament* (New York: Praeger, 1975); and Mortimer J. Adler, *We Hold These Truths: Understanding the Ideas and Ideals of the Constitution* (New York: Macmillan, 1987).

33. Whittle Johnson, "Little America—Big America," *Yale Review* 58 (Autumn 1968): 11.

34. Phillip E. Hammond's contribution in "Forum: American Civil Religion Revisited," *Religion and American Culture* 4 (Winter 1994): 7.

35. Sidney E. Mead, *The Nation with the Soul of a Church* (New York: Harper & Row, 1975), 65.

36. Joseph Vining, *The Authoritative and the Authoritarian* (Chicago: University of Chicago Press, 1986), 64, 201, 190.

37. Hans Kohn, *American Nationalism: An Interpretive Essay* (New York: Macmillan, 1957), 8.

38. Kenneth L. Karst, *Belonging to America: Equal Citizenship and the Constitution* (New Haven: Yale University Press, 1989), 5, 194. When Karst explained the lack of success of the "cultural counterrevolutionaries" in changing the law in the Reagan-Bush years, he credited "the centrality and the endurance of the principle of equal citizenship in American law and the American civil religion." Kenneth L. Karst, *Law's Promise, Law's Expression: Visions of Power in the Politics of Race, Gender, and Religion* (New Haven: Yale University Press, 1993), 189.

39. Hugo L. Black, *A Constitutional Faith* (New York: Knopf, 1968), 66.

40. Eric Black, *Our Constitution: The Myth That Binds Us* (Boulder, Colo.: Westview Press, 1988), xiii.

41. Michael J. Perry, *Morality, Politics, and the Law: A Bicentennial Essay* (New York: Oxford University Press, 1988), 138–39. Perry expands on his sacred text analogy on pages 142–45, and he adds the following to his discussion of aspirations: "A central aspiration of the tradition has been to achieve justice, and justice has generally been seen to lie partly in the direction marked out by the more particular aspirations signified by various constitutional provisions regarding human rights. Put another way, a central aspiration of the tradition has been to keep faith with the more particular aspirations regarding the form of life of the polity, the life in common." (Ibid., 166).

42. Ibid., 138. Perry says that "members of the Supreme Court . . . are in an institutionally advantaged position to play a prophetic role: first, by taking seriously the prophetic potential of aspirational meaning of the constitutional text; second, by taking seriously the prophetic voices that emerge, from time to time, in the community." (Ibid., 147).

43. In *Lee v. Weisman*, 505 U.S. 577 (1992), the Court rejected the idea that the civil religion so defined could be any more accommodated under the establishment clause than could any traditional religion. Earlier some observers and even lower federal court judges read certain Supreme Court decisions accommodating certain religious practices within constitutional boundaries as implicitly recognizing the existence of an American civil religion. See, e.g., *Stein v. Plainwell Community Schools*, 822 F.2d 1406 (1987), in which the appeals court upheld graduation invocations and benedictions on the ground that they were within the ambit of the American civil religion.

44. "[M]oral progress . . . has less to do with the discovery or invention of new principles than with the inclusion under the old principles of previously excluded men and women." Michael Walzer, *Interpretation and Social Criticism* (Cambridge: Harvard University Press, 1987), 27.

45. See the letters of Abigail Adams to John dated March 31 and May 7, 1776, in *The Book of Abigail and John: Selected Letters of the Adams Family, 1762–1784*, ed. L. H. Butterfield, Marc Friedlaender, and Mary-Jo Kline (Cambridge: Harvard University Press, 1975), 120–21, 126–27.
46. See Samuel P. Huntington, *American Politics: The Promise of Disharmony* (Cambridge: Belknap Press of Harvard University Press, 1981), in which the author charts episodes of creedal passion in American politics, where reformers sought to reduce the gap between principle and practice in the society.
47. Gunnar Myrdal, *An American Dilemma: The Negro Problem and Modern Democracy* (New York: Harper & Brothers, 1944), 13, 3.
48. James B. White, *Justice as Translation: An Essay in Cultural and Legal Criticism* (Chicago: University of Chicago Press, 1990), 202.
49. Kenneth L. Karst, *Belonging to America: Equal Citizenship and the Constitution* (New Haven: Yale University Press, 1989), 233.
50. Gary J. Jacobsohn, *The Supreme Court and the Decline of Constitutional Aspiration* (Totowa, N.J.: Rowman & Littlefield, 1986), 136.
51. Henry J. Abraham and Barbara A. Perry, *Freedom and the Court: Civil Rights and Liberties in the United States*, 7th ed. (New York: Oxford University Press, 1998), 449.
52. Michael J. Perry, *The Constitution in the Courts: Law or Politics?* (New York: Oxford University Press, 1994), 202–3.
53. James B. White, *Justice as Translation: An Essay in Cultural and Legal Criticism* (Chicago: University of Chicago Press, 1990), 174.
54. James B. White, *When Words Lose Their Meaning: Constitutions and Reconstitutions of Language, Character, and Community* (Chicago: University of Chicago Press, 1984), 264. See also, Winnifred Fallers Sullivan, *Paying the Words Extra: Religious Discourse in the Supreme Court of the United States* (Cambridge: Harvard University Press for Harvard University Center for the Study of World Religions, 1994), 167, in which the author says: "The Supreme Court is an important location in the United States for the creation and expression of American identity."

CHAPTER ONE

1. Sacvan Bercovitch, *The American Jeremiad* (Madison: University of Wisconsin Press, 1978), 11.
2. Beginning as early as the 1790s a rift between republican thinkers and clerics would develop and widen with profound implications for the future. The clerics would seek to move the nation in the direction of defining itself as a Christian country against the rekindled worries of political leaders that such a move would have divisive effects. See Harry S. Stout, "Rhetoric and Reality in the Early Republic: The Case of the Federalist Clergy," in *Religion & American Politics: From the Colonial Period to the 1980s*, ed. Mark A. Noll (New York: Oxford University Press, 1990), 62–76.
3. Clinton Rossiter, *Seedtime of the Republic: The Origin of the American Tradition of Political Liberty* (New York: Harcourt, Brace, 1953), 328.
4. Patricia U. Bonomi, *Under the Cope of Heaven: Religion, Society, and Politics in Colonial America* (New York: Oxford University Press, 1986), 208.
5. Robert A. Ferguson, " 'We Hold These Truths' : Strategies of Control in the Litera-

ture of the Founders," in *Reconstructing American Literary History*, ed. Sacvan Bercovitch (Cambridge: Harvard University Press, 1986), 20.

6. "We have it in our power to begin the world over again. A situation, similar to the present, hath not happened since the days of Noah until now." "Appendix to 'Common-Sense,' " in *The Complete Writings of Thomas Paine*, ed. Philip S. Foner (New York: Citadel Press, 1945), 45.

7. "The long list of rights reflects economic as well as religious interests." Although a religious aura "serves to strengthen the moral and political claims of property, it also makes it impossible to focus exclusively on those claims." Michael Walzer, "Constitutional Rights and the Shape of Civil Society," in *"The Constitution of the People": Reflections on Citizens and Civil Society*, ed. Robert E. Calvert (Lawrence: University Press of Kansas, 1991), 116.

8. Robert A. Ferguson, " 'We Hold These Truths' : Strategies of Control in the Literature of the Founders," in *Reconstructing American Literary History*, ed. Sacvan Bercovitch (Cambridge: Harvard University Press, 1986), 21.

9. John Adams and George Washington are quoted to this effect in David Chidester, *Patterns of Power: Religion and Politics in American Culture* (Englewood Cliffs, N.J.: Prentice Hall, 1988), 66.

10. Robert A. Ferguson, " 'We Hold These Truths' : Strategies of Control in the Literature of the Founders," in *Reconstructing American Literary History*, ed. Sacvan Bercovitch, 21.

11. For a treatment of this evolution, see Nathan O. Hatch, *The Sacred Cause of Liberty: Republican Thought and the Millennium in Revolutionary New England* (New Haven: Yale University Press, 1977).

12. The Declaration of Independence, July 4, 1776.

13. John Phillip Reid in *Constitutional History of the American Revolution: The Authority of Rights* (Madison: University of Wisconsin Press, 1986) emphasizes the seriousness of this talk of rights by Americans and gives it substance within the Anglo-American tradition leading up to the Revolution.

14. See Gordon Wood, *The Creation of the American Republic, 1776–1787* (Chapel Hill: University of North Carolina Press, 1969).

   Much recent scholarly dispute has focused on assessing the influences upon, and characterizing the thought of, the founding generation. For instance, the influence of John Locke on the Declaration of Independence seems clear, but, as the pre-Revolutionary arguments were more closely inspected, they much more commonly revealed another source—the protests of the radical Whigs in England earlier in the century as they challenged the Walpole government. The picture that emerged was of a conspiracy against the people's liberties led by a self-serving government. Each British action during the period from 1763 up to the Revolution was interpreted by American colonials as part of this conspiracy to undermine the rights of Englishmen. (See Bernard Bailyn, *The Ideological Origins of the American Revolution* [Cambridge: Belknap Press of Harvard University Press, 1967].)

   What the emphasis upon the radical Whigs also brought to the fore was a new focus on classical republicanism as an alternative to the liberalism associated with Locke. To the rediscoverers of this American republican heritage, liberalism was a limited ideology that stressed rights, often economic rights, to the detriment of a common good. On the other hand, republicans embraced civic virtue and insisted that individuals reached their highest stage of development in a commitment to the public good itself.

Much of the writing of the neorepublicans caricatured rather than characterized liberalism and most often implicitly lamented the loss of what they saw as a republican heritage that would limit the pursuit of individual self-interest. In addition to Bailyn, the argument for the dominance of republicanism can be traced in the following: Gordon Wood, *The Creation of the American Republic, 1776–1787* (Chapel Hill: University of North Carolina Press, 1969); Gerald Stourzh, *Alexander Hamilton and the Idea of Republican Government* (Stanford: Stanford University Press, 1970); J.G.A. Pocock, *The Machiavellian Moment: Florentine Political Thought and the Atlantic Republican Tradition* (Princeton: Princeton University Press, 1975); Pocock, "*The Machiavellian Moment* Revisited: A Study in History and Ideology," *Journal of Modern History* 53 (March 1981): 49–72; Pocock, "Between Gog and Magog: The Republican Thesis and the *Ideologica Americana*," *Journal of the History of Ideas* 48 (April–June 1987): 325–46; Pocock and Terence Ball, eds., *Conceptual Change and the Constitution* (Lawrence: University Press of Kansas, 1988); and Lance Banning, "Jeffersonian Ideology Revisited: Liberal and Classical Ideas in the New American Republic," *William and Mary Quarterly*, 3d ser., 43 (January 1986): 3–19.

For some criticism of the above and similar work, see Joyce Appleby, "Republicanism in Old and New Contexts," in ibid., 20–34; James T. Kloppenburg, "Christianity, Republicanism, and Ethics in Early American Political Discourse," *Journal of American History* 74 (June 1987): 9–33; and Isaac Kramnick, *Republicanism and Bourgeois Radicalism: Political Ideology in Late Eighteenth Century England and America* (Ithaca: Cornell University Press, 1990).

After the dust cleared, the defenders of a liberal tradition rescued it from caricature and showed that civic virtue, among other republican traits, was not incompatible with an emphasis on individual rights. (For instance, see Jeffrey C. Isaac, "Republicanism vs. Liberalism? A Reconsideration," *History of Political Thought* 9 (Summer 1988): 349–77; Frank Michelman, "Law's Republic," *Yale Law Journal* 97 (July 1988): 1493–537, and Cass R. Sunstein, "Beyond the Revival," in ibid., 1566–69.)

Evidence among eighteenth-century Americans of a willingness to sacrifice their rights for the public good was hard to find. In fact, though differences existed in the thought of Americans, those differences were housed within a liberal consensus that emphasized the rights of individuals. As one writer has put it, "republican goods are constrained by liberal rights," and civil virtue can best be defined as "a disposition among citizens to engage in activities that support and maintain a just political order." (Richard C. Sinopoli, *The Foundations of American Citizenship: Liberalism, the Constitution, and Civic Virtue* [New York: Oxford University Press, 1992], 5, 13.) The author evaluates the recent scholarship and concludes that Louis Hartz's interpretation in *The Liberal Tradition in America: An Interpretation of American Political Thought Since the Revolution* (New York: Harcourt, Brace and World, 1955) largely survives the challenge. Sinopoli says "that central to the liberal tradition has been the idea that each person should be free to pursue his or her own conception of the good while granting a like freedom to others. . . . The liberal state . . . provides a useful means of living together with our differences, and it is morally defended for respecting the dignity of each individual. It is a denigration of this dignity to coerce some to conform to the majority's conception of the good—whether religious or political—despite their deepest convictions." (Richard C. Sinopoli, *The Foundations of American Citizenship: Liberalism, the Constitution, and Civic Virtue* [New York: Oxford University Press, 1992], 12.)

15. In arguing that "the Revolution was the most radical and most far-reaching event in American history," Gordon Wood said that "it made the interests and prosperity of ordinary people—their pursuits of happiness—the goal of society and government." Gordon S. Wood, *The Radicalism of the American Revolution* (New York: Knopf, 1992), 8.

On the antecedents and history of the Declaration, along with its subsequent veneration, see Pauline Maier, *American Scripture: Making the Declaration of Independence* (New York: Knopf, 1997).

16. Garry Wills titled his book on the Declaration of Independence, *Inventing America* (Garden City: Doubleday, 1978). On the concept of invention, see Werner Sollors, ed., *The Invention of Ethnicity* (New York: Oxford University Press, 1989), x–xiii; and E. J. Hobsbawm and Terence Ranger, eds., *The Invention of Tradition* (New York: Cambridge University Press, 1983), 4–12.

17. For a brief description of this process, see Martin E. Marty, *Pilgrims in Their Own Land: 500 Years of Religion in America* (New York: Penguin Books, 1985), 154–66.

18. "While traditional religions have, at least in the West, taken politics very seriously, they have generally done so in the name of something sacred. Civil religions, on the other hand, train their gaze on politics. Political life is the source of their concerns and provides the raw material for rituals, moments and imagery. Civil religions are created in response to new political arrangements and are devoted to making sense of and justifying those arrangements in terms that all members of the polity can understand and find compelling and meaningful. Though not sacral in itself, the transcendent case of civil religions differentiates them from ideologies in that the latter have none of the ultimacy or formal structure of traditional, sacred religions. A civil religion gathers and expresses the most deeply felt, abiding ideals and attitudes of a society's political life." Yehudah Mirsky, "Civil Religion and the Establishment Clause," *Yale Law Review* 95 (May 1986): 1237, 1250–51.

The latter twentieth-century retreat from party politics and the declining participation of Americans in elections should not be interpreted as a decline in the importance of basic political ideals in the society. There is concern about the effectiveness and responsiveness of political leaders and even the institutions that they staff, but there is little questioning of the standards by which they are judged.

19. David Chidester, *Patterns of Power: Religion and Politics in American Culture* (Englewood Cliffs, N.J.: Prentice Hall, 1988), 88.

20. "American historical experience becomes refracted through a prism of religious thought and ideas. While each individual bit of myth or memory is not a whole religion, taken together they do take on the lineaments of one." Yehudah Mirsky, "Civil Religion and the Establishment Clause," *Yale Law Review* 95 (May 1986): 1252.

21. Samuel P. Huntington, *American Politics: The Promise of Disharmony* (Cambridge: Belknap Press of Harvard University Press, 1981), 85–129.

22. See Catherine L. Albanese, *Sons of the Fathers: The Civil Religion of the American Revolution* (Philadelphia: Temple University Press, 1976).

23. For a treatment of voluntarism as a source of religious strength in America, see Seymour Martin Lipset, *The First New Nation: The United States in Historical and Comparative Perspective* (New York: Basic Books, 1963), 159–69.

24. George Washington, First Inaugural Address, April 30, 1789, in *Speeches of the American Presidents*, ed. Janet Podell and Steven Anzovin (New York: Wilson, 1988), 4.

25. A symbol can be defined as a word or particular thing that represents something

greater, usually having ultimate or transcendent value. The symbol bridges the gap between the concrete thing and that to which it refers and is "supremely important for the proper functioning of the life of any particular society.

"This reference to society leads at once to another fundamental truth about symbols: they are intimately related to social cohesion and to social transformation." F. W. Dillistone, *The Power of Symbols in Religion and Culture* (New York: Crossroad, 1986), 13, 15.

26. These are President Woodrow Wilson's words in a Flag Day address on June 14, 1917, in *The Papers of Woodrow Wilson*, vol. 42, ed. Arthur S. Link (Princeton: Princeton University Press, 1983), 504.

27. "Legal language was the founders' chief tool for crafting their new civic world. The security of constitutionalism through the rule of law provided the vocabulary not just for revolution, but for constructing the framework of virtue. Republicanism is, in large part, constitutionalism recycled under another label." John Phillip Reid, *Constitutional History of the American Revolution*, abr. ed. (Madison: University of Wisconsin Press, 1995), xvi.

28. "In America the law is king." Paine, "Common Sense," in *The Complete Writings of Thomas Paine*, ed. Philip S. Foner (New York: Citadel Press, 1945), 29.

29. In Robert N. Bellah and Phillip E. Hammond, *Varieties of Civil Religion* (San Francisco: Harper & Row, 1980), 121–37, Hammond seeks to isolate the characteristics of a society that gives rise to a civil religion. He places emphasis on religious pluralism and a universalist legal system that provides the means to resolve differences and the potential to create a meaning system for the diverse people in the society.

30. See Willi Paul Adams, *The First American Constitutions: Republican Ideology and the Making of State Constitutions in the Revolutionary Era*, trans. Rita and Robert Kimber (Chapel Hill: University of North Carolina Press, 1980).

31. See John Phillip Reid, *Constitutional History of the American Revolution*, abr. ed. (Madison: University of Wisconsin Press, 1995).

32. Donald S. Lutz, *The Origins of American Constitutionalism* (Baton Rouge: Louisiana State University Press, 1988), 55–56.

33. More than half of what was in the Articles was incorporated into the Constitution. Ibid., 133.

34. The major work challenging the traditional nationalistic interpretation is Merrill Jensen, *The Articles of Confederation* (Madison: University of Wisconsin Press, 1940).

35. Liberty tied to natural rights had "no counterpart anywhere in classical republicanism." Locke's liberty depended "on a sober sense of individual self-respect, bolstered by or rooted in the possession of private property and the reasonable hope of bettering one's condition through private enterprise. Locke envisaged, and in his wonderfully influential writings helped to foster, a new conception of the property-based dignity of man as human being and citizen. In America that conception became predominant." Thomas L. Pangle, "The Philosophic Understandings of Human Nature Informing the Constitution," in *Confronting the Constitution*, ed. Allan Bloom and Steven J. Kautz (Washington, D.C.: The AEI Press for the American Enterprise Institute, 1990), 11, 76. See also, William B. Scott, *In Pursuit of Happiness: American Conceptions of Property from the Seventeenth to the Twentieth Century* (Bloomington: Indiana University Press, 1977).

36. Merrill Jensen, *The Articles of Confederation* (Madison: University of Wisconsin Press, 1940), 244–45.

37. *Paul v. Virginia*, 75 U.S. (8 Wall.) 168, 180 (1869). The Court cited *Lemmon v. People*, 20 N.Y. 562, 607 (1860).
38. For an argument that this clause precluded the development of any constitutional philosophy concerning religion, see Gerard V. Bradley, "The No Religious Test Clause and the Constitution of Religious Liberty: A Machine That Has Gone of Itself," *Case Western Reserve Law Review* 43 (1986–87): 674–747.
39. U.S. Constitution, Article VI.
40. Staughton Lynd, in *Class Conflict, Slavery, & the United States Constitution* (Indianapolis: Bobbs-Merrill, 1967), 153–213, argues that the most fundamental compromise at Philadelphia was with the proposition that all men were created equal.
41. Max Farrand, *The Records of the Federal Convention of 1787*, rev. ed., 4 vols. (New Haven: Yale University Press, 1937), 2:417, 415.
42. U.S. Constitution, Article I, Section 2.
43. Ibid., Article IV, Section 2.
44. Ibid., Article I, Section 8.
45. Ibid., Article I, Section 9.
46. For instance, see Frederick Douglass's speech, "The Constitution of the United States: Is it Pro-Slavery or Anti-Slavery?," March 26, 1860 in *The Life and Writings of Frederick Douglass*, 5 vols. (New York: International Publishers, 1950–55, 1975), 2:467–80. Douglass had moved from condemning the Constitution to finding within it the seeds of freedom for slaves. For his earlier view, see "The Constitution and Slavery," *The North Star*, March 16, 1849, in ibid., 1:361–67.
47. In the treatment here, I am indebted to Michael Zuckert, "Epistemology and Hermeneutics in the Constitutional Jurisprudence of John Marshall," in *John Marshall's Achievement: Law, Politics, and Constitutional Interpretations*, ed. Thomas C. Shevory (New York: Greenwood Press, 1989), 202–5.
48. Jacob E. Cooke, ed., *The Federalist* (Middletown, Conn.: Wesleyan University Press, 1961), No. 51, 347–48.
49. U.S. Constitution, Article VI.
50. In reviewing the evidence, both Raoul Berger, in *Congress v. The Supreme Court* (Cambridge: Harvard University Press, 1969), 188, and John Agresto, in *The Supreme Court and Constitutional Democracy* (Ithaca: Cornell University Press, 1984), 63, come to this conclusion. Most of the relevant discussion at the Convention came in response to the proposal to unite the justices with the chief executive in a Council of Revision.
51. Iredell to Richard Dobbs Spaight, August 26, 1787, in Griffith J. McRee, *Life and Correspondence of James Iredell*, 2 vols. (New York: Appleton, 1858), 2:172.
52. Jacob E. Cooke, ed., *The Federalist* (Middletown, Conn.: Wesleyan University Press, 1961), No. 78, 522.
53. James B. White, *When Words Lose Their Meaning* (Chicago: University of Chicago Press, 1984), 244, 246.
54. Jefferson to Madison, March 15, 1789, in *The Papers of James Madison*, vol. 12, ed. Robert A. Rutland and Thomas A. Mason (Charlottesville: University Press of Virginia, 1979), 13.
55. Madison's speech in the House of Representatives introducing the proposed amendments, June 8, 1789, *Annals of Congress*, 1st Cong., 1st sess., 439.
56. Ibid., 435, 437, 434.
57. The submitted proposal dealing with compensation for senators and representatives, as was generally true of amendments until the twentieth century, had no time limit,

and after decades of neglect, new states began to ratify it in rather recent times. In 1992 it was proclaimed ratified and became the Twenty-Seventh Amendment to the Constitution.

58. Leonard W. Levy, "Bill of Rights," in *Essays on the Making of the Constitution*, 2d ed. (New York: Oxford University Press, 1987), 274–89.

59. The concern of course was that the new government would interfere with religious liberty, but by excluding religious norms from the public sphere, the provisions tended to privatize religion. Ruti Teitel, in "A Critique of Religion as Politics in the Public Sphere," *Cornell Law Review* 78 (July 1993): 747–821, argues that the attempt of certain religious groups in recent times to project such religious norms into the public sphere, if successful, would not only reverse two hundred plus years of history but also substantially endanger the nation's constitutional democracy.

60. For useful coverage of Puritan, evangelical, Enlightenment, and civic republican views in the late eighteenth century and the way in which they pointed in the direction of a set of characteristics encompassing religious liberty, see John Witte Jr., "The Essential Rights and Liberties of Religion in the American Constitutional Experiment," *Notre Dame Law Review* 71 (1996): 371–445.

61. In introducing the proposed amendments and seeking to counter the arguments of opponents, Madison gave most credit to the contention that any such listing would be incomplete, thereby leaving open the possibility that there was some implicit recognition of the federal government's power to invade the individual rights not listed. Specifically to preclude this implied power and to provide the possibility for future protection, Madison proposed what became the Ninth Amendment. *Annals of Congress*, 1st Cong., 1st sess., 439.

62. Leonard W. Levy, "Bill of Rights," in *Essays on the Making of the Constitution*, 2d ed. (New York: Oxford University Press, 1987), 306.

63. Michael Walzer, "Constitutional Rights and the Shape of Civil Society," in *"The Constitution of the People": Reflections on Citizens and Civil Society*, ed. Robert E. Calvert (Lawrence: University Press of Kansas, 1991), 113–15.

64. Jacob E. Cooke, ed., *The Federalist* (Middletown, Conn.: Wesleyan University Press, 1961), No. 37, 238.

65. Jefferson to John Adams, August 30, 1787, in *The Papers of Thomas Jefferson*, vol. 12, ed. Julian P. Boyd (Princeton: Princeton University Press, 1955), 69.

66. Quoted in Frank I. Schechter, "The Early History of the Tradition of the Constitution," *American Political Science Review* 9 (November 1915): 729.

67. Quoted in ibid., 720.

68. George Washington, First Inaugural Address, April 30, 1789, in *Speeches of the American Presidents*, ed. Janet Podell and Steven Anzovin (New York: Wilson, 1988), 3–4.

69. Lance Banning, "Republican Ideology and the Triumph of the Constitution, 1789 to 1793," *William and Mary Quarterly*, 3rd ser., 31 (April 1974): 184–88.

70. Alfred North Whitehead, *Symbolism: Its Meaning and Effect* (New York: Macmillan, 1958), 88.

71. For an interpretation of the series of essays in support of the Constitution, done by Alexander Hamilton, James Madison, and John Jay under the name of Publius and collected as *The Federalist*, that stresses the idea of the Constitution creating a national community, see Edward Millican, *One United People: The Federalist Papers and the National Idea* (Lexington: University Press of Kentucky, 1990).

72. Sylvia Snowiss, in *Judicial Review and the Law of the Constitution* (New Haven: Yale

University Press, 1990), argues that John Marshall was responsible for transforming the fundamental law as outlined in the Constitution into a supreme civil law whose words would then become the focal point of constitutional adjudication, thus legalizing the fundamental law and ensuring its interpretation by the courts. Earlier judicial review, she maintains, was largely seen as a political act undertaken by judges in cases where no doubt existed as to the unconstitutionality of the challenged act. The justification then was found in the separation of powers and the need to eliminate the possibility of revolution.

73. In Michael Kammen, *A Machine That Would Go of Itself: The Constitution in American Culture* (New York: Knopf, 1986), the author documents that Americans have not been knowledgeable about the specific text of the Constitution.

74. In Sanford Levinson, *Constitutional Faith* (Princeton: Princeton University Press, 1988), the author questions whether faith should be placed in a document whose meaning is so unclear.

75. E. L. Doctorow, "A Citizen Reads the Constitution," in *America in Theory*, ed. Leslie Berlowitz, Denis Donoghue, and Louis Menand (New York: Oxford University Press, 1988), 292–93.

76. "Protecting 'private rights,' we enjoy an unprecedented degree of 'public happiness.' Our diversity protects our unity." Michael Novak, "How to Make a Republic Work: The Originality of the Commercial Republicans," in *"The Constitution of the People:" Reflections on Citizens and Civil Society*, ed. Robert E. Calvert (Lawrence: University Press of Kansas, 1991), 105.

77. Richard C. Sinopoli, *The Foundations of American Citizenship: Liberalism, the Constitution, and Civic Virtue* (New York: Oxford University Press, 1992), 171.

78. After a painstaking study of popular reaction to the Constitution throughout its history, one writer concluded that the most "significant phenomenon in our culture" has been the tendency of American constitutionalism to "discover new imperatives in these two simple words, personal liberty." Michael Kammen, *Sovereignty and Liberty: Constitutional Discourse in American Culture* (Madison: University of Wisconsin Press, 1988), 100. This volume presents some of the author's conclusions stemming from his earlier study, *A Machine That Would Go of Itself*.

79. Martin Diamond, "The American Idea of Equality: The View From the Founding," *Review of Politics* 38 (July 1976): 315–16.

80. Sanford Levinson, *Constitutional Faith* (Princeton: Princeton University Press, 1988), 191.

81. Kenneth L. Karst, *Belonging to America: Equal Citizenship and the Constitution* (New Haven: Yale University Press, 1989), ix. The author argues that equal citizenship should be a conscious principle that cuts through the myopia that often precludes empathetic interpretations of a claim.

82. For instance, despite his personal indication of faith, look at Sanford Levinson's agonizing in *Constitutional Faith* (Princeton: Princeton University Press, 1988).

83. Justice William Johnson in *Elkison v. Deliesseline*, 8 F. Cas. 493, 495 (C.C.D.S.C. 1823) (No. 4,366), quoted in Edward S. Corwin, "The Worship of the Constitution," *Constitutional Review* 4 (1920): 10.

84. Barbara Jordan and Shelby Heron, *Barbara Jordan: A Self-Portrait* (Garden City, N.Y.: Doubleday, 1979), 187.

85. See, for instance, Max Lerner, "Constitution and Court as Symbols," *Yale Law Journal* 46 (June 1937): 1290–1319.

86. W. Y. Elliot, "The Constitution as the American Social Myth," in *The Constitution Reconsidered*, rev. ed., ed. Conyers Read, with preface by Richard B. Morris (New York: Harper & Row, 1968), 223.

87. The tendency is further reinforced because "a certain consonance exists between the American Constitution's regard for the rights of individuals and a much older broader Western tradition which has particular regard for the integrity of the individual's experience and conscience." J. R. Pole, *The Pursuit of Equality in American History*, rev. ed. (Berkeley: University of California Press, 1993), xvii.

88. Hannah Arendt, *On Revolution* (New York: Viking Press, 1963), 154–56. Arendt argues that the American Revolutionary experience was unique in its devotion to limited government and in its separation of the sources of power and law. Because of their colonial experience, "the framers of American constitutions . . . were never tempted to derive law and power from the same origin. The seat of power to them was the people, but the source of law was to become the Constitution . . . an endurable objective thing." (Ibid., 155–56.)

89. Irving Kristol, " 'The Spirit of '87,' " *The Public Interest*, 86 (Winter 1987): 4.

90. Alexander Bickel, *The Morality of Consent* (New Haven: Yale University Press, 1975), 24.

91. James Madison, "Charters," *National Gazette*, January 18, 1792, in *The Papers of James Madison*, vol. 12, ed. Robert A. Rutland and Thomas A. Mason (Charlottesville: University Press of Virginia, 1979), 192.

92. George Washington, Farewell Address, September 17, 1796, in *Speeches of the American Presidents*, ed. Janet Podell and Steven Anzovin (New York: Wilson, 1988), 16.

93. Abraham Lincoln, speech entitled "The Perpetuation of Our Political Institutions," January 27, 1838, in *The Collected Works of Abraham Lincoln*, 8 vols., ed. Roy P. Basler (New Brunswick: Rutgers University Press, 1953), 1:112.

CHAPTER TWO

1. For instance, not until 1875 was the full range of jurisdiction, as outlined in the Constitution, conferred on the federal courts.

2. William M. Wiecek, *Liberty under Law: The Supreme Court in American Life* (Baltimore: Johns Hopkins University Press, 1988), 42–43.

3. See William R. Casto, *The Supreme Court in the Early Republic: The Chief Justiceships of John Jay and Oliver Ellsworth* (Columbia: University of South Carolina Press, 1995), for coverage of the 1789 act and the work of the early Court.

4. The judicial oath as stipulated by Congress quoted in *Marbury v. Madison*, 5 U.S. (1 Cranch) 137, 180 (1803).

5. The idea that circuit riding made education a two-way street was most clearly expressed during one of the congressional discussions that responded to the continued requests of the justices to be relieved from the onerous duty. Ralph Lerner, "The Supreme Court as Republican Schoolmaster," in *Supreme Court Review 1967*, ed. Philip B. Kurland (Chicago: University of Chicago Press, 1967), 179, captures this combination teaching-learning experience by interspersing quotations from a Congressional debate in 1826 with his own words: "One of the reasons Congress persisted in requiring members of the Supreme Court to ride circuit . . . was a fear of the political consequences of isolating the Court from its public. The argument that was

made pointed perhaps as much to judges learning as to judges teaching. It is precisely because judges have 'political functions to discharge' that they should be attentive to their political support; 'they should be conversant with public opinion, and imbibe the spirit of the times.' But it is not alone important that the judges have a clear and vivid sense of being 'tethered . . . but not shackled' to public opinion. It is perhaps even more important, in the long run, that the people at large have a clear and vivid sense that there is 'a harmony of opinion and of action' between the Supreme Court and the inferior courts, and between the judiciary and the people for whom it is meant to establish justice. 'In a Government founded on opinion, it is necessary that the People should be satisfied with judicial decisions.' "

6. For a discussion of the early justices in their role as educators, see ibid., 127–80.
7. Alexis de Toqueville, *Democracy in America*, ed. J. P. Mayer and Max Lerner (New York: Harper & Row, 1966), 137.
8. Wilson's Grand Jury Charge in Philadelphia, April 12, 1790, in *The Documentary History of the Supreme Court of the United States, 1789–1800*, vol. 2, ed. Maeva Marcus (New York: Columbia University Press, 1988), 33–34, 40.
9. Jay's Grand Jury Charge in New York, April 12, 1790, in ibid., 27, 30.
10. Iredell's Grand Jury Charge in Augusta, Ga., October 17, 1791, in ibid., 218, 219.
11. Iredell's Grand Jury Charge in Trenton, N.J., April 2, 1793, in ibid., 350.
12. Wilson's Grand Jury Charge in Boston, June 7, 1793, in ibid., 400.
13. Wilson's Grand Jury Charge in Richmond, May 23, 1791, in ibid., 190.
14. Blair's Grand Jury Charge in Dover, Del., October 27, 1794, in ibid., 490, 489.
15. Paterson's Grand Jury Charge in Trenton, N.J., April 2, 1795, in *The Documentary History of the Supreme Court of the United States, 1789–1800*, vol. 3, ed. Maeva Marcus (New York: Columbia University Press, 1990), 12–13.
16. Ellsworth's Grand Jury Charge in Savannah, April 25, 1796, in ibid., 119.
17. Iredell's Grand Jury Charge in Boston, October 12, 1792, in *The Documentary History of the Supreme Court of the United States, 1789–1800*, vol. 2, ed. Maeva Marcus (New York: Columbia University Press, 1988), 310.
18. Iredell's Grand Jury Charge in Savannah, April 26, 1792, in ibid., 271.
19. Iredell's Grand Jury Charge in Augusta, October 17, 1791, in ibid., 219.
20. Iredell's Grand Jury Charge in Savannah, April 26, 1792, in ibid., 264.
21. Wilson's Grand Jury Charge in Richmond, May 23, 1791, in ibid., 190.
22. Wilson's Grand Jury Charge in Philadelphia, August 15, 1791, in ibid., 202–3.
23. Cushing's Grand Jury Charge in Providence, November 7, 1794, in ibid., 491.
24. Iredell's Grand Jury Charge in Boston, October 12, 1792, in ibid., 310.
25. Ibid., 311.
26. Jay's Grand Jury Charge in New York, April 12, 1790, in ibid., 26.
27. Iredell's Grand Jury Charge in Savannah, April 26, 1792, in ibid., 271.
28. Ellsworth's Grand Jury Charge in Savannah, April 25, 1796, in *The Documentary History of the Supreme Court of the United States, 1789–1800*, vol. 3, ed. Maeva Marcus (New York: Columbia University Press, 1990), 120.
29. Iredell's Grand Jury Charge in Philadelphia, April 11, 1799, in ibid., 350–51.
30. The Chase story is well told in Richard E. Ellis, *The Jeffersonian Crisis: Court and Politics in the Young Republic* (New York: Oxford University Press, 1971), 76–107.
31. Alexander Hamilton to John Jay [November 13, 1790], and John Jay to Alexander Hamilton, November 28, 1790, in *The Correspondence and Public Papers of John Jay*, 4 vols., ed. Henry P. Johnson (New York: G. P. Putnam's Sons, 1890–93), 3:404–55, 409–11.

32. George Washington to Justices of the Supreme Court, April 3, 1790, in *The Documentary History of the Supreme Court of the United States, 1789–1800*, vol. 2, ed. Maeva Marcus (New York: Columbia University Press, 1988), 21.

33. Justices of the Supreme Court to George Washington, September 13, 1790, in ibid., 90.

34. *Stuart v. Laird*, 5 U.S. (1 Cranch) 299 (1803).

35. *Hayburn's Case*, 2 U.S. (2 Dall.) 409 (1792).

36. See Charles Warren, *The Supreme Court in United States History*, rev. ed., 2 vols. (Boston: Little, Brown, 1926), 2:69–83.

37. Jay and Associate Justices to President Washington, August 8, 1793, in *The Correspondence and Public Papers of John Jay*, 4 vols., ed. Henry P. Johnson (New York: G. P. Putnam's Sons, 1890–93), 3:448.

38. U.S. Constitution, Article III, Section 2.

39. In *John Jay, the Nation and the Court* (Boston: Boston University Press, 1967), 49, Richard B. Morris corrected previous errors as to the claim in this case.

40. In *Judicial Review and the Law of the Constitution* (New Haven, Conn.: Yale University Press, 1990), Sylvia Snowiss argues that the judicial view of the Constitution as higher ordinary law came only with John Marshall.

41. *Chisholm v. Georgia*, 2 U.S. (2 Dall.) 419, 454–55, 461, 464 (1793).

42. Ibid., 465.

43. Ibid., 471, 474.

44. Ibid., 475, 476.

45. At the very time this case was being heard Georgia was prosecuting a case against two citizens of South Carolina. See *Georgia v. Brailsford*, 2 U.S. (2 Dall.) 402 (1792).

46. *Chisholm v. Georgia*, 2 U.S. (2 Dall.) 419, 477, 479 (1793).

47. Ibid., 478.

48. Charles Warren, *The Supreme Court in United States History*, rev. ed., 2 vols. (Boston: Little, Brown, 1926), 1: 96–101.

49. *Chisholm v. Georgia*, 2 U.S. (2 Dall.) 419, 468 (1793).

50. Clyde E. Jacobs, *The Eleventh Amendment and Sovereign Immunity* (Westport, Conn.: Greenwood Press, 1972), 66–67.

51. For a survey of *Chisholm* and the interpretation of the amendment it inspired, see John V. Orth, *The Judicial Power of the United States: The Eleventh Amendment in American History* (New York: Oxford University Press, 1987).

52. Jay made his feelings about the Court clear in refusing to accept the position of chief justice. Jay to President John Adams, January 2, 1801, in *The Correspondence and Public Papers of John Jay*, 4 vols., ed. Henry P. Johnson (New York: G. P. Putnam's Sons, 1890–93), 4:285.

53. As early as 1824 in *Osborn v. Bank of the United States*, 22 U.S. (9 Wheat.) 214, the Court reached this conclusion.

54. *Ware v. Hylton*, 3 U.S. (3 Dall.) 199, 236, 237 (1796).

55. *Hylton v. United States*, 3 U.S. (3 Dall.) 171, 175 (1796).

56. *Calder v. Bull*, 3 U.S. (3 Dall.) 386, 388–89 (1798).

57. Ibid., 399.

58. Sylvia Snowiss argues, in *Judicial Review and the Law of the Constitution* (New Haven: Yale University Press, 1990), that while other justices continued to find sustenance for their views in natural rights, Marshall increasingly tended to base his decisions on the text of the Constitution, thereby transforming it, subtly, into higher ordinary law.

59. *Chisholm v. Georgia*, 2 U.S. (2 Dall.) 419 (1793).

60. Julius Goebel Jr., *Antecedents and Beginnings to 1801*, vol. 1 of *The Oliver Wendell Holmes Devise History of the Supreme Court of the United States* (New York: Macmillan Publishing Co., 1971), 792.

61. Paschal Larkin, *Property in the Eighteenth Century with Special Reference to England and Locke* (Port Washington, N.Y.: Kennikat Press, 1969), 241, 62.

62. James B. White, *Justice as Translation: An Essay in Cultural and Legal Criticism* (Chicago: University of Chicago Press, 1990), 206.

63. James Madison, "Property," *National Gazette*, March 27, 1792, in *The Papers of James Madison*, vol. 14, ed. Robert A. Rutland and Thomas A. Mason (Charlottesville: University Press of Virginia, 1983), 266.

64. For a brief treatment of the property right in American constitutional history from the colonial period to the present, see James W. Ely Jr., *The Guardian of Every Other Right: A Constitutional History of Property Rights* (New York: Oxford University Press, 1992). And for a treatment of the place of property in the drafting of the Constitution and its continuing importance, see Jennifer Nedelsky, *Private Property and the Limits of American Constitutionalism: The Madisonian Framework and its Legacy* (Chicago: University of Chicago Press, 1990).

65. *Vanhorne's Lessee v. Dorrance*, 2 U.S. (2 Dall.) 304, 307, 310, 311 (1794).

66. *Talbot v. Jansen*, 3 U.S. (3 Dall.) 133 (1795).

67. This decision, though illustrative of a concern for individual rights, is only the first of many grappling with the complex question of citizenship in a federal state. During the early years of the Marshall Court, the justices confronted the matter in many diverse fact situations and there was some support for the idea that the sovereign had a claim to allegiance which could not be rejected unilaterally by the individual. See George Lee Haskins and Herbert A. Johnson, *Foundations of Power: John Marshall, 1801–15*, vol. 2 of *The Oliver Wendell Holmes Devise History of the Supreme Court of the United States* (New York: Macmillan Publishing Co., 1981), 493–525; and James H. Kettner, *The Development of American Citizenship, 1608–1870* (Chapel Hill: University of North Carolina Press, 1978): 267–86. In fact, Kettner argues, in ibid., 343–44, that the issues of state sovereignty and slavery precluded a formal acceptance of the right of expatriation until the civil war resolved those issues.

68. Paterson's charge to the jury is printed in Francis Wharton, *State Trials of the United States During the Administrations of Washington and Adams*, reprint ed. (New York: Burt Franklin, 1970), 177. The coverage of the trials runs from 102–84.

69. Ibid., 591.

70. Quoted in its entirety in James Morton Smith, *Freedom's Fetters: The Alien and Sedition Laws and American Civil Liberties* (Ithaca: Cornell University Press, 1956), 441–42.

71. Iredell's Grand Jury Charge in Philadelphia, April 11, 1799, in *The Documentary History of the Supreme Court of the United States, 1789–1800*, vol. 3, ed. Maeva Marcus (New York: Columbia University Press, 1990), 347, 346.

72. See Leonard W. Levy, *Emergence of a Free Press* (New York: Oxford University Press, 1985), 297–349.

73. Jay to President Adams, January 2, 1801, in *The Correspondence and Public Papers of John Jay*, 4 vols., ed. Henry P. Johnson (New York: G. P. Putnam's Sons, 1890–93), 4:285.

74. A lame duck Federalist Congress enacted the Judiciary Act of 1801. Such reform, so long desired, was now perceived by the Republicans, who had swept the elections of 1800, as a measure designed to entrench the politically repudiated Federalists in the

judicial branch. The act was repealed by the Republican Congress in 1802, and the justices would have to wait for ninety years to be freed completely from circuit court responsibilities.

75. John Marshall to Joseph Story, 1827, in *The Documentary History of the Supreme Court of the United States, 1789–1800*, vol. 1, ed. Maeva Marcus (New York: Columbia University Press, 1985), 928–29.

76. Thomas Jefferson, First Inaugural Address, March 4, 1801, in *Speeches of the American Presidents*, ed. Janet Podell and Steven Anzovin (New York: H. W. Wilson Co., 1988), 39.

77. Leonard Baker, *John Marshall: A Life in Law* (New York: Macmillan Publishing Co., 1974), 68–69, 95, 195–96, 207–78.

78. Ibid., 282–83, 290–91, 303, 304, 328, 348, 358, 359.

79. That the Court had not yet established its visibility as one of the three branches of the federal government was evidenced by the fact that no thought had been given to providing it a home in the District of Columbia, the new seat of the federal government. Eventually, the House and Senate consented to have the Court occupy some basement rooms in the Capitol.

80. Actually, the movement in this direction seemed clear under Chief Justice Ellsworth. In his opinion in *Bas v. Tingy*, 4 U.S. (4 Dall.) 37, 43 (1800), Justice Chase implied that the justices had agreed that a unanimous result would be announced in a single opinion by the chief.

81. *Marbury v. Madison*, 5 U.S. (1 Cranch) 137 (1803).

82. For an extended historical argument that a modern myth was created around *Marbury v. Madison* to justify expanded judicial power, see Robert Lowry Clinton, *Marbury v. Madison and Judicial Review* (Lawrence: University Press of Kansas, 1989).

83. Quoted in William E. Nelson, "The Eighteenth-Century Background of John Marshall's Jurisprudence," *Michigan Law Review* 76 (May 1978): 937. Nelson claims that Marshall's work on the Court can be best explained in terms of his writing commonly held values into constitutional law and of his attempt to separate law from politics.

84. *Marbury v. Madison*, 5 U.S. (1 Cranch) 137, 163, 166 (1803).

85. For instance, see the hypothetical dissenting opinion in Michael Zuckert, "Epistemology and Hermeneutics in the Constitutional Jurisprudence of John Marshall," in *John Marshall's Achievement: Law, Politics, and Constitutional Interpretations*, ed. Thomas C. Shevory (New York: Greenwood Press, 1989), 195–99.

86. *Marbury v. Madison*, 5 U.S. (1 Cranch) 137, 176, 177.

87. Ibid., 178, 180.

88. Leonard Baker, *John Marshall: A Life in Law* (New York: Macmillan Publishing Co., 1974), 377–81.

89. *Stuart v. Laird*, 5 U.S. (1 Cranch) 299 (1803). On the basis of *Marbury*, a claim of a removed judge that he had unconstitutionally been deprived of his office would seem strong, but the case did not present this issue, and it was never brought to the Court.

90. Ibid., 309.

91. Chase's charge is quoted in George Lee Haskins and Herbert A. Johnson, *Foundations of Power: John Marshall, 1801–15*, vol. 2 of *The Oliver Wendell Holmes Devise History of the Supreme Court of the United States* (New York: Macmillan Publishing Co., 1981), 218.

92. U.S. Constitution, Article II, Section 4.

93. George Lee Haskins and Herbert A. Johnson, *Foundations of Power: John Marshall,*

1801–15, vol. 2 of *The Oliver Wendell Holmes Devise History of the Supreme Court of the United States* (New York: Macmillan Publishing Co., 1981), 234.

94. Marshall to Chase, January 23, 1804, quoted in Leonard Baker, *John Marshall: A Life in Law* (New York: Macmillan Publishing Co., 1974), 422.

95. In *The Jeffersonian Crisis: Courts and Politics in the Young Republic* (New York: Oxford University Press, 1971), 102–5, Richard E. Ellis attributes Jefferson's failure to push for a conviction as a decisive factor in the outcome.

96. G. Edward White, *The Marshall Court and Cultural Change, 1815–35*, vols. 3–4 of *The Oliver Wendell Holmes Devise History of the Supreme Court of the United States* (New York: Macmillan Publishing Co., 1988), 964.

97. *United States v. Peters*, 9 U.S. (5 Cranch) 115, 136, 141 (1809).

98. *Martin v. Hunter's Lessee*, 14 U.S. (1 Wheat.) 304, 325, 326, 328, 351 (1816).

99. *McCulloch v. Maryland*, 17 U.S. (4 Wheat.) 316, 405, 407, 415, (1819).

100. Ibid., 426.

101. Ibid., 421.

102. Ibid., 429, 436–37.

103. Ibid., 401.

104. The decision was so important to Marshall that he felt compelled to respond to attacks upon it printed in the *Richmond Enquirer*. Under the alias, "A Friend of the Constitution," he wrote his rebuttal in the pages of the *Alexandria Gazette*. The story is told and the attacks and responses printed in Gerald Gunther, *John Marshall's Defense of McCulloch v. Maryland* (Stanford: Stanford University Press, 1969).

105. James B. White, *When Words Lose Their Meaning: Constitutions and Reconstitutions of Lanuage, Character and Community* (Chicago: University of Chicago Press, 1984), 260.

106. "Despite its magisterial tone, this opinion turns to the reader it has instructed in its methods and says to him: it is now time for you to remake our language, to constitute and reconstitute our community and culture anew, as I have done: you must build on what I have made." (Ibid., 263).

107. *Cohens v. Virginia*, 19 U.S. (6 Wheat.) 264, 380, 382, 383–84 (1821).

108. Ibid., 389.

109. Ibid., 442, 443.

110. G. Edward White, *The Marshall Court and Cultural Change, 1815–35*, vols. 3–4 of *The Oliver Wendell Holmes Devise History of the Supreme Court of the United States* (New York: Macmillan Publishing Co., 1988), 965–66.

CHAPTER THREE

1. U.S. Constitution, Article I, Section 10.

2. *Fletcher v. Peck*, 10 U.S. (6 Cranch) 87, 138 (1810). For an extensive treatment of the case and the controversy from which it arose, see C. Peter Magrath, *Yazoo, Law and Politics in the New Republic: The Case of Fletcher v. Peck* (New York: Norton, 1966).

3. *Terrett v. Taylor*, 13 U.S. (9 Cranch) 43, 50–51 (1815).

4. *Dartmouth College v. Woodward*, 17 U.S. (4 Wheat.) 518, 628 (1819).

5. Ibid., 712, 713.

6. Story is a most interesting and important figure on the Court during the period from 1811 to 1845. For a thoughtful treatment of his contributions, see R. Kent Newmyer,

Supreme Court Justice Story: Statesman of the Old Republic (Chapel Hill: University of North Carolina Press, 1985).

7. *Providence Bank v. Billings*, 29 U.S. (4 Pet.) 514, 561 (1830).

8. James L. Kainen sees just this problem at the heart of the demise of the contract clause. See his "Nineteenth Century Interpretations of the Federal Contract Clause: The Transformation from Vested to Substantive Rights against the State," *Buffalo Law Review*, 31 (Spring 1982): 381–480.

9. *Ogden v. Saunders*, 25 U.S. (12 Wheat.) 213, 334 (1827).

10. Ibid., 331.

11. *United States v. Hamilton*, 3 U.S. (3 Dall.) 17 (1795).

12. *Ex Parte Bollman*, 8 U.S. (4 Cranch) 75, 95, 127 (1807).

13. *United States v. Hudson & Goodwin*, 11 U.S. (7 Cranch) 32 (1812). The Court seemed willing to determine how much of a general bar the 1812 case had imposed, but because the attorney general was not willing to argue the matter, the Court affirmed the earlier decision. See *United States v. Coolidge*, 14 U.S. (1 Wheat.) 415 (1816).

14. *Reynolds v. McArthur*, 27 U.S. (2 Pet.) 417, 434 (1829).

15. *Cherokee Nation v. Georgia*, 30 U.S. (5 Pet.) 1, 17 (1831).

16. *Mitchel v. United States*, 34 U.S. (9 Pet.) 711, 746 (1835). Not until much later did the rights of Native Americans receive sympathetic hearings in the courts.

17. *Cherokee Nation v. Georgia*, 30 U.S. (5 Pet.) 1, 41, 50 (1831).

18. Thompson cited *Osborn v. Bank of the United States*, 22 U.S. (9 Wheat.) 738 (1824).

19. *Cherokee Nation v. Georgia*, 30 U.S. (5 Pet.) 1, 78 (1831).

20. G. Edward White, *The Marshall Court and Cultural Change, 1815–35*, vols. 3–4 of *The Oliver Wendell Holmes Devise History of the Supreme Court of the United States* (New York: Macmillan Publishing Co., 1988), 729–32.

21. *Worcester v. Georgia*, 31 U.S. (6 Pet.) 515, 561 (1832).

22. Ibid., 562, 596.

23. G. Edward White, *The Marshall Court and Cultural Change, 1815–35*, vols. 3–4 of *The Oliver Wendell Holmes Devise History of the Supreme Court of the United States* (New York: Macmillan Publishing Co., 1988), 737–38.

24. *Barron v. Baltimore*, 32 U.S. (7 Pet.), 243 (1833).

25. *Permoli v. New Orleans*, 44 U.S. (3 How.) 589, 609 (1845).

26. U.S. Constitution, Article I, Section 8.

27. *Gibbons v. Ogden*, 22 U.S. (9 Wheat.) 1, 186–87 (1824).

28. Ibid., 191, 210, 221, 222.

29. Ibid., 223, 231.

30. See Donald G. Morgan, *Justice William Johnson: The First Dissenter* (Columbia: University of South Carolina Press, 1954), 192–202.

31. This analogy had been drawn by counsel in *Gibbons* and again in *New York v. Miln*, 36 U.S. (11 Pet.) 102 (1837), which involved a state regulation requiring a written report on each passenger arriving in the state. Counsel for New York argued that an invalidation here would necessitate a similar decision in regard to cases dealing with "the laws of the Southern States in relation to the intercourse and traffic with slaves, and to the introduction of coloured persons into those States." (Ibid., 111–12.)

32. *Passenger Cases*, 48 U.S. (7 How.) 283 (1849).

33. For a useful short synthesis of the Marshall and Taney Courts coming to this conclusion, see R. Kent Newmyer, *The Supreme Court under Marshall and Taney* (New York: Thomas Y. Crowell Co., 1968).

34. *Charles River Bridge v. Warren Bridge*, 36 U.S. (11 Pet.) 420 (1837). For discussion of how the decision paved the way for technological change, see Stanley I. Kutler, *Privilege and Creative Destruction: The Charles River Bridge Case* (New York: J.B. Lippincott Co., 1971).

35. *Passenger Cases*, 48 U.S. (7 How.) 283, 492 (1849).

36. *Swift v. Tyson*, 41 U.S. (16 Pet.) 1 (1842). In *Erie Railroad Co. v. Tompkins*, 304 U.S. 64 (1938), the Court overruled *Swift* and directed the federal courts to use the state's common law.

37. *Louisville, Cincinnati and Charleston R.R. Co. v. Letson*, 43 U.S. (2 How.) 497 (1844).

38. *Genesee Chief v. Fitzhugh*, 53 U.S. (12 How.) 443, 457 (1851).

39. Ibid., 465.

40. *New York v. Miln*, 36 U.S. (11 Pet.) 102, 139 (1837).

41. *Luther v. Borden*, 48 U.S. (7 How.) 1 (1849).

42. *Pennsylvania v. Wheeling & Belmont Bridge Co.*, 54 U.S. (13 How.) 518, 576, 592 (1851).

43. *Davis v. Police Jury*, 50 U.S. (9 How.) 280, 296 (1850).

44. *Talbot v. Seeman*, 5 U.S. (1 Cranch) 1, 44 (1801).

45. *Sturges v. Crowninshield*, 17 U.S. (4 Wheat.) 122, 200 (1819).

46. *Henderson v. Poindexter's Lessee*, 25 U.S. (12 Wheat.) 530, 535 (1827). The sacredness of such a right was again reiterated in *Delassus v. United States*, 34 U.S. (9 Pet.) 117, 133 (1835).

47. *Wilkinson v. Leland*, 27 U.S. (2 Pet.) 627, 657 (1829).

48. *Lessee of Grignon v. Astor*, 43 U.S. (2 How.) 319, 343 (1844).

49. *Maryland v. Baltimore & Ohio R.R. Co.*, 44 U.S. (3 How.) 534, 542 (1845).

50. *Rundle v. Delaware & Raritan Canal Co.*, 55 U.S. (14 How.) 80, 99 (1852).

51. *Northern Indiana R.R. Co. v. Michigan Central R.R. Co.*, 56 U.S. (15 How.) 233, 251 (1853).

52. *Philadelphia, Wilmington, and Baltimore R.R. Co. v. Quigley*, 62 U.S. (21 How.) 202, 219 (1859).

53. *Dodge v. Woolsey*, 59 U.S. (18 How.) 331, 356, 375 (1856).

54. *Ward v. Peck*, 59 U.S. (18 How.) 267, 271 (1855).

55. *Jackson v. Steamboat Magnolia*, 61 U.S. (20 How.) 280, 307 (1858).

56. *Mitchell v. Harmony*, 54 U.S. (13 How.) 115, 138, 147 (1851).

57. *Waring v. Clarke*, 46 U.S. (5 How.) 441, 493 (1847).

58. *Luther v. Borden*, 48 U.S. (7 How.) 1, 66–67, 69, 85 (1849).

59. *Holmes v. Jennison*, 39 U.S. (14 Pet.) 540, 564, 575–76, 579 (1840). Some of the dissenters worried about the ability of the Court to enforce its decision, but the Supreme Court of Vermont deferred to the judgment of the justices.

60. *Ex parte Wells*, 59 U.S. (18 How.) 307, 319 (1856).

61. *Lytle v. Arkansas*, 50 U.S. (9 How.) 314, 333–34 (1850).

62. *Wilson v. Rousseau*, 45 U.S. (4 How.) 646, 692 (1846).

63. *Charles River Bridge v. Warren Bridge*, 36 U.S. (11 Pet.) 420 (1837).

64. The full episode and its context are well presented in Carl B. Swisher, *The Taney Period, 1836–64*, vol. 5 of *The Oliver Wendell Holmes Devise History of the Supreme Court of the United States* (New York: Macmillan Publishing Co., 1974), 158–171.

65. *Kendall v. United States ex rel. Stokes*, 37 U.S. (12 Pet.) 524, 586 (1838).

66. Ibid., 613, 620.

67. For instance, see *Scott v. Ben*, 10 U.S. (6 Cranch) 1, 7 (1810), in which Marshall acknowledges that the case presents a contest between liberty and property.

68. G. Edward White, *The Marshall Court and Cultural Change, 1815–35*, vols. 3–4 of *The Oliver Wendell Holmes Devise History of the Supreme Court of the United States* (New York: Macmillan Publishing Co., 1988), 739–40, is critical of the Marshall Court's handling of cases involving Native Americans and African Americans, saying that a willingness to read natural law principles into the law did not extend to racial minorities.

69. *Dred Scott v. Sandford*, 60 U.S. (19 How.) 393 (1857).

70. The cases divide as follows: for emancipation—*Le Grand v. Darnall*, 27 U.S. (2 Pet.) 664 (1829), *Fenwick v. Chapman*, 34 U.S. (9 Pet.) 461 (1835), *Wallingsford v. Allen*, 35 U.S. (10 Pet.) 583, 592 (1836), and *Adams v. Roberts*, 43 U.S. (2 How.) 486, 495 (1844); for retrial—*Lee v. Lee*, 33 U.S. (8 Pet.) 44 (1834), and *Vigel v. Naylor*, 65 U.S. (24 How.) 175 (1861); and against emancipation—*Scott v. London*, 7 U.S. (3 Cranch) 324 (1806), *Scott v. Ben*, 10 U.S. (6 Cranch) 1 (1810), *Wood v. Davis*, 11 U.S. (7 Cranch) 271 (1812), *Queen v. Hepburn*, 11 U.S. (7 Cranch) 290, 295 (1813), *Henry v. Ball*, 14 U.S. (1 Wheat.) 1 (1816), *Davis v. Wood*, 14 U.S. (1 Wheat.) 6 (1816), *Mason v. Matilda*, 25 U.S. (12 Wheat.) 590 (1827), and *Miller v. Herbert*, 46 U.S. (5 How.) 72 (1847).

71. *Queen v. Hepburn*, 11 U.S. (7 Cranch) 290, 298–99 (1813).

72. *Wood v. Davis*, 11 U.S. (7 Cranch) 271 (1812).

73. For instance, see *Adams v. Roberts*, 43 U.S. (2 How.) 486 (1844), and *Vigel v. Naylor*, 65 U.S. (24 How.) 175 (1861).

74. *Le Grand v. Darnall*, 27 U.S. (2 Pet.) 664 (1829).

75. *Wallingsford v. Allen*, 35 U.S. (10 Pet.) 583, 592 (1836).

76. *The Antelope*, 23 U.S. (10 Wheat.) 66, 114, 120, 121 (1825).

77. *United States v. The Schooner Amistad*, 40 U.S. (15 Pet.) 518, 595, 596 (1841).

78. *Groves v. Slaughter*, 40 U.S. (15 Pet.) 449, 508 (1841).

79. Ibid., 516–17.

80. Such authority rested upon Article IV, Section 2 of the Constitution: "No Person held to Service or Labour in one State, under the Laws thereof, escaping into another, shall, in Consequence of any Law or Regulation therein, be discharged from such Service or Labour, but shall be delivered up on Claim of the Party to whom such Service or Labour may be due."

81. Quoted in Russel B. Nye, *William Lloyd Garrison and the Humanitarian Reformers* (Boston: Little, Brown & Co., 1955), 143.

82. *Somerset v. Stewart*, 98 Eng. Rep. 499 (King's Bench, 1772).

83. *Prigg v. Pennsylvania*, 41 U.S. (16 Pet.) 539, 610, 619, 623 (1842).

84. Ibid., 628, 629.

85. Ibid., 660.

86. Ibid., 671.

87. For a perceptive discussion of the dangers inherent in overriding the words of the law by a discovery of intent dealing with *Prigg v. Pennsylvania* and *Dred Scott v. Sandford* as examples, see James B. White, *Justice as Translation: An Essay in Cultural and Legal Criticism* (Chicago: University of Chicago Press, 1990), 113–40.

88. *Jones v. Van Zandt*, 46 U.S. (5 How.) 215, 230, 231 (1847).

89. *Jones v. Van Zandt*, 13 F. Cas. 1047, 1048–49 (C.C.D. Ohio 1843) (No. 7,502).

90. *Moore v. Illinois*, 55 U.S. (14 How.) 13, 17, 18 (1852).

91. Ibid., 21, 22.

92. *Menard v. Aspasia*, 30 U.S. (5 Pet.) 505, 512 (1831).

93. Ibid., 510–17.

94. *Strader v. Graham*, 51 U.S. (10 How.) 82 (1851).

95. To view the decision in a wide-ranging historical context, see Don E. Fehrenbacher, *The Dred Scott Case: Its Significance in Law and Politics* (New York: Oxford University Press, 1978). See also Walter Ehrlich, *They Have No Rights: Dred Scott's Struggle for Freedom* (Westport, Conn.: Greenwood Press, 1979).

96. *Dred Scott v. Sandford*, 60 U.S. (19 How.) 393, 454–55 (1857).

97. Ibid., 407, 416.

98. This, for instance, is the view expressed in Kenneth L. Karst, *Belonging to America: Equal Citizenship and the Constitution* (New Haven, Conn.: Yale University Press, 1989).

99. *Dred Scott v. Sandford*, 60 U.S. (19 How.) 393, 538, 550, (1857).

100. Ibid., 582, 575, 574.

101. The reasons for Curtis's resignation go beyond the *Dred Scott* decision, but it certainly was a contributing factor.

102. This was the holding of a famous English decision by Lord Mansfield in *Somerset v. Stewart*, 98 Eng. Rep. 499 (King's Bench, 1772), that had considerable weight in American law.

103. A good treatment of the episode and its aftermath can be found in Carl B. Swisher, *The Taney Period, 1836–64*, vol. 5 of *The Oliver Wendell Holmes Devise History of the Supreme Court of the United States* (New York: Macmillan Publishing Co., 1974), 653–75.

104. *Ableman v. Booth*, 62 U.S. (21 How.) 506, 517 (1859).

105. Ibid., 518, 521, 525 (1859).

106. *Piqua Branch of the State Bank of Ohio v. Knoop*, 57 U.S. (16 How.) 369, 392 (1853).

107. *Dodge v. Woolsey*, 59 U.S. (18 How.) 331, 357, 358 (1856).

CHAPTER FOUR

1. The two rival views of union are summarized well in James H. Kettner, *The Development of American Citizenship, 1608–1870* (Chapel Hill: University of North Carolina Press, 1978), 334–40.

2. For a useful treatment of these years and events, see James M. McPherson, *Ordeal by Fire: Volume I: The Coming of the War*, 2d ed. (New York: McGraw-Hill, Inc., 1993).

3. Harold Hyman, *A More Perfect Union: The Impact of the Civil War and Reconstruction on the Constitution* (New York: Alfred A. Knopf, 1973), 57.

4. See, for instance, ibid., 50–64, 124–40; and Mark E. Neely Jr., *The Fate of Liberty: Abraham Lincoln and Civil Liberties* (New York: Oxford University Press, 1991).

5. *Ex parte Merryman*, 17 F. Cas. 144 (C.C.D. Md. 1861) (No. 9487).

6. The episode is recounted in Carl B. Swisher, *The Taney Period, 1836–64*, vol. 5 of *The Oliver Wendell Holmes Devise History of the Supreme Court of the United States* (New York: Macmillan Publishing Co., 1974), 844–54.

7. Ibid., 851.

8. Speech in Independence Hall, Philadelphia, February 22, 1861, in *The Collected Works of Abraham Lincoln*, 8 vols., ed. Roy P. Basler (New Brunswick, N.J.: Rutgers University Press, 1953–55), 4:236.

9. Lincoln asserted that the authors of the Declaration "meant simply to declare the *right*,

so that the *enforcement* of it might follow as fast as circumstances should permit. They meant to set up a standard maxim for free society, which should be familiar to all, and revered by all; constantly looked to, constantly labored for, and even though never perfectly attained, constantly approximated, and thereby constantly spreading and deepening its influence, and augmenting the happiness and value of life to all people of all colors everywhere." Abraham Lincoln, Speech at Springfield, Illinois, June 26, 1857, in ibid., 2:406.

10. Abraham Lincoln, Gettysburg Address, in ibid., 7:23.

11. See Garry Wills, *Lincoln at Gettysburg: The Words That Remade America* (New York: Simon & Schuster, 1992), 145–47.

12. Abraham Lincoln, Second Inaugural Address, March 4, 1865, in *The Collected Works of Abraham Lincoln*, 8 vols., ed. Roy P. Basler (New Brunswick: Rutgers University Press, 1953–55), 8:333.

13. See Richard V. Pierard & Robert D. Linder, *Civil Religion & the Presidency* (Grand Rapids: Academie Books, Zondervan Publishing House, 1988), 87–113.

14. Harold M. Hyman and William M. Wiecek, *Equal Justice under Law: Constitutional Development, 1835–1875* (New York: Harper & Row, 1982), 234.

15. For a good treatment of Reconstruction, see Eric Foner, *Reconstruction: America's Unfinished Revolution* (New York: Harper & Row, 1988).

16. For a treatment of citizenship prior to the Civil War, see James H. Kettner, *Development of American Citizenship, 1608–1870* (Chapel Hill: University of North Carolina Press, 1978).

17. Quoted in Harold M. Hyman and William M. Wiecek, *Equal Justice under Law: Constitutional Development, 1835–1875* (New York: Harper & Row, 1982), 400. The authors make a forceful argument for the theoretical sufficiency of the Thirteenth Amendment as a basis for ensuring equal rights. The failure they see as one of will. See ibid., 386–438.

18. For instance, see *Yick Wo v. Hopkins*, 118 U.S. 356, 370 (1886).

19. U.S. Constitution, Article IV, Section 2.

20. For an introduction to the literature on this question, see Raoul Berger, *Government by Judiciary: The Transformation of the Fourteenth Amendment* (Cambridge: Harvard University Press, 1977) [against incorporation], and Michael K. Curtis, *No State Shall Abridge: The Fourteenth Amendment and the Bill of Rights* (Durham, N.C.: Duke University Press, 1986) [against Berger and for incorporation].

21. "Any recognition of substantive content in a constitutional guarantee of equality places on the courts a weighty burden of judgment." Kenneth L. Karst, *Belonging to America: Equal Citizenship and the Constitution* (New Haven: Yale University Press, 1989): 237.

22. Harold M. Hyman and William M. Wiecek, *Equal Justice under Law: Constitutional Development, 1835–1875* (New York: Harper & Row, 1982), 241–42, 262–63.

23. Charles Sumner to Abraham Lincoln, October 12, 1864, quoted in Stanley I. Kutler, *Judicial Power and Reconstruction Politics* (Chicago: University of Chicago Press, 1968), 21.

24. See ibid., 48–63.

25. William M. Wiecek, "The Reconstruction of Federal Judicial Power," *American Journal of Legal History* 13 (1969): 334.

26. Felix Frankfurter and James M. Landis, *The Business of the Supreme Court: A Study in the Federal Judicial System* (New York: Macmillan Co., 1928), 65.

27. Quoted in William M. Wiecek, "The Reconstruction of Federal Judicial Power," *American Journal of Legal History* 13 (1969): 344.

28. Felix Frankfurter and James M. Landis, *The Business of the Supreme Court: A Study in the Federal Judicial System* (New York: Macmillan Co., 1928), 96–102, 255–94.

29. *Prize Cases*, 67 U.S. (2 Black) 635 (1863).

30. *Ex parte Vallandigham*, 68 U.S. (1 Wall.) 243 (1864).

31. *Ex parte Milligan*, 71 U.S. (4 Wall.) 2, 109, 119, 120–21 (1866).

32. Ibid., 121, 123, 124, 126, 127.

33. During the war, the Democrats, often in contending for office, rarely passed up the opportunity to attack the Republican administration's invasion of civil rights. For instance, see Mark E. Neely Jr., *The Fate of Liberty: Abraham Lincoln and Civil Liberties* (New York: Oxford University Press, 1991), 185–209.

34. *Ex parte Milligan*, 71 U.S. (4 Wall.) 2, 142 (1866).

35. *Ex parte McCardle*, 73 U.S. (6 Wall.) 318 (1868).

36. *Ex parte McCardle*, 74 U.S. (7 Wall.) 506, 514 (1869).

37. *Ex parte Yerger*, 75 U.S. (8 Wall.) 85 (1869).

38. On the Yerger case, see Charles Fairman, *Reconstruction and Reunion, 1864–88: Part I*, vol. 6 of *The Oliver Wendell Holmes Devise History of the Supreme Court of the United States* (New York: Macmillan Publishing Co., 1971), 558–91.

39. *Cummings v. Missouri*, 71 U.S. (4 Wall.) 277 (1867).

40. *Ex parte Garland*, 71 U.S. (4 Wall.) 333 (1867).

41. *Cummings v. Missouri*, 71 U.S. (4 Wall.) 277, 318, 319, 321–22 (1867).

42. Ibid., 327, 328, 330, 331.

43. *Ex parte Garland*, 71 U.S. (4 Wall.) 333, 380–81 (1867).

44. *Mississippi v. Johnson*, 71 U.S. (4 Wall.) 475 (1867); and *Georgia v. Stanton*, 73 U.S. (6 Wall.) 50 (1868).

45. *Texas v. White*, 74 U.S. (7 Wall.) 700, 725 (1869).

46. The evidence on Field's view can be found in Charles Fairman, *Reconstruction and Reunion, 1864–88: Part I*, vol. 6 of *The Oliver Wendell Holmes Devise History of the Supreme Court of the United States* (New York: Macmillan Publishing Co., 1971), 467–80.

47. *Bean v. Beckwith*, 85 U.S. (18 Wall.) 510 (1874).

48. *Beckwith v. Bean*, 98 U.S. 266, 294, 297 (1879).

49. For a discussion of the rise and evolution of the jeremiad in American culture, see Sacvan Bercovitch, *The American Jeremiad* (Madison: University of Wisconsin Press, 1978).

50. *Blyew v. United States*, 80 U.S. (13 Wall.) 581, 601 (1872).

51. *Robertson v. Baldwin*, 165 U.S. 275, 303 (1897).

52. *Clyatt v. United States*, 197 U.S. 207 (1905).

53. *Bailey v. Alabama*, 219 U.S. 219, 245 (1911).

54. For the Court's delineation of the respective spheres of the two amendments, see *Civil Rights Cases*, 109 U.S. 3 (1883).

55. *Slaughter-House Cases*, 83 U.S. (16 Wall.) 36, 71, 82 (1873). This significant decision will be covered in the next chapter.

56. *United States v. Cruikshank*, 92 U.S. 542, 554 (1876).

57. *United States v. Harris*, 106 U.S. 629 (1883).

58. *Civil Rights Cases*, 109 U.S. 3, 22, 24, 25 (1883).

59. Harlan's dissents, so many of which would later be vindicated by majority opinions of

the Court in the mid-years of the twentieth century, have been responsible for his rising reputation in the last generation or so. For instance, his biographer ranks Harlan as "perhaps the great judge of the whole period following Marshall's death until at least the accession of Justice Holmes." Loren P. Beth, *John Marshall Harlan: The Last Whig Justice* (Lexington: University Press of Kentucky, 1992), 271. For further analysis of Harlan's thought and how his advanced views on civil rights and civil liberties could be placed within the tradition of an equalitarian republicanism, see Linda C. A. Przybyszewski, "The Republic According to John Marshall Harlan: Race, Republicanism, and Citizenship" (Ph. D. diss., Stanford University, 1989 [Ann Arbor, Mich.: University Microfilms, 1993]).

60. *Civil Rights Cases*, 109 U.S. 3, 26, 35, 48 (1883).
61. Ibid., 50, 53, 56.
62. Ibid., 58–59, 61.
63. *Hall v. De Cuir*, 95 U.S. 485 (1878).
64. *Louisville, New Orleans & Texas Ry. v. Mississippi*, 133 U.S. 587 (1890).
65. For a full treatment of the case, see Charles A. Lofgren, *The Plessy Case: A Legal-Historical Perspective* (New York: Oxford University Press, 1987).
66. *Plessy v. Ferguson*, 163 U.S. 537, 543, 544, 550, 551–52 (1896).
67. Ibid., 555, 559.
68. Ibid., 560, 562, 563–64.
69. *Brown v. Board of Education*, 347 U.S. 483 (1954).
70. *Hodges v. United States*, 203 U.S. 1, 16, 37 (1906).
71. *Berea College v. Kentucky*, 211 U.S. 45, 67, 68, 69 (1908).
72. The story of the NAACP's role in this litigation is traced in Roger L. Rice, "Residential Segregation by Law, 1910–1917," *Journal of Southern History* 34 (May 1968): 179–99.
73. *McCabe v. Atchison, Topeka & Santa Fe Ry.*, 235 U.S. 151, 161 (1914).
74. *United States v. Mosley*, 238 U.S. 383 (1915).
75. *Buchanan v. Warley*, 245 U.S. 60, 81 (1917). See Roger L. Rice, "Residential Segregation by Law, 1910–1917," *Journal of Southern History* 34 (May 1968): 179–99.
76. *Strauder v. West Virginia*, 100 U.S. 303 (1880).
77. Ibid., 306, 307–8.
78. *Virginia v. Rives*, 100 U.S. 313 (1880).
79. For instance, in *Brownfield v. South Carolina*, 189 U.S. 426 (1903), blacks outnumbered whites by four to one in the county in which the trial was held, and although the Court said that the case raised grave questions, it held that no evidence was provided to support the bare assertion of discrimination.
80. *Ex parte Virginia*, 100 U.S. 339, 344–45 (1880).
81. *Yick Wo v. Hopkins*, 118 U.S. 356, 370, 373, 374 (1886).
82. See Charles J. McClain, *In Search of Equality: The Chinese Struggle against Discrimination in Nineteenth-Century America* (Berkeley: University of California Press, 1994).
83. *Baldwin v. Franks*, 120 U.S. 678 (1887).
84. *Chinese Exclusion Case*, 130 U.S. 581, 609 (1889).
85. *Wong Wing v. United States*, 163 U.S. 228, 237 (1896).
86. *Fong Yue Ting v. United States*, 149 U.S. 698, 764, 760 (1893).
87. For speculation on why this was so, see Michael J. Brodhead, *David J. Brewer: The Life of a Supreme Court Justice, 1837–1910* (Carbondale: Southern Illinois University Press, 1994), 107–8.

88. *United States v. Sing Tuck*, 194 U.S. 161, 181, 182 (1904).
89. A brief summary of this history can be found in *United States v. Wong Kim Ark*, 169 U.S. 649, 701–2 (1898).
90. *Elk v. Wilkins*, 112 U.S. 94, 106 (1884).
91. Ibid., 114, 120, 122.
92. For a discussion of the Court's response to Native American claims, see John E. Semonche, *Charting the Future: The Supreme Court Responds to a Changing Society* (Westport, Conn.: Greenwood Press, 1978), 81–2, 109, 185–86, 219, 270.
93. For a brief survey of the citizenship issue, see John R. Wunder, *"Retained by The People": A History of American Indians and the Bill of Rights* (New York: Oxford University Press, 1994), 45-51.
94. *United States v. Wong Kim Ark*, 169 U.S. 649, 674, 688, 694, 701, 703, 704 (1898).
95. This was the first of what would eventually become four amendments placing restrictions upon states in making the franchise available to its citizens. The other three are the Nineteenth, barring sex as a qualification; the Twenty-fourth, outlawing the poll tax in federal elections; and the Twenty-sixth, imposing eighteen as the minimum voting age.
96. *United States v. Reese*, 92 U.S. 214, 218 (1876).
97. Ibid., 253.
98. *Habeas Corpus Cases*, 100 U.S. 371, 394 (1880).
99. *Neal v. Delaware*, 103 U.S. 370 (1881).
100. *Ex parte Yarbrough*, 110 U.S. 651, 658, 667 (1884).
101. In *Williams v. Mississippi*, 170 U.S. 213 (1898), the Court saw no impermissible discrimination in the use of literacy tests and poll taxes.
102. *Guinn v. United States*, 238 U.S. 347 (1915); and *Meyers v. Anderson*, 238 U.S. 368 (1915).
103. *Guinn v. United States*, 238 U.S. 347, 360 (1915).

CHAPTER FIVE

1. *Leffingwell v. Warren*, 67 U.S. (2 Black) 599, 603 (1862).
2. *Gelpcke v. Dubuque*, 68 U.S. (1 Wall.) 175, 206–7 (1864).
3. *United States v. Muscatine*, 75 U.S. (8 Wall.) 575, 581, 582 (1869).
4. *Poindexter v. Greenhow*, 114 U.S. 270, 306 (1885).
5. Ibid., 290, 291.
6. Ibid., 292.
7. This description of the surrounding circumstances of the case is drawn from Charles Fairman, *Reconstruction and Reunion, 1864–88:* Part II, vol. 7 of *The Oliver Wendell Holmes Devise History of the Supreme Court of the United States* (New York: Macmillan Publishing Co., 1987), 710–12.
8. *United States v. Lee*, 106 U.S. 196, 208–9, 218 (1882).
9. Ibid., 220, 223.
10. *Chisholm v. Georgia*, 2 U.S. (2 Dall.) 440 (1793).
11. *Slaughter-House Cases*, 83 U.S. (16 Wall.) 36, 72 (1873).
12. Ibid., 77, 78.
13. Ibid., 87, 93.
14. Ibid., 96, 109–10, 111.

15. Ibid., 113–14, 119, 116, 122, 123.
16. Ibid., 125, 129.
17. Regarding the Southern states, see Suzanne D. Lebsock, "Radical Reconstruction and the Property Rights of Southern Women," *Journal of Southern History* 43 (May 1977): 195–216.
18. *Bradwell v. Illinois*, 83 U.S. (16 Wall.) 130, 141 (1873).
19. *Ex parte Lockwood*, 154 U.S. 116 (1894).
20. *Minor v. Happersett*, 88 U.S. (21 Wall.) 162 (1875).
21. *Bartemeyer v. Iowa*, 85 U.S. (18 Wall.) 129, 136 (1874).
22. Ibid., 139.
23. Ibid., 140.
24. *Munn v. Illinois*, 94 U.S. 113, 130, 134, 140 (1877).
25. *Davidson v. New Orleans*, 96 U.S. 97, 104 (1878).
26. *Stone v. Farmers Loan & Trust Co.*, 116 U.S. 307, 331 (1886).
27. *Santa Clara County v. Southern Pacific R.R.*, 118 U.S. 394 (1886).
28. See *Munn v. Illinois*, 94 U.S. 113 (1877).
29. As an illustration, see *Adams Express Co. v. Ohio State Auditor*, 166 U.S. 185, 225 (1897).
30. *Chicago, Milwaukee & St. Paul Ry. v. Minnesota*, 134 U.S. 418, 458 (1890).
31. *Smyth v. Ames*, 169 U.S. 466 (1898).
32. *Powell v. Pennsylvania*, 127 U.S. 678, 691, 692 (1888).
33. *Budd v. New York*, 143 U.S. 517, 551 (1892).
34. *Gulf, Colorado & Santa Fe Ry. v. Ellis*, 165 U.S. 150, 160 (1897).
35. See John E. Semonche, *Charting the Future: The Supreme Court Responds to a Changing Society, 1890–1920* (Westport: Greenwood Press, 1978).
36. The resolution of the matter took two decisions of the Court; the first time the justices evenly divided on a number of questions. The comments that follow are drawn from both decisions.
37. The oral arguments are more fully reported in *United States Supreme Court Reports: Lawyers' Edition*. The quoted words can be found in *Pollock v. Farmers' Loan & Trust Co.*, 39 L. Ed. 759, 786 (1895).
38. *Pollock v. Farmers' Loan & Trust Co.*, 157 U.S. 429, 583 (1895).
39. Ibid., 652.
40. *Pollock v. Farmers' Loan & Trust Co.*, 158 U.S. 601, 664–65, 685 (1895).
41. Ibid., 695.
42. *United States v. E. C. Knight Co.*, 156 U.S. 1 (1895); and *In re Debs*, 158 U.S. 564 (1895).
43. Bryan grew bolder in contending with recent Supreme Court decisions as the campaign progressed. His most thorough airing of his views on this subject, in response to continued Republican criticism, came in speeches in Brooklyn and in Detroit as printed in William J. Bryan, *The First Battle: A Story of the Campaign of 1896* (Chicago: W. B. Conkey Co., 1896), 479–82, 563–65.
44. See John E. Semonche, *Charting the Future: The Supreme Court Responds to a Changing Society, 1890–1920* (Westport: Greenwood Press, 1978).
45. Ibid.
46. *Welton v. Missouri*, 91 U.S. 275, 282 (1876).
47. *Allgeyer v. Louisiana*, 165 U.S. 578, 589 (1897).
48. *Holden v. Hardy*, 169 U.S. 366, 391 (1898).

49. *Lochner v. New York*, 198 U.S. 45, 61 (1905).

50. This prevailing view has been challenged. For instance, see Michael Les Benedict, "Laisser-Faire and Liberty: A Re-Evaluation of the Meaning and Origins of Laisser-Faire Constitutionalism," *Law and History Review* 3 (Fall 1985): 293–331; and Howard Gillman, *The Constitution Besieged: The Rise and Demise of Lochner Era Police Powers Jurisprudence* (Durham: Duke University Press, 1993), 199. Gillman says that "the story of the *Lochner* era is not about how reactionary justices . . . exploit[ed] legal materials in order to protect or promote their class biases. Rather, the *Lochner* era is the story of how . . . an ideology that was fairly . . . inclusive around the time of the founding became more and more exclusive as . . . capitalistic forms progressed." See also Paul Kens, *Judicial Power and Reform Politics: The Anatomy of Lochner v. New York* (Lawrence: University Press of Kansas, 1990).

51. *Lochner v. New York*, 198 U.S. 45, 76.

52. For a useful analysis of Holmes's views in the first dozen years of his service on the Court, see G. Edward White, *Justice Oliver Wendell Holmes: Law and the Inner Self* (New York: Oxford University Press, 1993), 322–53.

53. *Muller v. Oregon*, 208 U.S. 412 (1908); and *Bunting v. Oregon*, 243 U.S. 426 (1917).

54. *Stettler v. O'Hara*, 243 U.S. 629 (1917). The Court did uphold a congressional act passed to head off a railroad strike that had the effect of fixing wages in interstate commerce. *Wilson v. New*, 243 U.S. 332 (1917).

55. The cases can be traced in John E. Semonche, *Charting the Future: The Supreme Court Responds to a Changing Society, 1890–1920* (Westport, Conn.: Greenwood Press, 1978), 295–97, 324–28, 369–73.

56. For instance, see *Missouri Pacific Ry. v. Mackey*, 127 U.S. 205; and *Minneapolis & St. Louis Ry. v. Herrick*, 127 U.S. 210 (1888).

57. *Knoxville Iron Co. v. Harbison*, 183 U.S. 13 (1901).

58. *German Alliance Insurance Co. v. Lewis*, 233 U.S. 389 (1914).

59. *Adair v. United States*, 208 U.S. 161, 180 (1908).

60. Ibid., 186, 190.

61. John E. Semonche, *Charting the Future: The Supreme Court Responds to a Changing Society, 1890–1920* (Westport: Greenwood Press, 1978), 430–31.

62. *Coppage v. Kansas*, 236 U.S. 1, 40, 42 (1915).

63. *Adams v. Tanner*, 244 U.S. 590, 597 (1917).

64. *Truax v. Raich*, 239 U.S. 33, 41 (1915).

65. *United States v. Cruikshank*, 92 U.S. 542 (1876); and *Walker v. Sauvinet*, 92 U.S. 90 (1876).

66. *In re Kemmler*, 136 U.S. 436 (1890).

67. *Hurtado v. California*, 110 U.S. 516, 533 (1884), quoting *Walker v. Sauvinet*, 92 U.S. 90, 93 (1876). For a treatment of *Hurtado* and some subsequent cases, see Richard C. Cortner, *The Supreme Court and the Second Bill of Rights: The Fourteenth Amendment and the Nationalization of Civil Liberties* (Madison: University of Wisconsin Press, 1981), 12–37.

68. *Hurtado v. California*, 110 U.S. 516, 541, 547, 557–58 (1884).

69. *Maxwell v. Dow*, 176 U.S. 581, 608, 609, 614 (1900).

70. Ibid., 615, 616.

71. Ibid., 617.

72. *Patterson v. Colorado*, 205 U.S. 454, 465 (1907).

73. *Twining v. New Jersey*, 211 U.S. 78, 113 (1908).

74. Ibid., 123.
75. *Chicago, Burlington & Quincy R.R. v. Chicago*, 166 U.S. 226 (1897). In the decision the Court on the eminent domain protection implicitly overruled *Davidson v. New Orleans*, 96 U.S. 97 (1878).
76. *O'Neil v. Vermont*, 144 U.S. 323, 371 (1892).
77. For a useful discussion of the position and its rivals, see Henry J. Abraham and Barbara A. Perry, *Freedom & the Court: Civil Rights & Liberties in the United States*, 7th ed. (New York: Oxford University Press, 1998), 31–93.
78. *Ex parte Lange*, 85 U.S. (18 Wall.), 163, 178 (1874).
79. *Kring v. Missouri*, 107 U.S. 221, 224, 229, 232, 233–34 (1883).
80. *Watson v. Jones*, 80 U.S. (13 Wall.) 679, 728 (1872).
81. To a Mormon's claim that the free exercise of religion insulated him from prosecution for polygamy, the Court relied on the words of Thomas Jefferson—that man "has no natural right in opposition to his social duties"—to establish the original understanding of the free exercise clause. "Congress," the Court continued, "was deprived of all legislative power over mere opinion, but was left free to reach actions which were in violation of social duties or subversive of good order." Then, rejecting the claim that personal religious conviction provides an exception to the general obligations of the law, the Court said otherwise personal religious belief would make the individual "superior to the law of the land, and in effect . . . permit every citizen to become a law unto himself." *Reynolds v. United States*, 98 U.S. 145, 164, 167 (1879).
82. *Church of the Holy Trinity v. United States*, 143 U.S. 457, 470 (1892).
83. *Logan v. United States*, 144 U.S. 263, 295 (1892).
84. This story is told in greater detail in John E. Semonche, *Charting the Future: The Supreme Court Responds to a Changing Society, 1890–1920* (Westport: Greenwood Press, 1978), 51–56.
85. *Boyd v. United States*, 142 U.S. 450, 458 (1892).
86. *Hicks v. United States*, 150 U.S. 442, 452 (1893).
87. For instance, see Brewer's dissenting opinion in *Allen v. United States*, 150 U.S. 551, 562–66 (1893).
88. *Hickory v. United States*, 160 U.S. 408, 425 (1896).
89. *Starr v. United States*, 153 U.S. 614, 628 (1894).
90. Specifically, regarding the death penalty, the Court in *Furman v. Georgia*, 408 U.S. 238 (1972), ruled 5–4 that capital punishment was so arbitrarily imposed by the states that it could not survive the Eighth Amendment's ban on cruel and unusual punishment made binding by the Fourteenth Amendment. States responded by passing one of two types of law: the first made capital punishment mandatory for conviction of certain crimes; and the second split the trial into two parts, leaving for the post conviction portion the weighing of specified factors in mitigation and aggravation that could then lead to the imposition of the death sentence. The Court invalidated the first type of law in *Woodson v. North Carolina*, 428 U.S. 280 (1976) but upheld the second in *Gregg v. Georgia*, 428 U.S. 153 (1976). Only Justices William J. Brennan Jr. and Thurgood Marshall were willing to rule that all capital punishment was unconstitutional.
91. *Ex parte Jackson*, 96 U.S. 727, 733 (1878).
92. *Boyd v. United States*, 116 U.S. 616, 630, 631–32 (1886).
93. Ibid., 635.
94. *Union Pacific Ry. v. Botsford*, 141 U.S. 250, 259, 251 (1891). The first legal article,

which argued for the recognition of such a right, is Louis D. Brandeis and Samuel D. Warren, "The Right to Privacy," *Harvard Law Review* 4 (December 1890): 193–220.

95. *Hale v. Henkel*, 201 U.S. 43 (1906). This early decision was confirmed in *Silverthorne Lumber Co. v. United States*, 251 U.S. 385 (1920), in which the Court said that to allow the government's action would violate the corporate officers' rights.

96. For a discussion of the evolution of the exclusionary rule and its early relationship to the property right, see James B. White, *Justice as Translation: An Essay in Cultural and Legal Criticism* (Chicago: University of Chicago Press, 1990), 203–14.

97. *Weeks v. United States*, 232 U.S. 383, 393, 394 (1914). The Court continued to give effective force to the individual's protection under the Fourth Amendment, saying it should be construed broadly to prevent individuals from having their rights invaded "by imperceptible practice of courts, or by well-intentioned but mistakenly over-zealous executive officers." *Gouled v. United States*, 255 U.S. 298, 304 (1921).

98. James B. White, *Justice as Translation: An Essay in Cultural and Legal Criticism* (Chicago: University of Chicago Press, 1990), 208. Extending his discussion, he says: "More than any other single constitutional provision it stands between us and a police state, for its central premise is that police (or other governmental) conduct that interferes with a person's liberty, bodily integrity, or right to exclude others from what is hers shall be subject to judicial control." (Ibid., 177).

99. *Counselman v. Hitchcock*, 142 U.S. 547 (1892).

100. *Brown v. Walker*, 161 U.S. 591, 627 (1896). Their worries were confirmed when the Court read an immunity in the federal bankruptcy law to apply only to oral testimony and allowed a state prosecution based upon written materials supplied under command of the federal law. See *Ensign v. Pennsylvania*, 227 U.S. 592 (1913).

101. *Brown v. Walker*, 161 U.S. 591, 637 (1896).

102. *Burdick v. United States*, 236 U.S. 79 (1915).

103. For instance, when the Court concluded that an area had been incorporated into the United States, as it did in regard to Alaska, it applied the full protections of the Bill of Rights. See *Rasmussen v. United States*, 197 U.S. 516 (1905), in which the justices decided that a twelve-person jury was mandated by the requirements of the Sixth Amendment.

104. *Downes v. Bidwell*, 182 U.S. 244, 379, 380 (1901).

105. For instance, see David J. Brewer, *The Spanish War: A Prophecy or an Exception?* Address before the Liberal Club, February 16, 1899, Buffalo, N.Y. (New York: Anti-Imperialist League, n.d.); and Brewer, "Two Periods in the History of the Supreme Court," *Report of the Eighteenth Annual Meeting of the Virginia Bar Association* (1906), 144–45.

106. *Hawaii v. Mankichi*, 190 U.S. 197, 218 (1903).

107. Ibid., 247.

108. *Crowley v. United States*, 194 U.S. 461 (1904).

109. *Kepner v. United States*, 195 U.S. 100 (1904).

110. *Trono v. United States*, 199 U.S. 521, 537 (1905).

111. *Gavieres v. United States*, 220 U.S. 338 (1911); and *Diaz v. United States*, 223 U.S. 442 (1912).

112. *Weems v. United States*, 217 U.S. 349, 364, 362, 373 (1910).

113. See Jesse H. Choper, *Judicial Review and the National Political Process* (Chicago: University of Chicago Press, 1980), in which he argues that protection of individual rights provides the best justification for judicial review in American democracy.

CHAPTER SIX

1. For a useful treatment of the general subject, see Paul L. Murphy, *World War I and the Origin of Civil Liberties in the United States* (New York: Norton, 1979).
2. *Selective Draft Law Cases*, 245 U.S. 366, 390 (1918).
3. *Schenck v. United States*, 249 U.S. 47, 52 (1919).
4. *Frohwerk v. United States*, 249 U.S. 204, 208 (1919).
5. *Debs v. United States*, 249 U.S. 211 (1919).
6. For an excellent treatment of the case in its social, political, legal, and human context, see Richard Polenberg, *Fighting Faiths: The Abrams Case, the Supreme Court, and Free Speech* (New York: Viking, 1987).
7. *Abrams v. United States*, 250 U.S. 616, 628, 629, 630 (1920).
8. *Schaefer v. United States*, 251 U.S. 466, 477, 495 (1920).
9. *United States ex. rel. Milwaukee Social Democratic Publishing Co. v. Burleson*, 255 U.S. 407, 414, 423, 417, 436, 438 (1921).
10. *Pierce v. United States*, 252 U.S. 239, 273 (1920).
11. For a useful treatment of Brandeis's views on individual liberty, see Phillipa Strum, *Brandeis: Beyond Progressivism* (Lawrence: University Press of Kansas, 1993), 116–49.
12. Although a number of others, including Judge Learned Hand and Holmes's friend and correspondent Harold Laski, contributed to Holmes's education, it was the young Harvard University teacher of law, Zechariah Chafee, who, in an article and apparently in person as well, seemed to convince the justice of the social utility of a broader interpretation of the protections of the First Amendment. Richard Polenberg, *Fighting Faiths: The Abrams Case, the Supreme Court, and Free Speech* (New York: Viking, 1987), 218–28.
13. In G. Edward White, *Justice Oliver Wendell Holmes: Law and the Inner Self* (New York: Oxford University Press, 1993), 412–54, the author traces the justice's views on free speech through three discrete stages.
14. *Gilbert v. Minnesota*, 254 U.S. 325, 327, 331, 333 (1920).
15. Ibid., 337, 343.
16. See Joan Hoff, *Law, Gender, and Injustice: A Legal History of Women* (New York: New York University Press, 1991), 206–9.
17. *Muller v. Oregon*, 208 U.S. 412 (1908).
18. Sutherland had spoken publicly in favor of women's suffrage as early as 1915 and had introduced the proposal for an enfranchisement amendment in the Senate. His words in the instant case were far from being only a cloak to mask an opposition to governmental regulation of the employment relationship. See Hadley Arkes, *The Return of George Sutherland: Restoring a Jurisprudence of Natural Rights* (Princeton, N.J.: Princeton University Press, 1994), 3–14, 71–80.
19. *Adkins v. Children's Hospital*, 261 U.S. 525, 553 (1923).
20. *Bunting v. Oregon*, 243 U.S. 426 (1917).
21. For instance, less than a year after *Adkins*, Sutherland wrote for a unanimous Court in upholding a New York law prohibiting women from working in restaurants between 10 p.m. and 6 a.m. See *Radice v. New York*, 264 U.S. 292 (1924). For the modern feminist perspective on such protective legislation, see Laura A. Otten, *Women's Rights and the Law* (Westport, Conn.: Praeger, 1993), 66–74.
22. That precedent was *Lochner v. New York*, 198 U.S. 45 (1905).

23. The story of Taft's successful lobbying can be found in Alpheus Thomas Mason, *William Howard Taft: Chief Justice* (New York: Simon & Schuster, 1965), 133–37.

24. Robert Shnayerson, *The Illustrated History of the Supreme Court of the United States* (New York: Harry A. Abrams, Inc., 1986), 178.

25. For a full treatment of the evolution and provisions of the new legislation, see Felix Frankfurter and James M. Landis, *The Business of the Supreme Court: A Study in the Federal Judicial System* (New York: The Macmillan Co., 1928), 255–94.

26. For a brief treatment of these changes, see John E. Semonche, *Charting the Future: The Supreme Court Responds to a Changing Society, 1890–1920* (Westport, Conn.: Greenwood Press, 1978), 419–26.

27. The Iowa and Ohio cases are collected in *Bartels v. Iowa*, 262 U.S. 404 (1923). The written dissent by Holmes, joined by George Sutherland, is included therein.

28. *Meyer v. Nebraska*, 262 U.S. 390, 398 (1923).

29. Ibid., 399, 400, 401, 403.

30. Ibid., 401.

31. *Pierce v. Society of Sisters*, 268 U.S. 510, 534–35 (1925).

32. Henry J. Abraham, *Justices & Presidents: A Political History of Appointments to the Supreme Court*, 2d ed. (New York: Oxford University Press, 1985), 175–78.

33. *Prudential Insurance Co. v. Cheek*, 259 U.S. 530, 543 (1922).

34. *Gitlow v. New York*, 268 U.S. 652, 666, 671 (1925).

35. Ibid., 673.

36. *Whitney v. California*, 274 U.S. 357, 372 (1927).

37. Ibid., 376, 377, 378.

38. See, for instance, *New York Times Co. v. Sullivan*, 376 U.S. 254, 270 (1964).

39. Charles A. Miller, *The Supreme Court and the Uses of History*, Clarion ed. (New York: Simon & Schuster, 1972), 97–99.

40. *Fiske v. Kansas*, 274 U.S. 380 (1927).

41. *Stromberg v. California*, 283 U.S. 359, 361, 369 (1931).

42. *United States v. Schwimmer*, 279 U.S. 644, 648 (1929).

43. Liva Baker, *The Justice From Beacon Hill: The Life and Times of Oliver Wendell Holmes* (New York: HarperCollins, 1991), 621. Schwimmer wrote to Holmes to thank him for his opinion in the case, an overture that led to a later meeting.

44. *United States v. Schwimmer*, 279 U.S. 644, 649, 650, 653 (1929).

45. Ibid., 654–55.

46. As to what happened to Schwimmer, see Ronald B. Flowers and Nadia M. Lahutsky, "The Naturalization of Rosika Schwimmer," *Journal of Church and State* 32 (Spring 1990): 343–66.

47. *United States v. Macintosh*, 283 U.S. 605 (1931); and *United States v. Bland*, 283 U.S. 636 (1931).

48. *United States v. Macintosh*, 283 U.S. 605, 627, 631, 634 (1931).

49. *Hamilton v. Regents of the University of California*, 293 U.S. 245, 267 (1934).

50. *Carroll v. United States*, 267 U.S. 132, 163, 169 (1925).

51. *Olmstead v. United States*, 277 U.S. 438, 468 (1928).

52. Ibid., 470. For an illustration of Holmes's earlier views, see *Kepner v. United States*, 195 U.S. 100, 134 (1904).

53. *Olmstead v. United States*, 277 U.S. 438, 488 (1928).

54. *Weeks v. United States*, 232 U.S. 383 (1914).

55. *Olmstead v. United States*, 277 U.S. 438, 476, 478, 479 (1928).

56. Ibid., 485. As to the issue in *Olmstead*, Congress passed the Communications Act of 1934, which in one of its sections sought to proscribe wiretapping. Not until 1967, in *Berger v. New York*, did the Court formally declare that electronic surveillance came within the Fourth Amendment's purview. Of course, a properly drawn warrant could authorize the search and seizure.

57. *Boyd v. United States*, 116 U.S. 616 (1886).

58. James B. White, *Justice as Translation: An Essay in Cultural and Legal Criticism* (Chicago: University of Chicago Press, 1990), 156, 157.

59. For a full treatment of the surrounding circumstances and the case itself, see Fred W. Friendly, *Minnesota Rag* (New York: Random House, 1981).

60. *Near v. Minnesota*, 283 U.S. 697, 707, 716, 722 (1931).

61. *Grosjean v. American Press Co.*, 297 U.S. 233, 243, 248, 250 (1936).

62. *De Jonge v. Oregon*, 299 U.S. 353, 365 (1937).

63. For a full treatment of the episode, see Dan T. Carter, *Scottsboro: A Tragedy of the American South* (Baton Rouge: Louisiana State University Press, 1969).

64. *Powell v. Alabama*, 287 U.S. 45 (1932).

65. See *Johnson v. Zerbst*, 304 U.S. 458, 465 (1938); and *Walker v. Johnson*, 312 U.S. 275 (1941).

66. *Norris v. Alabama*, 294 U.S. 587. 590 (1935). The second case involving the same situation is *Patterson v. Alabama*, 294 U.S. 600 (1935).

67. *Smith v. Texas*, 311 U.S. 128, 130 (1940).

68. *McCabe v. Atchison, Topeka & Santa Fe Ry.*, 235 U.S. 151 (1914).

69. *Missouri ex rel. Gaines v. Canada*, 305 U.S. 337, 351 (1938).

70. *Hebert v. Louisiana*, 272 U.S. 312 (1926). The Court would continue to quote this formulation. For instance, see *Mooney v. Holohan*, 294 U.S. 103 (1935).

71. *Brown v. Mississippi*, 297 U.S. 278, 286 (1936).

72. Black had survived the revelation of an early association with the Ku Klux Klan and would go on to amass a notable record on the Court. For a comprehensive study of the justice's life, see Roger K. Newman, *Hugo Black: A Biography* (New York: Pantheon Books, 1994).

73. *Chambers v. Florida*, 309 U.S. 227, 237, 236, 238, 240, 241 (1940).

74. *Smith v. O'Grady*, 312 U.S. 329, 334 (1941).

75. *Herndon v. Lowry*, 301 U.S. 242, 263–64 (1937).

76. *Perry v. United States*, 294 U.S. 330, 381 (1935).

77. *Sterling v. Constantin*, 287 U.S. 378, 398 (1932).

78. *Snyder v. Massachusetts*, 291 U.S. 97, 127–28 (1934).

79. Fireside Chat of March 9, 1937, in Russell D. Buhite and David W. Levy, *FDR's Fireside Chats* (Norman: University of Oklahoma Press, 1992), 87, 89, 93, 95.

80. For a comprehensive treatment of the episode, see Leonard Baker, *Back to Back: The Duel between FDR and the Supreme Court* (New York: The Macmillan Co., 1967).

81. Burton K. Wheeler with Paul F. Healy, *Yankee from the West* (Garden City, N.Y.: Doubleday, 1962), 335.

82. Quoted in William E. Leuchtenburg, "Roosevelt's Supreme Court Packing Plan," in Harold M. Hollingsworth, comp., *Essays on the New Deal* (Austin: University of Texas Press, 1969), 84, 82.

83. Ibid., 87.

84. *National Labor Relations Board v. Jones & Laughlin Steel Corp.*, 301 U.S. 1 (1937); and *Steward Machinery Co. v. Davis*, 301 U.S. 548 (1937).

85. For a useful summary on the negative impact of FDR's move against the Court, see William E. Leuchtenburg, *The Supreme Court Reborn: The Constitutional Revolution in the Age of Roosevelt* (New York: Oxford University Press, 1995), 156–62.

86. In *United States v. Darby*, 312 U.S. 100, 123–24, the unanimous Court repudiated any reading of the Tenth Amendment that would impose limitations upon congressional power, saying that "the amendment states but a truism." In fact, the Court would so totally accept Congress's reading of the extent of its regulatory power under the commerce clause that its decision in 1995 invalidating a federal law criminalizing the possession of firearms in a school zone came as a quiet surprise to Court watchers. See *United States v. Lopez*, 115 S.Ct. 1624 (1995).

87. *Palko v. Connecticut*, 302 U.S. 319, 325, 326–27, 328 (1937).

88. Henry J. Abraham and Barbara P. Perry, *Freedom and the Court: Civil Rights and Liberties in the United States*, 7th ed. (New York: Oxford University Press, 1998), 57, n. 125.

89. *Buck v. Bell*, 274 U.S. 200, 207 (1927).

90. 211 U.S. 78 (1908).

91. *Palko v. Connecticut*, 302 U.S. 319, 325, 326 (1937).

92. *United States v. Carolene Products Co.*, 304 U.S. 144, 152, n.4 (1938).

93. See Alpheus Thomas Mason, *Harlan Fiske Stone: Pillar of the Law* (New York: The Viking Press, 1956), 511–17.

94. *Nixon v. Herndon*, 273 U.S. 536, 541 (1927).

95. *Nixon v. Condon*, 286 U.S. 73, 88, 89 (1932).

96. Ibid., 104.

97. *Grovey v. Townsend*, 295 U.S. 45 (1935).

98. The importance of the case is highlighted in Richard Claude, *The Supreme Court and the Electoral Process* (Baltimore, Md.: Johns Hopkins Press, 1970), 27–36.

99. *United States v. Classic*, 313 U.S. 299, 316 (1941).

100. ibid., 318, 319, 320, 324. stone had distinguished the Louisiana primary from the Texas one upheld earlier, but the days of the Texas exclusion were numbered. The Court dealt it a fatal blow in *Smith v. Allright*, 321 U.S. 649 (1944).

101. See Margaret A. Blanchard, *Revolutionary Sparks: Freedom of Expression in Modern America* (New York: Oxford University Press, 1992), 167–69.

102. For instance, see *Truax v. Corrigan*, 257 U.S. 312 (1921).

103. *Dorchy v. Kansas*, 272 U.S. 306 (1926).

104. *Senn v. Tile Layers Protective Union*, 301 U.S. 468, 478 (1937).

105. *Davis v. Massachusetts*, 167 U.S. 43 (1897). The Court upheld a decision made by Oliver Wendell Holmes Jr., when he was serving on the Massachusetts Supreme Judicial Court.

106. *Hague v. Committee for Industrial Organization*, 307 U.S. 496, 515 (1939).

107. *Thornhill v. Alabama*, 310 U.S. 88, 95, 100, 102, 105 (1940).

108. *American Federation of Labor v. Swing*, 312 U.S. 321, 326 (1941).

109. *Milk Wagon Drivers Union v. Meadowmoor Dairies*, 312 U.S. 287, 293, (1941).

110. Ibid., 294.

111. Ibid., 301, 319, 320.

112. *Bakery & Pastry Drivers v. Wohl*, 315 U.S. 769 (1942).

113. *Carpenters & Joiners Union v. Ritter's Cafe*, 315 U.S. 722, 728, 738 (1942).

114. In G. Edward White, *Justice Oliver Wendell Holmes: Law and the Inner Self* (New York: Oxford University Press, 1993), 355–63, the author argues that the recognition of Holmes as a "great judge" was "the conscious product of a systematic campaign of

publicity. . . . The story of Holmes' rise to 'greatness' is to an important extent the story of his friendship with Felix Frankfurter, whose own rise to prominence in the years between 1912 and 1931 bore a symbiotic relationship to the emergence of Holmes as an eminent judge." (Ibid., 356).

115. For a comprehensive history of the organization's commitment to the struggle, see Samuel Walker, *In Defense of American Liberties: A History of the ACLU* (New York: Oxford University Press, 1990).

116. William S. McAninch, "A Catalyst for the Evolution of Constitutional Law: Jehovah's Witnesses in the Supreme Court," *Cincinnati Law Review* 55 (1987): 997–1077.

117. *Lovell v. Griffin*, 303 U.S. 444, 452 (1938).

118. *Schneider v. Irvington*, 308 U.S. 147, 161 (1939).

119. *Cantwell v. Connecticut*, 310 U.S. 296, 304, 307, 310 (1940).

120. Ibid., 310.

121. Ibid., 309–10.

122. *Chaplinsky v. New Hampshire*, 315 U.S. 568 (1942).

123. *Patterson v. Colorado*, 205 U.S. 454 (1907); and *Toledo Newspaper Co. v. United States*, 247 U.S. 402 (1918).

124. *Bridges v. California*, 314 U.S. 252, 265, 263 (1941).

125. Ibid., 270–71.

126. For how the justices differed during their respective tenures on the Court, see James F. Simon, *The Antagonists: Hugo Black, Felix Frankfurter and Civil Liberties in Modern America* (New York: Simon & Schuster, 1989).

127. For a treatment of how FDR's appointees, while agreeing on the existence of broad congressional power under the Constitution, differed in other matters, see Robert Harrison, "The Breakup of the Roosevelt Supreme Court: The Contribution of History and Biography," *Law and History Review* 2 (Spring 1984): 165–221.

128. *Baldwin v. Seelig*, 294 U.S. 511, 523 (1935).

129. *Edwards v. California*, 314 U.S. 160, 173, 174, 175, 176, 177 (1941). The old precedent to which the Court alluded is *New York v. Miln*, 36 U.S. (11 Peters) 102 (1837).

130. *Edwards v. California*, 314 U.S. 160, 181 (1941).

131. Ibid., 182, 184, 185.

CHAPTER SEVEN

1. For the defendant's recollections of this episode and a subsequent one, see William Schneiderman, *Dissent on Trial: The Story of a Political Life* (Minneapolis: MEP Publications, 1983).

2. During his limited time of service on the Court (1940–1949), Frank Murphy was the most forceful defender of individual rights and the American tradition of tolerating diversity. In the 1920s he had been a trial judge in a Michigan recorder's court, but most of his life had been spent in politics, as he moved from being mayor of Detroit, to governor of Michigan, to United States attorney general. As a Supreme Court justice, he instinctively grasped the Court's civil religious role. For a treatment of his work on the Schneiderman case, see J. Woodward Howard Jr., *Mr. Justice Murphy: A Political Biography* (Princeton: Princeton University Press, 1968), 309–22; and Sidney Fine, *Frank Murphy: The Washington Years* (Ann Arbor: University of Michigan Press, 1984), 408–22.

3. *Schneiderman v. United States*, 320 U.S. 118, 121, 120 (1943).

4. Ibid., 122, 132, 134, 137–38, 139.

5. Ibid., 139, 159.

6. Ibid., 165, 166.

7. In Sanford Levinson, *Constitutional Faith* (Princeton, N.J.: Princeton University Press, 1988), 122–54, the author uses this decision to demonstrate that attachment to the principles of the Constitution, a requirement for naturalization, has little substantive meaning.

8. *Baumgartner v. United States*, 322 U.S. 665, 674, 673 (1944).

9. *Girouard v. United States*, 328 U.S. 61, 64, 66 (1946).

10. *Knauer v. United States*, 328 U.S. 654, 674, 677 (1946).

11. Ibid., 676.

12. Quoted in Liva Baker, *Felix Frankfurter* (New York: Coward-McCann, 1969), 290.

13. For a treatment of both flag-salute cases in their historical context, see David R. Mainwaring, *Render Unto Caesar: The Flag-Salute Controversy* (Chicago: University of Chicago Press, 1962).

14. *Minersville School District v. Gobitis*, 310 U.S. 586, 594 (1940).

15. Ibid., 596, 597, 598, 600.

16. Ibid., 596, quoting *Halter v. Nebraska*, 205 U.S. 34, 43 (1907). That decision upheld a state law prohibiting the use of the flag in advertising.

17. *Minersville School District v. Gobitis*, 310 U.S. 586, 596, 598 (1940).

18. The episode is described in Alpheus Thomas Mason, *Harlan Fiske Stone: Pillar of the Law* (New York: The Viking Press, 1956), 525–33.

19. *Minersville School District v. Gobitis*, 310 U.S. 586, 601, 604, 605 (1940).

20. Ibid., 606–7, 604.

21. This acknowledgement was made by the trio in *Jones v. Opelika*, 316 U.S. 584, 623–24 (1942). Each of the three justices—Hugo L. Black, William O. Douglas, and Frank Murphy—either wrote or joined in concurring opinions seeking to explain their change of mind.

22. *West Virginia State Board of Education v. Barnette*, 319 U.S. 624, 637, 638 (1943).

23. Ibid., 640, 641.

24. Ibid., 641–42.

25. Ibid., 646.

26. Ibid., 646, 654, 662.

27. "Frankfurter would not have said that his personal experience as an immigrant and a Jew was irrelevant to his conception of himself as a judge. I surmise that he believed his successful passage from alien to fully assimilated citizen gave him special insight as a judge into fundamental American values because he embodied those values in his own experience. He drew no protective mandate or special sympathy for outsiders, however, from this experience. He instead derived a mandate zealously to protect the values and status of insiders, such as he had become." Robert A. Burt, *Two Jewish Justices: Outcasts in the Promised Land* (Berkeley: University of California Press, 1988), 45–46. Burt contrasts Louis D. Brandeis, who was comfortable and tolerant as an outsider, with Felix Frankfurter, who saw the rejection of his leadership in the reversal of *Gobitis* as a denial to him of his insider status.

28. *United States v. United Mine Workers of America*, 330 U.S. 258, 308, 311, 312 (1947).

29. *Jones v. Opelika*, 316 U.S. 584, 610 (1942). For a detailed treatment of this litigation, as well as *Marsh v. Alabama*, 326 U.S. 501 (1946), see Merlin Owen Newton, *Armed*

with the Constitution: Jehovah's Witnesses in Alabama and the U.S. Supreme Court, 1939–1946 (Tuscaloosa: University of Alabama Press, 1995).

30. *Murdock v. Pennsylvania*, 319 U.S. 105, 117 (1943).
31. For a survey of the relevant cases and a recognition of the role Jehovah's Witnesses have played in constitutional adjudication, see William Shephard McAninch, "A Catalyst for the Evolution of Constitutional Law: Jehovah's Witnesses in the Supreme Court," *Cincinnati Law Review* 55 (1987): 997–1077.
32. *Prince v. Massachusetts*, 321 U.S. 158, 176 (1954).
33. *Hartzel v. United States*, 322 U.S. 680, 689 (1944). Murphy spoke for four members of the Court, and Jackson agreed that the evidence was insufficient to sustain the conviction. The Court came to a similar conclusion with regard to German Bund members in *Keegan v. United States*, 325 U.S. 478 (1945).
34. *Ex parte Kumezo Kawato*, 317 U.S. 69, 73, 78 (1942).
35. An extensive treatment of the legal cases generated by this episode can be found in Peter Irons, *Justice at War* (New York: Oxford University Press, 1983).
36. For a treatment of the case and the personal recollections of the defendant, see Peter Irons, *The Courage of Their Convictions: Sixteen Americans Who Fought Their Way to the Supreme Court* (New York: The Free Press, 1988), 37–62.
37. *Hirabayashi v. United States*, 320 U.S. 81, 93, 99, 100 (1943).
38. Ibid., 110, 111, 114.
39. *Korematsu v. United States*, 323 U.S. 214, 220 (1944).
40. Ibid., 226, 232, 233.
41. Ibid., 235, 239–40, 242.
42. Ibid., 243, 245–46.
43. Ibid., 247, 248.
44. *Ex parte Endo*, 323 U.S. 283, 302, 307, 310 (1944).
45. Peter Irons, *Justice at War* (New York: Oxford University Press, 1983), 345–46.
46. Peter Irons, *The Courage of Their Convictions: Sixteen Americans Who Fought Their Way to the Supreme Court* (New York: The Free Press, 1988), 47.
47. For a discussion of the reversal of the wartime convictions, see Peter Irons, ed., *Justice Delayed: The Record of the Japanese American Internment Cases* (Middletown, Conn.: Wesleyan University Press, 1989), 3–46. The volume also contains the text of legal opinions in the original cases and in the reversals.
48. *Duncan v. Kahanamoku*, 327 U.S. 304, 322 (1946).
49. Ibid., 325, 330, 331, 334.
50. Ibid., 338.
51. *Terrace v. Thompson*, 263 U.S. 197 (1923); and *Porterfield v. Webb*, 263 U.S. 225 (1923).
52. *Oyama v. California*, 332 U.S.633, 647 (1948).
53. Ibid., 649–50, 673, 674.
54. *Takahashi v. Fish and Game Commission*, 334 U.S. 410 (1948).
55. *Asakura v. City of Seattle*, 265 U.S. 332 (1924).
56. See *Truax v. Raich*, 239 U.S. 33 (1915).
57. *Takahashi v. Fish and Game Commission*, 334 U.S. 410, 427 (1948).
58. *Ex parte Quirin*, 317 U.S. 1 (1942).
59. *Cramer v. United States*, 325 U.S. 1, 21, 45 (1945).
60. *Haupt v. United States*, 330 U.S. 631, 635, 647 (1947).
61. *Buck v. Bell*, 274 U.S. 200 (1927). A treatment of the case in its historical context can be found in William E. Leuchtenburg, *The Supreme Court Reborn: The Constitutional Revolution in the Age of Roosevelt* (New York: Oxford University Press, 1995), 3–25.

62. *Skinner v. Oklahoma*, 316 U.S. 535, 541 (1942).
63. Ibid., 544, 546.
64. *McNabb v. United States*, 318 U.S. 332, 343 (1943).
65. *Goldman v. United States*, 316 U.S. 129, 138, 142 (1942).
66. *Feldman v. United States*, 322 U.S. 487, 502 (1944).
67. *Thomas v. Collins*, 323 U.S. 516, 530, 531 (1945).
68. *Hannegan v. Esquire*, 327 U.S. 146, 158 (1946).
69. *Winters v. New York*, 333 U.S. 507, 510 (1947).
70. *Butler v. Michigan*, 532 U.S. 380, 384 (1957).
71. *Screws v. United States*, 325 U.S. 91, 93, 160–61 (1945).
72. Ibid., 135, 107. The plurality acknowledged that it was extending the rule announced in *United States v. Classic*, 313 U.S. 299 (1941).
73. *Adamson v. California*, 332 U.S. 46, 89 (1947). In James F. Simon, *The Antagonists: Hugo Black, Felix Frankfurter and Civil Liberties in Modern America* (New York: Simon & Schuster, 1989), 170–80, the conflict between Black and Frankfurter over *Adamson* is described in some detail.
74. The differing views of Black and Frankfurter are drawn out in Mark Silverstein, *Constitutional Faiths: Felix Frankfurter, Hugo Black, and the Process of Judicial Decision Making* (Ithaca: Cornell University Press, 1984).
75. *Adamson v. California*, 332 U.S. 46, 62, 67, 68 (1947).
76. For a treatment of Frankfurter focused on his views on judicial restraint, see Melvin I. Urofsky, *Felix Frankfurter: Judicial Restraint and Individual Liberties* (Boston: Twayne Publishers, 1991).
77. The Court primarily relied upon *Twining v. New Jersey*, 211 U.S. 78 (1908), and *Palko v. Connecticut*, 302 U.S. 319 (1937).
78. *Pennekamp v. Florida*, 328 U.S. 331, 335, 346, 370 (1946).
79. *Jacob v. City of New York*, 315 U.S. 752–53 (1942).
80. *Thiel v. Southern Pacific Co.*, 328 U.S. 217, 220, 223–24 (1946).
81. *Ballard v. United States*, 329 U.S. 187, 193, 194–95 (1946).
82. *Davis v. United States*, 328 U.S. 582, 594, 597, 615 (1946).
83. *Harris v. United States*, 331 U.S. 145, 157, 173 (1947).
84. *Wolf v. Colorado*, 338 U.S. 25, 27 (1949).
85. Ibid., 46.
86. See James Boyd White, *Justice as Translation: An Essay in Culture and Legal Criticism* (Chicago: University of Chicago Press, 1990), 203–14.
87. *Brock v. North Carolina*, 344 U.S. 424 (1952). Black did not participate in the case.
88. *Bute v. Illinois*, 333 U.S. 640 (1948).
89. *Bartkus v. Illinois*, 359 U.S. 121, 155–56 (1959).
90. See *Benton v. Maryland*, 395 U.S. 784 (1969).
91. In Leonard L. Levy, *The Establishment Clause: Religion and the First Amendment*, 2d ed. rev. (Chapel Hill: University of North Carolina Press, 1994), the author argues that the clause was designed to prevent government from aiding religion even on a non-preferential basis. For a contrary view, see Gerard V. Bradley, *Church-State Relationships in America* (Westport, Conn.: Greenwood Press, 1987).
92. *Everson v. Board of Education*, 330 U.S. 1, 18 (1947).
93. Ibid., 15–16, 18.
94. Ibid., 27.
95. Ibid., 33, 47, 59.

96. *Illinois ex. rel. McCollum v. Board of Education*, 333 U.S. 203, 256 (1948).

97. Ibid., 215–16, 217, 231.

98. *Zorach v. Clauson*, 343 U.S. 306, 313, 314, 315 (1952). Douglas would later conclude that he had erred in the case and would oppose all such accommodation. See *Engel v. Vitale*, 370 U.S. 421, 443 (1962).

99. *Zorach v. Clauson*, 343 U.S. 306, 319–20 (1952).

100. Ibid., 323.

101. Ibid., 324, 325.

102. *Mutual Film Corp. v. Industrial Commission*, 236 U.S. 230 (1915).

103. *Burstyn v. Wilson*, 343 U.S. 495, 501, 505 (1952).

104. Both the federal law proscribing the mailing of obscene matter and state obscenity laws were the products of the latter third of the nineteenth century. See Margaret A. Blanchard, *Revolutionary Sparks: Freedom of Expression in Modern America* (New York: Oxford University Press, 1992), 15–22.

105. *Roth v. United States*, 354 U.S. 476, 484–85, 487, 489 (1957).

106. Ibid., 509, 514.

107. *Terminiello v. Chicago*, 327 U.S. 1, 4–5 (1949).

108. *Kunz v. New York*, 340 U.S. 290, 296 (1951).

109. *Feiner v. New York*, 340 U.S. 315, 323 (1951).

110. *Beauharnais v. Illinois*, 343 U.S. 250, 251, 266 (1952).

111. Ibid., 284, 287.

112. Ibid., 270, 275.

113. See Stanley I. Kutler, *The American Inquisition: Justice and Injustice in the Cold War* (New York: Hill and Wang, 1982). For a more generalized treatment of this red scare, see David Caute, *The Great Fear: The Anti-Communist Purge under Truman and Eisenhower* (New York: Simon & Schuster, 1978). And for the effect of the second red scare on freedom of expression in the country, see Margaret A. Blanchard, *Revolutionary Sparks: Freedom of Expression in Modern America* (New York: Oxford University Press, 1992), 230–78.

114. *Bridges v. Wixon*, 326 U.S. 135, 148 (1945).

115. Ibid., 159, 160, 162.

116. *American Communications Association v. Douds*, 339 U.S. 382, 421 (1950).

117. Ibid., 439, 442.

118. Ibid., 444, 445.

119. Ibid., 452–53.

120. *Joint Anti-Fascist Refugee Committee v. McGrath*, 341 U.S. 123, 179 (1951).

121. The Smith Act prosecutions are well handled in Michal R. Belknap, *Cold War Political Justice: The Smith Act, the Communist Party, and American Civil Liberties* (Westport: Greenwood Press, 1977).

122. *Dennis v. United States*, 341 U.S. 494, 509, 510 (1951).

123. *Breard v. Alexandria*, 341 U.S. 622, 650 (1951).

124. *Dennis v. United States*, 341 U.S. 494, 580, 581 (1951).

125. Ibid., 589, 591.

126. Ibid, 584–85, 590.

127. *Adler v. Board of Education*, 342 U.S. 485, 497, 511 (1951).

128. *Carlson v. Landon*, 342 U.S. 524 (1952).

129. *Harisiades v. Shaughnessy*, 342 U.S. 580, 598, 599, 601 (1952).

130. *Wieman v. Updegraff*, 344 U.S. 183, 191 (1952).

131. Ibid., 193, 194.

132. *Ullman v. United States*, 350 U.S. 422, 445 (1956). Sixty years earlier in a dissenting opinion, Justice Stephen J. Field essentially took the same position, arguing that a promise of immunity was a poor exchange for the self-incrimination protection. *Brown v. Walker*, 161 U.S. 591, 631–32 (1896).

133. *Black v. Cutter Laboratories*, 351 U.S. 292 (1956).

134. Brennan's long and illustrious career on the High Bench is chronicled in Hunter R. Clark, *Justice Brennan: The Great Conciliator* (New York: Carol Publishing Group, 1995).

135. *Jencks v. United States*, 353 U.S. 657 (1957).

136. *Watkins v. United States*, 354 U.S. 178, 185 (1957).

137. Ibid., 187, 188, 197–98.

138. Ibid., 202, 204, 209.

139. *Sweezy v. New Hampshire*, 354 U.S. 234, 250, 251, 265 (1957).

140. *Beilan v. Board of Public Education*, 357 U.S. 399, 412–13, 416, 418–19 (1958).

141. *NAACP v. Alabama*, 357 U.S. 449, 460–61, 462, 466 (1958).

142. *Shelton v. Tucker*, 364 U.S. 479, 487, 490 (1960).

143. *Barenblatt v. United States*, 360 U.S. 109, 143, 144, 145, 146 (1959).

144. *American Communications Association v. Douds*, 339 U.S. 339, 449 (1950).

145. *Barenblatt v. United States*, 360 U.S. 109, 153, 162 (1959).

146. For the full story on this legislative attempt to curb the Court's power, see Walter F. Murphy, *Congress and the Court: A Case Study in the American Political Process* (Chicago: University of Chicago Press, 1962).

CHAPTER EIGHT

1. *Brown v. Board of Education*, 347 U.S. 483 (1954).

2. *Plessy v. Ferguson*, 163 U.S. 537 (1896).

3. *Bailey v. Alabama*, 219 U.S. 219 (1911).

4. *McCabe v. Atchison, Topeka & Santa Fe Ry.*, 235 U.S. 151 (1914); *Guinn v. United States*, 238 U.S. 347 (1915); and *Buchanan v. Warley*, 245 U.S. 60 (1917).

5. *Moore v. Dempsey*, 261 U.S. 86 (1923).

6. *Brown v. Mississippi*, 297 U.S. 278 (1936); and *Chambers v. Florida*, 309 U.S. 227 (1940).

7. *Powell v. Alabama*, 287 U.S. 45 (1932).

8. The exception to this general ruling allowed in *Grovey v. Townsend*, 295 U.S. 45 (1935) was finally closed in *Smith v. Allright*, 321 U.S. 649 (1944).

9. *United States v. Classic*, 313 U.S. 299 (1941).

10. For a treatment of the cases in a broader social context, see John P. Roche, *The Quest for the Dream: The Development of Civil Rights and Human Relations in Modern America* (New York: The Macmillan Co., 1963). And for a short survey of Afro-Americans and the Constitution, see Donald G. Nieman, *Promises to Keep: African-Americans and the Constitutional Order, 1776 to the Present* (New York: Oxford University Press, 1991).

11. For instance, on the matter of racial attitudes, see Michael J. Klarman, "*Brown*, Racial Change, and the Civil Rights Movement," *Virginia Law Review* 80 (February 1994): 7–150.

12. Gunnar Myrdal, *An American Dilemma: The Negro Problem and Modern Democracy* (New York: Harper & Brothers, 1944).

13. *Dred Scott v. Sandford*, 60 U.S. (19 How.) 393 (1857).

14. Charles Evans Hughes, *The Supreme Court of the United States* (Garden City: Garden City Publishing Co., 1936), 50.

15. *Brown v. Board of Education*, 347 U.S. 483 (1954).

16. *Missouri ex. rel. Gaines v. Canada*, 305 U.S. 337, 349 (1938).

17. *Fisher v. Hurst*, 333 U.S. 147 (1948). In *Sipuel v. University of Oklahoma*, 332 U.S. 631, 633 (1948), the Court ruled that the state had to provide a legal education for qualified black applicants "as soon as it does for applicants of any other group."

18. *Sweatt v. Painter*, 339 U.S. 629, 632 (1950).

19. Ibid., 634–35.

20. *McLaurin v. Oklahoma State Regents*, 339 U.S.637, 641–42 (1950).

21. Ibid., 635.

22. *Pierre v. Louisiana*, 306 U.S. 354, 358 (1939).

23. *Smith v. Texas*, 311 U.S. 128, 130 (1940).

24. *Hill v. Texas*, 316 U.S. 400, 406 (1942).

25. *Akins v. Texas*, 325 U.S. 398, 410 (1945).

26. *Cassell v. Texas*, 339 U.S. 282 (1950).

27. *Patton v. Mississippi*, 332 U.S. 463 (1947).

28. *Avery v. Georgia*, 345 U.S. 559 (1953).

29. See *Brunson v. North Carolina*, 333 U.S. 851 (1948). If the position of the Court was not made clear by such cursory reversals, the justices specifically drew the conclusion in *Moore v. New York*, 333 U.S. 565 (1948).

30. *Fay v. New York*, 332 U.S. 261, 296, 299, 300 (1947).

31. *Moore v. New York*, 333 U.S. 565, 569 (1948).

32. *Hernandez v. Texas*, 347 U.S. 475, 478 (1954).

33. *Shelley v. Kraemer*, 334 U.S. 1, 10–11, 22, 23 (1948). The Court's reference was to the *Slaughter-House Cases*, 83 (16 Wallace) 36, 81 (1873).

34. *Hurd v. Hodge*, 334 U.S. 24 (1948).

35. *Barrows v. Jackson*, 346 U.S. 249, 257, 254, 258, 259–60 (1953).

36. Quoted in *Mitchell v. United States*, 313 U.S. 80, 95 (1941).

37. *McCabe v. Atchison, Topeka & Santa Fe R.R.*, 235 U.S. 151 (1914).

38. *Mitchell v. United States*, 313 U.S. 80, 97 (1941).

39. Ibid., 94.

40. Ibid., 95.

41. *Bob-Lo Excursion Co. v. Michigan*, 333 U.S. 28, 40 (1948).

42. Ibid., 40, 41.

43. *Railway Mail Association v. Corsi*, 326 U.S. 88, 94, 98 (1945).

44. For detailed treatments of how the NAACP waged its judicial campaign before and after *Brown*, see Mark Tushnet, *The NAACP's Legal Strategy against Segregated Education, 1925–1950* (Chapel Hill: University of North Carolina Press, 1987); and Mark Tushnet, *Making Civil Rights Law: Thurgood Marshall and the Supreme Court, 1936–1961* (New York: Oxford University Press, 1994).

45. The fullest treatment of the case in context can be found in Richard Kluger, *Simple Justice: The History of Brown v. Board of Education and Black America's Struggle for Equality* (New York: Knopf, 1976).

46. G. Edward White, *Earl Warren: A Public Life* (New York: Oxford University Press, 1982), 218.

47. Critics complained that Warren was unschooled in constitutional law, but one scholar has harmonized the chief justice's approach with the long history of equity jurisprudence. See Peter Charles Hoffer, *The Law's Conscience: Equitable Constitutionalism in America* (Chapel Hill: University of North Carolina Press, 1990), 1–21.
48. *Brown v. Board of Education*, 347 U.S. 483, 492–93, 494 (1954).
49. Ibid., 495.
50. *Bolling v. Sharpe*, 347 U.S. 497, 500 (1954).
51. *Brown v. Board of Education*, 347 U.S. 483, 494 (1954).
52. *Brown v. Board of Education*, 349 U.S. 294, 298, 300, 301 (1955).
53. See Albert P. Blaustein and Clarence Clyde Ferguson Jr., *Desegregation and the Law: The Meaning and Effect of the School Segregation Cases*, 2nd ed. rev. (New York: Vintage Books, Random House, 1962), 240–71. For the political reaction to the decision in the South, see Numan V. Bartley, *The Rise of Massive Resistance: Race and Politics in the South During the 1950's* (Baton Rouge: Louisiana State University Press, 1969); and also Michal R. Belknap, *Federal Law and Southern Order: Racial Violence and Constitutional Conflict in the Post-Brown South*, new ed. (Athens: University of Georgia Press, 1995).
54. *New York Times*, March 12, 1956, sec. A, p. 19.
55. J. Harvie Wilkinson III, *From Brown to Bakke: The Supreme Court and School Integration: 1954–1978* (New York: Oxford University Press, 1979), 88–90.
56. Ibid., 90–91.
57. *Cooper v. Aaron*, 358 U.S. 1, 7 (1958).
58. Ibid., 16, 18, 19, 20.
59. Ibid., 20, 24, 25, 26.
60. In the short run Faubus's action was not condemned by Arkansas voters, who elected him to four more two-year terms as governor, but by 1972 Central High had become a model for successfully integrated schools. J. Harvie Wilkinson III, *From Brown to Bakke: The Supreme Court and School Integration: 1954–1978* (New York: Oxford University Press, 1979), 95.
61. *Griffin v. School Board of Prince Edward County*, 377 U.S. 218, 225 (1964).
62. *Mitchell v. United States*, 313 U.S. 80 (1941).
63. *Henderson v. United States*, 339 U.S. 816 (1950).
64. *Boynton v. Virginia*, 364 U.S. 454 (1960).
65. *Burton v. Wilmington Parking Authority*, 365 U.S. 715, 724, 726 (1961).
66. *Watson v. City of Memphis*, 373 U.S. 526, 530, 532–33, 537 (1963).
67. *Johnson v. Virginia*, 373 U.S. 61 (1963).
68. *Peterson v. City of Greenville*, 373 U.S. 244, 250 (1963).
69. Ibid., 248.
70. *Lombard v. Louisiana*, 373 U.S. 267 (1963).
71. Ibid., 283.
72. *Civil Rights Cases*, 109 U.S. 3 (1883).
73. *Bell v. Maryland*, 378 U.S. 226, 286, 287, 288, 311, 312 (1964).
74. Ibid., 243, 244, 245, 260.
75. "Radio and Television Report to the American People on Civil Rights," June 11, 1963, *Public Papers of Presidents of the United States: John F. Kennedy, 1963* (Washington: Government Printing Office, 1964), 469.
76. For a comprehensive treatment of national policy and resulting legislation under Presidents Kennedy, Johnson, and Nixon, see Hugh Davis Graham, *The Civil Rights Era:*

Origins and Development of National Policy 1960–1972 (New York: Oxford University Press, 1990).

77. "Radio and Television Remarks upon Signing the Civil Rights Bill," July 2, 1964, *Public Papers of Presidents of the United States: Lyndon B. Johnson, 1963–64*, vol. 2 (Washington: Government Printing Office, 1965), 842, 844.

78. *Heart of Atlanta Motel v. United States*, 379 U.S. 241, 261, 257 (1964). In a companion case, *Katzenbach v. McClung*, 379 U.S. 294 (1964), the Court said that the selling of food that had come to the restaurant through the channels of interstate commerce was sufficient to bring a restaurant under the provisions of the 1964 act.

79. *Heart of Atlanta Motel v. United States*, 379 U.S. 241, 286, 291 (1964).

80. *Hamm v. City of Rock Hill*, 379 U.S. 306 (1964).

81. *South Carolina v. Katzenbach*, 383 U.S. 301, 337 (1966).

82. *Katzenbach v. Morgan*, 384 U.S. 641, 652 (1966).

83. *Breedlove v. Suttles*, 302 U.S. 277 (1937).

84. *Harper v. Virginia State Board of Elections*, 383 U.S. 663, 669, 668, 670 (1966).

85. *Jones v. Alfred A. Mayer Co.*, 392 U.S. 409, 412, 438, 442–43 (1968).

86. Critics complained that the Court was rewriting the past to conform to the sensibilities of the present, but Harold M. Hyman has argued that the way the Court interpreted the Thirteenth Amendment here was the way it was intended to be interpreted at the time of its addition to the Constitution. See Harold M. Hyman and William M. Wiecek, *Equal Justice under Law: Constitutional Development, 1835–1875* (New York: Harper & Row, 1982), 386–438.

87. *Runyon v. McCrary*, 427 U.S. 160, 164, n. 1, 173 (1976).

88. *McDonald v. Santa Fe Trail Transportation Co.*, 427 U.S. 273 (1976).

89. *Saint Francis College v. Al-Khazraji*, 481 U.S. 604, 613 (1987); and *Shaare Tefila Congregation v. Cobb*, 481 U.S. 615 (1987).

90. *Saint Francis College v. Al-Khazraji*, 481 U.S. 604, 614 (1987).

91. *Loving v. Virginia*, 388 U.S. 1, 12 (1967).

92. *McLaughlin v. Florida*, 379 U.S. 184, 190 (1964).

93. *Palmore v. Sidoti*, 466 U.S. 429, 432, 433 (1984).

94. *Green v. School Board of New Kent County*, 391 U.S. 430, 437–38, 442 (1968).

95. *Alexander v. Holmes County Board of Education*, 396 U.S. 19, 20 (1969).

96. *Swann v. Charlotte-Mecklenburg Board of Education*, 402 U.S. 1, 15 (1971).

97. *Milliken v. Bradley*, 418 U.S. 717, 744, 745, 747 (1974).

98. Ibid., 762, 780, 782.

99. Ibid., 783.

100. Ibid., 806, 814–15.

101. Douglas was referring to *San Antonio School District v. Rodriguez*, 411 U.S. 1 (1973).

102. *Gaston County v. United States*, 395 U.S. 285 (1969).

103. *Griggs v. Duke Power Co.*, 401 U.S. 424 (1971).

104. *Regents of the University of California v. Bakke*, 438 U.S. 265 (1977).

105. For a treatment of the case and its implications, see Bernard Schwartz, *Behind Bakke: Affirmative Action and the Supreme Court* (New York: New York University Press, 1988).

106. *Regents of the University of California v. Bakke*, 438 U.S. 265, 298–99 (1977).

107. Ibid., 327.

108. Ibid., 398, 400.

109. Ibid., 403, 405.

110. For a perceptive historical treatment of affirmative action and the problems involved in shifting from the individual to the group, see Herman Belz, *Equality Transformed: A Quarter-Century of Affirmative Action* (New Brunswick, N.J.: Transaction Publishers, 1991).

111. *Lau v. Nichols*, 414 U.S. 563, 566 (1974).

112. *United Jewish Organizations v. Carey*, 430 U.S. 144, 161 (1977).

113. Ibid., 172, 173–74, 175.

114. Ibid., 187.

115. *Wright v. Rockefeller*, 376 U.S. 52, 67 (1964). In its decision the Court approved an apportionment scheme designed to empower a minority, in this case Puerto Ricans in New York City.

116. *Gomillion v. Lightfoot*, 364 U.S. 339 (1960) was the decision in which the Court condemned the racial gerrymandering that had sought to exclude black voters from the redrawn boundaries of the city of Tuskegee.

117. *Shaw v. Reno*, 509 U.S. 630, 658 (1993). The case returned to the Court in 1996; with President Bill Clinton's nominees—Ruth Bader Ginsberg and Stephen Breyer—now agreeing with the dissenting position of the now departed Byron R. White and Harry A. Blackmun, the majority by the same five to four count found North Carolina's attempt to justify the district constitutionally insufficient. *Shaw v. Hunt*, 116 S.Ct. 1894 (1996).

118. *Shaw v. Reno*, 509 U.S. 630, 647, 657 (1993).

119. Ibid., 675.

120. Ibid., 678.

121. *Miller v. Johnson*, 115 S.Ct. 2475 (1995).

122. *Abrams v. Johnson*, 117 S.Ct. 1925 (1997).

123. *Lawyer v. Department of Justice*, 117 S.Ct. 2186 (1997).

124. *Fullilove v. Klutznick*, 448 U.S. 448, 490 (1980).

125. *Richmond v. Croson Co.*, 488 U.S. 469, 493, 505–6, 510 (1989).

126. Ibid., 520, 527–28.

127. Ibid., 553, 562.

128. *Wygant v. Jackson Board of Education*, 476 U.S. 267, 314, 315 (1986).

129. Ibid., 316, 319, 320.

130. *Metro Broadcasting v. FCC*, 497 U.S. 547, 553, 564–65, 602, 633, 638 (1990). Justices White and Stevens joined the former dissenters in the Richmond case to create a bare majority.

131. *Adarand Constructors, Inc. v. Peña*, 515 U.S. 200 (1995).

132. *Missouri v. Jenkins*, 495 U.S. 33, 81 (1990).

133. *Board of Education of Oklahoma City Public Schools v. Dowell*, 498 U.S. 237, 251 (1991).

134. *Freeman v. Pitts*, 503 U.S. 467 (1992).

135. *United States v. Fordice*, 505 U.S. 717 (1992).

136. The precedent is *Swain v. Alabama*, 380 U.S. 202 (1965).

137. *Batson v. Kentucky*, 476 U.S. 79, 86, 87 (1986).

138. Ibid., 95, 99.

139. *Brown v. North Carolina*, 479 U.S. 940, 941–42 (1986).

140. *Holland v. Illinois*, 493 U.S. 474 (1990).

141. *Powers v. Ohio*, 499 U.S. 400, 402, 407, 409 (1991).

142. Ibid., 411, 412, 413–414, 415–416.

143. *Edmonson v. Leesville Concrete Co.*, 500 U.S. 614, 620, 624, 627, 628 (1991).

144. Ibid., 628, 630.
145. During his confirmation hearings Clarence Thomas indicated that his shared Afro-American heritage with the justice he would replace should lead no one to believe that his beliefs, approach, and votes would mirror those of Thurgood Marshall. To illustrate the difference, see Thomas's lengthy concurring opinion in *Holder v. Hall*, 512 U.S. 874, 893 (1994), in which he attacks the Court's work that reflected Marshall's views in the area of voting rights, calling it "a disastrous misadventure in judicial policymaking."
146. *Georgia v. McCollum*, 505 U.S. 42, 70 (1992).
147. Scalia's position here illustrates how he denies law an aspirational character and tends to place it in the service of the status quo. For a thoughtful appraisal of the justice along these lines, see Richard A. Brisbin Jr., *Justice Antonin Scalia and the Conservative Revival* (Baltimore, Md.: Johns Hopkins Press, 1997).

CHAPTER NINE

1. In Richard C. Cortner, *The Apportionment Cases* (Knoxville: University of Tennessee Press, 1970), the author not only focuses on the issue of reapportionment and the Constitution but also the political situation in both Tennessee and Alabama, the two states that furnished the key reapportionment cases.
2. Earlier, in *Colegrove v. Green*, 328 U.S. 549 (1946), the Court had ruled that such matters were political questions, that is, ones entrusted to the discretion of the other branches of government.
3. *Baker v. Carr*, 369 U.S. 186, 211 (1962).
4. Ibid., 259, 261, 262.
5. *Gray v. Sanders*, 372 U.S. 368, 380, 381 (1963).
6. *Wesberry v. Sanders*, 376 U.S. 1, 6, 7 (1964).
7. Ibid., 8, 17.
8. *Reynolds v. Sims*, 377 U.S. 533, 555 (1964).
9. Ibid., 566, 567.
10. Ward E. Y. Elliott, *The Rise of Guardian Democracy: The Supreme Court's Role in Voting Rights Disputes, 1845–1969* (Cambridge: Harvard University Press, 1974), 252–55.
11. This story is told in Chapter 8.
12. For a useful survey of the position of women in American society, see William H. Chafe, *The Paradox of Change: American Women in the 20th Century* (New York: Oxford University Press, 1991). A more thorough treatment of recent history, and one which focuses more on the legal battles, is found in Flora Davis, *Moving the Mountain: The Women's Movement in America Since 1960* (New York: Simon & Schuster, 1991).
13. Fifteen years earlier, in *Ballard v. United States*, 329 U.S. 187 (1946), the Court had insisted that women could not be excluded from federal jury selection.
14. *Hoyt v. Florida*, 368 U.S. 57, 62 (1961).
15. *Reed v. Reed*, 404 U.S. 71, 76 (1971).
16. For example, see *Goesaert v. Cleary*, 335 U.S. 464 (1948).
17. *Frontiero v. Richardson*, 411 U.S. 677, 684, 685, 686–87 (1973).
18. *Craig v. Boren*, 429 U.S. 190, 208–9 (1976).
19. *Dothard v. Rawlinson*, 433 U.S. 321 (1977).
20. *Brown v. General Services Administration*, 425 U.S. 820, 835 (1976).

21. *Davis v. Passman*, 442 U.S. 228, 235, 242 (1979).
22. In this decision the Court relied also on *Bivens v. Six Unknown Narcotics Agents*, 403 U.S. 388 (1971), in which an individual right of action was seen to arise from the Fourth Amendment's protection against unreasonable searches and seizures. Usually these cases came to the Court through the claim that evidence so seized was improperly used at trial. Here there was no trial, for there was no evidence of any guilt. The Court concluded that the Fourth Amendment did independently provide the individual with a right that could be enforced in the courts.
23. *Michael M. v. Superior Court of Sonoma County*, 450 U.S. 464 (1981); and *Rostker v. Goldberg*, 453 U.S. 57 (1981). In the latter case in dissent, Justice Marshall criticized the majority's premises, its perpetuation of stereotypes, and its categorical exclusion of "women from a fundamental civic obligation." (Ibid., 86).
24. The justice cited *Califano v. Webster*, 430 U.S. 313 (1977), which allowed women to drop more low-earning years than men in computing social security benefits, and *Schlesinger v. Ballard*, 419 U.S. 498 (1975), which allowed women, for whom fewer command positions were available, thirteen rather than nine years to achieve a certain rank in the armed services.
25. *Mississippi University for Women v. Hogan*, 458 U.S. 718, 724–25, 745 (1982).
26. *United States v. Virginia*, 116 S.Ct. 2264, 2284 (1996).
27. *Orr v. Orr*, 440 U.S. 268, 283 (1979).
28. *Kahn v. Shevin*, 416 U.S. 351, 353 (1974).
29. *Personnel Administrator of Massachusetts v. Feeney*, 442 U.S. 256, 285 (1979).
30. Such a role is championed by Kenneth L. Karst, *Belonging to America: Equal Citizenship and the Constitution* (New Haven, Conn.: Yale University Press, 1989), 112–13.
31. *Stanley v. Illinois*, 405 U.S. 645, 651, 656–57 (1972).
32. *Cleveland Board of Education v. LaFleur*, 414 U.S. 632, 640, 644 (1974). For the case with reflections by LaFleur, see Peter Irons, *The Courage of Their Convictions: Sixteen Americans Who Fought Their Way to the Supreme Court* (New York: Free Press, 1988), 305–29.
33. *Geduldig v. Aiello*, 417 U.S. 484, 501 (1974).
34. *General Electric Co. v. Gilbert*, 429 U.S. 125, 159–60, 161–62 (1976).
35. *Nashville Gas Co. v. Satty*, 434 U.S. 136, 142 (1977).
36. *California Federal Savings & Loan Association. v. Guerra*, 479 U.S. 272 (1987).
37. *Weinberger v. Wiesenfeld*, 420 U.S. 636, 645 (1975).
38. *Los Angeles Department of Water & Power v. Manhart*, 435 U.S. 702, 708 (1978).
39. Ibid.
40. *Johnson v. Transportation Agency*, 480 U.S. 616, 642 (1987). The case is treated in detail and placed in the context of the Court's work in this area in Melvin I. Urofsky, *A Conflict of Rights: The Supreme Court and Affirmative Action* (New York: Charles Scribner's Sons, 1991).
41. *Automobile Workers v. Johnson Controls*, 499 U.S. 187, 192, 211 (1991).
42. *Stanton v. Stanton*, 421 U.S. 7, 15 (1975).
43. *Duncan v. Louisiana*, 391 U.S. 145 (1968).
44. *Taylor v. Louisiana*, 419 U.S. 522, 530 (1975).
45. See *Ballard v. United States*, 329 U.S. 187 (1946).
46. *J. E. B. v. Alabama ex. rel. T. B.*, 511 U.S. 127 (1994).
47. Ibid., 131, 140.
48. Ibid., 142, 145–46.

49. Ibid., 153.
50. Ibid., 160.
51. *Hishon v. King & Spalding*, 467 U.S. 69, 81 (1984).
52. *Meritor Savings Bank v. Vinson*, 477 U.S. 57, 63, 68 (1986).
53. *Harris v. Forklift Systems, Inc.*, 510 U.S. 17 (1993).
54. *Cannon v. University of Chicago*, 441 U.S. 677 (1979).
55. *Franklin v. Gwinnett County Public Schools*, 503 U.S. 60 (1992).
56. *San Antonio School District v. Rodriguez*, 411 U.S. 1 (1973).
57. Rodriguez had more success under the Texas constitution when the state supreme
    court in 1989 ruled in favor of equalizing state funding. Not until 1993, however,
    did the Texas legislature comply. Peter Irons, *Brennan v. Rehnquist: The Battle for the
    Constitution* (New York: Knopf, 1994), 290–91.
58. *San Antonio School District v. Rodriguez*, 411 U.S. 1, 62 (1973).
59. Ibid., 111, 109.
60. Ibid., 59.
61. Although there is no federal constitutional right to an education, numerous states have
    established such a right in their own constitutions.
62. These two Texas cases are placed in context in Rosemary C. Salomone, *Equal Educa-
    tion under Law: Legal Rights and Federal Policy in the Post-Brown Era* (New York: St.
    Martin's Press, 1986), 78–111.
63. *Plyler v. Doe*, 457 U.S. 202, 216, 220, 221–22 (1982).
64. Ibid., 223.
65. *Harper v. Virginia State Board of Elections*, 383 U.S. 663, 668 (1966).
66. *Griffin v. Illinois*, 351 U.S. 12, 16, 19 (1956).
67. *Douglas v. California*, 372 U.S. 353, 357 (1963). The decision was announced on the
    same day as *Gideon v. Wainright*, 372 U.S. 335 (1963).
68. *Boddie v. Connecticut*, 401 U.S. 371, 374, 375, 383 (1971).
69. *Shapiro v. Thompson*, 394 U.S. 618, 629, 631 (1969).
70. *Levy v. Louisiana*, 391 U.S. 68, 70, 72 (1968). The dissent is printed in a companion
    case, *Glona v. American Guarantee & Liability Insurance Co.*, 390 U.S. 73 (1968).
71. *Labine v. Vincent*, 401 U.S. 532, 541 (1971).
72. *Weber v. Aetna Casualty & Surety Co.*, 406 U.S. 164, 169, 173, 175, 176 (1972).
73. The Court, however, would continue to subject each individual claim to scrutiny
    with results that seemed far from consistent. For instance, in *Jimenez v. Weinberger*, 417
    U.S. 628 (1974) the Court by an eight-to-one count found a portion of the Social
    Security Act that discriminated against illegitimate children unconstitutional, but in
    Mathews v. Lucas, 427 U.S. 495 (1976), by a six-to-three vote it permitted a discrimi-
    nation in another portion of the act on the basis of it being administratively conve-
    nient. Then, a year later, the Court by a five-to-four vote in *Trimble v. Gordon*, 430
    U.S. 762 (1977) invalidated a provision in the Illinois probate code that allowed ille-
    gitimate children to inherit from the mother but not the father in the absence of a
    will.
74. The Court reviews its precedents in this area in *Graham v. Richardson*, 403 U.S. 365
    (1971). The problems of aliens in the country illegally is the focus of Elizabeth Hull,
    Without Justice for All: The Constitutional Rights of Aliens (Westport: Greenwood Press,
    1985).
75. *Graham v. Richardson*, 403 U.S. 365 (1971).
76. Ibid., 374. Two years later in *Sugarman v. Dougall*, 413 U.S. 634 (1973), the Court
    invalidated a New York law seeking to exclude aliens from the state's civil service.

77. *Foley v. Connelie*, 435 U.S. 291 (1976).

78. *Ambach v. Norwick*, 441 U.S. 68, 77, 88 (1979).

79. See *In re Griffiths*, 413 U.S. 717 (1973).

80. *Bernal v. Fainter*, 467 U.S. 216 (1984).

81. These words are engraved on the facade of the building that the Court has occupied in Washington, D.C., since its completion in 1935.

82. *Everson v. Board of Education*, 330 U.S. 1 (1947); and *Zorach v. Clauson*, 343 U.S. 306 (1952).

83. *Engel v. Vitale*, 370 U.S. 421, 425, 429 (1962).

84. Ibid., 431, 432.

85. Ibid., 450.

86. *Abington School District v. Schempp*, 374 U.S. 203, 226 (1963).

87. Ibid., 241–42.

88. Ibid., 281.

89. Ibid., 293.

90. A short history of this campaign can be found in Rodney K. Smith, *Public Prayer and the Constitution: A Case Study in Constitutional Interpretation* (Wilmington, Del.: Scholarly Resources Inc., 1987), 261–94.

91. *Epperson v. Arkansas*, 393 U.S. 97 (1968).

92. *Edwards v. Aguillard*, 482 U.S. 578 (1987). See Lawrence Rosen, "Continuing the Conversation: Creationism, the Religion Clauses, and the Politics of Culture," *Supreme Court Review 1988* (Chicago: University of Chicago Press), 61–84, for a treatment of this case in a cultural context that emphasizes the Court's setting the terms of a conversation that seeks to incorporate all and gain their acceptance of the process of adjudication as legitimate and binding.

93. *Stone v. Graham*, 449 U.S. 39 (1980).

94. *Walz v. Tax Commission*, 397 U.S. 664, 681, 687, 689 (1970). The following year in *Tilton v. Richardson*, 403 U.S. 672 (1971), the Court upheld the provisions of a federal act providing construction funds to sectarian institutions of higher learning to be used only for secular educational purposes. The Court did invalidate a twenty-year limitation on the federal government's interest in seeing that its terms were followed. Douglas, joined by Black and Marshall, dissented and so did Brennan in a separate opinion, all contending that the establishment clause was violated by the statute.

95. *Marsh v. Chambers*, 463 U.S. 783, 792 (1983).

96. Ibid., 805–6, 813.

97. Ibid., 819, 821, 822.

98. *Lynch v. Donnelly*, 465 U.S. 668, 674, 680, 684 (1984).

99. In Winnifred Fallers Sullivan, *Paying the Words Extra, Religious Discourse in the Supreme Court of the United States* (Cambridge: Harvard University Press for Harvard University Center for the Study of World Religions, 1994), 167, 183, the author centers on the opinions in this case, which, she says, taken together "affirm values we hold in common: the continued importance of religious culture in American life, the primacy of political equality, and a respect for privacy and for the value of religious diversity and particularity," something she goes on to characterize as "a certain kind of American religion." The author, however, is critical of all of the opinions, arguing that the Court should deconstruct the term "religion" and, as a cultural location for a discourse and practice about the role of religion in American public life, . . . talk and act about American religion in a way that acknowledges the varied and changing religiousness of Americans without establishing religion."

100. *Lynch v. Donnelly*, 465 U.S. 668, 687–88, 691 (1984).

101. Ibid., 697, 700, 701, 703–4, 709.

102. *Allegheny County v. Greater Pittsburgh ACLU*, 492 U.S. 573, 582 (1989).

103. Ibid., 610, 620.

104. Ibid., 628.

105. Ibid., 655.

106. Ibid., 655, 657, 662–63, 679.

107. *Lee v. Weisman*, 505 U.S. 577, 583, 587, 588 (1992).

108. Ibid., 589.

109. Kennedy dealt with an apparent anomaly in the First Amendment's protection of speech and religion. If, as the justice conceded, the constitutional protection of speech calls upon the individual "to endure the speech of false ideas or offensive content and then counter it . . . [as] part of learning how to live in a pluralistic society," then why should individuals not be asked to tolerate the expression of religious sentiments in the same spirit and for the same desirable end? The answer, the justice continued, lies in the history behind the establishment clause in the First Amendment—"that in the hands of government what might begin as a tolerant expression of religious views may end in a policy to indoctrinate and coerce." While government is certainly not precluded from participating as a speaker in a debate over public policy, Kennedy added, it is expressly forbidden to enter into religious debate. (Ibid., 590–91.)

110. Ibid., 592.

111. Ibid., 595, 596.

112. Ibid., 594.

113. Civil religion so defined is the target of Deborah K. Helper in "The Constitutional Challenge to American Civil Religion," *Kansas Journal of Law & Public Policy* 5 (Winter 1996): 93–120.

114. For an argument that the Court might make more sense in its establishment clause decisions if it took as its guide the standards of the civil religion, essentially as described here in this book, see Michael M. Maddigan, "The Establishment Clause, Civil Religion, and the Public Church," *California Law Review* 81 (January 1993): 293–349.

115. For the view that coercion is a better indicator than that of governmental interference because the person or persons coerced are deprived of a civil fellowship to which all are entitled, see Timothy L. Hall, "Sacred Solemnity: Civic Prayer, Civil Communion, and the Establishment Clause," *Iowa Law Review* 79 (October 1993): 35–93.

116. *Lee v. Weisman*, 505 U.S. 577, 606–7, 609 (1992).

117. Ibid., 617–18, 616–17, 630.

118. Ibid., 631, 632.

119. Ibid., 638, 641–42, 646.

120. *Widmar v. Vincent*, 454 U.S. 263 (1981). The Court has continued to rely upon the analysis in this case, as in 1993, in *Zobrest v. Catlina Foothills School District*, 509 U.S. 1, when it ruled that the denial of school facilities to a religious group violated the First Amendment, and two years later in *Rosenberger v. Rector and Visitors of the University of Virginia*, 115 S.Ct. 2510 (1995), when the Court approved the funding of a religious publication put out by students. In *Rosenberger*, Justice Souter, for four dissenters, protested what he and the others who joined him saw as a departure from precedent against such funding of religious activities.

121. Equal Access Act, 98 Stat. 1302 (1984).

122. *Wallace v. Jaffree*, 472 U.S. 38 (1985).

123. *Westside Community Schools v. Mergens*, 496 U.S. 226 (1990).

124. *McGowan v. Maryland*, 366 U.S. 420 (1961).

125. *Braunfeld v. Brown*, 366 U.S. 599 (1961); and *Gallagher v. Crown Kosher Super Market*, 366 U.S. 617 (1961).

126. *Torcaso v. Watkins*, 367 U.S. 488, 496 (1961).

127. *Sherbert v. Verner*, 374 U.S. 398, 403, 404, 406 (1963).

128. Ibid., 412.

129. For an argument that seeks to justify such exemptions on the basis that American society has become more religiously pluralistic and that law, which reflects mainstream religion, does substantially burden religious believers who are not in the mainstream, see Stephen L. Carter, *The Culture of Disbelief: How American Law and Politics Trivialize Religious Devotion* (New York: Basic Books, 1993), 124–35.

130. *United States v. Seeger*, 380 U.S. 163, 171, 172 (1965).

131. Ibid., 174, 184, 185.

132. Ibid., 192.

133. In fact, Congress had responded to the *Seeger* decision by changing the draft law in 1967 to read as follows: "Religious training and belief does not include essentially political, sociological or philosophical views, or a merely personal moral code." Quoted in Henry J. Abraham and Barbara A. Perry, *Freedom & the Court: Civil Rights and Liberties in the United States*, 7th ed. (New York: Oxford University Press, 1998), 233.

134. *Welsh v. United States*, 398 U.S. 333, 341, 342–43, 344 (1970).

135. Ibid., 357–358, 365–66, 367.

136. William A. Clebsch, *From Sacred to Profane America: The Role of Religion in American History* (New York: Harper & Row, 1958).

137. *Sherbert v. Verner*, 374 U.S. 398 (1963).

138. For instance, consider the diverse groups behind the movement that led Congress to pass the Religious Freedom Restoration Act in late 1993.

139. *Thomas v. Review Board*, 450 U.S. 707 (1981).

140. *Hobbie v. Unemployment Appeals Commission*, 480 U.S. 136, 141, 145 (1987).

141. *Frazee v. Employment Security Department*, 489 U.S. 829, 834 (1989).

142. *Garber v. Kansas*, 389 U.S. 51 (1967).

143. *Wisconsin v. Yoder*, 406 U.S. 205, 209 (1972).

144. Ibid., 212–13, 215, 219, 221, 222, 226, 236 (1972).

145. Ibid., 243, 245.

146. *Bowen v. Roy*, 476 U.S. 693, 696, 700 (1986).

147. Ibid., 708, 727.

148. *Lyng v. Northwest Indian Cemetery Protective Association.*, 485 U.S. 439, 442 (1988).

149. Ibid., 447, 449, 453.

150. Congress sought in the act to give these different beliefs mainstream recognition and pledged "to protect and preserve for American Indians their inherent right of freedom to believe, express, and exercise the traditional religions of the American Indian, Eskimo, Aleut, and Native Hawaiians, including but not limited to access to sites, use and possession of sacred objects, and the freedom to worship through ceremonials and traditional rights." (American Indian Religious Freedom Act, 42 U.S.C. sec. 1996.) See also John R. Wunder, *"Retained by The People": A History of American Indians and the Bill of Rights* (New York: Oxford University Press, 1994), 193–98.

151. *Lyng v. Northwest Indian Cemetery Protective Association*, 485 U.S. 439, 456 (1988).

152. Ibid., 459, 460, 461, 467.
153. Ibid., 469, 472, 474, 477.
154. *Employment Division v. Smith*, 494 U.S. 872, 884, 885 (1990).
155. Ibid., 891, 897.
156. Ibid., 890, 902.
157. Ibid., 909, 921.
158. Peter Steinfels, "Clinton Signs Law Protecting Religious Practices," *New York Times*, 17 November 1993, sec. A, p. 18.
159. See Robert F. Drinan and Jennifer I. Hufman, "The Religious Freedom Restoration Act: A Legislative History," *Journal of Law and Religion* 10 (1993–94): 531–41.
160. *Sherbert v. Verner*, 374 U.S. 398 (1963).
161. This was the conclusion reached by a number of legal scholars. For instance, see Eugene Gressman & Angela C. Carmella, "The RFRA Revision of the Free Exercise Clause," *Ohio State Law Journal* 57 (1996): 65–143; and William Van Alstyne, "The Failure of the Religious Freedom Restoration Act under Section 5 of the Fourteenth Amendment," *Duke Law Journal* 46 (November 1996): 291–326.
162. The fact that a reasonable attempt to discern the original understanding of the free exercise clause would probably lead to finding little support for an exemption from generally valid civil law apparently did not bother those groups that generally saw original intent or understanding as the means to bridle the Court's power. For an inspection of the original understanding of the free exercise clause, see Michael J. Malbin, *Religion and Politics: The Intentions of the Authors of the First Amendment* (Washington, D.C.: American Enterprise Institute for Policy Research, 1978).
163. *City of Boerne v. Flores*, 117 S.Ct. 2157 (1997).
164. See *United States v. Seeger*, 380 U.S. 163 (1965); and *Welsh v. United States*, 398 U.S. 333 (1970).
165. See *Everson v. Board of Education*, 330 U.S. 1, 15 (1947), in which the Court says that the establishment clause prohibits government from aiding all religions or preferring belief over disbelief.
166. *City of Boerne v. Flores*, 117 S.Ct. 2157, 2172 (1997).

CHAPTER TEN

1. For a useful survey of this development, see Richard C. Cortner, *The Supreme Court and the Second Bill of Rights: The Fourteenth Amendment and the Nationalization of Civil Liberties* (Madison: University of Wisconsin Press, 1981); and Henry J. Abraham and Barbara A. Perry, *Freedom and the Court: Civil Rights and Liberties in the United States*, 7th ed. (New York, Oxford University Press, 1998), 31–93.
2. *Betts v. Brady*, 316 U.S. 455 (1942).
3. See James E. Simon, *The Antagonists: Hugo Black, Felix Frankfurter and Civil Liberties in Modern America* (New York: Simon & Schuster, 1989).
4. For a comprehensive treatment of their relationship on the Court, see Howard Ball and Phillip J. Cooper, *Of Power and Right: Hugo Black, William O. Douglas and America's Constitutional Revolution* (New York: Oxford University Press, 1992).
5. *Wolf v. Colorado*, 338 U.S. 25 (1949).
6. *Rochin v. California*, 342 U.S. 165, 169, 170–71, 171–72, 173, 174 (1952). The first

quotation Frankfurter took verbatim from *Malinski v. New York*, 324 U.S. 401, 416–17 (1945).

7. *Rochin v. California*, 342 U.S. 165, 172 (1952).

8. *Irvine v. California*, 347 U.S. 128 (1954).

9. Ibid., 144, 145–46, 147.

10. *Breithaupt v. Abram*, 352 U.S. 432, 442, 444, 439 (1957).

11. See *Byars v. United States*, 273 U.S. 28 (1927); and *Gambino v. United States*, 275 U.S. 310 (1927).

12. *Elkins v. United States*, 364 U.S. 206, 217, 223 (1960).

13. *Boyd v. United States*, 116 U.S. 616 (1886).

14. *Mapp v. Ohio*, 367 U.S. 643, 647 (1961).

15. Ibid., 654–55, 660.

16. The first use of Madison's quotation in the record of the Supreme Court came in Black's dissenting opinion, joined by Douglas and Murphy, in *Galloway v. United States*, 319 U.S. 372 (1943). The case involved a war veteran's disability claim, which the Court denied by upholding the lower federal court's direction of a verdict. Black argued that this ruling invaded the function of the jury, which through the Seventh Amendment had been entrusted with the determination of facts as "an essential bulwark of civil liberty." (Ibid., 397).

17. See Richard C. Cortner, *The Supreme Court and the Second Bill of Rights: The Fourteenth Amendment and the Nationalization of Civil Liberties* (Madison: University of Wisconsin Press, 1981); and for a broader but shorter survey, see David J. Bodenhamer, *Fair Trial: Rights of the Accused in American History* (New York: Oxford University Press, 1992).

18. *Mapp v. Ohio*, 367 U.S. 655 (1961).

19. *Olmstead v. United States*, 277 U.S. 438 (1928).

20. *Berger v. New York*, 388 U.S. 41, 62–63 (1967).

21. *Katz v. United States*, 389 U.S. 347, 352, 351 (1967).

22. *Robinson v. California*, 370 U.S. 660, 678 (1962).

23. *Powell v. Alabama*, 287 U.S. 45 (1932).

24. *Betts v. Brady*, 316 U.S. 455 (1942).

25. See Anthony Lewis, *Gideon's Trumpet* (New York: Alfred A. Knopf, 1964).

26. Laura Kalman, *Abe Fortas: A Biography* (New Haven, Conn.: Yale University Press, 1990), 180–83. Justice William O. Douglas praised Fortas's argument in the case and later welcomed him as a fellow justice. Fortas was appointed by Lyndon Johnson and served from 1965–69.

27. *Gideon v. Wainwright*, 372 U.S. 335, 342, 344 (1963).

28. *Douglas v. California*, 372 U.S. 353, 357 (1963).

29. *Fay v. Noia*, 372 U.S. 391, 400–402, 441 (1963).

30. *Malloy v. Hogan*, 378 U.S. 1, 5, 11 (1964).

31. *Murphy v. Waterfront Commission of New York*, 378 U.S. 52, 54, 55 (1964).

32. *Escobedo v. Illinois*, 378 U.S. 478, 492, 490 (1964).

33. *Miranda v. Arizona*, 384 U.S. 436, 439, 440, 441–42, 444 (1966).

34. Ibid., 444, 445, 457–58.

35. Ibid., 460, 467, 468.

36. *Pointer v. Texas*, 380 U.S. 400, 403, 405, 413 (1965).

37. *Lamont v. Postmaster General*, 381 U.S. 301, 302, 305, 307 (1965).

38. Ibid., 308, 310.

39. *Kent v. Dulles*, 357 U.S. 116 (1958).

40. *Aptheker v. Secretary of State*, 378 U.S. 500, 506 (1964).

41. *Perez v. Brownell*, 356 U.S. 44 (1958).

42. *Afroyim v. Rusk*, 387 U.S. 253, 262, 267 (1967). The key vote in the reversal was that of William Brennan, who in 1958, his first term, had voted with the majority in *Perez*.

43. *Washington v. Texas*, 388 U.S. 14, 23 (1967).

44. *Klopfer v. North Carolina*, 386 U.S. 213, 223 (1967).

45. *Duncan v. Louisiana*, 391 U.S. 145, 149, 156 (1968).

46. *Palko v. Connecticut*, 302 U.S. 319 (1937).

47. *Benton v. Maryland*, 395 U.S. 784, 796 (1969).

48. For a sensitive treatment of loyalty oaths in the pluralistic society, see Sanford Levinson, *Constitutional Faith* (Princeton: Princeton University Press, 1988), 90–121. A history of loyalty oaths in American society to the mid-1950s can be found in Harold H. Hyman, *To Try Men's Souls: Loyalty Tests in American History* (Berkeley: University of California Press, 1959).

49. *Keyishian v. Board of Regents*, 385 U.S. 589, 603 (1967). The decision quoted is *Sweezy v. New Hampshire*, 354 U.S. 234, 250 (1957).

50. *Keyishian v. Board of Regents*, 385 U.S. 589, 606 (1967).

51. *Pickering v. Board of Education*, 391 U.S. 563, 574–75 (1968).

52. *Perry v. Sindermann*, 408 U.S. 593, 598 (1972).

53. The dissenting opinions are in the companion case of *Board of Regents v. Roth*, 408 U.S. 564, 588, 589, 591–92 (1972).

54. *Tinker v. Des Moines Independent Community School District*, 393 U.S. 503 (1969).

55. Ibid., 506, 508–9, 511.

56. *Goss v. Lopez*, 419 U.S. 565, 574, 576 (1975).

57. *Ingraham v. Wright*, 430 U.S. 651, 670, 680 (1977).

58. Ibid., 684–85.

59. *Board of Education v. Pico*, 457 U.S. 853 (1982), only came to the Court because the four dissenters had voted to hear the case. When Chief Justice Burger realized that he could not get a fifth vote, he sought to head off the plurality opinion by having the Court declare the case moot. William J. Brennan to Chief Justice Warren Burger, June 22, 1982, Brennan Papers, Library of Congress.

60. *Lamont v. Postmaster General*, 381 U.S. 301 (1965).

61. *Board of Education v. Pico*, 457 U.S. 853, 865 (1982).

62. Ibid., 867, 868.

63. *New Jersey v. T. L. O.*, 469 U.S. 325, 342 (1985). Ten years later in *Vernonia School District 47J v. Acton*, 115 S.Ct. 2386 (1995), the Court widened the arena for such searches by approving the random drug testing of student athletes. Justice O'Connor, joined by Justices Stevens and Souter, dissented, arguing that such indiscriminate drug testing did not meet the standards of reasonableness. She argued that a suspicion-based testing system would not only reduce the wholesale intrusion but also give the students control over their own situation.

64. *New Jersey v. T. L. O.*, 469 U.S. 325, 354, 355, 357, 361 (1985).

65. Ibid., 371, 373.

66. Ibid., 373–74, 385–86.

67. For more detail on this case, see Ellen Alderman and Caroline Kennedy, *The Right to Privacy* (New York: Knopf, 1995), 36–49.

68. *Tinker v. Des Moines Independent Community School District*, 393 U.S. 503 (1969).

69. *Hazelwood School District v. Kuhlmeier*, 484 U.S. 260, 269, 270–71, 273 (1988).

70. Ibid., 278, 280, 285, 290.

71. *In re Gault*, 387 U.S. 1 (1967).

72. Ibid., 20.

73. Ibid., 28–29, 50.

74. In *Roth v. United States*, 354 U.S. 476, 489 (1957), the Court read obscenity out of the First Amendment and established this test: "whether to the average person, applying community standards, the dominant theme of the material taken as a whole appeals to prurient interest." The further requirement that the material be "patently offensive," was suggested by Justice Harlan in announcing the judgment of the Court in *Manual Enterprises v. Day*, 370 U.S. 478, 487 (1962). That the standards for judgment should be national and not local standards and that the words in *Roth*, "utterly without redeeming social importance," should constitute an independent test were added by Justice Brennan's opinion announcing the judgment of the Court in *Jacobellis v. Ohio*, 378 U.S. 184, 191 (1964).

75. See *Miller v. California*, 413 U.S. 15 (1973) in which the Court revised the definition by saying that the community standards used to test obscenity were not nationally but rather locally determined.

76. *Butler v. Michigan*, 352 U.S. 380, 383 (1957).

77. *Ginsberg v. New York*, 390 U.S. 629 (1968).

78. *FCC v. Pacifica Foundation*, 438 U.S.726 (1978).

79. Ibid., 776–77.

80. Ibid., 767.

81. *Erznoznik v. City of Jacksonville*, 422 U.S. 205, 213–14 (1975).

82. *FCC v. Pacifica Foundation*, 438 U.S.726, 771 (1978).

83. *Sable Communications v. FCC*, 492 U.S.115, 135 (1989).

84. *Reno v. American Civil Liberties Union*, 117 S.Ct. 2329 (1997).

85. Ibid., 2329, 2346, 2350, 2347, 2351.

86. For a useful discussion of symbols and their relationship to social cohesion, see F. W. Dillistone, *The Power of Symbols in Religion and Culture* (New York: Crossroad, 1986), 13–15.

87. For an assessment of the votes of Scalia and Kennedy, see Mark Tushnet, "The Flag-Burning Episode: An Essay on the Constitution," *University of Colorado Law Review* 61 (1990): 43–46.

88. *Texas v. Johnson*, 491 U.S. 397, 407, 416, 417, 418, 419, 420 (1989).

89. Ibid., 420–21.

90. Ibid., 422, 429, 432, 435 (1989).

91. Ibid., 437, 438, 439.

92. See, for instance, Sheldon H. Nahmod, "The Sacred Flag and the First Amendment," *Indiana Law Journal* 66 (Spring 1991): 511–47.

93. In fact, in ibid., 513, Nahmod argues that the dissenters confused the signifier with what is signified. But in seeking to transform the flag into a sacred object, the dissenters needed to merge the referent into the symbol. They were ready to sacrifice the flag's symbolism to protect it from desecration.

94. For a discussion of the priestly and prophetic roles within the civil religion, see Martin E. Marty, "Two Kinds of Civil Religion," in Russell E. Richey and Donald G. Jones, eds., *American Civil Religion* (New York: Harper & Row, 1974), 144–45.

95. Flag Protection Act of 1989, Pub. L. 101–13, 103 Stat. 777 (1990). It now read: "Whoever knowingly mutilates, defaces, physically defiles, burns, maintains on the

floor or ground, or tramples upon any flag of the United States shall be fined under this title or imprisoned for not more than one year, or both." The new statute still contained the old exception for disposing of worn flags.

96. *United States v. Eichman*, 496 U.S. 310, 316, 317 (1990).

97. Ibid., 317, 318, 319.

98. Ibid., 322, 323.

99. For a detailed treatment of the conflict in the mid-1950s, see Walter F. Murphy, *Congress and the Court: A Case Study in the American Political Process* (Chicago: University of Chicago Press, 1965).

100. F. W. Dillistone, *The Power of Symbols in Religion and Culture* (New York: Crossroad, 1986), 6.

101. *R. A. V. v. City of St. Paul*, 505 U.S. 377, 380 (1992).

102. Ibid., 386, 394.

103. Ibid., 413.

104. *Cohen v. California*, 403 U.S. 15, 24–25 (1971).

105. *McIntyre v. Ohio Elections Commission*, 514 U.S. 334 (1995). Scalia, joined by Rehnquist, argued in dissent that the widespread condemnation of anonymous electioneering material by preexisting law revealed a general governmental practice that "bears a strong presumption of constitutionality" that "must be given precedence . . . over historical and academic speculation." (Ibid., 375, 377). Scalia's opinion not only takes the majority to task but also his usual ally, Clarence Thomas. Thomas had concurred in the result, saying that, because anonymous political material circulated freely at the time the First Amendment was added to the Constitution in 1791, the intent must have been to protect such material under the guarantee of free speech.

106. *Virginia Pharmacy Board v. Virginia Consumer Council*, 425 U.S. 748, 764, 770 (1976).

107. For instance in a recent decision, although they could not agree on a Court opinion, all nine justices did agree that Rhode Island could not ban the advertisement of liquor prices. *44 Liquormart v. Rhode Island*, 116 S.Ct. 1495 (1996).

108. *City of Ladue v. Gilleo*, 512 U.S. 43, 46, 54 58 (1994).

109. *Pierce v. Society of Sisters*, 268 U.S. 510 (1925); and *Meyer v. Nebraska*, 262 U.S. 390 (1923).

110. *Griswold v. Connecticut*, 381 U.S. 479, 482–83, 484, 485–86 (1965).

111. For a treatment of the Ninth Amendment that builds on Goldberg's opinion to find justification in such constitutional reliance, see Calvin R. Massey, *Silent Rights: The Ninth Amendment and the Court's Unenumerated Rights* (Philadelphia: Temple University Press, 1995). For a useful collection of articles both for and against such an expansive view of Ninth Amendment protection, see Randy E. Barnett, ed., *The Rights Retained by the People: The History and Meaning of the Ninth Amendment*, 2 vols. (Fairfax, Va.: George Mason University Press, 1989, 1993).

112. *Griswold v. Connecticut*, 381 U.S. 479, 490, 493 (1965).

113. See Tinsley E. Yarbrough, *John Marshall Harlan: Great Dissenter of the Warren Court* (New York: Oxford University Press, 1992), 310–13.

114. *Poe v. Ullman*, 367 U.S. 497, 539, 540, 542 (1961). In a recent concurring opinion in *Washington v. Glucksberg*, 117 S.Ct. 2258 (1997), in which the Court saw no constitutional bar to states banning physician-assisted suicide, Justice David H. Souter pays tribute to Harlan's justification for the Court's engagement in this type of due process review.

115. For a study of the historical evolution of a right of privacy and a tracing of its subse-

quent application, see Darien A. McWhirter and Jon D. Bible, *Privacy as a Constitutional Right: Sex, Drugs, and the Right to Life* (New York: Quorum Books, 1992).

116. *Eisenstadt v. Baird*, 405 U.S. 438, 453 (1972).

117. *Carey v. Population Services International*, 431 U.S. 678, 693, 715 (1977).

118. For a treatment of abortion law and the women's movement culminating in *Roe v. Wade*, 410 U.S. 113 (1973), see Flora Davis, *Moving the Mountain: The Women's Movement in America Since 1960* (New York: Simon & Schuster, 1991), 157–83.

119. *Brown v. Board of Education*, 347 U.S. 483 (1954).

120. *Roe v. Wade*, 410 U.S. 113, 152 (1973).

121. *Union Pacific Ry. Co. v. Botsford*, 141 U.S. 250, 251 (1891).

122. *Roe v. Wade*, 410 U.S. 113, 152 (1973).

123. Ibid., 162, 164–65.

124. Ibid., 210–13.

125. Barbara Hinkson Craig and David M. O'Brien, *Abortion and American Politics* (Chatham, N.J.: Chatham House Publishers, 1993), 173–92.

126. *Thornburgh v. American College of Obstetricians and Gynecologists*, 476 U.S. 747, 759 (1986).

127. Ibid., 771–72.

128. Ibid., 781–82.

129. Ibid., 787.

130. *Vasquez v. Hillery*, 474 U.S. 254, 265–66 (1986).

131. *Webster v. Reproductive Health Services*, 492 U.S. 490, 538, 560 (1989).

132. Ibid., 566–67, 571.

133. *Planned Parenthood of Southeastern Pennsylvania v. Casey*, 505 U.S. 833 (1992).

134. Ibid., 940, 943.

135. In David Sadofsky, *The Question of Privacy in Public Policy: An Analysis of the Reagan-Bush Era* (Westport: Praeger, 1993), the author puts the abortion matter in the context of a larger political campaign against a right of privacy. See also, Christopher E. Smith, *Justice Antonin Scalia and the Supreme Court's Conservative Moment* (Westport: Praeger, 1993).

136. *Planned Parenthood of Southeastern Pennsylvania v. Casey*, 505 U.S. 833, 851, 844, 847, 852 (1992).

137. Ibid., 854, 856, 864.

138. Ibid., 865, 866, 868.

139. A useful overview of the abortion issue is provided by Lawrence H. Tribe, *Abortion: The Clash of Absolutes* (New York: Norton, 1990).

140. *Planned Parenthood of Southeastern Pennsylvania v. Casey*, 505 U.S. 833, 901 (1992).

141. Ibid., 912, 916.

142. Both of President Clinton's appointments to the Court, Ruth Bader Ginsberg and Stephen G. Breyer, are strongly pro-choice.

143. *Bray v. Alexandria Clinic*, 506 U.S. 263, 309 (1993). The dissenters were Stevens and Blackmun.

144. James Boyd White, *Justice as Translation: An Essay in Cultural and Legal Criticism* (Chicago: University of Chicago Press, 1990), 203–14.

145. *Mapp v. Ohio*, 367 U.S. 655 (1961).

146. *Stanley v. Georgia*, 394 U.S. 557, 564, 565 (1969).

147. *Bowers v. Hardwick*, 478 U.S. 186 (1986).

148. Ibid., 195–96.

149. Ibid., 201.
150. *Thornburgh v. American College of Obstetricians & Gynecologists*, 476 U.S. 747, 772 (1986).
151. *Bowers v. Hardwick*, 478 U.S. 186, 205 (1986).
152. Ibid., 206, 208, 211, 213, 214 (1986).
153. In retrospect, Powell felt that the dissenters were right in the case. For his views on the issue and case, see John C. Jeffries Jr., *Justice Lewis F. Powell, Jr.* (New York: Charles Scribner's Sons, 1994), 511–30.
154. The justices decided the case on free speech grounds, saying that the parade organizers could not be forced by the state to include a message that they chose not to. *Hurley v. Irish-American Gay, Lesbian, and Bisexual Group of Boston*, 115 S.Ct. 2338 (1995).
155. *Romer v. Evans*, 116 S.Ct. 1620, 1627 (1996)
156. Ibid., 1627, 1629.
157. Ibid., 1637.
158. Of the justices who decided *Bowers*, only three remained on the Court in 1996: Rehnquist, Stevens, and O'Connor. Only Stevens was in dissent, but now, in *Romer*, O'Connor joined him, as did four of the six new justices. For a treatment of *Bowers* from the standpoint of the message of exclusion it sent and the suggestion that it will not long survive, see Kenneth L. Karst, *Belonging to America: Equal Citizenship and the Constitution* (New Haven: Yale University Press, 1989), 201–10.
159. *Cruzan v. Director, Missouri Department of Health*, 497 U.S. 261 (1990).
160. Ibid., 302, 303, 305, 313, 316, 326, 328, 330.
161. Ibid., 289, 292.
162. Ibid., 300–301.
163. Ibid., 330–331, 338.
164. Ibid., 339, 343, 344.
165. Ibid., 345, 350, 351, 355, 356, 357.
166. In a book stimulated by the Cruzan case, Melvin I. Urofsky, *Letting Go: Death, Dying, and the Law* (New York: Charles Scribner's Sons, 1993), the author deals with the issues the case raises and appears comfortable with the role of the courts in coping with such problems.
167. For some discussion of these issues, see James M. Hoefler and Brian E. Kamoie, *Deathright: Culture, Medicine, Politics, and the Right to Die* (Boulder, Colo.: Westview Press, 1994); and G. Steven Neeley, *The Constitutional Right to Suicide: A Legal and Philosophical Examination* (New York: Peter Lang Publishing, 1994).
168. *Mutual Film Corp. v. Industrial Commission of Ohio*, 236 U.S. 230 (1915).
169. *Olmstead v. United States*, 277 U.S. 438 (1928).
170. *Estes v. Texas*, 381 U.S. 532 (1965).
171. *Washington v. Glucksberg*, 117 S.Ct. 2258 (1997); and *Vacco v. Quill*, 117 S.Ct. 2293 (1997).
172. *Washington v. Glucksberg*, 117 S.Ct. 2258, 2290 (1997)
173. Ibid., 2310.

CONCLUSION

1. William J. Brennan Jr., "The Constitution of the United States: Contemporary Ratification," Speech at Georgetown University as part of Text and Teaching Symposium, October 12, 1985, in *University of California at Davis Law Review* 19 (Fall 1985): 14.

2. *Chisholm v. Georgia*, 2 U.S. (2 Dall.) 440 (1793).

3. David A. J. Richards, *Conscience and the Constitution: History, Theory, and Law of the Reconstruction Amendments* (Princeton: Princeton University Press, 1993), 17.

4. *United States v. Lopez*, 115 S.Ct. 1624, 1637–38, 1639 (1995). In fact, the Court in 1985 said the judiciary has "no license to employ freestanding conceptions of state sovereignty when measuring congressional authority under the Commerce Clause." State representation in Congress was deemed to provide sufficient protection. *Garcia v. San Antonio Metropolitan Transit Authority*, 469 U.S. 528, 550 (1985).

5. American federalism has had a political basis, but not a constitutional one. H. Jefferson Powell, in "The Oldest Question of Constitutional Law," *Virginia Law Review* 79 (April 1993): 633–89, supports this conclusion but then notes that some justices have been trying to remedy that perceived deficiency.

   Although he then concluded that they had not yet succeeded, a majority of five has formed, seemingly intent upon reviving the Tenth Amendment and making it a constitutional testament to federalism. Actually, six members of the Court decided, in *New York v. United States*, 505 U.S. 144 (1992), that Congress lacked the power to command the states to come up with plans to dispose of radioactive waste or take title to it. That majority, which included Chief Justice Rehnquist and Justices Sandra Day O'Connor, Antonin Scalia, William Kennedy, and Clarence Thomas dwindled to five, with the defection of Souter, in *Garcia* but has held firm in *Prinz v. United States*, 117 S.Ct. 2365 (1997). In *Prinz*, the five-person majority found that a provision in the Brady Handgun Violence Prevention Act that called upon state and local law enforcement officers to make background checks invaded the sovereignty of the states. Justices John Paul Stevens, David H. Souter, Ruth Bader Ginsburg, and Stephen Breyer continued to protest the majority's niggardly view of federal power.

6. The following books are a representative sampling of the nature and extent of the debate: Robert H. Bork, *The Tempting of America: The Political Seduction of the Law* (New York: Free Press, 1990); Michael J. Perry, *The Constitution in the Courts: Law or Politics?* (New York: Oxford University Press, 1994); Jesse H. Choper, *Judicial Review and the National Political Process: A Functional Reconsideration of the Role of the Supreme Court* (Chicago: University of Chicago Press, 1980); John Hart Ely, *Democracy and Distrust: A Theory of Judicial Review* (Cambridge: Harvard University Press, 1980); Bruce Ackerman, *We the People, I: The Foundations* (Cambridge: Belknap Press of Harvard University Press, 1991); Christopher Wolfe, *The Rise of Modern Judicial Review: From Constitutional Interpretation to Judge-Made Law*, rev. ed. (Lanham, Md.: Rowman & Littlefield Publishers, 1994); John Arthur, *Words That Bind: Judicial Review and the Grounds of Modern Constitutional Theory* (Boulder: Westview Press, 1995); and Earl M. Maltz, *Rethinking Constitutional Law: Originalism, Interventionism, and the Politics of Judicial Review* (Lawrence: University Press of Kansas, 1994).

7. See Ethan Bronner, *Battle for Justice: How the Bork Nomination Shook America* (New York: Norton, 1989), 343–52. For Bork's own account of the confirmation fight and a delineation of his views on the Court's role in interpreting the Constitution, see Robert H. Bork, *The Tempting of America: The Political Seduction of the Law* (New York: Free Press, 1990).

8. Ethan Bronner, *Battle for Justice: How the Bork Nomination Shook America* (New York: Norton, 1989), 275–76.

9. Michael J. Perry, *The Constitution in the Courts: Law or Politics?* (New York: Oxford University Press, 1994), 202.

10. For an interesting discussion on constitutional interpretation, regarding who should interpret what, see Sanford Levinson, *Constitutional Faith* (Princeton, N.J.: Princeton University Press, 1988), 9–53.

11. For a brief description of the rulings reversed by the Civil Rights Act of 1991, see Henry J. Abraham and Barbara A. Perry, *Freedom and the Court: Civil Rights & Liberties in the United States*, 7th ed. (New York: Oxford University Press, 1998), 443–48.

12. William J. Brennan Jr., "The Constitution of the United States: Contemporary Ratification," Speech at Georgetown University as part of Text and Teaching Symposium, October 12, 1985, in *University of California at Davis Law Review* 19 (Fall 1985): 4.

13. For instance, see Gunnar Myrdal, *An American Dilemma: The Negro Problem and Modern Democracy* (New York: Harper & Brothers, 1944), 3–25.

14. David A. J. Richards, *Conscience and the Constitution: History, Theory, and Law of the Reconstruction Amendments* (Princeton, N.J.: Princeton University Press, 1993), 188, 257.

15. "Toleration is . . . the central constititutional ideal. . . . Substantitive and procedural constitutional guarantees are . . . ways in which we express and preserve the moral force of this ideal of equal respect in our political life." David A. J. Richards, *Toleration and the Constitution* (New York: Oxford University Press, 1986), x.

16. Robert N. Bellah, "Civil Religion in America," *Daedalus* 96 (Winter 1967): 1–21.

JUSTICES OF THE SUPREME COURT

Name (Dates of Service)	Nominated by
Henry Baldwin (1830–1844)	Andrew Jackson
Philip P. Barbour (1836–1841)	Andrew Jackson
Hugo L. Black (1937–1971)	Franklin D. Roosevelt
Harry A. Blackmun (1970–1994)	Richard M. Nixon
John Blair (1790–1795)	George Washington
Samuel Blatchford (1882–1893)	Chester A. Arthur
Joseph P. Bradley (1870–1892)	Ulysses S. Grant
Louis D. Brandeis (1916–1939)	Woodrow Wilson
William J. Brennan (1956–1990)	Dwight D. Eisenhower
David J. Brewer (1890–1910)	Benjamin Harrison
Stephen Gerald Breyer (1994–)	Bill Clinton
Henry B. Brown (1891–1906)	Benjamin Harrison
Warren E. Burger (Chief: 1969–1986)	Richard M. Nixon
Harold Burton (1945–1958)	Harry S Truman
Pierce Butler (1923–1939)	Warren G. Harding
James F. Byrnes (1941–1942)	Franklin D. Roosevelt
John A. Campbell (1853–1861)	Franklin Pierce
Benjamin N. Cardozo (1932–1938)	Herbert Hoover
John Catron (1837–1865)	Martin Van Buren
Salmon P. Chase (Chief: 1864–1873)	Abraham Lincoln
Samuel Chase (1796–1811)	George Washington
Tom C. Clark (1949–1967)	Harry S Truman
John H. Clarke (1916–1922)	Woodrow Wilson
Nathan Clifford (1858–1881)	James Buchanan
Benjamin R. Curtis (1851–1857)	Millard Fillmore
William Cushing (1790–1810)	George Washington
Peter V. Daniel (1841–1860)	Martin Van Buren
David Davis (1862–1877)	Abraham Lincoln
William R. Day (1903–1922)	Theodore Roosevelt
William O. Douglas (1939–1975)	Franklin D. Roosevelt

Gabriel Duvall (1811–1835)	James Madison
Oliver Ellsworth (Chief: 1796–1800)	George Washington
Stephen J. Field (1863–1897)	Abraham Lincoln
Abe Fortas (1965–1969)	Lyndon B. Johnson
Felix Frankfurter (1939–1962)	Franklin D. Roosevelt
Melville W. Fuller (Chief: 1888–1910)	Grover Cleveland
Ruth Bader Ginsburg (1993–　)	Bill Clinton
Arthur J. Goldberg (1962–1965)	John F. Kennedy
Horace Gray (1882–1902)	Chester A. Arthur
Robert C. Grier (1846–1870)	James K. Polk
John M. Harlan (1877–1911)	Rutherford B. Hayes
John M. Harlan (1955–1971)	Dwight D. Eisenhower
Oliver Wendell Holmes Jr. (1902–1932)	Theodore Roosevelt
Charles E. Hughes (1910–1916)	William Howard Taft
(Chief: 1930–1941)	Herbert Hoover
Ward Hunt (1873–1882)	Ulysses S. Grant
James Iredell (1790–1799)	George Washington
Howell E. Jackson (1893–1895)	Benjamin Harrison
Robert H. Jackson (1941–1954)	Franklin D. Roosevelt
John Jay (Chief: 1789–1795)	George Washington
Thomas Johnson (1792–1793)	George Washington
William Johnson (1804–1834)	Thomas Jefferson
Anthony M. Kennedy (1988–　)	Ronald Reagan
Joseph R. Lamar (1911–1916)	William Howard Taft
Lucius Q. C. Lamar (1888–1893)	Grover Cleveland
Brockholst Livingston (1807–1823)	Thomas Jefferson
Horace H. Lurton (1910–1914)	William Howard Taft
John Marshall (Chief: 1801–1835)	John Adams
Thurgood Marshall (1967–1991)	Lyndon B. Johnson
Stanley Matthews (1881–1889)	James A. Garfield
Joseph McKenna (1898–1925)	William McKinley
John McKinley (1838–1852)	Martin Van Buren
John McLean (1830–1861)	Andrew Jackson
James C. McReynolds (1914–1941)	Woodrow Wilson
Samuel F. Miller (1862–1890)	Abraham Lincoln
Sherman Minton (1949–1956)	Harry S Truman
William H. Moody (1906–1910)	Theodore Roosevelt
Alfred Moore (1800–1804)	John Adams
Frank Murphy (1940–1949)	Franklin D. Roosevelt
Samuel Nelson (1845–1872)	John Tyler
Sandra Day O'Connor (1981–　)	Ronald Reagan
William Paterson (1793–1806)	George Washington

Rufus Peckham (1896–1909)	Grover Cleveland
Mahlon Pitney (1912–1922)	William Howard Taft
Lewis F. Powell Jr. (1972–1987)	Richard M. Nixon
Stanley Reed (1938–1957)	Franklin D. Roosevelt
William H. Rehnquist (1972–1986)	Richard M. Nixon
(Chief: 1986–)	Ronald Reagan
Owen J. Roberts (1930–1945)	Herbert Hoover
John Rutledge (1790–1791)	George Washington
(Chief: 1795–1795)	George Washington
Wiley B. Rutledge (1943–1949)	Franklin D. Roosevelt
Edward T. Sanford (1923–1930)	Warren G. Harding
Antonin Scalia (1986–)	Ronald Reagan
George Shiras Jr. (1892–1903)	Benjamin Harrison
David H. Souter (1990–)	George Bush
John Paul Stevens (1975–)	Gerald Ford
Potter Stewart (1959–1981)	Dwight D. Eisenhower
Harlan Fiske Stone (1925–1941)	Calvin Coolidge
(Chief: 1941–1946)	Franklin D. Roosevelt
Joseph Story (1812–1845)	James Madison
William Strong (1870–1880)	Ulysses S. Grant
George Sutherland (1922–1938)	Warren G. Harding
Noah Swayne (1862–1881)	Abraham Lincoln
William Howard Taft (Chief: 1921–1930)	Warren G. Harding
Roger B. Taney (Chief: 1836–1864)	Andrew Jackson
Clarence Thomas (1991–)	George Bush
Smith Thompson (1823–1843)	James Monroe
Thomas Todd (1807–1826)	Thomas Jefferson
Robert Trimble (1826–1828)	John Quincy Adams
Willis Van Devanter (1911–1937)	William Howard Taft
Fred M. Vinson (Chief: 1946–1953)	Harry S Truman
Morrison R. Waite (Chief: 1874–1888)	Ulysses S. Grant
Earl Warren (Chief: 1953–1969)	Dwight D. Eisenhower
Bushrod Washington (1799–1829)	John Adams
James M. Wayne (1835–1867)	Andrew Jackson
Byron R. White (1962–1993)	John F. Kennedy
Edward D. White (1894–1910)	Grover Cleveland
(Chief: 1910–1921)	William Howard Taft
Charles E. Whittaker (1957–1962)	Dwight D. Eisenhower
James Wilson (1789–1798)	George Washington
Levi Woodbury (1845–1851)	James K. Polk
William B. Woods (1881–1887)	Rutherford B. Hayes

CASE INDEX

Passenger Cases, 48 U.S. (7 How.) 283 (1849), 78

Patterson v. Alabama, 294 U.S. 600 (1935), 191

Patterson v. Colorado, 205 U.S. 454 (1907), 157, 209

Patton v. Mississippi, 332 U.S. 463 (1947), 268

Paul v. Virginia, 75 U.S. (8 Wall.) 168 (1869), 23

Pennekamp v. Florida, 328 U.S. 331 (1946), 239

Pennsylvania v. Wheeling & Belmont Bridge Co., 54 U.S. (13 How.) 518 (1851), 80

Perez v. Brownell, 356 U.S. 44 (1958), 362, 458n42

Permoli v. New Orleans, 44 U.S. (3 How.) 589 (1845), 76

Perry v. Sindermann, 408 U.S. 593 (1972), 365

Perry v. United States, 294 U.S. 330 (1935), 196

Personnel Administrator of Massachusetts v. Feeney, 442 U.S. 256 (1979), 314

Peterson v. City of Greenville, 373 U.S. 244 (1963), 282

Philadelphia, Wilmington, and Baltimore R.R. Co. v. Quigley, 62 U.S. (21 How.) 202 (1859), 81

Pickering v. Board of Education, 391 U.S. 563 (1968), 364–65

Pierce v. Society of Sisters, 268 U.S. 510 (1925), 179, 382

Pierce v. United States, 252 U.S. 239 (1920), 173

Pierre v. Louisiana, 306 U.S. 354 (1939), 266

Piqua Branch of the State Bank of Ohio v. Knoop, 57 U.S. (16 How.) 369 (1853), 98

Planned Parenthood of Southeastern Pennsylvania v. Casey, 505 U.S. 833 (1992), 387–90

Plessy v. Ferguson, 163 U.S. 537 (1896), 122–25, 134, 263, 266–67, 275–77, 292–94

Plyler v. Doe, 457 U.S. 202 (1982), 322

Poe v. Ullman, 367 U.S. 497 (1961), 383

Poindexter v. Greenhow, 114 U.S. 270 (1885), 136

Pointer v. Texas, 380 U.S. 400 (1965), 361

Pollock v. Farmers' Loan & Trust Co., 157 U.S. 429 (1895), 146–47

Pollock v. Farmers' Loan & Trust Co., 158 U.S. 601 (1895), 147–49

Porterfield v. Webb, 263 U.S. 225 (1923), 232

Powell v. Alabama, 287 U.S. 45 (1932), 191, 263, 357

Powell v. Pennsylvania, 127 U.S. 678 (1888), 145

Powers v. Ohio, 499 U.S. 400 (1991), 303

Prigg v. Pennsylvania, 41 U.S. (16 Pet.) 539 (1842), 89–91

Prince v. Massachusetts, 321 U.S. 158 (1954), 224

Prinz v. United States, 117 S.Ct. 2365 (1997), 463n5

Prize Cases, 67 U.S. (2 Black) 635 (1863), 112

Providence Bank v. Billings, 29 U.S. (4 Pet.) 514 (1830), 71–72

Prudential Insurance Co. v. Cheek, 259 U.S. 530 (1922), 180

Queen v. Hepburn, 11 U.S. (7 Cranch) 290 (1813), 86

Ex parte Quirin, 317 U.S. 1 (1942), 233

R. A. V. v. City of St. Paul, 505 U.S. 377 (1992), 378–79

Radice v. New York, 264 U.S. 292 (1924), 436n21

Railway Mail Association v. Corsi, 326 U.S. 88 (1945), 274

Rasmussen v. United States, 197 U.S. 516 (1905), 165, 435n102

Reed v. Reed, 404 U.S. 71 (1971), 310–11

Regents of the University of California v. Bakke, 438 U.S. 265 (1977), 292–94

Reno v. American Civil Liberties Union, 117 S.Ct. 2329 (1997), 372–73

Reynolds v. McArthur, 27 U.S. (2 Pet.) 417 (1829), 73

Reynolds v. Sims, 377 U.S. 533 (1964), 309

Reynolds v. United States, 98 U.S. 145 (1879), 161, 434n81

Richmond v. Croson Co., 488 U.S. 469 (1989), 298, 449n130

SUBJECT INDEX

ABOUT THE AUTHOR

John E. Semonche is professor of history at the University of North Carolina at Chapel Hill. He received his A.B. from Brown University, his M.A. and Ph.D. in history from Northwestern University, and his LL.B. from Duke University. He has held a joint appointment with the School of Law at UNC-CH and is a member of the North Carolina and the United States Supreme Court bars. Among his many articles and books are *Charting the Future: The Supreme Court Responds to a Changing Society* and *Religion & Constitutional Government in the United States: A Historical Overview with Sources.* He has also been a pioneer in harnessing the computer to the study of history, both in terms of developing historical simulations as student exercises and of transforming lectures into multimedia presentations. His computer program entitled "1912: Can You Get Your State to Approve a Woman's Suffrage Amendment" was a EDUCOM/NCRIPTAL Higher Education Software Winner, and his simulations are highlighted in Judith V. Boettcher, ed., *101 Success Stories of Information Technology in Higher Education: The Joe Wyatt Challenge.*